We Are Not Slaves

Justice, Power, and Politics

COEDITORS
Heather Ann Thompson
Rhonda Y. Williams

EDITORIAL ADVISORY BOARD
Peniel E. Joseph
Daryl Maeda
Barbara Ransby
Vicki L. Ruiz
Marc Stein

The Justice, Power, and Politics series publishes new works in history that explore the myriad struggles for justice, battles for power, and shifts in politics that have shaped the United States over time. Through the lenses of justice, power, and politics, the series seeks to broaden scholarly debates about America's past as well as to inform public discussions about its future.

More information on the series, including a complete list of books published, is available at http://justicepowerandpolitics.com/.

We Are Not Slaves

State Violence, Coerced Labor, and
Prisoners' Rights in Postwar America

ROBERT T. CHASE

The University of North Carolina Press
Chapel Hill

The publication of this book was supported in part by a generous grant from the William R. Kenan Jr. Charitable Trust. This book was also published in association with the William P. Clements Center for Southwest Studies at Southern Methodist University by the University of North Carolina Press.

The University of North Carolina Press has been a member of the Green Press Initiative since 2003.

Library of Congress Cataloging-in-Publication Data
Names: Chase, Robert T., author.
Title: We are not slaves : state violence, coerced labor, and prisoners' rights in postwar America / Robert T. Chase.
Other titles: Justice, power, and politics.
Description: Chapel Hill : University of North Carolina Press, 2020. | Series: Justice, Power, and Politics | Includes bibliographical references and index.
Identifiers: LCCN 2019019416 | ISBN 9781469653570 (cloth : alk. paper) | ISBN 9781469653587 (ebook)
Subjects: LCSH: Prisoners—Civil rights—Texas—History—20th century. | Prisoners—Civil rights—Southern States—History—20th century. | Convict labor—Southern States—History—20th century. | Prisoners—Violence against—Southern States—History—20th century. | African American prisoners. | Mexican American prisoners. | Southern States—Race relations—History—20th century.
Classification: LCC HV9475.T4 C65 2020 | DDC 365/.65—dc23 LC record available at https://lccn.loc.gov/2019019416

Cover illustration: Bruce Jackson, *Ramsey Prison, Field Labor* (1978). Courtesy of the artist.

To the loving memory of my parents
John Terry Chase
Sara Hannum Chase

To the incarcerated people in Texas who demanded that
institutions of criminal justice also be spaces of social justice

At the time of the creation of Auburn and the Philadelphia prison, which served as models for the great machines of incarceration, it was believed that something indeed was produced: "virtuous" men. Now we know, and the administration is perfectly aware, that no such thing is produced. That nothing at all is produced. That it is a question simply of a great trick of sleight of hand, a curious mechanism of circular elimination: society eliminates by sending to prison people whom prison breaks up, crushes, physically eliminates; and then once they have been broken up, the prison eliminates them by "freeing" them and sending them back to society; and there, their life in prison, the way in which they were treated, the state in which they come out insures that society will eliminate them once again, sending them to prison. . . . [Prison] is a machine for elimination, a form of prodigious stomach, a kidney that consumes, destroys, breaks up, and then rejects, and that consumes in order to eliminate what it has already eliminated.

—Michel Foucault, after visiting Attica prison, 1991

I will be as harsh as truth, and as uncompromising as justice. On this subject [slavery] I do not wish to think, to speak, or to write with moderation. I am in earnest—I will not equivocate—I will not excuse—I will not retreat a single inch—and I will be heard.

—William Lloyd Garrison

What about this matter of crime and punishment, anyhow? You can trace it all down through the history of man. You can trace the burnings, the boilings, the drawings, and quarterings, the hanging of people in England at the crossroads, carving them up and hanging them as examples for all to see. We can come down to the last century where nearly two hundred crimes were punishable by death. You can read the stories of hanging on a high hill, and the populace for miles around coming out to the scene, that everybody might be awed into goodness. Hanging for pick pocketers, and yet more pockets were picked in the crowd that went to the hanging than had been known before. . . . Cruelty breeds cruelty. If there is any way to kill evil and hatred and all that goes with it, it is not through evil and hatred and cruelty; it is through charity and love and understanding. . . . You cannot cure the hatreds and maladjustments of the world by killing and punishment. You may here and there cure hatred with love and understanding; but you can only add fuel to the flames by cruelty and hate. What is our society's idea of justice? "Give criminals the same mercy they give to their victims." If the state is not kinder, more humane, more considerate, I am sorry I have lived so long.

—Fred Cruz, as prisoner of Texas, diary entry, 1966

Slavery Man, Human Slavery.

—Anonymous Texas Prisoner, 1978

Contents

Graphs, Illustrations, Maps, and Tables

Maps

Tables

Abbreviations in the Text

AB	Aryan Brotherhood
ACLU	American Civil Liberties Union
Ad Seg	administrative segregation
APPLE	Allied Prisoners Platform for Legal Equity
BPP	Black Panther Party
BT	building tender
CERT	Correctional Emergency Response Team
CO	correctional officer
CORE	Congress of Racial Equality
CURE	Citizens United for Rehabilitation for Errants
DCC	Dallas Community Committee
FAM	Free Alabama Movement
FIRST	First Inmate Reform Strike in Texas
IWW-IWOC	Industrial Workers of the World's Incarcerated Workers Organizing Committee
JCPR	Joint Committee on Prison Reform
JHLA	Jailhouse Lawyers Association
JLS	Jailhouse Lawyers Speak
LDF	Legal Defense Fund
LEAA	Law Enforcement Assistance Administration
LULAC	League of United Latin American Citizens
MAYO	Mexican American Youth Organization
NAACP	National Association for the Advancement of Colored People
NAPO	New Afrikan Prisoner Organization
NCF	National Committee to Combat Fascism
NLG	National Lawyers Guild
NOI	Nation of Islam

PIP	Point Incentive Program
PLRA	Prison Litigation Reform Act
PSC	Prison Solidarity Committee
RUP	La Raza Unida Party
RVP	Revolutionary Vanguard Party Platform
SAT	state-approved trusty
SCORE	Student Congress on Racial Equality
SLA	Symbonese Liberation Army
SNCC	Student Nonviolent Coordinating Committee
SORT	Special Operations Response Teams
SSIs	support service inmates
TCDL	Texas Criminal Defense Lawyers Association
TDC	Texas Department of Corrections, 1957–1989
TDCJ	Texas Department of Criminal Justice, 1989–present
TPS	Texas Prison System, 1867–1957
TS	Texas Syndicate
TSEU	Texas State Employees Union
TYC	Texas Youth Council
UCF	United Community Front
VISTA	Volunteers in Service to America

We Are Not Slaves

Introduction

At daybreak on October 4, 1978, the prisoners of the Ellis prison, situated in the heart of the cotton-growing region of East Texas, shuffled out of their prison cells for another day of grueling hard labor. Expected to pick between two hundred and three hundred pounds of cotton per day, the prisoners worked the field in racially segregated lines of African Americans, whites, and Mexican Americans. A prison guard high rider, what prisoners referred to as the "cap'ain," sat perched above them on horseback, with a .30-caliber rifle clutched in his hands and his face shaded by the broad brim of his Stetson. On this particular day, however, 9 prisoners sat down and refused to work. Despite the guards' sharp barks and insistent demands that the prisoners return to work, they remained steadfast, and by midafternoon, 408 prisoners joined them in a coordinated work strike. As news spread across the prison system, the prisons at Coffield, Ellis, Clemens, Darrington, Eastham, and Ramsey I and II erupted into disturbances and work strikes of their own. By the end of the week, the work stoppage and prison uprising engulfed six of the prison system's fifteen units, and involved nearly 1,500 prisoners, approximately 15 percent of the total prison population of 29,000, leaving 34 prisoners and 18 guards injured.[1]

Butch Mendez, one of the first to initiate the strike, defined the prisoners' resistance as a "slave uprising" mounted within an interracial coalition. "On Oct 4th 8 comrades and myself threw off our cotton sacks while out in the cotton fields and told the overseer that we refused to work. All of us 9 quit at the same moment, for the same reason, which was to show our support for the brothers in court (David [Ruiz] vs. Estelle) . . . Chicanos, blacks, whites! It was a united front to show support for the trial."[2] First filed in 1972, *Ruiz v. Estelle* was a massive omnibus lawsuit that demanded that Texas outlaw the practice of having prisoners act as guards over other fellow prisoners and seeking to alleviate prison overcrowding, improve prisoner health care, and grant prisoners access to attorneys and legal representation. It was the culmination of nearly a decade of struggle where prisoners initiated a legal, social, and political campaign against the southern prison's labor regime that divided prisoners through racial privilege and sexual assault.

As the first statewide, coordinated, interracial prison work strike in Texas history, the administrators of the prison system and the court overseeing the

Ruiz case feared that Texas was, for the first time in the postwar period, vulnerable to a rising tide of prisoner unrest that had gripped other parts of the nation. This series of nationwide prison revolts was seen by many "law-and-order" politicians and journalists as an epidemic of lawlessness and violent criminality.[3] There were five prison uprisings in 1967; fifteen in 1968; twenty-seven in 1970; thirty-seven in 1971; and forty-eight in 1972, the most prison uprisings in any single year in U.S. history. The September 1971 Attica prison uprising, in particular, alarmed the nation's prison managers as nearly 1,300 of the prison's approximately 2,200 prisoners seized control of the prison, taking 39 correction officers hostage for over four days. Occurring only a month after George Jackson was killed under extremely questionable circumstances by California prison guards at Soledad prison, New York's subsequent Attica uprising riveted the nation. After only four days of negotiations, Governor Nelson Rockefeller ordered state police to retake the prison in a bloody state assault that ended with 39 people killed and 89 wounded, including 29 prisoners and 10 correctional officers and civilians. As the state-appointed commission noted in 1972, the "state police assault which ended the four-day prison uprising was the bloodiest one-day encounter between Americans since the Civil War."[4]

In Texas, the prison work strike of 1978 caused great consternation. Robert DeLong, general counsel for the Texas Department of Corrections (TDC), admitted as much: "Never before in the history of TDC has there been a work stoppage that spread to more than one unit," DeLong warned. "We don't want to have another Attica or anything of that sort in Texas if it can be helped."[5] DeLong's admonition struck fear in the heart of Texas prison administrators, who during the *Ruiz* trial jealously guarded southern prison labor as the critical centerpiece of state efficiency, control, and discipline.

The *Ruiz* trial over the state use of abusive convict guards subsequently became the largest and longest civil rights trial in the history of U.S. jurisprudence up to that point. It convened in October 1978 and adjourned in late December 1980 and included testimony from 349 witnesses, of which over 100 were prisoners, and lengthy expert testimony from activists, academics, psychiatrists, and penologists. As a regional model, the *Ruiz* case inspired prisoners across the South to wage a campaign to convince the courts and the wider public that southern prisoners suffered terrible abuses at the hands of southern prison systems. On the national level, it challenged the once protected realm of state control over prisons systems with the threat of federal court intervention that could declare an entire state system as unconstitutional and place it into federal receivership. Doing so challenged the "policing powers" of the states, as enumerated as "residual powers" in the Tenth

Amendment to the Constitution, which granted exclusive control over prison conditions to the state.[6] As such, it pitted national judicial power against state executive and legislative control, while also extending civil rights and constitutional protections even to those convicted of a crime.

At the heart of the *Ruiz* case, then, was a struggle over state violence, coerced labor, and an internal labor division that privileged some prisoners, particularly white prisoners, while castigating others to the bottom ranks of hard field labor. Across the U.S. South, the southern prison system depended upon prison labor. The convict lease system from the end of Reconstruction through the early Progressive era denied African Americans full citizenship and dehumanized them within a Jim Crow construct, even as the coerced labor that they performed modernized the infrastructure and economy of the New South within new capital and industrial interests.[7] After the collapse of the convict lease, field labor structured the day-to-day work of southern prisoners and bound them to the South's coercive work discipline. As a matter of daily practice, prisoners incarcerated on southern prisons worked in grueling field conditions and conducted roadwork that required ten-hour work days and six days of hard labor.[8] In Texas, prisoners worked on former slave plantations where they picked the cash crop of cotton, cleared the land, and harvested so many agricultural goods that they became one of the state's greatest agribusinesses during the post–World War II period.[9] As prison systems outside of the South experienced cost overruns due to expensive rehabilitative programs and the decline of prison labor, Texas prison administrators could point to a nearly self-sufficient and extremely low-cost model. In 1951, the average daily cost of maintaining a prisoner in forty-four states was $2.23, and the cost increased to $3.59 in federal prisons, while the cost per prisoner in Texas was a very low $0.49. The low-cost prison remained a steady feature through the late 1970s.[10] In 1978, the year of the Texas work strikes and the opening of the *Ruiz* case, the state of Texas spent only $47 million to hold 23,614 prisoners, far less than what New York and California spent on 18,000 and 20,000 prisoners, respectively. New York's prison system costs were $218 million, and California, $269 million; a sum five times as much as Texas. Moreover, Texas was one of only seven states that did not pay its prisoners for their labor, and they maintained the lowest guard-to-inmate ratio at twelve prisoners to every guard, whereas the national average was three prisoners to every guard.[11] Such a labor regime allowed southern prison managers to claim that their emphasis on efficiency, order, low cost, and productivity yielded a modernized prison system that rivaled nonsouthern prison systems that were wedded to either the idle warehousing of prisoners or those that employed costly rehabilitative models, both susceptible to "prison riots" in a way that Texans claimed that they were not. Out of these statistics, Texans constructed a modernization narrative that positioned the southern prison at the center of a "New, New South" rising.

For prisoners, however, the modernization narrative was more mythology than truth. Prisoners understood full well the definition of myth offered by the literary scholar and historian Richard Slotkin that "myth describes a process, credible to its audience, by which knowledge is transformed into power" and that, once constructed thus, such "myths reach out of the past to cripple, incapacitate, or strike down the living."[12] Among prisoners, the *Ruiz* case was about a longer struggle over how the prison system divided its prison labor through racial privilege and power, rewarding its enforcers while subjecting the regular prison population to harsh labor regimes, routine corporal punishment, and state-orchestrated sexual violence. To maintain order within prisons and keep the costs so low, the southern system heavily relied on the "inmate trusty" system that provided some prisoners greater freedom of movement and privilege than others. In Louisiana, Mississippi, and Alabama, trusty shooters openly carried firearms and operated as prison guards to fire upon any fellow prisoner who attempted escape. Within prison dormitories, Mississippi and Louisiana deputized some trusties as so-called walkers, who maintained prison authority, discipline, and order within the barracks. In Texas, prisoner field drivers drew on the slave heritage of East Texas cotton plantations to drive the work of fellow prisoners.[13]

The Texas prison modernization narrative of competence and efficiency obfuscated the reality of a brutal system of internal prison management in which prisoners acted as guards, employing coercive means to maintain control over the prisoner population. The Texas prison administration allowed selected trusties to openly carry hand-made weapons so that they could ensure prisoner discipline and administrative control. In return for their service, the prison administration provided these trusties with certain privileges that allowed them control over the prison system's sub-rosa internal economy. The prisoners whom the prison system placed in charge also ran an internal prison economy in which money, food, human beings, reputations, favors, and sex all became commodities to be bought and sold. While prisoners worked the fields as coerced slave labor, privileged prisoners known as "building tenders" constructed an internal slave trade economy where they bought and sold the bodies of other prisoners as sexual slaves, subjects of rape, and as domestic cell servants. The building tender system was a hierarchical labor regime that constituted a vicious sex trade in which building tenders were given tacit approval from the prison administration to use their power to rape other prisoners and engage in the buying and selling of prisoner bodies as a sexual commodity that signified cultural standing and societal power. Moreover, it constructed racial hierarchy within the prison by privileging whites as the only prisoners who could act as "head building tender," a prisoner whose comprehensive power over fellow prisoners super-seded correctional officers and who answered only to the prison's warden, assistant warden, or major. It was this hidden division of labor connoting racial, gender, and sexual power that prisoners sought to expose over two decades of prisoner litigation and political organizing.

In this work, I analyze both how the Texas prison system managed to maintain its high external reputation for so long in the face of the internal real-ity and how that reputation collapsed when prisoners—inspired by the civil rights, Black Power, and Chicano movements—revolted. The prisoners' civil rights rebellion forged an alliance with the National Association for the Ad-vancement of Colored People (NAACP) and contested the constitutionality of Texas prisons in federal court, while behind bars an interracial prisoner coalition worked in tandem with external political allies as part of a shared public campaign to reveal the deplorable conditions of southern prisons and their prisoners as "slaves of the state." *We Are Not Slaves* reexamines the *Ruiz* case, then, as a process of prisoner consciousness, individual transformation, group organization, documentation, testimonial, and collective resistance. It repositions the *Ruiz* case through the historical lenses of prison rape, pris-oner organizing, rights, and labor. As such, it is the first history of prisoner organizing in the South around prisoner litigation. As a southwestern state, the Texas prison system crafted disciplinary traditions that drew directly from Texas's history as both a slave state and a state that heavily policed and criminalized Mexicans and Mexican Americans within the borderlands be-tween the United States and Mexico. Yet while prisoner organizing in Texas provides the driving narrative because it had one of the most comprehensive and controversial civil rights trials, the broader context of this southern pris-oners' rights struggle required some historical comparison with several foun-dational court cases and prisoner uprisings in other states. The cases that connected most often to the Texas narrative include Arkansas, Alabama, Louisiana, Tennessee, and Mississippi. But as a social movement history of prison litigation, the intricate prisoners' rights movement in Texas remains the book's driving narrative.

In the southern context, collective prisoner organizing grew out of legal work and a major shift in U.S. law that allowed prisoners to be included in the ongoing civil rights efforts of the mid-1960s. Prior to World War II, the courts, at both the state and federal level, maintained a "hands off" doctrine of nonintervention regarding the conditions of state captivity. But beginning in the 1960s, prisoner activists turned to section 1983 of the 1871 Civil Rights Act, which allowed citizens to sue the states in federal court for violations of their constitutional rights. Prisoners were never outside of events that occurred in the "free world" beyond prison walls, and they watched carefully the shift toward rights-based decisions by the U.S. Supreme Court under Chief Justice Earl Warren.[14] As the "rights revolution" in the courts progressed, the gulf between prisoners' rights and legal redress began to recede. In *Robinson v. California* (1962), the court ruled that state governments, as well as the federal government, were susceptible to the Eighth Amendment's prohibition against cruel and unusual punishment.[15] The court's decision to make states accountable to the Eighth Amendment opened the door for prisoners to seek legal redress for the abuses they experienced in state prisons. Extending civil rights to prisoners became a national issue in 1964 when the Supreme Court ruled that a Muslim prisoner in Illinois named Thomas X Cooper could not be barred from having access to the Koran. Since the 1940s, the Nation of Islam had been actively organizing Black prisoners around religious, racial, and personal transformation—the story of Malcolm X's conversion to Islam in a Massachusetts penitentiary during the early 1950s was shared by many imprisoned African American men across the nation.[16] The Illinois case over religious freedom for prisoners, *Cooper v. Pate*, found that prisoners could challenge the practices of prison officials in federal court.[17] The 1964 *Cooper* decision ignited a nationwide civil rights movement for prisoners, doing for prisoner rights what *Brown vs. Board of Education* had done ten years earlier for education and civil rights. Within a decade, the Supreme Court's Justice Byron White had struck down the legal silence imposed on prisoners when he declared in the 1974 prisoners' rights case *Wolff v. McDonnell* that "there is no iron curtain drawn between the Constitution and the prisons of this country."[18] In the aftermath of *Cooper v. Pate*, the number of prisoners' rights suits dramatically increased, from 218 in 1966 to almost 18,477 in 1984. Between 1970 and 1996 the number of prisoner civil rights lawsuits leaped an astonishing 400 percent.[19]

Importantly, sweeping federal court intervention yielded some monumental court victories against southern state prison systems. From 1965 to 1995, federal courts found eight of the eleven states of the U.S. South as having unconstitutional prisons, including six "totality of conditions" cases in Alabama, Arkansas, Mississippi, South Carolina, Tennessee, and Texas, while Georgia and Louisiana had comprehensive orders against their flagship maximum-security prisons.[20] Florida and North Carolina also faced sweeping court orders on overcrowding and the unconstitutionality of the southern prison dormitory and housing barracks at roadwork camps.[21] Only four of the thirty-nine states outside of the South, however, have been subject to a similar "totality of conditions" intervention from the federal courts—Alaska, Delaware, New Mexico, and Rhode Island. While nonsouthern prisons also suffered from prison abuse and severe brutality, the penetrating gaze of the federal courts was firmly fixed on the southern prison system because prisoners and their civil rights attorneys were able to successfully cast southern prisons as anachronistic examples of southern brutality that denied civil and constitutional rights.

This prison-made civil rights rebellion, while mounting a successful legal challenge, was countered by a new prison regime—one that utilized paramilitary practices, promoted privatized prisons, endorsed massive prison building programs, and embraced twenty-three-hour cell isolation—which established what I call a "Sunbelt" militarized carceral state approach that became exemplary of national prison trends.[22] Since the *Ruiz* decision, Texas grew its prison population more than any other state in the nation. During the 1990s, Texas led the nation with an average annual growth rate of 11.8 percent, an astounding annual increase that was almost twice the average annual growth rate for other states' prisons (6.1 percent).[23] In the 2000s, the incarceration rate in Texas has consistently placed the state in the top ten ranking, and during the early 2000s Texas had the nation's highest rate of incarceration, at 730 prisoners per 100,000 residents. Texas is also at the forefront of new developments in prison management since the 1980s, as Texas leads the nation in its number of privatized prisons, the number of people in super-maximum twenty-three-hour-a-day lockdown cells, prison construction, and state sanctioned executions. In 2016, Texas had 5,832 people in full cell isolation for twenty-three hours a day, seven days a week, making the state second only to Florida in the total number of people held in such restrictive cages. Of the 2,976 people throughout the nation in total cell isolation for more than six years, the state of Texas alone had more than half of that desperate prison population, incarcerating 1,587 people for six years or longer in total restricted cell isolation.[24]

Robert Perkinson's sweeping survey of Texas prison history from 1843 to the governorship of George W. Bush in the 1990s saw this growth through a southernization narrative that grounded the origins of mass incarceration in the fields of the Texas prison farm, where Perkinson hoped to "redirect the spotlight from the North, the birthplace of rehabilitative penology, to the South, the fountainhead of subjugationist discipline."[25] What Perkinson offered historians was a masterful reorientation of prison history that refuted the emphasis on the Foucauldian discourse analysis of the northern rehabilitative ideal to take up the raw brutality of southern prison practices. But when viewed from a more narrow base of specific labor and control systems having to change due to prisoner litigation, the time-specific narrative of the *Ruiz* case demonstrates that these startling growth numbers that constitute a "prison empire" in fact reflect a prison system torn from its southern roots to hastily construct atop its ashes the new militarized prison.

This book departs from recent studies of Texas prisons through its close examination of three critical understudied aspects of the southern postwar prison and the *Ruiz* case. First, prison labor in southern prisons during the postwar period was more than work; it was a regime of carceral discipline and power that ordered prison society, sexuality, and racial hierarchy. As such, this book considers the intersectional nature of prison labor as a cite of power that intersected with spatial control, gender identity, sexuality and sexual violence, and race and racial privileges. Even within the space of prison, where most might think that incarceration leveled every prisoner equally disempowered, there was a pronounced system of empowered privilege and disempowered dehumanization. By narrowing the temporal focus, this book aims to reveal how time-specific changes in the Texas carceral state shaped both how the prison wielded discipline and power, and the means by which prisoners confronted the time-specific labor regime.

Second, scholars of the *Ruiz* case have presented its origins as emanating from federal power and the judiciary system, where the presiding judge, William Wayne Justice, has been characterized as the one who initiated and orchestrated *Ruiz*. The literature on litigated Texas prison reform in the postwar period has approached the subject from the perspective of the prison administration, civil rights attorneys, and the federal court, but none of them tell the story of prison reform from the perspective of a social movement and in the context of interracial social and political organizing.[26] Perhaps the most important study in this field is the seminal *Judicial Policy Making and the Modern State: How the Courts Reformed America's Prisons*, by Malcolm M. Feeley and Edward L. Rubin. While a monumental work of policy history, their near sole focus on the federal court and the decisions of federal judges obscured the work of the prisoners themselves. Indeed, Feely and Rubin offered the dismissive conclusion that the "prisoner petitions were probably no more of an influence on the pattern of decisions than the Supreme Court or Congress. It was the federal courts themselves that not only initiated the prison reform movement but established its specific contours."[27] While David Ruiz is brilliantly humanized in the historian Robert Perkinson's *Texas Tough: The Rise of America's Prison Empire*, the story of how the case came to trial is told mostly through the lens of the courtroom drama, where Perkinson offers a similar conclusion to Feeley and Rubin that it was Judge Justice who, "to no small extent . . . had created [*Ruiz*]. . . . It was Justice who set this 'little case' in motion."[28]

Scholars of public policy, meanwhile, have cast litigation over prison conditions as a "paradox" because the unintended consequence of intervention by federal judges and liberal civil rights attorneys was to inadvertently contribute to the onset of mass incarceration by increasing the prison system's

capacity to incarcerate more people. According to the public policy narrative, the eventual acceptance of federal court orders against state prison systems allowed state leaders to claim that they removed the prison system's
most vicious and brutal features, that the state now recognized the rights of
prisoners, and that its prisons were humane. A prison system that claimed it
was free of brutality became less susceptible to alarmist charges against its
ever expansive growth. As Margo Schlanger has provocatively suggested, "by
promoting the comforting idea of the 'lawful prison,' the litigation movement
may have smoothed the way for even harsher sentences and criminal policies."[29] Similarly, in her policy study of Florida's prison litigation case concerning overcrowding, *Gideon v. Wainwright*, Heather Schoenfeld argued
that "the paradox of prison conditions litigation in Florida, therefore, is that
reform litigation on behalf of state prisoners aimed at reducing incarceration
ultimately led to a massive increase in prison capacity."[30] Schoenfeld termed
this interpretation of federal judicial intervention as a matter of unwittingly
expanding "carceral capacity," where court orders inadvertently created "new
bureaucratic structures, new frontline and administrative positions, new staff
training, and new protocols across the institutions of the criminal justice system" that directly contributed to mass incarceration.[31] While the *Ruiz* case
shared some similarities with the Florida narrative, what sets them apart is
the degree to which Texas followed the path of what I call *carceral massive
resistance*, where southern Democrats actively resisted federal court orders
and where new southern Republicans consciously thwarted judicial intentions to reduce prison populations in favor of retrenched political designs
that knowingly and quite openly constructed mass incarceration within the
Reaganesque "law and order" and "get tough" political context. By placing
prisoner litigation under the lens of social movements and prisoner-based civil
rights rather than the top-down lens of public policy and political elites, this
book thus reconsiders the degree to which the path to mass incarceration was
politically uncontested.

Critics of the *Ruiz* decision, meanwhile, have frequently blamed the intervention of the federal court on the rise of prison violence and gang organization in Texas. The *Ruiz* case, they argue, created a social breakdown within
prison society, diminished the guards' subculture, and created such agitation
among prisoners that many felt entitled to confront their keepers through violence, riot, and misrule.[32] Sociologists have appraised the building tender
system as initially a benevolent system of elite prisoner "mediators" and "managers" until it became a "co-option of the kept" and "out of control" when the
prison system grew too large in the mid- to late 1970s.[33] But prisoners had been
complaining about the building tenders and documenting abuses throughout the postwar period, particularly during the mid-1960s, before the prison

system experienced the massive prison expansion of the post-1977 period. Little attention is paid to the prisoners themselves and their claim that a divided prison labor regime encouraged sexual violence and physical abuse. This absence mutes the voice of the prisoners and their claims against the prison labor regime, while it also leaves prisoners' rights suits vulnerable to conservative critics who castigate federal-court-ordered intervention as an unwanted and disastrous intrusion into state management.[34] *We Are Not Slaves* reconsiders such court-bound approaches by returning the focus to the prisoners themselves and by chronicling the prisoners' rights movement through the lens of prisoner-initiated civil rights complaints, social protest, and political organizing. As Risa Goluboff reminds us in her work *The Lost Promise of Civil Rights*, "Legal change does not begin with the doctrines courts create or even the rhetorical strategies lawyers employ. It begins with the injuries individuals experience. When those individuals complain to lawyers, they invoke the machinery of the law on their behalf."[35] By placing the prisoners' rights movement squarely in the labor organizing and civil rights mobilizing traditions, *We Are Not Slaves* reconceptualizes what constitutes civil rights and to whom it applies. Historians have long been drawn to studies of citizenship to discern how different groups' inclusion and exclusion from citizenship shape race, ethnicity, gender, and sexuality.[36] To those categories, this study adds criminality and the demand from prisoners that prison cannot deny citizenship, constitutionality, and civil rights.

Prisoner documentation, litigation, and legal testimony was not just a legal product; rather, it fostered a transformative and political process that evolved through cumulative phases of individual consciousness, truth telling, solidarity, and collective resistance. Buried underneath the prison's power to effect the social death and dehumanization of people, African American and Mexican American prisoners had to embrace a transformative evolution that the historian Robyn Spencer has called "mind change" and what the Chicana/o scholar Louis G. Mendoza has named a "deliberate process of *conscientización*, a feature that undermines the framework of pathology that stamps the popular representation of prisoners."[37] In Texas, prisoners housed in a racially segregated and antagonistic labor regime underwent personal conscientización and mind change to then collectively construct an interracial alliance to invoke the machinery of the law on their own behalf as the process of legal documentation became what I call public rituals and testimonies of resistance. This book draws upon Mario T. García's conceptualization of oral histories as *testimonios*, which are "collective in nature because they address collective struggles."[38] To that definition, this book adds the interracial and prison-made legal testimonies of resistance as "the politics of truth" that revealed the stark brutality that made the southern prison function.[39] As Mendoza has noted, testimonios have the power "to render the 'often invisible' abuses of power visible as it seeks to realize a politics of solidarity."[40] Prisoners and their testimonies, whether in the courtroom or through oral histories, are at the center of this book's narrative. Revealing prisoner testimonies repositions the prisoners' rights movement firmly within the concurrent and interconnected movements for civil rights, Black Power, and the Chicano movement. Mumia Abu Jamal has called this process of "jail house" legal work as "law learned in the bowels of the slave ship, in the hidden, dank dungeons of America—the Prisonhouse of Nations. It is law learned in a stew of bitterness, under the constant threat of violence, in places where millions of people live, but millions of others wish to ignore or forget."[41]

The third difference that marks the narrative and analytical framework of this book as different is to reframe the Texas prison narrative around *Ruiz*, which fundamentally dismantled the southern model. In the post-*Ruiz* prison system, as my book will demonstrate, prisoners no longer toiled in fields of agricultural labor for ten-hour days; nor did they live under the threat of state-orchestrated racial and sexual violence perpetrated by the prisoner trusties' attempt to instill order and control. Instead, the prison system increasingly turned away from agricultural labor and instead gave prisoners makeshift garden work that barely resembled the field labor that created the state's agribusiness empire of the 1950s, 1960s, and 1970s. Since the *Ruiz* decision of 1980, the prison administration has increasingly emphasized industrial labor, housed prisoners in privatized prisons, and warehoused them in maximum security prison wings (called "supermax" in other states), where entire administrative segregation wings cage people twenty-three hours a day in isolated cell lockdown. Under the auspices of the 1977 *Lamar v. Coffield* consent decree, Texas prisons were no longer racially segregated, and its guard force was no longer exclusively white, largely rural, and entirely male.[42] Rather than rely on the southern trusty system to police and brutalize prisoners, the new militarized prison makes war on the prisoner insurgent through gang intelligence units, SWAT-like paramilitary units to make unannounced cell shakedowns, and gang injunction laws that sentence prisoners to "prisons within prisons" in administrative segregation's total cell isolation. In short, nearly all the aspects that made the Texas prison system uniquely southern were dismantled after 1985. The prison system that Texas fashioned after the *Ruiz* case ended the "control penology" labor model and what emerged from its ashes was neither the rehabilitative penitentiary of the Northeast nor the plantation prison model of the mid-twentieth-century U.S. South. Instead, I will argue, Texas was at the forefront of a new prison Sunbelt landscape of militarized prisons that eclipsed the scale of the southern plantation prison labor model of the past to initiate a massive prison building program that advanced Texas as the nation's largest carceral state in the era of mass incarceration.

To take readers behind prison walls and reveal the rapacity of prison economies, this book relies on prisoner testimonies, letters, affidavits, depositions, and the oral histories of prisoners who desperately wanted to expose the worst horrors of the prison economy to public view. The sixty oral histories that I conducted allowed me to visit the Texas prison system, spend time within its walls, and interview the prisoners who created within the prison a social and political upheaval. In the course of these interviews, some prisoners related the most intimate and traumatic details of their rape at the hands of trusty prisoners. These were not easy stories for them to recount, but they felt it necessary to renounce the violence done to them by naming the system that allowed it to happen. In addition to my own oral histories and letters with prisoners, I have collected forty additional oral histories from a variety of archival and privately held collections. Although oral histories are sometimes criticized as being susceptible to the whims of memory and the dangers of romanticization, they remain important sources to document those on the fringe of society whose stories and voices are often overlooked by traditional archival documentation.[43] The oral histories of prisoners create an alternative testimonial against the prison's sole stake on what constitutes "truth," where the carceral power charts a selective narrative that all too often dismisses and silences prisoner complaint. Importantly, the *Ruiz* case generated over one hundred prisoner testimonies that corroborated many of my oral histories. Finally, in an effort to document prison abuse, the prisoners themselves left a paper trail of letters, affidavits, and depositions that they sent to prison activists and state politicians. The papers of governors and state politicians have archived and preserved many of these letters. In other cases, my work was informed by private sources and the families of prisoners who shared private letters, writings, poetry, and the unpublished memoir of David Ruíz, whose lawsuit challenged the Texas prison system. By reading legal and state documentation through the lens of prisoner resistance, this book combines traditional sources with what Kelly Lytle Hernández has called "the rebel archive," where the oral histories and private papers of prisoners reveal how the southern prison attempted to hide how carceral power operated.[44]

––––––––

In prisons, names carry great significance. Prisons strip prisoners of their identity and make them legible to the state only through inmate number, while prisoners often know one another through prison nicknames or the tattoos inscribed on their skin that make their experiences and affiliations known to others. As part of the mid-twentieth-century effort to profession-alize southern prisons, Texas adopted the best criminal justice practice to re-name itself from the Texas Prison System (TPS) to the Texas Department of Corrections (TDC). TDC then named its individual prisons with either the bucolic southern nomenclature of "farms" or called them "units" to convey the criminal justice principle that prisoner rehabilitation was always scien-tifically observed, measured, and calculated. No such measurement existed on southern prisons, most especially in Texas, so this book uses none of those false euphemisms. Instead, I name the southern labor system that existed in Texas during the post–World War II period as a perfected "prison plantation." As this book will show, the mid-twentieth-century southern prison planta-tion worked prisoners as coerced field labor in a system that replicated the work of antebellum slavery, while it prioritized white prisoner power to con-struct an internal prison economy as slave market. The external political economy of high-yield productive prison labor was thus intrinsically tied to the prison's internal economy in a mutually reinforced system that comprised the southern prison plantation.

As a narrative of prisoner resistance and litigation as civil rights, this book uses the terminology of *prisoner* over *inmate* because the latter term renders people within prison as a numerical category that lacks humanization. Simi-larly, *convict*, as a term, is used sparingly and most often in reference to the convict guards. Within Texas prisons, the use of racial epithets was designed to uphold racial hierarchies and remind prisoners of their subservient condi-tion. When offering quotes drawn from oral histories and legal testimonies, I do not refrain from showcasing the rough and sometimes crude language of the prison because racial epithets established relations of power and au-thority. Guards and prison authorities used racial language to belittle pris-oners, while prisoners used similar language when they attempted to confront the power of the prison. Texas prisoners came from a diverse border state, and they maintained cultural, ethnic, and racial heritages that went beyond the prison system's simple classification system of "white," "Black," and "Mex-ican." In my own terminology, I employ the terms *African American* and *Black* interchangeably to discuss prisoners of color. As a racially segregated prison system, Texas classified all Latina/os simply as "Mexican" or "Mexi-can American," and although there were Latina/o prisoners within that overly broad categorization, most of the prisoner activist narratives come from Mex-ican Americans, and they are named here as such. Once prisoners became politicized within a cultural nationalist framework in the late 1960s, the term *Chicano* is also used. Anglo prisoners are referred to simply by using the term *white*, although whiteness and white privilege could also be lost within the context of a southern hierarchial prison labor regime. In my explication of internal prison society and culture, I depict some graphic instances of rape and sexual violence. Although these stories may sometimes make for difficult reading, I believe that only direct appraisals of prison society can fully convey the power of the prison and how prisoners experienced the reality of prison rape as a matter of state acquiescence, power, and control.

Over the course of nearly three decades, prisoners turned to law as a means to document the abuses of the southern prison plantation that the administration wholeheartedly denied. Texas prisoners wrote and filled legal affidavits, depositions, and testimonials to document how often they were severely beaten, brutally tortured, inhumanely starved, punitively isolated, sleep deprived for weeks at a time, and viciously raped. The culmination of these separate acts of state violence are what I term "carceral violence," as their cumulative power of daily human degradation for years on end is characteristic of how prisons deny prisoners not only civil rights and constitutional protections but their humanity. The prisoners' efforts to document carceral violence was more than a legal invocation of civil rights and the U.S. Constitution; it represented a collective politicizing and organizing process that I name "testimonials of resistance."

The struggle over the southern prison modernization narrative reveals what I call the *carceral dialectic*, where prisoner rebellion waged a campaign to make the southern prison's coercive labor regime legible to the wider public. James Scott has defined *legibility* as a state-initiated "condition of manipulation" that renders people as "units that are visible" to the state and thus clearly "identified, observed, recorded, counted, aggregated, and monitored."[45] In his analysis of political metaphor among California's Black prisoner radicals, Dan Berger has argued that prisoners engaged in what he calls "a strategy of visibility."[46] My work draws on these two concepts to show that southern prisoners engaged in a carceral dialectic where they countered the state's modernization narrative by flipping state legibility on its head. *We Are Not Slaves* reveals the centrality of prison labor as the means through which the southern prison secured coerced field labor and through which the division of that labor structured racial inequality, enforced corporal punishment, and bought and sold prisoner bodies to be raped and dehumanized. Because labor was constitutive of the southern prison's coercive power, labor was also the focal point of southern prisoner resistance. Southern prisoners therefore unmasked the abusive labor arrangements behind the southern modernization narrative and made it legible to the courts and the wider public as coerced slavery within a prison plantation.

Until recently, historical and sociological scholarship had been dismissive and critical of prisoners' rights movements. In his assessment of California's prisoner movement and its alliance with the radical Left during the late 1960s, the historian Eric Cummins summarily dismissed it as a "naïve casting of prisoners as society's potential leaders" and as "one of the fatal mistakes leading to the demise of radical politics" in the world outside of prison.[47] Sociological studies of prisoner uprisings, meanwhile, tended to cast the rising tide of racial unrest and demands for prisoners' civil rights as something that endangered the tranquility of an otherwise ordered and authoritarian prison community. In his study of the Illinois Stateville Penitentiary during the postwar period, the sociologist James Jacobs offered the provocative conclusion that prisoners yearned for authoritarian practices. In his assessment of the shift from authoritarian prisons to the "rehabilitative ideal," Jacobs argued that the rising tide of racial unrest and demands for civil rights caused social unrest in prison societies. In his telling, prisoners felt more "secure" under the authoritarian regimes of the 1940s than they had under the "liberal" prison of the postwar period. By viewing prisoner anxiety over "security" as the principal cause of the Stateville riot, Jacobs turned social control theory on its head and argued that rehabilitative reform led to riot and disorder.[48] His work contributed to sociological explanations for prison violence and misrule that emphasized internal economies as central to good order, discipline, and control.[49]

However, the past decade of prisoner and Black Lives Matter protest has occurred within the context of recent historical scholarship that has begun to reassess the prisoner organizing of the 1960s through the 1980s. Building on previous analyses that offered intellectual histories of the cultural production of prison radicalism, Dan Berger's *Captive Nation: Black Prison Organizing in the Civil Rights Era* presented a reinterpretation of the role of George Jackson and the Soledad Brothers in the history of prison organizing.[50] Berger offered a trenchant study of political metaphor to "connect the prison to other sites of black activism, whether the public housing project, the struggle against police brutality, or the anticolonial revolutions around the world."[51] Berger's reinterpretation of George Jackson as an "American Frantz Fanon" demonstrated how his death at the hands of California prison authorities in the summer of 1971 elevated Jackson as a cause célèbre by New Left activists outside prisons and a continuing source of political mobilization as a palimpsest among African American prisoners who looked to him as a martyr for the cause of Black liberation.[52]

Heather Ann Thompson's monumental study of the 1971 Attica uprising, *Blood in the Water: The Attica Prison Uprising of 1971 and Its Legacy,* navigated the jutting shoals of violence that punctuate Attica's narrative by making the case that carceral systems depend on violence and that state prevarication allowed such violent systems to continue unabated. In addition to offering a gripping narrative that repositioned Attica as a politically organized uprising, what Thompson delivered was a stark reminder that the carceral state depends on false narratives and prevarications for its reproduction. After Governor Rockefeller ordered the bloody retaking of Attica, the state succeeded in preventing the public from learning that nearly all casualties were caused by state forces storming the prison, not by the prisoners. Indeed, the state would undertake a conspiracy to blame the deaths on the prisoners so as to paint them as butchers and discredit their political demands. By chronicling the three-decades-long prisoners' civil suit against the state, Thompson revealed the effort to seek justice through historical truth. Despite these important accounts of prisoner radicalism, most accounts have concluded that state repression and the encroachment of mass incarceration effectively ended late-1960s and early-1970s prisoner organizing. In her assessment of Attica's legacy, Thompson concluded that the state assault and its aftermath had a "Janus-like" effect where prisoners looked to Attica's memory as a source of inspirational resistance and where Attica simultaneously created "a historically unprecedented backlash against all efforts to humanize prison conditions in America."[53]

But rather than serve as the denouement of the prisoners' rights movement and herald the beginning of post-1960s declension narratives, the tragedies at the Attica and Soledad prisons served instead to inspire two decades of struggle by prisoners across the nation, to demand that institutions of criminal justice also act as spaces of social justice. While most studies of prison radicalism have typically looked either to California or New York as the intellectual and pioneering spark for prison rebellion, *We Are Not Slaves* shifts the terrain from the West Coast and urban Northeast to the more rural U.S. South and Southwest. This 1970s and 1980s struggle over prisoners' rights erupted in both the courtroom and in the prison courtyard through peaceful work strikes, civil rights protests, and efforts to turn prison hostage situations into a call for media visibility to highlight the abusive conditions of mass incarceration. During the late 1970s and early 1980s, prisons experienced unprecedented levels of overcrowding due to the punitive turn in sentencing and drug laws. Overcrowding worsened prison conditions, exacerbated racial tensions, and accelerated state-orchestrated sexual and physical violence. Indeed, prisoners of the 1970s and 1980s understood the dangers of mass incarceration before many on the outside realized it. To ameliorate these worsening conditions, the southern prisoners' rights movement developed a two-pronged strategy that used mass protest tactics alongside civil rights cases and class action lawsuits to demand public visibility. They asked the courts to reconsider how the state punished those who committed a crime while also reminding the public of the prisoners' humanity and their constitutional rights. In all these cases, prisoners sought to be visible, both seen and heard, in a public campaign to elevate their voice in a crucial national debate over the growing power of the United States' rising carceral state. In his analysis of political metaphor among radical California prisoners, Berger concluded that prisoner organizing "was less a claim to expand rights than it was a critique of a rights-based framework."[54] But the southern prisoner critique of the state was a directed regional criticism of the southern state's particular apparatus as a prison plantation. *We Are Not Slaves* presents the southern prisoners' voices to consider how their legal documentation against the Texas carceral state was a political practice that took rights-based claims seriously. Southern prisoners relied on the courts to do more than mock the state; they appealed to federalism itself by making the southern prison carceral state legible to federal courts.

Integral to the southern prisoners' rights campaigns was a language of resistance that claimed that southern prisons, in particular, were explicit examples of twentieth-century slavery. Texas prisoners resisted their field work as slave labor and the state-orchestrated sex trade as a slave market that bought and sold prisoner bodies and cell servitude. As scholars of prisoner resistance have documented, the rhetorical strategy of equating prisons with slavery was shared among prisoner resistance groups nationwide. During the Attica uprising, New York prisoners employed the prisons-as-slavery discourse when their demands for releasing hostages included "Apply the New York State minimum wage law to all State Institutions. STOP SLAVE LABOR." Moreover, Berger's study of George Jackson and the San Quentin Six in California argued that prisoners employed the political language of "slavery as confinement" as "a metaphor that symbolized the endurance and enormity of white supremacy."[55] Southern prisoners drew on such strategies of resistance and applied them against the southern plantation prison. But while southern prisoners shared a national language of resistance, the lived experience of regional difference structured by historical change created important variation in regional and state prison practices that also structured how prisoners resisted and which, quite importantly, made southern prisons particularly vulnerable to the slavery-as-prison discourse.

We Are Not Slaves draws on the historiography of slavery to offer the important lens of change over time, region, and space as an intervention to carceral studies. From popular documentaries, like the recently released *13th*, to scholarly narratives, there has been a tendency to stress uniformity as a means to achieve collective resistance. While this effort is entirely laudatory for contemporary resistance projects, it runs the risk of flattening historical difference, region, and space by making the carceral state into a singular expression of racial oppression that operates the same way in all places and at all times. Framed in this way, resistance against the carceral state is similarly flattened, and regional struggles against particular kinds of state repression are collapsed. In his work *Slaves of the State*, Dennis Childs offers a powerful critique of the contemporary prison system as neoslavery that is bound to a timeless "ritualized, predicament of living death wrought through the mutually constitutive state-terror modalities of temporal dislocation, structural dehumanization, and collectivized natal alienation." In Childs's estimation, the South casts a great shadow over the dual processes of slavery and incarceration that are intimately linked across time in such a way that "the civil death of penal entombment performs the horrifying repetition of the social death of chattel enslavement."[56] Childs proposes that carceral studies should adopt a "concentric/accumulative view of history rather than a linear/sequential one," which considers "the time-bending power of the racialized carceral" as "an experientially informed conception of the dynamic interfacing of penal time, racialized carceral space, and terrorized Black unfree experience that discerns grim congruence."[57] In a similar vein, Berger's metaphorical use of "slavery of confinement" as a term of prisoner resistance moved away from a southerncentric or labor-oriented approach to offer the conclusion that "dissident prisoners maintained that slavery was a permanent feature of black life, less as a regime of labor than as a system of injustice. . . . These prisoners were not concerned about forced labor."[58]

While there is a danger in allowing histories of southern prison violence to become "blinded by a Barbaric South," as Heather Thompson eloquently put it, and in following what Khalil Muhammad called a liberal-progressive and bourgeois "modernizing narrative" that casts criminal justice as rehabilitative science in the North and racial criminalization in the South, what *We Are Not Slaves* offers is a study of how regional difference in time and space shaped a variety of different carceral states and resistance against it.[59] As historians of the carceral state are often steeped in the historiography of slavery, perhaps it might be valuable to consider Ira Berlin's seminal essay "Time, Space, and the Evolution of Afro-American Society on British Mainland North America." In Berlin's estimation, "scholars of all persuasions have held time constant and ignored the influence of place" in slave scholarship. Berlin advanced the argument that African American history "cannot be understood merely as a function of the dynamics of slavery or the possibilities of liberty, but must be viewed within the specific social and cultural traditions . . . that varied from time to time and from place to place."[60] By analyzing different forms of slavery and slave labor at particular times and places, Berlin reminded scholars of slavery that "slavery was first and foremost an institution of coerced labor" and "because work was both the source of the slaves' oppression and a seed of liberation, it became the terrain upon which slaves and masters battled for the wealth that the enslaved produced."[61] But the collapse of regional difference and historical time has denied prison labor as a crucial organizing feature of incarceration. In the U.S. South, however, the mid-twentieth-century prison plantation depended on coerced work that structured its control regime around the division of that labor.

As a study of urban Chicanos and African Americans incarcerated on rural prison plantations, *We Are Not Slaves* demonstrates that the "criminalization of urban space," as Heather Thompson named mass incarceration's contribution to the urban crisis, applies equally as well to Chicano/a and Black populations in southwestern cities.[62] Indeed, geographic dislocation was especially integral to the politicization of urban prisoners of color who were forced to labor on rural prison plantations. When urban youths found themselves forced to work on these rural prison plantations, they imagined their coerced geographic dislocation as analogous to the ways in which slavery uprooted African communities. In the U.S. South and Southwest, the coerced dislocation of urban minorities also meant that rural prisons received a growing number of people who had witnessed and were shaped by the urban social protest movements of the late 1960s and 1970s.

Most histories of prisoner radicalism have located the animus for resistance among Black prisoners inspired and connected to the Black Power movement. *We Are Not Slaves* also considers prisoner organizing within the framework of civil rights activism and Black Power critique, but one of its critical contributions is to reposition Mexican American prisoners within a clear Chicana/o movement framework.[63] As recent work on urban politicization during the 1970s has shown, southwestern cities erupted in this era with the politics of social justice stemming from a vibrant Chicano movement.[64] In urban Southwest and Midwest neighborhoods, particularly Chicago, Los Angeles, Denver, Albuquerque, Dallas, and San Antonio, a growing Chicano urban movement drew on the experiences of farmworkers during Cesar Chavez's California and Texas farmworkers strikes of 1965–66.[65] Recent scholarship, particularly newly published studies by David Montejano, Arnoldo de León, and Guadalupe San Miguel, has demonstrated that urban youths and college students joined together with gang members, known colloquially as *loco vatos* and *pachucos* (flashy toughs), to broaden the farmworkers' La Causa, or "the cause," to include urban concerns centered on citywide racial segregation, urban poverty, police brutality, and demands for local city control and political power.[66] Drawing on the Chicano movement's conceptualizations of La Raza Unida (the united people), *carnalismo* (masculine brotherhood), and the revitalization of Aztlán (a cultural and historical connection to ancestral pre-Columbian Mexican lands stretching from Mexico to the U.S. Southwest), these urban Chicanos fostered a political and cultural movement that connected the economic demands of striking rural farmworkers to the political and cultural second-class status of urban dwellers.[67] Similarly, the prisoners' rights movement in the U.S. Southwest made connections to la causa and fashioned an analogous brand of carnalismo between urban prisoners of color laboring in rural prison fields of hard agricultural labor. The geographic displacement of urban Chicanos from Southwest cities to the Cotton Belt of Texas prisons demonstrates that, while the system itself may have been southern, many of its prisoners, particularly Chicanos, straddled a southwestern and borderland world where the state struggled to make Chicanos legible and disciplined within a black-white Jim Crow South framework.[68] The borderland policing practices that were dependent on state violence and criminalization thus followed Mexican Americans into Texas's southern prison arrangement, as their geographic dislocation occurred within a settler colonial political project that Kelly Lytle Hernández has called "elimination in the service of establishing, defending, and reproducing a settler society."[69]

By offering an analysis of the ways in which Mexican Americans pioneered the prisoners' rights movement in Texas, this book contributes to new scholarship on the Chicano movement of the 1960s and 1970s, which explores the degree to which this movement made possible opportunities for interracial organization, particularly between Mexican Americans and African Americans.[70] Recent studies by such scholars as George Mariscal, Max Krochmal, and Laura Pulido have moved the study of the Chicano movement beyond what Mariscal has called a "narrow nationalistic straightjacket," toward a broader understanding of El Movimiento as both an era of "cultural nationalism" and an opportunity for coalition building and interracial solidarity.[71] On the streets outside of prison, the late 1960s produced a Black-brown coalition that simultaneously demonstrated genuine opportunities for interracial cooperation as well as moments of conflict.[72] Mexican Americans living in the Texas southwest and along the borderlands experienced different forms of state and racial oppression than African Americans, particularly true of the Mexican American encounter with the repressive and violent practices of Texas Rangers and the U.S. Border Patrol.[73] For the postwar generation that Mario T. García has named the "Mexican American Generation," their pursuit of civil rights depended on a whiteness strategy to achieve full citizenship status.[74] As Brian Behnken, Neal Foley, and Ian F. Lopez have collectively demonstrated, the pursuit of whiteness by Mexican Americans severely limited genuine opportunities for a broad and vibrant interracial coalition with African Americans in their civil rights pursuit to end Jim Crow segregation.[75] Even for the "Chicano Generation" interracial alliances with African American civil rights groups and Black Power organizations were attempted, but they remained fraught with political and personal fissures.[76]

Within prisons, however, the immediate need to fuse Black and brown coalitions was made more urgent by the ways in which incarceration rendered both Black and brown as subjects of carceral violence and as "slaves of the state." With the onset of mass incarceration in the mid-1960s, Chicano prisoners in Texas experienced their incarceration through the lens of shared criminalization against people of color—both brown and Black. But even in the extreme oppression of prison, there were times within the Texas prisoners' rights movement when Chicano cultural nationalism clashed with the aims of African American civil rights and political leaders who were attempting prison reform.[77] While some histories of Mexican American and African American civil rights struggles have seen them through separate lenses, where each group "engaged in their own civil rights battles," the history of a vibrant prisoner alliance in Texas corresponds with the Black-brown coalition in Texas civil rights and electoral politics that Max Krochmel has called "a *process* rather than making totalizing claims about inherent cooperation or mutual discord."[78] As a study of male prisoner organizing, We Are Not Slaves also takes up Lorena Oropeza's discovery of a repositioning of Chicano masculinity during the Vietnam War to reveal the complicated and nuanced portrait of Chicano prisoners who redefined machismo as a sense of carnalismo between prisoners of color who shared the same dehumanization of the prison planation.[79]

The division of prison labor in Texas constructed an internal economy centered on sexual violence and prison rape. We Are Not Slaves therefore situates prison masculinity and sexual violence within recent historiography that has powerfully explored the centrality of rape to systems of racial oppression and the ways in which the state defined homosexuality as outside the benefits of U.S. citizenship and constitutional protections. Historians of sexuality and gender, particularly Regina Kunzel, Sharon Block, Danielle McGuire, Kali Gross, Cheryl Hicks, Estelle Freedman, Sarah Haley, and Talitha LeFlouria, have provided haunting documentation of the ways in which sexual violence was used to construct racial subordination and how women and their communities responded to sexual violence through mobilization.[80] Talitha LeFlouria's study of African American women bound to the convict lease system in Georgia is particularly influential to my book as her compelling work did not shy away from narratives that offered stark and often difficult-to-read instances of white men's rape of Black women prisoners. In her clear-eyed and trenchant assessment of such sexual violence, LeFlouria framed these intimately personal violations of a woman's body alongside the convict lease's ability to deny gender identity and womanhood through what she termed "social rape." Scholars of sexuality and the state, meanwhile, have revealed—through what Margot Canaday has called a "social history of the state"—how the early twentieth-century state policed, surveilled, and ultimately constructed a legal definition of "homosexuality" as outside of the rights and guarantees of full U.S. citizenship.[81]

We Are Not Slaves draws on the historiographies of sexual violence and literature on the postwar state's response to homosexuality to analyze sexual violence in prison as a function of what I term "state-sanctioned prison rape" rather than as a function of prisoner pathology. The buying and selling of Texas prisoners constituted an internal sex trade where hypermasculine predators were given unofficial state sanction to deny young men control over their bodies through vicious rape. The building tender system redefined young men as "property" and as "wives," which served to sever these men from their sense of gender identification, personhood, and reputation. Wielding comprehensive control over their intrinsically linked labor regime, high-ranking prison officials knew that the building tender system that upheld their low-cost prison model also privileged trusties with the ability to "own" another prisoner as a sexual object and a domestic cell servant. Prison rape was thus constitutive of the southern prison plantation and the trauma and horror of such wanton acts of sexual violence eventually became the catalyst for prisoner resistance. As Danielle McGuire concluded in her pathbreaking study *At The Dark End of the Street: Black Women, Rape, and Resistance,* "if we understand the role rape and sexual violence played in African Americans' daily lives during the modern civil rights movement, we have to reinterpret, if not rewrite, the history of the civil rights movement."[82] *We Are Not Slaves* contributes to the scholarship of sexual violence as critical to white supremacy by advancing the argument that we cannot fully assess the carceral state nor the prisoners' rights movement that struggled mightily against mass incarceration until we also come to terms with the centrality of prison rape as a state-orchestrated design that privileged white prisoners with the power to use sexual violence to dehumanize and terrorize prisoners of color and more vulnerable white prisoners that they derisively claimed as "punks" and "wives."

As a study of prison masculinity and sexual violence, this book centers its narrative on male prisoners, but it also considers how women prisoners experienced the southern trusty system and the state's attempt to isolate and target women that the prison classified as the "aggressive female homosexual." As such, the otherwise hidden internal prison economy operated differently in male and female prisons. To reveal the sub-rosa economy that is often obscured within traditional archival documentation, this book is based on over sixty oral histories as well as prisoner testimony, affidavits, depositions, and letters. Because the social structure was so different for the women's prison and its trusty system, the research for this book was conducted mostly on male prisoners. Until the mid-1970s, approximately four hundred to five hundred women prisoners were incarcerated at Goree, the only women's prison in Texas. For women prisoners, the southern trusty system operated on a different power arrangement. Women trusties, for instance, were known as "key girls," because they controlled the keys to the various cells and wings, and the exhibition of their power revolved around different racial, gender, and sexual dynamics. Goree, for instance, was racially integrated, whereas the men's prisons were mostly segregated before 1980. A comparison of the differences between men's and women's prison labor and the powers of the prisoner trusty can be found in chapter 3. As anticarceral feminist scholarship has shown, women have always been critical organizers of prisoner resistance on the outside as well as on the inside.[83] Indeed, there were women jailhouse attorneys, as well as men, and a few women prisoners testified at the *Ruiz* trial. As a politicized prisoner and jailhouse attorney, Martha Quinlan, who has too often been left out of narratives of *Ruiz*, is an important subject of this book. Women outside of the prison, particularly the civil rights attorney Frances Jalet, were integral allies that made the prisoners' legal claims publicly visible. Sometimes, love and relationships blossomed as much as politicization. That was the case in several critical relationships during the prisoners' rights era between male prisoner organizing and women civil rights attorneys.

At nearly the same moment that the southern prisoners' rights movement effectively dismantled the southern prison plantation, the very ground shifted under their feet as the rising tide of mass incarceration erected a new and much larger prison regime defined by militarized policing tactics, gang intelligence units, prison overcrowding, privatization, the super-maximum prison, and the onset of violent prison gangs. Recent historical scholarship has argued that dissident urban gang culture should be understood within the larger Black Power critique of the late-1960s because urban gang formation represents an important organizational stepping stone in the process of urban racial politicization.[84] The gaze of most scholars of gang formation is thus focused on cities outside of the U.S. South and on gang formation within African American and Latina/o communities as a movement toward community control, racial empowerment, and radical politicization.[85] These studies point to the spatial construction of race as constitutive of the twentieth-century U.S. city where racial constructions of blackness and whiteness structured urban segregation in nonsouthern city spaces.[86] An analysis of Texas prisons, however, shifted my research lens from urban cityscapes to rural prisons, where some of the first prison gangs were rural, white supremacists who initiated an assassination campaign aimed against African American prisoners, while Mexican American gangs turned towards insurgent militarized hierarchies as "Soldiers of *Aztlan*." *We Are Not Slaves* is also a book about the moments when the Cold War intersected with the carceral state as the postwar period launched into strategies of containment over prison homosexuality and where defeat in Vietnam brought home military personnel to take on a new war on the prisoner insurgent.[87]

Even when prisoners' rights cases have ended in far-reaching victories, they all still occurred within the shadow of mass incarceration. Because of that daunting political reality, scholars of prisoners' rights cases have depicted even courtroom victories as having decidedly mixed results. Critical legal and policy scholars have offered important studies that collectively demonstrate how few prisoners' rights cases make it to court and how the initial radical intent of some prisoners' rights cases are narrowed as civil rights attorneys and courts reinterpreted civil rights suits through grievance boards and within limited "winnable" margins and strict legal confines.[88] In truth, comprehensive totality of conditions cases like *Ruiz* were rare, especially outside of the South.

Critical policy and political historians, meanwhile, have shown how Cold War and Great Society liberalism had as much to do with the punitive turn as did conservative Republicans steeped in "backlash" politics.[89] The historians Naomi Murakawa and Elizabeth Hinton have offered histories of the 1960s-era liberalism that advanced an earlier periodization of mass incarceration, where the Great Society's antipoverty programs contributed as much to the War on Crime as the concurrent War on Poverty.[90] In her evaluation of the Law Enforcement Assistance Administration (LEAA) and its programs, Hinton demonstrated that liberals pursued "get tough on crime" measures even as the Johnson administration built crime surveillance programs into its antipoverty measures. Both the Kennedy and Johnson administrations, according to Hinton, associated poverty with civil unrest and urban riots with crime. What made the subsequent mass incarceration so inevitable, however, was not simply that Johnson signed the1968 Safe Street and Crime Act but that Johnson's antipoverty programs established federal power in local urban spaces that stripped Black communities of decision making and any significant role they might play in how their communities could address poverty and reduce crime. Hinton thus concluded that liberalism was as much to blame for mass incarceration as the more revanchist conservative law-and-order politics that came after it.

Despite the critical role of federal largesse to the states, the era of mass incarceration has largely been driven by state prisons that incarcerate more than 1.35 million people. Among the states, however, the growth of mass incarceration during the 1970s, 1980s, and 1990s unfolded unevenly, with some states and regions incarcerating much more of its population than others. The incarceration rate in southern states, for example, is approximately 550 people per 100,000 people in the population, while in the Northeast its closer to 300 per 100,000 people. Indeed, southern states make up seven of the ten states with the highest incarceration rates, and the other top three are Sunbelt states.[91] Within specific regions, the scale is also uneven, with some states, like California and Texas, with far higher incarceration rates than others—where the incarceration rate of Texas approached 900 at the height of mass incarceration during the late 1990s.

Even when taking into account the ways in which the federal government contributed to prison growth in the states, the amount of federal largesse was also uneven. During the decade of the 1970s, from 1969 to 1979 at the very height of the LEAA before its 1982 dismantlement, the amount of federal expenditure that went to individual states varied. The states receiving the least amount of funding for prisons, policing, corrections, and rehabilitation were southern states. Alabama, for instance, received only $66 million, Louisiana $70 million, and Mississippi $44 million over the 1970s. By contrast, California, the state that received the most money from the LEAA, received $366 million, while Texas received $216 million, and New York $337 million.[92] The four states receiving the most from the LEAA were California, New York, Texas (the one southern state with heavy expenditure), and Illinois. Despite having the smallest federal grants, southern states have the nation's largest prisons systems.[93]

Some scholars of post-1960s politics have characterized the 1970s "as the decade of nightmares" and a period of declension for civil rights, Black Power, and Chicano activism. In these largely political accounts, the eventual conservatism and state repression of the 1980s is often cast as an inevitable byproduct of the "backlash" against the social unrest of the 1960s.[94] But recent scholarship has demonstrated that the 1970s should be viewed as more than simply a transitional decade wedged between the revolutionary 1960s and the revanchist 1980s. Instead, new studies have stressed historical contingency and the degree to which state repression attempted to silence otherwise vibrant social movements during a decade of continued protest.[95] Political and policy historians have also stressed state repression through explorations of the nearly simultaneous dismantlement of welfare with the concomitant rise of mass incarceration.[96] As mass incarceration worsened prison conditions during the 1970s and 1980s, gang violence accelerated as new groups vied for the drug trade within a rapidly growing prison population that only added to the prison's porousness and drug economy.[97] Prisoner resistance against the southern prison labor regime eventually led to the effective dismantlement of the prison plantation, but it did so at the very moment that mass incarceration delivered the new regime of super-maximum prisons that created what Loïc Wacquant has called "the warehousing of the poor" and what Ruth Wilson Gilmore has called "the incapacitation of incarceration."[98] This book concludes with the moment that the carceral terrain in Texas shifted away from a southern labor regime and toward a Sunbelt militarized prison arrangement.[99]

We Are Not Slaves has a three-part organization. Part I, "A Biography of State Violence and Coerced Labor," begins with an analysis of prison reform through the lens of sexualized containment, where elite northern reformers sought to replace the notorious 1940s prison farm and open dormitory system with the best practices of northern criminal justice and blended with a southern work model to create an efficient, business-oriented agricultural enterprise system. The first chapter considers how such a Cold War–era reform plan stressed the social quarantine of prisoners through the adoption of the northern penitentiary's design of cells and wings as a way to contain the prison rape that occurred all too frequently in open southern dormitories. The second chapter offers an analysis of how the reforms refashioned prison labor as the new tool of disciplinary control and racial hierarchy within a Jim Crow framework. When this new system was fully operational in the 1960s, Texas garnered plaudits as a pioneering, modern, efficient, and business-oriented enterprise. What fueled the modernization narrative, however, was coerced field labor and a regime of labor division that prioritized prisoners through gender, racial, and sexual power. As an analysis of prison labor as carceral power, chapter 2 analyzes how prisoners carved out hidden transcripts of resistance and survival that constructed a dissident culture to trouble the southern modernization narrative. Chapter 3 moves from the field to the prison building to reveal how hierarchial prisoner labor arrangements structured an internal prison economy that bought and sold prisoner bodies and services as cell slavery. Within the southern convict guard framework, prison rape is analyzed as a state-orchestrated design rather than as an individual act of prisoner pathology. Taken together, the first three chapters collectively offer a biography of systematic state violence.

Part II, "Resistance," offers five chapters on the prisoners' evolution from individual consciousness to legal documentation, solidarity, and eventually collective resistance. Chapter 4 offers an intimate narrative of how a single prisoner, Fred Cruz, underwent a process of intellectual transformation, mind change, and concientización to launch the beginning of the prisoners' rights movement in Texas. Importantly, this chapter charts Cruz's transformation within the broader legal turn in the law that allowed prisoners to turn to federal courts as a matter of civil rights. As such, it places the "slaves of the state" narrative in proper legal context, where prisoners were not slaves but entitled to civil rights, even as prisoners experienced de facto conditions of abuse and racial power that rendered their prison labor and lives as akin to slavery. Chapter 5 broadens Cruz's story to include a collective of fellow prisoners, particularly Muslims, within an interracial alliance to make prisoner litigation and legal documentation as politicization and a prison-made civil rights revolution. Chapter 6 offers the simultaneous narrative of African American politicians elected in the wake of the civil rights movement who sought prison reform, alongside radical Black political organizing against the prison plantation. Chapter 7 takes up the state's most famous prison hostage crisis to analyze the prisoner Fred Carrasco as an Aztlán outlaw who drew on nationalist and Chicano ideologies to critique the prison plantation, while also showing how this moment of carceral violence contrasted with and derailed the hopes of African American political reformers. To conclude the section on resistance, chapter 8 analyzes how legal testimonies and documentation became "testimonios of resistance" that crafted an effective narrative that southern prisons and prison labor constituted slavery. This chapter concludes its examination of the two-decade era of resistance by showing how prisoners organized the first ever statewide prison work strike in support of the *Ruiz* courtroom trial and to demonstrate that carceral power was derived from their labor.

Part III, "Collapse of the Prison Plantation and the Carceral Phoenix," considers the nearly simultaneous victory of the southern prisoners' rights movement and the refashioning of mass incarceration, where the new militarized prison arises like a carceral phoenix from the ashes of the prison plantation. Chapter 9 analyzes the *Ruiz* trial itself as drawing from prisoner-initiated narratives, but it situates even the most far-reaching courtroom victory within a political arrangement of carceral massive resistance, where southern Democrats resisted court orders and new southern Republicans consciously reinterpreted the court's intent as part of mass incarceration's broader political project. Chapter 10 reinterpets how the prison responded to the *Ruiz* victory with a new regime of militarization dedicated to waging war on what it considered to be the new class of prisoner insurgent. In the militarized climate, the new development of prison gangs erupted from the challenges of prison-made civil rights and racial struggle to initiate a new era of political assassination within the prison that constituted a carceral version of 1980s outsourcing and violence. Finally, the epilogue reflects on what happened to the prisoners who brought civil suits to Texas and frames the legal and political legacy of *Ruiz* within the current political moment of national prison strikes and the ongoing struggle over mass incarceration.

This history of concomitant resistance and new kinds of oppressive state building demonstrate that carceral regimes are simultaneously intractable yet malleable. Nonetheless, histories of prisoner resistance and the concurrent construction of carceral states must attempt the difficult task of disentangling geographies that create temporal variety and strategies of resistance bound to the physical reality of region and historical difference. *We Are Not Slaves* considers major shifts in the post–World War II period to show how southern prisoners adopted the slavery discourse to make the definitive legal argument that prisoners were not subjects of civil death without rights. From Attica to the Texas work strike of 1978 to the most recent nationwide prison strikes in 2016 and 2018, prisoners have offered a repeated historical refrain that prisoners are not slaves, that incarceration cannot deny people their right to humanity, and that coerced prison labor remains a constitutional fixture that requires a reconsideration of what constitutes a prisoners' civil rights.

PART I

A Biography of Coerced Labor and State Violence

Chapter 1

Fears of Contagion, Strategies of Containment

Pathologizing Homosexuality, Incarcerating Bodies,
and Reshaping the Southern Prison Farm

Alongside the new penitentiaries, built quickly in response to the public's
desire, the old prison remained and housed a great number of the guilty.
These seemed to become more unhealthy and more corrupting at the same
rate as the new ones became healthy and devoted to reform. This double
effect is easily understood: the majority, preoccupied with the idea of
founding a new establishment, had forgotten the already existing ones.
Everybody's attention was turned away from the matter that no longer held
their master's, and supervision ceased. The salutary bonds of discipline
were first stretched and then broken. And beside some prison that stood
as a durable monument to the gentleness and enlightenment of our age,
there was a dungeon recalling the barbarities of the Middle Ages.

—Alexis de Tocqueville, *Democracy in America*

Don't nobody know how much hell a man catch back in this lost valley.
When I was leavin' the Walls a man shook hands with me. He said,
"Well, friend, where you goin', I don't go much." That was Mr. Jesus
Christ shook hands with me. This place was one lost valley. People with
no understandin', don't know what understandin' is. They think a man
is a mule, don't ever get tired. But I done some days I'd sooner been dead
in hell with the wicked than hear that damned big bell ring. They'd make
you go ahead on from sun to sun.

—Anonymous prisoner of the Texas Prison System recorded in 1964,
    Wake Up Dead Man: African American Worksongs from Texas Prisons

In 1947, Marvin Brazer, a seventeen-year-old prisoner held at the Sugarland
Prison Farm just outside of Houston, Texas, lay nude in his unlit solitary cell
in "which there was no light and inadequate air." A car thief from Dallas with
a two-year sentence, Brazer was not a violent offender and had committed
no disciplinary offense. Upon his arrival at the Texas Prison System (TPS),
Brazer was sent to the Darrington Farm, but after his protestations that his
life was in danger there, the prison officials moved him to Sugarland, a prison
farm where prisoners lived in open dormitories called "the tank." When

Brazer first entered the Sugarland tank, another prisoner approached him with a knife in hand and asked Brazer if he "was going to be good to him tonight." When Brazer denied his request, the other prisoner told Brazer that he would sexually submit or be killed. In fear for his life, Brazer refused to return to the tank after dinner; in response, E. F. Brewer, the convict guard of the tank, beat him. Desperate, Blazer asked "to be put in solitary confinement" to protect him from "those men abusing" him "in the form of sodomy" or even killing him.[1]

Brazer's harrowing tale highlights the ways in which sexual violence as prisoner control stood at the very heart of the Texas carceral regime. Solitary was used as a punishment, since it meant being confined in a dark and dank cell, nearly bare except for a bed and concrete hole in the floor that prisoners used as their sole toilet. For a prisoner to request to be placed in solitary was rare indeed. Postwar reformers would have seen Brazer's desperate plight as yet another example of how the South's reliance on open dormitories for prison life hastened what they called the "spread of perversions."

The pages that follow will reveal how the postwar nation-state responded to a "perversion discourse" that excluded homosexuals from full U.S. citizenship and defined homosexuality as a growing social disease. Conceptualizing the federal state through the divisions of welfare, immigration, and the military, Margot Canady has argued in *The Straight State* that, from the Progressive era to the New Deal, the state constructed a legal apparatus that "explicitly regulated" homosexuality within a legal framework that increasingly defined homosexuality as outside of normative citizenship.[2] Historians of urban sexuality, meanwhile, have demonstrated that national and state authorities initiated a crackdown on urban vice during the 1930s, when antigay policing expelled open homosexuality from public spaces.[3] The subsequent Cold War employed "domestic containment" to shift political paranoia from routing out communism in the interests of the national-security state to removing homosexuals from federal service, urban spaces, and the welfare state.[4]

But as antigay policing ended in convictions, criminologists turned the scrutiny of their sex crime paranoia toward the postwar prison, where they feared that state incarceration itself was a site for the active reproduction and spread of homosexuality.[5] The decades of the 1940s and 1950s witnessed a shift among criminologists and sexologists from their early twentieth-century definition of prison homosexuality as largely "situational" to a medicalized diagnosis that exposure to prison homosexuality could create a more fixed sexuality. Postwar criminologists, according to cultural historian Regina Kunzel, employed "metaphors of disease and contagion" that warned that prison sex between men contributed to the "notion that homosexuality was catching."[6]

In the U.S. South, the practice of housing prisoners in labor camps and shared dormitories contributed to the metaphor of disease and contagion, a particular fear that the South's open living spaces hastened the southern prison's production of homosexuality. The response was a northern reform impulse to eradicate the southern prison system's attachment to open living spaces in favor of an enclosed cell penitentiary system. This can be seen in the investigations and reports of Austin MacCormick, the director of the Osbourne Association, who was a leading northern penologist and the War Department's chief consultant on military prisons. Following World War II, every southern state hired MacCormick and the Osbourne Association to assess their prisons systems and to offer a reform plan. Of all the prison reports he wrote, however, MacCormick considered his investigation of Texas prisons as the crowning achievement for southern prison management. For Texas reformers, however, the pressing concern centered on a mounting crisis concerning the efficiency and profitability of southern prison labor.

Southern Prison Labor in Crisis

Between the 1870s and World War II, contract labor and private markets for prison-made goods came under increasing legislative scrutiny, which culminated during the New Deal with the labor movement's successful lobbying effort to restrict the profitability of contract prison labor.[7] When President Herbert Hoover signed the Hawes-Cooper Bill on January 19, 1929, he initiated a new era in prison labor that rejected the South's reliance on prison labor for private profit. With the subsequent passage of the Ashurst-Sumners Act of July 24, 1935, which prohibited the transportation of prison-made goods into states that barred them, and the Sumners-Ashurst Act of 1940, which barred interstate commerce in prison-made goods, prison administrators became increasingly concerned that prisons would fall idle as industries producing for the open market were shut down.[8]

Between 1932 and 1940, the implementation of these acts caused prison labor to decline nationwide, as the number of prisoners productively employed decreased from 52 percent of the nation's total prison population in 1932 to 44 percent in 1940. The value of that labor, moreover, experienced a precipitous decline of 25 percent, from $75 million in 1932 to $57 million in 1940, even as the total number of prisoners nationwide increased from 158,947 in 1932 to 191,776 in 1940.[9] Prisons outside the South, in particular, turned increasingly to therapeutic rehabilitation over labor and adopted such practices as probation, parole, psychiatry, group therapy, secondary and college education, "bibliotherapy," social work, and even recreation. Indeed, during the postwar era, California even sought to encourage civic activity, employing prisoners in forestry and firefighting duties.[10] But as Heather Thompson uncovered in her history of the 1971 Attica prison uprising, prisons outside of the U.S. had uneven prison labor conditions and access to rehabilitative programs, with the best job positions and rehabilitative programming reserved for white prisoners. For instance, white prisoners incarcerated in New York's Attica prison accounted for only 37 percent of the prisoner population but held more than two-thirds of the highest-paid jobs, while prisoners of color held 76 percent of positions in the low-paid metal shop.[11] Prisoner access to rehabilitative programs and the harshness of prison labor conditions outside of the U.S. South were thus often uneven and favored white prisoners to the detriment of prisoners of color.

Southern states, however, were wedded to productive agricultural prison labor, and while state and federal laws forbade the sale of prison-made goods, there was no prohibition on prison labor geared toward the prison system's own self-sufficiency or for state use. Thus, by 1940 southern prisons still employed 60 percent of their total prison population, while northeastern prison states employed only 31 percent of theirs.[12] Southern states maintained higher rates of prison labor than anywhere else in the nation. In Kentucky, a border state, the prison population increased from 3,575 to 4,731 from 1932 and 1940, while its rate of productively employed prisoners fell precipitously from 67 percent to 9 percent. Alabama's prison population, by contrast, grew from 4,837 in 1932 to 6,940 in 1940 while its prison labor rate remained relatively high and stable, dropping from 78 percent productively employed in 1932 to 72 percent in 1940.[13] Reflecting on the new era for state-made prison labor for state use, U.S. attorney general Robert H. Jackson offered a bold pronouncement on what these New Deal–era laws would portend for the future of prison labor: "With the passage of these laws, the Industrial Prison was eliminated. In 1935, for the great majority of prisoners the penitentiary system had again reverted to its original status: punishment and custody."[14]

Yet across the post–World War II South, prisoners continued to perform grueling agricultural labor and roadwork, cordoned together in fenced encampments and open dormitories. By World War II, Virginia had only a single walled industrial penitentiary and operated instead an industrial farm for women, three prison farms for men, and a series of road camps in which nearly two thousand men labored on public projects. North Carolina also had a single prison, but over 80 percent of the state's prisoners worked on eighty-eight road camps and prison farms. With the onset of the Great Depression, Arkansas closed its sole penitentiary, "The Walls," by an act of the legislature under Govern J. M. Futrell. After 1933, all prisoners were moved to state farms as part of what the state historian John L. Ferguson called a "penal plantation as the heart of the correctional system of Arkansas."[15] Similarly, the state of Alabama maintained four prison farms and a cattle ranch over 11,000 acres, as well as twenty-one road camps where over one thousand prisoners worked on public projects scattered across the state. Their industrial operations were mostly focused on the cotton that prisoners picked, with two cotton mills and a small plant for license plates and road signs, as well as a shop that turned prisoner-picked cotton into prisoner clothing and bedsheets. In southern states, the state expenditure for prisons often did not meet the cost of running them, and the value of the agricultural labor that the prisoners performed made up the cost difference. In Alabama, for instance, the total appropriation for the prison budget in 1948 was $471,000, but the salaries and reimbursement for county courts alone was $871,000. The work of the prisoners therefore had to make up the $400,000 difference while also producing enough to feed, clothe, cover meager medical services, and provide building maintenance for forty-five hundred prisoners.[16]

The onset of World War II caused southern prison systems to lurch into yet another period of crisis as prison systems became more violent, less productive, and unable to retain qualified personnel. Despite the prison administrators' emphasis on prison labor and self-sufficiency, southern prisons remained inefficient and operated at a financial loss. Texas's expenditure for prisoners fell by 40 percent during the 1930s, but the inefficient prison system still operated at a deficit. Locked into a brutal and violent prison system, forlorn prisoners increasingly attempted escape and engaged in desperate acts of self-mutilation.

The Texas prison system's reliance on agricultural prison farms with open dormitories was at the heart of its postwar prison crisis. In 1945, the only prison in Texas that had cells similar to those in most northern penitentiaries was the "Walls" penitentiary, located in Huntsville. White prisoners were housed at the Walls penitentiary and the Central Farm and worked in the industries that made license plates, shoes, and printing.[17] Black and brown prisoners, however, were sent to prison farms. In 1939, most of the system's seven thousand prisoners (78 percent) lived on these farms in dormitories. In the 1940s, Texas had twelve prison farms dispersed around a two-hundred-mile radius of Huntsville, along the cotton-growing region of East Texas and the sugar land Gulf Coast region near Houston, where prisons lined the riverbanks of the Brazos and Trinity Rivers. The largely farming and agricultural prison system had its roots in the plantation and cotton-growing estates of the late 1880s.[18] By 1947, the prison system's sprawling farms encompassed 73,010 acres on rich farming soil that was worth over $5,000,000.[19] The system employed over five hundred people, including prison administrators, wardens, officers, and guards. A general manager governed the prison system and reported to the Texas Prison Board, made up of nine members

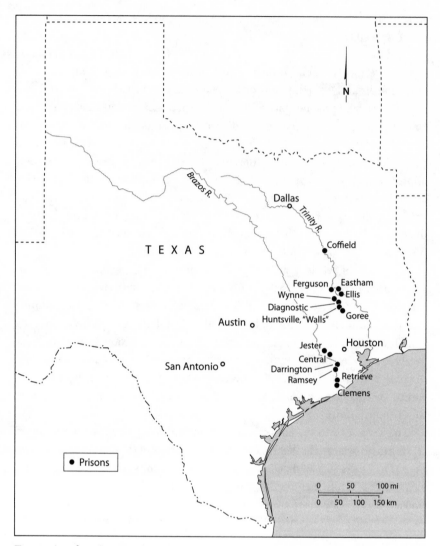

Texas prison locations, 1978

appointed by the governor. Each farm, however, constituted a small fiefdom from which the governing warden ruled the field labor with a staff of
guards following a military-style chain of command.

The dormitories consisted of cavernous rooms originally designed for 60
men, but habitual overcrowding meant that as many as 150 prisoners might
be housed in a single "tank."[20] Each of these tanks encompassed approximately 2,500 square feet of floor space and resembled "the hold of a ship" in
the words of the penologist Austin MacCormick. That meant that each man
was provided only 16 to 25 square feet of floor space, including toilet,

Table 1 Prison farms, acreage, locations, population, 1947

Institution	Location	Prison Population	Number of Employees	Acreage
Blue Ridge	Hobby	12	2	n/a
Central	Sugarland	829	68	5,203
Clemens	Brazoria	527	33	8,118
Darrington	Sandy Point	326	31	6,770
Eastham	Weldon	172	21	12,910
Ferguson	Midway	14	2	4,344
Goree	Huntsville	131	7	967
Harlem	Richmond	603	67	n/a
Huntsville	Huntsville	1,141	160	n/a (walled penitentiary)
Ramsey	Otey	744	59	15,089
Retrieve	Snipe	475	37	7,455
Wynne	Huntsville	522	160	1,913

Sources: The data was compiled from two sources: Letter to George W. Cox, MD, State Health Officer from D. W. Stakes, General Manager, Texas Department of Corrections, November 4, 1947, Jester, TSLA, Box 115/60-2; "Texas Prison System Runs Gauntlet of Bad and Best in Nation's Penal Institutions," Tyler Courrier-Times, Tyler, Texas, December 20, 1947.

washing, recreational, and passage space.[21] Rows of double-deck bunks were jammed together, allowing prisoners to cross from one to the other without touching the floor. The tanks extended from a central corridor with individual wings running perpendicular through the center hall. At each wing of the prison, there was a "picket"—a space through which guards could roll a gate and enclose prisoners within each wing.

Guards also lived in the dormitories, sometimes in rooms directly adjacent to the prisoners' living quarters. Such close living arrangements between keepers and kept meant that contraband was easily passed from guard to prisoner. The porous nature of near cohabitation between guard and prisoner worsened with the onset of World War II as conscription and the lure of better-paying jobs in military industries decimated the ranks of the guard force, and morale plummeted.[22]

The trusty system also contributed heavily to the abundance of contraband. In Texas, prisoners with better disciplinary records earned trusty status, affording them more freedom and tasks that often took them off the prison farm. Trusties could therefore easily move contraband from the fields to the prison farm. The flow of actual currency also contributed to a steady trade of contraband, as trusties' families were allowed to deposit money in individual prisoners' accounts, which could then be spent at the commissary.

"You could buy whiskey from the trusties traveling back and forth outside," recalled one prisoner. "Use to be whiskey hid all in the fields, buried in the fields. Stash it out where you could go get a pint when you needed it. Send a trustee to get it."[23] Indeed, the prison system's lack of accountability was so poor that D. W. Stakes, the system's manager, complained in the 1944 annual report that items were often missing from the prison, and he surmised that trusties sold these items on the outside for contraband. Items as large as a truck had gone missing and were never found.[24] Marijuana, whiskey, cigarettes, and other contraband easily passed from hand to hand through the walls, over the fields, and past the gate.

Trusties included those prisoners who worked inside the dormitories and on the prison farm. Those whose job was to help the prison administration enforce discipline and maintain control were known as "building tenders." This practice of employing prisoners in a "sub-boss" system dated back to the Reconstruction era.[25] Indeed, until convict lease was outlawed in 1910, the sub-boss system was praised as a kind of job-training program.[26] Texas followed a southern tradition of having trusties be openly armed. In Arkansas and Mississippi, such prisoners were "trusty shooters," who oversaw field work and ensured that no prisoner attempted escape.[27] In Texas, the prison guards oversaw field labor, and the trusties or building tenders maintained oversight of the dormitories. This practice continued from the era of nineteenth-century convict leasing through the mid-1980s.[28] Albert Race Sample's memoir of prison life concluded that building tenders maintained discipline and authority in the tanks through "their gang rapes, beatings and harassment of the weaker cons."[29] The building tenders, then, ruled the dormitories. Their power and influence in the prison system would only increase once the prison system replaced dormitories with cells in the postwar period.[30]

The prison administration also divided and organized the prison farms through racial segregation. In 1909, the legislature formally segregated prisoners, putting African American ("Negroes") and Mexican American prisoners ("Mexicans") on separate farms or in racially segregated dormitories on the same prison farm. Clemens, Darrington, and Retrieve, for instance, housed only African Americans. Blue Ridge was "Mexican," and Eastham and the Walls housed only "Anglos." Sequestering all the Mexican and Mexican American prisoners on a single prison farm, Blue Ridge, until World War II produced among Méxicano prisoners what the historian George Díaz has called a "prison *colonia*" and an incarcerated "Mexico de Afuera" (Mexico Abroad). Until the prison system closed Blue Ridge during World War II, Mexican prisoners housed together retained Mexican culture, language, and community as a cultural survival tool that allowed these prisoners to circumvent the isolation of a Texas prison farm.[31] The Central and Ramsey Farms held both Black and white prisoners, and later in the postwar period they held Mexican Americans as well. Goree was the only women's prison, holding three hundred prisoners through the first decade of the postwar period. The Wynne Farm, referred to by prisoners in characteristically hypermasculine terms as the "broke dick" farm, was for older prisoners and those who could not keep up with the harsh labor regime.

A new prisoner classification program introduced in 1936 ensured that the growing prison system would continue to segregate its prisoners and their work assignments by race.[32] This system organized and housed African Americans and Mexican Americans by race, age, and whether the prisoner was a first offender or a recidivist. White prisoners, however, entered a much more complex classification system that assessed them on the basis of their physical ability, mental acuity and sanity, drug addiction, and sexuality identity ("homosexual" or "heterosexual"). As the cultural historian Regina Kunzel revealed in her study of prison sexuality, social science during the decades of the 1930s and 1940s had created a series of "sex crime panics" that criminalized homosexuality by "collapsing and conflating sex psychopathy, violent crime, and male homosexuality."[33] In Texas, prison administrators used the sexual classification of only white prisoners to protect young white men from being housed with those classified as "homosexual," while Black and brown bodies were not considered worthy of such protection. White prisoners could also fall into a "rehabilitative group," an intermediate group of those who were "doubtful cases for rehabilitation," and a maximum risk group that included "those who have indicated extreme viciousness" and held "little regard for human life."[34] Before the World War II, women prisoners were segregated by race but underwent no additional classification.

The detailed classifications for whites were meant to identify those who could be given better and more responsible positions in the prison system. Only white prisoners were considered eligible for industrial jobs and for placement in the prison's flagship institution, the Walls. While some whites also worked the fields doing the same "scoop" labor as African American and Mexican American prisoners, they were usually assigned to live on the prison farms that offered the best living space. African American and Mexican American prisoners meanwhile got the worst conditions, finding themselves posted to harsh cotton and sugar farms along the Gulf Coast. Edward Ayers has argued that nineteenth-century southern prisons and the process of punitive justice was so transformative that it leveled racial markers and ethnic difference such that white prisoners "were considered the lowest of their race" and that "racial lines blurred" to the point where whites and other minorities were treated equally as bad.[35] White prisoners did face the prospect of losing their preferred status following their release from captivity, but within Texas prisons they maintained a claim to white superiority. As the prison system entered the World War II era, Texas mapped its prison farms through racial difference and distributed its prison labor and rehabilitation services through prioritized skin privileges.[36]

In designing both work patterns and discipline through corporal punishment, Texas prisons drew on the heritage of slave plantations. A 1911 law authorized prison guards and wardens to whip men on the bare back and buttocks. Prison guards beat prisoners with a leather strap, called the "bat," which was typically two inches wide and twenty-four inches long and attached to a wooden handle. The use of the bat was so routine that "Boss" Lee Simmons (1930–35), the Depression-era director of the TPS, once proudly bragged that "the bat to a prison warden was like spurs to a cowboy."[37] The use of such corporal punishment clearly harkened back to the slave lash.[38] "As the leather'd leave, the hide'd leave with it," recalled one African American prisoner who lived through more than one disciplinary session with the infamous bat. The prisoner vividly recalled that one man's whipping with the bat served as a fateful reminder to the general prison population: "You could tell all them what got whipped. They couldn't set down, had to lay on their stomach and other that he couldn't lay no other way. All the back part there would be just raw blood."[39] Recalled another African American prisoner, "One time Captain Powell was whipping a boy with that bat, and he [the whipped prisoner] kept a hollerin', 'Oh lordy, Oh lordy!' And finally he [Captain Powell] bust him again and he [the prisoner] say, 'Oh lordy, Captain!' And captain said, 'I thought you'd get around to me directly.' Cause he wanted him to know that Jesus wasn't whippin' him, it was *him* [Captain Powell] whippin' him. And Jesus couldn't help him neither."[40] Under pressure from the publication of *Deep Secrets behind Grey Walls* in 1940 and *Flood Lights behind the Gray Walls: An Exposé of Activities* in 1942 by the prison board member C. V. Compton, the Texas Prison Board outlawed whipping as an official punishment in 1941. Still, brutality persisted within the prison dormitories, where building tenders and guards delivered unrecorded corporal punishment.

While dormitory lifestyle dominated the prisoners' nights, it was field work that dominated the prison day. At first light, the early morning bell rang, and the prisoners rose, ate their breakfast, and then trotted as much as five to seven miles to the fields for a full day's labor. "The way we had to walk and work then," recalled one prisoner. "We had to walk seven or eight miles to work, seven or eight miles back to dinner, same thing after dinner, same thing at quitting time. That was from sunup to sundown. Wasn't no letup. And we worked Saturdays." The pace of work after a long day meant that the five- to seven-mile trek back to the prison farm took its toll. As another prisoner re-called,

> you hit that road, boy, you're on the way: you don't tarry, and that was all day. You didn't let up. The weak fell out, they'd haul them back. If one was just too weak to make it walking, he'd just hang on to his buddy's shirttails or belt loop. Sometimes they'd hang onto the horse's tail. Man, I seen as many as six or seven of them hanging onto his shirt, hanging on the boss's stirrup and he says, "Latch onto that stirrup and hang on," and all of them would practically be dragging along though they were still on their feet. They could barely even fall down.[41]

Prisoners labored in a racially segregated line of white-suited prisoners. Perched on his horse overlooking the prisoners was a prison guard, who pris-oners of all races characteristically called in slave idiom their "Cap'ain" or "Boss." This prison high rider watched over field work with a .30-caliber rifle clutched in his hands. As one prisoner joked, "During that old time you work ten to twelve hours, as long as there was sun. Eight hours—I didn't know what eight hours was then, you heard about it on the radio or something."[42] Prison labor included clearing the land, picking cotton, flat weeding, and logging. Cotton picking, however, was the prison's chief cash crop. By 1940, Texas prisoners toiled on 16,990 acres of land dedicated to cotton's cultivation. The six-day workweek was rarely interrupted, as prisoners worked through sick-ness, exhaustion, the Texas heat, summer storms, or winter frosts. Although sometimes the prisoners ran back to the farm for supper, often they simply ate in the field. "Stand out in the field and eat your dinner," recalled an Afri-can American prisoner. "Be raining hard like it was before, raining hard like a cow pissing on a flint rock, wash the beans out a your plate. There wasn't no sick. You don't have a fever of 202, then you ain't sick. Used to work people dead in the underworld down here."[43]

The deplorable living conditions, violence, and harsh field work only be-came worse during World War II. Wartime and the draft caused a precipi-tous drop in prison population, the number declining from 7,000 in 1939 to a wartime low of 3,394 prisoners in 1944.[44] Even so, wartime production de-mands remained high. Guards worked twelve-hour days and the state paid them low wages compared to those for military and industrial work, usually between $100 and $130 a month.[45] A demoralized guard force increasingly brutalized prisoners as the prison system demanded more labor out of fewer convicts. Beleaguered by press reports of guard incompetence, the prison manager D. W. Stakes admitted in 1946 that his guard force was "aged and infirm," "illiterate," and "others [were] sadists; others so unintelligent and in-capacitated that they were a distinct menace to safety or society at large."

Despite such slim pickings, Stakes pleaded that "our need was such that we were forced to employ them and as a consequence, suffer escapes and other unnecessary reverses."[46]

A demoralized, skeletal guard structure led to an increase in disciplinary problems. Throughout the 1940s, Texas prisons witnessed an increase in escapes, prison violence, work stoppages, and self-mutilations in which prisoners slashed their Achilles tendons so that they could avoid harsh prison labor, an act of desperation and defiance euphemistically known as "heel stringing." Desperate prisoners also went to such extremes as cutting three fingers off one hand, breaking a leg, or placing lye in an open wound so as to ensure infection and a festering abscess. Such desperate acts earned prisoners a month or more of prison hospital bed rest away from sweltering fields of labor. The practice of self-mutilation was a prison farm tradition with roots in prisoner resistance to convict lease labor and resemblance to practices of suicide and self-destruction among enslaved captives during the Atlantic slave trade.[47] However, incidents of self-maiming increased during World War II and in the immediate postwar period. Between 1936 and 1940 there was 174 cases of self-mutilation, but between 1944 and 1948 the incidents of self-destruction nearly doubled to 341 such incidents.[48] In 1940, the variety of self-mutilations included twenty prisoners with broken arms and two foot and one hand amputations. As the war progressed, self-mutilation increased. In 1942, ten prisoners broke their arms, sixty-five committed heel stringing, and six used lye in their open wounds. By war's end in 1945, the prison hospital recorded a record high 126 self-mutilations.[49]

Rising escape attempts and increased incidents of prisoner violence contributed to a mounting prison crisis. In 1939, there were 54 escape attempts, but by 1945 the number of escapes more than doubled to 115. Escaping prisoners faced the threat of being shot by the guards, beaten by building tenders once recaptured, or drowned in the Brazos River bottoms in what would be inevitably described as a failed "escape" attempt. Prisoner-on-prisoner violence was also on the rise. The prison administration allowed money in the prisons, which gave rise to an internal prisoner economy that contributed to violence and corruption. As one prisoner recalled, "there was a lot of cash, everything was cash money," leading to "a lot of killing over little petty debts, petty thefts, money, hustling money to gamble."[50] Perhaps the most publicized incidence of violence was the December 1948 decapitation of the prisoner Charles Redwine. While sitting at dinner, Redwine was beheaded in a single stroke with a cane knife by Earnest Jones, a kitchen convict worker, who harbored a grudge against Redwine. The press sensationalized the story and added to prison lore by reporting that the guards found Redwine's body still seated at the dinner table with his lit cigarette still poised between lifeless fingers.[51]

Such was the frequency of violence and the fear of "snitching" in the dormitory environment that not a single prisoner among the 200 fellow diners admitted to having witnessed such a brutal and swift decapitation. Jones, meanwhile, was punished by an extension of his sentence and simultaneously "rewarded" by Carl Luther "Beartrack" McAdams, a guard at the time of the incident, who made Jones a trusty when he became warden at Ramsey in 1951 because he felt that Jones was "a pretty good inmate. He had to kill him [Redwine] or be killed."[52] Murderous prison violence thus led to internal control and prisoner promotion.

Although the prison population was half the prewar size, the costs remained almost as high. In 1948, the prison industries and farm operations covered only 57 percent of the system's operating cost, leaving the remaining 43 percent to the taxpayers. The marked increase of violence and disruptions among a smaller prison population caused some politicians and citizens groups to declare that the Texas prison system bordered on crisis and calamity. Indeed, in a December 1947 article, the *Tyler Courier-Times* proclaimed the Texas prison system the "worst in the nation," one that reeked of "brutality, self-mutilation, sexual perversion, incompetency, and petty graft, a cesspool of humanity." The media claimed that the Texas prison system "poisoned society" and served as "a source of shame and disgrace to the Lone Star State."[53] Indeed, the *Tyler Telegraph* declared the Texas prison farm as "the system that had grown up backwards."[54]

Northern Penology in a Texas Prison: Austin MacCormick's Reform Vision

On January 24, 1934, Austin H. MacCormick, New York's newly minted commissioner of correction, gathered together a collection of armed wardens, including his first deputy, David Marcus, and Warden Joseph McCann, for an early-morning surprise raid at the Welfare Island State Penitentiary in New York. To ensure wide newspaper coverage, a gaggle of reporters were embedded alongside the posse. The newspapers reported that MacCormick led the early-morning raid with "utmost secrecy" and "with military precision" upon on unsuspecting Welfare Island prison as part of a raid to uproot drug trafficking and racketeering.

As they armed themselves, MacCormick admonished his raiding party that there should be "no rough stuff unless it's necessary, but if it is necessary make it good and rough. If you have to smack a man, smack him so hard the other prisoners can hear the blow." The subjects of the raid were the prisoner Joseph Rao, a member of the Dutch Schultz gang and, according to MacCormick, part of the "Italian mafia," and Edward Cleary, who MacCormick charged as head of "the Irish mafia." Rao and Cleary had relied on homing pigeons to breach the prison walls and to traffic heroin, distributing it both within the prison and on the outside. The deputy warden, Daniel Sheehan, housed these two gang leaders along with sixty-six "henchmen" prisoner accomplices in the prison's hospital ward, though none of them were sick, where they "had been living lives of ease and luxury." MacCormick's raiding party uncovered heroin, knives, hatchets, and lengths of pipe, as well as expensive radio sets, rugs, canes, glass-topped tables, and electric stoves. The private quarters of Rao and Cleary contained silk undershirts and underwear, expensive dress clothes, high-end cigars, monogrammed writing paper, and Cleary's pet German Shepherd, "Screw Hater," so-named derisively to demean guards. As an administrative accomplice, Deputy Warden Daniel Sheehan was placed under "military arrest," and the ringleaders and henchmen were "dragged out of comfortable hospital dormitories and put into cells."[55]

Appointed by the New Deal mayor Fiorella LaGuardia, MacCormick set out to uproot powerful convicts and their control over other less powerful prisoners. In language that was made to grab the attention of the public in newspaper headlines, MacCormick charged that gangster control of the prison administration and fellow prisoners constituted "a vicious circle of crime and depravity that is almost beyond the ability of the imagination to grasp." Big shots like Rao and Cleary had other prisoners waiting on them and performing their menial chores while "they lived like kings." As part of the raid, MacCormick also had his men target the southern cell block, even though that wing was not part of the drug ring. There, the deputy wardens reported to the press that they found the contraband of rouge, powder, mascara, perfume, a woman's wig, and silk undergarments and that prisoners on this block "affected long hair." With the blaring headline "Welfare Island Raid Bares Gangster Rule over Prison" on the front page of the *New York Times*, MacCormick was vaunted into celebrity as a tough-minded prison reformer. But the target of his reform centered on two aspects of prison life—a prisoner-controlled prison and prejudiced fears over prison homosexuality.[56] In Texas, he would find these two issues at the very forefront of his reform designs.

Texas's prison reform effort began during the war, but it was not until the postwar period that reform gained popular and political momentum, especially as the Texas Prison Board realized that returning veterans would likely trigger a return to prewar levels of crime and a concomitant rise in the prison population. Nationwide, in 1946 aggravated assault offenses increased 47 percent above the prewar average (1938–41); rape, 43 percent; negligent manslaughter, 11 percent; and murder, 22 percent. Nonviolent offenses also increased. In 1946, auto theft offenses increased 29 percent above the prewar average; burglary, 19 percent; robbery, 19 percent; and petty larceny, 4 percent. The crime rate seemed to be growing fastest in Texas. At the war's close in 1945, Texas recorded a total 53,000 criminal offenses. In 1946, however, the number of criminal offenses jumped to 60,650, which constituted a hefty increase of new prisoners that threatened to overwhelm Texas prisons.[57] The press linked the postwar increase in crime rates with the prison crisis when one newspaper charged that the "crime wave" was the "handiwork of Texas Prison 'graduates'" who returned to prison following their initial release.[58]

In response to the wartime prison crisis and anticipating a postwar crime wave, the prison board in 1944 asked MacCormick, who was then serving as director of the progressive Osborne Association in New York, to develop a long-term prison strategy to modernize the Texas prison system.[59] By the end of his sixty-five-year career as a penological expert, MacCormick had visited every state prison in the nation and had served as an investigator and chief reformer for the prison systems in Alabama, Arkansas, Louisiana, Mississippi, North Carolina, and Texas.[60] The board's choice of a New York–based, Progressive-era penological association to reform Texas's southern prison farm system was a nod toward northeastern supremacy in penology and rehabilitation.[61] MacCormick's national reputation depended most on his writing as an intellectual reformer who relied on social science to rethink the postwar prison. In a speech entitled "The Future of Correctional Work in America," MacCormick addressed a UN committee and European audiences with the admonition that "the debate on the punitive versus the rehabilitative theory has filled the pages of penological literature for generations. . . . So far as the United States is concerned, however, it is ended." Viewing the history of U.S. imprisonment as evidenced by the authority of the stockade, the lash, convict lease, and punitive brutality, MacCormick concluded that "punishment as retribution belongs to a penal philosophy that is archaic and discredited by history." Seeing his generation's penal reform work as heralding a new modernity, MacCormick concluded that "the merits of the philosophy of rehabilitation . . . should take unquestioned precedence in current penal thought."[62]

To advance his rehabilitation initiatives, MacCormick's thinking went beyond the purely rehabilitative to include his proposal that postwar prisons might operate as "research centers." MacCormick thought of these prison laboratories as a testing ground for researchers, experts, and students of psychopathology with a keen focus on the study of "sexual perversion and deviancy." As a research center, prisons would collect together experts to observe, surveil, and perform newly developed psychopathology tests on prisoners for "intensive research—carefully planned, adequately financed, and well-staffed." For instance, MacCormick cited the study of psychopaths at Federal Reformatory in Chillicothe, Ohio, and another study of sex offenders at Sing Sing Prison in New York under the supervision of the State Psychiatric Institute.

MacCormick's preoccupation with sexuality was part of the postwar transition among social scientists and psychiatrists to redefine homosexuality through the lens of criminality and social contagion. With Freudian psychology ascendant by midcentury, psychiatrists like Frederic Wertham, Robert Lindner, and Benjamin Karpman associated criminal behavior and subsequent incarceration as a regressive return to the uninhibited desire that Freudian psychopathology associated with infancy. Outside of prisons, expert concern over postwar crime rates and a new youth culture fueled a 1950s "moral panic" and "cycle of outrage," as the cultural historian James Gilbert aptly put it, that associated youthful sex, drug use, comic books, rock-'n'-roll, and radio and television programs with juvenile criminal delinquency. The shared concerns of the Children's Bureau, the Federal Bureau of Investigation, and Freudian psychology resulted in the 1950 Senate Crime Committee's investigation of juvenile delinquency. During the Senate hearing, Dr. Frederick Wertham, author of *The Seduction of the Innocent*, testified that comic books that depicted the pairing of older male heroes with juvenile boys, including the *Batman* and *Captain America* comics, promoted homosexuality as a "criminal perversion."[63] The advent of Freudian psychopathology coupled with societal concerns over the need to return society to a postwar order effectively criminalized homosexuality as a psychopathology.

Troubled state legislators responded by passing new sex psychopath laws that armed local law enforcement with the ability to aggressively police homosexuality.[64] Postwar criminologists, psychologists, and sociologists feared that prisons served as incubators for homosexuality and that prison society produced more "sexual perverts." As an intellectual history of this socioscientific discourse, Kunzel's *Criminal Intimacy* concluded that midcentury social scientists employed diagnoses that drew on medicalized metaphors of disease and contagion, where "sexual perversions long associated with prison life were not just habit-forming but subject-forming," which led these experts to believe that in prisons "homosexuality was catching."[65]

In his role as the architect of postwar prison reform in Texas, MacCormick sought to employ these very same techniques to observe, surveil, and quarantine the world of southern prison farm dormitories. After observing the prison in 1944, MacCormick's report addressed what he saw as four major problems in the management of Texas prisons: the outdated practice of agricultural work without industrial machinery; the tank lifestyle, where prisoners lived in large and open dormitories rather than cells; the prevalence of "perverts" and homosexuality; and an overwhelming amount of violence and brutality, particularly the desperate practice among prisoners of self-maiming. The report addressed the internal problems of prison society and life, most "notably escapes, perversion, assaults, self-mutilation, the bad influence of the worst prisoners on others." It drew attention to the "vicious circle of offenses and punishments," in which prison guards routinely engaged in savage beatings, causing prisoners to rebel with their very bodies through attempted escape and self-mutilation. To reform the prison system and help it cope with the expected postwar increase in prison population, the report recommended overhauling the system by reforming the agricultural program, constructing facilities for seven hundred prisoners, creating a vocational industrial training program for the prisoners, and upgrading prison personnel.[66]

The report was especially critical of the inadequate and poorly trained prison guard workforce. MacCormick charged that the prison guards were "unreliable" and "heavy drinkers" who "quit their jobs without warning." Those who remained were "too inexperienced or incompetent to handle prisoners," and "others are brutal and use methods that bring a wave of disciplinary problems." The report complained that the armed services had taken some of the "best men" and that those who did not join the war effort as soldiers often left the prison for better-paying jobs in the war industries. MacCormick concluded that "when almost anyone can get a job at higher wages," prison guards would inevitably abandon the prison system, and "very few men of the superior type are looking for a job in the prison field." MacCormick's experience as chief consultant to the War Department on military prisons buoyed his hopes that returning soldiers who "learned how to handle men" may well be "well suited to prison work." In terms of administrative personnel, the report found that "many of those occupying administrative positions fall below the level of combined ability, training and experience required in a prison system." Those whom MacCormick did consider as capable administrators were constrained by their unfamiliarity with the "more advanced prison methods" that existed in northeastern penitentiaries.[67]

A second personnel recommendation was to depoliticize the prison system and place all prison employees under civil service, "from the General Manager to the least important employee." MacCormick's recommendation to move the prison out of Texas's political patronage system was one of the more controversial aspects of his report. He believed strongly that "the prison systems of the country will never fulfill their true functions economically and effectively until they are taken out of politics." The report listed the "leading prison systems of the country" that were administered strictly by civil servants as the federal prison system and the state systems of New York, New Jersey, Michigan, and California. In MacCormick's mind, the path to modernization for Texas prisons ran north and west to the rehabilitative models of California and New York.[68]

MacCormick hoped to end agricultural work for most prisoners and establish instead "a variety of productive industries, particularly those having direct or indirect vocational training value." The report concluded that "it is an indefensible policy to operate what is practically a one-occupation employment program for the great majority of prisoners." Employing men in the field failed to provide anything resembling rehabilitation or vocational training, and, according to MacCormick, it also contributed to serious discipline problems. The report noted that prisoners working in the industries of Central Farm No. 2, for instance, "present few disciplinary problems, although the work is hard and hours are long." The report concluded that putting men to work in industry instead of agriculture would cause other "men who have been chronic disciplinary cases" to "drop off the punishment rolls" and would start to pull "their weight in the boat instead of trying to scuttle it."[69]

In spite of the force of MacCormick's report and his sweeping reform vision, the Texas Prison Board ignored his recommendations, largely because there was no political will and no financial well deep enough to overhaul the prison system.[70] Yet the MacCormick report remains a valuable source of information on the life of prisoners.[71] MacCormick conducted his work on the prison system largely unimpeded, a fact that diminished prisoner fears of being labeled a "stool pigeon," an act that would earn them a "tune-up," convict slang for a beating, at the hands of prison guards. The MacCormick report stressed that "no attempt has been made by the prison authorities to conceal or belittle the serious disciplinary problems." Further, the MacCormick report emphasized that "records of all types have been thrown open to the undersigned," and "personnel have been encouraged to talk frankly and appear to have done so." Even rarer, MacCormick reported that the prison system gave him "complete freedom" to interview prisoners "privately or in the presence of others." In a system that typically demanded loyalty among its staff and threatened prisoners who spoke against the prison system with severe punishment, the promise to openly review prison records and speak directly and unimpeded to prison staff and prisoners alike was indeed a rare opportunity.[72]

MacCormick's report was especially revealing about three aspects of 1940s life in Texas prisons: homosexuality, self-mutilation, and the control of space. The report's emphasis on the "spread" of prison homosexuality, which MacCormick referred to as a "perversion," shows the ways in which reformers believed that social behavior, particularly sexuality and sexual violence,

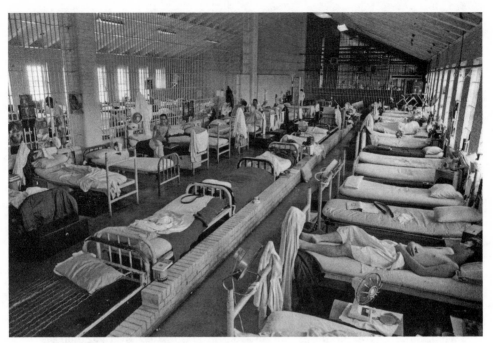

Open dormitory Texas prisons, Clemons prison, 1984 (in the postwar era, these beds would be typically double bunked). Courtesy of Alan Pogue.

operated like a "disease" and "contagion." MacCormick was also concerned and fascinated with acts of bodily self-mutilation. The solution to "perversion" and self-mutilation was to separate prisoners from each other in cells. Reformers rejected common social space and embraced instead individualized space. Such an effort was aimed at containing, segregating, and quarantining "contagious" prisoners and bad behavior.

MacCormick wrote that housing prisoners in dormitories led to "the problem of perversion," which "is always present in dormitories" because the "free mingling of men of varied types" caused "perversion" to "spread" from one prisoner to the next. "The pervert," continued the report, "get their weaker, more suggestible, or more impulsive fellows into trouble." McCormick did not distinguish between consensual homosexual relations and rape. Homosexuality was simply a perversion and could be nothing less than coerced or an act of "bestiality" by depraved criminals.[73] MacCormick's emphasis on "the crime of sodomy" and his inability to separate rape from consensual relationships showed the ways in which prison reform expressed sexual anxiety over the fear of prison homosexuality. MacCormick likened the "bad influence" of "perverts" to a contamination that "spreads through a tank-full of prisoners as a few drops of powerful poison spreads through a tank-full of water."[74] The media also covered prison homosexuality as if it was contagious. In a special newspaper series on prison life in the tanks, the *Tyler Morning Telegraph* pointed out that "only a small percentage of admissions are perverts but they force themselves on others who in turn become addicted" to prison homosexuality. The media warned its readers that "perverts" are "diseased and they spread the disease" and thus threaten the prison's overall "security."[75]

MacCormick's fear that "perverts" threatened "security" mirrored a similar postwar argument in Washington, DC, among national politicians. Historians of gender and sexuality have revealed how the postwar "red scare" campaign to remove communists from the federal government was intertwined with an even more aggressive political crusade to expose, persecute, and expunge homosexual workers from federal positions.[76] The result of this "lavender scare" was that more homosexuals were purged from the federal government than suspected communists. The fear that "perverts" in government positions posed serious "security risks" permeated postwar political culture. As David Johnson concluded in his study of the 1950s purge of homosexuals from government jobs, Republicans in Congress paired their "moral panic" over homosexuality with Cold War anxiety over national security.[77] The result, according to Johnson, was that the "containment of sexuality was as central to 1950s America as containing communism."[78] Like the federal administrators who purged homosexuals from federal government, Texas prison reformers warned of a "moral panic" in their effort to "contain" and stop the "spread" of prison homosexuality. In light of the convergence over red scares and "sexual panics," Regina Kunzel offered the astute observation that Cold War anxieties shared "the subversive ability of both to pass undetected, their tendency to form underground subcultures, and allegedly contagious and seductive quality of both communism and homosexuality."[79]

A second major impetus for prison reform was the concern with self-mutilation. MacCormick called such acts "a common practice in the Texas prison System" and "almost unheard-of in other prison systems." MacCormick called this practice "the most baffling" problem in Texas prisons because "of the difficulty of putting a stop to the practice under present conditions without recourse to punishment which seem to have the effect of increasing rather than reducing it." Self-mutilation, MacCormick realized, was not simply an act of self-destruction; it also served as a way of escaping for a time the physical brutality of convict keepers. McCormick cited "an inevitable pattern" and a "vicious circle of offenses and punishments" that prisoners "working in the fields and living in dormitories would inevitably attempt escape," only to have the prison guards capture them and subject the prisoners to corporal punishment. The beaten convict then "register[s] his bitterness and gets away from the farm for a while by self-mutilation; by cutting his heel-string, breaking his arm, slashing his wrists." The report called these self-mutilating men "psychopaths, but not insane," because their primary motivation was to "get away from the farm." Further, the report correctly ascertained that self-mutilation was "an expression of their feeling of resistance toward the whole prison system, their bitterness over their sentences, resentment toward police, prosecutors, judges, and jailers in general, and the underlying, smoldering sense of frustration and defeat that so many prisoners have without being able or willing to express it in words."[80] MacCormick was simply appalled at how common and public the practice was:

> The reason behind most of our troubles is due to the whole life in the tanks . . . and it results in something that is not encountered anywhere else in the country except Georgia, —self-maiming—and they claim that some ex-Texan prisoner started it there. They break their arms, cut their heel strings and there is on record a case of where men cut off hands and feet. . . . They all give reasons but there are plenty of reasons that they do not give. Sometimes, a man does it to get away from the farm; sometimes to get out of the tanks; sometimes because of activities of perverts; sometimes they are forced to do it by others who are going to keep the mutilations going on; sometimes, apparently, a bunch draw names out of a hat and the loser has to do it. There have been as high as a hundred in the last year. And none anywhere else that I know of. It has attacked Texas like a peculiar tropical disease; it is as contagious as can be.[81]

MacCormick's diagnosis of self-mutilation divided self-mutilating prisoners into two types. The first were those "who are physically not up to the demands of long hours of hard outdoor work." The report considered this type of prisoner "weighted down and depressed" and someone who had fallen to the "influence of a chronic trouble-maker" or, worse, had "fallen prey to an aggressive pervert." MacCormick considered these prisoners a "pitiable group" and categorized them as either "psychopaths," "homesick boys," or "older weaklings," who should be dealt with "humanely" and "understandingly" rather than from the "punitive viewpoint."[82]

The second type included those physically strong enough for the field work and "mentally tough enough" to survive in prison society but resistant to prison work and guard brutality. These prisoners, according to the report, developed resistance from a well of "deep lying," and they therefore lacked "the necessary moral stamina even if they have the necessary physical strength."[83]

Although race was not a major theme or consideration of the report, MacCormick did offer the intriguing suggestion that the "problem convict" was usually white and urban. Minority prisoners, according to the report, were "used to farm work or to hard manual labor," and they therefore "accept it as an inevitable part of the prison sentence." Minority prisoners, however, were anything but docile and accepting of their predicament. The majority of work stoppages and hunger strikes through the 1940s occurred on the Harlem, Ramsey, and Retrieve farms, which housed largely African American and Mexican American prisoners. The sit-down and hunger strikes of the 1930s were nearly always short-lived acts of rebellion that lacked organization and systemwide leadership. Still, their absence in the MacCormick report betrays his inclination to view rural minorities as less threatening and more accepting of their convict role. By protecting young, white prisoners and ignoring what must have been a similar threat of sexual violence against minorities, MacCormick revealed the degree to which white bodies were deserving of protection while Black and brown bodies earned no consideration whatsoever.

MacCormick's observations concerning the "pattern" of resistance and subjection between prisoner and prison authority resembles acts of resistance that theorists and historians Michel de Certeau, James C. Scott, and Robin D. G. Kelley have termed as working-class "everyday" resistance, a "hidden transcript," and a pattern of "infra-politics" in which the disenfranchised and less powerful practiced defiance, struggle, and conflict through everyday life and working-class culture against those holding power, authority, and mastery over their lives and work.[84] Living under the control and authority of their keepers in a comprehensively authoritarian and brutal prison regime left prisoners' little recourse other than to rebel with the one thing that they still owned and controlled—namely, their own bodies. Still, though self-mutilation may have confounded and frustrated the power of prison keepers, it must also be understood as a self-destructive act that wrought physical and sometimes lasting harm to prisoners' bodies.

The best means to "contain" self-mutilation and "perversion," according to MacCormick, was the foreclosure of the southern prison dormitory in favor of the separation, quarantine, and containment of prisoners into enclosed spaces. MacCormick believed that building cells would protect the "weak" prisoner while simultaneously isolating "manipulative" prisoners. "Texas has paid dearly for that policy," MacCormick wrote, for the policy of "employing on its prison farms" and "housing in open dormitories, men who in most prison systems would not be permitted, let alone required, to work and live outside a walled institution of the maximum security type."[85] Individualized cells and the closure of public and shared space would, MacCormick believed, lead to stability through prisoner segregation and containment.

Legislative Response

In response to the MacCormick report, the state legislature convened in April 1947 a special legislative committee, the Legislative Committee on Investigation of State Penitentiaries and the Farm System. Three senators and nineteen representatives composed the committee. State Senator Wardlow Lane and State Representative Sam Sellars served as its chairs. The committee visited the farms, freely interviewed prisoners, and toured both the regular tanks and the prisoners in solitary confinement. The legislative committee delivered a series of sharply critical observations with far more examples of individual brutality than the MacCormick report. In particular, the report cited rampant brutality, filthy living conditions, overly cruel treatment in solitary confinement, sodomy, and self-maiming. The state legislature committee couched the argument for prison reform in humanitarian and personal terms by providing a more intimate abuse narrative full of individual examples of brutality that provide a rare portrait of the prison farm.

The legislative committee cited the tanks and the housing of prisoners in dormitories as major contributors to what they considered a "deplorable prison system" where acts of "human depravity," where homosexuality was cast within a criminally perverse discourse, reigned over convict's everyday lives. On the Wynne farm, for instance, the committee noted that the tanks constituted a space where "crime is further bred" and that the worst of these crimes was sodomy, which was "committed regularly and consistently." In its visit to the Darrington prison farm, which the committee called the farm with the "most desperate criminals in the whole system," the legislators reported that the "greatest crime going on in the prison was the crime of sodomy among the men."[86]

The committee went to great lengths to reveal their view that homosexuality and violence were intrinsically linked. The committee reported that "one man related he was attacked at night by 28 men—had been held at point of a knife at his throat and made to submit." After relating the rape, the committee concluded that many men "have their 'girls' and fight over them," making sodomy "the crime of crimes" that was "prevalent at every place." The prison board member B. A. Stufflebeame similarly described the dormitory lifestyle in the metaphorical language of disease and contamination. The prison tanks were filled with "older prisoners, incurably hardened criminals" who depended on their veteran position of relative power and authority to claim the bodies of younger prisoners. "There, on their bunks, were 12 or 15 of these veteran prisoners, each with a young man on his lap, being caressed and fondled," proclaimed Stufflebeame. "These, I learned from the warden, these boys were their 'sweethearts' . . . That was my first observation, my first knowledge, of the most degraded and vicious sex-perversion to which human beings can sink. But it pervades the entire system." Stufflebeame claimed that his first visit to Texas prisons had "hounded me since that hour" and that he "bawled like a baby" after first viewing the "indescribable degradation" of the dormitory lifestyle. As a critic of the southern dormitory system, Stufflebeame described how these young men lived as if they were caged animals in a human zoo:

> Another tank contained only young men, aged 20 to 25, at another unit. I was warned not to go in there, for it was dangerous. Upon my entrance, there as elsewhere, the convicts came running to their bars like chickens coming for corn. Each one hopes faintly for some slight relief from any visitor. The stench was terrible. Toilets were stopped up. Overhead water pipes leaked copiously. There were 75 men in there, and only 66 bunks. How could they manage to bed down 75 men in 66 bunks? One of the boys explained it. He said there always were enough of them up walking in an effort to keep warm and to take up surplus.[87]

The committee's report cited the conclusion of Captain Hinds of the Darrington Prison that "only when separate cells are provided would the crime of sodomy be stamped out." Mirroring the MacCormick report, state legislators concluded that the only thing that would stop the "spread of homosexuality" was closing the farms and building cells and walls instead.[88] Reformers therefore responded to sexual "contamination" with "strategies of containment" that borrowed from medicalized discourse to control homosexuality and secure the prison through spatial isolation and social quarantine.[89]

Prison guards still routinely used corporal punishment without granting an official disciplinary hearing. The men on the Wynne prison complained that they were routinely subjected to "severe beatings and of continuous cursing by the guards." At the Darrington prison farm "brutality was very prevalent." The prisoners reported that the guards "routinely cursed" them and "beat them in the fields with rubber hoses." Mrs. Lillie B. Atchison, whose brother was a prisoner on the Retrieve prison, pleaded in a letter to the governor that "the boys" are "treated like animals" without recourse to complain to state authorities as the building tender system ensured that "if they talk they are beat nearly to death or worse."[90] In another letter, a Mrs. Riley wrote about her husband, who was used as human bait so that the prison administration's trained dogs might learn to better track escapees:

> I visited my husband Easter Sunday at Harlem Farm C 2 Richmond, Tex. I noticed peces [sic] of flesh torn out his lefs [sic] by dog's there. They are using him as dog trainer. He runs while the dogs run after him. He is

forty-nine yrs of age. He is afraid to say any-thing—afraid that they will mistreat him. Please send some one out there to investigate his condition. It is'ant [sic] that he doesn't want to do what is required of him it is that he wants some better job where he wouldent [sic] be eaten on by these dogs.[91]

This letter also offers evidence that prisoners caught up in the racialized classification system could lose their status as "white." Written as if it occurred to Mrs. Ripley as an afterthought, she included in the letter's "P.S." that her husband was wrongly classified as an incorrect "race." "Most these folks out on prison farm call my husband a Mexican. But he is no Mexican. He is French. I know he bourne out in LA. Of course a Mexican is a human same any other. But Frank Ripley is French."[92] Frank Ripley's plight highlights the importance of the racial classification system and the ways in which prioritized skin privilege shaped a prisoner's condition and safety. Indeed, had the prison system chosen to classify Frank Ripley as a French "white" prisoner as opposed to a French "Mexican," it would be unlikely that his job position would have rendered him as human fodder for trained hunting dogs.

Prisoners also complained that the guards frequently used tear gas as a means to punish the entire prison farm for one man's violations. "If any one man causes trouble," stated the legislative report, "tear gas in large quantities is shot in the cells and all the men suffer for the wrongs of one man. This was the most consistent gripes of all the men." At night, silence was enforced, and there was no talk allowed above a whisper "without the use of tear gas by the guards." On the Darrington prison farm, the use of tear gas against all prisoners was even more widespread. Tear gas was used "every night," and canisters were put into the air circulators so that it could "blow down on them over the entire building." It was an atmosphere in which "men were treated worse than animals." One man who had served time in a German prison camp alleged that "all indications were that this farm was far worse than a German or Jap prison camp during the entire war."[93]

In addition to its brutality, the Texas prison farm and dormitory system was also inefficient and costly. S. E. Barnett, a former superintendent of printing with the TPS, offered an open letter when he tendered his resignation on August 31, 1946, after having worked in the prison system for fifteen and a half years. Addressing his open letter to M. Riley Wyatt, the chairman of the Texas Prison Board, Barnett charged that the prison system possessed a "unequalled record" of financial mismanagement, citing the 1944 annual report, which showed a net loss of $1,500,675, amounting to a per man loss for the year of $436 for every prisoner in the prison system. Barnett's vituperative letter was especially damaging because it showed the public that many of the prisoners' complaints concerning brutality were indeed justified and centered on the unaddressed building tender system:

> You certainly cannot lay a claim to rehabilitation or a reformative institution. You should know that building tenders have beat the heads of their fellow prisoners almost to a pulp. You should know that inmates have had knives plunged into their hearts while others slept by because they were some farm managers' "stool pigeons." You should know that inmates have been almost devoured by dogs in the fields and have been brutally handled in other ways. You should know that inmates have been taken from the farms by the farm managers, or their wives, to work on nearby personal property. You should know that inmates on the farms were forced to live and sleep in dirt and filth and slime that bed bugs and other vermin almost took over some of the farm barracks.[94]

Barnett warned that prison reform can erect "the finest buildings that money can buy" but that the failure to end the practice of prisoners serving as guards (building tenders) would mean that Texas would "still have the rottenest system on earth." "It takes more than fine buildings to make a modern prison system," Barnett admonished.[95]

An equally dreaded punishment was the prison's reliance on solitary confinement. Prisoners found guilty of a disciplinary offense were put into the "hole," a small, unlit cell without toilet where they subsisted on only bread and water and one full meal every thirty-six hours. The cases of the prisoners Kenneth Clem and Cecil Bear reveal the nature of the solitary experience. The committee found Clem on the Darrington farm in his pitch-dark solitary cell where he was "handcuffed for the period of two days with no blanket to sleep on, and his hands behind his back in such a way that sleep must have might near impossible." The guards gave Clem water and one piece of bread every eight hours and a full meal only once every thirty-six hours. A full meal, according to the committee report, consisted of "4 spoonfuls of water gravy, 1 spoonful of beans, small piece of dry salt bacon, 3 biscuits and water. No milk or coffee." This was the standard solitary diet until 1971. It is no wonder then that the committee described Clem as a "pitiful sight," who "cringed from fear of the committee," and was just "a boy who almost cried when being talked to by the committee." In the next cell, the committee found Cecil Bear, from Houston, who was confined to solitary because he refused to work and attempted self-mutilation. Bear reported that in addition to being fed only once every thirty-six hours, the prison guards had repeatedly beat him with a rubber hose. Bear also claimed that Captain Easton had told him that he would remain in solitary for thirty days, handcuffed. Bear also related how the guards "cursed the men continuously and beat them in the fields with rubber hoses for talking to each other and for other minor reasons." Prisoners in the field at Darrington corroborated Bear's claims that men were put in solitary confinement for little or no reason and that prison guards left them handcuffed and naked in solitary cells for days on end.[96]

A particularly acute problem in confinement was the inability to sleep. The solitary cells were often overcrowded with as many as six men handcuffed together, making sleep impossible because, as the committee reported, there was "not enough room to lie down—its too crowded." The wearing of handcuffs for such long periods of time also led to deep sores on the wrists of the offending prisoners, which, the committee reported, "were horrible to look at." The committee cited one case in particular of a prisoner who had been in solitary confinement for four days and had deep sores on his wrists caused by the "rubbing of the handcuffs when he attempted to lie and sleep." Prison guards and officials showed little interest in the physical suffering or maladies of such prisoners. After showing the captain the sores, the captain told the offending prisoner to "dash some mercurochrome" on the sore and "get to work in the fields." The committee found that "there were too many of these types of sores and blisters and raw rubbed sores on feet going unattended to and appearing infected and in horrible condition."[97]

Even outside of solitary confinement, health conditions were poor. The clothing on the Darrington prison farm, for instance, was "filthy," and clean clothes were given out only once a month. Shoes, furthermore, were "old and worn out" or improperly fitted, causing massive blisters. Blisters on many of the men's feet resulted in "horrible, dirty, open infected sores with no evidence of medical care." The committee further reported that "the skin was rotting away and yet the men were forced to work all day standing on these sore feet." Others simply worked barefoot because "their feet were so infected and they couldn't wear shoes." For those who did receive medical attention, the committee found it "poor" at best and administered by a reportedly incompetent physician. Dr. Austin, an eighty-year-old resident physician, was the only prison physician, and the committee found him simply "too old to give the proper attention to the men" and "the worst hated man in the institution." Even the unit's captain reported that Dr. Austin was "about useless as a doctor." As an example of the poor medical care, the committee cited the case of one man who had his teeth pulled out twenty-four months before the committee visit, and yet he still had no false teeth. The prison guards forced the prisoner to eat regular meals without being given neither "teeth nor soft foods to compensate." "Medical attention surely is needed at this institution," the committee concluded.

The committee also cited the near ubiquity of self-mutilation that had "spread" across the prison system. "Many men had cut off their fingers, mutilated their feet and cut the tendons of their legs in hopes of getting shipped from this institution," reported the committee. Another man who had cut three of his fingers off was "taken directly to the dispensary and bandaged, but was then beaten for 30 minutes with a hose for mutilating himself." The prisoners' reasons for self-mutilation, according to the report, had less to do with psychological self-destruction than a practical desire to escape constant beatings and the fear of death in the cotton fields of East Texas. The prisoners claimed that they could not "stand the beatings of the guards and took this way out to keep from being killed in the fields by the guards." The committee concluded that "this story was told over and over again word for word by many of the convicts."[98]

Conclusion

The MacCormick report and the conclusions of the legislative committee represent a rare moment when prison reform was taken seriously by both reformers and politicians as both a humane and a modernizing endeavor for southern prison management. In his cover letter for the committee report, Representative Sam Sellar lamented that after reviewing "many penal institutions throughout the nation," he was forced to come to the sad conclusion that "we have the worst prison system of any State." Although the committee acknowledged that "these men [prisoners] have violated the laws of society" and should therefore "be punished for their crimes," the legislators also conveyed their humane impulse that insisted that prisoners are still "human beings and should be treated as humans and not beasts."[99]

The severity of the postwar prison crisis highlighted the "backwards" condition of southern prison farms. By calling on a northeastern reformer to overhaul their system, the prison board hoped to counter negative images of the prison farm with a modernized penitentiary. MacCormick, steeped in progressive penology, offered a reform vision that perceived the prison crisis in medical and clinical terms. By drawing on the new sexology field of psychopathology, MacCormick pathologized homosexuality as criminally violent and socially contagious. He concluded that dormitory and communal living threatened to "spread" homosexuality and brutalization to a "contaminated" general prison population. The reformers' solution was to contain and isolate "perverts" and "aggressive" prisoners by building cell blocks and enclosed spaces. As such, prison reformers reimagined southern prison dormitories as celled penitentiaries that would reshape young men away from "peversions" and transform prisoners into wards of what Margot Canaday has called a "straight state." The campaign to end the southern practice of dormitory living and embrace instead the northern walled penitentiary should thus be seen within the Cold War context of subversion, containment, and "sex crime" panic. Anxiety over prison homosexuality was not the only motivation for reform. The reformers also displayed a genuine interest in protecting prisoners from sexual violence and physical abuse, but the fear of "sexual peversions" made the construction of walls and cells that might protect younger prisoners from those perceived as "wolves" as the postwar era's most pressing reform.

Moving prisoners from public living spaces to separate cells had an unintended consequence, however. While the reformers hoped to control and safeguard prisoners through spatial reconstruction, they failed to consider how the movement from farms to cells might shift the balance of power within prison society, for, while the prison warden and his officers controlled field labor, the control of the prison building was dependent on building tenders. And yet both the committee and MacCormick failed to address the building tender system in their reform vision. This is particularly striking because MacCormick began his career as New York's prison commissioner by ferreting out gang and convict control of the Welfare Island prison. Their approach to prison reform thus focused on reshaping the prison farm into a modern penitentiary rather than addressing the social structures that ordered and controlled prison society.

Such an external emphasis on prison space and containment had profound consequences. As the geographical theorist Edward Soja reminds us, "space can be made to hide consequences from us, how relations of power and discipline are inscribed into the apparently innocent spatiality of social life, how human geographies become filled with politics and ideology."[100] Reformers, however, never foresaw that their spatial reform agenda might actually end up accelerating internal brutality and corruption.

Chapter 2

A Fine Southern Plantation

Perfecting Prison Slave Labor as the Agribusiness Model

A great problem in American prisons is finding something constructive for
the inmates to do. In many prisons, especially in the north and east, they
warehouse convicts—they keep them in cells and permit them to lie around
all day long. Every able man in our department works. And he works
hard. . . . If we don't do anything else in the Department of Corrections we
at least teach them the dignity of work and the necessity of work.

—George Beto, Director of Texas Department of Correction, 1962–1972

They've got this place so regulated that there's no chance to screw up. Here,
every decision, even the tiniest one, is made for you. . . . It's like running a
poultry farm. There's good feed, the cages are clean, they wash down the
animals, but it's all mechanical. Honor, integrity, decency—these are
the human things that there is no attempt to instill. It's the antithesis of the
outside world, where you have to take some measure of responsibility for
yourself. They turn out great prisoners here—but broken people.

—Frank Leahy, Texas Prisoner, 1978

In 1961, Jack Kyle, the steely-eyed warden of the newly built Ferguson prison,
looked out over the 1,222 acres of prison fields where 1,122 young men, first
offenders between the ages of seventeen and twenty-three, worked in a tightly
managed agricultural labor system that Kyle believed to be "foolproof" and
"perfectly designed." Ferguson prison, known by the prisoners as the "Glad-
iator farm," held youthful first offenders new to the Texas Prison System. As
new entrants to the prison system, these young offenders were at the bottom
of the internal prison ranks and had to work their way up the hierarchical ladder to earn better work positions that came with attendant privileges. Field
labor was the lowest-ranking work assignment that a prisoner could receive,
and it constituted the rank position that held many young men and prisoners
of color bound to coerced field labor on a well-ordered and tightly controlled
twentieth-century prison plantation. Prisoners understood how promotion
and demotion of job assignment meant all the difference in how they might
experience the pain of their incarceration. As the first warden of Ferguson,

Warden Kyle, explained: "Well, that made sense to the convict as well as the officer, because they knew that if they were going to get a job, they had to please the officers. That's all they had to do—just do a good job. . . . That system worked fine because it allowed those people to know that if they worked, did what they were told, stayed out of trouble, they were going to get out of that field."[1]

In the postwar period, the national reputation of Texas's prison system went from the "worst in the nation" to that of an ambitious reformer. The state's $4.2 million outlay in 1948 was the nation's largest single appropriation for the reorganization of a prison system, with the exception of the reorganization of the federal prison system in 1930. When this new system was fully operational in the 1960s, Texas garnered plaudits, becoming "the best in the nation" and the "national prison yardstick" according to Austin Mac-Cormick, the nation's leading post–World War II penologist.[2] The "national prison yardstick" that measured Texas prisons against other systems used a metric that considered work, order, control, productivity, economic self-sufficiency, and low-cost government as the measure of good prison management. These were the key elements that comprised what the historian Robert Perkinson termed "control penology," the guiding philosophy of Texas prison management during the post–World War II era.[3]

What undergirded the national reputation of prison order in Texas, however, was a coerced regime of tight labor discipline, where a narrative of modernization and low costs served the prison farm's transition to efficient prison plantation while disguising its internal labor discipline and control apparatus. By moving beyond control penology's external modernization narrative and dissecting how prison labor disciplined, ordered, and controlled every aspect of southern incarceration, this chapter shows how incarceration on the Texas prison plantation rendered Black, brown, and even white bodies as slave labor, where the state relegated prisoners to coerced and entirely unpaid labor, daily acts of bodily degradation, and the perpetual denial of civil and human rights.

By emphasizing prison labor and work, Texas reenergized the southern tradition of prison labor, which convict leasing had stained.[4] The conventional narrative of the southern prison concluded that the turn toward convict leasing from 1870 to 1920 left the southern economy mired in an inefficient tradition of plantation agriculture.[5] More recent literature on the New South, however, has documented that convict leasing was not simply an anachronistic "barbarous relic." Rather, historians of the convict lease system have linked coerced convict labor to the development of a capitalist political economy that modernized the South's infrastructure, roads, and railroads by coercing convict labor in the emerging industrial sectors of mining, steel, and coal. As the historian Alex Lichtenstein so aptly put it, convict leasing and labor were thus associated with "the process of modernization itself."[6] Subsequent historians of convict lease have analyzed how racial oppression and the industrialized convict lease system placed southern incarceration at the center of Jim Crow's racial oppression.[7] Historians of the twentieth-century southern prison have emphasized the transition from the convict lease system to prison roadwork to demonstrate that southern prisons barely "inched their way toward penal modernism."[8] But just as convict leasing was intrinsic to the development of both the Jim Crow South and capitalist modernization, the Texans' effective use of state-made prison labor during the post–World War II era allowed Texas to stake a claim on what the labor historian Robert Zieger termed the "New, New South," a period from the 1950s to the 1980s where the South "trumpeted the region's low wages, low taxes, and anti-unionism" as a more business-friendly mid-twentieth-century agribusiness model.[9]

By charting the state's attempt to perfect coerced prison labor to achieve a fully functioning twentieth-century plantation system, this chapter offers prison labor as the critical instrument to achieve carceral discipline and order social privilege and power. By examining the organization and regimentation of field work and how prisoners found means to resist what they saw as enforced patterns of "slave labor," this chapter maps the political economy of the prisons' successful agribusiness model and the ways in which that success allowed Texas to stake a claim to low-cost government, order, and efficiency that connoted a New, New South modernity.

Implementing the Reform Design: The Ellis Plan

Although Texas did not immediately implement MacCormick's recommendations from his 1944 report, his state-by-state review of southern prisons had earned national attention. In June 1947, J. Edgar Hoover, the director of the Federal Bureau of Investigation, personally wrote to MacCormick and forwarded to him a prisoner's letter from Mississippi's Parchman prison farm. Hoover felt that it would be "useless to refer this to the prison officials and we hesitate to send it to any of the state authorities" because they would not respond, but he felt that MacCormick's interest in reforming southern prisons might yield better results. The letter, signed anonymously by a "crusader" who feared retribution from Parchman trusties and guards, asked the FBI to investigate and intervene against "the horrible cruelty that is being practiced in our Southern prisons." The letter highlighted the degree to which heel stringing and self-cutting were staples of the southern prison farm and how self-mutilation amounted to a desperate plea shared by desolate prisoners mired in the Deep South's coerced labor system. "The boys cut their muscles to try to bring attention to the inhumane treatment," the letter pleaded. Moreover, the pains of starvation diets, sixteen-hour workdays, the heat of summertime field labor, and corporal punishment defined the southern prison experience. "Isn't it terrible," the letter rhetorically asked, "that these boys are given food that dogs wouldn't eat, worked 14 to 16 hours a day in unmerciful heat, never being allowed to stop for breath, and beaten unconscious, even to death on two occasions, for the slightest infraction of the rules, whether intentional or not?"[10] By forwarding this letter, Hoover acknowledged that MacCormick's northern penology reform vision was attempting to refashion the southern prison system.

Despite MacCormick's national notoriety as a reformer of the South, Texas did not immediately advance his 1944 reform vision during wartime. But the 1946 election of Beauford Jester, a well-connected corporate lawyer and a prominent member of the state railroad commission, provided Austin MacCormick with opportunity to implement his reform designs.[11] MacCormick continued to press for reforms in Texas, despite the prison board's initial failure in 1944 to implement his suggestions. In the spring of 1947, MacCormick begin a letter-writing campaign to Texas newspapers and sent an urgent telegram directly to the governor. In his telegram, MacCormick informed the governor-elect that Texas had "more self mutilations than all other prison system in the country put together" and "more escapes in a few months than the whole federal prison system has in a year." Moreover, MacCormick cited the "rampant sex perversion" and "frequent stabbings and occasional murders" as having resulted in an "intolerable state of affairs." Noting the political sensitivity of his telegram, MacCormick admitted that he "would not have wired you except for conviction that present split board may not agree."[12] In response, Governor Jester called a general meeting in his office on March 3, 1947, which included MacCormick, all the members of the prison board, the prison's general manager (D. W. Stakes), and the secretary of state. During the meeting, MacCormick reiterated, point by point, the conclusions of his report and repeated to the governor and the board that the Texas Prison System had an "extraordinary and a critical problem."[13]

By going around the board and directly to the public and the governor, MacCormick triggered a political reform movement that swept across the state. State legislators interested in MacCormick's claims and discontented prison board members who wanted to take the issue directly to the public joined MacCormick's growing reform crusade. In response to the governor's

March meeting with MacCormick and the board, the state legislature convened in April 1947 the Legislative Committee on Investigation of State Penitentiaries and the Farm System. The committee report, issued in April, mirrored MacCormick's conclusions and added significant political weight to the calls for reform. By the fall of 1947, the prison board felt the mounting pressure for prison reform and, after several testy letter exchanges, fired the TPS's general manager, Major D. W. Stakes, in early November. "There will be no peace for any of us until we obtain the services of a forceful, fearless, conscientious, energetic executive for this position," confided the board chair, W. C. Windsor, in a private letter to Jester. But, continued Windsor, "with the right man, all our troubles will dry up quickly."[14]

The board's nationwide search for a new prison manager centered on O. B. Ellis, the forty-five-year-old manager of the Shelby Prison Farm in Tennessee. Ellis's management of Shelby earned the board's attention because it served as an example of southern agricultural efficiency combined with discipline and order. The Shelby farm had few incidents of guard brutality, escapes, or prison riots. Moreover, its operation was profitable.[15] When Ellis had started as manager, it had held six hundred prisoners on a 5,000-acre farm with cash receipts of $54,000. By the time Ellis received his visit from the Texas Prison Board, however, he had turned it into a remarkable agribusiness operation with $403,487 in cash receipts, resulting in a $173,287 profit.[16] The board pinned their hopes on Ellis, so much so that Windsor compared Ellis to the Texan legends Sam Houston and Davey Crockett, who had "made their name immortal in Texas history. Mr. Ellis has a similar opportunity, and it is my belief that he will fulfill our greatest expectations."[17] The board member B. A. Stufflebeame told the press that Ellis's prison "looks more like a fine southern plantation than a prison farm. The buildings are spotless, the grounds attractively landscaped and the morale of the prisoners high. The whole layout is the most impressive I've ever seen."[18]

The board hired Ellis in November, and he pledged with much publicity and fanfare that he would make "the Texas prison system the best in the nation." Memphis residents were so familiar with Ellis's success that their own *Commercial Appeal* declared that his "creative accomplishments at Shelby Penal Farm have been so many, so far reaching and so widely known that it is almost unnecessary to comment on them."[19] The *Tyler Morning Telegraph* praised Ellis's "missionary spirit" and declared that Texans should look forward to his ability to "operate independently of the tax dollar" and that the board's selection of Ellis "may well go down into the annals of Texas history as an important milepost."[20] Windsor similarly chimed to the press that he expected "a new era of outstanding achievement."[21]

On February 21, 1948, Ellis delivered to the board his ambitious reform plan, with the carefully worded title "To Protect Society from the Criminal and the Criminals from Each Other." The lengthy report and memorandum included a "five point plan," which stressed rehabilitation and vocational training; new buildings with cells, segregation wings, and better classification; increased salaries for guards; the modernization and mechanization of Texas prison farming; and a commitment to operate a low-cost, "self sustaining" prison system. Ellis's five-point plan came, however, with a costly $4.2 million price tag, including a $1.6 million outlay for building cell blocks on the various prison farms.[22]

The press applauded the Ellis plan. The *Tyler Daily* summarized the public's reception of the Ellis five-point plan when it called it "more modern, more humane, and more nearly self sustaining."[23] In an editorial titled "Give Ellis a Chance," the *Houston Press* addressed the high price tag of reform from a business perspective: "If the blueprint of such an investment were to be laid before the directors of a private corporation, a board of business men would jump at the chance to put up their money. Investors, given free labor with materials and equipment produced at cost, would get two dollars in value for every dollar cash they spent on their plant. It seems hard to believe that any reasonable body of men could reject such a proposal."[24] The passage of the Ellis plan in 1948 marked the beginning of the nation's most ambitious reform program to replace a notoriously inefficient prison farm system with an efficient, business-oriented agricultural enterprise and plantation system.

"From the Gutter to a Level of Respectability": The Construction of a Prison Business Plantation

Between 1948 and 1961, the year of the prison director O. B. Ellis's death, Texas approved nearly $19 million to improve and "modernize" its prisons. Drawing from such state largesse, Ellis launched a major penal reform program that modernized agricultural production and initiated industrial production, while also hardening Texas's penal discipline. In an acknowledgment of Ellis's success with the Texas legislature, Austin MacCormick trumpeted in a 1949 letter to Ellis, "This is a very momentous time in the history of the Texas prison system."[25] MacCormick's excitement over the reform package was especially valuable to Texas prison administrators as MacCormick had previously been the nation's foremost critic of the Texas prison farm system, and he served as the state's chief architect and reformer during the immediate postwar period. Over the course of the next twenty years, the success of Texas prisons was measured through the prism of control penology's central tenets. Control penology established four indices of improvement: (1) self-sufficiency and a low-cost prison; (2) building cells over farms; (3) efficient farm production; and (4) low rates of escapes, self-mutilations, work strikes, and riots.

Prison upheaval became a particularly important issue as overcrowded prisons nationwide erupted into postwar riots. In 1952 and 1953, there were over forty prison riots across the country, which amounted to more prison riots during that eighteen-month period than there had been over the past twenty-five years.[26] Texas, however, suffered from no riots or unrest at this time. The prison system could also point to a significant decline in self-mutilations and prison escapes, both of which had been perennial problems during the war. Following the 1948 reforms, heel stringing declined from 119 cases in 1946 to zero in 1953, while prison escapes decreased from 126 in 1947 to 16 in 1953.[27]

Further, Texas prisons were nearly self-sufficient and extremely low cost, facts that caught the eye of cost-conscious politicians leery of rehabilitative programs with high price tags. In 1951, the average daily cost of maintaining a prisoner in 44 states was $2.23, and the cost increased to $3.59 in federal prisons, while the cost per a prisoner in Texas was a very low $0.49.[28] The low-cost prison remained a steady feature through the late 1970s. In 1963, for instance, the prison system operated at a cost to the taxpayers of $1.47 per man per day, while the national average was $3.50 per man per day.[29] Other southern state prison systems were also less costly than those outside of the South but none as cost effective as Texas. Florida, for instance, spent in 1977 $115 million to maintain 19,269 prisoners, twice as much as Texas but half as much as California for roughly the same number of prisoners.[30]

Texas prisons were also productive, which explains the prison system's low cost. In 1948, the prison industries and farm operations covered 57 percent of the system's operating cost. Three years into the Ellis program, the prison experienced an increase in work productivity that amounted to 77 percent of the prison system's total cost. When asked about these astounding numbers by a journalist, Ellis remarked that his successes were due to his emphasis on work: "The solution is to give them both the incentive and knowledge of how to work." And Ellis noted that, from the prisoner's perspective, "the more you produce the more you will have to eat and the better you will live. Soon men who had picked 60 to 70 pounds of cotton a day started picking 300 pounds."[31] Over the course of the next decade, agricultural improvements led to a more productive and a more diversified produce base. In 1947, the TPS had 22,000 acres under cultivation, and the crop schedule called for 7,000 acres of corn, 7,000 acres of cotton, 7,000 acres in feed crops, and 1,000 acres in edibles. By 1959, however, the TPS had 36,000 acres under cultivation, and

Table 2 Prison population, escapes, mutilations, deaths, 1939–1963

	Average Population	Escapes	Mutilations	Prisoners Killed by Prisoners	Prisoners Killed by Guards
1939	6,992	54	n/a	3	8
1940	6,687	55	n/a	3	3
1941	6,011	81	n/a	5	6
1942	5,433	92	n/a	4	1
1943	4,292	151	n/a	3	1
1944	3,461	103	n/a	2	6
1945	3,275	115	126	7	2
1946	3,850	124	87	4	3
1947	5,099	126	87	5	9
1948	5,760	91	49	8	7
1949	5,987	49	28	6	2
1950	6,302	56	18	4	3
1951	6,616	25	15	3	3
1952	6,828	29	n/a	2	0
1953	7,414	16	0	4	1
1954	8,248	28	n/a	2	0
1955	8,715	9	0	1	1
1956	8,995	18	n/a	0	0
1957	9,781	24	0	3	2
1958	10,550	18	n/a	1	0
1959	10,953	5	0	0	3
1960	11,308	n/a	n/a	n/a	n/a
1961	11,820	15	0	0	1
1962	12,203	n/a	n/a	n/a	n/a
1963	12,304	16	0	0	2

Sources: Data compiled from Texas Department of Corrections, "Annual Report, 1963," Texas Department of Criminal Justice, TSLA; TDC Board meeting minutes, November 1963, TDCJ, TSLA.

the crop schedule included a far more diversified produce base with fifty-two different crops, including 3,700 acres of edibles.[32]

Texas prisons had become one of the state's biggest agribusinesses, so much so that the *County Farmer*, which conducted a statewide poll of agricultural-ists and state farmers, recognized Byron Frierson, the prison's agricultural director, as "Texas Farmer of the Year" for 1957.[33] The prison's greatest cash crop by far was cotton. By 1962, the prison system yielded $2,000,000 from its 10,000 acres of cotton cultivation. In that year, Texas prisoners harvested 12,000 to 14,000 bales of cotton from the system's five gins, which ran twenty-four hours a day and turned out 700 bales daily. The increase in cotton

Table 3 Cotton and cotton seed production, 1947–1967

Fiscal Year	Cotton Average	Bale Yield	Average Yield per Acre	Cotton	Cotton Seed	Total Production
1947	4,650	2,215	0.476	$266,955.93	$70,157.79	437,113.72
1948	7,160	3,441	0.481	548,898.26	101,698.79	650,597.05
1949	10,850	3,821	0.352	432,291.79	55,927.53	588,219.32
1950	7,200	4,031	0.56	817,097.40	157,462.04	974,559.44
1951	11,419	10,409	0.912	1,809,834.23	272,753.05	2,082,587.28
1952	13,135	10,980	0.84	2,020,808.24	370,016.66	2,390,824.90
1953	14,770	12,352	0.84	1,939,381.89	267,720.08	2,207,101.97
1954	9,135	10,929	1.196	1,863,175.94	296,966.41	2,160,142.35
1955	7,283	11,512	0.158	1,786,731.75	200,690.89	1,987,322.64
1956	6,927	9,580	1.383	1,504,568.76	234,787.92	1,739,356.68
1957	6,954	9,924	1.427	1,483,255.62	235,400.19	1,728,655.81
1958	6,724	8,755	1.302	1,416,030.86	154,560.21	1,570,591.07
1959	8,625	7,727	0.895	1,028,267.99	125,338.02	1,153,606.01
1960	12,504	10,111	0.809	1,466,710.65	186,257.57	1,652,968.22
1961	12,050	6,394	0.53	1,031,695.66	131,349.85	1,163,045.51
1962	10,000	11,604	1.16	1,879,703.90	272,847.98	2,152,551.88
1963	9,503	9,893	1.041	1,574,652.39	252,388.67	1,827,041.06
1964	9,347	11,381	1.217	1,626,420.66	238,518.90	1,864,939.56
1965	9,421	10,587	1.124	1,522,021.40	225,547.01	1,747,568.41
1966	7,813	6,916	0.886	709,629.46	234,002.08	943,631.54
1967	7,855	8,047	1.024	893,659.62	179,087.89	1,072,747.51
Totals	193,325	180,619		$27,831,792.40	$4,263,379.53	$32,095,171.93
Average Per year	9,250.90	8,600.90	0.934	$1,325,323.44	$203,018.07	$1,528,340.56

Source: Department of Corrections, *Twenty Years of Progress: 1947–1967* (Huntsville: Texas Department of Correctional Justice, 1967).

production was the key to the system's profitable success. During the twenty-year period from 1928 through 1947, the TPS planted 258,748 total acres of cotton for a total yield of 113,148 bales, or an average of 0.44 bales per acre. From 1947 to 1967, however, the TPS reduced its total acreage planted to 188,675 acres, and yet production increased to 178,404 bales for an average per-acre production of 0.945 (table 2). Such high production levels meant that individual prisoners picked between two hundred and three hundred pounds of cotton per a day.[34]

The high productivity levels caused notice among the media, who praised the Texas system for having moved from "one of the most barbarous hellholes in the nation" to a system that was now "pulling itself up by its own bootstraps."[35] Similarly, a 1955 *Houston Post* editorial entitled "The Prisons: In Seven Years They've Gone from Bad to Good" proclaimed that "no longer are there scenes of old-fashioned, worn out equipment. Instead, everything points to an operation that is in keeping with modern practices established by free-world 'enterprises.'"[36] Some newspapers practically beamed with state pride over the improvements. "The Huntsville unit shines, it is so clean," gushed the *Dallas News*. "Even the old brick, some of it laid in the walls before the turn of the century, is shellacked and glistens like brass. Flowers grow on every available spot on earth."[37] The prison also engaged in cost-effective industrial work, although this aspect of Texas prison labor received less attention. During the convict lease era, Edward H. Cunningham, the "Sugar King of Texas," had run a large sugar milling and refining plant at Sugar Land, in Fort Bend County some thirty miles from Houston, where the state leased prisoners to harvest, grow, cut, and process sugarcane through industrial prison labor and arduous field harvesting work.[38] Following the cessation of leasing convicts to private businesses, Texas turned to state-made industrial labor that included license plate production, shoe making, wagons, and wooden furniture. In his study of life and labor on Texas prison farms during the New Deal, Ethan Blue noted that industrial output remained significant throughout the Great Depression but remained inefficient, operating each year at a steady loss.[39] By 1962, the prison system had thirteen industries employing on average eight hundred prisoners, nearly all of them white until 1968. The industries included textiles, shoes, garments, mop and broom, mattresses, pillows, brick manufacturing, canning, meat packing, and manufacture of all license plates. The industrial sector was also economical. In 1962, industrial prisoner labor cost was estimated at $0.15 an hour, which was based on the $1.50 per day cost per prisoner divided by the ten-hour workday. Unlike most prison systems, however, the state did not pay Texas prisoners for their labor. This kept production costs extremely low. License plates, for instance, were produced at $0.13 a set. More than six million sets were produced

Table 4 Texas prisons: year founded, location, size

Prison	Year Founded	Location	Size (acreage)	Prison Capacity	Type of Prisoner
Central (Imperial)	1908	Sugarland	4,459	700	First-time offender over 20
Clemens	1901	Brazoria	8,116	1,000	First-time offenders, 17–23
Coffield	1965	Anderson County	22,433	4,000	Nonviolent offenders
Darrington	1918	24 miles south of Houston	6,770	780	Recidivists, 22–25
Diagnostic	1964	Huntsville	93	790	All incoming prisoners
Eastham	1917	Walker County	12,970	2,224	Maximum security
Ellis	1963	Walker County	11,672	1,722	Maximum security multiple recidivist
Ferguson	1962	Midway	4,355	1,122	First-time offenders, 17–23
Goree	1900	Huntsville	889	585	Female
Huntsville (Walls)	1849	Huntsville	47	2,013	First-time offender over 25, with good records
Jester (Harlem)	1885	Richmond	5,011	924	Ones whose release dates are near
Ramsey	1908	Brazoria County	16,844	1,879	Recidivists over 25
Retrieve	1918	Brazoria County	6,754	1,000	Multiple recidivist
Wynne	1883	Walker County	1,412	2,300	Older prisoners, recidivist
Mountainview	1975	Gatesville	97	645	Female

Sources: Department of Corrections, *Twenty Years of Progress* (Huntsville: Texas Department of Correctional Justice, 1967); Department of Corrections, Annual Reports, 1945–76 (Huntsville: Texas Department of Correctional Justice, 1967).

in 1963, which was almost twice as many as the 3.5 million produced in 1940.[40] Other items were equally as low. A pair of prison trousers cost $1.60 to produce; a shirt cost $1.55; dresses ranged from $2.60 to $4.15. A standard prison mattress (single-bed size) cost only $8.13 and a pillow $0.85. In 1962, the canning plant turned out more than 85,000 cases of thirteen different types of canned vegetables.[41]

This productive prison system was also expanding, and MacCormick's reform design had initiated the architectural transition that moved prisoners from dormitories to cells, wings, and walls. In 1959, the prison opened a new mental hospital at Wynne Farm outside Huntsville, called the Wynne Treatment Center. In 1962, the vision of segregating youthful offenders from older convicts came to fruition when the prison system opened the Ferguson prison, near Huntsville, for younger prisoners. Like most construction projects, the new prison was built almost entirely by convict labor, and, according to its architect, George L. Duhl, the new Ferguson prison was built for a third of the cost of what a similar prison would cost if they had contracted with a private construction company.[42] In 1963, the prison system dedicated a new prison to O. B. Ellis with the 1963 completion of the Ellis prison in Walker County, some twelve miles northeast of Huntsville. TPS purchased 7,951 acres of land for the Ellis prison in 1959 from the Gabriel Smither estate of Huntsville. The new prison cost $4.5 million to build, although TPS estimated it would have cost nearly $15 million had they not used prisoner labor.

A Taylorized Prison Plantation: The Ellis Work Regime, Field Labor, and Control Penology

The Ellis reform plan reorganized the prison administration with a blend of business administration, strict paramilitary hierarchy, and Jim Crow racial subordination. The director of the prison system reigned over all divisions. Underneath him were four assistant directors, who were responsible for agriculture, construction, custody, and treatment. Beneath the assistant directors were the individual wardens. Each warden ran his unit as a fiefdom, in which his officer corps was organized from assistant warden to major, captain, and lieutenant. Before the Ellis plan, guards had no uniforms, morale was low, brutality was frequent, and corruption and graft were common. During the first eighteen months of his tenure, Ellis replaced over fifty prison staff from guard to warden with his own handpicked prison personnel. Ellis outfitted the new prison staff in paramilitary gray uniforms and developed in them a sense of camaraderie and pride.[43] By implementing such administrative incentives as a "Warden of the Year" award, Ellis contributed to high morale among the prison staff, many of whom spent their entire careers in the prison system. The wardens similarly demanded loyalty from their officers, who often followed them from prison to prison when a warden transferred.

One of the key elements of control penology was a tightly knit kin network of loyal employees drawn from local East Texas communities who guarded the prison system from both the prisoners on the inside and from any intrusion by unwanted outsiders. Ellis retained life-long career employees to ensure high morale and an intense sense of esprit de corps among prison staff. Promotions came almost exclusively from within the ranks of prison guards, who were almost entirely white men from the rural communities surrounding Huntsville and Houston. The prison system frequently bypassed the minimum hiring and educational requirements for its wardens so that it could continue to ensure employee loyalty by promoting from within. In 1974, for instance, the Joint Committee on Prison Reform found that 29 percent of the wardens did not possess a college degree, and one had not completed high school. Moreover, 53 percent of the assistant wardens did not possess the state's minimum educational qualifications for their position. The discrepancy between educational requirements and rank was even sharper when considering the prison officers, in which 81 percent of the majors, 91 percent of the captains, and 94 percent of the lieutenants did not meet the state's minimum educational requirements for their positions. The same was true for those working more directly in counseling and rehabilitation. The legislative committee found that over 67 percent of the prison's psychologists, psychiatrists, and social worker staff did not meet the state's requirement to have a college degree from a four-year college or university with a master's degree in psychology or sociology.[44]

Although prison wages remained low, Ellis offered other informal incentives and emoluments to ensure loyalty. Texas prisons were unique in that the agricultural bounty from prison labor allowed prison officials and staff access to free food. Moreover, senior prison officials earned community prestige and respect when the prison system gave them free homes that were staffed by "house boys," a job position filled only by African American prisoners, who provided the families of senior officers, wardens, and prison officials with a full-time, live-in domestic servant. The Joint Committee on Prison Reform found a series of informal work incentives and unaccounted perks to prison officials that "included free housing, laundry and dry cleaning services, haircuts, shoe shines, a tremendous amount of food at an extremely low rate, for example, prime beef at thirty cents a pound or eggs at fifty cents a dozen."[45] The Joint Committee for Prison Reform estimated that in 1974 the value of such benefits for higher-ranking officials was $21,000 a year. For the lower-ranking officers, "who were entitled to generally having their uniforms cleaned, possibly being able to have a space in a trailer park, if there was room, or living in bachelors quarters, in addition to a limited number of surplus vegetables that they would buy, the value of that would be about $18,000.00 a year."[46] Prison guards were thus more than employees; rather, they were part of a tightly knit community that derived their societal rank, status, and livelihood from their position within the prison. Such benefits encouraged an insider mentality that jealously guarded Texas prisons from outside intervention and investigation.

Securing loyalty among his staff allowed Ellis to create a prison environment where order and control ensured effective prison labor. Behind the programmatic recommendations and the massive economic request of the 1948 Ellis plan was a new correctional philosophy based on Ellis's firmly held conviction that work was necessary as both rehabilitation and as effective management. Work represented more than an occupation and a time-oriented task to fill the prisoner's day and keep him out of trouble. Labor regimented and controlled every aspect of prison life, and it became the prison system's raison d'etre. "The prison day should be divided into three parts, a time for work, a time for sleep and a time for profitable use of leisure hours," insisted Ellis. While Texas law forbade more than ten-hour workdays, Ellis made it clear that

> I BELIEVE ABLE-BODIED MEN ARE ENTITLED TO NO CONSIDER-
> ATION UNTIL THEY HAVE WORKED THIS TEN HOURS [emphasis in
> the original]. After the man has done his work and had his sleep, there
> are still six hours left in the prison day. It is this six hours that creates
> most prison problems. It is this six hour period that has branded some
> institutions as schools of crime. I believe that all educational, recre-
> ational and religious training should be carried on as extracurricular
> activities, something in addition to the work period.[47]

In addition to working prisoners ten hours a day, six days a week, Texas was one of fewer than half a dozen states that did not pay prisoners even a nominal wage for their work.[48] In 1978, for instance, the states that did not pay prisoners even a nominal wage included Texas, Arkansas, Mississippi, Georgia, and Maine. Within a few years of the survey, Mississippi and Maine started a pay program for their prisoners. By way of comparison, California paid prisoners between $0.50 and $2.60 an hour and New York between $0.25 and $2.30 and Illinois paid the most at $0.40 up to $7.00 an hour. On the Texas prison plantation, however, coerced, unpaid labor shaped the prisoner's everyday experience.

A key tenet of control penology was to work the newly arrived prisoners in the field and use the system of "promotions" to building and indoor factory work as incentives for hard labor. From 1948 to 1978, more than half of the prison population labored in prison fields. Field work acted as a kind of boot camp for new convict recruits and a proving ground where prisoners could demonstrate their work ethic and productivity levels. When Billy Wayne "Redbird" McCarter was first incarcerated at the age of eighteen in 1955, his first introduction to the centrality of field labor came from Warden Hal Husbands. Incarcerated at Central, one of the prisons for younger first offenders, Redbird recalled that Warden Husbands had the new prisoners brought to him so that he could make clear what Texas incarceration was all about. "What are you down here for?" Husbands would bark at eighteen-year-old youthful offenders like McCarter. When the assembled prisoners responded with their convictions of car theft, burglary, and the like, Husbands would roar back at them: "That's a damn lie! You down here to work, that's what you down here for and that's what you better learn and you better learn it right now!"[49]

Prisoners who worked hard, remained obedient, and showed leadership might earn a promotion to an inside job. As the first warden of the Ferguson Unit, Jack Kyle recalled that job assignments were under the absolute control of prison staff, where all first-time offenders were assigned field work, and "if they worked, did what they were told, stayed out of trouble," then they would "please the officers" and earn a promotion out of the plantation fields.[50] If a prisoner disrespected the guards' authority, however, the prisoner could be kept in the field indefinitely.

In the two decades after World War II, Texas experienced a demographic shift of African American and Mexican Americans moving to the urban centers of San Antonio, Austin, Dallas, and Houston. Correspondingly, the prison population reflected this demographic shift as prisoners of color from urban areas were geographically dislocated after their conviction to work far afield on the rural prison plantations of East Texas. In 1940 the state population was 45 percent urban and 55 percent rural, but by 1980 the urban population had grown to 80 percent and rural population dwindled to 20 percent.[51] Convictions in the postwar period were therefore increasingly drawn from urban populations. By 1970, for instance, the prisoner population of 14,000 was overwhelmingly populated by former urban dwellers, with the urban areas of Harris and Dallas Counties alone accounting for 2,536 of the total 3,904 of new prisoners.[52] Most of these prisoners were young and had little in the way of education or job skills. A 1971 survey of the prison population found that "of the total population of 16,500, 96 percent were school drop outs, 60 percent (using a strict definition) came from broken homes; 18 percent were illiterate; the average grade level of achievement being the 5th, with an average I.Q. of 80; 20 percent were mentally retarded, almost 1 percent actively psychotic, 40 percent with no sustained record of prior employment, 50 percent under the age of 25; 42 percent Black, 38 percent Anglo and 20 percent Mexican." As historians of criminology have shown, however, such statistical and numerical accounts were often strewn with implicit racial bias.[53]

Geographic dislocation from urban communities to the rural fields of East Texas was intrinsic to the criminalization process, where Texas prisons drew on familiar historical patterns of achieving racial oppression through disorientation and dislocation. As a tactic of racial oppression, geographic dislocation confirmed the process of "social death," which the historian Vincent Brown poignantly defined as a process that "annihilate[d] people by removing them from meaningful relationships that defined personal status and belonging, communal memory, and collective aspiration."[54] The centralization of Texas prison plantations in East Texas created a similar process of annihilation that relied on geographic dislocation and disorientation that bound former urban people to rural plantation work that must have seemed to them as if they had been ripped from the very pages of antebellum history. Such dislocation was more than geographic, as the transition from urban communities to field work relied on disarticulating the prisoner from his previous sense of self to reconceive of himself as a prison slave. The former Houston resident and African American prisoner Arthur Johnson recalled with shock his first visit to Texas prison fields in 1962 at the age of nineteen for a conviction of burglary: "You know, I had never seen no cotton in my life. Well, I mean except in books or on TV. So you had to get a certain weight. If the officer told you he wanted two hundred pounds of cotton at the end of the day you had to get two hundred pounds of cotton, or they was going to whip you or make you stand on the wall all night with no breakfast and catch you out the next morning."[55] The reliance on slave practices and customs purposefully reoriented prisoners toward the urgency and centrality of work.

Importantly, however, the disarticulation of their former selves as free people was shared among all races who worked in the prison fields. White prisoners, for instance, experienced incarceration as the loss of their white skin privilege as they too were forced to take up degrading customs drawn from antebellum slavery and the racial degradation of Jim Crow. Bobby Lee Mudd, a white prisoner who first entered the prison system at age nineteen in 1969 with a five-year drug conviction for possession of a single marijuana cigarette, spent ten of his thirty years of incarceration working in the field, a labor that he called "the purest form of slavery existing in this country today." "The [field] line is not considered a job," Mudd continued. "It has historically

Prison guard high rider overseeing African American field labor, Ramsey prison, October 1965. Courtesy of Bruce Jackson.

been used as a form of reprisal for misconduct or, for the newly arrived, it was used to condition you. Not physically, but mentally. Borrowing from slave terms, prisoners working in the line are 'field niggers.' Once they feel they have you conditioned then you're given a job—many times in factories—and then you become a 'house nigger.'"[56] In the minds of many white prisoners, the rigors of southern prison labor and the debasement of prison life made their experience one of "enslavement" that caused them to surrender their perceived sense of white skin privilege.

Field work consisted of a range of outdoor labor that can be divided into four main tasks: cotton crop, lesser crops, logging, and flat weeding. Cotton cultivation was a year-round endeavor.[57] Prisoners plowed the fields in January and planted cotton during the months of February and March, while plowing and hoeing of the cotton crop continued through June. The harvesting of the crop began in the late summer and continued through December. Prisoners also cultivated lesser crops, such as garden vegetables, potatoes, and all the prison's edibles. Additionally, prisoners fed, penned, branded, and butchered the prison system's vast herd of livestock, including hogs, chickens, and cattle. During the winter months, prisoners cleared the land by using hand saws and axes to cut down the area's thickly rooted trees. When prisoners were not involved in the cotton or sugarcane crop, they engaged in what they called "flat weeding," which was a predominant type of field labor done with a hoe (an "aggie" in prison terminology). Flat weeding included such labor as clearing brush, digging ditches, irrigation, building roads, uprooting ground before planting, following a tractor to break up clods of collected earth, and chopping cotton.

Drawing on the historical practice in Texas to rely on enslaved "drivers" to oversee slave labor, prisoners worked under strict supervision and a tightly managed work regime that included prisoner oversight and discipline over the labor of their fellow prisoners.[58] Prisoners worked from "can see to can't see" or, in prisoners' ominous reformulation, from "can shoot to can't shoot." Prisoners rose at 5:00 to 5:30 A.M. for breakfast, which generally finished by 5:45 A.M., and they assembled to work in the fields by 7:00 A.M. The workday was a full ten hours and lasted until late afternoon, when they returned to the building for supper. Prisoners worked a six-day week until 1953 when Ellis changed the work policy so that prisoners worked six-day workweeks for only a month in the spring planting season and for two months during the fall harvest. While in the field, prisoners worked in squads, or lines, that were segregated by race. The order, regimentation, and production demands of prison labor were shared by all prisoners, regardless of race. The prison administration selected a pair of veteran prisoners, known as the tail and lead row, to keep the line moving apace and production levels high. The lead row, usually a man of some stamina who moved quickly through the field, would lead the line constantly forward by doing his work at a rapid pace. The tail row, meanwhile, would also be a fast worker, and he would press the line from its rear so that those in the middle, known as "the swing," would never have a chance to fall behind or slow the line. An armed guard watched over the prisoners on horseback, while a prisoner called the "striker," who was one of "the biggest and roughest guys in the squad," ensured that other prisoners continued working and did not fall behind.[59]

When the line produced too little, it was the line leaders who would answer to the field major. These line leaders, in turn, exacted their own brand of prisoner discipline when production quotas remained unmet. Lawrence Pope, a white prisoner during the 1970s, described the tail/lead row as "enforcers. Like in—under slavery, they had the drivers that were blacks, slaves and their job was with whips, to whip the other slaves into working harder and faster. Well, you had the tail row and lead row out in the field, and that was precisely what they were there. They had no whips, but if you did not go fast enough to satisfy them, they had a perfect authority to go back and jump on you right in the field with the officer looking on, and it was condoned."[60] The sociologist Ben Crouch, who worked as a Texas prison guard in the 1970s, concurred that field officers allowed prisoners to rely on corporal punishment to exact productive yields. The common utilization of violence to achieve field efficiency was never recorded as acts of corporal punishment but was instead dismissed simply as "inmates fighting." "Field officers seem also less

Prisoners running to field work, Ramsey prison, 1978. Courtesy of Bruce Jackson.

concerned about the fights that occur regularly," admitted Crouch. "It is not uncommon for the two inmates to be allowed to 'duke it out.'"[61]

Field guards demanded a frantic work pace, and when the line did not move swiftly enough, punishment was assured. Robert Mudd described his first working day as a Texas prisoner in 1969 at the Ferguson Unit for young offenders as a moment of frantic activity, disorientation, and physical exhaustion. His words and recollection capture the experience that so many new prisoners faced, and his recollection of that experience is recorded here at length:

The steel door opened with such force it jarred me awake. . . . Out the cellblock we ran. From there we ran out an exit door to the back stab and came to stop at the backgate. Here the individual hoe squads lined up in order—1, 2, 3, 4, etc. I was in 4 hoe. Pairing up we walked through the backgate. An inmate in front of me had his cap knocked off his head by the field lieutenant. Slaves are to remove their hats when walking by the master. This was not a written policy but it was a policy nevertheless. Once out the gate we were at a run again. . . . We ran down a dirt road where the field officer (the boss as he was called) yelled at us to keep up with each other. . . . We ran for what seemed to be several miles. We were told to line it up. . . . The lead row set the pace and the others had to keep up. The wooden handle ripped the skin from your hands. You had blisters on top of blisters. It was 6:30 in the morning and we would work till eleven and stop for lunch. You got two water breaks in the morning and two in the afternoon. You turned back out at 1 P.M. and worked til 5 P.M. That morning three inmates collapsed from heat exhaustion. They were dragged away from their squad and, if they were lucky, the waterboy would throw cold water on them. That afternoon others would collapse as well. I remember my clothes were dripping wet with sweat. My hand bleeding.[62]

Despite physical exhaustion and work-related ailments, prisoners had to continue working. If a prisoner attempted to call attention to work-related injuries, what prisoners referred to as "falling out," his pleas fell on deaf ears. Prisoners who failed to keep up with the frantic work pace faced the constant threat of corporal punishment where prison high riders would have their horses ride and stomp over indolent or exhausted prisoners who tarried. Michael Eubanks, a white prisoner who first came to prison in 1975 from Houston with a four-year conviction for auto theft, recalled how the work would leave his body callused and constantly sunburned. Eubanks spoke of the price that prisoners paid if they tried to fall out and avoid the field:

If you fell out [stopped working], the first thing they'd do is the guard would ride over there with his horse and try to get the horse to step on you. If the horse stepped on you, and you moved—you were in trouble. You weren't hurt—you were faking. If you didn't move, well you got stepped on, and then they'd have the water boys come over and get you and drag you over by the water trailer or somewheres and wait till the pick-up come down and pick you up. What we called the taxi. And they'd take you into the building. Guys suffered from heat stroke, heat exhaustion, and some guys just couldn't handle it anymore.[63]

Once prisoners became used to the labor, they could earn promotions and "compensations." One African American prisoner displayed pride concerning his squad, which often received work outside of the field because it was composed of veteran workers with a valued reputation. "After you get broke in, it still can wear you down, but it's not the same. It's not impossible any more. And something else: the higher squads that these guys are in, they get other breaks. Like maybe they got some trucks to load or something while the rest of them are working, well they go unload the trucks. You get some compensations." Owning very little else, prisoners sometimes felt that they could at least own the reputation that they were "strong men" who could master hard work while other men were seen as "weak." As one African American prisoner confided, "A guy says, 'Well, I can do it a little better than Bill, and it makes me feel that's the only consolation I can get.'"[64]

Beyond the threat of "tune-ups" (corporal punishment), prison guards and assistant wardens would devise competitive "rewards" that simultaneously incentivized prison labor even as it mocked the prisoners' antiauthority aspirations. In order to instill effective work and high production demands, the field guards often initiated cotton-picking contests that offered coveted consumer items. Guadalupe Guajardo, who first came to prison in 1966 for killing a police officer during a disputed Pan de Campo celebration in San Diego, recalled, "They use to have contests for Stacy Adams shoes. Whoever picked the most cotton during the season—we'd compete, and if there was a tie they would put you out there in the row—two of you picking, see how—how much you would pick, see. I won me a pair."[65] As part of the signature style of the urban zoot suiters, Stacy Adams shoes allowed urban Pachuca/os to distinguish themselves with barrio fashion, which created an alternative street argot through colorful dress that combined urban style with cultural defiance.[66] Prison guards and wardens, however, dangled the footwear of the zoot suiters to simultaneously induce prison labor while openly mocking the symbolism of the Pachuca/os antiauthoritarianism because it was only won by yielding to hard prison labor.[67]

Petty awards were also given as a means to ridicule the prisoner and remind him of his lowly status. During a 1964 interview, one African American prisoner spoke with pride about how hard he worked picking cotton so that he might gain rewards or a promotion. But his effort ended when he "won" one of the cotton-picking contests: "The captain called us up to the picket. He said, 'Give me my three best cotton pickers here.' Me and Willie Lawrence and old Foots, we three went up there. 'Seein' the way you picked, I'm gonna give you all the prize.' He say, 'You split this.' He gave us a quarter. After that I never picked for no prize, that broke it up."[68]

In an Ellis-run prison, recreational time and rehabilitative activities were rare. Ellis's notion of education was almost purely vocational and geared toward practical approaches to work. The master plan given to the board in 1948 envisioned two objectives for education in which there would be a formal school for illiterates and a "second directed study correlated with work assignments." Ellis's educational philosophy was that learning should contribute to the work of a prison farm. "A boy working in the welding shop should be taught how to read blueprints and some physical characteristics of metals. A boy working with dairy cattle should have a course in feeding, breeding and the like," explained Ellis. Indeed, in the new era of Texas prisons, work became "rehabilitation." Although Texas prisons had always practiced hard field labor, Ellis developed a correctional philosophy that advocated labor as rehabilitation.[69]

At the heart of the labor regime was a seemingly innocuous classification mechanism, known as the "good time" law, that southern prison administrators used to control the length of a prisoner's sentence. As part of the progressive movement to individualize punishment and sentencing decisions, most states outside of the U.S. South had implemented indeterminate sentencing, probation, and parole laws by the 1920s. Texas, like many southern states, had no such system.[70] Until 1957, there was no court-monitored or board-appointed system that would hear a prisoner's appeal to shorten his sentence.[71] Instead of relying on a formal board, Texas employed a point system administered exclusively by prison officials. Prisoners with good prison records could earn earlier release from their initial sentence. Under this so-called good time law, prisoners earned additional time taken away from their sentence for every day they labored. At the behest of the prison administration, the state legislature established three classes of good time. Class 1 provided that a prisoner earned twenty extra days' time for each month served on his sentence, as long as that prisoner maintained a clear conduct and work record. The prison administration immediately placed newly arrived prisoners in class 1. Class 2 allowed prisoners to receive ten extra days time for each month served. Class 3 required that prisoners serve their full sentencing time day for day without any allowances.[72] Although classification initially placed every prisoner into one of the three classes, administrators could change a prisoner's classification and move them either up or down the scale. More than a classification system, what the assignment of classes provided the prison administration was an internal control mechanism that they could use as reward, payment, or punishment to incentivize prisoners with the promise of early release and the prisoner's freedom or the punitive extension of a prisoner's captivity.

Beyond good time, a second internal point system, known as the point incentive program (PIP), geared one's work and placement assignment according to the labor regime. To implement his program, Ellis institutionalized PIP, which graded all prisoners on work, conduct, attitude, and participation in the various prison programs. Prison administrators required a score of 80 to promote a prisoner for parole or for a trusty position. Ellis's new disciplinary methods depended on an assessment of a prisoner's labor and work ethic. "A system of promotion and demotion could be cycled," explained Ellis. "In other words, if a prisoner is in Class 1, assigned to Huntsville with a good job and then made a mistake or was indifferent to his job assignment, he would be demoted to a farm unit and a boy on a farm unit who had built a good record could be promoted to his place. The same thing would be true at Central. A man who did not appreciate his job and who not do a good job would be demoted to Ramsey and a man from Ramsey promoted to take his place."[73] Work therefore determined how prisoners were classified and their placement on one prison or the next.

The PIP program proved to be a potent tool, and sometimes weapon, in the prison system's struggle with rebellious prisoners in the 1960s and 1970s. By promoting or demoting a prisoner based on his work ethic, Ellis's vision prioritized one prison plantation over the other and thereby ensured that prison administrators might consider some prisons as more habitable and hospitable than those that contained "hard cases." Prisoners with a history of disobedience and a poor work record could expect to be moved to the "toughest" prison plantations, assigned with field labor, and receive the lowest classification that would ensure that they served the full length of their sentence. Seemingly innocuous classification designations and internal point systems determined displacement and reassignment, and therefore these numerical systems replaced the bat and the rubber hose as Ellis's disciplinary tools.

No prisoner, inside or out, could leave his job once he was reassigned. The two hundred prisoners who worked in the cotton textile mill, for instance, had to suffer noise, extreme heat, and lint-filled air, no matter the health effects. Even the prison board member Dr. George J. Beto admitted "that textile mill works night and day—seven days a week. It never shuts down and it's a beastly place to work—noisy, hot and those men draw 2 for 1 [2 days off their sentence for each day served]. And I think it would be extremely difficult for us to secure the cooperation from the inmates and to secure the production which we secure without this liberal good time law."[74] The prison administration therefore rewarded such hazardous work assignments with the promise of potential freedom. Prisoners working in the mill earned two days' credit for every day that they worked in the mill; any day that the prisoner did not work, he was denied the extra days' credit toward his prison sentence.

Prison officials could also revoke a prisoner's PIP points. Prisoners who lost PIP points faced restrictions on their ability to go to school or take part in other recreational activities. Worse, however, was the loss of good time. Prisoners who refused to work or participated in a work strike or any other form of collective action faced charges of "mutiny" or "aggravation to mutiny," which could result in a month or more in the hole and the permanent loss of good time. The price of collective organization was a prisoner's potential freedom. When prisoners initiated civil rights suits in the 1960s and 1970s, this same work discipline arrangement targeted those that claimed their civil rights as prisoners by denying them their accrued good time and assuring politically inspired prisoners that they would not receive early release and that their freedom would not be easily won.

Rockin' Easy: The Hidden Transcript of Field Labor

Despite the prison's comprehensive labor discipline, field prisoners found both overt and less obvious means to resist the harsh prison labor regime. Laboring prisoners left behind a hidden record of daily acts of unorganized resistance in the fields of prison plantations.[75] The fact that much of this record of hidden resistance comes from the fields of prison labor demonstrated what the ethnographer Lila Abu-Lughod has called the "diagnostic" of power, where the prison system derived its authority and reputation from their labor discipline.[76] As the engine of southern carceral power, an excavation of southern prison fields reveals not only that labor served as the epicenter of carceral oppression but that it can also be mined to reveal how the oppressed resist through a "dissident political culture" as a precedent to political organization.

As has been extensively documented, prisoner work songs provided prisoners some relief and escape from their labor and provided the historian with a hidden transcript of resistance.[77] In 1964 at the very height of control penology's productive labor regime, the folklorist Bruce Jackson visited Texas prisons to record African American work songs that existed only in the field lines of Black prisoners. Then twenty-eight years old, Jackson was a junior fellow in the prestigious Harvard Society of Fellows. As a fellow, Jackson pursued his abiding interest in folk music and collecting human stories and followed the path of the Depression-era folklorist Alan Lomax and travel to prisons in Indiana, Michigan, and Missouri to collect folk toasts and tales from African American prisoners. After writing a letter request to the prison director, TDC gave Jackson permission in 1964 to come to Texas and record prison work songs on the Ramsey II, Retrieve, Eastham, and Ellis prisons. Hailing from Brooklyn with a working-class Jewish background, Jackson was received by the TDC and African American prisoners as someone who was both foreign to Texas prisons and yet an intriguing observant of prison culture. Jackson considered prison work songs as a living but finite "artifact of slavery" that could only "exist in the prison system that is closest to slavery." In an oral history on his folkloric sojourn to Texas, Jackson reflected on the shared heritage that work songs created across the nineteenth and twentieth centuries between the enslaved and the incarcerated. "Blacks work elsewhere, but they don't sing elsewhere. The work songs existed on a plantation. . . . They were a survival technique in the plantation, and they became a survival technique in the penitentiary. And that trajectory of a literal single-formed expression going back all the way to Africa, to 19th century slavery, to the 20th century prison, fascinated me. I wanted to see what it was like. It was like being in touch with time."[78]

African American prison work songs drew upon the slave tradition of communal song as a way to time and control labor, belittle their keeper, and earn a much needed respite from a long day's work.[79] The rhythm of axes and hoes hitting the ground in unison provided the beat for these work songs, and the lead singer provided lyrics that spoke to loss, heartache, and secreted resistance. Although there was always a lead singer, someone who knew the words by heart and who could improvise with ease, the entire line engaged in a "call and response" rhythm that told personal stories with communal understanding and empathy. As one prisoner revealed, "In the river songs you tell the truth about how you feel, you know, but can't express it, see, to the boss. They really be singing about the way they feel inside. Since they can't say it to nobody they sing a song about it." Tools of survival, community, and resistance, the work songs also provided a shared space to sing of individual isolation, loneliness, and despair. The song "I'm in the Bottom" carries a double meaning that places the singers in the geographical location of their labor—namely, the alluvial riverbed bottoms of East Texas—and the symbolic "bottoms" of endless work, fatigue, and anguish:

I'm in the bottom, oh lord
I'm shovelin dirt
I'm getting tired
It's in the mornin'
I'm shovelin' cinder
It's in the evenin'
It's for the captain
I started achin'
All in my shoulder
The boss don't believe it
Here in my side man
I'm hurtin all over
Take me to the buildin'
I need some water
My heart is achin'
Boss say I'm fakin'
What I'm gonna do, man
Gonna write my mother
Tell her see the governor
Ask him do somethin'
I can't move now.[80]

Work songs also subverted and confronted the authority of their keepers without the knowledge of the guards. While the song "Jody" is mostly about

African Americans working in unison to the rhythm of prison work songs, where chopping axes striking wood become the music's beat and cadence. Courtesy of Bruce Jackson.

the loss of a prisoners' girlfriend to a free man, its lyrics also belittle the guard above them on horseback by questioning the value of his work and the ease of his job as opposed to the prisoners' hard field labor:

> Boss on a horse and he's watchin' us all
> Better tighten up, [if you] don't we'll catch the hall
> Wonder if the major will go my bail
> [Or] give me twelve hours standing on the rail
> I see the captain sittin' in the shade
> He don't do nothin' but he get paid
> We work seven long days in a row
> Two packs a Bull and a picture show.[81]

Resentment over punishments are featured in the words "standing on the rail" and "catch the hall," which refer to the punishment of standing on a long piece of wood for hours at a time or standing in the hall overnight for failure to work hard enough, both common punishments in such a work-oriented culture. Similarly, the stanza "two packs a Bull and a picture show" ridicules the system of incentives, as that stanza refers to two packs of cigarettes (Bull Durham) and the weekly Saturday film night. Such resentments could not be heard in regular speech, and the work songs provided the rare opportunity to air discontent against the guards without fear of reprisal. As one prisoner revealed, "I mean, you know, long time ago when the penitentiary was kind of rough they used to sing songs about the bosses, captains, sergeants, lieutenants, whatever they think about them, that's what they'd sing about them."[82] Like slave drivers of a prior generation, the guards seemed content to have the work songs control the day's work rhythm, despite the content of the lyrics. Albert "Racehoss" Sample, an African American prisoner from 1955 to 1972, observed in his published prison memoir that the work songs provided the community with a sense of control over their labor and a surreptitious contempt with the work demands of their keepers: "Boss Deadeye [the overseeing guard] sat on his horse contented. 'When them ol' nigguhs is sangin, ever thang's awgiht [sic].' With his shot gun laid across his arms, he listened as we sang and sang."[83]

Black prisoners also relied on the rhythm of the songs to control the labor and make work a community effort that would leave no single man behind. Controlling the timing of work and slowing it down when necessary with the rhythm of the hoes was called "rockin' easy." Among African American prisoners, these songs also gave them a kind of singular wisdom and pride in their work that they felt none of the white or Mexican American prisoners could claim. As one prisoner proudly observed, "They call it 'rockin, rockin dead easy.' That's what they call it when they start singin' the river songs. Did you ever notice that when they really doin' it white guys never did do it? Why didn't they? The way they work, they works a lot different. The way we do it, we do it by time. We have a steady rock. Everybody raise their axe up and come down at the same time, just rock . . . I guess work by time. I can do a whole lot more work workin' by time than I can workin' loose." Maintaining a tandem rhythm could also be an opportunity to get a much needed rest without raising the suspicion of the guards:

> When you're working the convicts get tired and they say, "Come on, you all, let's rock awhile," and they get together, you know, and that's the way they fool the boss. They come down with their axe and they work like it's stuck, they be resting, see. Then they take it, carry it out, hang it, carry it over their head real high: they resting. And they drop. But they ain't hitting as hard as they would if they's working. . . . They ain't doin' much. They rocking. That's called "Rocking along easy." And it's a lot different than just a steady hack. We're the ones that ever rock, you know. Mexicans, white guys, I don't think they know nothing about it 'cause I think it originated from us.[84]

African American prisoners relied on communal labor and helped one another in their work. Field guards and officers typically demanded production quotas for each line. When an individual could not meet his share of the quota, African American prisoners might revert to "weighin' up" the scale of picked cotton, which meant placing rocks and other heavy items into the cotton sack to increase its weight. As one prisoner recalled, "they'd weigh up rocks and this and that, they weigh up dogs. They'd have an old pet hound out there and they'd weigh that hound up in the sack. They had that old hound out there that they weigh forty or fifty times a week. They'd put him in there to make their weight and that old hound would never say a word until they dumped him out of the sack." The fact that African American prisoners could "weigh up" the sacks without having any other prisoner "snitch" to the field guard is testament to racial solidarity. New field laborers with less experience, stamina, and skill to keep up with the field work sometimes paid faster workers with commissary goods, usually a "blue bag," which referred to the blue bags of Maxwell House coffee. Although African American prisoners shared a communal response to prison labor, the practice of sharing weight, particularly picked cotton weight, could also entrap another prisoner in unwanted sexual debt if he habitually relied on another's work. As one prisoner explained: "The average man back in those days, generally, he'd pick around five or six hundred [pounds of cotton]. That was 'steppin' it.' On the average he'd pick three-fifty, four hundred. And he have trouble there if didn't get up there and give a bit more weight. . . . A man would pick three or five hundred pounds for himself and he'd pick four or five hundred pounds for his sissy, so you wouldn't tell how much he was picking."[85] Owing another prisoner for his labor often meant that that he had to give something in return, and if that prisoner had nothing to give, he sometimes had to pay in sexual favors and with his body.

In addition to recording work songs, Jackson also conducted interviews with African American field workers that provide examples of prisoner resistance and agency. African Americans found unique ways to defy the power of their keepers by playing to the supposed superiority of their white captors. Whenever confronted by white guards demanding deference, African American prisoners put on a false portrayal of their own supposed inferiority by engaging in what Black prisoners termed "playin' the Jeff game" or "playin' at Sambo." During one of his recordings with an African American prisoner, a guard, apparently threatened by Jackson's presence, attempted to exert his authority over the prisoner by asking him if he was "going home" that weekend, which was a play on words intended to remind the prisoner of his lasting confinement. The prisoner responded first to the guard and then privately to Jackson: "No suh, I don't think I'm goin home this weekend. The warden told me I had to work, boss, I can't make it." And then privately to Jackson: "See, that's what I tell you. When you been in the joint a long time you know how to address all the officers and bosses like that. That boss, he asked me was I goin' home this weekend. He know I can't go home. So I told him, 'No, boss, I can't go. I got to work this weekend.' That's the way things go like that. You get smart with 'em."

The songs therefore provided African American prisoners some control over their labor while also providing them the freedom to collectively express spiritual hope, personal resentment, collective resistance, and physical exhaustion. Work songs were, as Lawrence Levine has called them, a "communal instrument" that created for prisoners, just as it had once done for slaves, "an improvisational communal consciousness." And, as Bruce Jackson has theorized, prison work songs gave prisoners a sense of ownership over their labor that was otherwise denied. "The songs change the nature of the work by putting the work into the worker's framework," observed Jackson. "By incorporating the work with their song, in effect, co-opting something they are forced to do anyway, they make it *theirs* in a way it is otherwise not."[86]

Prisoners in the white and "Mexican" lines, meanwhile, found different ways to resist the labor regime. They did not employ the work song tradition, but they did help one another in their work in exchange for commissary items or simply as an act of racial solidarity. The practice of self-maiming had become less frequent since the 1948 reforms, but it had not disappeared altogether. As late as July 1977, Michael Jewell, a white prisoner, wrote to Senator Chet Brooks and explained why he had turned to the tradition of self-mutilation:

> I found an old razor blade in my cell and severed the main tendon in my left leg that runs up from the heel, cutting into it. I did so deliberately so that I would not have to continue working in the fields and suffering the abuses already mentioned. This was not an original idea. I merely followed the example of many men before me, who chose to maim themselves rather than suffer the abuses of field work. . . . Senator, please consider how disagreeable a thing must be for one to chose self-mutilation as a preferable alternative. In prison slang, the act is popularly known as "heel stringing." Dozens of men have done it over the years. A factual record which poignantly suggest that there must be some truth to the charge that field work as it exists on the Ellis Unit is a form of cruel and unusual punishment. Senator, please consider how disagreeable a thing must be for one to chose self-mutilation as a preferable alternative.[87]

Some prisoners continued the practice of self-maiming as a means to confront prison authority and as a way to avoid prison labor, although it occurred with far less frequency than before the reform period.

The most direct and confrontational form of resistance was the work strike, what prisoners referred to as a "work buck." Prior to 1978, these work strikes were uncoordinated, lacked leadership, and were relatively rare, but given the totality of the work regime these brief moments of collective resistance suggest a deep undercurrent of discontent. White, Black, and Mexican American prisoners engaged in short-lived work strikes throughout the postwar period. Mexican American prisoners, in particular, engaged in some of the period's most notable work strikes, particularly the work bucks of 1957 and 1961.

On the first day of cotton-picking season, on a Saturday in March 1957, three hundred Mexican American prisoners on the Harlem Prison Farm No. 1 in Sugar Land, just southeast of Houston, sat down on a humid Texas summer day and refused to work. The prisoners had a minimal quota that day to pick 160 pounds of lint cotton, but this was Saturday and the prisoners were determined to make demands for a five-day workweek. Four years previously, in 1953, Ellis had changed the six-day-a-week work policy so that prisoners worked only five days a week, except for a month in the spring planting season and two months during the fall harvest. The prisoners felt that even the restricted six-day workweek remained unfair, especially because the planting and harvesting seasons made for particularly hard work. In response to the prisoner unrest, Ellis notified the board members H. H. Coffield and George Beto about the strike, and they both immediately traveled to the Harlem farm to help calm the situation. While the strike was put down after only one day, it represents a rare moment of prisoner solidarity and collective action against the Ellis work regime.

These acts of daily resistance and communal agitation allowed prisoners to find ways to survive the rigors of prison work and life. These unorganized daily acts of resistance did not yet represent an open prisoner rebellion. But they were also more than individual acts of survival because the site of their resistance was the labor fields where the prison plantation took great pride in their ability to avoid prison riots, prolonged work strikes, and any semblance of disorder or organized resistance. The ordered, controlled, and thoroughly disciplined prison field provided the very signification of the prison plantation's power. While this unorganized form of daily resistance did not overturn the prison plantation, it did disrupt and trouble its sense of comprehensive control. For the prisoners, their acts reveal that they knew precisely where the prison's power resided.[88] In the 1970s, the prisoners' rights movement would build upon these acts of daily resistance to forge an inter-racial coalition who engaged in sustained, coordinated, and organized acts of collective resistance aimed at upending the prison system's power hierarchy.

"Houseboys" and Domestic Servitude

The prison system also divided African American men by making some of the longer-term prisoners serve as live-in domestic servants to the system's top administrators and wardens. These domestic servant positions, known by prison officials and guards as "houseboys," could only be staffed by African American men. The practice has its origins in the East Texas slave plantation in which enslaved women waited on tables, cleaned clothes, and did household chores and enslaved men served as gardeners, hostlers, and carriage drivers.[89] By the early twentieth century, male African American prisoners had been pressed into both the male and female service roles that enslaved African Americans had provided during slavery.[90] The practice survived until 1980, when the prisoners' rights movement turned to the courts to dismantle the southern prison plantation.

The use of houseboys was prevalent in the 1940s, 1950s, and 1960s, even though prison directors viewed the tradition with caution. In 1951, the director Ellis issued a memorandum to all wardens warning them that "the use of houseboys is hazardous at its best. Through the years there have been a number of prison officials killed, or members of their families killed, by trusty servants." Houseboys, according to the 1951 memorandum, should not be allowed to become too familiar with the family that they served. Incidents of impropriety and rule infractions centered on white sexual anxieties and on Jim Crow fears that cultural patterns of racial subservience were not thoroughly obeyed. The rule infractions listed in the 1951 memo included employee wives who drove prisoners "to the building for their grocers," a "wife and houseboy sitting in the living room conversing," a prisoner listening to radio and television programs with the prison employee's family, and the case of a houseboy who interrupted a "business conversation about prison operations" to "give his views." Indeed, sexual anxiety over prisoner domestic servants nearly threatened to end the houseboy practice. In 1965, a TDC memorandum to all wardens cited "two serious incidents" that involved "houseboys and sex." The memorandum did not state the specific nature of the incidents, but they were serious enough that the prison director, Dr. George Beto, promised to remove all prisoners as domestic servants if there was "another serious houseboy incident."[91] Instead of ending the practice, however, Beto permitted a grandfather clause that allowed officials who kept houseboys at the time of the memorandum to continue the practice. As late as 1978, there were fifty-five remaining homes that used houseboys, all of whom were male African American prisoners, as live-in servants.[92] Available records on the houseboy system are few. Personal recollections and oral histories are among the few means available to reconstruct the existence and operation of the system.

The Combs family and their relationship with the family houseboy provides an intriguing glimpse into the shared life of keeper and kept that maintained the domestic tradition of racial subservience through much of the twentieth century. Charlie Combs III grew up with a houseboy, as his father, Charlie Combs Jr., was superintendent of prison construction at various units, including Diagnostic, Eastham, Goree, Darrington, and Ferguson, from 1955 until his death in 1968. Most houses near the prison were a two-story duplex with an adjoining garage that could be converted into an apartment or have an upstairs room where the prisoner lived. Typically, houseboys had a life sentence, often for murder, because the prison administration believed that these prisoners were more trustworthy and less likely to attempt escape than prisoners with shorter sentences. Combs recalled that most houseboys had "good records in prison, but they were usually doing a long time like life. Murderers made good trustees because you knew that they going to be around for a long time." Houseboys were a precious commodity and a status symbol for high-ranking TDC employees. A particularly "good houseboy," one with a trustworthy reputation, might earn the attention of other high-ranking prison officials who would arrange to have that houseboy as their own servant. "If you got a real good house boy," Combs recalled, "you usually lost him shortly because the warden would get him. And he'd get reassigned."[93]

A prisoner with the racially charged nickname of "Coon" worked for the Combs family for nearly a decade, from 1958 to 1968. Coon, or "Coonie," as the family often referred to him, had earned that nickname because he captured wild animals, from raccoons to armadillos, and barbecued them; it seems just as likely that the name had a double meaning given its racial connotation. Coonie lived in the upstairs apartment over the family garage, and everyday he made breakfast for Charlie Jr. at 4:30 A.M. Coonie then spent his day cleaning, doing laundry, gardening, and preparing for supper. Charlie Combs III reflected on the tension between the family's general affection for Coonie and for the prisoners' role as the family's live-in servant and houseboy. "In a sense they were a slave, and I mean I never thought about that when I was a child and we had this 'house boy' . . . but as a child, you don't really see it from that standpoint. That's just somebody that puts your dirty shoes out on the back porch in the evening and you get up the next morning, and they're all cleaned and shined . . . but you never did think of them as a slave—they became a member of your family." Indeed, Coonie even shared a place among the Combs family on Christmas morning, although he had to stand at the entryway to the family room. Combs remembered, "We got up at the crack of dawn on Christmas Day and he would already be there. And, I guess have the coffee ready and then when mom and dad got up, then when we started opening presents, he'd just move his chair in. . . . And he'd just come put his chair right in the doorway . . . and he was just included in this semi-circle. And he had his presents under the tree and as everybody got a present, he got his present. One of the main things was a carton of cigarettes." After the death of Charlie Combs Jr., Coonie was reassigned to Jack Kyle, the former warden of the Ferguson Unit and later the TDC's assistant director of business, a high-ranking position second only to the director of the TDC. The Combs family continued to stay in contact with Coonie, and when he was paroled, the Combs family arranged to have him work for one of the Combs boys' brother-in-laws at Hardy Lumber Company near Huntsville.[94]

From the perspective of African Americans who served as houseboys, their work required that they masked themselves through the complicated practice of feigning subservience within the mid-twentieth-century persistence of the "house slave" tradition. First incarcerated in the mid-1950s, Benny Wade Clewis started his incarceration as most prisoners did, as a cotton field laborer, which he characterized in an oral history simply as "slavery, you know. You had cotton fields. . . . They wasn't interesting in nothing but the white gold. They wanted that cotton, you know." Desperate to work his way out of the cotton fields, Clewis saw the opportunity to earn a job position in a prison administrator's home as a step up on the southern prison's hierarchical ladder. To gain the houseboy position, Clewis knowingly engaged in what he considered to be the performative art of "playing at Sambo" that required African American men to perform domestic duties within the prescribed role of Jim Crow subservience. "Me and a few more, we could dance and do that ham bone," as a way to impress and please senior prison wardens, Clewis admitted. "By our actions they knew that we could along with the Mrs." Ensuring that white housewives remained comfortable with having an African American male prisoner as live-in domestic servant required houseboys to engage in a delicate but always servile performance. In his role as houseboy to the warden Carl Luther McAdams, Clewis learned to remove his hat whenever the warden's wife came into the room and to come running to attention whenever he heard the ring of a small bell that the warden's wife used to call Benny into service for whatever household task she might demand. Clewis described his typical workday as a litany of household chores: "They had a wash house back there. When you get through with your chores, you go to wash house. If she said, 'go in there and make up the bed,' you make up the bed, when you get through with that bed, you go to the wash house. . . .

If you cookin', you stay in that kitchen. And she had a little bell, had a little ol' yellow top on it . . . and she wanted something, she'd ring the bell. You go, 'Yes, ma'am,' you'd take your hat off. 'Yes, ma'am.' Stick your head through the door. And she'd tell you what she want." In his eyes, such subservient practices required a deep knowledge of Jim Crow practices and southern culture. "You just had to be a Southern boy," Clewis admitted. "I mean all the way southern, just Mississippi and Georgia and Alabama, you know, even ask permission to laugh or giggle, anything you know. You had to be there."[95] For Clewis and other African American male prisoners, the price of escaping cotton field labor and the prison cell was a return to the slave practice of domestic servility and gendered subservience.

As the press, politicians, and out-of-state prison administrators extolled the economic success of Texas prisons, few proponents took the time to look into the homes of prison officials who maintained Black prisoners as personal servants. Indeed, among proponents of the prison system, the role of houseboy was considered a privilege and a rare opportunity to leave the confines of the cell block for the partial freedom of a prison official's home. Within the extended prison community that included the homes of prison officials, houseboys were used as a status symbol that conferred respect and authority among white families who were prison officials. And, as the case of the Combs family suggests, some measure of familial relationship was established between keeper and kept, although always as a measure of supposed white superiority and as a means to belittle African American men. The prison fields replicated the slave plantation, and the warden's homes replicated the slave master's "big house."

The South Has Risen: The Agribusiness Prison Narrative as Southern Modernization

In recognition of the sea change in Texas prison management, the penological establishment heralded Texas as a regional leader to advance southern prison management. E. R. Cass, the general secretary of the American Prison Association, for instance, suggested in a letter dated July 6, 1953, to Governor Gordon Persons of Alabama that Texas was a model for prison improvement. Cass noted that the Texas system had gone from being "justly condemned" and a "vicious prison system" to a "very remarkable change for the better." Indeed, Cass also wrote a congratulatory note to Governor Allan Shivers of Texas that the TPS "had been raised from the gutter to a level of respectability." Cass saw such progress as occurring not just state by state but as a regional movement across the South in which Texas was the leader. "One by one the southern states are moving forward in prison affairs.

Louisiana is on the march; so in Georgia; and I am sure you want Alabama to do likewise."[96] As Cass had predicted, other southern prison systems had taken note that Texas now stood as the model for southern prison management. Frank Lee, commissioner of the Alabama prison system, wrote Austin MacCormick in 1969 to praise the Texas system after he received a copy of the "Texas Report of Twenty Years of Progress." Lee wrote with passion about the progress that Texas had made, calling it "terrific" and a model for Alabama, where Lee felt that "we in Alabama have gained much from what gone on in Texas." Indeed, Lee considered himself "the strongest booster of the Texas system outside of the Texas Department of Corrections." But, he confessed, "it certainly does make you feel insignificant when you return home and realize how little we have done and how hard it is going to be to accomplish anything like what they have done there."[97]

While Texas served as the model for southern advancement, MacCormick and the Osbourne Association had castigated Louisiana's and Arkansas's prison systems for still relying on the southern practice of deputizing armed prisoners as favored trusties to oversee their fellow prisoners. In a 1964 Osbourne report on the "unpleasant truths" of the Louisiana prison system, MacCormick found that the system was "critically in need of corrective action" because the state had made an unjustifiable cut of a million dollars to the Department of Institutions, most of it cutting the penitentiary's operation. In the early 1950s, the Angola prison farm was rocked by a series of prison uprisings, and three dozen prisoners maimed themselves to "attract public attention to the conditions under which they lived and worked." Following the 1952 Angola uprising, the Louisiana state legislature appropriated $8 million to build what MacCormick thought was a "modern institution that would be a credit to any State," with an expected prison population of 2,160 that was expected to house 240 prisoners in cells and 1,920 in 60-man dormitories surrounded by eleven guard towers and security fences.[98]

However, at its 92nd Annual Congress in 1962, the American Correctional Association passed a resolution expressing "deep concern that the drastic cut" would amount to a "disastrous reversal of the significant reform" that was initiated after the 1952 prison disturbances. Such deep funding cuts had rendered Louisiana's modernization of Angola in utter disarray. Angola's dirty and overcrowded barracks, what MacCormick's report characterized in racialized language as "jungle camps," housed hundreds of men in bed space for only 100 people. The 1964 report cited overcrowded and deplorable living conditions, routine brutality and corporal punishment, the use of armed prisoners as guards, the "almost complete absence of rehabilitation programs," and "preferential granting of releases to prisoners with political influence and/or hard cash." The report cited that there were currently

262 armed prisoners acting as guards, with 66 prisoners overseeing the field prison labor, and 196 armed prisoners manning the towers and gates. Inside the prison buildings, prisoners also acted as guards, known as "watchers," who "patrolled the dormitories and were reportedly unarmed." As a prisoner at Angola in 1965, Albert Woodfox placed the southern trusty system at the heart of a white disciplinary regime at Angola. "Inmate guards, for the most part, oversaw prisoners of their own race," recalled Woodfox. "However, in some cases white inmate guards worked over Black prisoners— in the field, the guard towers, and the dining hall."[99] The report cited that the prisoner-guard system violated "every principle of sound prison custody" but was employed only in Arkansas, Louisiana, and Mississippi. MacCormick denounced Louisiana's "indefensible" prisoner-as-guard system in no uncertain terms: "There should be no more temporizing, in the name of false economy, in providing funds for sufficient security officers to eliminate the prisoner-guard system entirely."[100]

In another scathing Osbourne Association report on Arkansas's prison system, MacCormick once again pointed to the use of prisoner-guards as a uniquely southern problem. In a letter to an Osbourne financial contributor, MacCormick called the Arkansas prison "the worst I have ever seen in my career of 50 years, during which we have surveyed every prison system in the country." Writing that he had "concentrated on Southern prisons," MacCormick noted that whenever he went to Arkansas's Cummins Farm, he would first head directly "to the Negro barracks and get hold of a Negro lifer named Hosea Robinson, who really ran the barracks." Under Hosea Robinson's protection and guidance, MacCormick had the opportunity to see how the prisoner-guard system operated.[101] In the 1967 report, MacCormick concluded that "trusties were assigned to positions with duties and responsibility which in most prisons would be given only to civilian personnel." These armed prisoner trusties were "responsible for custody and discipline in the barracks," as well as manning gun towers and the gates. In an ironic twist of armed custodial authority, whenever state troopers had to visit an Arkansas prison camp, they "had to turn over their loaded weapons to the gate trusties, who were themselves armed." The report cited that the Cummins prison farm, the largest prison in Arkansas, had 145 armed trusty guards, 155 unarmed trusties, 105 "do-pops" half trusties to oversee a prison population of 845 "rank men," who were unarmed prisoners subject to the arbitrary corporal punishment of armed prisoner trusties. The report concluded that these prisoner-guards were "brutal by nature, trigger-happy, and unstable enough to shoot recklessly."[102]

While MacCormick castigated the trusty-shooter and convict guard systems of Mississippi, Arkansas, and Louisiana, he remained silent on Texas's building tender system. The administration's effort to disguise the system by calling these trusties custodians seemed to have effectively blinded MacCormick from discerning similar patterns of abuse within the newly made prison cells of Texas. MacCormick returned to Texas in 1954 for another review. Following his visit, MacCormick went before the American Prison Association's annual convention in Philadelphia and announced that Texas ranked alongside California and the federal prison system as one of the three best prison programs in the nation. In a letter dated November 2, 1954, to Ellis, MacCormick wrote that the Texas prison system had experienced "progress which has probably not been surpassed in an equal period of time by any other prison system in the country." What impressed MacCormick "most immediately and forcibly" was the improvement in business management.

> I am so accustomed to seeing, as I visit prisons in various parts of the country, listless and inefficient or partially idle prisoners, and little effort to keep prisoners productively employed for their own good and in the interests of the taxpayers that it was a welcome relief to see the opposite of those conditions in your system.

> To prison administrators in other sections of the country, especially in the many prisons where idleness is widespread and earnings from prison labor do not come within gunshot of the annual budget, it will seem almost unbelievable that the cash revenue of your system since 1951 has averaged more than $2,000,000 a year, in contrast with an average amount of less than $500,000 a year deposited in the treasury by the system prior to 1948.

MacCormick proudly told Ellis that "prison administrators in states where only a handful of prisoners work on farms would view with admiration and envy" the Texans' production value.[103]

MacCormick's final note of praise, which he "kept until the end of this letter for extra emphasis," was an invitation to Ellis and the prison board to stake a symbolic claim to modernity and national success. "The Texas Prison System (TPS) has now reached a level of quality and a degree of dignity where its title and your title of General Manager are no longer appropriate," explained MacCormick. "Texas now has more than a *prison* system [emphasis in the original], and you have far more than the managerial functions your title implies. As you know, a correctional system as large and important as yours in other states would frequently be in a Department of Corrections, and the executive head would have the title of Commissioner or Director. The former of these two titles seems to me to be the better one." The board pursued MacCormick's recommendation, and by 1957 the legislature changed the name of the Texas Prison System to the Texas Department of Corrections

(TDC); the Texas Prison Board became the Texas Board of Corrections; and the title of general manager was changed to director. These appellations, in MacCormick's evaluation, were more than mere euphemisms. Indeed, they were titles that staked a claim to modernity and heralded the rise of Texas from punitive prison farm to the modern age of "correctional justice." Texas gained national recognition in 1958 when O. B. Ellis became the first southerner to be elected as president of the American Correctional Association.[104] By 1968, some twenty years after his initial foray into Texas prison reform, MacCormick reflected on the two decades of progress. "I saw the Texas Prison System come up from close to the bottom of the rating list to its present position in the top half-dozen, and in many ways in the 'top half of the top half.' . . . Nothing in my entire career of 50 years in the correctional field has given me such satisfaction as the remarkable transformation that has taken place."[105]

By the early 1960s, the control penology model had become a fixture of prison labor management that extended beyond the tenure of any single prison director. As a labor control system, control penology reigned over Texas prisons from 1947 to 1980 and included the prison administrations of Ellis (1947–61), Dr. George Beto (1961–71), and Ward James Estelle (1972–83). As the first successor, Beto remained true to the Ellis conviction that "prisons furnished an opportunity to introduce the individual to the benefits of the disciplined life" and that "rehabilitation should include a constructive work experience." Beto repeatedly stressed in his speeches and meetings with the press that "confinement serves a constructive purpose in teaching the dignity and necessity of labor."[106] The system remained just as productive, cost efficient, and orderly under Beto as it had been under Ellis, perhaps more so since Beto emphasized industrial production and had the political acumen and wherewithal to convince the fifty-eighth legislature to support and pass Senate Bill 338, The Prison-Made Goods Law, on September 1, 1962. This law required other state institutions to buy prison products, if the State Board of Control certified that they were competitive in quality and price. The law permitted the prison system to establish a revolving fund for revenues from these sales, using the funds to purchase supplies, equipment, and other necessities. This law propelled prison production through the 1970s and ensured that Texas prisons would continue their cost-effective business plan. By the time of Beto's retirement in 1972, the cost per prisoner remained one of the nation's lowest, at $3 per prisoner per day. In 1970, the Texas prison industries put 1,300 men to work and grossed $2 million a year. By 1972, the system's seven industrial factories had tripled to twenty-one shops and produced goods well in excess of $6 million. In 1976, for instance, TDC industries produced more than $8.5 million in outside sales to state agencies and turned a profit of $900,000.[107] Prison industries relied on the system's agricultural resources to make such items as shoes from the leather of prison-owned cows, clothes from its cotton fields and textile mills, and boxes, brushes, brooms, and mops made of prison-produced wood, straw, and cotton fibers. The bulk of prison labor, meanwhile, remained dedicated to high-yield farm work on over 100,000 acres of land that grossed over $5 million annually.[108]

Unbeknownst to the public, however, such high-yield prison production remained reliant on the trusty building tender system. Over the course of his administration, Beto continued the Ellis policy of relying on the good-time law and the PIP system as an effective control mechanism to ensure a highly diffuse level of prison labor, hierarchy, and order. Beto understood that "liberal good time laws" were not so much for the prisoner's benefit, as for the prison administration's ability to control and motivate prison labor:

> The most important commodity to a convict is time. In Texas if a man comes to the penitentiary, the day he comes—he's made a first class prisoner, which means he earns 20 extra days a month as long as he behaves himself. For every 30 he serves, in other words, he knocks 50 off his sentence. And then if he's a second class prisoner, he earns 10 extra days a month. If he's recalcitrant, he serves it day for day, 30 days. And he can build up this time—we can take away from him and we can also restore it. It makes an excellent lever or motivation device for us. In addition to that, the law allows us to make certain men what is known as state approved trustees, which does not mean that we place confidence in them, it means because of their willingness to behave themselves in the type of work that they do—we can give them 30 extra days a month and they can knock off 60 days for every 30 they serve. And in an operation such as ours—where we are geared to production, this device is extremely important.[109]

Beto thus continued the building tender system, despite the fact that he publicly declared that he did not "believe in any form of brutality or corporal punishment."[110] Building tenders not only ensured control and discipline within the prison building, but it had become economically imperative to retain the building tender system so as to ensure continuity with the Ellis regime's low cost. By having prisoners serve as guards and turnkeys, the Texas prison system maintained the nation's lowest guard-to-prisoner ratio.

When Beto retired in 1971, the prison board replaced him with Ward James (W. J.) Estelle, who, at the age of forty-one, had more than twenty years of experience in corrections. Estelle continued the prison system's emphasis on labor and discipline. Control penology therefore governed Texas prison management through three successive administrations. The apogee of control penology occurred between the mid-1950s through the late-1970s. Assessing the cumulative administrations of Ellis, Beto, and Estelle, the *Christian Science Monitor* declared that Texas was under the tutelage of "a highly disciplined industrial dynasty." Similarly, the *Dallas Morning News* enthusiastically declared, "The Texas system has been lifted to a top position." Such high praise vaunted Texas prisons as a model for other states. "Texas prison authorities are host to a continual stream of visitors from other states looking for their secret. Because its Department of Corrections is autonomous, and because unions do not oppose the prisoner work program, Texas is able to run its shops like a business," crowed a *Houston Chronicle* article in October 1977.[111] Declaring that Texas had "the best operation in prisons today," Wesley Bolin, Arizona's governor, fired his prison administrators in 1977 and borrowed two top Texas prison administrators to reorganize the Arizona system along the lines of the control penology model. Other administrators also expressed their interest in the control penology model. "Frankly, I'm envious of a lot of their programs," confessed David Evans, the head of the Georgia Correctional System. "They have a unique situation down there—they have a lot of land and strong legislative support—so there are things you just can't duplicate anywhere else." C. Paul Phelps, the head of the Louisiana prison system, similarly concluded that "a lot of states have a lot of things to learn from Texas, if they will only listen." Indeed, Lewis Fudge, the senior planner for California's Department of Corrections, visited the Texas prison system in 1973 and 1976 as part of an effort to reduce California's prison costs, which were four times as high as the Texas prison budget to hold nearly the same number of prisoners. Fudge concluded that comparing Texas to other state systems was "like comparing the General Motors Corp with a local department of welfare."[112] In a letter to Jim Estelle, Fudge wrote to his former colleague, "I cannot extol the Texas virtues too strongly," saying that he was "mightily impressed" by the Texas "system that bears close examination." Fudge remained "convinced that a part of our medications must be along Texas lines."[113] Indeed a 1978 *Corrections Magazine* feature article crowned the Texas prison system "as the greatest system in the nation. George Beto and Jim Estelle sit, in a sense, as the crown prince and archduke of American corrections."[114] Once an object of scorn among penologists, Texas therefore had shed its "backward" reputation in the postwar period and was heralded as a model for the nation and the "crown jewel of corrections."

The claims that Texas made for productive correctional management applied to a wider vision of a modernized and resurgent U.S. South. Indeed, when Beto addressed the members of the Southern States Prison Association in 1964, he articulated the role of the prison in the South's resurgence:

> Last year in Boston, at the annual meeting of the American Correctional Association, a distinguished and revered penologist was reported to have said: "South of the Mason-Dixon line, there are no corrections."
>
> We resent that observation. While we are unwilling to make any invidious comparisons between Northern and Southern corrections, we are of the firm persuasion that corrections in the South have entered a new day. . . . I want to plea with all of you to hold your heads high, to rid yourselves of the feeling of inferiority which has in the past character-ized Southern corrections and accept with pardonable pride the work you are doing—for the future of American corrections belongs to you and your colleagues.
>
> I have a college boy son who on occasion facetiously states, "The South will rise again." As far as corrections are concerned, the boy is wrong; the South has risen.[115]

The South had indeed risen and its dominance of prison management set a standard of expansive and cost-efficient state power that the nation was soon to follow. The vast expansion of the Texas prison state in the last quarter of the twentieth century has its roots in the 1940s prison reform movement that created a planned prison success story. Unlike the Progressive-era reform movement, the postwar reform effort fashioned a governing philosophy of Texas prison management that resulted in high-yield agricultural production, cost efficiency, and absolute order. When prison administrators implemented control penology over the course of thirty years, the result was an agribusi-ness operation that was so successful that state leaders and penologists could claim that they had successfully modernized the South and vanquished the ghosts of their past. Although the prison plantation was the engine of the agri-business model, the prison administration cast its success not as a barbarous relic of the state's slave past but as a modernized New, New South. Rather than accept the albatross of their slave heritage and a prison system that served as a living symbol of southern "backwardness," Texans created instead a prison where such "bottom line" and business-like results as production, cost efficiency, and external images of order allowed the state to stake a claim to modernity.

While penologists, politicians, and much of the public heralded the Texas prison system as a harbinger of modernity, the internal prison society bris-tled under the authoritarian grasp of a brutal and violent prison regime. The creation of walls and cells resulted in a spatial formation that organized, disciplined, and controlled prisoners outside of the prying eyes of the public. Many external observers, particularly southern politicians and penologists, viewed the Texas prison system only through a narrow business model. From an external vantage point, it seemed that prison administrators had embarked on a remarkable thirty-year period of success from 1948 to 1978 in which Texas prisons became a regional and national model of efficiency and order that marked a "golden age" for Texas prison management. Externally, the prison plantation was a model of business efficiency, but the internal control mechanism of prisoners controlling and disciplining other prisoners remained disguised and hidden.

Work performance therefore determined where prisoners lived, how they were categorized, and whether they were favored. The PIP program, good time, and the trusty system allowed the prison administration to maintain control, discipline, and order. It also gave an unfree and unpaid labor force the incentive to meet the high production demands of prison overseers who expected nothing less than a high-yield and effective crop. Daily acts of resistance drew on the folk practices of slavery and work slowdowns, where the site of such resistance was the prison plantation's coveted emphasis on work, but the language of dissent remained a hidden transcript that tested the boundaries of southern practice but could not yet mount a full challenge to prison labor discipline. Control penology thus depended on slave labor traditions and disguised their internal control mechanisms with the narrative trope that the Texan brand of discipline, order, and prison labor had modernized and reshaped the prison toward effective, low-cost, high-yield productivity. The prison thus operated as a fully functioning twentieth-century plantation, but the trope that the prison administration embraced was not slavery but instead their carefully constructed narrative of low-cost government and effective agribusiness that allowed them to stake a claim on New, New South modernity. So long as profit, order, and cost effectiveness remained the measure of success, there was little public desire to probe behind prison walls.

Chapter 3

Enslaving Prison Bodies

Labor Division, Prison Rape, and the
Internal Prison Economy

> See, the whole thing [internal prison society] is a pretty physically-based
> thing. It's a very predatory system and this, I think, is a very important
> thing to note, that predatory is the common denominator for all of it. The
> strong prey upon the weak, and the weak are in a terrible position. . . . If
> they succumb to the predation, it only gets worse, and predation is social;
> it's sexual; it's economic.
>
> —Lionel Lippman, former prisoner of the Texas Prison System

On the Eastham prison during the month of April 1978, a twenty-three-year
old prisoner was repeatedly raped by a building tender turnkey, Charles Robertson. Through his position as building tender, Robertson arranged to have
the prison major's bookkeeper, a prisoner named McChristy, move Robertson into the cell with the younger prisoner. For the next five to six weeks, the
young prisoner was forced to engage in coerced sexual activity with Robertson "many times." On July 1, 1978, Robertson arranged to have the young prisoner run into him in the washroom so that he could reclaim his "property."
The young prisoner's affidavit claimed:

> Robertson began to fondle me all over and when I failed to get an erection
> he got angry. He told me that since I was not going to cooperate with him,
> he would get his pleasure in other ways. He hit me several times in the
> stomach and chest and knocked me back into the commode. Robertson
> then told me to turn around and bend over on the commode, I hesitated
> and he again hit me. He pulled me to my feet and spun me around;
> grabbed my pants and pulled them down. I struggled to get away, it was
> then that Robertson pulled a home-made knife from his pocket. Placing
> the knife at my throat, he forced me to bend and proceeded to rape me.[1]

In a 1978 letter to W. J. Estelle, the Texas Department of Corrections director, the prisoner David Ruíz forwarded this affidavit. Disgusted but resolute,
Ruíz explained that the literal owning of one prisoner by another was an issue
that he intended to expose. "You and your high ranking staff have opposed
prisoner rights' activists with all the force you can muster and in some cases

brutal force have been used," wrote Ruiz. "This is to inform you that I will continue in seeking prison reform, regardless of the hardships I must endure."[2]

What David Ruíz understood was that the new arrangement of cells over dormitories hid the extent to which southern prison administration relied on state-orchestrated sexual violence. The postwar reform effort to house prisoners in cells rather than dormitories and to build new and modern prisons had the unexpected and unplanned effect of enhancing the power, prestige, and influence of the prisoner trustees known as building tenders (BT). When George Beto became prison director in 1961, 75 percent of the prisoners still lived in dormitories, what prisoners called the tanks. By 1964 that number dropped to 60 percent, and by the late 1970s, the majority of prisoners lived in cells rather than dormitories.[3] Building tenders used the new spatial formation to move freely when other prisoners could not, to control more effectively the internal prison economy by stockpiling commissary goods in their private cells, and to use their influence and power to change the living arrangements of other prisoners from one cell or wing to another in a vicious sex trade. The cell block living arrangement, in short, enhanced their power.

By narrating southern prisons' shift from dormitories to cells, this chapter will show how the power and control of prisoner trusties was strengthened by the changes. In Texas, prisoners had to contend with two sets of unwritten social rules. The first was dictated by what the sociologist Gresham Sykes called the "total power" of their keepers, who insisted on prisoner acquiescence to the work hierarchy that separated those who worked in the prison building from those that labored in the field. Sykes defined the total power of prisoner administrators as the ability to shape prisoner behavior with a system of rewards and punishments that was so absolute that "no inmate could afford to ignore their demands for conformity."[4] According to a pioneer in the study of prison society, Donald Clemmer, an unwritten "inmate code" governed behavior and measured prison identity against perceptions of manly honor and respect, which prisoners earned through violence and physical confrontation. Moreover, such an inmate code, according to Clemmer, constructed a "prison community" where prisoners "are to refrain from helping prison or government officials in matters of discipline, and should never give them information of any kind, and especially the kind which may work harm to a fellow prisoner. Supplementary to this, and following from it, is the value of loyalty among prisoners in their dealings with each other. This basic idea constitutes the 'prisoner's code.'"[5] The "defects of total power," according to Sykes, were that the prisoner code and a sense of "con loyalty" mitigated the prison administration's absolute rule.

In Texas prisons, however, the building tender system bridged the gap between the "defects" of the prison administration's government and the supposed solidarity among prisoners. There was little defect in the total power of Texas prison keepers because the prisoner code was made less cohesive than in other prison systems because of the building tender system, which was an orchestrated division of the prison society. Clemmer's prisoner code, therefore, does not consider how prison societies differ over time and space. Different regional and state practices shaped how prison administrators empowered trusties, and that empowerment, in turn, changed the nature of a variety of different prison societies. As such, it does not adequately describe the evolution of the Texan building tender system within a changing southern prison labor system. In Texas, the internal BT system functionally and systematically divided the prison society against itself by empowering one smaller and elite group of prisoners against the general prison population, which thereby rendered such a code of collective con solidarity as meaningless. Such a regime of power and control forged an ethic of violence, sexual rapaciousness, and hierarchy that defined the internal society of Texas prisons.

Through an analysis of sexual violence in male prisons as a social construct of the southern trusty system, this chapter joins in a historical turn toward placing sexual violence at the very center of racial oppression. Seeking to take prison rape seriously as evidence of evolving state control and orchestration, this chapter pushes against the criminological view that has cast prison rape as a timeless function of the prisoners' own pathology. The buying and selling of Texas prisoners constituted an internal sex trade where hypermasculine predators were given state sanction to deny young men control over their bodies through vicious rape that rendered young men as "property," "wives," and as "slaves," which served to sever these men from their sense of gender identification, personhood, and reputation. The construction of gender identity through sexual commodifaction and power is a more coercive version of what the historian George Chauncey termed the "third sex," where contemporary hegemonic society's binary between hetero- and homosexual was absent in gay and working-class culture in the pre–World War II period. While Chauncey concluded that "the state built a closet in the 1930s and forced gay people to hide in it," studies of prison societies have revealed that the state's effort to enclose an increasing number of working-class males behind prison walls may well have created prison societies that replicated and mirrored some of the working-class sexual habits, argot, and society of prewar New York City.[6] Even so, sexual violence suffused the cell blocks and working-class world of southern prisons during this period.

To take readers behind prison walls and reveal the rapacity of prison economies, this chapter relies on prisoner testimonies, letters, affidavits, depositions, and oral histories of prisoners who desperately wanted to expose the worst horrors of the prison economy to public view. These prisoners wanted to make themselves seen and their plight plain and clear in the light of public scrutiny. The lawyers who took up the prisoners' cause documented this system, and this chapter relies on their work to map the internal prison economy through the *Ruiz v. Estelle* documents.

The southern trusty system therefore constructed a hierarchial and tiered prison society where more vulnerable prisoners were subjected to prison rape and domestic cell service, a process of subjugation that constituted carceral violence. The building tender's power rested on this system of carceral violence that determined a prisoner's gender, their identity and reputation, and the degree to which they might suffer doubled enslavement—a slave for the state in prison fields and an enslaved body and servant within prison cells.

Entering the Prison Plantation: Geographic and Temporal Dislocation

Chained together, leg by leg, traveling usually on a bus without air conditioning, prisoners arrived at the designated prison, where classification officials documented and stripped them of their former identity, family, friends, and home. Prisoners typically describe the first-time journey and arrival as a jolting introduction to the prison marked by confusion and fear. This bus-ride journey from freedom to incarceration aboard the "Blue Bird" bus was one of self-transformation, a process that prisoners termed "up on the chain" or "riding the chain bus." Benny Wade Clewis, an African American prisoner first incarcerated in 1955, described the chain bus as a journey not only through space but through time, where chains of newly convicted men bound for the Texas prison plantation replicated the iconography of bondage within the slave trade. "They had a long chain they would take and put, like you seen back in the slavery days, when they had those chains around they neck with the big hook," Clewis recalled. "And they would run these chains through there and run 40 or 50 inmates, run them through all they necks. Then, they would handcuff you here and have chains here with a big ring through it. . . . Then, they'd bring another chain from that second loop there and hook it through your waist and hook it to that wall. Then, they would bring another chain and hook it down on the floor and bring it and put it around your legs through another ring. And that's where you'd stay." Transporting prisoners across the Texas landscape to the cotton fields of East Texas, prisoners of all races experienced the same chained geographic and temporal dislocation. "See, all those slave drivers [prison administrators] back during that time," Clewis continued, "he didn't treat the white no better than he treated the black, you know. You was just a convict, you know, and that's what you were to him, whatever color you were. And, as far as having a chain that run black inmates to the penitentiary, one that runs whites to the penitentiary, and one that run Mexicans, we was all the same when it came to that."[7]

Upon arrival, prisoners confronted two walled gates crowned by rings of barbed wire. The reforms of 1948 and heavy state investment in prison construction created new prison buildings, made of a characteristic red brick with a design that featured a long, straight, and wide main hall through the entire prison. Wings of cells and dormitories ran perpendicularly through the great hall's center, a layout that prisoners and guards called the "telephone pole" design.[8] Hard concrete constituted the prison floor. A bright yellow line ran down the center of the main hall, representing the carefully guarded line that divided the walking space between guards and prisoners.

Once inside, prison guards demanded each new arrival's name, age, conviction, and sentence so that each could be recorded. Many prisoners felt that this process caused them to leave their prior identity at the prison threshold to be recovered only upon their exit. Once registered and documented, prisoners were then stripped of their clothes, given a full body search, and told to file down a nearby hall to have their heads shaved. Stripped of anything that might suggest individuality, guards provided prisoners with the all-white prison uniform. This process became for some a ritual that reinforced the feeling that their past identity had been written over by a new white outfit of "blankness" and uniformity. At the end of the intake process, many prisoners experienced a near total loss of identity. They became unknown persons without a history, a community, or even a name and donned instead their new identity as products of the prison.[9]

Brutality and corporal punishment welcomed new entrants into the southern prison. In some of the toughest prisons, a line of guards met prisoners at the "back gate" with brutality and threats of violence. Billy Wayne "Redbird" McCarter, a white prisoner who spent more than twenty years in prison, remembered his introduction to the Ellis Unit during the 1960s as calculated violence meant to show newly arrived prisoners that no disorder would be tolerated: "When the chain bus arrived at the back gate, the first thing that happened is that they had what they called a 'Welcoming Committee.' It was about six bosses and they'd come out to the back gate, and they had pick handles or axe handles. Some of them had baseball bats. . . . Blam! They start right on in, beatin' that ass. I'm talking that they would give you a real good whoopin' too. There wasn't no doubt in your mind what was gonna happen to you if you done wrong."[10]

Similar tales of immediate disorientation to a southern and brutal past are strewn across prisoner narratives from other southern states. In the first draft pages of his autobiography, Robert Hillary King, the cofounder of the first Black Panther chapter in a Louisiana prison, who was placed in solitary for twenty-seven years as one of the falsely accused Angola Three, described his first day

at Angola in 1971 as an experience of temporal disorientation where the historical memory of antebellum southern violence merged with his present reality.

> Upon entering Angola for the first time. I immediately got the impres-
> sion that I had been hurled backwards, in another time zone. Those who
> ran it [all southern white men] was from a bygone era, mannerism,
> speech and attire all attested to this. But it was their actions towards the
> prisoners that gave them their high mark in barbarity. Corporal punish-
> ment, and cruel and unusual punishment were administered by them
> with impunity. Extreme emphasis was placed on the "work ethic." The
> work consisted mostly of farming. . . . Other than the right to work,
> prisoners had no other rights that the prison was bound to respect.[11]

At the most notorious prisons like Louisiana's Angola and Texas's Eastham,
the southern prison looked, felt, and sounded like a slave plantation. In the
documentary of his life and art, the artist and former prisoner Winfred Rembert recalled how the prison experience as slavery extended beyond prison
walls. Rembert described his working experience on the Georgia prison roadwork chain gang during the 1960s as "probably the worst thing you can to a
human being. They say slavery was tough, but I just can't believe it was any
tougher than the chain gang. The chain gang is just inhuman. It's a place
[prison] where all dignity is taken for you. You are not a man anymore. It's
designed to break you down physically and mentally. It's so tough of a life. It
makes you feel like you need to be more than one person in yourself."[12] Once
inside, what ordered prison society was the southern trusty labor system, as it
divided up and coercively governed the prison wings, cells, and dormitories.

Internal Government: Prison Politicians and the Building Tender System

Although the press and penologists pointed to business productivity and ad-
vances as the reasons for the improving reputation of Texas prisons, a critical reason for Texas's rise in corrections was its internal government of
prisoners ruling other prisoners. The prison system divided the prison population between those who worked in the field and those who worked in the
building. Lawrence Pope, a former banker turned bank robber and a prisoner
of both the federal and Texas systems, noted that the Texas prison system was
based on a "slavery type of operation." With the characteristic racialized language of the Texas prison plantation, Pope bluntly told an interviewer, "You
had the field niggers, and then they had the house niggers. Well, the building
tenders in the building were—had the role of being the house niggers
under the old slavery system, you see."[13] The use of stark racial stereotypes,

particularly coarse images of enslavement, became the political language that prisoners used when they wanted to call public attention to the divided nature of Texas prison society and the conditions of their imprisonment.

The BT system was a hierarchical, almost feudal, system of violence and domination in which prisoners owed allegiances to other more powerful prisoners who, in turn, owed fealty to prison guards and officers. The Texas prison system relied on a closely knit, nearly all-white guard structure with kin networks drawn from the local community. It divided prison society by race and ruled it with prisoner "snitches" and specially selected BTs, who served the prison administration as openly armed security forces. BTs were typically allowed homemade weapons, such as prison knives, known as "shanks" and bats, and with these weapons they acted as guards, enforcers, spies, and turnkeys. As the prison system's internal security force, they could engage in routine but unreported beatings and maimings of fellow prisoners, an enforcement process known euphemistically as "tune-ups" or "head strumming." In return for their service, the prison administration gave BTs almost total control of the prison wing and certain privileges. Most importantly, BTs received the promise of an early release, as they received the highest rating of good time. They also received informal rewards, such as private cells in a vastly overcrowded prison system, which allowed them to "run a store," which in prison argot meant that BTs used their private cells to stock commissary items that they resold to other prisoners at loan shark barter prices. They also had separate shower times, which allowed them to avoid any threat of physical retribution from other prisoners, as the common room shower was often the site of prisoner violence. Perhaps the most odious informal reward was the system of sexual domination in which building tenders could participate. As the system's unofficial guards, prison administers allowed building tenders to move prisoners from one cell or wing to another cell. This informal reward from the prison administration allowed building tenders to rape other prisoners and to construct an internal slave trade in prisoner bodies, where a powerful prisoner could "own" another prisoner.[14]

Building tenders drew their ranks from a racially segregated prison society, in which members of any of the three major racial classifications—"Blacks," "Whites," "Mexicans"—could become a building tender. White prisoners, however, ruled the hierarchical building tender system as typically white convicts served as the prison's "head building tender," a prisoner whose comprehensive power and influence within prison society was derived from his close working relationship with a prison administrator, usually a warden, assistant warden, or a prison major. Moreover, prisoner bookkeepers and office administrators, who in some instances had the influence and power to move prisoners from one cell or wing to another, were often white prisoners. White prisoners therefore had a greater ability to exert power through the abuses of the building tender and trusty system. As one white prisoner at the Ramsey prison confided to his mother in a letter, "They call the wings integrated—but it is only token—which I dig. We have about eight blacks on the wing—about twenty Chicanos—and the rest are white. We have an all-white building crew. Would you believe eight (8) building tenders? Now, they are right out front police-men!"[15]

Prisoners who worked inside the building usually had some influence and seniority and were known as "politicians," and together they formed a "building crew." A building crew was composed of such positions as building tender, porter, turnkey, floor boy, bookkeeper, hall tender, count boy, and dorm tender or attendant. At the Ramsey prison, Frank Leahy described in a private letter the powers granted to each job position:

> For the record the building tender are the convict guards in the wings. Turn Keys are the convict guards in the halls, and the Count Boys are the convict guards at work. So called Count Boys patrol out at the Furinture Factory the exact same way guards [correctional officers] patrolled. . . . They even write up their own disciplinary reports which the supervisor then signs. They yoke people out and take them to lock up—then come back and write their report—giving it to the free world guard—which is usually the first he has even seen or heard of anyone being locked up. If the building tender locks one up from the wing, then they usually get an ass whipping by the BTs and Turn Keys on the way to lock up—ditto from the factory, only by the Count Boys and Turn Keys.[16]

The court-appointed special master who oversaw the enforcement of the *Ruiz* decision in the 1980s defined a building tender as a prisoner "responsible for the smooth administration of a given wing or dormitory," who acted as "middle management," and whose function was "both administration and enforcement."[17] The building tender Bertrand Jerome Bennett provided a more apt description: "I was like the police in that tank, you know."[18] Michael Wayne Eubanks, a white prisoner who first came to prison in 1975, further defined building tenders as "the forerunners of today's prison gangs. Except they didn't fight for color or club name or anything like that. They fought just as their clique to protect their authority that they had over prison."[19] Typically, each unit had a head building tender, who worked directly for the highest-ranking prison officer, usually the major or the assistant warden, and he had a crew of subordinate building tenders. Head building tenders were almost always white prisoners. Each row of cells along a prison wing had at least one building tender, which typically meant that there was usually one building tender for every sixty prisoners. Although the number varied on each unit and in each wing, there were typically three to five building tenders for every cell block. Beneath building

Table 5 Support service inmates (formerly building tenders) by prison unit, 1981

Unit	Number of SSIs	Total Prison Capacity	Percent of SSIs to General Population
Beto	270	1,595	18
Central	61	700	6.8
Clemens	172	1,000	14
Coffield	283	4,000	9
Darrington	114	780	9.3
Diagnostic	79	790	9.5
Eastham	189	2,224	6.1
Ellis	233	1,722	8.8
Ferguson	164	1,122	7.5
Gatesville	143	900	15.6
Goree	36	585	4.1
Grimes County	0	n/a	0
Hilltop	14	240	5.8
Huntsville (Walls)	195	2,013	9.3
Jester I	12	924	2.5
Jester II	52	340	14.5
Mountainview	77	500	15
Retrieve	193	1,000	20.2
Ramsey I	277	1,879	13.1
Ramsey II	117	1,460	7.9
Wynne	295	2,300	13.1

Sources: "First Monitor's Report of the Factual Observations to the Special Master," report on section 2, D of the Amended Decree Granting Equitable Relief and Declaratory Judgment, *Ruiz*, 2004/016. The report spanned the period April 20, 1981, to October 9, 1981.

tenders were porters, turnkeys, and floor boys. In each prison, there were usually one hundred fifty to two hundred of these so-called trusty politicians.

Prior to 1980, there were few available records that provided an exact count of how many building tenders there were in each prison unit. The 1980 *Ruiz* decision, however, resulted in a series of court-ordered studies that provided some sense of the size and proportionality of the building tender system. Once court-appointed monitors started to inspect the prison units, the prison administration changed the name of BTs to support service inmates (SSIs), which was a euphemism meant to disguise building tenders as janitors. In 1981, the court monitor's first report on the building tender system provided the number of BTs throughout the prison system. It listed 2,976 support service prisoners, 9.75 percent of the total prison population of 30,523.[20] The number of support service inmates for each prison is represented in table 5.

A prisoner became a politician through a complicated set of informal networks, bribery, reputation, or just simply size and brute strength. Walter Siros, for instance, was a white prisoner in the Texas prison system from the late 1950s until the late 1980s, and his ability to become a building tender was entirely dependent on a prisoner patron. Paul Lux, a fellow convict, was never a building tender himself, but he ran the domino game in the evenings on the Eastham prison, which allowed him to earn a series of reciprocal favors to amass power and influence. After working six months picking cotton in the fields, Siros desired an inside job. He sought Lux's help. Lux explained to Siros that during the next visit with his grandmother, he should instruct her to leave twenty dollars behind a mirror in the visiting room bathroom, which a trusty (another prisoner politician) would then pick up. After taking a portion of the money for himself, the trusty would then present the remainder to the count boy, who would then place Siros's name on the job list. A week later Siros became an Eastham building tender.[21]

Prison administrators selected building tenders based on their ability to administer brutal force. Warden Hal Husbands offered the blunt admission that carceral violence and hypermasculinity determined that "we chose 'em [building tenders] the biggest and strongest and toughest. Everybody always chose 'em that way. If you chose a little sissy, it wasn't any use in puttin' him in as a building tender, 'cause the rest of 'em'd whip him, you see."[22] If the building tender did not please his supervising officers, he could be demoted to field work. As Warden Robert M. Cousins put it, such demotion would "tighten up" any indolent or complacent building tender. "You might have to just take him off his job as building and teach him some more agriculture, about six months of field with a hoe, or a shovel. Maybe that'll help him a whole lot. . . . That would tighten any of 'em up."[23] The disciplined trusty could then return to their inside building tender job, now that the onus of field work had "tightened them up" and assured their devotion to the divided labor regime.

Perhaps the most important distinction between BTs and the rest of the prison population was that the BTs were armed. The prison administration did not provide guns but made baseball bats, riot batons, and regulation hunting knives regularly available. Building tenders also made their own weapons and were allowed to keep such weapons as lead pipes, shanks (pieces of lose metal sharpened hard enough to make a two-inch blade), and "slapjacks" (a loose leather pocket filled with lead). The court-appointed special monitor W. David Arnold noted in his September 21, 1981, interview with the building tender Benny Hudson that the prisoner showed him a series of weapons given to him by the prison administration. The building tender told Arnold, "Now when I first got this job several years ago at that particular time I was given a weapon. Something like this, except it was a billy-club, riot club." Arnold went on to report that the "inmate is showing me a long wooden toilet brush. Now he is showing me a very sharp knife that he just pulled out from under his bed. . . . Hudson is handing me a lead pipe with tape at the end of it. It's about 8–10 inches long. Another knife is also under his mattress."[24] BTs were able to keep their weaponry, despite periodic shakedowns on their unit. James Lagermaier, a former BT, pointed out that "politicians were notified prior to a shakedown, and in most cases their weapons were removed to another cell block or to another location or even to the major's office until the shakedown was completed and then returned to them afterwards."[25] Building tenders could also hide the weapons of prisoners during a shakedown and then give them back to that prisoner if they met their price.[26] In an affidavit, the prisoner William M. Smith reflected on the prison society of the 1970s and summed up the comprehensive nature of a building tender's power: "The job of the 'B.T.' is to do the job of the paid guard. They, the 'B.T.', don't get paid in money, but they receive many special things, such as full freedom to go about the farm as they wish. They don't haft to go by any rules of TDC . . . they have compleat [sic] control over the inmates. They use their authority to gain commissary from others, to get forced sex from others, to beat others as they wish. They are to keep us inmates 'in line', so to speak."[27]

Prisoner guards used their homemade weapons to mete out punishment. "There is also the most brutal type of punishments, physical force, brutal because it leaves mental as well as physical scars for the rest of the inmates' life," concluded the 1973 Joint Committee on Prison Reform (JCPR). "Here the prison officials and Building Tenders use their fists, axe handles, billy clubs, leaded rubber hose, horse bridles and reins, gun butts, black jacks and baseball bats."[28] One building tender admitted that their relationship to turnkeys provided them the power to open, close, and lock cell doors on any given wing, which provided them the ability to time their attacks by isolating the targeted prisoner and physically overwhelming him in his cell: "If a building tender wanted to whip one of them he'd just go up there and shut all the doors and open that one and run in there and if it took three or four building tenders to whip him, then that's what happened."[29] The JCPR provided the following blunt conclusion that building tenders are "totally ignorant of mental and emotional problems" and that their work as convict guards was circumscribed "in strict accord with limited concepts and impulsive opinions or judgments." In their investigations, the JCPR concluded that prison officials were not just culpable for the actions of their convict guards but that they knowingly empowered them to punish other prisoners:

Prison officials are only concerned about the B.T.'s willingness to inform on other inmates, to enforce rules, and to suppress any form of resistance by the prison population when it tries to resist, protest or appeal for outside relief (e.g. to officials of this Committee, the Courts, State Officials, or their families). The administration guarantees the B.T.'s prosecution immunity, provisions or weapons, and physical assistance by other armed inmate guards. Prosecution immunity includes granting an inmate guard the arbitrary power to convict and punish any inmate suspected of any rule infraction even when a suspicion never goes beyond the rumor stage.[30]

In return for maintaining control in the tanks and doing the bidding of the prison administration, the prison hierarchy, particularly the prison major and warden, granted building tenders privileges, both formal and informal. First, prisoner politicians were considered a trusty of the prison system and earned higher rates of good time than other prisoners, which reduced their overall sentence.[31] Second, prisoner politicians worked inside the building and therefore avoided the grueling "sun-up to sun-down" work regime in Texas cotton fields. The third perk was a series of day-to-day informal privileges, including freedom of movement. "Most of them had the run of the building," explained the prison guard James Eckles. "They could go just about anywhere they wanted to inside the compound. They had commissary privileges whenever they wanted them. They had cooking utensils within the wings. They had stereos, radios, record players, tape decks, things that a regular inmate would not have."[32] Typically, building tenders carried "blue cards" that stated that they were "pass runners," who could freely move from cell block to cell block. In the Ramsey prison farm, for instance, Assistant Warden D. A. Christian signed these cards, which provided building tenders with unlimited access to various prison wings.[33]

Prisoners could often differentiate a building tender from another prisoner simply by his appearance. BTs characteristically wore their shirts untucked, and they often wore knit skull caps or had BT emblazoned on the back of their shirt. Correction Officer Francisco Guerra Jr. recalled, "Inmates were not supposed to walk down the hall in, say, house shoes. They were supposed to be properly dressed. A BT could walk up and down the hall with a shirttail untucked, with a tee shirt, with house shoes, with his shirt unbuttoned, with a cowboy hat and cowboy boots and never be stopped by an officer and never run the chance of being written up."[34] While the prison denied freedom, the ability to express oneself freely in dress was a point of pride among the prison population and accorded individual BTs a certain measure of respect and exclusivity.

Table 6 Trusty status, 1977

| Class | Building Service | | All Other Prisoners | |
	Number	Percent	Number	Percent
SAT 3	519	75.99	7,875	38.5
SAT 2	4	0.58	1,758	8.59
SAT 1	2	0.29	469	2.29
Class 1	142	20.79	9,075	44.36
Class 2	1	0.15	144	0.7
Class 3	14	2.05	556	2.72
Unknown			98	0.48
Total	683		20,458	

Source: Office of the Special Master, "Monitor's Reports," *Ruiz v. Estelle.*

Building tenders also received more PIP points, which allowed them to engage in more rehabilitative and recreational activities. Walter Siros, the former building tender, recalled: "You got three points for going to church. You got points for school if you could get in it. Then you got points for going to the craft shop which was almost unbelievable to get in to—I mean, cause you know, where you build saddles and spurs and rings and purses, but building tenders automatically got a hundred and nineteen points a month by just being a building tender."[35]

In addition to PIP, trusties could gain time off their criminal sentence for early release. Texas's unique good-time law allowed prisoners to earn additional time taken away from their sentence for every day they labored. While rank-and-file prisoners were classified within three classes of good time, building tenders were generally considered a state-approved trusty (SAT), providing them even more good time. There were three categories of state-approved trusty classifications, and all three classes earned thirty extra days for each month served as opposed to the twenty days of good time that the highest rank-and-file class 1 prisoners received. In 1977, 75 percent of all prisoners that worked in the building were designated as SAT 3, the highest class, while only 38 percent of those that worked outside held that high classification.[36]

The close relationship between building tenders and the guards, particularly the officer staff, allowed the BTs to administer nonviolent punishments as well. Prisoners were often cited for such minor offenses as not working hard enough (cited as laziness), talking in the squad, leaving grass in the picked cotton, disrespecting an officer, disrespectful acting, "bad eyeing" the officer, refusing to obey an order, and, most often, fighting with another prisoner. The punishments were calculated efforts to cause the offending prisoner public humiliation and to ensure control through public example. Building tenders who accused other prisoners of stealing, for instance, could initiate the punishment of "advertising." The prisoner Stephan Thompson explained that "advertising was where inmates had to wear signs on their chest and on their back with certain slogans or things wrote [sic] on it. For instance, an inmate would be out in the field, and if he got caught eating a strawberry or cucumber or something like that and he got caught, he went before a disciplinary committee for that, and they would sentence him to, say, eight hour or twenty-hours or forty-eight hours advertising, and they would have inmate bookkeepers tape signs on the inmate's back."[37] Thompson related one incident in which a hungry prisoner who stole a chicken had to stand against the wall for thirty-six-hours and hold a dead chicken by the neck until it started to decompose in his hands. Other minor punishments included "standing on the wall," in which a prisoner stood with his toes and nose touching a brick wall for four to six hours; "riding the rail," in which a prisoner stood on a two-by-four that was placed edgewise approximately a foot from the floor; "riding the box," in which he stood on top of a box that was stood on its edge; "hugging the barrel," which involved having dozens of prisoners pressed together on top of a fifty-five-gallon barrel overnight; or "shelling peanuts," which was a common punishment in which a prisoner had to shell a "Texas gallon" of peanuts overnight.[38] Prisoners found with minor contraband, according to prisoner testimonies, received "the lighter punishment" of standing on the soda water boxes for a few hours. But frequently punishments of public humiliation were paired with brutality. "They would set that Coca Cola case up under that. They call that the rail," one prisoner recalled. "And you stood up on that water case, and if you fall off of that soda water case, you gonna get whooped, and they gonna add another hour on it."[39] Prisoners who were caught in homosexual relationships might be humiliated by having to hold each others' penis in the open hallway for all to see. For prisoners in the general population, the BT system surveilled, policed, and punished homosexuality through public humiliation and degradation of a prisoner's ability to retain respect within the general population.

Other public punishments took the form of torture. In his memoir recounting his prison experience from 1955 to 1972, Albert "Racehoss" Sample depicted in gruesome detail how he and other African American prisoners were frequently punished for small infractions by being cuffed and left hanging from cell bars with "toes barely touching the floor" for hours at a time. "After an hour, a couple of the cuff hangers started groaning," Sample wrote of the first time he experienced such torture. "I bit my lip to keep from crying out too. I thought about what that lying boss told the captain, 'All this nigguh's dun all day long is look up in the sky an count birds. Cap'n, I had to beg this nigguh to git him to go to wek [sic].' The pains shot through my arms; I dug my teeth deeper into my bottom lip until I tasted the blood inside my mouth." After the sixth hour of this punishment, one of the other prisoners hanging alongside Sample could take such torture no longer. He began "moaning louder and louder, violently jerking and pulling against his cuffs" and "pitching, straining, and pulling as hard as he could" in the futile hope that he might break free and end the agony of hanging from cell bars. After struggling for several minutes and crying out in pain, the frustrated prisoner "bit into his wrists as if they were two chocolate éclairs, growling and gnawing away like a coon, with its foot caught in a steel trap."[40] Benny Wade Clewis, an African American prisoner during the 1950s and 1960s, described painful memories of how hanging from the handcuffs caused the metal to "mash into your flesh" as prisoners hung under that picket as their "foots would barely touch that ground, just barely touch it."[41] "Hanging from the cuffs" was thus a racialized punishment that put mostly Black and brown bodies on display as public symbols of carceral power.

In one case, Sample related how a fellow African American prisoner, Kotch Tom, was forced to hang from the cuffs all night for having a photograph of a white woman in his locker. The woman, however, was Kotch Tom's wife, whom he had met and married in Germany while serving overseas in the U.S. Army. Kotch Tom had gone to prison for sitting next to his wife on a bus leaving from the Fifth Ward of Houston, a largely poor and working-class African American community. When the bus driver stopped the bus and demanded that no Black man should sit next to a white woman, Tom attempted to explain that she was his wife. Dismayed by such outright defiance of white superiority, the bus driver reacted to this claim of racial miscegenation by slapping Tom, causing Tom to draw his pocketknife and stab the driver to death, which was an act of humiliated rage that caused the state to sentence Tom to a lifetime in Texas prisons. Both outside and inside the prison, Sample wistfully observed, the Texas criminal justice system policed the parameters of white superiority.[42]

Lawrence Pope, a prisoner who spent time in both the federal prison system and the TDC, noted that the single most important difference between the federal and state prison systems was that the traditional "convict code" against snitching was absent in Texas. "In the Federal, it was just anathema to snitch," Pope recalled, "and it was a killing offense if they could get to you. But in TDC I went down there and sitting there shelling [peanuts as punishment] and this inmate got up and hollered at the officer there, 'Hey Boss!'

Then he pointed to this inmate such-and-such and he was snitchin' him off right there, to everybody around him. Man, in the Federal, that would be—you would be dead."[43] Public punishments were intended to mock the prisoner and make him look foolish in the eyes of other prisoners. In an environment where prisoners owned so little and fought over so much, the need to protect their reputation could mean the difference between life and death. Damaging a prisoner's reputation was therefore a potent tool that lent building tenders and bookkeepers credibility while diminishing the reputation of rival prisoners.

The BTs enforced their own brand of the convict code, and the unwritten rules of order and complicity changed, depending on the personality of the BT and the situation. In recalling his first trip to Eastham, the prisoner Eubanks felt the arbitrary nature of building tender authority keenly. On arrival, the head building tender on the cell block "tells you how it's going to be," which meant that "you're going to do what you're told down on the cellblocks. You were going to go in your cell when you're supposed to, come out when you're supposed to, and when they call work, you take off running when they call your squad. You go to chow when you're supposed to. You follow the rules. And those rules were not written down. Those were the convict rules. And those rules changed whenever they felt like changing them."[44]

Although the BTs were prisoners, they often carried greater authority within the prison cells than the guards. Francisco Guerra, a former prison guard, angrily lamented in his resignation letter, "An officer even daring to object to BT conduct is subject to heavy rebuke, censor and transfer to the least desirable units." Further, Guerra explained that although the prison hierarchy was based on military rank that went sequentially from correctional officer (CO) 1 and 2 to sergeant, lieutenant, captain, and major, the real prison hierarchy was different. "Most of us," noted Guerra, "felt that it really should have went C.O. I, C.O. II, building tender, sergeant, lieutenant, count boy, captain, major."[45] Even then, a particularly powerful head building tender often carried more sway than anyone besides the prison major. Charlie Combs, a prison guard in the 1970s, similarly recalled that building tenders trained and controlled low-ranking guards: "when the building tender told you to open a cell, you opened the cell. I mean you basically worked for the building tender. . . . The inmates trained you."[46] The Joint Committee on Prison Reform observed the comprehensive power of BT governance with the following conclusion:

> The Building Tenders not only control the daily prison work production, noise level in the unit, daily personnel activities of the inmate population, amount of food consumption by inmates in solitary

Jerry Ray Bolden, building tender. Robert R. McElroy/ Getty Images.

confinement, selection of radio and T.V. entertainment, freedom of movement in the wings of the prison, sanitation conditions in the inmate and guard living quarters, the spread of rumors and the degree of medical assistance—but they also possess more keys to open and close the doors and gates inside the prison walls than all of the prison guards put together.[47]

From the prison administration's perspective, the TDC and the building tenders themselves frequently defended the trusty guard system by claiming that such an arrangement protected weaker and younger prisoners. In the view of Warden Hal Husbands, who served as a TDC administrator from 1952 to 1978, the role of building tenders was to "see that the young ones don't get run over and mistreated and abused, and sexually abused."[48] James Willet, who, as a thirty-year career TDC employee, worked his way up at the flagship Walls prison from correctional officer to warden, felt that building tenders served as peacekeepers.[49] For instance, incessant and loud noise is always a great point of frustration in prisons, where many conversations are interspersed across echoing halls and compete with dozens of blaring radios and the occasional screams and taunts of other prisoners at all hours of the night. But when Willett wanted to control the noise on one African American wing, he simply went to the building tender from that wing, who the prisoners might listen to when they otherwise ignored Correctional Officer Willett. "He was a great big fellow," Willett recalled of the Black building tender. "I told him, I said, 'Hey, that guy up there with that radio playing loud,' I said, 'I done told him to turn it down and it's still up.' He said, 'I'll take care of it.' And he went up there, and I watched him and he never went inside the cell. He stood at the cell door and he said something to that convict. I never had no problems out of that radio being loud for the rest of that day."[50] As warden of the Walls, Willett found that the flagship Walls penitentiary relied less on the building tender system than the prison farms that required building tenders to help maintain order for the labor regime. "I think it was probably different at the Walls in that it was more of a light scaled version of it [BT system] than what you had out on the farms," Willett reflected. "They depended on those building tenders [on the farms], the wardens did more I think than the warden did at the Walls. From what I saw, I think—I just didn't see [abuse]—it seemed to be a good system to me."[51]

BTs also depicted themselves as protectors and as peace administrators, but within a labor regime that required constant discipline. Certainly, not all building tenders abused their privilege and power, and some may well have protected vulnerable prisoners. But the benefits of accruing more privilege and economic advantage than other prisoners within the labor regime made abuses routine. In a 1981 interview, one building tender argued that despite his record of violence, he received no punishments because he was busy "keeping the peace." The BT had four official violations for "fighting with a weapon; fighting without a weapon; creating a disturbance, use of abusive language," and yet he never lost his job; nor had he ever served any time in solitary. The building tender Benny Hudson admitted in a 1981 interview that during the 1970s his power within the prison cell was comprehensive and could be exercised with arbitrary authority.

Nobody knows what's going on other than the building support service, building tenders, you know. And if there's anything that goes on in here that we feel like the man should know then we're supposed to go out there, or [go to] this head building tender, with the problem. Now it's his discretion as to whether he takes this problem to the man or not. I mean, if I want to make me two or three gallons of chaulk [homemade alcohol] I just make it, and I get drunk, I don't beat nobody up, you know, but at the same time if I want to get drunk and beat somebody in the head, I can do that too.[52]

As a head building tender during the 1960s, Cecil Alexander affirmed the TDC explanation that the trusty guard system shielded the first-time youthful offender from sexual abuse from older, more seasoned prisoners. "I didn't want to see nobody taking no kids [youthful offender]," Alexander professed, "and jumping on a kid, or four or five of 'em jumping on one little kid. No, I ain't never liked that in my life and I won't never like it." Despite Alexander's claim to the contrary, prisoners under his charge claimed that "Alexander and his lieutenants continuously robbed other prisoners, forced them to submit to homosexual acts and forced them to pay for protection."[53] A more honest admission from Alexander, however, revealed how his role as convict guard entrapped him within the building tender system as much as those prisoners under his rule. "I was an everyday survivor in the penitentiary," Alexander admitted. "You survived 24 hours a day and if you wasn't a little animal, you was made one . . . to survive."[54] Corrobating Alexander's admission, the building tender Benny Hudson similarly confessed to the court monitor, Arnold: "I've seen rape, I've seen murder, I've seen assaults, I've seen abusive assaults, and taking other people's commissary away from them, you know when they get the money. I've seen these weaker type inmates wash peoples' clothes and, well, abused in every form of degradation that a man could be put through."[55] These building tenders sought to escape grueling field labor but found that their privileged positions obligated them to a labor system that depended on carceral violence for its survival.

Not only did the BT system rely on disguise, but the promise of informal rewards or the constant threat of demotion to field labor created an incentive for BTs to file false prison charges. As one BT admitted to *Corrections Magazine* in their prison exposé, "you're granted privileges only when you have something to tell [the warden]. When you run out of things to tell, you're no use to them, and they send you back to the fields. So you turn to lying. You have to keep it going so you can keep your job. They always want to hear about some kind of . . . revolution." TDC's reliance on state-controlled informants thus established carceral discipline through a rewards system that incentivized prevarication and outright lying.[56]

Table 7 Comparative murder rate, 1973–1976

State	Period	Homicides	Year Average	1974 Prison Population	Homicide Rate per 100,000
California	1973–76	66	16.5	22,163	74.4
Colorado	1973–76	10	2.5	1,987	126
Florida	1973–76	30	10	8,414	118
Minnesota	1973–76	5	1.67	1,387	120
Missouri	1973–76	23	5.7	3,243	177
New York	1973–76	7	1.75	12,684	14
Oklahoma	1973–76	14	3.5	2,984	117
Texas	1973–76	4	1	16,683	6

Sources: U.S. Department of Justice, *Sourcebook for Criminal Justice Statistics* (Washington, DC: Government Printing Office, 1973, 1974, 1975, 1976); Bruce Jackson to Alvin J. Bronstein, November 23, 1978, Clements Papers, Texas A&M; "Readings on Violence," Treatment Directorate Research and Development Division, TDC, Special Project No. 16 May 77, Texas A&M, Clements Papers, Box 10.

As an unofficial and illegal arrangement, building tenders and the high-ranking prison staff who relied on them could sometimes have a tenuous relationship that made prison administrators wary of ending the practice. In a letter to his closest associates, which included his mother, Fay Morris, and his former cellmate Michael Chase, Frank Leahy confided that the newly arrived Warden Walker at the Ramsey prison "never did believe in using building tenders, turn keys, count boys, etc," but that when Walker attempted to dislodge BTs from authority over other prisoners, he faced "a total buck on his arrival and realized he didn't have the manpower or frankly the control to enforce his decisions or take over the farm." Worse was the threat that dislodged building tenders might present as snitches and whistle-blowers against the system. "For so many years," Leahy revealed, "these headstrummers [violent BTs] run things and there were so many atrocities—literally murders—for the man—and these convict guards are holding that over the administrations' head. In other words, if the administration tries to mess with the convict guards' playhouse—then the convict guards blow the whistle on past atrocities and the whole thing blows up."[57]

In defense of the building tender system, the prison administration liked to point out that Texas prisons had the nation's lowest homicide rate. While this was true, the incidents of rape and beatings often went unreported for fear of retribution from the building tenders. For instance, California had 66 prison homicides between the years 1973 to 1976 for a homicide rate per 100,000 of 74.4 percent. Under the building tender system, Texas had the nation's lowest prisoner murder rate with only four homicides between 1973 and 1976 with a homicide rate per 100,000 of only 6 percent.[58]

The administration's response to charges of abuse often shifted the blame from the building tender to the uncontrollable nature of the general prison population. The prison system's attempt to dismantle the psychiatric ward at the Wynne prison in 1961 offers one example of such a response. When Warden "Beartrack" McAdams took over the Wynne Unit in 1961 as warden, the "most distressing problem" was the 382 psychotic patients who were not working and remained "locked away in cells" at what was then the Wynne Treatment Center. Some of these prisoners had been confined in a cell for as long as six years and many, according to McAdams, had been used "for experimental purposes" by the Texas Research Institute of Mental Science, a branch of Baylor Medical School. McAdams wanted to return these prisoners to the fields in what he called a "modified work program." In developing his back-to-work plan, "inmate helpers were recruited, most of them former patients themselves," whose job was to "chase down" other prisoners "who suddenly decide to runoff across the field, without hurting them." McAdams defined the "chief function" of building tenders in the treatment center as "providing protection for weaker patients from the stronger, more violent ones, seeing after the patients' basic needs and guiding them in normal civilities." In less than a year, McAdams's program dismantled the treatment center and reintegrated the 382 patients back into the general prison population. But, as McAdams noted in his report, the "very nature of 2 tank" and its patient inhabitants "practically guarantees incidents of unexpected violence." When one of these "guaranteed incidents of unexpected violence" erupted, one prisoner named Melvis Austin Sadler died and another was badly injured. In defense of his building tenders, McAdams argued:

> Our main concern is to protect all the other patients from the few who become periodically dangerous. It is for that reason that we have selected capable building tenders and nurses who live right in the dormitory with the patients and sleep side by side with them. . . . When patients like Melvin Austin Sadler become manic, it is for the building tenders to whom the weaker, more timid patients turn to for protection. It is the building tender's job to subdue the manic patient, without injuring him, if at all possible, and to restrain him until he becomes manageable. Melvin Austin was subdued in such a fashion, without any bodily injury being inflicted upon him. He died from overexertion, which no one could prevent.

Put more simply, Sadler was "subdued in the only manner available—outfighting him."[59] The prison administrators' defense of the southern trusty system as a benevolent force that protected weaker prisoners hid the reality that the prison's internal labor and economic system was predicated on its ability to prey on vulnerable prisoners without public knowledge or scrutiny.

Internal Economy: Running a Store and Managing a Corporation

The internal prison economy in Texas was centered on the BT system and on three mechanisms of exchange and control: scrip and a barter system; a system of respect and reciprocity; and outward displays of power, brutality, and extortion. After the 1948 reforms, the TDC forbade currency and "hard money" among prisoners. Instead, scrip or "coupons" served as money in the prisons. Every two weeks, each prisoner could draw as much as $20 from his account, which was divided into scrip ledgers, called "chocho books," of $1, $5, $10, and $20 denominations.[60] Of course, only prisoners lucky enough to have outside family members or friends place money in their account could draw scrip. The scrip allowed prisoners to buy and trade commissary goods and served as currency in card or domino games.

Regular prisoners, however, did not visit the commissary. Instead, the building tender on the cell block took a shopping list from each prisoner and filled it as the other prisoners worked in the fields. No matter how many items the BT bought for each prisoner, it was customary that prisoners leave one dollar blank on their scrip book so that the BT could fill it with an item of his choice. Even though Texas prisons were vastly overcrowded, building tenders almost always had their own cell, unless they chose to fill it with the derisively named "punk"—a prisoner that they considered as their property or "wife." The BTs stockpiled commissary goods in these cells. As supplies dwindled in the two-week interval between the arrival of new scrip, the building tender would then sell his items to other prisoners at a two-for-one or three-for-two price, depending on the physical size of the purchaser and his reputation. This was called "running a store."[61]

—————

The prisoner Kenneth Hayes testified that running a store was a privilege granted only to BTs. "Running a store is illegal at TDC," he explained. "The building tenders on Ramsey were licensed by the Building Captain and the Major and everybody in a position of authority to run a store. They would buy from the regular commissary, the TDC commissary, and they would sell to the convicts in the tank for the interest rate from draw day to draw day."[62]

Further, the BTs used their relationship and authority with the guards to ensure that no competition would arise. James Lagermaier recalled:

> Well, the politicians ran what we call the stores. This was the distribution of cigarettes, selling items two for one, loaning an inmate items on credit based on commissary or a promissory note, and they controlled the stores. They controlled any distribution of tobacco or borrowing at all in that particular cell block they live in, and if they thought somebody else was in the business other than themselves, they would oftentimes initiate a shakedown just so that particular inmate's store could be confiscated and turned over to the politicians.[63]

In addition to stores in each row of cells, there were also "corporations," which was a series of stores made into one economic unit that comprised a line or an entire wing. Typically, a "corporation" consisted of five to six building tenders who banded several stores together so that they might share in the profit and have greater numbers when it was necessary to use physical brutality for enforcement and debt collection. Moreover, building tenders had access to a prisoner's accounts through the bookkeeper, and they could therefore keep a prisoner in perpetual debt. The prisoner Michael Eubanks explained how one building tender by the name of "Oilcan" Harry had access to the withdrawal box that contained the withdrawal slips of other prisoners. Harry would remove and throw away the slips of those "he figured he could prey upon." Once those prisoners ran out of money, Harry would offer to lend them items at a two-for-one price over the course of several months until they fell deeply into his debt. Eubanks explained how revolving debt worked in prison: "If you had a twenty dollar scrip book or a thirty dollar scrip book, all you could spend was half of it per a week. So you'd owe more than you were going to get—more than you had coming in. Eventually, after they did this to you two or three times, you would owe more money than you were going to get in even if you got a thirty dollar scrip book. You may owe fifty or sixty dollars. . . . So, he's got to still borrow some more."[64]

Prisoners who did not pay their debt were punished swiftly and often in public. Through their close association with count boys and bookkeepers, BTs often knew just how much money each prisoner had in his account. The building tender Siros recalled an incident in 1963 where one prisoner owed $100 to one of the corporations, and he continued to plead penury, despite the fact that the corporation on the unit knew that he had over $300 in his account. The result was that the BTs took the prisoner into the washroom, a space that was exclusive to BT control, and they "whupped him, I mean really whupped him. And he was a pretty boy too. But they pound his face down on the knobs of the sink. They really missed his face up. Knocked his teeth out. Twenty or thirty stitches. But an example was made and ain't nobody cheated that store again."[65]

Stripped of all other possessions, prisoners fought over commissary items or seemingly small slights. Even so, the only acts of possession a prisoner was allowed were personal items, such as a gallon of ice cream, cigarettes, a jar of peanut butter, sandwich meat, or even chewing gum—small everyday items that accorded a prisoner a semblance of self-control, ownership, and even dignity. Establishing a "reputation" meant asserting masculinity, control over one's body, and declaring a willingness to use violence to maintain that control. Prisoners who willingly used violence to prove their "manliness" earned a reputation demanding respect and the title "character" or "good people," whereas prisoners who did not resort to violence were seen as "weak." In the external world outside of prison, the accumulation of material goods, homes, and domestic lifestyle conferred middle-class respectability.[66] Prisoners, by contrast, embraced their own working-class ethic of "toughness," where status and identity were determined by one's public "reputation," willingness to fight for "respect," and the ability to maintain sexual control over one's body.[67] "Anybody who came down here in the sixties," insisted the prisoner Arthur Johnson, "and tell you that they didn't have to fight, then they lying. Because everybody got to fight."[68] The building tender system worked within that hypermasculine prison ethic, and yet its sexual rapaciousness also mitigated working-class honor by empowering an elite group that threatened the general population's ability to retain perceptions of "respect" and control over their own bodies.

Owning Prison Bodies: The Sex Slave Trade and Sexual Violence

The most odious feature of the internal economy was the BTs' trade in sex and human ownership, a process of physical domination and symbolic power. The vicious prison sex trade provided building tenders the unofficial but tacit approval of some prison administrators to use their informal power to rape other prisoners and buy and sell other prisoners' bodies.

In Texas, the intake and classification process not only determined a prisoner's placement and work position, but it also made a key determination on a prisoner's sexual and gendered identity. The only wing that was fully racially integrated before 1980 was what the prison administration termed the "protective custody" wing, which was a separate and isolated wing on every prison. As an isolated wing, protective custody segregated those that the prison system classified as too vulnerable to be incarcerated among the general prison population. If classification determined that a prisoner was "openly gay" or determined to be excessively "weak" and vulnerable, the prison administration would house these prisoners, many of them young men and first-time offenders, in protective custody. Such classifications were often arbitrary and capricious decisions. Nonetheless, prisoners so classified were housed in the protective wing of the prison, known by prisoners by the derisive term "sissy" or "punk wings."

For the Texas prisoner Steven Blanchard, who was sentenced to prison in 1969, the initial intake considered him for the protective wing because he was openly gay. Blanchard, who was from California, had long hair that he cherished as it provided him a sense of control over his own self-identity. "During processing they wanted to cut my hair," Blanchard explained. "And I took exception to wanting to cut my hair. . . . I was labeled a communist, hippy, pinko fag from California because of my long hair. And a couple of bossess and a couple of convict guards minions picked me up, and they cut my hair. . . . And within moments I was beaten."[69] Thereafter, Blanchard was then put in general population, where he later become an object of sexual reprisal at the hands of building tenders for his prisoner activist allegiance with Black and brown prisoners.

The former prisoner Ray Hill described the response he received when he openly expressed in 1970 his sexuality to a classification psychologist during the intake process: "They bark; we respond. They make notes on your responses and bark some more. When I responded to the question: 'Do you get fucked by other men?' with 'Sometimes but there is usually more to it than that,' he was a little taken aback. He was not expecting a no-guilt response. In 1970, he had never encountered an out and proud gay person."[70]

Prior to his 1970 conviction, Ray Hill was a gay rights activist who cofounded in 1967 Houston's branch of the gay rights organization the Promethean Society. Hill was an early proponent of gay pride, and he came out to his parents while still in high school in 1957, a decision he made after his high school librarian had coyly given him as a gift a brown-paper-bag-wrapped copy of Walt Whitman's *Leaves of Grass*. Following a brief career as a teenage evangelist, Ray Hill traveled the country and spent time in the early to mid-1960s on the campuses of Tulane University and Columbia, where he was influenced by the lectures of such leftwing stalwarts as Salvador Allende, C. Wright Mills, William S. Woods, and Haley Thomas. Beginning in the late 1960s, however, Hill created an interstate fencing operation, which he used to continue the lavish lifestyle he had become accustomed to as a popular evangelical speaker. Hill thought of himself as the "gay Robin Hood," as he used some of the proceeds from his fencing operation to fund antiwar and gay rights activism. His fencing operation, in his words, "specialized in something queens know something about, antiques, art, jewels, and electronics."[71]

In 1969, however, Hill's operation was discovered, and he was arrested in San Diego. Extradited to Texas, he was convicted in 1970 on a twenty-eight-year concurrent sentence. While sentenced to the Ramsey II prison in Otey, Texas, Hill became a bookkeeper for construction, a position of some influence that insulated him temporarily from the reach of building tenders. By utilizing the law library and making a cogent legal argument, Hill was able to reduce his sentence on appeal, and he was released from prison in 1975. Since his release, Hill has remained out of prison, and he became a local prison celebrity as the host of Houston's *Prison Radio Show*, broadcast from Pacifica's KPFT station. Many of the prisoners held in the Gulf Coast region eagerly tune in each Friday night from 9:00 to 11:00 P.M. During the program's first hour, the *Prison Radio Show* features a guest and a themed topic for discussion on prison issues. The second hour of the show, however, has callers calling in from across the state to send messages to family members in prison, as Texas prisons still do not allow prisoners to have access to telephones of any kind. After his prison release, Hill remained a lifelong advocate for both prisoners' rights and gay rights, as he helped to found such organizations as the Montrose Counseling Center, the Montrose Activity Center, the Gay and Lesbian Switchboard and the Montrose Clinic, and the Conference for the Futures of Lesbian, Gay, Bisexual, Transgender, Intersexed, Questioning and Allied Residents of the Houston Metropolitan Area. As a former prisoner, Hill advanced the notion that gay rights did not constitute a separate and isolated sphere of white, middle-class gay interests but that gay liberation requires what the historian Alan Berubé termed "the roots of my antiracist desires and gay desires" that are intrinsically intertwined with the fate of the most vulnerable in society, both within prisons and on the streets.[72]

However, Hill's memory of his self-identification as an "out and proud gay person" was a rarity in 1970s prison culture. The 1970s represent, according to the historian Regina Kunzel, a moment in which "to be *homosexual* and to be *gay* were emerging as two different things—the first simply descriptive of a sexual orientation and the second embodying a set of norms and values." In her analysis, the effort among gay activists in the 1970s to educate prisoners on the difference between sexualized roles and a "gay identity" and consciousness was confounded by varying concepts of what constituted homosexuality. "Prison sexual culture," Kunzel concluded "could be more capacious, heterogeneous, and troubling in its queerness than could be easily accommodated by an emerging gay rights movement."[73] Such an apt historical assessment certainly applies to the social history of Texas prison sexuality during the post–World War II period.

While not advancing gay liberation within the prison, Ray Hill did rely on the internal prison economy to try to shield more vulnerable prisoners from

Ray Hill at Houston's 1979 Gay Pride March with "TRUSTEE" emblazoned on his prison "whites" uniform alongside the Gay Pride pink triangle button. Courtesy of the JD Doyle Collection of Houston LGBT History and the Charles Botts Collection of LGBT History, Inc.

the prison's capriciousness. During his incarceration, Ray was held on the Ramsey II Unit, which during the 1960s and 1970s gay prisoners called "Montrose," a playful allusion to Houston's upscale gay neighborhood. Ramsey II had six wings and two cell blocks to house nine hundred prisoners, but the protected wing was a closed off space that only building tenders could access. Unlike the other wings of the prison, the protective custody wings like the one on Ramsey II, what other prisoners derisively called "punk wings," collected prisoners of all races. It was the only genuinely integrated space of the Texas prison system prior to the 1980s. Hill explained that in "Montrose" prisoners were less likely to face racist animosity and the exploitation that prisoners experienced in the regular population: "Because we had black inmates, we had Hispanic inmates, we had people that couldn't even speak English, and we also not only got the gay ones, but we also got the crazies—if you weren't crazy enough to be sent to the limited space in the treatment center which was a unit for people with severe mental handicaps then where you lived was in the punk wing. Because otherwise, if you were . . . mentally hand-icapped, you would be tragically exploited by other inmates. But in the 'punk wing,' we weren't so exploitive."[74] Once on the protective custody wing, how-ever, prisoners, no matter their sexual identity, were most often known within the prison as having what was known as a "homosexual jacket." The Joint Committee on Prison Reform reported that "one of the most salient com-plaints" among prisoners with mental health problems was that housing them in the "punk wing" resulted in "disrespect to his manly pride" that left them with a permanent "homosexual jacket," which was a reference to both their official prison record and their overall reputation in prison society.[75] Within "Montrose," however, Hill operated a cigarette-rolling business in which he employed the mentally handicapped prisoners to roll cigarettes that he would then sell for commissary items. The cigarette rollers kept half the profit, and Hill took the other half. Hill described his cigarette-rolling operation as a "family" and as a way to protect prisoners from sexual exploitation: "Uncle Ray, you know, he'd put you in the cigarette business and that way you were independent. You didn't have to depend on those other people for necessi-ties. Then if you wanted to sell or give your ass away, then that was your deci-sion. You know, that's not my business. But what was my business is I didn't see any need for you to have to do that to survive."[76]

The photograph below taken at the Clemens protective custody prison wing by the photographer Alan Pogue in 1981 is a rare photographic exam-ple that depicts youth, sexuality, and racial integration within the protective custody wing. In 1981, Allan Pogue received permission to take photographs in the TDC during the compliance phase of the 1980 civil rights case *Ruiz v. Estelle* as part of the effort to document compliance with federal court orders. At the Clemens prison, Pogue wanted to take photographs of the protective custody wing, where prisoner activists charged that building tenders had se-lected youthful offenders to be moved from protective custody into their pri-vate cells, where they raped these boys. Because of those charges, Pogue asked the youthful offenders, who all self-identified as gay, if they would be willing to take a group photograph. The youths willingly gathered to take photographs that put their gay identity on display, where some carried purses to the photograph shoot, though the purses were not photographed. Others primped themselves for the picture, as in the case of the young blond man in the front who plucked his eyebrows and offered the camera what Pogue de-scribed as his "best Lauren Becall pose."[77] This rare glimpse into the protec-tive custody wing depicts a gathering that humanized these young men and offered a self-conscious documentation of gay pride, "punk" solidarity, and interracial fellowship in a prison system that was extremely hostile to all three.

Protective custody wing of young men who self-identified as gay, Clemens prison, 1984. Courtesy of Alan Pogue.

Outside of the protective custody wings, the prison administration attempted to put homosexuality on public display as a kind of mocking celebration. Prisoners recall that in the late 1960s and mid-1970s several prisons, particularly Eastham and Ramsey, had an "Open House" on Christmas Eve in which "drag queens" held a public and open procession down the general population wing of cell blocks. Eubanks recalled Open House in Eastham this way:

> You could go in and visit your friends down on another cellblock or a dorm or anything. Well the homosexuals would be brought in dresses, blouses, bras and they'd stuff them with toilet paper, fishnet stockings, wigs, high heeled shoes, and they would get dressed out to the nines. And they'd make the rounds from one cellblock to another and everything— get on top of the domino tables—the game tables in the day rooms— dance—I mean they'd put on some shows. The New York City Rockettes got nothing on some of those old things man. . . . The sex was rampant during open house. Eastham was a strange world.[78]

Eubanks also claimed that prisoners received a marriage certificate and even a marriage ceremony from Eastham's Chaplain Solomon. Such a marriage certificate would often be accompanied by official TDC "property papers" that "showed ownership of the inmate." Other prisoners have also spoken of "field marriage" ceremonies, where a high rider would mockingly perform a marriage ceremony between two prisoners in the field.[79] In the African American tank on the Retrieve prison, Albert "Racehoss" Sample related how Retrieve's warden, who the Black prisoners called "Big Devil," married two African American prisoners because "sumtimes marryin has a way uv settlin crazy-assed nigguhs down [sic]." The ceremony between prisoners "Pork Chops" and "Flea Brains" was performed by the unit's reverend and included a pair of wedding bands made from old metal nuts. In attendance were the unit's warden, many prisoners, and guards. Sample recounted how they "put the rings on each other's fingers and Rev pronounced them 'man an wife.' After which, Big Devil ordered them to embrace," to which "most of the audience exploded in laugher" and "showered the newlyweds with food scraps." Sample explained, "The cons and bosses were really enjoying the warden's show. Especially us, because it afforded the opportunity, however short-lived, to go acceptably berserk without fear of punishment."[80] In an oral history, Floyd Patterson recalled that Warden McAdams, "Cap'n Mac," relied on a similar humiliation ceremony that entailed a forced public "wedding" and then subsequent "alimony." "That was one of the things he [McAdams] would do to humiliate guys. He would marry them, pay him alimony. If he [either of the prisoners] went to the store and I bought ten dollars' worth of commissary, he would me give five dollars of that to the 'homosexual.'" Patterson also confirmed that prisoners caught in same-sex relations went through the humiliation of having to "hold one another's private privats. During the 12 o'clock Sunday meal where everyone would file past them."[81]

When prisoners turned to the law to document abuses, one weapon that prison administrators had to quell "such documentation" was to charge prisoners that collaborated on legal work with "sex malpractice—committing, soliciting, or inciting other inmates to perform any unnatural or immoral sex act." When prisoners Frank X. Leahy and Michael Chase collaborated together on a lawsuit against Sheriff Clarence Jones for having illegally incarcerated them in TDC before their trial and subsequent conviction, they were charged with "sex malpractice" on December 10, 1976, which sent Frank Leahy to solitary. In a letter to the prison director, Chase pleaded "that they are not guilty of sex malpractice and that this charge is harassment to deprive them of legal research and place a tremendous burden on their access to the courts. A charge of 'sex malpractice' whether unfounded or not, leads to abusive treatment by correctional officers and other prisoners . . . the whole atmosphere surrounding the arrest and investigation has been highly emotional by all parties."[82]

The southern prison not only mocked homosexuality in Texas, but notorious prison farms in other southern states also drew on traditions from slavery's past to perform other sexualized rituals of racism and sexual debasement.

In Louisiana's Angola prison, for example, prisoners drew on the heritage of Deep South slave folk traditions and had prisoners "jump the broom" to signify their official-unofficial nuptials.[83] Prisoners who took up the role of "queens" in the TDC flouted the authority of their prison keepers while also calling the attention of other prisoners to their body by "tightening up," which meant tailoring their prison uniforms to make it tighter in the seat and around their calves while applying prison-made rouge makeup, made up of crushed rouge from the prison commissary, to distinguish high cheekbones. While it may seem improbable that southern prisons would sanction homosexual marriages or Christmas Eve drag queen shows, these "performed" acts of public mockery were intended to objectify and belittle "sissy" or "weaker" prisoners while asserting the supposed "maleness" of the more aggressive prisoners. Equal and consensual relationships, as Hill noted, are difficult in such a predatory environment because "if you're going to have a husband and a wife, that means you've got to have a relationship. To have a relationship you've got to have trust, and that's what's missing in prison is trust. Trust and privacy just do not exist. . . . There are no relationships there. Sex is a commodity."[84]

Becoming the sexual object of prison rape could change a person's sexual identity. Prisoners offered the hypermasculine argot that "punks" are distinguished from "fags" and "queens," who prisoners considered to be "true homosexuals" and born gay. A "punk," however, was a prisoner who submitted to coercive and violent rape and under such coercion accepted his sublimated role to hypermasculine dominance and sexual violence in exchange for goods, better living quarters, job assignments, or as protection from others. In his autobiographical essay, *A Punk's Song*, Stephen Donaldson, who took the name Donald Tucker as his pen name but "Donny the Punk" as his pseudonym, defined the meaning of "punk" as a prisoner who was "turned out" and thereby "made a homosexual" by the act of prison rape. After Donaldson was the victim of a gang rape in 1972 while incarcerated at a District of Columbia jail, he embraced the otherwise contemptuous prison nomenclature and thereafter became known as "Donny the Punk." Donaldson defined being "punk" as a "status symbol," where "in jail it is generally the youngest and smallest prisoners who get raped and 'turned' or 'turned out,' a phrase suggesting the inversion of their sexual role. In jail, the punks are distinguished from the queens—effeminate semitransvestite homosexuals to whom only feminine terms are applied." Punks, however, "generally retain some sense of masculinity and expect to resume relation with women when released. Punks are involuntarily recruited in the first place and adopt feminisms only when forced to."[85] In Texas, Ray Hill saw prison sex as monetized, especially outside of the punk wing, where a system of obligations, favors, and debts always conveyed a dangerous power structure, what Hill called "playing the sex game." Hill elaborated:

> These are people who were straight when they got to prison, but either fell into some kind of trap like, "Here, I've got a candy bar for you," or "Here, I've got a cup of coffee for you," or, "This is an illegal cigarette and I got it for you," whatever—you get obligated. That's how sex in prison gets started is with obligations. I'm going to protect you from somebody else. Guess what the cost of the protection is going to be? So the deal is that people get obligations and then they get pulled into a trap where they get into the sex game. And once you get in to the sex game, everybody knows it. No privacy. Where you going to hide?[86]

Prisoners like Donaldson and Hill understood the working-class world that Chauncy described, but with the critical distinction that in prisons, violence, economic exchange/extortion, and power upheld notions of who was considered a "man," and rape relegated otherwise "straight" men or disinterested gay men as disposable punks. "Most working-class guys, and thus most men coming into jail," Donaldson explained, "look at this differently than do the middle-class academics who write books. While the middle class thinks the most important thing is the *gender* of one's sexual partner, *the working class is more concerned with the power relationship, which is linked to role and masculinity*."[87]

The act of prison rape itself not only conferred gender identity, but such victimization constituted a system of domination and submission that amounted to extended periods of servitude. As a violent initiation to prison society, the initial rape served as only the first act of a prolonged exchange between the aggressive "man" and his victimized punk, where the punk becomes a sexual object and takes up the "feminine" role of domestic cell servant in exchange for goods, narcotics, protection from others, a better job assignment from a political prisoner (trusty), or even legal knowledge to assist with their case.

Prisoner ownership through sexual domination is not unique to the South, but when describing the southern prison economy, prisoners frequently used the slave terminology to describe sexual violence. On Louisiana's Angola prison, Wilbert Rideau, the editor of the *Angolite* prisoner news magazine, offered the racialized imagery that Angola represented a "sexual jungle," where prisoner bodies were bought and sold in an internal slave market. Rideau described Angola's internal prison economy as one where the use of the term "slave" was more than metaphorical; it represented instead economic and sexual subservience that had monetary value and was part of a thriving internal economy. "Slaves are 'property,'" Rideau explained, "and, as such, are gambled, sold, traded and auctioned off like common cattle. What results is a widespread system of slavery and exploitation created and maintained via the instrument of fear and violence." As a southern prison plantation, Angola prisoners were also subject to an internal economy where prisoner slavery and ownership claimed prisoners' bodies and domestic service. Rideau described the internal slave trade within Angola during the 1960s and early 1970s as similar to the horrors that Texas prisoners described:

> The Angola prisoner lived in a sub-human world in which the strong survived and ruled, while the weak served and perished. It was a time of cliques, lawlessness, and violence—anything was possible, including the ownership of as many "slaves" as a convict could claim and hold. The strong routinely enslaved the weak, and new inmates entering the prison had to pass a test of violence to determine the status they would have in the prison community—"man" or "slave." The younger slaves served as effeminate homosexuals, while the older slaves served as servants who were made to produce income for their owners. In keeping with prison tradition, slaves were bought, sold, and traded among the strong. This practice was accepted as a natural part of prison life by both inmates and security officials.[88]

A fellow Angola prisoner and Black Panther, Robert King corroborated Rideau's description when he wrote in his autobiography that "raping, selling of prisoners, and forced homosexuality of younger prisoner by inmate prison guards and prison officials was the order of the day."[89] Similarly, Albert Woodfox, also one of the "Angola Three," offered an even more direct indictment of Angola's rape culture as state orchestrated. "Sexual slavery was the culture at Angola," Woodfox wrote in his autobiography. "The administration condoned it. I saw men being raped . . . Freemen [correctional officers] didn't do anything to stop it. They wanted prisoners who had no spirit. They wanted prisoners to fear one another and abuse one another; it made them easier to control."[90]

One such example was James Dunn, whose conviction of burglary at the age of nineteen landed him at Angola with a three-year sentence. Within the first month of his incarceration, Dunn was raped while attending the prison library, where, in his words, another prisoner "shove me into a dark room where his partner was waiting. They beat me up and raped me. That was to claim me." Once claimed as a "slave," Dunn not only became the perpetual object of sexual assault, but he was further reduced to the role of domestic servant within his assailant's cell, where he was expected to be a "good housewife" and "take off his old man's clothing, fix the beds, prepare meals, bust pimples in his face and give massages." In shockingly candid language,

C. Paul Phelps, the secretary of the Department of Corrections, admitted in an interview with Rideau: "Sex and power go hand in hand in prison. Deprived of the normal avenues, there are few ways in prison for a man to show how powerful he is—and the best to do so is for one to have a slave, another who is in total submission to him."[91]

The term enslavement within southern prisons thus had a deeply gendered component as freedom was associated with masculinity and slavery was seen as feminine. When Dunn became frustrated in his subservient role in Louisiana's Angola, he characterized the breaking of his sexual bondage with gendered language that associated resistance and assertiveness with the return of his masculinity. "I made up my mind . . . I'd do something to stop this and become a man again, the kind of man I could respect. . . . I was being used. I was a slave." But as a slave, Dunn's body and services could be bought and sold within an internal slave market where "in an economic sense, a slave is capital stock, property that can be made to produce income." Because Dunn's "old man" needed money to maintain his heroin addiction, he sold Dunn to another prisoner for $150.[92] Incarcerated on prison plantations and bound to coercive slave labor, southern prisoners also found themselves treated as slave chattel to have their bodies and domestic services bought and sold within their own cells.

Prison gender identity was thus constructed through the prism of violence and rape. In order to be seen as a "man," a prisoner had to demonstrate that he had ownership over his own body, which could only be achieved through violence. Once a prisoner's identity as a punk/slave became public knowledge, which was almost immediate within prison's close quarters, it was nearly impossible for the general population to see that prisoner's identity otherwise unless the prisoner was willing to challenge this enslaved double jeopardy through routine displays of violence and fighting, which in rough prison argot meant to "fight or fuck." For the Texas prisoner Floyd Patterson, the TDC not only denied prisoners their freedom, but it denied them their identity as men and rendered "masculinity" as an identity circumscribed by violence. "The system was just designed, I feel, to take your manhood," Patterson explained. "You know, to stop you from being a man. I don't think a man is a measure by how we can fight, nothing along those lines. I think it's just respecting yourself, respecting other people, treating people the way you want them to treat you. They [TDC] try to put in a position where you don't have respect for yourself."[93] Another example of how carceral violence circumscribed prison masculinity can be found in Haywood Patterson's autobiography, *Scottsboro Boy*. As one of the nine Scottsboro Boys falsely accused and convicted of raping two white women on an Alabama train, Patterson was incarcerated at Alabama's Atmore State Prison. In *Scottsboro Boy*, Patterson stressed the number of times he had to fight other prisoners in order to not become their "galboy."[94] When Dunn wanted to shed his slave/punk identity at Angola, he complained that "they wouldn't let me be a man" and that to retain his manhood he had to fight between fifteen and twenty times over the course of two months, ending finally when he killed the prisoner Coyle Bell, who had attempted to "own" Dunn. Prosecuted for murder within Angola, Dunn's three-year sentence then became a life sentence, but while his freedom from the prison system was stripped from him, he felt that he had gained his own sense of freedom within the prison plantation. "Nobody tried to claim me anymore. I was finally free—but it cost like hell."[95] Carceral violence was therefore integral to prison society and constructed a prisoner's gender, his identity and reputation, and the degree to which he might suffer doubled enslavement—a slave for the state in prison fields and an enslaved sexualized body and domestic servant within prison cells.

What separated the slave trade at Angola from the Texan internal prison economy, however, was that Angola's slave trade did not have as structured an internal control mechanism as the state-directed system of building tenders. Yet the internal slave/sex trade was an aspect of prison societies that prison administrations in other southern states could still manipulate. C. Paul Phelps, the secretary of the Department of Corrections for Louisiana, admitted to the *Angolite* editor Rideau that the administration engaged in daily "trade-offs." In his interview with Rideau, Phelps noted that between 1966 and 1976 that "the inmate power structure at Angola was very, very powerful. And anytime that happens and high level of homosexual rapes and enslavement is taking place, there has to be a tacit trade-off between the inmate power structure and the administration." Phelps noted that when you have two prisoners in a cell that often fight and one of the prisoners claims that "there's another inmate farther down the line who he can get along with," then the prison guards and administration will often grant the request just to avoid the trouble, even though, in Phelps's words, "We know what's happening there. But officers would prefer to have two people in a cell who get along rather than fight . . . so they put them together." In Rideau's estimation, prison rape in Louisiana was not so much a function of state orchestration as it was a matter of "nonverbal" communication where prison guards would "encourage, definitely tolerate" the wolf-punk/slave dynamic in the hopes that it would avoid prisoner-guard conflict. But Angola officials did manipulate these wolf-punk/slave relations to their advantage as the rules prohibited homosexuality and the administration could use that against a prisoner when they wanted "to elicit information and/or induce cooperation with the administration."[96] Indeed, Albert Woodfox offered this devastating revelation about the intentionality of prison rape at Angola. "Freemen [correctional officers] also used violent rapists to intentionally hurt other prisoners, placing them in cells with a prisoner they wanted to punish or putting them in situations when they wanted to start lethal fights. Those prisoners were called 'rape artists.'"[97]

Prison guards and officials may have acquiesced to Angola's trade in prisoner bodies, but the building tenders' powers were more extensive and integral to the prison administration than the prisoner-initiated slave trade in Louisiana. In Texas, the prison administration denied that building tenders ruled the internal prison economy, and they maintained that no prisoner had supervisory power over another prisoner. As the director George Beto misleadingly professed to the press, he lived in "mortal fear of a convict ruled prison."[98] However, in Louisiana, Mississippi, and Alabama, there was no administrative attempt to disguise that the external presence of trusties served as obvious prison guards armed with guns as trusty shooters. Moreover, these trusty guards looked outward, and while they sometimes engaged in corporal punishment, their primary role was to prevent prisoners from escape. The internal prison economy within these prison farms was therefore not as tightly controlled as the state-sanctioned but publicly hidden building tender system. While other southern prison systems acknowledged the power that their trusties had, Texas administrations hid the power of building tenders and disguised them as custodians.

In reality, the BTs had the power as state-sanctioned guards to partake in sexual violence and human ownership as an unfettered reward for their service. This process of physical domination constituted symbolic capital that had the power within the prison to ascribe sexual and gendered identity to prisoners.[99] BTs relied on a system of reciprocal favors, scrip, and promises of protection to count boys and bookkeepers so that they could be kept abreast of available information on all prisoners. The close relationship with bookkeepers allowed BTs to move prisoners from one cell, row, or wing to another, which became a particularly powerful tool when the BT wished to use that privilege to turn out another prisoner and make him his punk/slave. In order to get another prisoner into his cell, BTs sometimes paid money to the count boy, or they might simply call in a debt or a favor to another prisoner politician working in the administrative office. In Texas, the long reach of the building tenders extended into the protective custody, to take a younger prisoner as their sexual victim. "These count boys (another trusty, often a building tender)," wrote a former building tender to the special master's office for the *Ruiz* case, "can move an inmate or get them moved to where they want them to go. Money is given to the count boy and then he will move this person. I paid one count boy to move someone off a protection tank (gym) to three tank when I had my job. It cost me sixty (60) dollars. These count boys do as they want and the major lets them. I have a homosexual in here who I care a lot about but I am told to stay away from him.

These count boys have them but nothing is said. And the man knows they have them. I even had one count boy threaten to 'dust me' if I didn't leave mine alone. This same count boy has his in the cell with him."[100] As the testimony points out, prison administrators, likely at the assistant warden or major level, knew that building tenders controlled the sexual trade, but they could not disrupt the trusties' abuse of their power, or they would disrupt the balanced nature of the inside and outside labor regime.

Similarly, Jerry Quate recalled how at Eastham the head building tender, Jack Friday, routinely pulled prisoners from the "punk wing" into his own cell just as he might any other commodity: "We have a wing for homosexuals. If Jack Friday, he was about half of a homosexual, wanted one, he would get one. He would walk over there and get one of them homosexuals out, take him to his cell and keep him all weekend if he wanted to."[101] As these oral histories attest, prisoners engaging in same-sex relations did not characterize themselves as gay nor as homosexual, but their victims were always cast either as "homosexual," whether they identified as such or not, or in derisively gendered terms as punks/slaves. Their legal testimonies and oral histories reveal what Regina Kunzel has called the capacious nature of prison sexual culture that relied on the continuance of George Chauncey's "third sex" designation where men could engage in homosexuality while not considering themselves gay but rather casting themselves as a "wolf," "trade," or "normal" straight man.[102] Prisoners that owned a punk saw the control over another human's sexuality and services as prison's ultimate status symbol. There was nothing a prisoner could own that was more valuable than their own body and the body of another, and flaunting such control over body ownership enhanced a prisoner's reputation as a "good character." The prisoner Jerry Quate recalled: "Back then, it was a front—a macho deal. If I had what I call my punk, well you know, I'm supposed to be a big macho man. And a lot of us had them, but now, a lot of them did have sex with them, but I wouldn't. Now see, I was married when I come to the penitentiary in '68. And in fact, she waited for me when I got out in 1971, she was still there for me. All right, but it was just an ego thing, you know. And we'd sit out in the day room and I'd go to the commissary and buy him ice cream and stuff, you know, anything he wanted, and just talk to him. And it was just an ego thing."[103] Whether or not Quate's denial about having sexual relations, forced or as an exchange, were truthful, his words speak to the prison's symbolic capital that accorded respect and status to a male who maintained control, dominance, supervision, and sometimes even care of another prisoner. The internal prison economy in Texas was therefore central to a power structure that ascribed identity to prisoners as either "strong" or "weak," masculine or feminine along gendered definitions of sexuality and sexual behavior that went beyond the literal act of homosexual sex.

The BTs' near immunity to official punishments, access to weapons, and control of the internal economy also gave them the power to rape without much fear of prisoner reprisal or official rebuke. Prisoners who resisted rape could expect severe consequences. When a prisoner named Gilbert resisted the BT Charles Robertson's repeated attempt to take away Gilbert's commissary along with unwanted sexual demands, Robertson paired with William "Butch" Ainsworth, another building tender, to force Gilbert to submit. Ainsworth was well known in the prison for his 1969 jail break in Galveston County when he and four other prisoners escaped from the jail and took hostages, including a sheriff's deputy, who was shot and left for dead. Although the sheriff's deputy survived, Ainsworth was tried and convicted for attempted murder and sentenced to thirty years. Despite his violent record, or quite possibly because he was so well known for terrible acts of violence, the TDC assigned Ainsworth to Eastham, one of the toughest prisons, where he was soon elevated as a trusty, to become one of the most notoriously violent building tenders so that even Eastham's Warden Bobby Taylor called him "the most violent inmate he had ever known."[104] Ainsworth was also a self-mutilator, and in 1974 he used an axe to chop off three fingers from his left hand. In a failed attempt to earn a transfer from Eastham, Ainsworth had his severed fingers delivered to a guard.[105] When Gilbert refused to submit to their sexual demands, Ainsworth and Robertson attempted to electrocute Gilbert by wrapping a wet blanket around him and pressing an exposed extension cord against the wet blanket. When this failed, Ainsworth and Robertson forced Gilbert's feet into the commode and then placed the exposed wires into the water, which caused Gilbert "to scream from extreme pain, to begin to tremble, even to cry, and to submit to the homosexual acts."[106] After torturing and raping Gilbert, Ainsworth and Robertson then forced Gilbert to sign his commissary book over to them.[107] This gruesome act of torture and sexual violence was part of the comprehensive power of building tenders, who used their position within the internal prison economy to assert a reign of sexual terror over fellow prisoners.

As the prison system's architectural shift from southern dormitories to cells and wings approached completion in the mid-1970s, prisoners felt that the power and abuses of the building tender system were accelerating with the construction of cells that hid prison rape. Moreover, as civil rights activism challenged the prison system in the late 1960s and 1970s, the building tenders responded to prisoner "agitation" with greater levels of violence, intimidation, and sexual control. While there are no statistical studies of prison rape in Texas during the 1970s, the evidence that the prisoners themselves produced and shared with civil rights attorneys indicated that prison rape was thoroughly controlled by the building tender system and that the hierarchy of the building tender system favored powerful white prisoners, not African Americans or Mexican Americans. During the late 1960s and 1970s, politically minded prisoners drew on civil rights tactics and legal ideology while also borrowing racial critiques of systemized police and prison oppression from the Black Power movement and the Chicano movement to document prison rape as part of a wider effort to substantiate how prison societies constituted "cruel and unusual punishment." In Texas, prisoners maintained that white building tenders engaged in prison rape both as a reward for their service and as a punishment against those prisoners who were known as "political agitators" and "civil rights workers." What the prisoners' rights movement hoped to highlight was that state-orchestrated prison rape was accelerating because trusty-guards waged a social war of escalation with prisoners of color who rebelled against a white-trusty-ruled prison. For instance, in a 1974 letter to State Senator Chet Brooks, the prisoner Michael Jewell explained that civil rights activism had angered white building tenders, who turned with frightening frequency to escalated levels of physical and sexual violence. "Every time I leave my cell, I do so with the feeling that I'm entering a jungle, and the beasts could spring from behind any bush. The building tenders here have created a situation wherein one cannot feel safe, where tension is so thick you can drive nails into it, where there is no peace, nor freedom from fear. We simply cannot live under such conditions."[108] But prisoners rendered as perpetual victims in the punk/slave caste had scant legal recourse to bring rape charges against building tenders, whose power and position remained protected within Texas prisons.

Some sociological studies have argued that the reported ubiquity of rape in prison is a social misconstruction and that the actual occurrence of rape is, in fact, rare.[109] When prison rape has been a serious subject of study, it is often cast as a function of a hypermasculine prison culture or a product of individual pathology.[110] These studies, however, rarely attempt to distinguish whether prisoners are engaging in consensual relationships, a sex trade, or rape. Nor do they consider the role of prison authorities as it might contribute to, whether indirectly or through willful state orchestration, the ubiquity of prison sexual violence. Consensual homosexual relationships in prison are rarely explored, while the category of "rape" is frequently misinterpreted as a "consensual relationship," which leads to lower tabulations of prison rape.[111] Moreover, the literature does not take into account the impact of underreporting, the reluctance of prisoners to discuss rape, and attitudes of indifference to rape allegations among prison staff.[112] Prison rape in Texas is even more difficult to assess by reviewing reported incidents because the informal power of building tenders routinized sexual exploitation. Moreover, the state did not punish the building tenders that upheld their internal security system, and thus their misdeeds were never recorded in the punishment ledgers. The legal affidavits and oral histories of prison rape that are offered here are a product of prisoner frustrations and their eventual politicization over the shame and fear they experienced. Indeed, one letter of an anonymous prisoner to the court-appointed monitor shows how shame, humiliation, and fear kept this particular prisoner from reporting his rape:

> I was a victim of a homosexual assault on two separate occasions while I was in disciplinary lock up by two building service inmates. These inmate had access to building keys and they had the authority to open my solitary door at any given time. . . . These building service inmates should never have had the power to open my cell door. This shows you that if these inmates had this kind of authority in lock up that they do as they want on the whole unit. . . . I am very ashamed of what happened and I have not informed my wife of what took place. I had also not told any TDC official of the assault because I feel my life would indeed be in danger if I remained on the same unit with these two inmates. . . . If the truth is known and I am not given a transfer, my life wouldn't be worth a nickel.[113]

During the mid- to late 1960s, prisoners inspired by the civil rights revolution began a campaign to document such abuses and leave behind a record that might give some proof to the truth of their claims. Invariably, the prison administration responded to such claims by denying that building tenders held anything more than custodial duties and that there were no such prisoner guards in Texas as there had been in Louisiana, Alabama, and Mississippi. Because building tenders could engage in sanctioned and state-orchestrated prison rape, the prison administration dismissed out of hand any charges of sexual assault by building tenders. But when prisoners considered homosexual engaged in sexual acts with another man, they could suffer arbitrary and humiliating penalties that resulted in symbolic or corporal punishments. A system built on rewarding building tenders with the power to rape effectively masked state-orchestrated sexual violence and denied sexual violence its history. But during the 1970s Texas prisoners well understood Estelle Freedman's definition that rape "encompasses a malleable and culturally determined perception of an act . . . the meaning of rape is thus fluid," where the fact of its occurrence could face historic erasure through racial, class, and social hierarchies.[114] Through the act of legal documentation and affidavit as intimate testimonial, prisoners hoped to not only expose the depravity of prison rape but to give it a history as a state-sanctioned enterprise.

Following the gains of the civil rights movement, sociologists and criminologists during the 1970s reported a higher incidence of prison rape as a consequence of a rising prisoner population and the construction of a "new breed of prisoner" that was associated with the critical influx of African American prisoners due to the onset of mass incarceration.[115] A 1968 study of Philadelphia's jails by District Attorney Alan J. Davis rang the alarm bells by declaring that there was an "epidemic" of prison rape at the hands of African American prisoners. Davis's study of 156 assaults by 3,034 prisoners reported that 56 percent of the rapes were Black-on-white, twenty-nine percent were Black-on-Black, while only fifteen percent were white-on-white. In his study of Connecticut reformates, *Rape in Prison*, Anthony Sacco concluded that prison societies were a social inversion of wider society's white hegemonic rule where prisons served as spaces of "Negro Rule" where the more statistically common Black-on-white prison rape validated African American prisoners' sense of "masculinity or dominance."[116] Similarly, Leo Carroll's study of a northern maximum security prison found that "75 percent or more of the sexual assaults involved black aggressor and white victims." Indeed, the concept of "slavery" itself was racially inverted by Dr. Frank L. Rundle, the Chief Psychiatrist of California's training facility at Soledad prison, who explained that "blacks often have a preference for white slaves" as part of a "conscious kind of revenge" for their second-class citizenship in white society and the "conscious status which it confers upon them in the eyes of other blacks."[117] To explain the rise of what they called the "violent prison," prison sociologists of the 1970s questioned the static nature of Clemmer and Goffman's cohesive "society of captives" that utilized "deprivation theory," which located the formation of prison culture within prison walls.[118] Sociologists of the 1970s countered the deprivation model with "importation theory," which argued that theories of deprivation deny the individual prisoner's preprison cultural and societal experiences, which could include political encounters with the civil rights and Black Power movements. Donald Cressey and John Irwin, two of the pioneers of importation theory, concluded that "there has been a glossing over of the older notion that inmates may bring a culture with them into prison."[119] In her insightful critique of social and criminological studies of rape in the 1970s, historian Regina Kunzel concluded that Black-on-white rape was represented as "either an expression of pathological rage enflamed by black nationals or as evidence of the primitive relationship to sexuality nurtured in black communities, these arguments fixed the responsibility for prison sex in black men."[120] Most of these studies, however, focused on prison rape in non-Southern institutions, such as Philadelphia, Rhode Island, Connecticut and California. Importantly, however, many southern prisons still had racially segregated cells and wings during the 1970s and in Texas the southern trusty system thoroughly structured internal prison hierarchies. When Texas prisoners influenced by civil rights, the Black Power movement, and the Chicano movement confronted the southern trustee system during the 1970s, they pointed to systematic rape by state empowered southern trustees who ruled through a racial hierarchy that favored white prisoners. The Texas prison plantation system therefore problematizes the 1970s rape discourse about the so-called rapacity of African American men because in a racially segregated prison it was state-sanctioned prisoners, often privileged whites, who were given the tacit power to rape other prisoners.

To make their predicament even worse, when a prisoner who was a victim of building tender rape attempted to fight back against the building tender system or call attention to sexual intimidation, they were labeled as "agitators" and given official punishments. Indeed, when the prisoner who was raped by the BT Charles Robertson attempted to file a civil rights suit against prison officials for neglecting his welfare, he found himself "written up" for "damaging or destroying state property" because his narrative of the incident was written on the college program's paper. For his attempt to tell the story of his rape, the building major and sergeant threatened him and told him that he could "look for a good whipping" when he returned to his cell.[121] Prisoners with little other choice often responded with violence against the building tender system. In a 1977 letter to Senator Chet Brooks, James Adams, who had been in prison since the 1948 reforms, described how over three decades he turned to violence to combat what he saw as the sexual violence of the building tender system: "My prison record shows that I had possession of a weapon in 1958, but it don't say that I obtained the weapon (a knife) to defend myself from assault by Rudolf Polk, a 270 pound building tender, who had threatened me with a blackjack because I told him to stay out of my cell trying to play with my penis and fondling my cell mate and trying to force him to commit sex acts."[122] James Adams's letter reveals how sexual violence shaped a prisoner's defense of his own body, where he had little other choice than to arm himself for self-defense. Prisoners fought for their own sense of individual honor and societal respect in a system that inherently accorded power through carceral violence.

Prison administrators were certainly aware that prisoners lived or died based on the ability to retain respect among other prisoners. A key element of earning and retaining respect was the ability to demonstrate one's sexual prowess and control over one's body. The prison administration sought to undermine this pursuit of control, often by exploiting the tenuous nature of a prisoner's reputation. Stephan Blanchard was a self-described liberal, openly gay, and one of the few white prisoners on the Ramsey prison farm who supported the efforts of prisoner activists of the 1970s. In 1974, Warden Lanier of the Ramsey prison farm offered Blanchard early release if he signed an affidavit against the prisoner activists. Blanchard recalled, "I was asked to sign statements against [activists] on saying that I had been coerced into joining them to give them legitimacy because of my race, because I was white, and at the time, it was just browns and the blacks on this farm that were really actively engaged." When Blanchard refused, he was moved to seven wing, which was an all-Black wing on the racially segregated Ramsey prison. Blanchard recounted what happened next:

> I was taken into an empty cell in seven wing, which was an all black line wing, and a few hours of listening to the various catcalls, and race crap that was coming from black inmates walking by, my door was rolled and . . . this black head building tender came into my cell, followed by many others and the fight was on. And I was raped. And I couldn't even see his face. I was raped by one guy, and this head building tender told me, "That's a gift, writ-writer."[123]

While Blanchard never turned away from prisoner activism, the use of racial animosity and sexual violence irrevocably changed him. "It turned me from being a socially aware liberal into, I don't want to say racist, but a racialist conservative," Blanchard admitted. "My whole life, the beatings couldn't do it, the promises couldn't do it, but that shit—that rape did it in a heartbeat."[124] Salvador Gonzalez, a former building tender turned prisoner activist, corroborated Blanchard's rape and recounted how the prison administration offered Blanchard to Gonzalez as a sexual object if Gonzalez would end his association with prisoner activists and return to work as a building tender.[125] Gonzalez turned down Assistant Warden Christian's offer, and thereafter he and the other activist prisoners attempted to document prison rape and expose the sexual trade and violence in the Texas prison economy and the building tender system.[126]

Key Girls, Row Tenders, and the "Aggressive Female Homosexual": Women's Prison Labor, Gender, Race, and Sexuality

Until 1975, Texas had a single prison for women, the Goree State Prison Farm, which held women prisoners on 889 acres of the southeast Texas cotton belt, approximately four miles south of Huntsville, Texas. The TDC purchased the land around Goree in 1892 for $5,000 from Joseph Baldwin and initially used the site as a convict labor camp for men, but soon the Texas Prison System moved a number of women convict laborers who had been contracted to work on the Bowden plantation to a new camp that became the Goree prison. From 1915 to 1954, Goree was overseen by male wardens, but in 1954 Velda Dobbs was named the first female warden, a position she held until her retirement in 1973. During the postwar Ellis reform and prison building plan, Goree received funding to add an additional 136 individual cells, and in 1961 they built an entirely new cell block that could incarcerate another two hundred women. From the 1930s through the postwar period, Goree worked women in crop fields, a henhouse, a fruit orchard, a cannery, a barn for dairy cattle, and most importantly a garment factory.[127]

In the popular imagination and even in state-level legislative committees formed to scrutinize the TDC, Goree was often cast as much softer and more feminine than the space of the rough and violent world of men's prison farms. In its description of Goree for its 1974 final report, for instance, the JCPR described Goree as "the most attractive of [all TDC] units" and remarked that the reception room was painted in pleasant bright colors with potted plants and "brightly colored furniture" that was "reminiscent of a doctor's waiting room." Rather than the cold, hard steel prison bars that separated prison buildings and male prisoners, the JCPR characterized the steel bars at Goree as "shaped in interesting geometrical designs and painted in pastel colors" without the armed gun towers that watched over male prisoners. Instead, women were penned into the area surrounding Goree with a fence that had three strands of barbed wire around the top.[128] The press offered similarly rosy depictions of Goree as a stereotypically "feminine" prison environment. Along the cell blocks, the *Dallas Times Herald* reported, "the walls were painted in pastel shades and festooned with art created by the prisoners and photographs of inmates' children."[129] Each of the cell blocks was named with garden and flower nomenclature, such as Azalea, Daffodil, Fern, Ivy, Magnolia, and Terwinkle. Unlike the male prisons where talking in the hallway was strictly forbidden, conversations rang through the hallways as people moved from mealtime to work assignments. While men had their long hair roughly shorn off their shoulders, women could express some identity by wearing their hair long and putting on makeup that they could purchase at the prison commissary. Whereas men could only engage in craftwork in what was known as the "piddling room" and unauthorized "piddling" was a punishable offense, women prisoners could do macrame, knit, and make arts and crafts in their cells and adorn their cell walls with photographs of their children and their prison-made artwork. Moreover, the TDC granted women a "ten-minute parole" once a month, which was an eagerly awaited telephone call with family. Men had no such telephone privileges. Special day programs also seemed to suggest an air of near frivolity, entertainment, and leisure with such days of special prison celebration as "Fun Day," "Baskin Robbins Day," "Carnival Day," and "Inmate vs. Staff Basketball." Drawing on the outward expression of a women's prison that presented itself as practically an amiable space of sisterhood, the JCPR in 1976 offered the public conclusion that Goree was "much more humane, relaxed and pleasant than perhaps any other unit we visited in the Texas Department of Corrections."[130] But as with all Texas prisons, there was the public view of what the TDC presented, and then there were the internal dynamics of how hierarchical labor systems structured race and power within prison society.

While men were sent to a separate classification unit, women were sent from jail directly to Goree, where they were initially placed in "quarantine" and assessed based on a battery of psychological and sociological exams. Women were held in quarantine for the classification and intake process out of fear of mixing women and male prisoners together. Once in quarantine, TDC staff placed women in white cotton robes while their body cavities were thoroughly searched, and afterward their bodies and body hair were greased with camphor oil. As part of their classification process, women underwent two sociological background interviews that made a record of their education, criminal history, and family history. The women were then put through six exams for mental acuity, including the Revised Beta IQ test, the General Aptitude Battery designed by the Department of Labor to measure ten different factors related to job suitability, the California Adult Basic Education Test, the Minnesota Multi-Phasic Personality Inventor, the Beder-Costale test for brain damage, and a battery of psychological tests. The first four tests men received as well, but the last two were given at the request of Goree psychologists. These exams determined a prisoner's classification level and work assignment.[131]

As with most Texas prisons, overcrowding at Goree was a growing problem beginning in the late 1960s. Goree was originally built to incarcerate 400 women, but by 1974 the general population was 660 women, representing 4 percent of the total state prison population. The JCPR final report found that a growing women prison population during the early 1970s had made Goree "extremely crowded and space for programming was at a premium."[132] Internally, Goree had three main wings that provided living quarters arranged into cell blocks, wards (similar to the open prison dormitory), and a small population in single-person cells. Along the three main cell blocks nearly all cells meant for just one person were double bunked and crowded.

Incarcerated in close spaces, most of the women were young, first-time offenders who had been convicted for nonviolent crimes, but quite strikingly Goree also had a much higher percentage of women convicted for murder than did the general population of men. Because Goree was the sole women's prison, there was no segregation based on security level, so the convicted murderers lived alongside those convicted of a nonviolent crime. In the early 1970s, the majority of women (56.8 percent) were incarcerated at Goree for nonviolent offenses, including 137 for drugs (21.27 percent), 69 for larceny (10.71 percent), 58 for forgery (9 percent), 53 for fraud (8.22 percent), and 49 for burglary (7.60 percent). Women convicted of particularly violent crimes (49.49 percent) included 115 for murder (37.85 percent), 74 for robbery

Table 8 Goree woman prisoner population by race, 1973

Racial Group	Number of Prisoners	Percent Prisoners
African American	351	54.50
Caucasian	192	29.81
Mexican American	68	10.56
Other	33	5.12
Total	644	

Source: Prisoner population based on race compiled by TDC for JCPR in "Table 2: Ethnic Group Classification of Inmate Population," in Esther Chavez, committee staff, "Women in Prison in Texas," working paper submitted to the Joint Committee on Prison Reform (JCPR), CAH, *Ruiz*, MAI 8/J103.

(11.49 percent), and one woman for rape (0.15 percent).[133] As such, the majority of women (362, at 56.2 percent) had a sentence of five years or less. At the other end of the sentencing spectrum, however, 131 women (20 percent) had a ten-year or more sentence and 78 prisoners (12 percent), many of them convicted for murder, had lengthy sentences of twenty years to life.[134] But whether the crime was murder or fraud, most women at Goree were in prison for the first time in their lives, with 540 women (83.85 percent) never having had a prior incarceration. Only 12 women (1.86 percent) had more than three prior incarcerations.[135] Most of the women had only ever been incarcerated in Texas (610, at 94.71 percent), but 34 other women (5.26 percent) had previous prison terms in other states.[136] Unlike many of the men, who had a lifetime of encounters with incarceration beginning with Gatesville's juvenile detention that primed them for recidivist lives in and out of the TDC, 90 percent of the women (582) had not had a prior incarceration at a reformatory. Only 62 women (10 percent) had been previously confined in a reformatory.[137] The age range of the population was wide but included mostly women under the age of forty-five. One hundred eight (28 percent) were under twenty-five, and 326 women (50 percent) were between the ages of twenty-six and forty-five. Only 41 women were above the age of 46 (6.31 percent).[138]

As Goree was the only prison for women, it differed significantly from the rest of the system because it did not racially segregate the prison; nor did it separate first-time and multiple offenders. Goree's guards and staff were 75 percent women, and whenever a male guard came through the block, a staff matron was supposed to travel the hall ahead of him, announcing, "Man on the hall." The JCPR described the staff and guard attitude toward the women as "patronizing," where women were typically referred to as "my girls" and "comments about how pretty and silly these 'girls' can be are common."[139] Perhaps the most striking difference with the male prisons was the fact that

Table 9 Number of times in solitary, for women prisoners

Times In	Prisoner Number	Percent of Prisoners
1	498	77.32
2	77	11.95
3	43	6.67
4	11	1.70
5	4	0.62
6	3	0.46
7	4	0.62
8	3	0.46
9	1	0.15
Total	644	

Source: Esther Chavez, committee staff, "Women in Prison in Texas," working paper submitted to the Joint Committee on Prison Reform (JCPR), CAH, *Ruiz*, MAI 8/J103.

84 percent of Goree's living areas were fully integrated. As table 9 indicates, Goree incarcerated 351 African American women (54 percent) followed by 124 white women (29.81 percent) and 68 Mexican American women (10.55 percent). As with the men's prisons, the staff was predominately white (88 percent), and as such prisoners reported to the JCPR that there was "differential treatment of inmates based on race." The report did also note, however, that it did not find the ubiquitous use of racial epithets at Goree as they did with the male prisoners, where prison staff routinely shouted the worst kinds of racial slurs, even in front of JCPR investigating staff.[140]

In the critical categories of punishment, job assignment, and trusty status, there were clear racial disparities, though there were some differences from male prisons. When compared to the male prisons that routinely used solitary confinement as harsh discipline, Goree seemed to rely on solitary less frequently. When the JCPR came to visit Goree on September 1, 1973, only two women, 0.31 percent of the total 642 general population, were in solitary confinement. As table 9 demonstrates, 77 percent (498) of the women had been in solitary only one or fewer (zero) times. Twelve percent of the women (77) had been in solitary twice, and 7 percent of the women (43) had been confined to solitary three times. Only 2 percent (15) had received five or more solitary sentences. But as with the male prisons, whites had the fewest trips to punitive solitary. Solitary confinement resulted in racial punishment disparities where only 20.1 percent of white women spent one or more terms in solitary compared to 37.8 percent of the Mexican American women, who had the highest rate as a racial group for solitary punishment.[141]

Women's prison field labor, Gatesville prison, 1996. Courtesy of Alex Lichtenstein.

Job positions revealed striking racial disparities. Most of the women worked at the least desirable jobs, which were the prison's garment factory and food service. In the factory, women worked long ten-hour days sitting at their sewing machines so that they could turn cotton that male prisoners had picked into clothing and bedding for the entire prison system, as well as all the uniforms for both prisoners and guards and all the underwear, caps, pillowcases, sheets, and nightshirts. The largest number of garment and food service workers were Black women, who held nearly half of all the positions at the garment factory and more than two-thirds of the kitchen and food service jobs. Seventy-eight African American women held the largest number of positions at the least desirable job in the garment factory, followed by fifty white women and thirty-six Mexican Americans. Similarly, Black women dominated the food service position with eighty-eight women compared to twenty-seven white women and nine Mexican Americans. White women held the most clerical positions (fifteen), while thirteen African Americans and only three Mexican Americans held similar jobs. While the domestic servant houseboy was always a Black male prisoner, the "house girl" domestic servant for high-ranking prison staff was overwhelming held by Black women (twenty-one), while five whites and two Mexican Americans were also house girls.[142]

For their small numbers in the general population, Mexican American women received the worst and least desirable work assignments. Sixty-five

Table 10 Job assignment positions by race, for women prisoners

	African American	White	Mexican American	Total
Garment factory	78	50	36	164
Food service	88	27	9	124
Landscaping	14	8	0	22
Hospital	10	6	0	16
Clerical	13	15	3	31
Hall girls	21	3	1	25
Trusties	21	10	5	36
Maintenance	9	5	0	14
Dormitory attendant	26	10	0	36
Key girls	25	11	3	39
Laundry	25	6	5	36
Building tenders	17	16	0	33
House girls	21	5	2	28
Totals	368	172	64	604

Source: Esther Chavez, committee staff, "Women in Prison in Texas," Working paper submitted to the Joint Committee on Prison Reform (JCPR), CAH, *Ruiz*, MAI 8/J103.

percent of the total Mexican American population was assigned to food services and the garment factory. The more desirable positions, meanwhile, went to African American women as the majority population and to white women in numbers steeply disproportionate to their relative general population. In clerical work, perhaps the most coveted job outside of hall girl and row tender, Mexican Americans had only three positions, while African American women, as the majority population, had thirteen positions and white women had the most disproportional number of such coveted positions with thirteen women.

Because African American women constituted the majority population, they also held the most trusty positions (59.5 percent). Importantly, however, the number of prisoners in the highest status of trusty 1 were disproportionately white. According to the JCPR, "sixteen of the thirty-three [trusty] positions are filled by whites although they comprise twenty-nine percent of the population. The remaining seventeen positions are held by Black women who comprise 54.5 percent of the population." The proportions shift higher for whites when trusty 1 is separated from the other levels. Whites as trusty 1 exceed their proportion of the entire population, while Black and Mexican American women fell below their overall percentages. As table 11 indicates, 6.7 percent of all white prisoners were classified as trusty 1, compared to 5.1 percent of all Black women and 4.1 percent of all Mexican American women. As the largest population, Black women held the most number

Table 11 Classification and trusty status by race, for women prisoners

Class	White		Black		Mexican American		Total
All trusty	110	28.9%	226	59.5%	44	11.6%	380
Trusty 1	12	37.5%	17	53.1%	3	9.4%	32
All line	69	33.8%	105	51.5%	30	14.7%	204
Line 3	2	10.5%	11	57.9%	6	31.6%	19
Total	179	30.7%	331	56.7%	74	12.7%	584

Source: Esther Chavez, committee staff, "Women in Prison in Texas," Working paper submitted to the Joint Committee on Prison Reform (JCPR), CAH, *Ruiz*, MAI 8/J103.

of trusty positions, but not at the highest rank, which was reserved for white women, while no Mexican American women held the senior politically powerful position of dorm attendant. For the most part, African American women held the lowest-ranking trusty position that equaled their overall proportion of the general women population. Women in the "line" category were nontrusty prisoners who received less good time on their sentence. Black women comprised the majority (53.1 percent) of that low ranking, followed by whites (33.8 percent) and Mexican Americans (14.7 percent). The lowest positon receiving the fewest privileges was line 3. African Americans (57.9 percent) were the most so classified, followed by Mexican Americans (31.6 percent), while only 10.5 percent of whites were stuck in the low-status positon.[143]

Just as in male prisons, in Goree whites occupied the highest positions within the hierarchical and racially privileged arrangement of the building crew, which constituted the positions of the hall girl, key girl, dormitory attendant, and the powerful row tender position that granted trusties direct power over their fellow prisoners. Half of all building tender row assignments went to white women, such that they held sixteen of the thirty-three positions. The remaining seventeen row positions all went to African American women, leaving Mexican American women without any claim to the most influential job in the prison. The key girls were also powerful trusties who controlled the keys to individual cells, which granted them the unique power of denying the free movement of prisoners or opening the cell door to other prisoners whether they wanted company or not. In this capacity, the key girl acted as prison gatekeeper. Twenty-five African American women held this position, eleven white women, and only three Mexican Americans.

The state legislative committee tasked with investigating Goree in 1973 speculated that Spanish-language barriers may have been the reason why

Mexican American women held so few of the crucial building crew positions. As the JCPR working paper noted, there were only two bilingual persons among the Goree staff, which presented little opportunity for Mexican American women to create the internal relationships with staff and other prisoner politicians that were necessary to cultivate. Worse, the "Rules and Regulations" that bound prisoners to disciplined conduct were printed only in English, and most testing and educational programs, which offered the rare coveted escape from prison labor, were also only in English. The JCPR concluded in its report that the lack of building crew job positions, and particularly being locked out of the building tender row position, was "very frustrating for most Chicanas."[144] As a Mexican American woman, Esther Chavez, the author of the JCPR's working paper on Goree, offered a clear-eyed perception of racial disparities and the plight of Mexican American women prisoners, who had little recourse to complain. As Chavez's report understood, the southern prison world for women was predicated on white privilege and a Jim Crow black-white binary that locked Chicanas out of the row tender power structure altogether and left them without any opportunity for the refuge of educational classes. African American women, meanwhile, received more trusty and building crew positions relative to their proportion of the prison population than did Black men, but white women shared with the white male building tenders a disproportionate share of the most privileged and powerful positions.

Even as labor hierarchies privileged some women and locked others out of better jobs and power, Goree targeted sexuality and prison lesbianism for surveillance, policing, and segregation. While 486 (84 percent) of the women lived in the general population in mostly racially integrated double cells, the TDC's classification process selected 93 other women (16 percent) to live in a segregated row in single cells known derisively by the guards and other female prisoners as "stud row" for holding what the prison determined to be the "aggressive homosexual." Alongside those labeled as "aggressive homosexuals" were a few women who had "outstanding institutional records and want to live alone" and women with sentences of twenty-five years to life. While gay and young, vulnerable men were incarcerated in protective custody ostensibly to protect them, despite the reality that they often became targets of building tender assaults, the women in "stud row" were placed there to protect the general population from the spread of "aggressive female homosexuality."

As the historian Estelle Freedman has documented in her study of the social science discourse that constructed the "aggressive female homosexual," there was a shift in the postwar decade away from the long-held view among criminologists that Black women held "the male aggressor role" in prison lesbianism. Prior to World War II, criminologists constructed the prewar "aggressive homosexual" within prisons as a Black woman whose object of desire and pathology was white women. Without men, white women, so the theory went, craved a more masculine relationship, which African American women provided. Black women, then, took up the social role of "husbands" while white women acted as their "wives." In this prewar sexuality schema, white women therefore retained "a semblance of femininity" because "white women were not really lesbians, for they were attracted to men, for whom Black women temporarily substituted for their white partners."[145] As Freedman made clear, this thinking did not necessarily reflect "women inmates' own erotic systems," but rather it was a discourse of social science that effectively "racialized the sexual pathology" of Black women, while retaining the virtue of seemingly hapless white women. As a result, a more liberal and forgiving attitude prevailed when it came to white women's prison lesbianism. However, once more white working-class women went to prison due to increased arrests of prostitutes during an era of postwar "sex crime panics" and amid fears that returning soldiers were susceptible to venereal diseases from prostitution, the previously forgiving attitude toward white prison lesbianism waned. As incarceration swept up more women during the postwar period, worried criminologists developed what Freedman called a "new consciousness" that cast "the prison lesbian as a dangerous sexual category." New fears that prison lesbianism among white, working-class women was a "serious threat to moral order" was made more grave within the cultural context of the postwar emphasis on patriarchal middle-class families and traditional domesticity. To respond to this new threat, prison systems turned to "greater surveillance and ultimately to condemnation" of the "aggressive female homosexual" as an unwanted source of both social disorder and perverse criminality. It was in this historical context that the TDC isolated, monitored, and harassed lesbian prisoners as "aggressive homosexuals."

As might be expected, women building tenders and key girls abused their power and targeted segregated lesbians. The story of the prisoner Martha Quinlan provides one such example. To maintain her $150/day drug addiction, Martha Quinlan had turned to theft and petty crimes that ended with six convictions resulting in prison terms in Louisiana, Illinois, and Texas that caused the *Dallas Times Herald* to label her a "six-time loser." On December 12, 1975, Quinlan began her prison term at Goree, where classification immediately consigned her to the "aggressive homosexual" segregation wing. "They told me I was a butch broad," Quinlan told a reporter. Once classified as an "aggressive homosexual," Martha faced frequent harassment from the guards, and when Martha cut her hair short, she was given what she felt was the "punitive job" of staying up all night to mop floors. Whenever she left her cell, Quinlan became a frequent target of the key girls and dorm floor attendants, who harassed her daily and threatened her with extortion demands for her commissary. Quinlan did not experience Goree as a cheery pastel-walled space of rehabilitation and sisterhood, but rather she maintained that the trusty labor system and internal prisoner hierarchy created an atmosphere that was "brutalized, pervaded with fear and oppression."[146]

In her explanation of the power of key girls, Quinlan detailed how these state-empowered trusties could use their key-wielding power to "lock us up and let us out and report what we do." Quinlan explained that row tenders were even worse. "If a BT takes a disliking to you, you can't take a shower or go to a job assignment." A fellow prisoner labeled an "aggressive female homosexual," Rosa Lee Knight similarly testified that key girls and row tenders worked together to misuse their power in ways similar to the men by controlling whether women could leave their cells. "If the building tenders don't like you for some reason, you have a hard time getting out," Knight testified. Extortion was another reward that building tenders and key girls gave to themselves. "Sometimes they demand commissary from you," Knight further testified. "Cigarettes and coffee and so forth in order to let you out of your cell."[147] For Knight, the correctional officers were as hostile to her sexuality as the key girls and row tenders. "I go down the hall more than twice with somebody, I'm constantly screamed at," she testified. For gay women, all relationships with other prisoners was under constant watch and scrutiny. In the hospital, prisoner trusties performed medical care, where some prisoners who did not even hold high school degrees performed sutures, pap smears, blood tests, and dental work in hospital conditions that Quinlan described as "outmoded, unsanitary, and unsafe." As a favorite target of row tender and key girl abuse, Quinlan felt that vulnerable women at Goree, particularly out lesbians, were purposefully targeted for punishment under "unwritten, unpublished, unpromulgated rules" and that grievance procedures calling out these punishments were merely "an empty formality."[148] Internal job positions and work hierarchies at Goree were thus central to a labor regime that prioritized white prisoners, reduced most Black women to the worst jobs in the factory and food work (despite some Black women having trusty positions), shut out Mexican American women from the best and most powerful positions, and targeted the prison lesbian with intimidation, humiliation, and extortion.

Conclusion

When David Ruíz and Salvador Gonzalez forwarded to the prison director James Estelle the affidavit of the building tender Charles Robertson's 1977 rape of a youthful prisoner, they consciously called attention to sexual assault not as solely a mark of individual prisoner pathology but as a product of state orchestration. Repeated violence against individuals spread "collective trauma" throughout the prison community, undermining communal trust and collective identity. But prisoners who lived in a shared community in which they similarly experienced, saw, or heard about the prison system's everyday systematization of sexual violence eventually experienced the solitary act of prison rape as an injury to the entire prison community. As Jeffrey C. Alexander has defined it, "'experiencing trauma' can be understood as a sociological process that defies a pain or injury to the collectivity, establishes the victim, attributes responsibility, and distributes the ideal and material consequences. Insofar as traumas are so experienced, and thus imagined and represented, the collective identity will become significantly revised."[149] Prisoners such as Ruíz and Gonzalez might not have personally experienced prison rape, but their words speak to a collective and shared sense of having lived in a traumatic environment in which they understood that what happened to another fellow prisoner might just as easily happen to them. Collective trauma in a prison environment becomes a means to understand how prisoner collectivity, outrage, and politicization resulted in the face of a comprehensive power structure that previously ruled prison society with little interruption and near absolute control. As Regina Kunzel has argued, historians must "situate" prison sexual culture in time and in a social setting that considers prison homosexuality alongside cultural shifts and external political pressures. By doing so, historians can reconsider what Kunzel has called the "rhetorical strategy" that has rendered prison rape as "inevitable and somehow therefore less troubling, an expression of nature rather than of a particular culture."[150]

The development of an internal prison economy created more than simply the subtle acquiescence of prisoners to prison authority. The exchange of goods, knowledge, services, sex, and even human beings was at the core of an economic system that depended on brutality, violence, graft, and extortion, leaving no room for anything resembling "rehabilitation." Sociologists may well be correct that prison hierarchies and attendant internal prison economies do, in fact, bring a certain measure of "order." The type of order that prison hierarchies offered, however, exacted its own price in terms of human suffering. "See, the whole thing is a pretty physically-based thing," observed prison bookkeeper Lionel Lippman. "It's a very predatory system and this, I think, is a very important thing to note, that predatory is the common denominator for all of it. The strong prey upon the weak, and the weak are in a terrible position. . . . If they succumb to the predation, it only gets worse, and predation is social; it's sexual; it's economic."[151]

Seen through the lens of the internal prison economy, the external economic success of the Texas prison system was built upon the foundations of the BT system and the hidden prison economy. Both were part of a power system that traded in not only commissary goods but also in human dignity and personhood. As prisoners influenced by the civil rights movement came to recognize how the internal prison economy and society operated as a mechanism of physical control, racialized hierarchy, and sexual violence, a prison-made civil rights revolution erupted and thereby challenged the public image of Texas as the South's model prison system.

PART II

Resistance

Chapter 4

From Pachuco to Writ Writer

The Carceral Rehabilitation of Fred Cruz

A convicted felon, whom the law in its humanity punishes by confinement in the penitentiary instead of with death, is subject while undergoing that punishment, to all the laws which the Legislature in its wisdom may enact. . . . He has, as a consequence of his crime, not only forfeited his liberty, but all his personal rights except those which the law in its humanity accords to him. He is for the time being a slave of the State. He is *civiliter mortuus*; and his estate, if he has any is administered like that of a dead man.

—*Ruffin v. Commonwealth*, 1871

Without resistance there can be no freedom and liberty, for the history of liberty is a history of resistance. The time to march is almost here, the fires must be rekindled, and the soul made ready for the trial. The theater is small but the objective is the survival of man within himself and nothing must be spared . . . to win.

—"Memo: Theater of Operations," 1966, the diary of Fred Arispe Cruz

In November 1966, Fred Arispe Cruz sat naked in the darkened cell of Ellis prison's solitary wing. Cruz was a frequent visitor to solitary, but this particular stay seemed truly unjust. He was there because guards had discovered a copy of the U.S. Constitution in his cell.[1] Cruz had been a prisoner since 1961, after a pair of thirty-five- and fifteen-year convictions for aggravated robbery. Within his first year in the Texas Department of Corrections, Cruz had petitioned the prison board to reduce his field labor so that he could concentrate on his legal effort to appeal his conviction. The prison board denied his request, but Cruz continued legal work on his appeal and became one of the earliest prisoner pioneers who learned the law and acted as his own jailhouse attorney. Texas prisoners who acted as their own attorneys wrote appeals and writs of habeas corpus that sought court-ordered intervention to seek relief from what they argued was an unjust and illegal detention.

Among fellow prisoners, Fred Cruz was known as a "writ writer," but among the prison administrators he was simply called an "agitator." As a young *pachuco*, Cruz arrived on the Texas plantation prison system as what the Mexican theorist Octavio Paz called an "instinctive rebel."[2] Within the bounds of control penology, however, Cruz's rebelliousness soon earned him the negative attention of the prison plantation where, as the Chicana/o scholar David Montejano put it, "the defiant *pachuco*, in other words, invited hostility and harassment."[3] Within a year of his incarceration, Cruz became an avid student of the law, mastering legal precedents, rules, and procedures, and other prisoners, particularly in the Mexican American wing and among Muslim prisoners, sought his help with the appeals process. While the prison administration assumed that Cruz and practicing Muslim members of the Nation of Islam would see one another as racial rivals competing for precious resources within the rapacious prison economy, the Muslims and Cruz formed an early alliance. As Cruz's notoriety for legal work grew from 1962 to 1966, so too did the animosity of his captors, who increasingly viewed him as a threat to the prison system's otherwise comprehensive control. Prison administrators barred Cruz, and any other writ writer, from keeping legal material in his cell. When the prison administrators found the U.S. Constitution in Cruz's cell, they argued that the framing document for U.S. government constituted "legal material" and cast Cruz once again into the darkness of solitary confinement. Placing Cruz in solitary for his legal activities sparked a prison-made civil rights movement that would dominate Texas prisons for the next twenty years.

Prison Minority: Urban Mexican Americans on the Rural Prison Plantation

Fred Cruz was born in 1940 and raised in San Antonio, Texas, in the Mexican American neighborhood of Alazan de Guadalupe, which was beset with poverty, street crime, youth street toughs and gang organization, and the underground drug trade. As a southwestern city, San Antonio's Mexican American neighborhoods experienced ideological differences along class lines. On the one hand, the New Deal and World War II generation produced a new, rising middle-class Mexican American community who were, in the words of the historian Richard García, "ideologically pragmatic, Americanist in its patriotism, and acutely conscious of its civic obligations."[4] On the other hand, deep economic inequalities stratified San Antonio between privileged whites, a small number of rising middle-class Mexican Americans, and a majority of poorer Latino/as who were subjected to racial segregation, police brutality, economic impoverishment, and the denial of political and legal power. In his study of the Chicano movement in San Antonio, the historian David Montejano described San Antonio in the late 1960s as "the poorest city in the nation," trapping indigent Latino/a citizens living in the west and southwest sides of San Antonio within a nearly inescapable "internal co-lonial" condition.

Trapped in the mire of poverty, Fred Cruz joined other barrio youths who eschewed the assimilationist ideology of middle-class Mexican Americans, instead adopting the pachucos ("outlaw") lifestyle that "developed a distinc-tive linguistic argot, flaunted a colorful dress style, and were aggressive in de-fending their neighborhoods."[5] A childhood friend of Fred Cruz, and later a fellow TDC prisoner, Rudy Portillo recalled that San Antonio's "Alazan de Guadalpe was a very unique barrio with its own individuality," where the young pachucos sported a style of "super pride. You can tell it in their shoes! . . . They'd always have a nice pair of khakis and a clean shirt and their shoes would always be shiny." Many of the neighborhood pachucos also contrib-uted to the drug trade, which offered a sense of rebellious and audacious pride. Portillo explained that drug dealing allowed defiant local youths to declare: "'Hey, I'm a Tecato, now!' You're shooting dope and you're at the echelon where now you become a shot-caller in the neighborhood, because you can choose to deal, associate, and have your own thing."[6]

San Antonio's street pachuco culture sought *el respeto* as a way to circum-navigate the indignities of a system of ubiquitous and racially targeted pun-ishment that criminalized street youth. Not only did criminalization render youth culture as perpetual targets of racialized policing; it also structured the terms of resistance, as pachucos like Cruz and Portillo embraced their crim-inalization and reframed it as a paradoxical dissident political culture.[7] In his historical analysis of youth zoot suit culture during World War II, Luiz Alva-rez called such street dissidence a struggle for "dignity" that constructed "a politics of refusal, a refusal to accept humiliation, a refusal to quietly endure dehumanization, and a refusal to conform."[8] Drawing from Victor Rios's con-cept of "racialized punitive control" and what Alvarez has called a sense of "dignity" as dissident street politics, we can begin to see how prisoners em-braced the need to retain notions of respect from the street corner to the cell block as a means to survive and even confront carceral regimes.[9]

While Cruz turned to street crime, his father abandoned the family, leav-ing his mother, Sarah Arispe Aguilar, to raise Fred and his older brother, Frank. Without any means of support, the family remained poor. The Cruz brothers turned toward drugs and then crime as an escape route from pov-erty. Fred Cruz discovered marijuana at an early age, dropped out of school by eighth grade, and became a heroin addict by age fifteen. Throughout his teen years, he engaged in small robberies to support his growing drug habit. Abusive policing practices and violence followed him. The police fired on Cruz's brother and killed him during a botched robbery. In 1957, at seventeen, Cruz engaged in a pistol-drawing contest with his best friend, accidentally

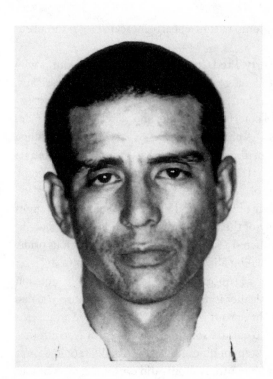

Fred Arispe Cruz,
mug shot, 1961.

shooting and killing him. The state did not charge him for this crime, but four years later the courts convicted him on two counts of aggravated robbery, sentencing him to the TDC with a pair of fifteen- and thirty-five-year sentences. The TDC sent Cruz to the Harlem prison, a unit near Houston along the Gulf Coast, where fertile ground produced bountiful harvests of sugarcane and cotton.

During the classification process, the TDC's battery of "intelligence" and behavioral diagnostic tests labeled Cruz a "hardened incorrigible" with an IQ of only 87, which cast him among many Mexican Americans whose abilities were similarly discounted based on racialized and culturally biased aptitude testing.[10] Even so, one classification psychologist thought that Cruz had "leadership potential," but rather than see such potential as meritorious, the TDC instead relegated him to field labor, lest he "most certainly be a disturbing influence."[11] Fred Cruz, who hailed from San Antonio's streets, would now work as a stoop laborer on a large agricultural prison farm that was once a slave plantation.

As a TDC prisoner from the same part of Alazan Courts (Alazan de Guadalupe) as Cruz, Rudy Portillo recalled that cotton picking did not come easily to urban pachucos. Portillo described how Warden Hal Husbands had an initiation ritual where he barked at all the incoming prisoners: "What are you down here for?" To which, the mostly urban prisoners would answer honestly with their conviction of "car theft or burglary or whatever," which would always earn a roaring response from Warden Husbands. "That's a damn lie!" the warden screeched. "You down here to work, that's what you're down here for and that's what you better learn."[12]

Portillo's introduction to cotton picking came through a jarring conversation with the prison guard high rider that he never forgot. "Okay, old thang!" the high rider barked, "you see these little plants here? . . . Well, this is cotton. It's my cotton. You see all this little grass and all these weeds, here? That's your grass, that's your weeds. I want you to get all your grass and all your weeds out of my cotton right now, man! I want you to get it right now, now-now-now!"[13] For Portillo, the first day of field work was an "awakening" that severed him from his urban pachuco upbringing and recast him as a Mexicano field worker and the lowest rung on the cotton prison plantation. This was the world of rural field labor against which Fred Cruz rebeled.

Cruz and Portillo were part of a growing Mexican American prison population during the 1960s who served the state's agribusiness interests at the same moment that the end of the Bracero program in 1964 created an opportunity for unpaid prison labor to replace some of the agricultural labor that poorly paid and nonunionized guest workers had once filled. Among all states that participated in the Bracero program, Texas experienced the nation's largest influx of guest workers, as 40 percent of all the Braceros in 1961 migrated to Texas.[14] Bracero programs offered international work contracts that legalized migration labor and racialized temporary foreign labor without providing an opportunity for citizenship or any chance to be fully integrated into the U.S. social fabric.[15] Meanwhile, the postwar "Operation Wetback" deportation program and the coercive powers of the U.S. Border Patrol policed what Kelly Lytle Hernández called "Mexicano mobility" as an international crime rather than as an act of "enforcing the political boundary between the United States and Mexico."[16] Mexican American citizens, meanwhile, remained racially connected to braceros and "wetbacks" in the public (white) imagination, but as citizens of color they were increasingly subject to domestic patterns of criminalization and imprisonment.[17] Incarcerated Mexican Americans, especially those from urban enclaves, increasingly found themselves as unpaid agricultural labor on large prison farms.

Although growing in numbers, Mexican American prisoners remained a minority within Texas prisons, constituting approximately 2,000 prisoners in a total prison population of 10,000 to 12,000 during most of the 1960s. From 1921 until World War II, Mexican prisoners were gathered together on the Blue Ridge State Farm, the system's only majority Mexican American prison, known as "Little Mexico."[18] Although geographic dislocation yanked

Mexican Americans from both urban spaces and the southwest borderlands, their shared incarceration as a racial group on a single prison farm allowed them to construct *"Mexico afuerra"* (Mexico Abroad) as a means of cultural resilience. On Blue Ridge, Mexican and Mexican American prisoners continued to speak Spanish and openly practiced Mexican folk traditions of song, sport, food, religious practices, and a Spanish-language prison newspaper, all of which sustained the south Texas prison farm as what George Díaz has called a *"colonia* within the carceral state."[19] Following World War II, Blue Ridge fell into disrepair, and during the mid-1940s instead "Mexican American" and "Spanish Speaking" as they dispersed the Mexican American prison across the system's twelve prisons.[20] Mexican American prisoners remained segregated in the 1950s and 1960s, and sometimes they occupied entire wings.

While field work and arduous agricultural labor ordered prison existence at the Harlem farm, most of these Mexican Americans hailed from the urban enclaves of Austin, Dallas, San Antonio, and Houston. Unlike the proliferation of prison gangs in California during the 1960s, the southern trusty tradition empowered building tenders to root out any organized prison gang, particularly gangs of minority prisoners. As a result, prison gangs did not exist as organized entities during the 1960s, leaving prisoners racially segregated and loosely congregated around informal and unorganized cliques based on home cities and neighborhoods. Incarcerated alongside Cruz, a fellow Chicano prisoner, Guadalupe Guajardo, experienced racial segregation as a kind of classification that denied individuality. "Really, no integration, none," Guajardo recalled. "You were Mexican, you were white, you were black, see that's the way it was."[21] Indeed, prison farms along the alluvial Brazos and Trinity Rivers, where sugar and cotton production were plentiful, were filled with Mexican American and African American prison laborers, but the two groups remained segregated within the same prison environment.

The Harlem prison, just outside of Houston, was known for its resistance to TDC authority, particularly during a pair of work strikes by Mexican American prisoners in 1957 and 1961. In one incident during 1957, a Mexican American prisoner was ripped from the embrace of his wife during a prison visit when he refused to stop kissing her. As a witness to the incident, Rudy Portillo described how "the guards literally got him by his ears, and pulled him out of the visiting area, which was right in front of the building, they just started whipping him" and "pounding him all over." Watching the beating from the nearby windows, other horrified prisoners began hitting the windows with their boots and shouting, "Ora, estos vatos de San Antone, cooperacion!" ("Hey, you guys from San Antonio, let's get a little cooperation here!") As a result, the prisoners broke into a near full-scale uprising. When the warden arrived to try to restore order, Portillo threw scalding hot water that hit the warden and badly burned his chest. In a rage, the warden had Portillo thrown to the ground and hand-cuffed, and he then ground his foot into Portillo's wrist. Portillo was then beaten unconscious and awoke later to find himself "hanging like a crucifix from the bars" of the mess hall windows on public display for all to witness.[22] At Harlem, incidents such as this one taught Mexican American prisoners that discipline was achieved through overwhelming carceral violence.

Beginning in 1961, Fred Cruz's incarceration coincided with the start of Dr. George Beto's term as prison director. On November 12, 1961, the prison system's director, O. B. Ellis, collapsed and suffered a fatal heart attack during a traditional Sunday evening dinner with prison board members. Ellis was only fifty-nine, and his death came as an unexpected surprise to the board, who soon thereafter commenced a search for a new director with the hope that they might maintain continuity and a smooth succession. Within eight days, the board turned to one of its former members, Dr. George J. Beto. At six feet, four inches and known for wearing his characteristic gray Stetson hat and a spur tie clasp with the initials GJB at its center, Beto was an imposing figure, both physically and intellectually.

Born a son of a Lutheran minister in 1916 in Montana, Beto was a product of Lutheran schooling, including Concordia College, a preparatory school in Milwaukee, Wisconsin (1930–35), and Concordia Seminary, St. Louis (1935–37). He earned a bachelor's degree at Valparaiso University, a private Lutheran university in Valparaiso, Indiana (1939), a master's degree in history at the University of Texas at Austin (1944), and a PhD in educational administration, also at the University of Texas (1955).[23] His educational career included twenty years at Concordia College in Austin, Texas, which was a college in name only and served since its founding in 1926 as a Lutheran prepatory high school for boys. While at Concordia Austin, Beto served as a history and religion teacher, what the school titled a "professor," from 1939 until 1949, and then as the school's president from 1949 to 1959. As president of Concordia Austin, Beto oversaw its transition to a junior college in 1951; admitted the college's first Black student, Henry Sorrel, in 1953; and started a modest program of coeducation, with the first women matriculating in September 1955.

The appointment of a theologian and educator as prison director for a system so grounded in the tenets of control penology and agribusiness initially was not without challengers. On only his second day in office, Beto's authority was threatened by thirty Mexican prisoners on the Number One Hoe Squad at Harlem who conducted a work strike. The prisoners sat down in the fields and insisted that they be allowed to speak to Beto. Soon thereafter, other prisoners joined their protest. The guards refused to give in to their demands and so the three hundred striking prisoners stayed in the fields overnight and remained surrounded by prison guards and officials. After failed talks with the striking prisoners, Beto called "five or six" wardens together to find a solution to the increasingly tense situation that had become, in Beto's words, a "test of me, because some of the wardens didn't know me, they didn't know what I would do." Beto responded forcefully and quickly by placing his wardens on horseback armed with wet rope and instructed them "to go out and put number one squad to work" and to "use whatever force was necessary," suggesting that Beto was prepared to have the prisoners whipped. Beto remembered that in his response to his order, "there was a flurry of excitement and then the number one hoe squad went to work in a hurry and the rest of the inmates followed."[24] Prison lore among the striking prisoners was that Beto arrived on the scene and pronounced, "Gentleman, I can go either way, with the bat or with Bible. Which would you prefer?" While Beto later averred that the "bible and bat" story was nothing less than convict legend, its truthfulness is less important than the image that Beto cultivated as being a religious and intellectual man while remaining a stern prison administrator committed to discipline, order, and work.[25] For the Mexican American prisoners, however, the lesson that they drew from this first encounter with Beto was that he was prepared to use corporal punishment and violent force to quell prisoner dissent. It is not clear from the prison archives whether Cruz participated in this strike, but over the course of the next decade, Cruz and Beto would become fierce adversaries.

Within his first year in the Harlem prison, Cruz initially received a string of disciplinary punishments. At first, the TDC frequently disciplined Cruz for his resistance to field labor with such punitive citations as "refusal to work" and "unsatisfactory work," while the TDC also exhibited great frustration with his cultural rebelliousness and punished him for "impudence," "disrespectful attitude," "insolence," and "insubordination." Under constant punitive threat, it did not take Cruz very long to find another means to resist by turning to the law, where he spent what little free time he had away from field labor on the legal appeal of his conviction. Each prison had a small law library—what prisoners and prison guards referred to as the "writ room," a reference to the legal practice of writing writs of habeas corpus—but no prisoner could retain legal material in his cell. Access to the law library was restrictive, its hours of operation irregular, and its depositories were not rich. Despite the limitations of the law library and its scant legal material, Cruz taught himself the law, wrote his own appeal, and acted as his own attorney. Although the TDC considered his legal work as "agitation," fellow prisoners referred to Cruz as a "writ writer." Cruz represented a new generation of prisoners who turned to the law and thereby confronted the TDC in the courtroom rather than in the fields of prison labor.

Beginning with his effort to appeal his conviction, Cruz studied Supreme Court decisions in the early 1960s that overturned the century-long legal silence imposed on prisoners. To place a term crucial to Cruz's legal activism, "slaves of the state," in proper historical legal context, we must turn to the term's evolution and how it epitomizes the southern prisoners' rights movement, even as the prisoners were not slaves without civil rights.

Not "Slaves of the State" and the End of the Hands-Off Doctrine: The Legal Evolution of Prisoners' Rights

During the year 1870 in Bath County, Virginia, the prisoner Woody Ruffin was sold under convict leasing to the Chesapeake and Ohio Railroad. In 1870, he attempted escape, and during his attempt he killed a guard. Once he was recaptured, the state sentenced Ruffin to be hanged. To avoid execution, Ruffin appealed based on his location at the time of the escape. Ruffin's defense looked to the state constitutional provision that a defendant must be tried within their "vicinage," which meant near a defendant's home rather than where the alleged crime took place. In the same stroke that the Thirteenth Amendment abolished the private ownership of human beings, it also expanded states' control over the lives and work of convicted criminals. By establishing that "neither slavery nor involuntary servitude, except as a punishment for crime whereof the party shall have been duly convicted, shall exist within the United States," the amendment allowed state slave labor to persist within prisons. The slave status of prisoners was seemingly confirmed by the 1871 Virginia decision *Ruffin v. Commonwealth*, which ruled that convicted criminals are "for the time being a slave of the State. . . . He is civiliter mortuus; and his estate, if he has any, is administered like that of a dead man."[26] In *Ruffin v. The Commonwealth of Virginia*, the Virginia Supreme Court dismissed Ruffin's claim with the conclusion that a prisoner's "vicinage" was "within the walls of the prison" and that the metaphorical "walls" extend beyond the institution itself to "surround him [the prisoner] wherever he may go."[27] Importantly, however, as the criminologist Donald Wallace pointed out, there was no "formerly held general view that prisoners were slaves of the state" and that legal scholars that frequently cited it as the basis of the dismissal of prisoners' civil rights offered an "erroneous historical view of the legal status of prisoners."[28]

Even as legal scholars have cited Ruffin's "slave of the state" framing as the predicate for the denial of prisoners' rights before 1964, this explanation has come to represent a prima facie narrative that substantiates the claim that twentieth-century prisons constitute neoslavery.[29] While twentieth-century prisons do replicate many of the traditions of slavery, made particularly visible by the agricultural nature of prison labor in the U.S. South, the "slaves of the state" narrative should be understood within a bifurcated framework under which prisoners claimed that the condition of their confinement rendered them as "slaves of the state" while the courts themselves denied hearing a prisoners' civil rights case based on practices having more to do with federalism than slavery. The distinction between the prisoners' lived experience of being treated as if they were slaves and how the law viewed prisoners as something other than slaves is important because it allowed federal courts to recognize that prisoners' were not slaves and that they were entitled to civil rights. That key distinction made possible civil suits based on the conditions of prisoners' captivity.

As a legal system framed by federalism, the individual state court decisions contradict one another; they do not uniformly embrace "civil death," and they very rarely cite "slaves of the state" as the defining language to deny a prisoner's complaint.[30] In the 1888 New York case *Avery v. Everett*, the court offered the stark admission that the civil death of prisoners was unevenly cited and often with contradictory decisions.[31] The court offered the analogy that following the legal history of civil death was like walking an unlighted path in the murky dark of contradictory law. "Anyone who takes the pains to explore the ancient and in many respects obsolete learning connected with the doctrine of civil death in consequence of a crime, will find that he has to grope along paths marked by uncertain flickering, and sometimes misleading lights; and he cannot feel sure that at some point in his course he has missed the true road." Between the 1871 *Ruffin* decision and 1964, the case *Ruffin v. Commonwealth* was only cited by other courts thirteen times, and these citations often refuted *Ruffin's* "slave of the state" language.[32]

The legal framing of "slaves of the state" as the basis for the denial of a prisoner's civil rights overstates *Ruffin's* national reach while it ignores a host of other state-level cases. Some state courts expressly claimed federalism as a reason to deny the "slaves of the state" claim. In the 1933 West Virginia case *State v. Dignan*, the court declared that "the principles of the *Ruffin* case are not the laws in this state. Here, all men are entitled to the protection of the Constitution, and this protection is not forfeited by even a convict."[33] In the North, the 1916 Rhode Island case *Anderson v. Salant* offered the blunt assessment that "the rights of a prisoner in Rhode Island are far wider than those of a slave. A slave had no property rights whatever and could neither sue, nor be sued. . . . Thus a convict can have an interest in property, while a slave cannot; a convict can sue, while a slave cannot."[34] In *Moss v. Hyer*, a prisoner in 1931 was struck by a driver while conducting roadwork in West Virginia and subsequently sued the driver for damages. As defendant, the driver cited *Ruffin* to argue that the prisoner was civiliter mortuus, and therefore no prisoner could bring suit against a citizen. In its ruling, the court cited cases where ex-convicts successfully sued for personal or property damages, as well the fact that a prisoner, unlike a slave, may hold property. The court believed that it would make for "an anomalous situation" if property rights were acknowledged but personal rights and bodily well-bearing were "to be treated as non-existent." The court expressed its dismay that "a third person would be subject to damages for injury to the convict's real or personal property, but if this same person should assault and beat the convict while working on a road gang with other convicts, or while as a 'trustee' acting as chauffeur or messenger for the warden of the penitentiary, there would be no liability."[35] The court therefore rejected the claim that prisoners have no ability to sue for damages. In its determination, the court cited *Westbrook v. Georgia* (1909) and its conclusion that "the convict occupies a different attitude from the slave toward society."[36] The *Westbrook v. Georgia* case is instructive because it reveals how the court could recognize that prisoners were not legally "slaves of the state" and thus entitled to some measure of rights, even as the decision fortified the practice of prisoners as slave labor through the chain gang system.

On January 22, 1909, Cleveland Westbrook, an African American prisoner, was part of a ten- to twelve-man chain gang when violence erupted between them that evening. George Walker, a white witness, offered his racially skewed testimonial of what occurred: "Ten or twelve of the boys were on a chain, all sitting around the fire, having a good time, like negroes usually do, singing and going on, cutting up," when a fight between them ensued. The camp warden (overseer), J. M. Davis, was called out to see what the matter was, whereupon he found Westbrook "sitting down quiet, with the knife between his legs." Davis then reportedly told Westbrook "that I would have to punish him for his conduct. He says, 'No Sir; you won't.' I says, 'I reckon I will; you are not running this business.' He says, 'I know that, but you ain't going to whip me.'" Davis then called upon his prisoner, the trusty Eugene Wilson, "a big negro I had there," to help him take Westbrook's knife as the prisoners on the chain called out, "You can't handle Big Boy." As a southern convict leasing camp, the prisoner trusty served as additional muscle for the overseer should the other prisoners ever resist. When the trusty Wilson lunged at Westbrook, he received a quick cut from the knife, and he retreated. According to Davis's account, Westbrook attempted to then stab Davis, but the other prisoners held Westbrook back by tightening the chain. Bound by his chains, Westbrook was helpless to stop Davis from stepping forward to repeatedly strike Westbrook with the sharp sting of a leather strap against his face "some eight or ten times." Westbrook continued to stab at Davis, but the prisoners "kept all the slack out of the chain," keeping Westbrook from cutting Davis, while Davis kept lashing Westbrook's face "lick for lick four or five times." In his frustration, Westbrook turned on his fellow prisoners and stabbed the closest one, who fell on all fours; Westbrook then "just stabbed him in the back," which killed him.[37]

At stake in the *Westbrook v. Georgia* case was whether the whipping of Cleveland Westbrook by the overseeing warden at a prison work camp was a justified part of enforcing labor or whether it was an unjustified act of corporal punishment that was "not of a character sufficient to authorize such punishment, . . . an assault." The state maintained that Westbrook was "a slave of the state" who had no right to resist. But the court decided in favor of Westbrook and offered a seemingly conclusive rebuke of *Ruffin* in its conclusion that "the convict occupies a different attitude from the slave toward society. He is not mere property, without any civil rights, but has all the rights of an ordinary citizen which are not expressly or by necessary implication taken from him by law." The crucial issue before the court, however, was whether the camp warden had a right to whip Westbrook when the ensuing fight was not over prison labor. The court decision stated that "a warden . . . has no authority to administer corporal punishment to a convict, except such as may be reasonably necessary to compel the convict to work or labor."[38] As a southern state, the Georgia Supreme Court jealously guarded the southern prisons' power to coerce Black labor through corporal punishment. The court therefore offered a two-sided decision that allowed the court to recognize a prisoners' constitutional rights while also upholding the southern prison's labor regime.[39] While the *Westbrook* decision upheld the South's labor regime, it is important to note that it also simultaneously acknowledged that prisoners did not occupy the legal category of "slaves of the state" and that prisoners could expect some measure of constitutional protection.

As the nation waged a global war in the name of democracy and freedom, the Supreme Court reevaluated the question of citizenship for prisoners during World War II, in a series of legal challenges that asked state and federal courts to reconsider whether the Eighth Amendment's "cruel and unusual punishment" clause applied to state prisoners. In 1945, the Supreme Court upheld in *Coffin v. Reichard* a federal appeals decision stipulating that a prisoner had a right to appeal for habeas corpus relief based not just on conviction but on the "conditions of confinement." A number of subsequent cases cited *Coffin v. Reichard*'s conclusion that "a prisoner retains all the rights of an ordinary citizen except those expressly, or by necessary implication, taken from him by law. While the law does take his liberty and imposes a duty of servitude and observance of discipline for his regulation and that of other prisoners, it does not deny his right to personal security against unlawful invasion."[40] The 1956 Stateville, Illinois, case, *Atterbury v. Ragen*, offered a clear declaration of the hands-off doctrine: "The Government of the United States is not concerned with, nor has it power to control or regulate the internal discipline of the penal institutions of its constituent states."[41] Most courts simply rejected *pro se* petitions out of the principle that the judiciary branch could not intercede against the state's oversight of prisoners. But a second case that challenged the hands-off doctrine was the 1958 case *Trop v. Dallas*. Trop, a soldier stationed in Morocco, left his post briefly, and the U.S. military summarily charged him with desertion, punished him with a dishonorable discharge, and later denied him a U.S. passport. The court ruled in favor of Trop, stating that denying his citizenship rendered him "stateless." Such an act, concluded the court, constituted "cruel and unusual punishment" as stipulated in the Eighth Amendment.[42] In 1961, the Supreme Court reconsidered the role of federal courts over individual states in *Monroe v. Pape* and concluded that federal courts had jurisdiction over state officials when the state infringed on individual rights protected by the Constitution.[43] Although that case was not about prisons or prison rights, it paved the way for state convicts to petition federal courts for more humane treatment by relying on an 1871 U.S. civil rights statue, article 42, section 1983, of the U.S. Code.[44] Then, the next year, the Supreme Court ruled in *Robinson v. California* (1962) that the Eighth Amendment's ban against "cruel and unusual punishment" applied to state as well as federal government.[45]

The decisions in *Coffin*, *Trop*, *Monroe v. Pape*, and *Robinson* opened the door to prisoners seeking to challenge the hands-off doctrine. In the 1963 *Jones v. Cunningham* decision, the Supreme Court had to decide the legal fate of prisoners themselves. Following the precedent established two years earlier in *Monroe v. Pape*, the court ruled that prisoners had the right to file a writ of habeas corpus to challenge both the legality and conditions of their imprisonment.[46] This ruling reversed the Supreme Court's nearly century-long hands-off policy regarding federal interference in state prisons.[47]

Once the Supreme Court established that prisoners possessed the right to file writs of habeas corpus appealing their convictions and conditions of confinement, prisoners began to identify civil rights that, they argued, the courts were obliged to protect. In 1964, Joe Ragan, the warden of Illinois's Stateville penitentiary and Dr. George Beto's mentor, barred a Black Muslim prisoner named Thomas X Cooper from having access to the Koran. Under the organization of the Nation of Islam, Muslim prisoners had brought civil suits against prisons that denied them their ability to practice Islam. The prisoners' rights movement took up Cooper's cause and prevailed upon the court to rule in favor of Cooper and to establish the rights of prisoners to challenge the practices of state prison officials in federal court.[48] The 1964 *Cooper* decision ignited a nationwide civil rights movement for prisoners, doing for prisoner rights what *Brown v. Board of Education* had done ten years earlier for education and civil rights.

Within a decade, the Supreme Court's Justice Byron White firmly declared in the 1974 prisoners' rights case *Wolff v. McDonnell* that "there is no iron

curtain drawn between the Constitution and the prisons of this country."[49]
In the aftermath of *Cooper v. Pate*, the number of prisoner rights suits dramatically increased from 218 in 1966 to almost 18,500 in 1984.[50] Behind many of these landmark cases was a network of outside legal organizations, such as the National Association for the Advancement of Colored People (NAACP) and the American Civil Liberties Union (ACLU), who pioneered these rights-based cases and pressed for the legal recognition of prisoners.[51] In a 1972 letter to David Hunter of the Stern Fund, the civil rights attorney Alvin J. Bronstein offered the rationale behind the ACLU's creation of the National Prison Project, which offered civil rights attorneys to represent prisoners in civil rights cases. Bronstein admitted that a "question on the minds of many people, including foundation trustees," might well be "why [develop] a program of litigation which may only cosmetically change an evil system rather than concentrating on alternatives to incarceration which do away with the system?" In response, Bronstein drew on his civil rights experience during the 1960s, asserting that conditions did not change in the South without "continuous assaults on the system with litigation as the major vehicle" alongside direct action and protest. "To the extent that things have changed in the South," Bronstein explained, "litigation, protecting and following direct action, and acting as a catalyst for national legislation forced the change." Bronstein explained that the ACLU were deluged with "dozens of letters each week" from prisoners asking for legal assistance in both their individual cases and "particularly when they act collectively, and [require] the protection of inmates against retaliation for the exercise of those rights." Bronsein concluded, "That is why we are engaged in the major litigation effort in this country." More specifically, the new civil rights initiative was "aimed at getting as many men and women out of the system as we can, making life more human for those who still remain in the system, and at the same time acting as one of the catalysts for the eventual institutional changes." For crusading attorneys, the prisoners' rights era that blossomed during the 1970s thus derived from two immediate sources, those stemming from incarcerated Muslims, many of whom converted through the prison prosletizing of the Nation of Islam during the 1950s and 1960s, and out of the context of civil rights litigation and direct action protest coming out of the U.S. South during the 1960s.

Solitary Revolution and Mind Transformation:
The Evolution of Fred Cruz

Inspired by the court's recognition of prisoners' rights and the wider civil rights movement in Texas, Cruz's turn toward civil rights for prisoners built on the decades-long civil rights struggle in Texas that sought equality for both African Americans and Mexican Americans, but each group often pursued their aim with historically distinct tactics and outcomes. In the pre-*Brown* era, the NAACP in Texas aggressively pursued civil suits in their effort to challenge school segregation and the all-white Democratic primary that the state initiated in 1923. In a series of civil litigation cases from the 1920s and 1930s, including *Nixon v. Herndon* (1927), *Nixon v. Condon* (1932), and *Grovey v. Townsend* (1935), the NAACP gained some legal victories, only to have the state legislature find loopholes that kept the Democratic primary all white in Texas.[52] The twin victories of *Smith v. Allwright* (1944) and *Sweatt v. Painter* (1950) offered successful challenges to the all-white Democratic primary and created an important legal precedent that racially segregated spaces for education was not equal.[53] During the early 1960s when Cruz first started to research civil rights law, African Americans in Texas had moved beyond the courtrooms to initiate direct-action campaigns that included sit-ins at lunch counters that were first organized by Texas Southern University students under the organizational banner of the Progressive Youth Association. Other organizations, such as the Dallas Community Committee (DCC), organized similar sit-ins across the state that drew on the tactics and practices of the Student Nonviolent Coordinating Committee (SNCC).[54]

Mexican American civil rights activism in Texas, however, had a historically distinct path that marked it as different than the Black freedom struggle because it drew on middle-class "whiteness politics." In the southwestern cities of El Paso and San Antonio, the middle-class organizations of the League of United Latin American Citizens (LULAC) and the American GI Forum encouraged civic nationalism, military service and patriotism, and cultural assimilation as the most effective means for Mexican Americans to stake a simultaneous claim to both whiteness and citizenship.[55] In such civil rights and segregation cases as in *re Rodriguez* (1897), *Delgado v. Bastrop* (1948), *Pete Hernandez v. Texas* (1954), and *Hernandez v. Driscoll* (1957), LULAC's whiteness strategy earned some key victories that secured Mexican American citizenship through the 1790 naturalization law that granted citizenship through "whiteness," while postwar litigation also acknowledged that Mexican Americans had the right to sit on Texas juries and questioned the educational segregation of Mexican Americans "as a class" rather than as a nonwhite "race."[56] In the early 1960s, middle-class Mexican Americans also turned to electoral politics in the hopes that the Democratic party might further the Mexican American claim on full citizenship. Political clubs such as Viva Kennedy! and the elevation of Henry B. Gonzalez from the state senate to the U.S. House of Representatives for San Antonio's Twentieth District even offered some hope that pressing for civil rights through electoral politics might yield political gains.[57] The whiteness strategy amounted to what the historian Brian Behnken aptly described as an "insistence on whiteness [that] had very little to do with classification as 'Mexican.' Rather, it had more to do with being viewed as 'colored' and [Mexican Americans] *not* being classified as white."[58]

But such whiteness strategies offered no hope to Mexican American prisoners whose incarceration on southern prison plantations equally denied Black and brown prisoners their constitutional rights, personal dignity, and humanity. Aware of the wider civil rights revolution beyond prison, Cruz's writ writing soon evolved beyond the effort to appeal his conviction to focus on the conditions of his confinement, which was a critical legal evolution that placed prisoners' rights within the wider struggle for civil rights.

Between the years 1966 and 1967, Cruz kept a meticulous record of his daily activities in a handwritten, two-volume diary that recorded every day of his confinement and his thoughts concerning his legal struggle, his place in American society as the son of Mexican immigrants, and his intellectual and political transformation. On the first page of the 1966 volume, Cruz pasted a picture of the Supreme Court and then individual photos of Justices Felix Frankfurter and Hugo Black. Underneath the photograph of the Supreme Court, Cruz copied the poem "Invictus," translated from Latin as the "unvanquished" (or "unconquered") by William Earnest Henley, which reads, in part, "Out of the night that covers me, Black as the Pit from pole to pole, I thank whatever gods may be for my unconquerable soul. In the fell clutch of circumstance, I have not winced nor cried aloud. Under the bludgeoning of chance, my head is bloody, but unbowed."

In prison, Cruz, who had dropped out of school by the eighth grade, became a voracious reader, devouring both legal and philosophical texts. In 1966 and 1967, his diary records that he had read such works as Jean Paul Sartre's *Existentialism and Human Emotion*, Martin Heidegger's *German Existentialism*, texts on Plato and Aristotle, and the socio-psychologist Frantz Fanon's *Wretched of the Earth*. In his diary, Cruz made a special note of Fanon's conclusion: "Violence is a cleansing force. It frees the native from his inferiority complex and from his despair and inaction; it makes him fearless and restores his self respect."[59] Cruz considered the kind of "transformative violence" that Franz Fanon advocated, but he chose instead a nonviolent path of resistance through legal confrontation rather than physical force. Even still, Cruz's studies to achieve self-actualization drew upon Fanon's psychopathology of colonization to help Cruz understand his incarceration on a prison plantation as similar to Fanon's internal colonization over Black and brown bodies.

Rather than embrace violence despite the harsh conditions of Texas prisons, Cruz instead offered a deeper philosophical and spiritual reflection that gave him the personal fortitude to withstand the prison administration's punitive animosity. Indeed, his writing reflected upon how the state ought to respond to criminals and the meaning of justice and citizenship for prisoners. His hunger for study, education, and written reflection caused Cruz to conclude that Texas prisons were entirely punitive and that his keepers abused their power. In the margins of his diary, Cruz jotted down quotes from such historical figures as Thomas Jefferson, William Jennings Bryan, and John F. Kennedy. In a series of entries with such titles as "Crime and Punishment" and "The American Commitment," Cruz wrote short pieces demonstrating artful prose, clarity of thought, and a growing sense of frustration with his captivity. He also demonstrated a sense of civic nationalism, rights, and obligations.[60] In his second-to-last entry for 1967, his piece on "Crime and Punishment" reads, in part, as follows:

> What about this matter of crime and punishment, anyhow? You can trace it all down through the history of man. You can trace the burnings, the boilings, the drawings, and quarterings, the hanging of people in England at the crossroads, carving them up and hanging them as examples for all to see. We can come down to the last century where nearly two hundred crimes were punishable by death. You can read the stories of hanging on a high hill, and the populace for miles around coming out to the scene, that everybody might be awed into goodness. Hanging for pick pocketers, and yet more pockets were picked in the crowd that went to the hanging than had been known before. . . . . Cruelty breeds cruelty. If there is any way to kill evil and hatred and all that goes with it, it is not through evil and hatred and cruelty; it is through charity and love and understanding. . . . You cannot cure the hatreds and maladjustments of the world by killing and punishment. You may here and there cure hatred with love and understanding; but you can only add fuel to the flames by cruelty and hate. What is our society's idea of justice? "Give criminals the same mercy they give to their victims." If the state is not kinder, more humane, more considerate, I am sorry I have lived so long.[61]

Cruz's studies focused on societal and historical tensions between rehabilitation and punishment and between rights and oppression. His writing reflected upon how the state ought to respond to criminals and the meaning of justice and citizenship for prisoners. Cruz read deeply into the law, and while he taught himself the technical nuances of the law and its rights-based shift, he also engaged philosophical texts that reflected his deep contemplation over quintessential and timeless human rights.

As Cruz sought to satisfy his intellectual curiosity, he also developed a spiritual hunger for a guiding philosophy and a personal religion. Cruz discovered

Eastern philosophy and spirituality as a source of inspiration and personal transformation. His readings on spirituality centered on a growing interest in Buddhism, and increasingly he appreciated and admired the ways in which Buddhism insisted on the pursuit of truth and an acceptance of reality. Cruz found these aspects of Buddhism particularly appealing given his predicament as a prisoner struggling to bring the reality of prison experience to the wider public. By 1966, Cruz converted to Buddhism, though his desire to practice it would become a new source of conflict with prison administration. For Cruz, the discovery of Buddhism coincided with his legal pursuit of civil rights for prisoners. Yet it also signaled his personal conversion to what George Mariscal has termed "international nationalism," in which many in the Chicano movement increasingly defined themselves as a colonized minority and looked outside of the United States for political, religious, and ideological inspiration.[62] Texas did not have a rehabilitative library program as voluminous as California's "bibliotherapy" program, which the historian Eric Cummins called a "hospital of the mind" in an institutional attempt to intellectually "up-lift" prisoners with Victorian classics and the Western canon. But even with a less ambitious library program, Cruz was able to read widely, and the volumes that he chose reflected his abiding interest in the subjects of both revolution and rights.[63] Indeed, Cruz's prison transformation followed a similar trajectory to Malcolm Little's transition to Malcolm X while incarcerated in Massachusetts, where both men experienced a concurrent process of personal and political transformation that reinscribed incarceration from the loss of self and individuality to become what the scholar of U.S. radicalism Dan Berger has called "a radical politics of survival."[64] Cruz's student David Ruíz would later describe Cruz as "cell taught, self taught," and his deeply personal, trenchantly intellectual, and profoundly religious transformation was part of what the Black Panther historian Robyn Spencer has called a "mind change," where personal transformation breeds political inspiration.[65] In a carceral system that offered coerced labor as the chief source of "rehabilitation," Cruz initiated his own rehabilitation through a carceral brand of mind change.

Inspired by Thomas X Cooper's legal battle at Stateville penitentiary over his constitutional right to religious freedom and his ability to read the Koran, Cruz began a similar campaign within the TDC.[66] Cruz's writs demanded access to legal counsel, the freedom of religious worship, and the ability to correspond with buddhists. However, his avid pursuit of the law and his keen ability to write writs for fellow prisoners soon earned the unwanted attention of Dr. George J. Beto.

Beto first encountered Fred Cruz in his second year as prison director in 1962 at the segregation unit of the Walls prison, a special unit that housed "300 to 350 alleged incorrigibles" in what Beto described as "a prison within a prison." Those housed in the segregation unit lived in permanent solitary, apart from the rest of the prison population in an isolated and desolate wing. Cruz had been temporarily placed there as a behavioral charge, but the more likely reason was the ongoing attempt to silence his writ writing. Prisoners referred to it as the "Little Shamrock," whose name mocked the inhospitality of prison because it was a perverse inversion of Houston's Shamrock, a premier hotel for high-rollers.[67] Despite its punitive purpose, Beto closed down "Little Shamrock" in June 1962 because it did not conform to the labor regime. "It bothered me," Beto confessed, "to see three hundred fifty people not working, locked up, listening to the radio—in bearing the label of incorrigible."[68] Beto was known for his daily surprise visits throughout the prison system, where he would inspect the various prisons and meet individually with prisoners to discuss their grievances, a habit that earned him the nickname of "Walking George" among the prison administration and "Promising George" among many prisoners for his failure to make good on his assurances. On one of his surprise tours of the "Little Shamrock" wing, he met with Cruz briefly to discuss his legal situation. Beto would later reflect that upon first meeting Cruz, he found him insolent and a "nonconformist who looked at other people as being stupid." As a prominent TDC board member, Beto had helped found the prison's Education Program, devised along with Dr. H. E. Robinson, of the Texas Education Board, and Dr. Elliott Bowers, of Sam Houston State Teachers College. As TDC director, Beto enacted the 1968 creation of the Windham School District, establishing a school at each prison.[69] As a theoligan and minister, Beto's directorship also expanded the prison's chaplaincy from just a single clinically trained chaplain in 1961 to thirteen trained chaplains.[70] Despite holding a PhD and having a successful career as an educator and minister, Dr. George Beto just could not perceive Fred Cruz's intellectual and spiritual journey as education or genuine rehabilitation, dismissing Cruz's intellectual trajectory as subversive nonconformity and as a sociopathic tool for "convict manipulation."[71]

By 1966, Cruz's legal work was gaining prisonwide notoriety at Harlem, so to silence him, Dr. Beto moved Cruz from Harlem to the dreaded Ellis prison plantation. The Ellis prison was a newly built, maximum security prison near Huntsville that housed recidivists, "agitators," the lowest classification of prisoners, and those on death row. When Beto took over the prison system in 1961, one of his first acts was to dismantle the isolation unit at the Walls (the "Little Shamrock" wing) and place prisoners with a poor disciplinary history at the newly constructed Ellis prison. Billy Wayne "Redbird" McCarter, a prisoner with over four decades of prison sentences in the TDC, recalled, "Everybody that come to this unit [Ellis] was brought from another unit. And they was classified as a malcontent, an escapee, an agitator, or an instigator, or a Muslim." Overseeing the Ellis prison was Warden "Beartracks" McAdams, who was a career TDC employee and Ellis loyalist, who bolstered the prison system's reputation among both prisoners and the press. When appearing before reporters, the imposing six-feet-two, 220-pound McAdams struck them as "a big man with a velvet voice, a cherub's face and a hulking frame," who, "despite the paunch," "can move like a mongoose when there is trouble brewing." Prisoners described McAdams in less benevolent terms as a "dead shot, hits like a mule kicking, and makes tracks like a big old bear." McAdams was born in the heart of the prison region in Walker County. He was a third-generation Texan whose family had come to Texas with Sam Houston. Although he became the system's most prominent warden in the 1960s, McAdams never finished high school and had left school by the eleventh grade. McAdams had first joined the prison system in March 1935 as a guard at Wynne, but he quit in protest in 1941 to become a Dow Chemical Company plant security agent. McAdams was "depressed" over the "lax manner" of the prison administrators; he was particularly distressed over internal corruption and the lack of hierarchical organization among his superiors. After Dow, McAdams became a Huntsville police officer from 1946 to 1948. But the Ellis plan "really convinced" him to return to the prison system. McAdams served the Texas prison system as guard, dog sergeant, field guard, assistant warden, and warden in a career that spanned nearly thirty years.[72] He received the name "Beartracks" while a guard at Wynne in the 1930s because the prisoners there thought he was as "big as a bear" and yet his constant patrolling of the tanks caused him to seemingly be "everywhere at once" while leaving "his tracks wherever he goes." Local newspapers heralded him as a hero when he reportedly "cleaned out a barricaded cellblock with a baseball bat" and for his ability to track down escaped convicts, causing one reporter to remark that "McAdams has brought in more than 30 of the escapees himself, and is still hunting the missing man."[73]

As a life-long career prison administrator, McAdams had a hard-earned reputation as the system's toughest warden, who attempted to tame the system's most "incorrigible" prisoners. Working his way up the ranks, McAdams earned his first warden position in 1949 overseeing the Retrieve prison, which at the time held, in McAdams's words, "incorrigible white men." Wherever McAdams went within the system, he took with him "all the incorrigibles," and as he moved from Retrieve to Ramsey to Ellis, he brought these men with him. "We moved all the incorrigibles to the Ramsey Unit," he told an interviewer. "And I moved at the same time. In other words, I moved 'em with me and put 'em in this big cellblock that we had, which was individual cells." When he took over the Ramsey and then the Ellis prisons, he oversaw Mexican American and African Americans prisoners, as well as white, but his life-long experience had taught him what he considered to be the value of racial segregation. "Well you take the Blacks and the Latin Americans, they're two different people," McAdams explained. "In other words, they're handled different. . . . I had my worst white men. . . . I had homosexuals. . . . I had colored . . . and you keep 'em separated. And if you didn't, you had trouble back then with the different races on there—trouble within on 'em. And that's why we kept 'em separated like that." But of all the prisoners, McAdams found the Mexcian Americans the most violent. "Well, Latin Americans or Chicanos is dangerous people with knives," McAdams contended. "They're knife people. . . .'course colored is not as bad. They just more or less with their fists. And whites is a lot like that. But Latin American, no ways. They believe in knives."[74]

To police the different races, McAdams employed his white "incorrigibles" as trusty building tenders, and he recruited only the most violent men to ensure discipline. For instance, Clyde Thompson was a convicted murderer of two people and had only just missed the electric chair when his death penalty conviction had been commuted to life. During his twenty-seven years of incarceration, Thompson had killed another five prisoners, and his reputation as a thoroughly violent prisoner was such that Beto had Thompson shipped to McAdams at the Ramsey prison. Although Thompson had killed fellow prisoners, McAdams thought he still might prove useful. At first Thompson worked in the field, but after Thompson had gone to McAdams to tell him that another prisoner had hidden a homemade knife in the pipe chase, he then earned McAdams's trust. Thompson told McAdams that in the past he "would'a just killed him [the prisoner who had made the knife]," but now he had changed and was willing to work for the administration. "Sure enough," McAdams recalled, "it [the knife] was in there [the pipe chase] like he said it was, and that made me believe that Clyde Thomson had changed his way of life because he was—like I say, he had killed two men before he ever got to the electric chair and that was commuted to life. Then after that, he killed five more in prison. And that made me believe more that he changed." McAdams never thought to consider the possibility that Thompson himself might have planted that knife in order to gain a trusty building position, but what mattered to McAdams was the degree of loyalty and control he could exert over violent prisoners like Thompson. For McAdams, such men, although violent themselves, were actually "peacekeepers" and defenders of the "weaker inmate." "They's the best help that's ever been in a prison," McAdams opined. "He [the building tender] can stop another inmate from running over the weaker inmates. The weaker inmates get run over, if you don't have somebody in there among 'em, to kind of protect 'em. And let the employees know what's going on." As a building tender, Clyde Thompson earned greater good time against his sentence, and despite having killed an additional five people in prison, the reward for his service to McAdams was to eventually earn his freedom, whereupon McAdams reported that he subsequently became a preacher in Lubbock, Texas.[75]

Attempting to curb the violent world of the Texas prison plantation, Cruz's writ writing was now under the watchful eyes of McAdams and his ruthless building tenders. The McAdams administration frequently sent Cruz to solitary for petty reasons as part of a concerted effort to silence his outreach beyond prison walls. Cruz chronicled McAdams's reliance on caceral violence, making special note of McAdams's "unwavering belief in the efficiency of brute force," where "unrestrained power is geared to expose inmates to a continuous process of humiliating degradation designed to repress," "destroy self-esteem," and "plunge men into darkest despair." "If he can succeed in convincing men that he has more authority in their lives than the courts," Cruz warned, "and if he can generate a constant state of fear, then, and only then, does he feel he is extracting payment from law violators."[76] In such an atmosphere, Fred Cruz quickly emerged as McAdams's foremost adversary.

Prisoners who wrote to outside organizations complaining of prison conditions and requesting assistance or investigation faced derision, scorn, and outright attempts to silence them from prison authorities. One of the earliest recorded attempts to reach civil rights organizations to enlist their support in a nascent prisoners' rights movement occurred from 1947 to 1952 when David C. Rook, an African American prisoner, attempted to tell the NAACP about the ways in which Black prisoners faced unrelenting brutality and discrimination. In one such letter, he asked NAACP director William White if their "debt to society" also included being "beaten and run like dogs or cattle merely because we are in prison?"[77] His outreach effort had reached such levels that the prison board's September 1952 meeting commented that Rooks's attempt to "file thousands of papers of photo static copies of material . . . at our expense" had just about "exhausted our patience." "He has written the President of the United States, the Attorney General of the United States, the Director of the Federal Bureau of Investigation, numerous federal courts, numerous state courts, the National Association for the Advancement of Colored People, legal aid clinics, lawyers, and others." The board concluded that Rooks must be silenced because "Rooks is an irresponsible, psychopathic Negro." To limit his correspondence, the Texas Prison Board cited two cases—*Homer B. Adams v. O.B. Ellis* and *Sigel v. Ragen*—involving prisoner correspondence rules in both Texas and Illinois, in defense of its decision to limit prisoners to five persons on their correspondence list and three letters a week. Only family members could appear on the correspondence list, however. Moreover, prisoner correspondence, even with a prisoner's attorney, was opened, read, scrutinized, and could subject a prisoner to violent punishment at the hands of building tenders.[78] Prisoners could not openly criticize the prison system in this correspondence, and no communication with media was allowed.

Prison officials considered writ writers as a threat to the discipline and security of the prison, particularly if the writ writer offered to assist a fellow prisoner on his case. On southern prisons, they ardently opposed the practice of jailhouse law and frequently established strict rules prohibiting it. Southern prisons made it particularly difficult for writ writers as they dedicated so few resources toward the establishment of an adequate law library. When southern prisons could not dissuade from lack of adequate legal materials, they outright forbade prisoners from practicing the law and issued harsh punishments. The 1965 Tennessee case *Johnson v. Avery* was one of the first successful challenges against such arbitrary prohibitions. When William Joe Johnson, an African American prisoner serving a term of imprisonment for life in Tennessee, was placed in solitary confinement for practicing jailhouse law in violation of a prison rule, he and his attorneys filed a complaint that eventually reached the U.S. Supreme Court. Johnson argued that denying him the right to file writs both for himself and on behalf of other prisoners was a constitutional violation of his right to access to the courts. In *Johnson v. Avery*, the Supreme Court ruled that unless the state provided legal assistance to prisoners in their postconviction pleadings, then prisoners had no other recourse but to assist one another with their cases. In a dissent that must have struck Fred Cruz as ironic, Justice Byron White charged that the "aim of the jailhouse lawyer is not the service of truth and justice, but rather self-aggrandizement, profit, and power."[79]

Though the Rooks precedent made it nearly impossible to enlist outside assistance, Cruz would not be deterred and continued to file writs for himself and on behalf of other prisoners. On Valentine's Day in 1967, Cruz was called before Major Wallace M. Pack, Assistant Warden Joseph Walker, and Warden McAdams for his attempt to send a certified letter to the ACLU attorney John Farra. McAdams told Cruz that "we know who you have been talking to and who you can't talk to." He accused Cruz of lying about the conditions of his confinement, and he promised that the letter would be sent to Dr. Beto. In his diary entry for that day, Cruz reported that at the meeting "the envelope with forty cents postage was returned to me. I accepted it with the clear understanding that I was not withdrawing my letter from the United State Mail depository and that letter was being seized against my will and without my consent." Cruz then related what transpired: "As I started to leave towards the door, Mr. Walker said: 'We are taking this letter away from you and keeping it. We may have some use for it later on.' To which I responded with: 'You probably will.' The Warden then rose to his feet shouting: 'Making threats! Put him in solitary!'" Cruz then spent the next fifteen days in solitary.[80]

Cruz records a deep and lasting sense of despair, depression, and illness from his time in the darkened and isolated solitary cell. Prisoners in southern solitary confinement were placed in a bare and unlit cell, with a steel bunk bed that on many occasions did not have a mattress, and a hole in the middle of the floor serving as the toilet. Until 1970, the prison administration placed prisoners in solitary on a strict bread-and-water diet in which guards gave prisoners a "full meal" only once every three days. Cruz's thoughts on those days spent in solitary provide a rare glimpse of the price that prisoners paid for any effort to reveal the inequities of captivity:

February 15, 1966, Tuesday, Solitary Confinement: Nothing to do. I just laid down and meditated. The printing crew was giving solitary a paint job. The paint fumes got real bad and started making everybody sick. I started experiencing cramps and severe pains in my stomach.

February 17, 1966, Thursday, Solitary Confinement: I got a breakfast tray this morning. It was practically nothing. All it had was one fried egg, a little gravy, and some oatmeal without any sugar; with two slices of bread. I have started suffering from diarrhea. My whole body system feels extremely weak and I feel so lazy I can hardly move. I just lay on the bed cursing the darkness not caring if the sun don't shine.

February 19, 1966, Saturday, Solitary Confinement: Tried to make sick call again this morning but everyone went by like a streak of lightening. I'm feeling pretty bad now. The doors are open and the noise is worse than having the doors closed. These people in here talk endlessly and don't say a thing worth listening to. *Thought for the day:* If a bus stopped in front of my cell and the devil was driving it one-way trip to hell, I would get right on it.

February 20, 1966, Sunday: Solitary Confinement: I got my second tray this morning. It was the same as Thursday's. I'm getting sicker than hell. The cell doors are still open. Everybody is busy talking about nothing at the same time. *Thought for the Day:* I wish somebody would come in and shoot us all dead.

As the days progressed, Cruz became more sick and his mental anguish such that he came to welcome the prospect of his own death as the only remaining escape.

Following his solitary stay, Cruz prepared himself for what he considered a "war" with the prison officials. By May 1967, Cruz's letter to the ACLU attorney Farra had still not been mailed, and Warden McAdams told Cruz that if he wanted to use the writ room again, he would have to sign a paper stipulating that if he did "anything wrong up there," he would never again request to use the writ room. Signing such a statement circumscribed Cruz's ability to practice law, and he knew that the threat was vague enough that any small infraction or unsubstantiated accusation would cost him his access to the law library for the duration of his confinement. This was an unacceptable proposition for Cruz, who refused to sign the statement and decided to up his resistance rather than capitulate. In a memo to himself titled "Theater of Operations," Cruz planned his next phase of resistance: "Under the circumstances the proper thing to do is first notify John Farra of existing conditions; second, consult with family to determine the strength of support; third, inform the court on the abridgements of my rights; fourth, maintain a state of readiness to cope with any eventuality that might arise because once the line is drawn I must stand prepared to defend it against invasion of all hazards." Beneath his meticulous plans was an inspirational piece of writing that conveyed Cruz's belief that his legal work should be seen within a broader framework of resistance to the prison plantation's oppression.

> For too long the guns have been silent and the fires within the camp have grown cold. The lesson of history has once more repeated itself: the desire for peace is mistaken for weakness and the child oppression is born. Tolerance at times is prudent but there is a point where tolerance must end and resistance to begin. Without resistance there can be no freedom and liberty, for the history of liberty is a history of resistance. The time to march is almost here, the fires must be rekindled, and the soul made ready for the trial. The theater is small but the objective is the survival of man within himself and nothing must be spared . . . to win.[81]

Chapter 5

Eight Hoe—Sowing Seeds of Dissension

Chicanos and Muslims Make a Prison-Made Civil Rights Revolution

During the cold months of October and November 1967, the TDC once again cast Fred Cruz into the deep dungeons of Texas prison solitary for two consecutive two-week terms, but Cruz refused to yield to despair. For while he was relegated to solitary, Fred Cruz knew that he was no longer alone. Cruz's intellectual journey from the streets of San Antonio as a young pachuco to the far-flung East Texas prison plantation did not exile him from the social, political, and cultural tumult of the 1960s. Even in the fields of prison plantations, prisoners could not be sequestered from learning about the civil rights revolution and El Movimiento for Chicana/o empowerment. Over the course of the next five years, Cruz joined other Texas prisoners in the late 1960s and early 1970s who collectively fused together the rights-based language that emanated from the nation's courts within an initial interracial prison coalition between Chicanos, Muslim prisoners, and a few white prisoners who also saw themselves as victims of carceral violence.

Cruz's first and most important ally came from outside of the prison through the Great Society's antipoverty law programs.[1] While Cruz's 1967 effort to notify the ACLU failed, he managed to get a letter to Frances T. Freeman Jalet, a white attorney who had graduated from Columbia and Georgetown law schools and who worked for the Office of Economic Opportunity. As a working practitioner of Lyndon Johnson's Great Society and antipoverty program, Jalet also held a prestigious Reginald Heber Smith fellowship, which allowed her to train in poverty law at the University of Pennsylvania Law School. Prior to coming to Austin, Jalet had raised five children from her first marriage, run her own private practice, and worked as a staff attorney for Cornell University's New York State Law Revision Commission. Jalet moved to Austin, Texas, in 1967 to begin work for the Legal Aid and Defender Society of Travis County. Shortly after her arrival, the *Austin American Statesman* dubbed this fifty-seven-year-old mother of five children and noted lawyer as the "Portia of the Poor," a reference to the character in Shakespeare's *The Merchant of Venice*, who disguised herself as a man and a lawyer so that she could defend an imperiled man in court. Cruz read the article with interest and, because of her work in antipoverty initiais and law, contacted Jalet and asked her to meet with him to discuss his case.

On October 26, 1967, Jalet arranged an initial visit with Cruz at the Ellis prison. Cruz's diary reported, "Her legal aid under Office of Economic Opportunities is restricted to civil cases. She is helping in her free time at personal expense." Jalet further told Cruz that she had discussed his case with Beto, who "stated that at one time he had felt sympathetic towards my cause because he felt that I had suffered unfairness, but that his inquiries had revealed that I was actually guilty, and that as a consequence he had changed his opinion on the matter." Moreover, Beto had "attempted to convey the impression to her [Jalet]" that Cruz was a "crafty individual." Cruz ended his diary entry on his first meeting with Jalet by noting that she had told him that she has a daughter in Thailand who was also studying Zen Buddhism. Cruz wrote that he "found her to be a very nice person with a charming personality. Her views are very liberal and seems to have a vast resource of understanding and compassion for the plight of man."[2] In a subsequent letter to Jalet, Cruz displayed an abiding intellectual and personal connection with the poverty attorney. In one passage of a fifteen-page handwritten letter, Cruz relayed his dismay that TDC had taken away from him Eric Fromm's *Man for Himself: Beyond the Chains of Illusion* and *Zen Buddhism and Psychoanalysis*. "Since Fromm is one of my favorite authors," Cruz reported, "you can imagine my surprise upon discovering that you also read him and that you have his book *Escape from Freedom*." In their intellectual exchange, Cruz then excitedly provided her a list of his very favorite titles, which conveyed his intellectual growth and maturity: *The Confessions*, by Jean-Jacques Rousseau; *The Confessions of St. Augustine*; *The Great Political Theories*, by Michael Curtis; Machivelli's *The Prince*; Marcus Aurelius's *Meditations*; *The Communist Manifesto* by Marx and Engels; Khalil Gibran's *The Prophet* (with the side note—"Have your read *The Prophet*? Its one of my favorites!"); Voltaire's *Philosophical Dichotomies*; Corliss Lamont's *The Philosophy of Humanism*; and Dante's *Divine Comedy*. The personal rapport was also nearly immediate; Cruz conveyed that he felt comfortable with Jalet from the outset of her visit: "You seem to have a very rare gifted capacity to employ your charm in such a tender fashion that while with you, a person feels very much at ease and comfortable in expressing their views. This is a virtue not possessed by many, and one which is really appreciated."[3]

For her part, Jalet saw that prisons represented an ideal opportunity for her to practice poverty law for those who needed help most. Jalet found Cruz impressive. In her notes concerning their first meeting, Jalet wrote: "Fred Cruz is handsome. He is witty. He is charming. . . . He can think. He can persuade. He can write. But he is human and makes mistakes and he admits them. He transcended doctrine. He worked with inmates where he could. . . . He is not afraid. He drew no limits for himself, including death. It didn't take much to arouse my interest in joining in with him . . . but even so my impression of Fred was that of an extraordinary man."[4] From the first moment they met, there was a personal and intellectual attraction, appeal, and mutual respect shared between Cruz and Jalet.

The remaining challenge, Cruz knew, was to pull back the veil over TDC's modernization narrative to make Jalet, the courts, and the public see what prisoners knew to be true. Cruz had to make TDC and its hidden labor regime legible to people who could not see it. "Most lawyers I have talked to," Cruz pointed out, "have agreed that something needs to be done, but have hesitated to make any kind of personal contribution to that end." Cruz's letter expressed great frustration over the difficulty of piercing TDC's public image but also great hope that Jalet might perceive what other outside attorneys had not seen:

> You are the first person that I know of who has actually inquired as to what is going on down here. I am almost persuaded that it is an impossibility for anyone to really find out the truth unless you have been down there personally. I would tell you what I have seen: what I know, but you probably would not believe me. I have thought about it many times and find it unbelievable myself. Yet how can you deny what your eyes have seen, when you have suffered all these things yourself. I have thought about George J. Beto and Warden McAdams. I can see them in the light that others see them, and you would never see them from my standpoint of view. They are masters of the art of deceit, they hide behind a cloak of respectability, they go to Church, on Sunday they speak before congregations, they smile and shake the hands of many, but they are maneuvering wolves in sheep's clothing. They eat their prisoners all day long and at night they wipe their mouths.[5]

Soon after the visit, Jalet wrote to Beto that she was in disbelief that the TDC had placed Cruz in solitary because of his desire to share his religious beliefs with other prisoners. "As a minister, I am sure you would be a champion of freedom of religious belief," Jalet noted with dismay, "but why is he forbidden to discuss Buddhism with others? If its tenets, which I'm told in some respects are akin to those of Christianity, offer solace to him, they may well do so for others."[6] Rather than earn sympathy, Jalet's letter only provoked Beto's ire. When McAdams first encountered Jalet when she came to visit Cruz, he offered the dismissive and derisive description that Jalet seemed to him a "witch, scary looking and all," out of his very nightmares. Once Jalet began working with Cruz, she provided him with additional legal readings on the Supreme Court's recent recognition of prisoners' rights. The two began a frequent correspondence where Cruz and Jalet discussed law and also shared details about their life's journey. In one letter, Cruz confessed to Jalet that his tough San Antonio upbringing placed him in "a community of criminals who are anti-social to the greatest extent" and that he had "always been among the worst." In his admission to street crime, however, Cruz hoped to relay "a better insight into the nature of my existence" so that she could understand his self-initiated carceral rehabilitation in the proper light: "I do not have anything to hide, nor do I have anything of which to boast."[7] He plainly told Jalet where he had come from, and that only made her want to help him more on his journey toward self-reformation and mind change. Through Cruz, Jalet was introduced to the Muslims, particularly Bobby Brown, who like Cruz was brutalized and punished for his religion, and Ronald Novak, a white writ writer whose struggle with mental illness was exacerbated with prolonged stays in solitary due to the TDC's effort to silence his legal activism. Over the course of the next year, twenty-seven more prisoners turned to Jalet in hopes that she could help them bring the abuses of the TDC to light. This marked the beginning of one of the most radical crusades in U.S. prison reform and jurisprudence history.

The initial result of Jalet's investigation was the Ellis Report, a fifteen-page typewritten report sent to Anthony G. Amsterdam of the NAACP Legal Defense Fund in New York City on the advice of the University of Pennsylvania law professor Howard Lesnick. In her November 6, 1968, cover letter to the document, Jalet wrote that she was "deeply distressed" over the "denial of their [prisoners'] constitutional rights," particularly its treatment of African American and Mexican American prisoners, and from "the mistreatment that they regularly receive," which constituted a "pattern of repression, harassment and even torture, that is shocking." She stated that prisoners live "in constant fear," "fear of punishment in the form of deprivation of privileges, loss of good time, humiliations and indignities, and beatings; fear of solitary where when incarceration is prolonged starvation or even death can result." Jalet believed that the Texas prison system maintained a mask over its brutality by presenting itself publicly as a national model for correctional management. She warned that despite the brutalities existing behind prison walls, the average visitor to Ellis "senses none of this" as the worst horrors of the prison system remained "hidden—much of it buried in the dungeon-like (all-dark) cells of solitary." Jalet believed that the prestige of Dr. George Beto among the public and penologists was a "mask of respectability" and that he used his good name and public presence "to obscure the truth from interested eyes."[8]

The Ellis Report drew upon Cruz's experience, which he disclosed in his meetings with Jalet. It therefore focused on aspects of prison abuse that Cruz knew all too well, including solitary, denial of religious freedom, denial of access to the courts, mail censorship, discrimination based on race, and the intimidation, brutality, beatings, and sadism that resulted from the building tender system. The report was culled from a number of prisoner accounts, interviews, and written testimonials, including one "beautifully presented report [which] is 60 pages long, naming about sixty prisoners who would testify." The report described solitary as a "subterranean windowless cell completely in the dark, with nothing to do and no equipment to keep oneself clean—no soap, toothbrush, etc; with no food except bread (three slices a day) and water with a 'repast' every 72 hours consisting of a few vegetables—no meat." Solitary confinement was never supposed to go beyond fifteen days, but her report cited instances in which "at the end of 15 days (the normal durational period) the outer cell door (made of solid steel) is opened—but the prisoner is still behind bars in the inner cell—and this is considered 'release from solitary.'" But after "one or two days and a few meals, the door is shut again and he is kept there another fifteen days." Jalet cited instances of prisoners being kept in solitary for over forty-five days.[9]

The report also highlighted the degree to which prison administrators denied prisoners access to the courts. "Legal assistance to prisoners is forbidden," the report concluded. "The presence of legal materials of any sort—books, papers, pleadings, is considered 'contraband' and confinement in solitary is the fate of the possessor." Not only were prisoners barred from keeping legal material in their cells, but the limited law library, the writ room, was not open during regular hours, and it was open for no more than "two hours some evenings or on Saturdays for the brief period." At other moments, the writ room might be closed "for weeks at a time," and most legal briefs and entreaties were censored and "many are never mailed."[10]

Jalet also cited religious intolerance as prevalent throughout the prison system, particularly in the denial of religious services for Muslim prisoners who had joined the Nation of Islam. The report noted that the prison's main house of worship, the Chapel of Reconciliation, was a "supposedly non-denominational religious edifice" but that in actuality it offered church services for "adherents of the Christian faith only." Drawing upon Cruz's frustrations to gain religious services as a Buddhist, Jalet wrote that "prisoners of the Jewish Faith go into town; those who profess Islamic or Buddhist beliefs are denied the right to worship." "Especially harsh," continued Jalet, "is the treatment accorded Black Muslims who are singled out for punishment in solitary and locked up in isolated pales 'until they get their thinking straight.'"[11]

In prisons throughout the nation, particularly in New York and California, thousands of African American prisoners seeking empowerment, community, and spiritual fulfillment amid the despair of prison's ever-present threat of violence joined the Nation of Islam (NOI), converted to Islam, and adopted the teachings of Elijah Muhammad. After converting to the NOI in prison, Malcolm X's 1957 defense of Johnson X. Hinton following a severe beating by the New York Police Department that left Hinton with a brain contusion and subdural hemorrhaging, catapulted Malcolm and the NOI into the public spotlight as an organized voice against police and prison brutalities.[12] The NOI seized on Malcolm's prison conversion and actively recruited African American prisoners on that basis. By 1960, registered adherents to the NOI numbered between 50,000 and 250,000.[13] Confined to the prison environment, many Black prisoners found good reason to join the NOI and partake in its promise of religious spirituality, a protective community, and martial techniques for self-defense.[14] Once converted, Muslim prisoners not only turned to Islam as their personal salvation but also as a means to collectively resist the prison's daily oppression. For instance, the historian Garrett Felber has documented how at New York's Attica prison, NOI prisoners engaged in a politicized strategy to fill solitary confinement, similar to the civil rights movement's "Jail, No Bail" strategy, when the prison administration attempted to limit their writ writing during the late 1950s.[15]

Fearing that Muslims might foment similar resistance in Texas, the prison administration struggled to reckon with the small but growing group of Muslims in the TDC. The comprehensive power of the building tender system rendered any attempt at gang organization nearly impossible. The TDC recorded very little gang activity prior to 1982. The Muslims, however, organized themselves around their religion and remained a difficult organization for building tenders to dismantle. Upon their initial encounter with the "Negro Muslim Movement," the prison board related their fears that this group was foreign to Texas and would foment violence in its prisons. During a March 1961 prison board meeting, the board received an overview on "Black Muslims" in the TDC, and they concluded that a "sizeable group of the Negro Muslims would like to do violence to the white people" and that "the black Muslims do not believe in heaven or hell and that it is their policy to get everything that they can out of life." Moreover, the prison board cast the NOI as an organization to foment Black criminality and that "the organization has been listed as subversive by the Federal Bureau of Investigation," and Elijah Muhammad himself "had been handled by law-enforcing officers on several occasions." As a response, the Ellis administration did not allow prisoners to correspond with Elijah Muhammad; they restricted their meetings and insisted that "such meetings should be under the supervision of security officers . . . as are all religious services." In addition to close surveillance, the TDC also enacted a policy that dispersed Muslims across the prison system in the hopes that isolating Muslims would restrict organization and demands for religious practice. When hearing the prison board's report on the "Muslim movement," the prison director, Ellis, called to the board's attention that California's Folsom prison had experienced riots "because of conflict between the whites and colored over the Muslim Movement."[16]

Dr. Beto's administration, however, changed the policy of disbursement when he collected the Muslims from across the system and placed them onto the same wing of the Ellis prison during the mid-1960s.[17] Doing so allowed Beto to claim that he was permitting the Muslims to freely practice their religion, while also strengthening the TDC's pattern of controlling prisoners through "segregation" and "isolation." The placement of the Muslims at Ellis placed them under the direct authority and control of "Beartracks" McAdams and his head building tender, Robert Barber, whose reputation for racial terror was known by every prisoner in the TDC. Whatever prison McAdams oversaw, he always brought with him the head building tender and white prisoner Robert Barber. As the prisoner Billy Wayne "Redbird" McCarter recalled, "He [McAdams] believed in them building tenders. Back when he was a warden . . . he had some rough building tenders that would literally beat people to death. Robert Barber . . . they furnished them baseball bats, brass knucks, shanks with brass knucks, they would literally beat you to death . . . or if you got cross ways with the administration and they put the word out to do something to you and they would."[18] Lawrence Pope, one of the prisoners at Ellis and a prison rights activist, noted that Barber "was Beartracks' right-hand man." Pope recalled that Barber "actually ran that unit" and that "he could himself fire just an ordinary officer you know, a correctional, CO 1, CO 2, and there are reports that he actually did fire these officers, just tell 'em 'Pack your shit and git, I don't want you on this farm.' And this he had the authority to do it, Bear Tracks backed him up 100%. And he was a psychotic killer type, and he had been into all kinds of brutality."[19] Carl Robbins, a white prisoner at Ellis, lived across from Barber's cell and he remembered the ways in which Barber's brutality was aimed against African Americans in a kind of prison-made white terror: "He'd come in at night, bloody, I mean just bloody, he would change his clothes in the cell. 'What'dya been doin'?' [Robbins would ask. And Barber responded,] 'I been whipping niggers all night, All night!'"[20] Al Slaton, a writ writer who was close to Cruz, put Barber's reputation even more bluntly "he was a bad person. This guy was a gun smoking hoodlum. He wasn't afraid of anything or anybody. He would kill you at the drop of a hat."[21]

McAdams took to the job of silencing Muslims through spatial isolation combined with the threat of building tender brutality. "The Muslims were harder to control than the others," confessed McAdams. "I had 'em segregated from the rest of 'em. In other words, that particular wing, put all them Muslims in and I had to control 'em with that."[22] When the Muslims did try to gain some legal relief from the restrictions against the practice of Islam, they faced administrative neglect and stubborn recalcitrance. Jalet concluded that "to my personal knowledge legal papers sought to be filed to enforce the religious rights of Muslims simply disappeared—were never mailed." One prisoner in particular who Jalet found to be "more persistent and courageous than the rest" sought permission to hold Muslim services, and for his efforts he was "brutally assaulted and is repeatedly placed in solitary charged with 'agitating.'"[23] The building tenders in the "Muslim tank" were not followers of Islam, and they included such notoriously violent African American building tenders as Ernest Rows, Benny Cole, and Cecil "Big Guinea" Smith.

The prospect of an alliance between the Muslims and Frances Jalet's clients was something the TDC hoped to avoid by closely monitoring and segregating the Muslims. Yet Cruz continued his efforts by relying on other prisoners to deliver legal materials and writs to the Muslims. On one occasion in 1967, "Redbird" McCarter was caught delivering one of Cruz's writs to Ace Miles, one of the leading Muslims. A fellow prisoner, Floyd Patterson, described Ace Miles as "a brother that everybody respected and admired because at the time he was the oldest Muslim on the farm . . . that hadn't been swayed. They [TDC] couldn't shake his foundation" of moral and religious convictions.[24] Although McCarter did not know the contents of Cruz's writ for Ace Miles, Warden McAdams was furious that it charged him as "passing out barbaric treatment" to prisoners of color. As punishment, "Beartracks" McAdams charged McCarter, a white prisoner, as a "civil rights worker" and moved his cell assignment to D-11, the Muslim tank. As the only white prisoner on D-11, the TDC high riders taunted McCarter, renaming him from "Redbird" to "Ole' Albino" and forcing the entire Muslim wing to work a seven-day workweek as punishment alongside McCarter. Despite the TDC's attempt to use racial animosity as an intimidation tactic to thwart interracial cooperation, McCarter's new African American cellmates assured him that no harm would come to him, particularly at the insistence of Ace Miles. Instead, Black and white worked together in an effort to "tear this tank up" and overthrow the building tenders by jointly attacking them, taking away their keys, locking themselves within their wing, and barricading the doors with mattresses and broken furniture.[25] The revolt was short-lived, and the guards recovered control over the tank through streaming tear gas and force, causing McCarter to suffer a broken collar bone and over sixty stitches. After a stay in the hospital, the TDC thereafter removed McCarter from the Muslim tank and sent him and several of the leading Muslims to solitary as "agitators," with stays that lasted nearly a month. When he was visited by Jalet, McCarter followed the convict code of silence and refused to admit that he had even been part of the riot, despite his arm cast and obvious wounds. The prospect of racial division and fear was a constant weapon in the arsenal of the TDC, but moments of interracial cooperation persisted. The strategy of whiteness was limited to the privileged white building tenders, leaving most other prisoners, particularly Mexican Americans and African Americans, as natural allies in their shared state of desperation and degradation.

Because of such incidents, Jalet remained particularly attuned to racial discrimination and the prison's practice of segregating the prisoners by race as a means to maintain racial authority through targeted, racialized violence. Her report offered several individual stories of racial brutality to make its point. In one incident, the guards terrorized an entire African American work gang when it failed to make a corn harvesting quota because a rainstorm made the cornfield extremely wet. Prisoners simply found it too difficult to drag the heavy sack filled with harvested corn across the muddied ground. When the prisoners could not meet the quota, "the angry guard knocked down some of the men with his horse, whipping them with the reins, he cursed them as he rode." After prisoners complained of the unfair beatings, Warden McAdams arrived with guards armed with "baseball bats, steel pipes, water hoses and black jacks" and "without warning" attacked the group of Black prisoners. After the "severe beating," the prisoners lined up across the road with a pick-up truck behind them, and the guards ordered them to run toward the field as fast as they could or face being run over by the speeding truck trampling up behind them. "Two prisoners couldn't make it and were knocked down; they were picked up and spread across the hood of the truck for all prisoners to see." The reporting prisoners then quoted Warden McAdams's response: "You niggers ain't bucking on me."[26]

Violence was meted out to prisoners in a knowingly public and brutal fashion for seemingly small infractions. The Ellis Report related one such incident in which a prisoner was arrested in the field for fighting with another prisoner, handcuffed, and then forced to run for two miles as "the Major rode his horse with his pistol pointed at me through the woods" and he "cussed me, threatened to kill me and tried to make me escape from his custody." When the prisoner refused to attempt escape, the major and another guard "stomped on the handcuffs that were on my wrists, kicked me, hit me and cussed me." Following the beating, the guards gave the prisoner solitary for twenty-one straight days.[27] Symbolic public punishment was often followed by the torture of long stays in solitary isolation.

Building tenders and the degree to which they used their power to foster racial animosity and enforce racial hierarchy earned a great deal of attention in Jalet's report. The report cited one case in particular that highlights the racial power of white building tenders. Jalet interviewed an unnamed

Mexican American prisoner who served as an eyewitness to a beating that rendered another Mexican prisoner mentally unrecognizable. The eyewitness reported that his fellow Mexican prisoner was "sitting in the hall waiting to be punished for some minor infraction of the rules" when a white building tender passed and called him a "sorry Mexican" and told him, "When I walk by you stand up, Mexican." When the prisoner told him "to go to hell," the building tender returned and brought with him a "negro turnkey" and the night warden and together the three, both prison guard and building tenders, beat the Mexican American prisoner until "he barely resembled a human being." The prisoner who reported the incident to Jalet claimed that the beaten man "would be much better off dead" because the beating incident rendered him "a stark, raving idiot now hidden from public view in the treatment center on the Wynne Farm. He doesn't even know who he is."[28]

At the NYC headquarters of the NAACP Legal Defense Fund (LDF), Anthony G. Amsterdam shared Jalet's alarming letter and the "Ellis Report" with his colleague William Bennett Turner. Fresh out of Harvard Law School, Turner first took a position with a Wall Street law firm, but he felt more drawn to poverty law after volunteering to work on civil rights cases through Mississippi's Farish lawyers group. Turning away from finance law, he was hired by the NAACP LDF in 1967 where he worked on school desegregation cases, title seven employment cases, and fair housing in Louisiana. Once Turner saw the extent of prisoner claims, he decided to travel to Texas to meet Jalet. Together Jalet and Turner developed a partnership where Jalet collected the prisoners' complaints and Turner tried the cases in court. In an oral history, Turner reflected that he viewed prisoners' rights "as a logical step from the civil rights movement . . . because of the disproportional number of African American prisoners across the country and their treatment by the criminal justice system. Since we were interested in race and criminal justice, it wasn't a big leap to go to civil rights."[29]

From 1968 to 1972, Jalet worked with Turner to pursue Cruz's complaints through a series of court challenges. The first was *Novak v. Beto*, in which Cruz and his fellow complainant Ronald Novak challenged solitary as "cruel and inhumane" punishment largely because of the restricted diet, length of solitary stay, and enclosure in total darkness. The case also revisited and challenged the constitutionality of prison rules that prohibited writ writers from giving legal assistance to fellow prisoners. During the trial, Judge Woodrow Seals, appointed by the Johnson administration in 1966, questioned Cruz's notion that solitary was "cruel and unusual" punishment as opposed to the alternative of whipping. True to his thoughtful nature, Cruz offered the court a trenchant reflection on the cycle of carceral violence that reproduces criminality. "When you use physical force on a man, the only thing you do is breed hostility. . . . He [the prisoner] takes that hostility and hatred with him, and that's why a lot of people go back in society and commit more crimes and it creates a cycle."[30] Despite Cruz's courtroom eloquence, Judge Seals handed the prisoners a bitter loss as the state district court decided in favor of the TDC on both charges, ruling that the Texan brand of water-and-bread diet on solitary did not violate the Eighth Amendment and that the prison's law libraries were sufficient enough that no prisoner need assist another in preparing legal appeals.[31] Other losses experienced by Turner and Jalet that year included *Rocha v. Beto*, in which Jalet unsuccessfully pursued for a second time the question of legal materials in a cell. Further, Jalet failed in *Woolsey v. Beto* to convince the court that punitive work assignments and solitary punishment were unconstitutional.[32]

Jalet and Turner's litigation to reform southern prisons was not work done in total isolation. As the civil rights movement exposed the brutality that upheld the South's Jim Crow system, the incarceration of so many activists in jails and prisons served as the site of both racial oppression and the space from which liberation and struggle would spring. The social and racial activism of the 1960s highlighted to the public, the courts, and to civil rights attorneys the degree to which prisoners' rights were a crucial feature of civil rights. With the 1961 formation of the SNCC, their student and activist members fanned out across the South to engage in the organization work of civil rights, which more often than not earned the unyielding scrutiny of local law enforcement, who increasingly targeted SNCC activists as unwanted, outside "agitators." As SNCC members ran afoul of local law enforcement, a group of northern attorneys offered pro bono services to defend SNCC members and poor southern African Americans when they faced arrest, harassment, and fines. When the left-leaning National Lawyers Guild (NLG) established the Committee for the Assistance of Southern Lawyers, they created a southern network of civil rights legal defenders that included attorneys from the ACLU, the NAACP's LDF, and the Lawyers Committee for Civil Rights Under Law— known as the President's Committee, a group of young attorneys that President Kennedy assembled for a White House meeting in 1963. Later that year, these young attorneys opened offices on North Farish Street in Jackson, Mississippi, to form the Farish Street Lawyers Group, which sought to defend civil rights activists and took on such cases as the attempt to integrate the Mississippi Highway Patrol, as well as cases to convince federal judges to issue federal injunctions against Jim Crow–era voter disenfranchisement practices.

The Farish Street Lawyers Group came of age during civil rights activism, and they watched the 1961 newscasts when Governor Ross Barnett incarcerated forty-five Freedom Riders in Parchman, a southern prison so notoriously dehumanizing that the historian David Oshinsky has called incarceration there "worse than slavery." As James Farmer, the leader of the Congress of Racial Equality (CORE), recalled, the introductory strip search of Freedom Riders at Parchman made clear how far freedom seemed from their grasp and how the southern prison extracted "a measure of dignity . . . We were consumed with embarrassment. We stood for ages—uncomfortable, dehumanized." Adding to the strip search's designed dehumanization, the Freedom Riders were then openly mocked by a prison guard's taunting order: "Y'all all a time wanna march someplace. Well y'all gon' march right now, right t'yo cells. An' ahm gon' lead ya. Follow me. Ah'm Martin Luther King."[33]

By 1970, Roy S. Haber, a thirty-one-year old attorney from Brooklyn, New York, took on the case of Matthew Winter, a prisoner at Parchman who had received poor legal counsel that did not advise him that the jury in his murder trial would be all white and subsequently received a life sentence at the Parchman farm. In his meetings with Winter, Haber was able to witness Parchman's brutal work regime and the way it conditioned Black prisoners through routine violence and cultural practices of subservience and degradation. When the warden invited Haber to a weekly luncheon with local plantation owners and businessmen, he saw firsthand how the prisoners had to act as the warden's servile domestic servants and how the pattern of such racial subservience extended from the prison to the warden's dinner table and all the way to the back kitchen. More startling was the clear evidence that Haber saw on a daily basis when visiting Parchman that violence stood at the center of Parchman's labor regime. In an oral history, Haber relayed how his first visits to Parchman felt like he had returned to the Deep South's slave past:

> It was an attempt on the part of Mississippi to be able to keep intact some of the vestiges of the slave culture. They could not keep African Americans any longer in slavery outside of prison, but in prison you can make people work without paying them. They set this prison up to maintain the slave culture, inside and out. Black prisoners were supposed to pick 200 pounds of cotton. They were housed in overcrowded dormitories that resembled slave barracks. They were subject to being beaten with a black strap called black Annie. And that was sanctioned by the State Legislature. The Warden could give them six lashes. . . . The prisoners would show me where they were beaten, their buttocks were scarred and all worn away by brass knuckles. The Black prisoners were treated as slaves and not as human beings, as not having worth, as being chattel, all the vestiges that you had on the plantation were brought onto the prison.[34]

After making observations of such brutality, Haber sorrowfully confessed that "each day, I would get in the car and start crying as I started driving."

From the confluence of civil rights and prisoners' rights came *Gates v. Collier*, a 1972 civil rights lawsuit for the prisoner Nazareth Gates filed by the attorney Roy Haber, who argued that the Parchman prison farm was the "last vestige of state-sponsored slavery."[35] The federal court that heard the argument eventually dismantled the southern trusty system of Mississippi through consent decree. The victory that prisoners had gained at Parchman was just what writ writers hoped to achieve in Texas, but the shadow of prison rebellion elsewhere made Texas cling even more tightly to its southern disciplinary regime.

Soledad's and Attica's Shadow: The Mortal Fear of a Convict-Run Prison

As Cruz and Jalet pursued a rights-based legal agenda, prisoners outside of the South embraced Black Power, organizing to resist the nation's incarceration system as a dehumanizing symbol of racial oppression. Inspired by the Black Power struggle that captured the national imagination, prisoners at Attica and across the nation increasingly became politicized and saw their captivity as crucial to the maintenance of white supremacy. During the 1960s and 1970s, prisoners made concrete demands to improve their immediate living and working conditions, which were generally deplorable, even as they simultaneously made claims that, as people under the full auspices of state control, they were entitled to both constitutional protections as citizens and basic human rights. Nationally, prison uprisings mirrored the urban unrest during the late 1960s as there were five prison uprisings in 1967; fifteen in 1968; twenty-seven in 1970; thirty-seven in 1971; and forty-eight in 1972—the most prison uprisings in any year in U.S. history. The cases gaining the most national notoriety, however, were instances of state violence in California's Soledad prison and New York's Attica prison.

While writing *Soledad Brother*, George Jackson became a cause célèbre of New Left activists outside prisons. California had incarcerated Jackson since 1961, and during his incarceration Jackson developed a leftist political philosophy and advocated Black political awakening behind prison bars. On January 16, 1970, the state of California charged that Jackson, along with fellow prisoners Fleeta Drumgo and John Clutchette, had murdered the guard John V. Mills in retaliation for the guard O.G. Millers's alleged murder of three Black prisoners. The state held the trio of suspects in Soledad's maximum security cell bock, and the case received nationwide attention as the press soon dubbed the three prisoners the "Soledad brothers."[36] Confined in a solitary cell for twenty-three hours a day, Jackson used the time to publish in 1971 the popular political tract of his prison letters, *Soledad Brother*, which earned him even greater notoriety and brought visibility to the condition of Black oppression. His death on August 21, 1971, during an alleged escape attempt brought further national attention to prison radicalism.[37] The state of California defended Jackson's killing by claiming that Jackson's attorney, Stephen Bingham, had smuggled a pistol concealed in a tape recorder into the prison and gave it to Jackson. Bingham was later acquitted from having played any part in the Soledad escape attempt. Administrators elsewhere, including Beto in Texas, used the Bingham case to warn the courts that "the seeds of unrest exist in every penal institution, and are being compounded by a few lawyers—some financed by federal anti-poverty funds—who make prison administration more difficult by stirring up malcontents behind the walls."

Jackson's death at the hands of California prison guards became a national rallying cry among prisoners who demanded humanity in an otherwise inhumane criminal justice system. Jackson became what Dan Berger has named "a palimpsest, an absent presence," whose untimely death granted prisoners everywhere a shared political ideology and a historical memory of critical resistance that allowed "the desperate and disenfranchised to locate themselves within a broader body politic."[38] In New York, the Attica Liberation Faction issued its prison manifesto first published in California's Folsom prison, declaring that prisons were being denied their humanity: "We are firm in our resolve and we demand, as human beings, the dignity and justice that is due to us by our right of birth. We do not know how the present system of brutality and dehumanization and injustice has been allowed to be perpetrated in this day of enlightenment, but we are the living proof of its existence and we cannot allow it to continue."

Occurring only a month after Jackson's murder, the September 1971 Attica, New York, prison uprising alarmed the nation's prison managers, as nearly 1,300 of the prison's approximately 2,200 prisoners rioted and seized control of the prison, taking 39 corrections officers hostage for over four days. While the immediate cause of the takeover was a struggle between a guard and prisoner, politicized prisoners quickly organized into a collective democratic expression that organized fellow prisoners, protected the hostages, issued a list of grievances, and called for 33 external observers to visit the prison. Such immediate prison organization was possible because the prison already had a number of grassroots organizations, whose leaders represented a broad spectrum of organizations, including the prominent speaker and Black Panther L. D. Barkley, the head of prisoner security Frank "Big Black" Smith, self-taught legal expert ("prison house lawyer") Roger Champen, NOI Muslim Richard X. Clark, Black Panther Tommy Hicks, activist Herbert X. Blyden, Young Lords leader Mariano "Dalou" Gonzalez, and Weatherman Sam Melville. The prisoners' demands included amnesty for actions during the takeover; an end to "slave labor" by applying the minimum-wage law to prisoners; the allowance of prisoners to remain politically active, without intimidation or reprisals; religious freedom; the end of media censorship; better education; a healthier diet; more effective medical care; and an institutional process to air prisoner grievances. After four days of negotiations, Governor Nelson Rockefeller ordered state police to retake the prison in a bloody assault that ended with 39 people killed and 89 wounded. Once the prison was retaken, prisoners were stripped naked, made to crawl through the mud, and then proceed through a police line where they were beaten with clubs. Perceived leaders of the uprising fared far worse, however. Some prisoners were tortured for hours, sodomized with foreign objects, and forced to play shotgun roulette. The historian Heather Thompson offered the disquieting conclusion that Attica's political legacy is "a historically unprecedented backlash against all efforts to humanize prison conditions in America."[39] In the U.S. South, prison administrators were determined not to have an Attica of their own, and their greatest fear was that radicalized prisoners wanted to create a "convict-run" prison. Among southern prisoners, however, Attica served as both inspiration and a lesson learned when it came to their keen interest in avoiding the kind of bloodbath that Attica prisoners experienced at the hands of the state.

Back in Texas, Dr. Beto followed these developments with great interest and some concern. The day of the New York state police assault at Attica, Beto was speaking before the national governors' conference at San Juan, Puerto Rico. Calling the Attica revolt a "tragic and horrible example of the convict-run institution," Beto associated the New York uprising with his growing anxiety over Cruz's dissension and Jalet's legal efforts. Unlike other states, Beto claimed that Texas experienced no prison riots and near absolute control over its prison population. The occasional "work buck" in Texas was quickly put down, usually by force, and such work strikes never spread beyond any single prison nor included more than a handful of prisoners during any given incident.

For Beto, Attica and Soledad represented the predictable outcome of a dangerous 1960s decade where antiwar student protest, civil rights demonstrations, Black Power demands, and Chicana/o empowerment threatened society's commitment to law and order and now had infected the nation's prisons. In speeches he gave across the state, Beto outlined his belief that prisons must instill in criminals what society failed to teach them. He believed that U.S. society was increasingly lawless, and the result was a "deterioration of American character." Beto also believed that modern society was experiencing "an erosion of moral fiber" in which "we worship the wrong gods; we burn incense at the wrong altars; we have misplaced values; we consider the wrong things important." He concluded that stemming the "rising tide of criminality" meant that prison management's crucial test was to successfully "reintegrate" the criminal back into society as a "law and order" citizen and thus "preserve ourselves as a nation." In his estimation, "America will last only as long as there are Americans. . . . Only as long as we as individuals and as a nation remain dedicated to these [law and order] concepts can we stem this rising tide of criminality, and at the same time preserve ourselves as a nation."[40] Beto linked the violence at Attica with his perception that the 1960s had become a movement decade of "long hairs" and "liberal do-gooders" who contributed to a "lawless" antiwar movement, a radical student protest movement, and "dangerous urban racial riots."[41] In a letter to Chicago mayor Richard Daley written in the aftermath of the 1968 Chicago Democratic Convention, Beto revealed his view that control penology could partner with law-and-order politics. When Mayor Daley insisted that Chicago would remain "The City That Works," despite the "lawlessness and disorder" from outraged student protestors, Beto supported Daley's hardline approach to putting down protest. "I am persuaded that your approach," wrote Beto, "which involved meeting insolent disrespect for law and order with force, is the only solution to the problem of lawlessness in this country."[42]

While Beto attempted to shore up law and order within Texas prisons, Cruz and Jalet continued their campaign against the TDC into the decade of the 1970s. The bloody events at Attica and Soledad prisons did not silence prisoners but rather inspired them to chart a new future for prisoners' rights during the decade of the 1970s. Undeterred by their initial losses, Jalet and Turner focused their next case on Cruz's access to legal material and his right to practice his religion freely. Initially filed on May 21, 1970, the case *Cruz v. Beto I* was decided in 1972 once again in favor of the TDC. Following Attica and Soledad, Beto instructed the TDC's attorneys to craft the argument that Cruz was attempting to "influence and control" other prisoners through his alleged proselytizing of Buddhism. In light of prisoner uprisings, the court agreed with Beto's charge when it offered explicit language that seemed to be drawn from Beto's own admonitions: "There are many reasons why one prisoner should not counsel another in legal and religious matters. One which comes to mind quickly is the 'influence' and 'control' which one inmate might gain over another. Such a situation on a large scale could lead to a 'convict-run' and not a state-controlled prison."[43] The court's ruling mirrored Beto's earlier testimony in *Novak v. Beto* that he did not want Cruz assisting prisoners in the preparation of writs because "he could develop an unconscionable control over other prisoners by setting himself up as a lawyer. I would like to amplify, your honor. I live in mortal fear of a convict-run prison."[44] But the Supreme Court overturned this reasoning in 1972 by declaring that no prison could deny a prisoner a right to worship in a manner consonant with his faith. Although Jalet and Cruz lost more often than they won in those early years, the mounting number of cases against the TDC grounded in claims of abusive prisoner treatment caused the previously vaunted reputation of the TDC to come under scrutiny.

The TDC struck back, orchestrating a counter lawsuit where three prisoners accused Jalet of "indoctrinating prisoners with revolutionary ideas" and conspiracy to commit violence against prisoners. These three prisoners alleged that Jalet orchestrated violence and directed her clients to beat those prisoners that refused to join them in their efforts against the TDC. The case, *Dreyer v. Jalet*, is remarkable for its target of an attorney rather than the prison system or the prisoners themselves. All three of the accusers were of the highest class of prisoner and therefore earned the highest rates of good time. Two of them were building tenders, and one of them was a trusty. The state paroled Freddie Dreyer, a building tender at Ellis, before the case went to trial, and he never testified. Donald Lock, a trusty, testified against Jalet and then later admitted that his testimony was false. Lock recanted his testimony and told the court: "It's a lie. Mrs. Cruz has done nothing. She's tried to help me. She's tried to help the entire prison population." Moreover, Lock claimed that the TDC assistant director W. Dee Kutach and Warden McAdams pushed him to make the false allegations by suggesting that filing such a suit might earn him his freedom. "They don't come out and tell you to do it," Lock confessed. "But you just get the way these people talk you know what they mean. I knew that filing was my only way out."[45] One of the state's means to defend itself was through use of the southern convict trusty system to reward prisoners with the promise of early freedom in exchange for false testimony.

———

As the *Dreyer* case was proceeding, the terror that building tenders created began to extend beyond the prison's walls. Following McAdams's retirement in 1971, his chief building tender, Robert Barber, was shortly thereafter released from TDC custody, despite having over a decade left on his sentence for having killed a police officer. Barber's role as the system's most notorious and powerful building tender made him a potential source for civil rights litigation against the prison system. Al Slaton, a writ writer and Cruz ally, had a tenuous and complicated friendship with Barber centered on equal parts respect and fear. In an oral history, Slaton claimed that William Kilgarlin, who served as Frances Jalet's attorney in *Dreyer vs. Jalet*, had reached out to Barber in the hopes that he might become an informant against the TDC. During a phone conversation between Barber and Kilgarlin, Slaton claimed that "Robert gave him [Kilgarlin] a lot of answers about how corrupt TDC was, how evil they were, all the years that he had participated in murder, brutality, and how sadistic the wardens had been in regards to some different inmates, including Fred Cruz and myself." But Barber never testified in *Dreyer* because, according to Slaton, "Robert didn't really turn against the system because he was the system. He was part of the system, and he was trying to be loyal, not only to himself, but to Warden McAdams." Barber, according to Slaton, had told Kilgarin that there was a TDC-orchestrated conspiracy to assassinate Frances Jalet outside of the prison system at the hands of a former prisoner and parolee, Billy Whitworth, who apparently backed out of the plot. But on January 4, 1972, Billy Whitworth was found dead, shot in the back three times in a vacant parking lot in Houston.[46] Barber privately confessed to Slaton that he had killed Whitworth "because he knew too much on him."

Once Slaton was released from TDC custody on December 8, 1971, he received a phone call from Barber, who tracked Slaton down in Houston and convinced him to come down to Austin. Thereafter, the two continued an inordinately complicated six-month relationship where Barber displayed depression and regret over what he had done within the TDC, even requesting that Slaton kill him. At one point, he told Slaton, "You better kill me, because if you don't, I'm gonna kill you," as he thrust a loaded and cocked .38 pistol into Slaton's hands. In that moment, Slaton confessed that "I almost shot him. But, all of a sudden, he started talkin'. He sorta let his guard down stated talkin' about the Ellis and the Ramsey and what he tried to do there. And why he was so mean and why he killed so many people. And how much he loved his daughter and how much he loved me, and cared about Fred Cruz and us." Over the next few weeks, Slaton became "very paranoid, extremely paranoid" that Barber was planning to kill Slaton and his wife without warning because Slaton knew that "the way Robert would kill you, you'd just be sitting and all of a sudden, bam, a bullet goes through your body." On June 7, 1972, Barber and his wife, Christine, joined Slaton and his girlfriend at the Chief Drive-In movie theater in Austin, Texas, for a double date. Christine Barber had told Slaton earlier that day, "Al, if you're gonna do it [kill Barber], you better do it tonight because he's goin' to do it to you." Robert Barber was sitting in the front seat of the car with a sawed-off shotgun in his lap and a .38 in his hand. When Barber turned around in the car with a .38 in his hand, Slaton was ready. "I shot him right in the forehead," Slaton vividly recalled. "Shot him five times. He fell out of the car."[47]

During Slaton's murder trial, the complex human relationship between TDC prisoners and building tenders was on full display. Slaton frequently professed, "I loved him. I still love him [Barber]." But in his defense he cited Barber's history of brutality and the fact that he had killed two former prisoners, Billy Whitworth and Paul Myers, since his 1971 release from the

TDC. Witnesses for the defense included the surviving police officer, A. L. Armstrong, who said that he had "never encountered a more dangerous man than Barber" during the "wild gun battle" that resulted in Barber's original 1952 conviction for killing the police officer Henry Cleveland.[48] In his final emotional closing statement, Slaton professed that he was tortured over having to kill Barber but that it was an act of self-defense: "Ladies and gentlemen of the jury, I couldn't wait until my wife was shot to death. I had to kill Robert Barber."[49] As a result of such stark testimony over Barber's dangerousness, the jury acquitted Slaton and determined that he did indeed kill Barber as an act of self-defense. For Slaton, however, his killing of the infamous building tender was an act of mercy against someone who was both inherently violent and a violent pawn of the prison system. "I don't think I murdered Robert Barber," Slaton reflected. "I killed Robert Barber. I gave him something he couldn't find here on planet Earth. I gave him eternal peace, you know. And I didn't do it through hate or malice. I did through caring and love. And that's hard for people to understand, but I was more crushed than I've ever been in my whole lifetime and held a lotta hardcore guilt for many, many years."[50] Barber's death provides a convoluted study of the shared humanity between activist prisoners and even the worst building tenders, who were both caught up in a system of carceral violence that sometimes stretched outside of the boundaries of prison gates. More directly, it raises the prospect of extending the reach of carceral violence beyond the prison, where Barber killed former prisoners amid strange circumstances and rumors of an external assassination plot against Frances Jalet.

Meanwhile, the *Dreyer* case against Jalet resulted in a series of charges and countercharges in which the TDC claimed that Jalet and Cruz were gaining an "immoral control" over other prisoners and in which Jalet and Cruz responded with lurid accusations of the TDC's reliance on brutality and racial violence.[51] During the trial, Cruz testified that his courtroom testimony against the TDC had caused the building tenders Jesse "Bay City" Montague and Cecil Alexander to threaten Cruz that "no fucking greaser is going to take over my cell block." Montague and Alexander were notoriously violent tenders who used their power to rape other prisoners, such that Jalet's attorney facetiously described Montague as "the best building tender of all" for "setting an employee on fire with a bottle of lighter fluid," "cutting another inmate's Achilles tendon, allegedly forcing other inmates to act as a passive partner in anal sodomy, and robbing other inmates [of their commissary]."[52] To silence Cruz, Montague and Alexander beat Cruz with prison-made blackjacks so badly that he was hospitalized with severe injuries for twelve days before the TDC subsequently incarcerated his broken body in solitary on the charges that Cruz was actually the one that had started a "fight" with the pair of building tenders. During the beating, the tenders told Cruz that Warden Robert Cousins and Assistant Warden J. V. "Wildcat" Anderson were "very upset over his testimony against prison officials."[53] The acrimony of the testimony and its revelations of stark carceral violence caused the presiding judge, Carl O. Bue, to remark, "Frankly I've never seen a case like this before. . . . For the past six weeks, as a member of the judiciary, I have felt that I have lived in another planet."[54] Judge Bue concluded that there was no evidence that Jalet was fomenting a prison revolution, and the court delivered the first victory for Jalet and Turner.[55]

Yet, during the *Dreyer* trial, Beto defended the building tender system as a prison institution that kept the peace. Whether Beto knew that the building tender system engaged in abuses and brutality is an issue of debate among his biographers and prison scholars. Within the first two years of assuming the directorship, Beto issued a memorandum to all wardens on November 8, 1963, stating that the use of building tenders was an acceptable "long standing policy," as long as his wardens adhered to the policy that "at no time are inmates to be used to perform duties in the area of punishment and discipline."[56] Beto's memorandum allowed the TDC to have an official policy that outlawed building tenders serving as "convict guards" while allowing the practice to continue at the discretion of individual wardens. As a hero of penology, many have characterized Beto as a "prisoner of an obdurate subculture he thought he had abolished" and a man who "was not a total master of his system because he was selectively informed by those that ran his system below him."[57] Scholars have argued that "to properly appraise Beto's contribution to penology, it is only reasonable to assume that his desire was to eliminate all abuses."[58] The social psychologist Hans Toch concluded that Beto was "a humane, civilized man, intolerant of brutality," who "did not know at the time of his tenure that his presumed well-oiled, benevolent regime encompassed lawless practices." Beto's biographer agreed that "it was the BT system that Ellis and Beto perpetuated that was most out of step with Beto's general philosophy."

Beto's testimony during *Dreyer* is revealing, however. Beto told the court that "building tenders are inmates who are carefully selected because of their attitude. They are inmates who recognize that the welfare of it all depends on a certain amount of peace in prison. They are people who have pretty well proven that they want conformity to the rules for themselves." Yet these were the very same prisoners who also ran an internal prison economy and upheld a racial hierarchy that was dependent on sexual violence as a tool of enforcement. Ironically, when Arkansas faced scrutiny over allegations that its trusty system abused prisoners, the state hired Beto in 1967 as its outside consultant. In his consultant role, Beto offered the bewildering suggestion that

Arkansas simply do away with its trusty system and hire more guards and expend the money to train them.[59] Beto insisted that "a stupid guard can undo in less than a minute what it takes a qualified psychologist or psychiatrist six months or a year to achieve."[60] Had Beto applied to his own administration the same professional advice that he offered the Arkansas prison system, then perhaps the court-ordered intervention of the 1970s might have been avoided. At the least, Beto's professional advice in the Arkansas prison case demonstrates that he was aware that the southern trusty system could be horribly abusive. Yet in defending his own use of trusties, Beto inverted the reality of prison society and turned the building tender system on its head, testifying: "I personally am strongly persuaded that the minimum amount of forced homosexuality in our department, the minimum amount of forcing inmates to give up their commissary, the items that they buy at the little canteens, is due to the presence of building tenders."[61] Indeed, Beto himself summed up the prison administration's rationale for the building tender system by offering the promise of control: "Either you pick their leaders, or they do. In any contemporary prison, there is bound to be some level of inmate organization, some manner of inmate society. . . . The question is this: who selects the leaders? Are the inmates to select them? Or is the administration to choose them or at least influence the choice? If the former, the extent of control over organized and semi-organized life is lessened, if the latter, the measure of control is strengthened."[62] The building tender system and the control it accorded over prisoners' behavior was thus at the very heart of Beto's "philosophy of corrections," and its removal had become unthinkable. In a strange, ironic twist, the continued economic success and the growing legend of Texas prisons made prison management beholden to preserving the building tender system.

Eight Hoe: Sowing Seeds of Dissent and Planting the Seeds of an Interracial Coalition

Less than a month after Attica and two months after the Jackson slaying, Beto barred Jalet from Texas prisons and from corresponding with Texas prisoners. The struggle between Beto and Jalet had become intensely personal, with allegations that Beto had used his influence to create problems between Jalet and the director of the legal aid office, which caused her to be transferred in 1968 to Dallas and eventually to lose her position. But Jalet continued working on prison reform through a Houston law clinic.[63] Beto argued that Jalet's "continued and frequent visits," as well as her "continued correspondence with inmates," made it "impossible" for him "to guarantee tranquility within the institutions and the protection of inmates." But within a month Beto was forced to lift the bar on Jalet's visitation and correspondence with her clients. Backpedaling, he insisted that the TDC collect her clients into a single prison and house them on a separate wing. Beto chose the Wynne prison and once again paired Cruz and "that whole writ writing crew" with Warden "Beartracks" McAdams.[64]

This collection of writ writers was designated "Eight Hoe Squad" for their field line number, and it contained all twenty-seven of Jalet's incarcerated clients. They lived and worked together from November 5, 1971, through October 1972, sowing the field in the day and sowing dissension at night. The TDC gave this group difficult job assignments and few privileges. Each prisoner lost his good time and thus faced longer sentences than the rest of the regular population. The TDC also denied these prisoners commissary privileges, sports, recreational activities, and access to education, while overmedicating them on psychotropic drugs, such as heavy tranquilizers, thorazine, and librium.[65] In response, Jalet and twelve of her clients filed *Cruz v. Beto II*, which claimed that the segregation of Eight Hoe and the denial of privileges to these prisoners were unconstitutional.[66]

Cruz v. Beto II was far more personal than Jalet's previous prison reform cases. Indeed, Jalet aimed her charges directly at its director, George Beto, and her suit demanded $750,000 in damages for her prisoner clients and $50,000 for herself. In a crushing blow to Beto's personal and professional reputation, Judge Carl O. Bue Jr. of the U.S. district court ruled in 1976 against the TDC and ordered Beto to pay $10,291 in damages to the prisoners and Jalet. Although the state of Texas paid the actual damages, the state was barred by law from paying the $27,825 in attorney fees, which Beto was required to pay from his own pocket. The case did little to promote prisoners' rights to the wider prison population. But what developed internally during the year of Eight Hoe's seclusion and isolation was a close-knit cadre of prisoner leadership and a mounting prisoners' rights movement.

Eight Hoe was unique in that it housed African American, white, and Mexican American prisoners together in an otherwise racially segregated prison system. Among these prisoners, Cruz had become more than just their legal teacher and prison-house lawyer; he had become a font of philosophical learning and a symbol of prisoner resistance. "Fred to me is like Cesar Chavez or Martin Luther King," remarked Rudy Portillo. "He helped me to learn to live for today, because if I hadn't learned to do that, I probably would have lost my melon while in isolation."[67] While the TDC hoped to isolate these writ writers from the general population, what developed instead was a tightly knit organization of radicals and prison attorneys who collaboratively shared their legal knowledge and dedication to prison reform. Among Jalet's twenty-seven clients was Eduardo Mauricio, who before Eight Hoe had considered his legal writ writing as that of a "lone ranger by myself, fighting my case, and then trying to find ways of fighting the prison conditions." But the collection of so many politicized prisoners into one group created for Mauricio a legal and political collective where like-minded writ writers "were able to put our heads together and come out with better civil rights complaints against the prison system, than when we were apart, because now we had the input of everybody."[68] With outside help from Jalet, these prisoners taught themselves how to confront the TDC in the courtroom, and they made it their goal to bring the internal prison economy to public attention. This interracial coalition of prisoners therefore carried the civil rights revolution from the streets to the cell block.

One of the leading members was Lawrence Pope, a white fifty-two-year-old former banker turned bank robber and a former prisoner originally sentenced to the federal prison system. Lawrence Pope was born in July 1918 and grew up in the shadow of the penitentiary in Huntsville, Texas. Pope followed his maternal grandfather into the banking industry and by the late 1950s had become executive vice president of the Gulfgate State Bank in Houston. Pope made $12,000 a year, a sum he felt was insufficient to support a family, especially since his wife, Geraldine, suffered from multiple sclerosis. Things become more difficult after Gulfgate Bank fired Pope for "inefficient operation." He then founded West National Bank and served as its president until his three partners sold their shares. Creditors and auditors of the bank then began to identify questionable loan and accounting practices. In 1960 Pope was pushed out of West and, at the age of forty-two, was on the verge of divorce and bankruptcy. Desperate, Pope bought a .38 revolver and a used black Ford and carried out a bizarre series of bank robberies. Without disguise, Pope walked into the First State Bank of Thornton and demanded at gunpoint all of the bank's cash. Pope then proceeded to take the female bank teller and the bank owners, Jack and Laurenne Bennett, into the vault, where he forced the two women to undress and assume lewd poses while he snapped pictures with a Polaroid camera. Pope threatened to provide the sexual photos to the newspapers if they tried to identify him. The following day Pope followed the same ritual at Farmers' State Bank in Schulenberg, Texas. He was tracked down by police the next day, and, following his trial, the state gave Pope a tough fifty-year sentence in federal prison.[69]

Housed in Leavenworth's federal penitentiary, Lawrence Pope became frustrated with his inability to seek information on his case, a problem he soon remedied by learning the law and writing writs. Pope thought of himself initially as a scribe. He and others similarly interested in writ writing would go to the law library and hand copy entire volumes of legal procedures. "We'd go up there and spend our whole time just copying stuff out of the law books—

to have it in handwriting so you could have it in your cell, and then you'd go back to your cell," Pope recalled. Within his cell, Pope accumulated fifteen handwritten notebooks of legal material—a true marker of what a difference access to law libraries and permission to have materials in one's cell could make. Pope's writ writing started in earnest when he attempted to write a letter to the U.S. probation office in San Antonio, Texas, to receive a presentence report on his case. The federal prison system refused to send his letter, however. In response, Pope wrote in longhand a suit against the federal prison system, which became *Hope v. Kavoi*. When his case was dismissed during trial, Pope took it to the Tenth Circuit Court of Appeals in Denver. This he lost, too, but not before Thurgood Marshall, who at the time was the solicitor general for the United States, ordered the warden of Pope's prison to guarantee his right to send a letter to his probation officer. The warden unhappily obliged. As his reputation as a writ writer grew, the federal prison system decided in 1969 to transfer Pope into the custody of the Texas prison system. With a copy of Pope's record and his noted writ writing, the TDC sentenced Pope to the Ellis prison, which was the same prison that held Fred Cruz and was known by Pope and other federal prisoners as "the Alcatraz of the TDC system."[70]

Upon Pope's arrival at Ellis on March 26, 1970, Assistant Warden Bobby Taylor, the field major Oscar Savage, and a "huge building tender" singled Pope out as an agitator and writ writer. Taylor assigned Pope to B3 Wing, which was an all–Mexican American wing in the segregated Ellis prison. Housing Pope in an all–Mexican American wing was yet another calculated attempt to use racial animosity and intimidation against writ writers. Pope recalled his first introduction to building tenders on that wing as an explicit warning from the TDC that his legal activities must cease. "There were three building tenders there. . . . It was just practically death to talk law—to discuss law, to discuss anything pertaining to law in T.D.C."[71]

Pope soon witnessed white building tenders targeting African American and Mexican American prisoners. Within a month of his arrival, Pope observed a struggle on April 12, 1970, between Mexican American and African American prisoners against a gang of white building tenders and guards. The struggle started when building tenders assaulted a pair of Muslims, and the resulting alliance between Mexican American and Black prisoners over the incident underscored how much the building tender system upheld the maintenance of white power and targeted racial oppression. Grabbing weapons from the "big sack full of baseball bats" at the guard picket, the building tenders "came in with their baseball bats and quelled them all." As witness to the toll of carceral violence, Pope reported that "I saw—not just some spots of blood, I saw pools of blood. And it lead all the way up to the B3

Lawrence Pope testifying and providing legal documentation to state legislature with Charlie Sullivan of the Citizens Advisory Committee on Prison Reform, 1974. Courtesy of Alan Pogue.

wing, right where I was going, and I followed this trail of blood up there . . . blood everywhere—even up on the ceiling—there was blood up there." Pope recalled this incident as the catalyst for his involvement in the prisoners' rights movement in Texas.[72]

Thereafter, Pope utilized his banking experience as someone who had a meticulous sense of detail to become the prisoners' chief documentarian. Pope regularly wrote Anthony J. P. Farris, a U.S. attorney in Houston, with a series of documented abuses concerning the building tender system. Even though Pope came from a middle-class white background, he felt a kinship with Black and brown prisoners, and he shared their radical critique of the TDC. When comparing his experience in the federal prison system with Texas, Pope felt that it was the harshness of the Texas system that created among prisoners a life-long anger and a sense of radicalism.

> In Texas, the concept of imprisonment is quite different from, say, in the Federal. In the Federal, they accept the fact that you are there as punishment. But in TDC they add another thing—that you are there

for punishment and they do make your life as miserable and just make it hell on earth. And this is why I feel that any person who is incarcerated in TDC has just minimum chances of ever becoming a halfway normal citizen and keeping out of trouble, because of the very nature of it, of incarceration. . . . You're so frustrated and so angered by the things that can happen to you over there in TDC that well, you have a bitterness, an anger, toward the society that put you in this position and subjected you to this treatment. And, to me, this is why so many inmates are radicalized while in prison—because of the very nature of the treatment they receive.[73]

Pope's level of activism also determined his good relations with the Mexican American and African American prison population. On the Mexican American B2 wing where TDC housed Pope, there were benches that were customarily reserved for different groups from various geographical locations with individual benches that were carefully guarded by those from El Paso, San Antonio, and Houston. Uncharacteristically, however, these different urban cliques allowed Pope to sit with them, and they opened up to him. "They looked on me with a little more favor," Pope recalled. "Anglo in that deal— ordinarily he was just the lowest of the low, but I had come as a writ writer— apparently some of them knew of some of my activities as a writ writer in the feds."[74] These prisoners were in touch with Cruz and Jalet, who soon thereafter took Pope as one of her clients.

The racial animosity that the TDC hoped to foster within Eight Hoe never materialized. Instead, the new living arrangement opened up previously closed avenues for interracial cooperation. Pope remembered that living with the other members of Eight Hoe created "a rigidly segregated bunch. It was a disciplinary offense for any inmate to be caught talking to us or passing us anything, or vice versa, for us to talk to or pass anything to any other inmate." Housing Jalet's clients together was an attempt by the TDC to segregate and isolate while hoping that racial animosity and in-fighting would break the group part. "They could've single-celled us," Pope recalled, "you know, put us just in there, the bunks were already there. They took out the first bunks— made those cells unusable—and move 'em back and double-bunked us, and they made it a definite point to mix the races and Black with white, Black with Chicano, Chicano with white, and so forth—and this was to cause friction— create friction and it did. Three inmates left our group and went over and they didn't want Frances Cruz for their attorney any longer, so they were removed from our group." Pope recalled that, despite the initial desertion of three members of Eight Hoe, the prisoners, for the most part, navigated the attempt to incite racial violence by fostering interracial cooperation instead:

We were very much in solidarity and with each other and well, whatever the squad decided to do, why, everybody went along with, there was no dissension or problems. They [TDC] tried to create it and did everything they could to create it, but it just didn't happen. And that disappointed them very much that it didn't happen. They thought we'd get into all kind of difficulties but we didn't. They wanted fights to start out and maybe even a cutting or something or other, you know, but it didn't. It didn't happen that way. We were very cohesive and cooperative with each other.[75]

Fellow Eight Hoe prisoner Guadalupe Guajardo, who first came to prison in 1966 for killing a police officer during a disputed Pan de Campo celebration in San Diego, agreed that living on Eight Hoe "was just like a family. That's the worst thing that the directors could have done. Dr. Beto done. He got all the best brains together. That's where he messed up. If he would have separated us, it would have been different, but he put all the brains together."[76] Pope also recalled the heightened level of legal activity within Eight Hoe. "We had all filed different lawsuits, and there many of them that were going on, and those of us who were the more or less writ writer types, well, we were just going night and day, you know, every chance we could, doing the bit of legal work on these different things."

Beginning in the early 1970s, four major class-action lawsuits emanated from Eight Hoe: (1) *Lamar v. Coffield*, challenging Texas's rigid system of racial segregation of prisoners and charging that the TDC practiced discriminatory hiring practices for its guards; (2) *Guajardo v. McAdams*, challenging the TDC's right to open an prisoner's legal correspondence; (3) *Corpus and Sellars v. Estelle*, demanding the right of prisoners to serve as their own legal counsel, thus eliminating the jailhouse lawyer prohibition; and, most importantly, (4) *Ruiz v. Estelle*, an omnibus lawsuit demanding decent medical care; the dismantling of the convict guard system; adequate protection for prisoners against unjustified beatings, sexual assaults, and extortion; adequate and hygienic living space; safe working conditions; and prisoner access to the courts and counsel.[77] *Ruiz v. Estelle* placed nearly all aspects of the TDC on trial.

Insurgency's Advance, Beto's Fall

After a year of confinement, the TDC disbanded Eight Hoe in October 1972, dispersing Jalet's clients throughout the prison system. George Beto had grown weary of the struggle with Jalet and her prisoner clients. The mounting number of cases filed against the system had damaged the TDC's reputation, but Beto always managed to remain a figure of statewide respect. Even when the court in *Cruz v. Beto II* determined that the TDC's punitive treatment of the prisoners of Eight Hoe was unconstitutional, the judge was careful in his decision to highlight Beto's otherwise "outstanding administration of Texas prisons."[78] Indeed, the penological community honored Beto when it elected him president of the American Correctional Association during its centennial celebration in 1970, and the University of Texas honored him the same year with a distinguished alumnus award. Nevertheless, Beto retired as director of the TDC in 1972, returning to education as a distinguished professor in the Criminal Justice Department of Sam Houston State University in Huntsville, Texas. After his retirement in 1991, Sam Houston State University honored Beto with the dedication of the George J. Beto Criminal Justice Center in his name. Although Beto later claimed that he had always set a ten-year time limit on his administration, the timing of his departure came at the height of his personal and legal battles with Jalet. Many prisoners of Eight Hoe viewed Beto's departure as a personal victory. "I always felt that this is the thing that broke Dr. Beto," admitted Lawrence Pope. "Right after that he—it was realized that he made a terrible, terrible mistake by putting us all over there together. Some of us were writ writers, some were not, but it was a very horrible mistake for him to put us all over there together and we certainly took advantage of it. . . . All the major litigation arose right out of that group. And, by putting us together, it enabled us to work together and to converse and to join our mutual knowledge and experience."[79]

The relationship that developed between Jalet and her clients on Eight Hoe also had a personal dimension. The prisoners on Eight Hoe enjoyed an abiding sense of camaraderie with one another, and their interaction with Jalet provided them with a teacher, a champion, and a friend. Although many of her clients might have had feelings for Jalet, it was Fred Cruz that developed a more intimate relationship with her. Cruz had a common-law wife, Bartola Perez Mendez, with whom he had a daughter. But Mendez was also incarcerated during the 1960s at Goree.[80] Separated from Mendez, Cruz and Jalet formed a bond of partnership, mutual respect, abiding trust, and love that surpassed the prison bars that separated them.

By 1974, Jalet had handed the broader prison reform effort over to William Bennett Turner so that she could concentrate on the defense of her clients and personal reputation in *Cruz v. Beto II*. With great legal skill, Jalet arduously pursued Cruz's appeals to get back the good time that the TDC stripped from him because they viewed his legal efforts as agitation. On March 9, 1972, Frances Cruz won an appeal of Cruz's robbery case. After ten years of imprisonment, Fred Cruz walked out of the TDC and into freedom. Later that month, Fred Cruz and Frances Jalet married. The marriage brought to fruition

Sharing culture, Fred Cruz and Frances Jalet-Cruz at the HemisFair in San Antonio, on April 22, 1973. Frances Jalet-Cruz Papers, di_11655, Dolph Briscoe Center for American History, University of Texas at Austin.

the connection and devotion that Cruz felt with Jalet from their first meeting, which he lovingly compared to the biblical predicament of Moses on the mountain. "During your visits in the Ellis Unit, I often experienced the same frustrations Moses must have felt on the mountains in being so close to godliness and not being able to make physical contact with it. Of course, I had an advantage over him because I could see you, but he could not lift up his eyes to see God."[81]

Following his 1972 release, Fred Cruz came home to a very different world than the one that he had left behind. During the decade of Cruz's incarceration (1962–72), the Chicano movement had erupted across southwestern cities and lit fire to a politicized youth that challenged white privilege and power with demands for local political control and an end to racial segregation, police brutality, and economic and educational inequality. In San Antonio, Cruz's hometown, El Movimiento fused college students, barrio youths, and pachucos in the spirit of *carnalismo* (brotherhood) and Raza Unida (united people) toward the collective effort of La Causa (the cause). The historian David Montejano aptly described this generational coalition as "the restlessness of barrio youths . . . channeled toward social protest under an identity greater than that of the neighborhood."[82] For instance, Juan Guajardo, once the leader of one of the largest urban street gangs—the Ghost Town—had become by the late 1960s the founding member of San Antonio's Brown Berets.[83] During the late 1960s, the fusion of students and former gang members led to the Mexican American Youth Organization (MAYO), which sought to gain local control of the Great Society's Volunteers in Service to America (VISTA) Minority Mobilization Program to address urban poverty while also establishing in San Antonio La Universidad del Barrios, an education alternative modeled after the freedom schools of the civil rights movement that sought to educate Chicano youth and turn gang members away from crime and drug use and toward ethnic pride and politicization.[84]

As an avid reader while in prison, Cruz had kept abreast with the unfolding Chicano movement even as he pursued his own brand of legal activism behind bars. Almost immediately after his release from prison, Cruz determined that he would bring the prisoners' rights movement to the attention of the wider Chicano movement. In June 1972, Cruz made a public announcement in the Chicano newspaper *Papal Chicano* that he had formed the Jail and Prison Coalition, with himself as president. The aim of Cruz's coalition was to educate Chicano youth on the prisoners' rights movement and to bring the issue of prison reform to the agenda of La Causa. In his appeal to Chicano readers, Cruz provided a trenchant observation that captured the stark contrast between the external image of Texas prisons and the reality that he and his fellow prisoners experienced. "There have been some external changes in the Texas prison system in the last 15 years. The buildings are more modern, housing conditions, food and clothing have improved. This is the scale on which Texas prisons are measured and rated as 'progressive.'" But, Cruz admonished, "this does not take into the account the treatment accorded prisoners as human beings." He promised to help launch a statewide effort "to bring about a humane prison system based on justice, tempered with mercy and compassion that will give men hope for the future."[85]

Later that year, he published a piece in the San Antonio *Chicano Times* titled "Remember the Prisoners." Drawing on México de afuera,[86] Cruz began his plea by building an association between the prisoners' rights movement and the Chicano Movement by noting that the TDC barred prisoners from celebrating Diez y Seis de Septiempre, a day to commemorate the Mexican War of Independence against Spain. In a reference to Attica, Cruz noted "recent rebellions in the nations' prisons have served the purpose of creating a public awareness" of prison abuse and that now was the time to fuse external political movements for racial and ethnic empowerment with the prisoners' rights movement. Cruz told his readers that he now represented a voice on the outside for "the voices inside; voices that will speak of systematic racial oppression and brutal treatment." Spanish-speaking prisoners, Cruz pointed out, were not able to communicate with family members because the TDC had too few Spanish speakers to read and censor their mail. Demonstrating how erudite study and Chicano empowerment were inextricably linked, Cruz particularly lamented that "the prison libraries are practically bare of any Chicano literature so that Chicanos in prison are at a loss to study their cultural history and to attain the pride that is essential in the struggle to preserve their self identity." The lack of Spanish-speaking films, Chicano newspapers, and the ability to write families in Spanish amounted to what Cruz thought was violation of the First Amendment rights of free speech and access to the press. Cruz also highlighted the fact that the TDC had no Chicano or African American wardens, and he pulled back the veil on the southern prison plantation system to reveal that "the penal system from its inception has been on a redneck philosophy steered by men afflicted with racist attitudes which still enables them to call Chicanos 'greasers, pepper bellies' and blacks 'niggers, coons.'" Highlighting the duality of Texas prisons, between the efficient agribusiness mask and the unseen reality of prison plantations, Cruz pointed out that "the scale on which Texas prisons are measured and rated as 'progressive'" was its agribusiness efficiency, but the TDC's false public image masked "the treatment accorded prisoners as human beings and personal attitudes [of racism] can never be measured by scales because they are elastic and not always susceptible to mathematical formulations."[87]

Cruz's personal and political transformation within prison from uneducated "convict" to "organic intellectual" and self-taught jailhouse lawyer served as an inspiration for the next generation of Chicano and Black Power prisoners who carried the struggle for prisoners' rights into the 1970s. Reflecting on Cruz's life, Floyd Patterson recalled wistfully how Cruz's legal brilliance came with the price of retributive punishment. "Probably in another life, Fred might have been a great attorney," Patterson reflected. "He was smarter than the law. He knew the law. He knew when the officials in the prison system was breaking the law. He knew their law, he knew their prison laws, he knew the American Constitution, he was just a lawyer. And he was a threat."[88]

Cruz grounded his legal work and demand for humanity and social justice on what he saw as correctable injustices within their own prison society. His struggle was in the courtroom, and his demand that prisons apply the just application of constitutional rights and the law. However, the deadly violence that the state had meted out at the Attica and Soledad prisons provided a lesson to Cruz and the remaining Eight Hoe prisoners. In response, they looked to Attica and revolutionary language and ideals for inspiration, but they also employed practical appeals to humane treatment that relied on constitutional rights-based language. Cruz and Jalet's shared legacy gave voice to the previously voiceless prisoners whose situation was dire but largely unknown by the wider public. Their collective effort served as notice to the other prisoners that prisoners had a champion outside of the prison and that the courts were paying attention. Over the course of the 1970s, the legal struggles of Cruz and Jalet inspired a prisoners' rights movement that spread across the prison system like wildfire.

Chapter 6

Attica South

Black Political Organizing against the Prison Plantation

The question of prisoner rights is a question of human rights, as well.
The Texas Department of Correction is a closed and arrogant system.
Prisoners in this state are not afforded their constitutional rights, nor are
they afforded their human rights. Despite all the propaganda of the TDC
and the constant posing of rehabilitation as the purpose here, the objective
fact is that constitutional rights is a joke, rehabilitation is a joke, and human
rights are a joke.

—Allen Lamar, prisoner of Texas, 1974

As Cruz and Eight Hoe confronted the TDC in the courtroom, out in the
fields of prison labor, a movement of Black radical prisoners was growing. The
TDC's steadfast dedication to coerced labor discipline and carceral violence
against African American prisoners was becoming more difficult to sustain
as the Black Power critique of the late 1960s outside of prison inspired new
levels of Black radicalism on the prison planation through the 1970s. An increasing number of Black Power proponents in Texas looked to the examples
of the Deacons for Defense and the Black Panthers, groups willing to carry
arms for self-defense and to openly oppose state violence and police brutality.[1] As the social tumult of the late 1960s reached cities in Texas, numerous
and deadly incidents of police brutality and state violence accelerated the
spread of Black Power consciousness. A 1967 standoff between police and protesting Texas Southern University students ended in a hail of over 5,000
rounds of police ammunition fired against a student dorm, the subsequent
arrest of 488 students, and the death of Houston police officer Louis Kuba,
killed by a ricocheting police round. A year later, Lee Otis Johnson, a charis-
matic Black Power organizer in Houston, was given a thirty-year sentence for
selling a single marijuana joint to an undercover police officer, sparking a
"Free Lee Otis" Texas-based campaign that mirrored the national "Free
Huey" campaign. In response to incidents of state violence and police brutality, Houston Black Power advocates formed their own version of the BPP,
known as the People's Party 2, which earned statewide notoriety when its
twenty-one-year-old leader, Carl Hampton, was killed by a police sniper following a rally, in what one member bluntly named a "police assassination."[2]

Into the 1970s, as a wave of mass incarceration cast more and more African Americans into prison, it also swept onto southern prison plantations a younger generation who not only had witnessed 1960s-era civil rights protest but several of whom were active veterans of the Vietnam War, the Student Nonviolent Coordinating Committee, the Black Panthers, and local Black Power groups. These men were part of a generation of Black Power advocates in Texas who criticized the alliance with Great Society Democrats by arguing that the passage of the Civil Rights Act of 1964 and the Voting Rights Act of 1965 did nothing to curb police brutality, economic inequality, Black political dependence on white Democrats, and the daily degradations of racism. While Fred Cruz and Eight Hoe had grounded their writ writing in the nonviolent civil rights tradition, a new generation of Black Power prisoners in Texas took up more radical traditions of self-defense. In response to growing fears that Attica might come South, Texas prison administrators doubled down on the southern trusty system and looked to "get tough" on civil rights agitation by bringing in new leadership with experience in quelling Black radicalism, civil rights suits, and gang organization.

Getting Tough on Prison Radicalism: The Appointment of James Estelle

When Beto retired in 1972, the prison board replaced him with Ward James (W. J.) Estelle, who, at the age of forty-one, had more than twenty years of experience in corrections. Estelle was a product of the California prison system, having worked his way up from his first position in 1952 as prison guard at Folsom State Prison to administrator of California's prison camp operations, an experiment in rehabilitation and conservation.[3] However, Estelle felt that the California rehabilitative model was too accommodating to its prisoners, and he grew impatient with the "tolerance that California had for violence in its system."[4] In the decades that followed, Texas would look to California's prison system with great trepidation as an example of what they saw as a liberally permissive, overly rehabilitative, and "convict-controlled prison." A TDC file titled "California's prison radicalism" records a series of documents that reflect TDC's growing concern that Texas prisoners might look to California and New York for radical inspiration. Prison administrators became increasingly concerned that 1960s-era social and racial unrest had become by the 1970s an era of "urban terrorism and guerilla warfare."[5]

In 1970 Estelle left the California Department of Corrections and became warden of Montana's Deer Lodge prison. The Montana prison was small, overseeing a total population of 276. Estelle first met Beto at the American Correctional Association that same year, and soon thereafter Beto contacted

Estelle about working for him as his assistant director. To the prison board, Beto presented Estelle as a successor who would ensure continuity and stability. As Estelle later reflected on his hire, he remarked, "I don't think I was brought in here to revolutionize or dramatically change a system that had already had some proven success in the way of efficiency and effectiveness."[6] He was a veteran of California's system and also had an excellent reputation for his work in Montana. Governor Forrest Anderson highlighted the fact that "Warden Estelle's success at Deer Lodge unquestionably has been his good relations with the news media. He trusted them and they have respected him. This good relationship has extended to guards and other members of the prison staff."[7] With so many prisoner civil rights suits making their way into court and onto the front pages of newspapers, Estelle's "good relations" with the press made him an attractive candidate to replace Beto.

It made sense, then, that the TDC selected Jim Estelle to replace the scholarly Dr. Beto. The Texas press seemed to approve, with such headlines as "Prison System Gets Good Man." One editorial acknowledged that "these are volatile times for prison systems" and that "there is more unrest among prisoner ranks than ever before in history." "Even in a well-operated system such as Texas boasts, a problem could flare suddenly," the editorial warned. The paper praised Estelle as a potential replacement for Beto as it cited his experience in California as "superb credentials," where he displayed "great skill and good judgment" in his twenty-year career in prison management.[8]

Estelle vowed to keep the control penology work regime intact while offering a very different approach to how the TDC handled writ writers. Within two months as director, Estelle disbanded Eight Hoe and dispersed Jalet's clients throughout the prison system. As Lawrence Pope recalled, Estelle employed disbursement as a new tactic against prisoner agitation. "He [Estelle] shipped us every which way, we just went into all points of the compass. Some of the guys went to Ellis, some stayed on Wynne, I went with two others down to Retrieve unit, and we were just scattered out."[9] Dispersing Eight Hoe militants across the prison system lessened the writ writers' ability to communicate and consolidate their efforts. But it also had the effect of spreading the prisoners' rights movement more broadly across the system.

The Father's Day Incident and the Ramsey Rebellion

Estelle faced his first great test as the new director when the tenuous labor arrangement of constant prison field work ruptured in 1973 during what was known as the Father's Day incident. On Sunday June 17, 1973, Warden Bobby Taylor ordered prisoners at the Retrieve prison to harvest a crop of nearly rotten sweet corn. Taylor's June 17 order to work on Sunday angered prisoners because TDC had always observed that day as a day of rest and visitation with families. The work order was even more egregious as it was Father's Day. Thirteen of the three hundred prisoners ordered to the field on Father's Day refused to work and remained in their cells. That night, Warden Taylor placed ten of the thirteen prisoners into administrative segregation. The ten men—five African American, two white, two Mexican Americans, and one Native American— had contested the prison plantation's labor regime and earned the warden's ire.

The following day, the men were rudely awakened with shouts of racial slurs and the swinging of riot batons by both building tenders and prison guards alike. Ernest McMillan, one of the ten prisoners who had refused to work, explained how he experienced that moment as racial terror. "I heard a clamor in that wing and heard people screaming and hollering, and words being shouted like 'Nigger get up! You are goin' to work!' And I felt very apprehensive and you could hear them approaching cell by cell. I could hear the sound of blows, and people being struck, screaming and shouting with all these racial epithets."[10] Most of the men ducked out of their cells as they frantically tried to dodge the hard blows, but McMillan remembered one Native American prisoner, a Lakota Sioux, who stoically withstood the violence as he marched down the line without flinching even as blood began to pour. After being driven from their cells with clubs, the guards then pressed the prisoners down a gauntlet of building tenders and guards armed with baseball bats and rubber hoses who beat them as they ran. Bloodied and only half dressed, some without shoes and others just in their undershorts, these prisoners were then taken to the cornfields and forced to pick wet corn with long heavy bags that became unwieldy as they filled with corn and slick mud. As the prisoners picked the corn, the guard high riders rode over them and beat them again while all the other prisoners were collected from their field assignments to watch them, as McMillan recalled, "seeing us getting beat—the example for all to see." When the prisoners returned to the cell blocks at the end of the day, the warden met with them individually and told them that "unless they caused more trouble that there wouldn't be anything like that happen again" and that "we would forget it."[11]

Marion Ernest McMillan Jr., a civil rights veteran, had been born in 1945 in one of Texas's oldest Black communities in North Dallas. He hailed from a middle-class home, where his grandfather, Dr. Walter Ree McMillan, was a well-known member of the local community. Dr. McMillan, the son of a former slave, was the founder of the McMillan Sanitarium, one of the first African American–owned mental health clinics in Dallas.[12] McMillan's father was a pastor of a United Methodist Church in Newnan, Georgia. In 1962, during his senior year at Booker T. Washington High School, McMillan joined the NAACP Youth Council and became active in local organizing. When he graduated from high school, he followed his father to Georgia and enrolled in Morehouse College. While there, McMillan became increasingly disenchanted with the NAACP because he found its level of protest to be "mediocre," "lukewarm," and "ho-hum." He later complained that the NAACP idea of protest was to "dress up in your tie, go down to the movie theater, stand in line, ask for a ticket, they would refuse to give it to you, you'd go back to the end of the line and come back up again. That was the extent of protest for desegregating the movie theater, for example."[13]

McMillan found more direct and vocal forms of protest in the SNCC. "SNCC," he observed, "was about organizing grassroots people and helping them to build their own structures and being a part of the community with them, and helping them realize their goals which may be, you know, freedom schools or voter registration and elected officials." At the age of eighteen, he became a SNCC field secretary and served as a community organizer for voter registration in Georgia, canvassing the more rural parts of the state. McMillan faced mounting racial violence and direct white resistance. "You had shootouts," he recalled, "people chasing you, running you off the road, shooting up houses, injuring people, beating people up in demonstrations, arresting you if you had your shirt tail out." When a friend and SNCC coworker was killed in Mississippi, McMillan began to embrace Black Power as a more effective means of effecting self-determination.

> There was no adequate response to address murders and false imprisonment and bombings and Ku Klux Klan activities, so we had to begin to become seriously engaged in organizing for our own destiny being built and shaped. And that meant self-determination, that meant organizing for the community, to get the improvements. So, it meant you just couldn't go about desegregating them and sitting next to people or having access to a college. You really had to have economic, political power to bring about those kind of changes. And that's what the Black Power movement is all about. Its just a natural, logical extension of the struggle to advance the people.[14]

McMillan's encounter with white terrorism and violence as an integral part of his political evolution toward Black radicalism mirrors the longer historical struggle that reaches from Reconstruction to civil rights to Black Power that Hasan Jefferies named "freedom rights" in his study of "bloody Lowndes" and white violence against SNCC's voter registration drive in Alabama.[15]

Following the passage of the Voting Rights Act in 1965, McMillan returned to Dallas so that he could enroll at the University State College, which later became the University of Texas at Arlington. While in school, McMillan retained his activist streak and founded and presided over the campus organization Student Congress on Racial Equality (SCORE), which aimed its activism against the practice of "Old South Week" on campus and against racial discrimination in the university environment, where the university routinely flew the Confederate flag, segregated its dorms, and in which professors practiced classroom and grading discrimination. For his efforts, the university suspended McMillan, and so he returned to community organizing in Dallas. As the movement against the Vietnam War gained momentum in 1966, McMillan turned his attention to military induction centers in Dallas, where his organization intercepted young men and provided them with antiwar leaflets that instructed them how to earn school deferments by preregistering two years in advance for divinity school. He then organized an SNCC chapter in South Dallas and published the local newspaper, *Black Discipline*, advocating Black history studies and the right to wear African garb on local Dallas campuses. At its height, McMillan's SNCC chapter in Dallas had over two hundred activist members.

The assassination of Dr. Martin Luther King in April 1968 caused McMillan to join with many other Black activists in the assessment that "things weren't working" and that greater militancy was sorely needed. In an effort to link civil rights to economic inequality, McMillan organized an economic boycott of the white-owned OK Supermarket. McMillan and the SNCC charged that the white-owned store was "ghetto gouging" and that it routinely profiteered from the local Black community by marking up prices and selling spoiled produce and meat. In the attempt to link economic and racial inequality, McMillan and Matthew Johnson, another SNCC activist, held a demonstration against the store in which they told their fellow thirty to fifty demonstrators to fill their shopping carts with food and then walk out of the store. Some other items, such as eggs and a single milk bottle in McMillan's case, were intentionally smashed and broken, causing over two hundred dollars in damages of store merchandise. The state charged McMillan and Johnson as leaders of the demonstration and found them guilty of destruction of private property over the value of fifty dollars, which was a felony offense with a normal sentence of two to twenty years, for which the state gave McMillan a ten-year sentence.[16]

After three months in the local jail, McMillan was temporarily released on bail, only to find that he was also wanted on draft evasion charges. As an avid antiwar protestor who saw the Vietnam War as an extension of U.S. imperialism to quash Third World independence, McMillan determined to avoid the draft and decided that he must flee to Canada and then Africa. McMillan was "romantic about Africa" and felt that "this is always the mother land." After stepping off the plane, he kissed the continent's soil. But not too long after his arrival, McMillan reconsidered his choice. He left the continent, renewed in his mission to organize Black resistance at home in the United States. Without

Ernest McMillan testifying to CURE with State Representative Eddie Bernice Johnson, 1976. Courtesy of Alan Pogue.

his passport, McMillan returned to the United States and was arrested in Cincinnati when an informant snitched on him. While in the federal prison system at Fort Leavenworth for draft evasion, McMillan served alongside Walter Collins, a New Orleans Black draft resister and Southern Conference Education Fund (SCEF) organizer, where he became committed to the belief that "only through organizing, principled political struggle and unity can we realize the power necessary to transform our situation."[17] McMillan was then transferred to the TDC in 1970 and housed at the Ramsey prison.

McMillan's arrival brought a veteran organizer and a political prisoner to the prison system, but on the day of the Father's Day incident, McMillan was not looking to achieve organization or active resistance. The efforts of those who refused to work were not coordinated. "This was an individual decision," McMillan insisted. "Hey, we're not going to work, for whatever reason. Somebody may have been up for religious reasons, somebody may not have felt well, somebody may have had their feet hurt, or maybe don't want to work period. But, I know what my reason was—I don't work on Sundays, you know. And I also expected a visit, so it's like, I guess call it religious grounds. I'm not going to work on Sunday."[18] Even so, McMillan and the others knew full well that their refusal to work was likely to elicit a punitive and possibly violent response. Once the beating occurred, it created a wider élan among the prisoners, particularly Black prisoners.

While the prison administration hoped to keep the incident quiet, McMillan determined to bring the "massacre" to light. As a Black Power proponent and community organizer, McMillan had followed the efforts of Jalet and Cruz with great interest. He had also followed state politics and the recent creation of a legislative committee to investigate the courtroom allegations against the TDC.

The Hope for Political Reform: The Citizens Committee and the Joint Prison Reform Committee

The notoriety of Jalet's court battles had raised the public's awareness concerning the full extent of the power that building tenders exercised within the prisons. Horrified by the courtroom revelations of brutality, Charlie and Pauline Sullivan, a former Catholic priest and nun, in 1972 formed Citizens United for Rehabilitation for Errants (CURE), a prisoner reform organization aimed at bringing rehabilitative ideas and practices into Texas prisons. The Sullivans had met in Minnesota when Charlie Sullivan took a leave of absence from the Church to attend the University of Minnesota. Pauline was a thirty-one-year-old nun teaching in Minneapolis, and soon after they met the two became romantically involved. Together they left the Church and married in 1970. Over the course of the next year, the couple engaged in various movement activities, from the May Day anti–Vietnam War strike in 1971 in Washington, DC, where they were among the more than 15,000 protestors arrested, to hunger strikes at the local San Antonio jail. Upon their return from the May Day demonstration, the Sullivans dedicated themselves to prison reform by organizing three-dollar bus trips to bring indigent family members to East Texas so that they could visit with prisoners who lived as far as two hundred miles away. Bishop Patrick F. Flores of San Antonio was CURE's biggest sponsor, and he helped raise their profile when he became archbishop of San Antonio and later the head of the Catholic Church in Texas. From a small apartment in San Antonio, the Sullivans produced a newsletter that advocated rehabilitative and humanitarian prison reforms. Drawing on the experience of transporting hundreds of indigent families to faraway prisoners, CURE emphasized "community corrections," which meant an emphasis on parole, halfway houses, work release programs, and the construction of smaller prisoners in urban areas across the state. Even the name of the organization was humanizing, emphasizing "rehabilitation" for those who were "errants," meaning those "who made mistakes."[19] They also created a lobbying effort to press the state legislature to pass a bill that would outlaw the use of building tenders. The Sullivans turned their chartered buses toward Austin and gathered family members of prisoners to lobby for prison reform at the state capitol, the very building that prison labor helped construct during the convict lease period.[20]

By the spring of 1973, the state legislature, under intense lobbying pressure from CURE, introduced a bill to ban building tenders and a second bill to create a legislative committee to investigate charges of abuse. Fred Cruz, whom Jalet had freed from prison in 1972, testified during a March 1973 hearing held by the House Committee of Criminal Jurisprudence on the proposed antitender bill. "If a prison guard beats up a prisoner," Cruz explained to the committee, "the prisoner has recourse through the federal courts by using the personal damage suit against the guard. If you file against another prisoner, there is not much recourse. The prison administration puts it off as just another fight between two prisoners."[21] Charlie Sullivan testified that he had arranged over "four thousand" visits between family members and that he was corresponding with over fifty prisoners. In all his contact with prisoners, Sullivan testified that "the biggest number of complaints has been with the building tenders." Estelle, meanwhile, supported the bill and claimed that the TDC already had such a policy that forbade building tenders from having authority over other fellow prisoners. In 1963, TDC director George Beto issued an internal TDC memorandum that stated to all wardens that "while it is no prohibition against the use of wing attendants or building tenders, at no time are prisoners to be used to perform duties in the area of punishment and discipline. This responsibility rests and must continue to rest solely with custodial officers."[22] Estelle pointed to that policy during the legislative debate and argued that the bill only "added statutory emphasis to what we consider a long standing policy." Estelle argued that the TDC banned the abusive power of building tenders as long-standing policy that had its origins in the Ellis reforms of 1948, and Beto in his 1963 memorandum reinforced that policy.[23]

Without much opposition, the legislature passed House Bill No. 1056, which prohibited any prisoner to act in a supervisory or disciplinary role over other prisoners. The successful passage of the bill did not conclusively end the building tender practice, however. It had the same loophole as Beto's 1963 memorandum as it did not outlaw the use of building tenders altogether or dismantle the hierarchical social structure internally. Indeed, the limited nature and specific wording of the bill allowed the TDC to continue employing prisoners as building tenders as long as they did not have "supervisory or disciplinary authority of inmates." The TDC claimed that building tenders were simply building janitors and turnkeys with no ability to punish or supervise any other prisoner. When the power of the building tender system continued despite the law, it placed the burden of proof back upon the prisoners.

A month after the House passed Bill No. 1056, the Senate passed Concurrent Resolution No. 87, which sanctioned a joint committee on prison reform to investigate allegations of abuse. The political will and pressure to pass such an investigative committee came from Texas state senator A. R. "Babe" Schwartz and the Houston Chapter NAACP president Reverend C. Anderson Davis. In 1972, Reverend Davis requested that the Texas Prison Board and TDC hire African American personnel at all levels, including two assistant directors, the next warden appointment, and one African American assistant warden at each unit. Davis also envisioned prisoner participation in the pursuit of civil rights. He requested that the board consider the establishment of a prisoner council for self-government and that the TDC allow prisoners to establish NAACP chapters at each prison. In a letter to Texas Prison Board chairman H. H. Coffield on December 20, 1972, the board member David Allen provided the board's disapproving response. The board argued that affirmative-action hires, particularly at the level of warden and assistant warden, "in and of themselves would be discriminatory" and that such a proposal conflicted with the TDC's current policy to hire "qualified personnel . . . without regard to race, religion, or creed."[24] Director Estelle, the prison board concluded, should decide if prisoners could form a prisoner council and NAACP prison chapters. Estelle vigorously opposed the establishment of NAACP chapters. Reverend Davis's request fell on deaf ears, and he turned instead to sympathetic politicians in the legislature to pursue an end to racial discrimination through the formation of a legislative investigative committee.

In April 1973 the state legislature established the Joint Committee on Prison Reform, which was chaired by the Texas reformer State Senator Chet Brooks and included such liberal stalwarts as Mickey Leland and Eddie Bernice Johnson. The creation and composition of the JCPR owed much to the successes of the civil rights movement in electing minority candidates who pursued a progressive agenda. Indeed, Leland and Johnson were among a group of recently elected minority politicians known as the People's Five. In 1972, Texas changed its districting rules and allowed state representatives and senators to be elected from single-member districts. This decision resulted in the election of five minority candidates, including Mickey Leland, Craig Washington, Anthony Hall, Benny Reyes, and Cecil Bush. Opportunities for African American candidates had grown since Barbara Jordan's 1966 victory in her state senate campaign, which made her the first African American state legislator in Texas since Reconstruction.[25] The election of the People's Five in 1973 brought numbers and strong advocates to political issues that mattered most to the African American community. Prison reform was foremost on the agenda of the People's Five, and although Leland was new to the halls of the capitol, he became its vice chairman and newly elected house representative Eddie Bernice Johnson joined him on the committee.

The JCPR produced a series of working papers and a final report. John Albach, a graduate of University of Texas's law school and formerly with the Center for the Advancement of Criminal Justice at Harvard Law School, served as the committee's staff director, and his staff produced a series of sixteen unpublished working papers on a variety of topics, ranging from prison homosexuality to the building tender system and prison education. Although these working papers remained unpublished, the staff presented them to committee members during its public hearings on the prison system. Under pressure from CURE's lobbying efforts, the state legislature also created the Citizens' Advisory Committee, which Charlie Sullivan chaired, and it included twenty-five prominent citizens with mixed racial and ethnic backgrounds hailing from the fields of law, medicine, education, the church, journalism, labor, and a homemaker. For good measure, the Citizens' Advisory Committee also included a former TDC prisoner and a former member of the Texas Board of Corrections. Both the JCPR and the Citizens' Advisory Committee were to each produce a final report with legislative recommendations after a one-year investigation.

The state legislature formed the JCPR only one month before the Father's Day beating, and McMillan saw his opportunity to bring the massacre into the political arena. Refusing to remain silent, McMillan instructed his mother, Eva McMillan, to write a letter about the incident to Frances Jalet, and she helped McMillan contact sympathetic committee members, particularly Leland and Johnson, who visited the beaten prisoners. Eva acted as a kind of confidant and matriarch to the SNCC Dallas organizers and had the endearing nickname among them as "Mama Mac." Reflecting on her son's political evolution and his experience at the hands of the Texas prison system, "Mama Mac" told a reporter, "It all had an impact in more ways than you can ever tell anyone. There are just some things we have to do in this society."[26] Visiting Retrieve just three days after the Father's Day massacre, Leland and Johnson witnessed prisoners who were still bruised and bloodied from state violence. In disgust, Leland remarked to the press that the TDC purposefully hid prisoner dehumanization behind external walls and conveyed a false public image that was "a beautiful picture from the outside. The yards are well-kept. The flowers are pretty. The place is clean."[27] Similarly, Representative Johnson found upon their arrival to the prison that she was initially "impressed with the cleanliness, the neatness, the attractiveness of the grounds," and since this was the first time that she had ever visited a prison, she was "very surprised to see it appear physically looking as pleasant." But once she had contact with the prisoners and heard their stories concerning the beatings, she felt "overwhelmed with the oppressive environment that seemed to prevail."[28] Stressing themes of human and civil rights, Leland argued that the truth of the matter was that "the human beings, the lives behind those walls," were subjected to such degradation that Leland could no longer "see how any citizen can sit idly by and not make any attempt to improve the plight of the prisoners." Moreover, Leland critiqued the plantation labor regime when he told the press "to say its [prison labor] rehabilitation is a fallacy—it's punishment." He questioned why so many urban people were put to work on the prison plantation. "What's so rehabilitative about teaching a man from an urban area to pick cotton or pull corn? He sure as hell isn't going to find a job picking cotton in the Third Ward."

Leland and Johnson defied the TDC's wishes to keep the incident a secret. Instead, the committee sent a press release that publicized the incident and provided prisoner narratives and allegations of abuse. During their visit, Johnson and Leland found two prisoners with their heads and Afros forcibly shaved and two others who had "bruises on their bodies, shoulders, and backs."[29] Leland and Johnson told the press that "each prisoner was beaten severely, two were bleeding, and one 58-year man with a known record of hearing pathology [was beaten so badly he] was unable to perform the work. He blacked out, in fact, and attempts by another prisoner to aid this person were rewarded by further beatings to both." One elderly prisoner with an ulcer on his shoulder was repeatedly beaten on that particular spot until it bled profusely. Another prisoner, the legislators reported, had a "tumor on his shoulder, the size of a baseball."[30] The prisoners reported that "they were beaten to the floor." Leland reported that the prisoners maintained that corporal punishment was "usually the task of the building tenders—the so-called 'inmate guards' who the inmates say have permission to carry knives and kill if necessary," but what "shocked the inmates . . . was the fact that the guards actually did the beating this time." Leland was visibly angry. "It's just inhuman to use any kind of baseball bat or ax handle or rubber hose to force somebody to work and say that work is rehabilitation instead of punishment," Leland admonished. "I think its absolutely horrible for people—whether they be prisoners or whatever—that they be subjected to the type of treatment that these men were subject to." McMillan's refusal to remain silent had prompted Black legislators to witness state violence, and the result was a genuine political impetus for prison reform. As Johnson explained, "reform is badly needed because I am of the firm belief that this kind of brutality is what causes a man to feel the system owes him something when he gets out. This is what causes high recidivism." For Leland, prison reform meant eradicating the armed building tenders because "beatings are ridiculous and grossly unnecessary" and "breeds hate and anger." Leland reminded the press "the prison is costing the state a very little amount of money" and that it must end field labor, where urban prisoners placed on agricultural plantations discover that "work is indeed punishment."[31]

In response, the warden issued a press release of his own that maintained that his men were responding to "a work buck" and that any such labor strike was an "act of mutiny" that substantiated state reprisal. As prison director, Estelle defended his warden and steadfastly denied the charges by characterizing the prisoners as "mutinous inmates" who were the ones that assaulted the prison guards first.[32] "When I see 265 men going to work and 10 others not going," Estelle admonished, "there is little question in my mind that you've got a mutinous situation." Estelle claimed that his people were in their right to use "necessary force" because, by law, "mutinous situations can be met with necessary force to put them down."[33] Moreover, Estelle refused to allow media their requests to interview the beaten prisoners.[34] Estelle angrily denounced the beaten prisoners and the ensuing investigation: "Those men [the beaten inmates] were fortunate that he [Warden Taylor] was their warden, and not the Director."[35] In a private memorandum to Estelle, Warden Taylor reported that he ordered the beating because of his fear that the work refusal of ten prisoners would lead to a prison wide strike. "It was found out that some of these ten inmates had spread the word through the building that if the rest of the inmates . . . would just quit . . . then the Administration couldn't mess on them," wrote Warden Taylor.[36] Warden Taylor continued: "Seeing the unrest it was causing in part of the inmate population I ordered [the officers] to arm themselves with rubber hose and night sticks and get ready to put the ten inmates to work. . . . Some of the inmates received cuts on their heads and bruises about their bodies, but all were able to go to work." Taylor reported that seven of the prisoners told him that "they would just rather try to forget what had happened" and that "they got what was coming to them." Three of the prisoners, however, remained unrepentant. One told Taylor that "he would work until he decided to quit again" and "that the only thing that I could do to him would be to whip him or kill him and that he had been beat a lot worse than this before and that he was not afraid to die." Another prisoner boldly told Taylor that "he would try to do everything in his power to see that I was paid back for it." A third prisoner, likely McMillan since he said his father was a minister, promised Taylor that "he would try to go through the courts the next time instead of taking matters in his own hands."[37]

————

McMillan was true to his word and contacted Frances Jalet to file a suit alleging that the beating constituted "cruel and unusual punishment." Jalet filed the civil rights lawsuit *McMillan v. Estelle* on behalf of McMillan. During the trial, Estelle continued to deny the veracity of the prisoners' account. "I don't believe in that. I don't believe it happened," Estelle testified.[38] Denial was the first line of defense for the TDC, where the state put the character and veracity of convicts as honest whistle-blowers into question. Despite the TDC's repeated denials, the court concluded that the assault upon the prisoners "constituted a flagrant deprivation of their civil rights."[39]

Imperialism Means Imprisonment: Allen Lamar and the Interracial Challenge against the Prison's Racial Segregation

At the heart of the prisoners' rights movement in Texas was a challenge to Jim Crow arrangements of labor and racial segregation. One of the major pieces of litigation that came out of the early-1970s post–Eight Hoe period was the lawsuit *Lamar v. Coffield*, a class-action lawsuit filed in 1972 that was written by Allen Lamar and Lorenzo Davis.[40] At thirty-six years old in 1972, Allen Lamar had a life-long history of institutionalization, where he shared with many Eight Hoe prisoners the experience of early incarceration through juvenile detention at the State School for Boys in Gatesville. Prior to his first term in the TDC in 1962 for theft of a purse, Lamar had prison sentences for car theft in California's San Quentin and the federal penitentiary in El Reno, Oklahoma. He also shared with other Eight Hoe prisoners a rebellious streak, as he had received disciplinary punishments at San Quentin and in the federal system for "insubordination and instigating a riot," "talking back," "instigating a mess hall strike," and for "refusing to work." In his first year of TDC incarceration, Lamar requested through a letter exchange a private meeting with the prison director, Dr. Beto, "to help eradicate erroneous treatment." Beto granted the meeting, and although there is no record of what they discussed, following the meeting Beto personally had Lamar's classification status changed with a handwritten note to TDC classification that Lamar must be "put on the Muslim list." As a classified Muslim and with a prison disciplinary record ending with multiple solitary sentences, Lamar was transferred to Ellis in 1963, where he was placed alongside other Muslims under the authority of "Beartracks" McAdams. As a budding writ writer, Lamar filed several appeals of his conviction based on his assertion that he was convicted by an all-white jury from an exclusive and segregated white community. Due to the ways in which he framed his legal appeal as a civil rights matter, Lamar soon earned the interest of Fred Cruz, who introduced Lamar to Frances Jalet; he soon became one of her clients. As with all of Jalet's prisoners, Lamar expressed his appreciation for Jalet's efforts through letter writing. In one letter, Lamar remarked that Jalet's legal foray into the mire of the TDC's prison plantation arrangements likely exposed her to "many perplexing situations since your commencement of assisting the incarcerated." Nonetheless, Lamar thought that Jalet offered prisoners the clear "illustration of the human goodness and diligent representation."[41]

As one of Jalet's clients, Lamar was sequestered with her other clients as part of Eight Hoe, where he befriended Jalet's Mexican American clients. Following the dispersal of Eight Hoe, Lamar wrote a manifesto, "Imperialism Means Imprisonment," which he dedicated to "Comrade Jackson," that is, George Jackson. In the document, he argued that prisons functioned as sites of imperialism that rendered prisoners as an internally colonized people.

In the manifesto, Lamar stressed that TDC was a site of "maximum repression" that incarcerated "Third World persons, racial minorities and poor persons" within the "impregnable hypocrisy" of TDC's prison plantation. Lamar offered over twenty specific instances that documented how incarceration was tantamount to colonization's destruction of the colonized psyche. Lamar contended that coerced prison labor made prisoners into "forced labor-slaves," and he cited the internal division of prison labor through the use of building tenders and their having abusive powers—able to enact physical brutality, sexual violence, and the subjugation of a prisoner's psyche—as elemental to the dehumanizing nature of TDC.

He found the trusty system, in particular, as a force of subjugation. Several of his examples recounted how prisoners who resisted violence or attempted to document it became the target of state-orchestrated prison rape. Lamar cited at length an incident on Mother's Day 1973 where eight building tenders, who operated as "agents of the authorities," assaulted another prisoner. When the prisoner attempted to report the building tenders' sexual assault, the whistle-blowing prisoner was then given over to the major's "head count boy," who claimed the whistle-blower as his "wife and that he [the head count boy] would get him [the whistle-blower] a favorable job assignment." If the whistle-blowing prisoner "accepts the marriage, then no official will abuse him and if he refused the proposal, things would be very difficult for him." When the threatened whistle-blower "agreed to the marriage," the prisoner received a highly sought after job assignment as the parole counselor's bookkeeper. Lamar further recounted how state-controlled sexual assault could also be frighteningly random when citing an incident in 1975 where an African American prisoner at Ellis was "laying in his bed in his cell when to his surprise the cell door opens and he is forced to perform in a sexual relation with a Building Tender . . . After the assault has been complete the door is locked" by the building tender who had keys and full access to another prisoner's cell.

The manifesto then connected TDC's division of labor and its attendant trusty privilege to Fanon's argument that "imperial control aims at the thorough domination and humiliation of the subjugated."[42] "Confined under these conditions," Lamar wrote, "prisoners [politically] organize their character or their character becomes weak and incapable of resistance. For such measures damage and destroy mind and spirit. For example, many prisoners who had resisted what they find to be immoral and inhuman, with ample justification, surrender their principles for favorable treatment and earlier possibility of parole." Lamar considered himself an "awakened" prisoner whose political consciousness was part of a new community of prisoner solidarity. He closed his manifesto with his concluding argument that incarceration itself was not a place but a *process* that aimed for nothing less than the total mental subjugation of colonized/incarcerated people. "The Department [TDC] is a process which colonizes women, minorities, the poor and Third World persons within the state," Lamar concluded. "It divides, rapes, exploits, and robs these persons of dignity, character, and spirit."[43]

Out of Eight Hoe's interracial camaraderie came the notion for a lawsuit that challenged the TDC's racial segregation practices. First filed in 1972, the *Lamar* suit cited segregation in living arrangements, work assignments, disciplinary practices, and access to medical care, free religion, recreational activities, dining, and showering. In all these areas, the suit claimed, race and racial segregation favored white prisoners over African American and Mexican American prisoners. As a suit aimed against the prison plantation's system of racial segregation, *Lamar* was joined by Jalet's clients, who had been disbursed across the prison system. The suit included the African American prisoners Lorenzo Davis, Leavy Campbell, and O'Neal Browning. Eight Mexican American prisoners joined the suit within two weeks of its filing. The group included many of the Eight Hoe writ-writing veterans, including Ernesto R. Montana, David R. Ruíz, Raul A. Rodríguez, Isaias Lara, Salvador Gonzalez, David Villalpandro, Eduardo Salazar Mauricio, and David Robles.[44] Within a year after Lamar's initial filing of the suit, the U.S. Justice Department filed a motion to join the class action. The TDC responded with its usual legal intransigence by fighting the case, and by 1975 they convinced two white prisoners, four African Americans, and two Mexican American prisoners to join their legal case in defense of racial segregation. Lamar would go on to file thirty more civil rights suits and help seventy-five prisoners file other suits against TDC.

As a racial integration case, the *Lamar* suit faced challenges beyond the TDC from white prisoners who resisted the idea of being celled with a prisoner of color. Chief among such white prisoner citics was Frank Xavier Leahy, a well-known and talented writ writer whom Sarah T. Hughes, a federal judge, had called "one of the best lawyers in Texas and one of the nation's most effective prison activists." Leahy had become a subject of media interest for his well-known civil rights suit against Sheriff Clarence Jones for having transferred Leahy and other prisoners in 1972 from the Dallas jail to be incarcerated in TDC before they had been tried and convicted.[45] In his brief, Leahy used ninety-four far-reaching legal quotations that earned such respect among

Dallas lawyers that one journalist called Leahy's legal brief "an act of mind numbing originality."[46]

The press called Leahy, who came from a good home in Memphis, Tennessee, a "rich-kid delinquent" with compulsory "military school as the solution," after which he eventually earned a conviction for armed robbery. To Leahy's mind, however, he was above other prisoners, especially those that were not white. "People like me," he told a reporter, "with some education, from decent family ties, shatter all of the 'norms' in prison. Prisons aren't made for us. They are made for the offspring of the ghettos, with ghetto rules, ghetto treatment, even guards with ghetto mentalities. I once had a prison chaplain tell me that my problem was that I couldn't think 'black.'"[47] When the *Lamar* case threatened to desegregate the cells, Leahy responded with a counter suit and formed the white prisoner organization the Advocates of the Ku Klux Klan (AOKKK). Leahy conceived of the AOKKK as "a patriotic, religious, educational and legal organization in support of the *original* ideals of the Ku Klux Klan," which he thought would fill a "tremendous void in the civil rights programs for poor white minority members." Leahy reasoned that "when a Chicano gets killed, the Brown Berets, La Raza, LULAC raise plenty of hell. If a Black gets killed, you've got NAACP, SDDL, Panthers, Muslims to deal with. But nobody, nobody, gets down for the poor whites."[48] Although Leahy frequently professed that he was no racist and that he was on "the front lines" with VISTA in 1968 working in Hope, Arkansas, to help integrate public schools and work with African American youth, his time in TDC made his racism clear. For instance, his "Christmas card" had a well-illustrated and hand-drawn depiction of an African American man in a prison cell with his pants unbuckled and a raised bat in his hands standing over a half-dressed, horrified white prisoner lying prone as a victim with the card's title "Christmas Eve—In Prison." White prisoners, according to Leahy, "got up and moving over the Klan," but Leahy's real purpose was to build a legal movement for white prisoners. "While loudly organizing the damned Klan," Leahy reported, "I am ever so quietly and seriously organizing the Texas Legal Action Group . . . which is a self-help legal co-op." In a letter to state senator Chet Brooks, Leahy laid out his plans to challenge *Lamar* based on legal precendent over a prisoner's right to privacy. "Cells are bedrooms," Leahy contended. "If the court's ruled tomorrow that every bedroom in America had to be black/white without exception, you would have civil war instantly, yet that *exactly* is what they have ruled for TDC inmates . . . What I am attacking in the *Lamar* decision is the arbitrary ruling that every white inmate MUST have a black cell partner."[49]

Although Lamar's case benefitted from an anti-racist interracial collaboration stemming from Eight Hoe, prison sexuality may have also played an important part of why this particular case was filed. In their research on the racial segregation in Texas, the sociologists Chad R. Trulson and James Marquart placed an ad in the prison newspaper *The Echo* asking for prisoner information on Allen Lamar. In response, one prisoner, whose identity they kept anonymous, responded, "Lamar did not care *one* bit about 'equality' in prison housing, nor did he believe segregated housing really 'disadvantage' black prisoners." Instead, the letter stated that what motivated Lamar's suit was that he "had a white, homosexual lover called 'Kiki" that Lamar wanted in his cell with him. The letter cited the trading power of the building tenders' internal prison economy, where normally "a couple packs of smokes or a bag of Max [coffee] to Major's Bookkeepr BT would 'fix' a cellmate assignment as long as the 'punk' you wanted in your cell was the same race . . . Since Lamar was black and 'Kiki' was white, no bribe would get Lamar's lover in the same cell with him."[50] The letter cannot be verified as true, but Lamar did have two prior official prison punishments for sodomy. While Marquart and Trulson dismiss Lamar as "no angel, nor a Rosa Parks–like trailblazer who sought to pull down a long standing barrier for the benefit of humankind," the fact that his earlier suits were focused on racial empowerment suggests that his effort to combat racial segregation was genuine.[51] Moreover, the wider context of prisoner politicization within the civil rights and Black Power era makes Lamar's personal reasons less salient than the shared goal among his interracial coalition to eradicate racial empowerment and white privilege on the prison plantation. For the prisoners, the lofty goal of "racial integration" was less important in and of itself than challenging the racial empowerment that derived from the southern prison's labor regime. What the letter does show, however, is the complicated nature of privilege in prison, which was simultaneously racialized and sexualized, where powerful white prisoners could use their trusty position to gain access to whomever they wanted, when they wanted, and to do with them as they pleased, whether their actions were consensual, brutal and coerced, or a matter of unbalanced economic exchange. A white prisoner could not easily move a prisoner of another race into his cell, but he could have access to him through his powerful connection to bookkeepers. Perhaps more salient, if Lamar did indeed have a relationship with "Kiki," then the intersectionality of racial and sexual liberation is deeply intertwined in the *Lamar* case. Prisoners like Lamar would have understood the historian Charles Payne's assertion that integration, as a term of acceptable comfort, and "'civil rights' becomes so popular precisely because it is narrow, precisely because it does not suggest that distribution of privilege is a part of the problem."[52]

Black Power and the Challenge to Carceral Violence:
Eddie James Ward and Black Prison Masculinity

Only days before the JPRC convened its hearings on the Father's Day incident, renewed Black Power organizing challenged the labor regime at Ramsey
prison in early November 1973. As word of the Father's Day massacre spread
across the prison system, a group of African American prisoners at the
Ramsey prison responded by plotting rebellion. Eleven prisoners, some of
them with a history of civil rights activism and Black Power organizing,
banded together and decided to confront the brutalities of the prison system
through collective refusals to follow the orders of building tenders. Ramsey's
prison administration was beholden to the building tender system. Indeed,
its warden, James "Wildcat" Anderson, had been named in *Dreyer v. Jalet* as
the prison official who recruited the building tenders to bring suit against
Jalet. His assistant warden, David Christian, was so infamous among the prisoners for utilizing building tenders that one prisoner characteristically
charged that "violence followed Christian like a shadow." The prisoners believed that Warden Anderson and Assistant Warden Christian responded to
the wave of prisoner litigation against the TDC by orchestrating building tender assaults against minority prisoners, particularly the Black population.
Beginning in mid-October 1973 and continuing for three weeks, there was at
least one savage beating a week. White building tenders, for instance, had
beaten Eddie Jeffrey and then used sharp razors to cut off his sizable Afro.
As a symbolic act, the sight of white building tenders forcibly shoring the
Black Power Afro hairstyle conveyed the message that the prison's internal
white power structure would humiliate and degrade any sign of Black self-
actualization and empowerment. The prisoner Eddie James Ward reported
that the building tenders had threatened him that "he was next to be beaten
up" because of how he wore his hair. Only the night before the attempted rebellion, another African American prisoner, named Simonton, was "jumped
on" by a pair of white building tenders, Billy White and Billy Preston. African Americans viewed these attacks as part of a larger pattern of increased
brutality aimed at quieting the disaffection among minority prisoners through
intimidation, humiliation, and violence.[53]

On November 8, 1973, at 10:30 A.M. the guards took these prisoners to the
writ room and granted them two hours of legal work. As Black Power advocates, these men hoped to use their time in the writ room to hold a meeting,
share how they were beaten, and document the abuses through a collective
class-action lawsuit. They had not gone to the writ room with the intention
of plotting a rebellion, but once there they discussed the beatings collectively
and decided, in Eddie Jeffrey's words, that "we're going to have to stop it the

best way we can." These Black Power prisoners were particularly vulnerable to building tender assault because their legal activities placed them in "administrative segregation," where they lived in individual cells apart from the general population. Building tenders, however, had full access to these individual cells. When the beatings would occur, typically five to six building tenders would storm into the cell, which gave the individual African American prisoners little chance to fight them off. Their time in the writ room represented the only opportunity that these prisoners had to converse with one another. After a brief discussion concerning the increased beatings, these prisoners decided that when they emerged from the writ room, they would turn the tables on the building tenders and "make them wup us or we wup them." Four of the prisoners opted out of the plot, but the other seven felt that they had no choice but to take up self-defense. Six of the prisoners were African American and one of them was Chicano.[54]

Although the prisoners knew that only seven prisoners could not possibly take over the prison, they felt they had no recourse other than to send the prison administration a message by attacking the white building tenders that had been terrorizing them. The prisoners planned to use a hidden knife and a body building weight bar to assault the building tenders when they exited the writ room. On the way out of the writ room, Eddie Jeffrey managed to hide a pocketknife in his boot, which escaped Officer Nichols's attempt at a strip search. Jeffrey first stabbed the building tender Lawrence Wynne, who was an African American prisoner whom the TDC classified as a fourth-class medical condition, meaning he was medically incapable of taxing physical work, and his official job was "wing barber." Jeffrey countered that Wynne "weighed about 300 pounds and was plenty strong" and that he had joined the other BTs in beating Jeffrey a week earlier. Other building tenders rushed to Wynne's defense, and the uprising was quickly put down with bats, clubs, and knives.[55]

Among the prisoners who had plotted the rebellion was Eddie James Ward, an activist on the campus of the University of Texas at Austin, a former marine and Vietnam veteran, and the defense minister for the Black Power organization the United Community Front (UCF). Ward was another prisoner who was swept up in the Vietnam War and the tumultuous struggle for civil rights. In the fall of 1962, at the age of seventeen, Ward joined a series of nonviolent sit-ins at Woolworth's lunch counters. Despite the racial injustice he witnessed in Texas, Ward remained nonviolent and thought of himself as a patriot. Inspired by President John F. Kennedy's 1960 inaugural address, Ward joined the marine corps to serve his country and to earn the education benefits that he would otherwise never afford. Following boot camp, Ward had a year-long combat tour in Vietnam from 1964 to 1965 that forever changed his outlook on violence and race. "I mean Vietnam exposed me to more violence than I ever even thought about seeing," Ward recalled. During his service in Vietnam, Ward and a group of soldiers captured a Viet Cong prisoner near Da Nang on the border with Laos. Following the prisoner's interrogation, Ward's fellow soldiers "pushed him [the prisoner] out of the helicopter," which, in Ward's words, "really threw me off" and "tripped me out." What caused Ward to go through a personal transformation in Vietnam was watching how white soldiers treated Vietnamese prisoners. "The way they treated the Vietnamese," Ward recalled. "The way they imprisoned them. I mean, man, it was terrible. I mean it was rough. . . . Why is it we trying to get these people to go with our way of thinking, why are we doing it this way? Them guys I was with on the tour, we went out, you know, and we captured prisoners and they'd be killing prisoners. We did a lot things we shouldn't have."[56] Ward's wartime experience in Vietnam politicized him, and he joined the ranks of many Vietnam veterans who felt disenchanted with the war and raised their voices in the antiwar effort as "new winter" soldiers.[57]

When Ward returned from Vietnam in 1966, the Black Power movement had captured his imagination and inspired Ward's renewed civil rights activity centered on Black political organizing. Back in Austin, Ward came into contact with Larry Jackson, a local community organizer and SNCC member. Together, Ward and Jackson formed the United Community Front, which was affiliated with SNCC. Like Houston's local PP2, the UCF also patterned itself on the local community control efforts of the national Black Panther Party (BPP), and they began in 1968 a local breakfast program and daycare center on Twelfth Street in their newly established headquarters, "the Revolutionary Club."[58] Ward was the UCF's minister of defense, and his job was to maintain the stockpile of weapons and help organize training classes in armed self-defense. Although the UCF patterned themselves on the Black Panthers, it was a local organization that eschewed national control, and its aim was autonomous local control within the immediate Black community. Ward explained, "We wanted control, see, because the Black Panthers, they wanted us to sell papers and stuff and send the proceeds to them. But we wanted local control. That's the one thing that I always pushed for."[59]

In 1969, however, Leonard Meadows, Tommy Ray, and Ray's wife approached Ward to participate in a burglary with them to steal the deposits of the Texas Warrant Company in Austin, which was a credit union for state employees. Neither Meadows nor Ray were part of the UCF, and the burglary for them was simply a way to maintain their heroin addiction. Ward had access to automatic weapons, particularly Soviet-made AK-47s, and they convinced him to be part of the crime so that he could gain more money to fund the UCF, which after three years of breakfast and daycare programs was rapidly running out of funds. Ward was the only one of the four who was caught for the robbery, as Tommy Ray and his wife tipped the police off against Ward after the couple had a fight over whether Ward was sleeping with Ray's wife. Demonstrating how the state criminalized Black Power advocates well beyond typical sentencing guidelines, Ward was given an astounding 101-year sentence for his part in the burglary. The prosecutor in Ward's case recalled that Ward's militance and cultural embrace of Black Power added to the sensationalism of his trial and his harsh conviction. "Eddie James Ward walked into that courtroom wearing a dashiki, an afro and a hostile attitude," recalled Ward's prosecutor, "and he scared those 12 white middle Americans to death, so they put him in the pen for 101."[60] Even though he was betrayed, Ward defiantly refused to turn over Meadows and the Rays to the police, and he turned down a 7-year sentence offered in exchange for a guilty plea. Ward conceived of his Black Power politics as an extension of Third World Left solidarity, and he felt that his steadfast refusal to turn on his coconspirators kept him true to his principles of Black solidarity. "I don't think no one in the world is to the left of me," he told a reporter at the time of his trial. "I can't be moderate. I realize there is a time for compromise, and sometimes a historical retreat is necessary. But I'm not going to accept a Jimmy Hoffa–type condition on any parole. I'm not going to sell out to oppress the masses for self-interest. I feel that anyone who does this is not really sincere in those things he professes, or those things he's running around telling everyone about or tying to expose to the masses. What is not good for him is definitely not good for the masses. . . . I'm not going to sell it out. I'm going to maintain."[61]

Once inside the prison, Ward understood that the prison plantation's reliance on racial violence ruled life within the TDC. "It was ruled by a mass—who was the baddest," Ward remembered. "You know, who had the most muscles. They should dominate. It was black on black and white on white and Mexican on Mexican." To combat the carceral mentality that set men against one another, Ward stressed collectivity instead, and he surrounded himself with a clique of fellow Black Power militants who advocated self-defense, a community ethos, and active resistance against the white hierarchy's building tender system. "The first thing I done was circle the wagons," Ward recounted. "Everybody knew me from Austin. And when I got there I just got those people together that I knew that I could trust and circled the wagons. No, I wasn't afraid. I was a Marine. I was never been afraid. You know, I've always been afraid of my activities, of myself. How far would I go. And when I was young, I had no boundaries of what I would do for justice. And that was my fear, but once I seen it [the prison] once my eyes set on that, I wanted to change it."[62]

Ward's self-defense philosophy and communitarian organizing sensibility left him particularly disturbed by the building tenders' ability to rape other men without reprisal. Ward and his collection of Black Power prisoners had witnessed firsthand how the building tender system earned as their reward for their service the bodies of other prisoners. They watched as building tenders reached into the administrative segregation wing and with their influence and power plucked out younger prisoners to have them celled with the building tender for their sexual violation and domestic cell service. As urban Black Power advocates, Ward and his small company witnessed what they perceived to be twentieth-century slavery as powerful building tenders bought and sold prisoners' bodies as sexualized objects that signified the building tenders' power. While Ward embraced a militant expression of Black masculinity, he also reinterpreted prison's hypermasculine predatory nature and reinvented masculinity to mean mutual protection and respect for the sanctity of another person's control over his own body. Upon witnessing prison slavery and rape, Ward determined, "I'm not going to sit around there and let the man, anybody in authority, rape, anybody that puts up resistance is not going to be raped in my presence."[63] Ward's self-defense philosophy and communitarian ethos extended to weaker prisoners whom he thought his Black Power clique should defend in a renewed sense of masculine protection, community, and working-class respectability. When a prisoner could own little else, Ward believed that the one thing he should be able to control was his own body. Ward thus reinterpreted Black masculinity in the Black Power era as a figure of communitarian protection rather than as one driven by false discourses of pathologies and prone to violence.[64]

Ward's disgust with state-orchestrated prison rape as a critical design of systematic racial degradation was shared by other Black Power prisoners caged on southern prison plantations. As a Black Panther at Angola, Albert Woodfox related that he witnessed a prison rape that subsequently allowed him to make the critical connection between his political awakening as a Panther to "the brutal consequences of rape." "I was seeing the face of a person who had his dignity taken, his spirit broken, and his pride destroyed. . . . Before, I had thought of rape as a physical violence and I felt it was my duty, as a Black Panther, to try to prevent it. Now, I saw that rape went beyond a physical act. Rape brought about the complete destruction of another human being." As a result, Black Panthers at Angola organized an "anti-rape" squad much as Eddie James Ward tried to do in Texas.[65]

Disgusted by the prison's sexual and racial rapacity, Ward looked beyond the prison for allies that might help him expose how the prison's internal economy operated. Ward developed a close and intimate relationship with Janet Stockard, who was a white University of Texas law student, a self-defined "hippie," and a "movement lawyer," who had come into contact with prisoners through CURE's social work.

Stockard visited Ward the day after the November 8 incident and found Ward badly beaten. Ward told Stockard that three building tenders had rushed into his cell the day after the incident to seek retribution by beating him. She immediately called Mickey Leland of the JCPR who had Ward moved to the prison hospital for his wounds and for protection. Leland then ordered JCPR staff to visit Ramsey and investigate. Warden Anderson met the JCPR investigators upon their arrival and asked them "to report that these building tenders risked their lives to save others and that this was a good example of the good in the building tender system."[66] Moreover, Warden Anderson emphatically insisted that the men on Ramsey were "violent and dangerous men" who were "not in here for singing too loud in church on Sunday."

The prisoners told a different story, however. What they wanted to stress was that as civil rights prison litigation mounted and as Black Power political organizing took hold, the white-controlled building tender hierarchy felt imperiled and responded by targeting Black and brown prisoners. As civil rights litigation and Black Power critiques began to mount, the state-orchestrated carceral violence, humiliation, degradation, brutality, and sexual assault accelerated. When the JCPR committee staff visited Ward, they found "his cell covered with blood caused by head wounds. Ward was transferred to the prison hospital at the Walls on Saturday." The other prisoners on his wing corroborated Ward's account about the building tender assault. The prisoner Lonnie Flowers, for instance, told JCPR staff that since Warden Anderson had taken over at Ramsey, he had "drastically cracked down on the inmates," and things had become "very explosive"; the prison environment was "very tense now at Ramsey, and without something to look forward to, the inmates are more likely to riot." The JCPR report stressed that there was "tremendous pressure on the inmates, pressure on the BTs to be hard on the inmates."[67]

Prisoners not only initiated civil rights litigation; they also pursued their own brand of politics by documenting state violence through letter-writing campaigns to enlist the support of politicians. In one letter to State Senator Ron Clower, Florentino G. Rangel placed the prisoner documentation effort as equally important as the nation's other momentous social movements. "Women are demanding their human rights, Blacks are demanding their rights, and the Chicanos too," Rangel pointed out. To make his case to state politicians, Rangel recounted the historical anachronism of the TDC's prison plantation. "We have landed men on the moon and will soon land one on Mars, but here at home are found some of the atrocities that occurred at the crucifixion of Jesus Christ, in Rome." Despite society's claims of advancement in the 1960s toward a "modern society, civilized we call it, today, right in the Texas prison system, human rights are denied to all prisoners except those who work and receive privileges from the weak personnel who work for the institution and have power." Calling attention to the rapacious nature of the southern system, Rangel related, "Today prisoners are still raped, beat, abused in all forms, mentally tortured, exploited and degraded, or made to feel lower than ugly dogs."[68] Simply put, Rangel's letter joined many other prisoner letters that defined carceral violence and made prisoners visible to politicians. Indeed, he sent multiple copies of the same long letter to Governor Dolph Briscoe; State Senators Clower, Chet Brooks, and Lloyd Dogget; State Representatives Mickey Leland, Joe Hernandez, and Chris Miller; and JCPR committee member Erasmo Andrade. His letter was among hundreds of others that offered similar testimony.

Others wrote letters as steadfast white allies to a Black-brown coalition, in which these white prisoners consciously rejected their claim to the racial privilege as expressed in the hierarchical trusty system. In a November 11, 1973, letter to State Senator Clower, the white prisoner Steve Blanchard described the tension at Ramsey, his hopes for peace and nonviolence within the prison, and pleaded for the legislature to intervene. Blanchard had previously been a victim of building tender rape. "It is fairly common knowledge what Warden W.V. Anderson is trying to do on this unit," Blanchard wrote. "His 'special' mission to break-up all of the 'writ writers and agitators' is resulting in people being seriously injured and may result in more serious incidents if the unbearable pressure does not cease. The main idea everyone had in mind was for a peaceful change in our archaic penal system. . . . We want peaceful change. But we need outside help. This is why we are imploring you to help us!"[69] Despite his whiteness, Blanchard viewed the prison plantation and the trusty system through the lens of 1960s-era radicalism. What animated Blanchard's alliance with Black and brown prisoner organizers and writ writers was Blanchard's feeling of regret that he was of the same age as the SNCC generation but that his incarceration during the 1960s had kept him from joining his generation's civil rights revolution. When asked why he joined the writ writers, Blanchard responded, "I keep thinking it was because of the news. I think it was Walter Cronkite live . . . the promises that the Kennedy brothers made, and even King's contribution to our nation, and I wanted to be part of the life that I was missing because of my criminal episodes that brought me to prison." The liberal hope to change the nation, however, foundered for Blanchard as the incarceration that had consumed his youth politicized him and he witnessed firsthand how little the civil rights movement had changed the southern prison. As a bisexual prisoner from California, Blanchard's sexuality also made him an outsider and target of sexual violence, despite his whiteness. To give his incarceration greater meaning, Blanchard determined that he would become "one of the more bombastic,

CURE celebrating Eddie James Ward's Release from the TDC with State Representatives Gonzalo Barrientos and Larry Bales (a state representative, but better known as owner of the Scholz Beer Garten, an Austin establishment for those working in the state capitol). Courtesy of Alan Pogue.

communist oriented people in the joint, and was actively trying to convert people to something different than the status quo that was America with a 'K.'" An alliance with Black and Chicano prisoners presented Blanchard with a critical opportunity to make up for having missed the 1960s by engaging the prison's structural racism during the 1970s. "I wanted to be part of something that I had thrown away, and it was my way of rejoining that life."[70]

When the JCPR's attempt to document abuse was stonewalled, Ward took up Fred Cruz's example and turned to the courts and the law. In response to Ward's beating, Janet Stockard filed a civil rights suit on behalf of Ward. In a narrative quite similar to that of Jalet and Cruz, Stockard alleged in her suit that the TDC barred her clients from correspondence with her and members of the state legislature. Moreover, her suit claimed that Warden Anderson and Assistant Warden Christian provided building tenders with authority over fellow prisoners and that the eleven building tenders who had assaulted her clients utilized "cruel and unusual" punishment against their fellow prisoners.[71] Stockard's suit, *Ward v. Estelle*, filed on December 19, 1973, was the first civil rights action aimed directly at the building tender system. In response, the TDC responded to Stockard nearly exactly as Beto had responded to Jalet. In their attempt to thwart Stockard's outside "interference," Estelle had her clients caged in solitary, censored their mail, made Stockard wait for hours to meet with her clients, confiscated her tape-recorded interviews, and moved her clients suddenly from one prison to another on the day of her visitation. Stockard's relationship with Ward also became intimate, mirroring the personal relationship between Cruz and Jalet.[72]

Stockard later claimed that her clients had also warned her that the TDC had gone so far as to plan her murder by having a car run her off the road on the late-night, two-lane return drive from rural Brazoria to Austin.[73] This incident recalled a similar strange occurrence in 1969 when Frances Jalet's car suddenly and uncontrollably veered into a ditch as she was driving home from a prison visit with her clients. Jalet emerged bruised but alive and somewhat suspicious of the circumstances. Although there is no documentation that Stockard's public allegation was ever true, it was clear that the TDC openly attempted to prevent Stockard from having access to her clients. The TDC followed the same line of attack against Stockard that Beto had used against Jalet, claiming that she was fostering "revolutionary insurrection." Warden Anderson and Assistant Warden Christian, for instance, alleged that Stockard's clients were members of the Symbonese Liberation Army (SLA) and that they had hatched a plot to murder prison officials. Mirroring the allegations that the California prison system made in the George Jackson shooting, the TDC charged that Stockard was plotting to smuggle guns to Ward as part of an open prison insurrection. Stockard countered the hyperbolic TDC allegations when she held a press conference during a July 3, 1974, demonstration on the steps of the state capitol in Austin. Stockard charged that prison officials would murder her clients during a TDC-orchestrated "riot."[74] While Ward was an active part of the Black Power movement, he was not an SLA member, and it was unlikely that Stockard, who was more a counterculture hippie than an armed insurrectionist, would supply her clients with weapons. Murder within Texas prison was always a possibility, but the Texas prison system maintained the nation's lowest murder rate, and it seemed unlikely that the TDC would attempt to murder Stockard or her clients when they had so many other means of intimidation at their disposal. But it was clear that the rapacious carceral violence of the building tender system was accelerating in response to civil rights litigation and Black political organizing. Incarcerated on prison plantations, southern prisoners watched in horror as the state of New York and California turned to deadly carceral violence to quell Black political organizing at the Attica and Soledad prisons. Southern prison administrators watched these events with no small amount of anxiety, and they were determined to avoid "Attica South."

Panthers on the Southern Prison Plantation: Angola and the Southern Prison Response to Black Radicalism

Texas was not the only southern state where prisoners had drawn inspiration from the Attica uprising. At the same time that Texas experienced Black prisoner radicalism, Louisiana's Angola penitentiary was buffeted by the near simultaneous forces of rights-based litigation, top-down liberal hopes for prison reform, and Black radicalism.

During the 1970s, Angola was Louisiana's largest prison, situated on a former plantation some sixty miles from Baton Rouge, with a population of approximately 1,200 prisoners. The land surrounding the prison produced rich soil amounting to 3,200 acres of soybeans, 850 acres of cotton, 400 acres of corn, and 300 remaining acres for assorted vegetables. The work regime at Angola was as long and brutal as Texas, and its prisoner newspaper, *The Angolite*, reported that Louisiana prisoners shared the Texan sentiment that "many, if not most, prisoners regard field work as punishment."[75] As a southern prison plantation, Angola prisoners were also subject to an internal economy where prisoner slavery and ownership claimed prisoners' bodies and domestic service. "Raping, selling of prisoners, and forced homosexuality of younger prisoner by inmate prison guards and prison officials was the order of the day," wrote Robert King in his memoir of his incarceration at Angola.[76]

Angola's work regime was threatened in the early 1970s by the combination of prisoners' rights lawsuits, and the development of the first prison chapter of the Black Panthers formed in the prison. In 1969–70, Billy Sinclair wrote several *pro se* petitions against the living conditions on death row that he argued constituted "cruel and inhuman" punishment.[77] Initially, his complaint was dismissed, but the dismissal was overturned on appeal by the Fifth Circuit Court.[78] Once the court recognized that the hands-off argument had been overturned, *Sinclair v. Henderson* secured due process rights in prison trials over disciplinary infractions and prohibited extended stays in solitary confinement that the court found as a violation of the protection from "cruel and unusual punishment."[79] As civil rights complaints challenged Angola's punitive practices in the courtroom, prisoners on the ground began to organize.

In 1970, twelve Black Panther members of the National Committee to Combat Fascism (NCF) barricaded themselves in an apartment complex in New Orleans's lower Ninth Ward as police raided their homes.[80] Without suffering a casualty, this group was arrested and their subsequent convictions conveyed them, along with a new militant critique, to Angola. As Angola prisoners they believed that they were thrown backward in time and held on a modern-day "slave plantation." Robert King, Herman Wallace, and Ronald Ailsworth (Faruq) started to organize Angola prisoners around the Black

Panther Party's sense of communitarian values and politicized action. "We rounded up other politically conscious brothers," Wallace explained, "and periodically met on the yard discussing prison conditions and how we were going to change them." In the aftermath of Attica and Black Panther organizing in New Orleans, Wallace felt that "the time has come, whereas the level of conscious[ness] of the inmates at Angola is at the stage of truly understanding the real functioning of this institution." At Angola, there were clear connections to the prison organizing in other states, as Woodfox had just been extradited from the Tombs jail in New York City where he had come in contact with three members of the Panther 21 and where he joined them as part of the 1970 Tombs jail uprising. For many Black prisoners, the early 1970s represented a moment of consciousness-raising where they recognized their incarceration within a systematic construct of white superiority and racial degradation. "We believed that being in prison we were at the forefront of social struggles and it was our responsibility to respond to the issues," Woodford acknowledged.[81] In a June 1973 letter to Director Hunt, Herman Wallace wrote that the consciousness raising had produced a true "understanding of the real function of their institution. For we have been kidnapped, ransom[ed] off, stripped of manhood, and throwned in a Neo-Slave camps."[82] Hailing from New Orleans, urban Black radicals experienced geographic dislocation to southern rural prisons as a modern-day Middle Passage that denied them their freedom, masculinity, and humanity within prison plantations that constituted "neoslavery." As the Black Panther prisoner Gilbert Montegut put it, his "mental engulfment in study" had allowed him "to assist in transforming the criminal mentality into revolutionary mentality to broaden the revolutionary culmination of Third World politics."[83]

————

As the political consciousness raising drew more followers, the group drafted a joint letter to the Black Panther Party's Organizing Committee in Oakland, California, and they successfully petitioned to have the nation's first officially recognized Panther chapter in a prison. In his autobiography, *Top of the Heap*, Robert King remarked with pride on how the Black Panthers had enacted a profound shift in mentality and prisoner temperament. "I felt as if I had entered a different Angola than the one I had entered years before; where prisoners were totally subservient," King noted with newfound pride. "Absent was the submissive, sycophantic behavior of bygone years."[84]

Once Angola's Black Panther chapter was established, Black prisoners found civil rights attorneys who had deep historical connections to civil rights struggles in the U.S. South during the 1960s and who hoped to make prisons the new terrain for struggle in the 1970s. David J. Dennis, once a leading organizer of the SNCC's activities in Mississippi, partnered with Lolis E. Elie, Alvin J. Bronstein, and George Stickler Jr. of the American Civil Liberties Union. Dennis appealed to prisoners because of his civil rights organizing in the South through the SNCC, and Bronstein appealed because he had just established the ACLU's National Prison Project in 1972.[85] For Bronstein, the Attica uprising had awakened an unconsciousness that the new struggle for civil rights must be in prison. "When Attica exploded," Bronstein wrote, "it created an unmatched awareness of prisons and their nature. It was no longer true that prisons and prisoners were 'out of sight, out of mind.' The prisoners' rights movement began in earnest."[86] To assist the movement, Bronstein advocated for the development of a cadre of civil rights attorneys to work on cases that pertained to "First Amendment rights of inmates, particularly when they act collectively, and the protection of inmates against retaliation for the exercise of those rights." As a civil rights attorney, Bronstein felt that his role was to elevate the prisoner complaint and their collective voice, "because people in prison are best equipped to tell the outside world what is actually happening and because, if they act collectively inside prison, they can have the ability to directly affect their lives."[87]

The mounting political dissent and the prisoners' new cadre of civil rights attorneys frightened prison administrators. To silence them, Louisiana drew on Beto and the TDC's tactic to claim that civil rights attorneys were unduly influencing prisoners to foment revolution. And true to the divided southern prison labor regime between trusty and line prisoner, the Angola prison administration turned to prisoner informants, what prisoners called "snitches," who offered intelligence on a plot to expose Angola's prison conditions. Based on these letters, the attorneys Dennis, Elie, Bronstein, and Stickler were barred from visiting their clients. The following description of Black Power organizing at Angola is drawn from prisoner informants to the administration, as such it sheds light on how the TDC and Angola officials shared similar tactics of carceral violence to repress prisoner organization.

Two letters written four months apart by the prisoner informant Robert C. Coney highlighted some discrepancies, however. In his first letter written in July 1971, Coney charged that plots were being hatched at "a special meeting . . . held by the people who are organized to attack the free personnel through the federal courts," where a writ that had gained six hundred signatures was circulated against Warden Dees. The strategy "is to get a federal grand jury or investigation of the Department of Justice" while bringing members of the media and the NAACP to witness a prison wide work strike to publicize their claims of abuse. According to the letter, there were over two hundred prisoners, both "youngsters and a few old heads," ready to protect the leadership of the prison cabal. "This thing is well organized," Coney marveled.

"I've never seen anything like it in all my prison years. . . . This thing is serious and these people are determined."[88] The first letter, written July 10, 1971, stressed a plot centered around a prisoners' rights suit and a work strike meant to bring media and political attention to Angola.

The second letter, dated September 30, 1971, warned of a violent revolt rather than a work strike. In the second letter, Coney claimed that the leaders of the group were Arthur Holland, L. Flannigan, E. Jackson, F. Johnson, Leotha Brown, and James Jumpkins. Written only nineteen days after the Attica uprising, the informant reported that the plan was to have no less than one hundred fifty prisoners "armed with knives and clubs to act as enforcers" strategically placed in all the dormitories to ensure that all prisoners were compliant with the pending revolt when the leaders gave the word. The plan was to burn down the license tag plant and the sugar mill, the sites of the prisoners' despised prison labor.[89]

Much like Ernest McMillan's attempt to reach newly elected Black politicians, the Angola prisoners planned to demand that Dorothy Taylor, the first African American elected to the Louisiana House of Representatives in 1971, along with NAACP members and the media, meet with a prisoner committee. Coney charged that prisoners planned to document the prison's corruption by stealing records from the prison and different warehouses and then supplying those documents to Representative Taylor through Dave Dennis. The informant then offered the claim that the aim of the revolt was to "improve the political position of Mrs. Taylor and for the leaders to get help in obtaining clemency once she was powerful enough to deal with state officials in high office." Written only nineteen days after the Attica uprising, the second letter's claims, whether true or a result of administrative machinations, seemed to fit the rising fears of southern prisons that they might experience an Attica of the South.

Drawing upon both California's and Texas's playbook to target the attorneys of radical prisoners, Angola officials claimed that David Dennis was orchestrating a prisoner uprising for political ends. These letters conveyed the fear that newly elected state-level Black politicians threatened how southern prisons maintained racial order. Another prisoner informant, David L. Clark, claimed that Dennis was trying "to help Mrs. Dorothy acquire the influence and power which she was seeking. . . . It was necessary to conduct a mass demonstration." Clark maintained that Dennis, who was "responsible for the organization of the entire idea," had instructed the prisoners to go on a hunger and work strike, because work was so central to Angola's disciplinary regime. Refusing to work in such a work-oriented prison would, above any other provocation, earn the anger and violent indemnity of the guards. "They wanted the security officers to come down and say beat up some guys," Clark explained. "You know, so these guys could come back and say, 'Yeah, I was beat up man, this was a peaceful demonstration and the free people beat me up with baseball bats and so forth.' This is what they wanted. They tried to provoke this."[90] The enemy of the southern prison was thus the prisoners' rights attorney, and the narrative that both Angola and TDC crafted was that the intrusion of civil rights attorneys was more than a nuisance; it was, to their mind, a subversive attempt to masquerade behind the law to foment violent rebellion. But these conspiratorial charges against Dennis and Representative Taylor were not only fabricated, but such false charges fit the narrative southern prisons wanted to tell about prison litigation formenting violence. Despite their obvious intent to cast aspersions on the prisoners, these informant letters reveal that Angola's prisoners were organizing politically and reaching outside the prison to make a collective case that they suffered degrading and inhumane treatment.

On April 17, 1972, prisoners staged a peaceful demonstration against the work conditions: a six-day workweek of sixteen hours a day at only $0.03 hourly pay. The warden responded with fifty guards, armed with bats, iron pipes, shotguns, and mace as they delivered the menacing admonition that the prisoners return to work or face a beating. Twenty minutes later, Brent Miller, a white prison sergeant, was murdered; he was found with over thirty-eight stab wounds from a mowing blade, which he had received while inspecting the Pine 1 dormitory. Miller, only twenty-three years old, was a generational product of Angola, as his father had also been a guard. The news of the murder was relayed to other prison guards and the local white community created an extremely violent lynch mob. In the shocked words of the prisoner Wilbert Rideau, the repeated stabbing of twenty-three-year-old Miller "turned Angola's undisciplined security force into an enraged mob seeking revenge. Lynch-fever burned in their brain." The prison guards gathered "local residents, barroom patrons, and area farmers" to deputize them and arm them with machine guns, shotguns, and baseball bats.[91]

The lynch mob then stormed the dormitories, where they unleashed tear gas and used mace upon their entrance, and then as the prisoners were succumbing to the gas, they "beat, tortured, and brutalized prisoners indiscriminately."[92] Robert King's memoir recalled that while he was held in solitary, prisoners from the general population were brought to solitary and forced to run through a gauntlet of guards "all wielding bats, clubs and other types batons." Rideau offered a similar report that Black prisoners were "interrogated for hours, routinely beaten and tortured for the slightest bit of information about the militants." In a July deposition, one African American prisoner maintained that since April 17 Angola had been in a constant "reign of terror" where African Americans were continuously "beaten, gassed, and intimidated in every way possible." As an example of how southern prisons manipulated the segregated prison and stoked racial animosity, the deposition stated that the white prisoners in solitary were removed from their cells and re-placed by African American prisoners. The prison guards then provided this notorious group of white prisoners with knives and put them back in general population "where they are told that it is open season on niggers! That nothing will be done to anyone if they kill a nigger." Following the white rage of the guards and deputized local community, the prison then charged Albert Wood-fox and Herman Wallace for Miller's death, and Robert King was subsequently charged with the killing of another prisoner. Despite an internal prison tribu-nal that denied due process, Angola incarcerated all three men in solitary for the next four decades, where they became known as the Angola Three, caged in the "longest period of solitary confinement in American prison history."[93] Falsely accused, King's conviction was overturned on appeal and he was re-leased in 2001 and Woodfox's conviction for Brent Miller's murder was over-turned in 2015. He was released in 2016 after pleading no contest to lesser charges of burglary and manslaughter, which he did so only because of his old age and desire to finally be free from the dungeons of Angola. State violence and solitary's incarceration within incarceration served as notice to southern prison administrators that no liberal reform agenda nor prison litigation nor even radi-cal political organizing would successfully interrupt the comprehensive power of the southern prison plantation and its attendant racial and labor regime.

During the postwar era, Austin MacCormick had advised Alabama's and Louisiana's prison systems to look to Texas as the model for southern advance-ment. When Texas faced the threat of prisoner litigation and political organ-izing among prisoners, a similar predicament faced Louisiana's prison administrators at nearly the same moment. Both adopted the shared tactics of targeting the attorneys of prison litigants with fomenting rebellion. In the context of the "get tough" politics of the 1970s, both states also shared a deep racial anxiety over the post–civil rights election of Black politicians to state office. When carceral power was countered by constitutional claims for pris-oners' rights and challenged by the southern prison work strike, Louisiana and Texas responded similarly by claiming that liberal civil rights attorneys and Black political leaders were part of an extensive "criminal" plot to upend the southern prison labor regime. More to the point, both states shared sim-ilar patterns of corporal punishment and the abusive use of solitary to mute prisoner complaint and to charge politically organized prisoners as "crimi-nal terrorists" fomenting "rebellious plots." When deadly violence did erupt in Texas with the Carrasco hostage crisis of 1974, which was the nation's longest-running prison hostage situation, it was not directed by the prison-ers' rights movement, Black politics, or the political organizing of prisoners.

Chapter 7

The Aztlán Outlaw and Black Reform Politics

The Carrasco Hostage Crisis and the Collapse of Political Reform

On the same day that the Supreme Court decided *United States v. Nixon*, paving the way for President Richard Nixon's presidential resignation, what grabbed people's attention in Texas was the beginning of the nation's longest prison hostage siege, led by three Mexican American prisoners: Frederico "Fred" Gómez Carrasco, Rudolfo "Rudy" S. Dominguez, and Ignacio "Nacho" Cuevas.[1] Fred Carrasco, known by law enforcement as a nefarious southwest drug smuggler but celebrated within borderlands Chicana/o culture as a "modern Pancho Villa," had arranged through his powerful underworld connections to smuggle several guns into the prison.[2] As the 1:00 P.M. prison whistle sounded, Carrasco pulled from within his white prison uniform a concealed .38-caliber pistol. He ordered the other prisoners in the library to get out and then fired upon two guards attempting to storm the ramp, hitting one in the foot. Dominguez and Cuevas brandished guns of their own and slammed shut the doors of the library, sealing themselves inside with fifteen hostages: four prisoners and eleven prison employees, eight of them women.

Over the course of the next eleven days, Carrasco made a series of flamboyant demands. Through the prison library telephone, Carrasco gave interviews to reporters in Spanish as he communicated his discontent with the prison and his set of demands to the prison administration. His demands stressed his Chicano pachuco sensibility when he requested three tailor suits, three pair of Nunn-Bush shoes, ties, and cologne. In a more practical nod to militant self-defense, he demanded bulletproof vests, walkie-talkies, and bulletproof helmets constructed like iron masks. Finally, situating his embrace of cultural nationalism within a wider array of international radicalism, Carrasco then demanded that he and his comrades be given an armored car and have a plane waiting for them to provide safe passage to Cuba—only then would they return the remaining hostages.[3]

The Carrasco hostage crisis did not occur in a vacuum. Sensationalistic journalistic accounts covered this moment of prison violence for voyeuristic media consumption and presented Carrasco as a "heroin merchant," who forced his hostages to endure "eleven days of hell."[4] More recently, Chicano/a movement scholars have revisited Carrasco's story, critiquing Carrasco's acts of violence, while exploring how his narrative symbolized, in Montejano's words, "the aspirations, desires, regrets, and weaknesses of the working and lower classes."[5]

The Carrasco hostage crisis also offers a critical historical parallel to Reies Tijerina's 1967 raid of a New Mexico courthouse to demand land grant rights. On June 5, 1967, Tijerina led twenty armed members of the Chicana/o organization, La Alianza of Pueblos and Pobladores (Alliance of Towns and Settlers), to the Rio Arriba County Courthouse in Tierra Amarilla, New Mexico, to make a "citizens arrest" of the local district attorney, Alfonso Sánchez, for incarcerating eleven Aliancistas and failing to respect their First Amendment rights of freedom of assembly. Although Sánchez was not there when they arrived and the eleven Aliancistas had already been released (unbeknownst to Tijerina), the ensuing armed confrontation resulted in the shooting injuries of Eulogio Salazar, a jail guard, and Daniel Rivera, a sheriff's deputy, while Tijerina's Alianza escaped with two hostages. The historian Lorena Oropeza has argued that Tijerina effectively "repositioned Chicana/os racially by insisting on their indigenous ancestry and hybridized identity" within a "legacy of conquest," war, and internal colonization.[6] But Tijerina's courthouse raid should also be understood within a larger borderlands carceral framework that Tijerina attempted to invert by claiming that unjust jail incarceration and the denial of rights by law enforcement was the thing that should be named and widely known as a criminal act.[7]

Two years later, when Corky Gonzalez hosted the National Chicano Liberation Conference in Denver, the 1969 crafting of El Plan de Aztlán rejected whiteness altogether and declared all people of Mexican heritage as a single La Raza (the race and the people) who, on both sides of the border, had been separated by a "brutal 'gringo' invasion of our territories." As such, the Chicano generation definitely embraced a *sin fontera* (without border) framework that no longer "recongnize[d] the capacious frontiers on the bronze continent" that held people on both sides of the border captive to a false national division.[8]

Both the Alianza courthouse encounter with criminal justice and the development of El Plan drew upon a history of violent border confrontation with border police and El Rinches, the Texas Rangers, that stretched across time and borders. In the course of the eleven-day hostage prison crisis, Carrasco made a borderlands outlaw claim to Aztlán in a series of Spanish-language interviews where he told reporters that what they saw as a criminal hostage crisis was for him an open and armed rebellion against an unjust system where incarceration of Mexican Americans represented a systematic denial of Mexican American rights, heritage, and culture that rendered Mexican Americans just as devastated and colonized as had war and land occupation. As this chapter will show, Carrasco presented himself as an Aztlán borderlands cultural hero who exposed carceral violence through the only means he felt available to him, which was armed resistance and public confrontation rather than through the courts or political reform.

That same summer of 1974, however, was also the critical moment for newly elected Black and progressive politicians to use the state legislature to enact prison reform to dismantle the southern building tender system and to address state violence against prisoners of color. In 1972, Texas for the first time enacted single-member districts to elect member to the state house of representatives and senate, which resulted in the election of several minority candidates known as the People's Five. These newly elected state representatives made common cause with Black prisoners, who themselves had ties to civil rights and Black Power organizations. First initiated in 1972, by 1974 the Joint Prison Reform Committee, led by State Senators Chet Brooks and Mickey Leland, had managed to gain political traction in Austin as it prepared its final report for public release. This political reform effort was interrupted by the violence surrounding the Carrasco hostage crisis.

This chapter looks at Carrasco through the lens of competing agendas between Carrasco's presentation of himself as cultural outlaw icon to frustrated Chicana/os outside of prison and the other agenda of those within prison who had fought and worked for over a decade to build a prisoners' rights movement whose claim to civil rights was based not just on the U.S. Constitution but on showing prisoner humanity. The Carrasco hostage crisis therefore simultaneously intersected with three critical narratives—the borderlands outlaw and Chicano hero of Aztlán willing to take up arms against police brutality; the divided prison labor system that accorded power and privilege; and the prisoners' rights movement. When seen from the vantage point of the prisoners' rights movement and through prisoners' eyes, we also learn something new about what the prisoners themselves witnessed the day that the hostage crisis came to a calamitous end.

The Hope of Political Reform: The Joint Prison Reform Committee and Citizens Report

As Texas prison administrators apprehensively watched the news and correctional reports of Angola's struggle with the Black Panthers alongside their own struggles with Black militants, they increasingly feared that Attica's shadow was now cast south. Out of this growing discontent between keepers and kept, the members of the JCPR, particularly Mickey Leland, still held out hope that they could reach a political solution that might avert similar uprisings in Texas. Over the summer and fall of 1974, both the JCPR and the

Citizens' Advisory Committee composed their comprehensive reports that included over 160 recommendations for prison reform. The JCPR report, which the staff culled together from over one thousand pages of interim reports and hearings, provided a comprehensive overview of the TDC. It focused its many recommendations on three areas of prison reform: lack of medical care, the building tender system, and racial segregation.

JCPR members felt confident that the issue of medical care might elicit enough public empathy to help their reform recommendations gain passage. On medical care, the report found that the TDC's employment of prisoners as "nurses" pointed to the "glaring need for more doctors." "When one considers that two physicians are the only full-time physicians serving TDC's over 17,000 inmate population, one must seriously question the priorities of the TDC administration," the report concluded. JCPR staff director John Albach later testified about his dismay when he first learned that prison "nurses" performed operations on other fellow prisoners. "Very frankly, I had come out of an operating room that I had walked into and suddenly found out that there was an inmate on the operating table, an inmate giving the anesthetic and an inmate performing the surgery. I asked about it, because inmates had told us about it, but, frankly, I didn't believe that such a thing happened."[9] The prison's Dr. Astone confirmed to Albach that prisoners did indeed perform surgery and that the "convict doctor" who performed the surgery was the prisoner Applegate, who was a former truck driver who had learned to operate "by watching and eventually by doing. He had absolutely no formal medical training."[10] The report cited the use of "convict doctors" and the lack of health care as one of the most pressing issues for humane treatment.

The TDC treatment center for the mentally ill was another "glaring example" of inadequate care in which "tranquilizer and hypnotic drugs are used primarily to control prisoners, not to treat them."[11] The TDC had attempted to build a hospital for the mentally insane in the 1950s, but its effort failed to pass muster in the state legislature. As a result, the TDC housed the treatment center at the Walls prison, and it offered eighty-two single cells with 132 beds. A JCPR working paper reported that these prisoners "were frequently prescribed medications" that kept them heavily sedated. The medications typically included the mood-altering drugs Thorazine (100–200 mg), Mellaril, Artane (2–5 mg), chloral hydrate (500 mg), and Valium. Because the treatment center housed so few prisoners, the TDC also placed mentally ill prisoners in the protected custody wings of individual prisons, that is, the so-called sissy wings and punk wings. The JCPR working paper reported that a chief complaint among mentally disturbed prisoners was that housing them in the punk wing resulted in "disrespect to his manly pride" that left them with a permanent "homosexual jacket."[12] As a potential "cure" for homosexuality, the prison board had sanctioned the work of Dr. John Kinross-Wright, the associate director of the Houston State Psychiatric Institute, "to use 96 inmates in a research study relating to the effect of tranquilizing drugs on Homosexuality" in the hopes that tranquilizers would "produce a temporary and reversible effect on sex function."[13] The treatment center also "experimented" with a device called the neurotone machine, which was a Soviet-made device that delivered a mild form of electroshock therapy to patients. Another JCPR working paper noted that an "inmate nurse" operated the neurotone machine and that "he did not have a background in psychology and he basically taught himself how to the run the machine."

The JCPR's allegations about electric shock therapy stirred up the recent discovery that an Alabama prison warden had used electric shock therapy in domestic prison torture. At the Cummins prison farm in Arkansas, Warden Jim Burton had used a device called the "Tucker telephone" as a means to torture and discipline prisoners. The "Tucker telephone," according to an Arkansas State Police investigation, was "an electric generator taken from a ring type telephone, placed in sequence with two dry cell batteries, and attached to an undressed Inmate strapped to a treatment table . . . by means of electrode to a big toe and the second to the penis, at which time, a crank was turned sending an electric charge into the body of the inmate."[14] Such horrific findings in Arkansas led to the nation's first "totality of prison conditions" lawsuit, known as *Holt v. Sarver*, decided in 1970 and affirmed in 1971, which caused the federal court to declare the Arkansas state prison unconstitutional and to place the state prison system into federal receivership.[15] The JCPR's findings on the TDC's poor medical care thus reminded the media and state legislators that prison reform was urgently needed if Texas was to avoid the kind of court-ordered intervention that Arkansas experienced.

The JCPR authors, including Leland and Johnson, saw their role in prison reform as bringing civil rights and humanity to prisoners. Much of its focus on racial discrimination can be attributed to Leland and Johnson's ability to successfully communicate with prisoners of color, who were victims of mounting racial violence. Although the TDC claimed that it was already well on the way to racial integration within the prison system, the JCPR concluded that more than 56 percent of all prisoners lived in racially segregated living units. The report noted that the degree of racial segregation varied on each unit as follows: Ramsey II (100 percent), Central (97 percent), Clemens (93 percent), Darrington (89 percent), Eastham (55 percent), Jester I (86 percent), Ferguson (82 percent), Jester II (74 percent), Retrieve (74 percent), and Ramsey I (53 percent).[16] Moreover, the JCPR stressed that field work assignments were entirely segregated and that "even in a wing which is racially and ethnically mixed, inmates who share a cell are almost always of the same race or ethnic background." The JCPR also cited that the TDC employed a largely white security staff, which the committee viewed as a detriment to race relations within the prison. The final report cited the racially discriminatory practices of low-level correctional officers as "especially critical" since prison guards "directly shape the inmates' environment." The report also found the highest levels of TDC officials as complicit in racial discrimination. "Rather than making an aggressive effort to stop discrimination and segregation at the unit level, the Department appears to tacitly support those practices. No real effort has been made to force unit Wardens to conform with the requirement of law or TDC policy." Moreover, the JCPR noted that while over 60 percent of the prison population was either African American or Latino, there were no Black or Mexican American chaplains. Eight of the system's sixteen chaplains were Baptist, and there was no imam to serve the needs of the Muslim community.

Estelle countered the JCPR's critique of racial segregation by arguing that the prisoners themselves were the source of resistance to racial integration. "We have Black Muslims who insist upon staying together," Estelle told the press. "If we mixed them with other inmates, we could expect trouble. We could also expect trouble if we put some whites with Blacks. But we do not practice racial discrimination." Warden Bobby Morgan, of Ferguson, similarly told reporters that the JCPR did not understand the stark racial reality of segregated prison life: "Inmates tend to segregate themselves by races during their free time." Upon the report's public release, an anonymous prison guard was quoted in the *Dallas Morning News* with the crude admission that summed up the TDC's response to charges of racial discrimination: "We don't practice discrimination here. We treat niggers just like whites."[17]

The JCPR also understood that racial violence and discrimination within the prison system was intricately linked to the building tender system. "Some wardens use racial segregation as another mode of punishment," the report concluded. "An inmate of one race was assigned to live in a wing with inmates all of another race. This was done to a number of so-called 'writ writers' as punishment. There is no excuse for this practice." The report also understood that the TDC's continued use of building tenders contradicted the 1974 63rd Legislature's House Bill 1056 that outlawed the use of supervisory prisoners. The report concluded that during the two-year study the staff "was told repeatedly that BTs are used to enforce discipline and to carry out physical punishment" and that "the staff has seen too many 'incident reports' . . . to believe that these allegations are unfounded."[18] The report acknowledged that "there are not an adequate number of TDC guards to properly supervise TDC's large prison population without considerable reliance on building tenders" and that the "complete elimination of the 'BT' system will require determination on the part of TDC to comply with the law and end the brutal system it sponsors." It would also require that the state legislature approve a large sum to hire new guards to replace the building tenders. The JCPR co-chair Leland expressed his desire that the prison reform consider the humanity of prisoners in its reevaluation of the TDC:

> We're still living in the dark ages, whether we want to accept it or not. Even though we talk about idealistic things like rehabilitation or correction, we still are faced with the fact that the public is grossly ignorant of the fact that the inmate population—even though its committed fouls against the society we live in—is still made up of human beings. We fail to treat them as human beings. I for one feel that all people, regardless of the mistakes they make in life, should at least be given the right to humane treatment.[19]

The Citizens' Advisory Committee report was similarly concerned with racial discrimination, poor health care, and the brutality of the building tender system. The report, however, provided a far sharper critique that was aimed against the TDC's agribusiness model and the clustering of prisons into a single geographic and rural area. Under Charlie Sullivan's guidance, the committee conducted a nine-month study of the TDC in which they "encountered substantial TDC opposition" from a "closed system, hidden from public view."[20] Despite the difficulties in investigating such a guarded prison environment, the committee made more than 150 recommendations in a 280-page report.

The committee criticized the state's prison system as "a victim of its own history" in which "large, rural prison farms, concentrated in a single part of the state" offered only "a single kind of maximum security correctional model." Moreover, the TDC used "unpaid prisoner labor" to farm "tens of thousands of acres of rich east Texas land" that resulted in no useful vocational training for prisoners in an increasingly urban and industrialized world. "For too many, manual field labor is the only work experience ever obtained in their stay at TDC," the report noted. The report concluded, "It is difficult to see how the ability to do field work equips ex-prisoners to compete for jobs in the urban labor markets to which they will return."[21]

The Citizens' Advisory Committee report argued that while the TDC may have become efficient since the 1948 reforms, it was not modern because it was inhumane and too focused on running an agribusiness rather than offering rehabilitation. The particular target of the report's ire was the Coffield prison. Although Coffield was the first TDC prison to utilize a modern wheel-spoke design, the prison followed the traditional East Texas agribusiness model. The TDC built the new prison near Huntsville on over 18,000 acres of land with a massive prisoner capacity of 4,000 and with the unusually large price tag of $20 million. The committee recommended a moratorium on construction of a "high-cost, traditional, rural prison farm facilities" that "dramatically restricts TDC's ability to recruit and hold able and diversified staff, especially minorities."[22]

To replace agribusiness prisons, the committee recommended "community corrections," by which it meant a "broad, modern corrections program" providing "diversified alternatives" such as probation, parole, halfway houses, and correctional centers located in local communities. It argued that "keeping the offenders in or near the community from which they come will provide a minimum of disruption of family life" and thereby "avoid the negative impact of massive institutionalization." Other recommendations from both the JCPR and the Citizens' Advisory Committee report included ending racial segregation, hiring employees of color, allowing prisoners (particularly African Americans) to grow their hair as they pleased, payment of wages to prisoners, a grievance system for prisoners, increased mail and visitation privileges, experimentation with conjugal visits, a provision for impartial disciplinary committees and for prisoner appeals, abolition of solitary confinement in its present "inherently cruel and debilitating" form, and an end to "corporal punishment, beatings, physical threats, and intimidation" at the hands of building tenders.[23] As Leland remarked to the press, what both committees hoped to achieve was to effectively "urbanize" the prison system. "We find that even though our system compares favorably to the other systems throughout the country," Leland reminded the press, "we're falling far short of being a correctional institution. We're falling far short of really doing the things that are necessary to return the inmate population back to the streets of our cities . . . and making them responsible citizens."[24]

The Citizens' Advisory Committee's emphasis on parole and "community corrections" had some support within the highest levels of the TDC. Indeed, the prison director Jim Estelle had repeatedly told the press that at least 40 percent of the 17,000 prisoner population did not need to remain in prison and that they could instead be paroled or transferred to a community-corrections model. "Communities and the state together have got to seek some alternatives to imprisonment," Estelle told the local press. He believed that prisons should be reserved only for those offenders whom the TDC deemed violent and dangerous to the community. "When we use them [prisons] for anything else, I think we are walking down a road of social and economic bankruptcy," Estelle declared.[25] Estelle continued to emphasize the TDC work tradition, but he believed that a rising prison population made a work-release system for prisoners increasingly necessary. "I am a believer in a system of restitution in which a convicted person has to work to repay the money he stole or embezzled. More prisoners should stay in local prisons and work at jobs in the community to make restitution."[26] Estelle had not abandoned his commitment to the control penology and agribusiness model in the East Texas prison system, but he was troubled by the growing prison population and interested in the possibility of experimenting with community corrections for prisoners with minimal criminal and behavioral records.

Initial press accounts and editorials, particularly those from large city papers, also responded positively to the committees' ideas. An editorial in the *Dallas Morning News* highlighted the stark difference between the committees' vision for prisons and the TDC's current management practices. "Texans must decide what they want their prison system to do: Punish, rehabilitate or both. And then they must either be prepared to support the system adequately or be prepared to live with the consequences."[27] The *Houston Post*, on the other hand, placed the Citizens' Advisory report in the broader historical trajectory and irony of postwar prison reform. "The irony of the citizens' committee report is that the TDC is itself the product of reform efforts. The Texas system has served as the model for other penal systems and has been widely praised for its efficiency and progressiveness. Now the advisory panel warns that those gains are jeopardized if still more reforms are not forthcoming." The *Houston Post* editorial admitted that some might see the recommendations as "coddling criminals." "But the most effective penology is that which returns the largest number of lawbreakers to society as productive, law-abiding citizens," the newspaper editorialized. "The legislature should not ignore the work of the citizens' advisory committee on prison reform."[28]

Others, however, condemned the JCPR and the Citizens' Advisory Committee reports. State Senator Walter "Mad Dog" Mengden, a disaffected JCPR committee member, argued that the recommendations, if implemented, "would cause the greatest crime wave in the history of the world because every person would have a tremendous incentive to want to go to prison in order that he could enjoy all the tremendous benefits in it." Calling himself a "strong believer in law and order," Mengden promised to do all in his power to see that many of the recommendations were not implemented. Mengden vituperatively charged, "The [JCPR] staff consisted of the most grotesque collection of radical activists ever put together under one roof east of Berkeley."[29] Mengden believed that the JCPR staff "displayed a profound sympathy for the criminal element and intense hatred for the (TDC)" and that the staff had "acted as cheerleaders for the convicted murderers, rapists, burglars, and armed robbers and showed no interest in protecting society from such individuals." Indeed, during the course of the year-long legislative investigation, the JCPR dismissed two staff members for "extremely strong emotional bias." The JCPR fired staff member Erasmo Andrade for being too sympathetic to the prisoners, and it similarly discharged staff member Wayne Oakes for being too quick to defend the TDC. JCPR committee staff director Albach felt that Andrade "was completely and totally blinded by his bias against TDC" and that "he was unable to discern the difference between what the inmates told him and what actually existed."[30] The cochair Leland later agreed that "Mr. Andrade appeared to be too pro-inmate" and that he "expressed an extreme support of the inmate population, those who appeared to be more dissident than objective." On the other hand, Leland also found that "Mr. Oaks tended to support almost wholeheartedly . . . the position of the Texas Department of Corrections."[31]

Although Leland later admitted that the committee staff suffered from bias on both sides, his comments to the press at the time of the report's release demonstrated his frustration with Mengden's allegations. Leland feared that public infighting on the JCPR committee might hurt the political chances for legitimate reform. "Senator Mengden is joking or he has lost his mind, for this was indeed an act of lunacy," Leland charged to the press. In his press conference, Leland claimed that Mengden had never once during the committee's many months of study "raised a point of disagreement over any staff member" and that the senator was maliciously "trying to destroy all our efforts." Leland issued a public challenge against such charges: "I defy Walter Mengden to prove any of his foul allegations and personal attacks against any member of our staff." Leland was particularly angered by Mengden's opposition to a JCPR recommendation that called for a ban on prison discrimination against prisoners on the basis of "political beliefs." Mengden countered by saying that there were certain prisoners preaching and organizing "revolution." When the committee questioned the proposed ban, Leland expressed disgust that it would "appease a reactionary like Walter Mengden" by tossing overboard "the basic American principles of democracy." Leland and Mengden also clashed over how to interpret the importance of Muslims in prisons. "The staff made a great deal of the fact that the Black Muslims form the largest religious group in the TDC," said Mengden. "I think that's sort of interesting when you compare that with the low percentage that Black Muslims have in society as a whole." Mengden thus hinted at a belief that race, Islam, and criminal activity were linked. Mickey Leland dismissed such statements as "ludicrous and ridiculous."[32]

The JCPR recommendations to pay prisoners a wage and to legislate the hiring of minority prison guards were also contentious issues. Mengden sharply criticized the JCPR recommendation that prisoners earn a small wage. "Prisoners are not working for a living—they are working as part of their punishment. Criminals are in prison for punishment," Mengden declared. David D. Allen, a former member of the Texas Board of Corrections and a member of the Citizens' Advisory Committee, made common cause with Mengden's critique. Allen charged that the citizens' report was "totally devoid of any recommendation relating to the tremendous progress" and the "good work" of Texas prisons over the past thirty years. Allen was particularly vocal over the report's "ridiculous and self defeating" recommendation that the TDC hire minority employees rather than hiring "qualified people."[33]

In light of these battles, the press wondered whether the "thinly veiled antagonism between state prison officials and the legislature's prison reformers" would result in any lasting legislation. The *Sunday Express News* editorialized that such open antagonism and perpetual intransigence "shows that the men in charge of our prisons believe that prison reform represents a direct, almost personal affront to themselves."[34] Some members of the Citizens' Advisory Committee also expressed their frustration with the TDC's intransigence and efforts to block the committee's desire for surprise prison inspections. "It said in the beginning that if we had to give prior notice [of visits], we wouldn't play. We said if we had to do that, we couldn't DO A GODDAM THING. I'm outraged," declared an unnamed University of Texas law professor and committee member.[35] On the other hand, the *Express News* editorial suspected that "much of the responsibility rests with the reform movement itself. The reformers have seriously crippled themselves with the adversary relationship they helped to create between their movement and the established prison system."[36] Attacked by journalists and betrayed by dissenting committee members, some members of the committee complained that they had been "treated like orphans all along" and that they should express "our resentment and anger at what's happening."[37] What ultimately doomed prison reform, however, was the specter of carceral violence.

Borderlands Outlaw: The Carrasco Transcript of Aztlán Resistance

Four months before the committees released their reports, the public was fixated on the Carrasco prison hostage crisis. The leader, Fred Carrasco, had a long storied history as a major narcotics trafficker and daring prison escapee across the Mexican and U.S. border. Raised in Victoria Courts just outside of San Antonio, Carrasco joined the local gang and experienced running gun battles with rival gangs, until he went to prison for the first time in 1958 at the age of only nineteen for having shot and killed a rival teenager. As a borderlands *narco-traficante*, Carrasco had prison sentences in both Texas and

Mexico, and he had become famous for his flamboyant prison escape in Guadalajara, when he stole a prison laundry truck to flee the prison. Carrasco's life revolved in and out of prisons, having served additional sentences in the federal reformatory at El Reno, Oklahoma; the federal penitentiary in Leavenworth, Kansas; and the federal penitentiary in Terre Haute, Indiana. On July 22, 1973, Carrasco's infamy came to a violent apogee when he was involved in a shootout with a dozen plainclothes officers and Texas Rangers at the Tejas motel in San Antonio. The police shootout and his subsequent apprehension led to a sensational trial in which the state convicted him on January 9, 1973, for assault with intent to murder.

Given a life sentence, Carrasco arrived in the TDC as a high-profile prisoner, but rather than place him at the bottom of the hierarchical labor regime as a field worker, he was instead housed at Huntsville's flagship Walls penitentiary. The media dubbed Carrasco the head of the "Mexican Mafia," an exaggerated Anglo construction that did not understand the role of the Mexican Mafia as a California prison gang that had not yet extended into Texas. Within the TDC, the staff psychiatrists conducted a psychological profile of Carrasco that diagnosed Carrasco as a "manipulative sociopath." The TDC "psychological summary" found that Carrasco possessed "high intelligence, cunningness, and total disregard for existing social and moral values." The report claimed that Carrasco "had been involved in the murders of 50 people" and that he "is a very smooth and polished individual who uses his confidence, graciousness, and gentlemanly manner to conceal his less desirable social traits." The psychological summary concluded that Carrasco was a "masterful manipulator of people" and "psychopathic to an extreme degree."[38]

But among Chicana/o communities, particularly those familiar with patterns of abusive policing along the borderlands, Carrasco symbolized the essence of Eric Hobsbawm's formulation of the "social bandit."[39] As a borderlands smuggler, Carrasco's smuggling was seen as a defiant challenge to the power of Texas Rangers and the Border Patrol to police what the historian Kelly Lytle Hernández has called "*Mexicano* mobility."[40] Upon his arrival at the Walls, Carrasco used his street influence to build a following among some Mexican American prisoners, although he had no connection to the budding interracial prisoners' rights movement. Carrasco convinced Dominguez and Cuevas to join in his plot to smuggle arms, hold hostages, and attempt a daring escape. On July 24, 1973, Carrasco, Dominguez, and Cuevas used their positions in the Windham School district library at the Walls unit to hold eleven hostages at gunpoint for an eleven-day hostage crisis that captured the state's attention.[41]

During the eleven-day standoff, Carrasco built upon his already legendary desperado status with a flurry of phone interviews where he made a series of outlandish demands that conveyed to the public that Carrasco was a defiant Chicano nationalist outlaw. Carrasco's initial demands included the practical defense implements of helmets for protection, walkie-talkie radios for communication, and M-16 rifles and bulletproof vests. But true to the pachuco's sardonic defiance, Carrasco also mocked the TDC's power and authority when he flamboyantly insisted upon "three tailored suits, three pairs of Nunn-Bush shoes, three shirts and ties, cologne and toothbrushes." He also had seventeen steak dinners, cooked medium, served with baked potatoes and tossed salad for $78.75, delivered from La Sire, "one of the city's finer restaurants."[42] The hostage negotiations were a flurry of phone calls where Carrasco engaged in defiant conversations with Ruben Montemayor, his attorney, and the TDC's chief hostage negotiator, as well as with Director Estelle and Governor Dolph Briscoe. At one point Carrasco told Estelle that he can "shove it up their ass" and called Briscoe "a redneck." Carrasco then subsequently cracked a joke when a reporter asked if Carrasco really had the audacity to call the governor such names, to which Carrasco responded, "I didn't call Briscoe a redneck, he is one. And a chewing tobacco redneck."[43] Carrasco was thoroughly bilingual and spoke English fluently, but he made the strategic choice in his conversation with the governor to speak only in Spanish and to have his attorney Ruben Montemayor translate for him. In his first emergency telephone conversation with the governor, Carrasco explained that he did "not want to eliminate the lives of these people that we have as hostages" but that if his demands weren't met, "you obligate us to pass them through fire."[44] In the background of that conversation, the hostages' cries for help included a flurry of frantic pleas: "Please, we have children," "We are only human beings, can't you help," "We only have a few minutes to live."

But there are two transcripts within the Carrasco prison crisis. The first is the English narrative between Carrasco and the TDC, and between the TDC and the hostages. That transcript is filled with terror, and Carrasco comes across as dangerous and morbidly glib, insulting the TDC and authority wherever he can and often stating that he expects to die. Then, there is the Spanish-language transcript, which reads quite differently. Throughout the hostage crisis, Carrasco expressed his cultural kinship to other Mexicanos by speaking directly to them in Spanish-language media interviews. In one conversation, a bilingual reporter offered to give the interview in both English and Spanish so that he could spread the reporting to both English- and Spanish-speaking news outlets. Carrasco, however, adamantly refused, stating that he had "about 15 names of reporters that I will speak in English with" and that he wanted to keep the interview in Spanish because "I would like Mexicans to know why I did it and all of that."[45] In another example, he told the reporter Amador Rodriguez that he preferred to speak in Spanish, to which Rodriguez agreed, because "I'd like our race [*nuestra raza*] to also know what's the situation."[46] Carrasco frequently conveyed that he had "acted as a man" and with honor by not touching any of the women hostages. "We have treated them well," he told a reporter in Spanish, "treated them with respect, like the women they are. We haven't laid a hand on them, we haven't mistreated them at all. Because we, as Mexicans, know how to respect the women." In another conversation he emphasized how he understood his masculine honor through his relationship to La Raza and Mexican *sangre* (blood). "If it had been another race that took over and held women hostages, they would've abused/assaulted these women. . . . But we have behaved like men. It hasn't even crossed our minds. Because we have honor. The blood that runs through our veins, doesn't allow us to do such things, we respect women too much."[47]

Throughout the many conversations with Spanish-speaking reporters, Carrasco and his coconspirators consistently raised their connection to La Raza and indicated that they behaved with masculine honor because they all shared "Mexican blood." For instance, Cuevas told one reporter he should not worry whether they had enough to eat, because "the Mexican, we have 'Indian blood' [*sangre india*], you may not understand. The Mexican can last. . . . The Mexican is not like whitey who wants to eat the second the clock hits noon."[48] Even their prisoner hostages when speaking to family and reporters in Spanish stressed that they felt safe in their shared Mexicano heritage with Carrasco. For example, the prisoner hostage Vera pointed out in one conversation: "Todos somos Mexicanos. El Mexicano siempre a sido pobre. Somos pobre Mexicanos" ("We are all Mexicans. The Mexican was born poor. We are poor Mexicans.").[49] To appeal to the hostage takers' sense of Aztlán kinship *sin fontera*, the attorney Montemayor stressed to Carrasco that if I was the one deciding [about meeting the demands], you know what my decision would be. I'm Mexican too [Yo soy Mexicano tambien]. My father came from Monterray. . . . Mexican blood runs through my veins. [Mi padre vino de Monterrey . . . Me corre la sangre Mexicana]."[50]

From the very beginning of the negotiations, Carrasco presented himself within a Chicano and wider Aztlán nationalist framework. Carrasco remarked to a reporter that ""I know what kind of system we have here in the United States" and that "I am a Mexican and I'd rather die than face humiliation"—although he did not elaborate, his words resonated with the Chicano and Mexicano critique against U.S. Anglo hegemony along the borderlands. In return for some of the hostages, Carrasco demanded an armored car and safe passage to Cuba. When asked by a reporter if he knew Fidel Castro and why he had chosen Cuba, Carrasco responded, "No, I do not know

Castro. I read about the man, he suffered a lot in his life, and I believe we would have a mutual feeling, a mutual experience and he would sympathize with me." To another reporter's question on why he thought Castro would allow him refuge in Cuba, Carrasco offered a somewhat sardonic response: "I read a lot about Mr. Castro's rise to power, and I know that he had a hard time, he suffered a lot, and I believe that if I was to ask for refuge, he would lend a hand."[51]

While Carrasco's English-language interviews focused more on the hostages and the demands, he saved his sharp critique of the TDC for those interviews only in Spanish. Carrasco pointed to the severe racial imbalance in the guard structure that led to the unequal treatment of Mexican Americans as yet another reason for his use of force in the hostage situation. Carrasco noted that at the Walls there were "2,000 [total] convicts. About 400 Mexicans. And about 4 or 6 guards (and I'm exaggerating) Mexican guards. Of these 6, one is a sergeant. That says it all. . . . So you grab your conclusions from there. If one rebels for the sake of it or out of necessity."[52] Just as Tijerina's 1967 courthouse raid attempted an inverse carceral logic that the DA was actually the criminal, Carrasco also offered a similar juxtaposition that it was the TDC that committed everyday crimes against prisoners. "The ones committing crimes are the ones running the place," he said angrily, "the fucking director, Estelle and all those snakes, you know. Against human rights. The blame lays with Estelle." In Carrasco's mind, his incarceration in Huntsville was an intrinsic part of internal colonization and tied to the Mexicans' loss of their land, heritage, and citizenship. "You know all these people, they stole everything," Carrasco reminded the Spanish press. "Everything. Texas and California, it was all ours, all the ranches, everything. They left them poor, people are doing nothing but suffering. So now it is their turn, see how they like it. These gringos took the ranches and called themselves pioneers. But they weren't pioneers, they were thieves."[53]

In Spanish only, Carrasco frequently expressed La Raza sentiment and anger over the treatment of Mexican American prisoners as opposed to the better treatment to the "favored." "In the 200 something years this prison has existed," Carrasco defiantly declared, "there has never been anything for the Mexican. Those that commit crimes, I'm not saying they should be given a medal. I understand that punishment is punishment. But when they take everything away from you and give to some, it's not just."[54] Importantly, Carrasco critiqued the prison as a space that offered white privilege. Carrasco clarified to one reporter how prison privilege operated: "When I say 'the considered' I refer to people within the penitentiary [who] are called 'relajes' [the relaxed or the privileged]. This people, they have good jobs, privileges."[55] Carrasco further explained, "We haven't had representatives from our language. I'll tell you something. Where we are, we don't have Mexican music. We don't have discs, if we do they are contraband. Well, those that are favored do. . . . We don't have any culture. . . . Listen, they take away food, they take away women, they take away our liberty, they take away our culture, listen, it'd be better to be killed. Understand?"[56] His reference to the "favored," publicized to Mexican Americans the stark truth that white privilege and power reigned even within the despised space of the prison.

Although not a field laborer, Carrasco had clearly heard stories from other prisoners, and he consciously chose to publicly name prison labor as both racial control and carceral violence. "These people [TDC] are willing to chase you with a horse and kick you, and you have to take off your hat and say 'yes boss, no boss.' Doesn't matter the race. . . . They treat us like we are nothing." Carrasco found some amusement in the TDC's fear of his kind of prison hostage rebellion, which he believed was the only available path when compared to the resistance of the prison work strike. "So now they are bothered, there were rebellion among 3 men," he told an interviewer, with some sense of irony. But with emphasis, he pointed out that his actions "were NOT [work] strikes. If it were a strike, they just come with bats, sticks and hit them over the head. They do what they want." In light of the carceral labor regime's comprehensive and violent power, Carrasco believed that work strikes would not accomplish prison reform, so he chose instead the path of taking up arms and creating a hostage crisis.

Despite his disdain for white privilege in prison through the building tender system, it is critical to note that Carrasco did not see himself as a member of the interracial prisoners' rights alliance. Quite likely, he may not even have known about their existence. For one thing, his placement at the Walls kept him from the field labor, which was the amalgam of prisoner oppression and resistance. As the prison that had fewer field laborers and fewer African Americans and Mexican Americans, the building tenders at the Walls were known to rely less on brutality to enforce labor discipline and racial control than at the tougher field prison plantations at Ellis, Eastham, Ramsey I and II, and Retrieve. In the English interviews, Carrasco never mentioned the prisoners' rights movement at all. In the Spanish interviews, he never mentioned Cruz or any of Jalet's Mexican American clients, and he mentioned the JCPR's legislative campaign only once to scoff at what he thought was the false allure of liberal reform that lacked "action."

> Now, I'm not saying I'm for reform or anything like that, because I didn't think I'd be here this long. My thing was to recover and get out. I'm leaving dead, but I'm leaving. So if I say this [referring to BTs and white prison privilege], it's because I hear it. People here say: "What are we

'gonna do'?" "What is the committee for penal reform doing?" "What is [unintelligible, possibly Leland] person doing?" And in the end, no one does anything. All they do is pure talk. Talk and talk. Nothing else."[57]

While Carrasco never mentions the prisoners struggling for rights or ever aligns himself with Cruz and Jalet's clients, he does specifically name the prison as a critical site of cultural repression against Mexican Americans. He explained that his rebellion was not just an act of crime but an act of defiance against a system that he saw as unjust and inhumane to an entire group of people. "And if we have rebelled," Carrasco explained, "we have rebelled for a reason. I don't want you to think we are just animals, that we do this for no reason. No sir. It's that we were treated unjustly and we have our reasons for doing this."[58]

In a twist of tragic irony, while the TDC publicly aired their fear that activist attorneys might smuggle guns to prisoners, the real threat came from the TDC's own insistence on maintaining a racially hierarchical and subordinate trusty system. Lawrence James Hall, an African American prisoner in the TDC on a life sentence, smuggled the guns to Carrasco by using his position as Assistant Director Alton Akins's houseboy. Prison officials frequently "lived off the state," as prisoners put it, by eating food from the prison commissary. Houseboys delivered the food without oversight from the prison commissary to the homes of prison officials. In the summer of 1974, Carrasco's out-of-prison operative Benito G. Alonzo pressed Hall into delivering the guns by making threats to expose Hall and have him lose his valued trusty status as a houseboy.

Under threat of exposure and with an additional threat made against his family members, Hall agreed. He packed rounds of ammunition in a pair of drained peach cans, placed the .38 in a rotted ham, and hid the two .357s in meat wrappers. Once at the gate, Hall told the attending guard that Assistant Director Atkins was returning the spoiled meat to the commissary, and he passed by the guard without arousing suspicion. Carrasco's reliance on a highly placed houseboy to deliver arms into the prison shows the ways in which these African American prisoners were anything but subservient to a trusty system geared toward instilling racial subordination. It also demonstrates that the real threat for smuggling arms to prisoners came not through activist attorneys but through the TDC's overreliance on a trusty system that depended on racially subordinate traditions of domestic service.[59]

On August 3, 1974, the Carrasco hostage crisis ended in tragedy. Direct telephone negotiations between Carrasco and Governor Briscoe, Director Estelle, Warden H. H. Husbands, and Carrasco's attorney, Montemayor, had continued throughout the eleven-day crisis and siege. Outside the Walls library, state police cars lined the street, Texas Rangers were positioned with high-powered rifles in strategic positions, TDC guards in full riot gear lay in wait, and a police helicopter circled anxiously overhead. The prisoners in the general population were kept in complete lockdown, held in their cells all day, and given hand-delivered brown-bag lunches. The tension at the Walls was palpable. In the course of the negotiations, Carrasco had demanded nothing less than his freedom. Through an interpreter, Estelle and Governor Briscoe gave in to the demand that they deliver an armored truck so that Carrasco and his fellow prisoner coconspirators could escape. Carrasco, Dominguez, and Cuevas, meanwhile, allowed two of the hostages to be freed as a sign of good faith. To get safely from the prison in the armored truck, the prisoners built a rolling shield that was constructed with portable blackboards and a thick set of law books that were draped by Mexican flags torn out of library books. The three moved down the library's ramp at 9:30 P.M. with eight of the remaining hostages tied to the makeshift shield.

Estelle and Governor Briscoe had no intention of allowing the hostage takers to escape. The TDC planned to use fire hoses with two thousand feet of highly pressurized water to press the hostages down to the ground while a thirteen-man team of Texas Rangers and a dozen police officers subdued Cuervas, Carrasco, and Dominguez. Inside the shield with the three prisoners were four hostages, three female librarians handcuffed to the prisoners and Father Joseph O'Brien, the prison's Roman Catholic priest. As the prisoners huddled behind their makeshift shield and wore welded steel masks, TDC guards turned the high-powered water cannons on the prisoners. Gunfire erupted, although from what quarter, whether from Rangers or prisoners, remains unclear.[60] In the ensuing firefight, the hostages Elizabeth Y. Beseda, who taught reading and math at the prison, and Julia C. Stanley, a prison librarian, were shot and killed while Father O'Brien sustained a critical gunshot wound. In a blaze of gunfire and mayhem, Carrasco and Dominguez were also shot and killed. Unhurt behind the shield were Novella Pollard, a hostage, and Cuevas.[61] In one of his last telephone conversations, Carrasco knew that he wasn't likely to leave the TDC alive. He instructed Montemayor to have his body cremated and to take care of his wife. His final request was that Montemayor tell his wife the following: "I died like a man and that I died with honor and with her and my children on my mind. She already knows that she was the only woman that I came to respect and love with all my heart."[62]

The press widely covered the Carrasco hostage crisis and its tragic conclusion. The Associated Press member newspapers voted the story as the number one newspaper item for 1974.[63] Occurring just six days before President Nixon's departure from office because of the Watergate scandal, the news of the Carrasco hostage crisis had crowded the front pages of the Texas press and made Nixon's untimely demise the second-class news story. The press portrayed Carrasco as a villainous murderer, a capricious drug lord, and a man without honor who killed two innocent women in a suicidal blaze. In Chicana/o folklore, however, Carrasco's confrontation with the law made him a cultural hero to some, and his story joined the *corrido* folklore tradition. Corrido folklore celebrated the manly honor of those who confronted the *rinches* [Texas Rangers], even if that confrontation ended in death. Carrasco's tale inspired a series of well-known corridos that celebrated Carrasco's masculine honor and his fatal fight against the overwhelming power of the state. The corridos cited Carrasco's promise during the hostage negotiations that "I can guarantee you that if I die, I die with honor."[64] Indeed, Carrasco's death inspired nearly a dozen corridos narratives.[65] Over the subsequent decade the many corridos written about Carrasco's defiance constituted what the Chicana/o literary scholar B.V. Olguín called "a palimpsest and floating signifier in competing Chicana/o and White narratives."[66] The poem by Richardo Sánchez, for instance, powerfully conveys Olguín's analysis of *la pinta* (prisoner) resistance: "I joyfully did laugh / to hear that he'd demanded / a pair of Stacey Adams / and good suits from the streets, / he made us realize / that he would die in freedom and not in pinto shoes / nor wearing prison whites."[67] In the Chicano press, articles with titles such as "Reflections on Chicano Folkheroes" and "Frederico Gómez Carraso—a Hero or a Criminal?" raised Carrasco to mythical status alongside the pantheon of Anglo hero worship of other violent men. "The American people have made folk heroes out of such people as Davy Crockett, James Bowie, Jesse James, and Billy the Kid. It is probable that Frederico Gómez Carrasco will join Juan Cortina, Joaquin Murieta, and Gregorio Cortez in the pantheon of Mexican American folk heroes."[68]

Among the prisoners, however, Carrasco's defiance may have signaled symbolic la pinta resistance, but his actual lived experience within the TDC was quite apart from the prisoners' rights movement. Housed at the Walls penitentiary, Carrasco was not subjected to the slave-like conditions of field labor; nor was he in a prison that had many of the prominent writ writers or Black political organizers. During the many hours of negotiations that were in English with the TDC and reporters, Carrasco did not signal that he was directly allied with or even aware of prisoners' rights advocates like Fred Cruz. But when speaking in Spanish to local Chicano reporters, Carrasco revealed more awareness of southern prison abuse, particularly that Mexican Americans were denied what favored and privileged white prisoners regularly received. Still, one newspaper reporter traveled to a popular dive bar on the west side of San Antonio's Guadalupe Street that former prisoners would frequent so that he could interview them. One prisoner shared his frustration that Carrasco had not raised the matter of prisoners' rights and prison conditions: "His complaint is not against the prison system, how it can be reformed or against conditions. He just wants out and will use other inmates if he has to." Moreover, Carrasco held as hostages the Chicano prisoners Martin Quiroz (twenty-six), Florencio Vera (twenty-nine), and Henry Escamilla (forty). In an interview with a Chicano San Antonio reporter, Quiroz confided to him: "You are a Chicano, like me. Chicanos here have a real hard time with the officials. I am afraid when this is over, if this is over, if Carrasco was going to let us go, I want some kind of assurance from the news media that those people [prison officials] will not take this out on us."

Nonetheless, Carrasco's death raised many doubts and furthered the narrative that Texas prisons constitute state violence and brutality without accountability. Huntsville's medical examiner, J. W. Beeler, claimed that Carrasco and Dominguez shot themselves after shooting and killing the two hostages. The Harris County Medical Examiner's Office determined that Carrasco was killed by a single magnum-class pistol shot that was fired from six inches to a foot away and that the bullet had entered his right temple and exited the rear of his skull. But upon examination, Beeler confessed to the press: "Your guess is as good as mine as to who fired that shot."[69] In order to shoot himself, Carrasco would have had to remove his steel helmet in the middle of being blasted by water hoses and caught in the crossfire of a gunfight. However, both the Texas Civil Liberties Union and John Albach, the staff director of the JCPR, received a letter from a prisoner that claimed that two other prisoners witnessed prison guards shooting the wounded Carrasco and Dominguez twice each in the head at point-blank range.[70] Frank X. Leahy, one of the writ-writing prisoners at the Walls, relayed a discussion to Senator Oscar H. Mauzy of three prisoner witnesses who claimed that Carrasco was allegedly killed by Ranger Captain G. W. Burk at point-blank range after the shooting had already occurred.

> Senator, I'm typing rather rapidly trying to simply get my thoughts on paper, exactly as these things were related to me. . . . Now it is not known—probably never will be, whether Carrasco and Dominguez were dead after the initial shooting, but—this Ranger Captain G.W. Banks ran up—Carrasco was laying on his back—the helmet still on, and kicked his helmet off, then at point blank range blew the top of Carrasco's head with his own (Capt. Burk) .357 magnum. He then turned and kicked Dominguez helmet off and blew the side of his head off with the same .357 magnum—and he then turned to where Ignacio Cuevas (the

survivor) lay, and aimed his pistol at him. By this time, however, two medical men were bending over Cuevas.

Such "convict stories" were typically dismissed out of hand, however, and the investigation sided with the official Ranger report that the hostage-taking prisoners were killed during the initial firefight. But what gave the letter from white writ writer Frank X. Leahy some credence was that it was written immediately after the incident, before the media announced who had died and who had survived during the hostage crisis. Moreover, many prisoners questioned why someone with Carrasco's violent and notorious record was placed at the Walls, which was reserved for prisoners with good records. Prisoners also wondered why a known drug kingpin with a long record of incarceration was given such a soft job at the Walls library.[71] The question of how the guns were smuggled into the prison was also not solved until September 1974 when Alonzo, captured on a drug charge, confessed to using the houseboy Hall to get the guns into Carrasco's hands.[72] Alonzo's confession was only gained after "a pair of burly Texas Rangers" had refused to give Alonzo treatment for his heroin addiction until he confessed after three days of painful withdrawal symptoms. For his role in delivering the guns to Carrasco, Benito Alonzo was given a life sentence, well beyond the normal second-degree felony sentence of two to twenty years for intent to facilitate an escape. Alonzo had two prior felony convictions, felony theft and burglary. Alonzo's confession also revealed Hall's role as the arms-delivery man. Hall was already serving a life sentence, and for his role in delivering the guns, he was given another life sentence in 1984. At age fifty-seven, Hall died while still confined in prison on April 6, 1993.

Aftermath—the End of Political Reform

Many prisoners correctly surmised that after the bloody Carrasco affair the TDC would ratchet up security and clamp down on "dissenters." "Already there is some deceptive cover-up," prisoner Frank Leahy warned in his letter to State Senator Ron Clower. Leahy felt that "the handwriting is pretty much on the wall that they [TDC] will attempt to manipulate this tragedy" and thereby "sabotage the legitimate Prison Reform efforts" and "tighten down the screws on all the dissenters."[73] With allegations of a conspiracy swirling in the air and fears that some prison guards might seek retribution against prisoners, the JCPR inserted itself into the state investigation. "We're not trying to investigate the situation as a criminal matter," Leland told an incredulous House Administration Committee that had previously warned the JCPR to suspend its inquiry. During the hearing, Representative George Preston of Paris, Texas, admonished Leland that "you were to study prison reform and not the criminal acts down there." Representative Bill Hollowell of Grand Saline threatened the committee's funding when he told Leland that "you're going to abide by the resolution [which created the JCPR to investigate prison reform] that was passed by the House or you're not going to get the money. A committee such as yours is purely for remedial legislation. We would not permit the state district attorney to come up here and interfere with legislative matters."[74]

Following the disastrous Carrasco crisis, the state legislature became increasingly hostile to prison reform. One of the freed hostages, Aline House, a sixty-one-year-old librarian, blasted the JCPR as "fighting tooth and nail for every right of prisoners but they didn't stick their nose in here when trouble was going on." In an open letter to the JCPR and the ACLU, House charged that both these groups "who are engaged in the so-called reform and rights movement, present to the public only the biased view of those incarcerated, the ones who could not abide by the laws of God and/or man." House pointedly asked why the JCPR only cared about "convict rights" and not the rights of the "11 [hostage] citizens [to] have their civil, legal or personal rights respected or protected."[75] A JCPR investigation of the hostage crisis, however, was beyond their mission and more than the legislature would allow. Lieutenant Governor Bill Hobby, a proponent of the TDC and a critic of the JCPR, felt that the committee had "exceeded their authority" by injecting themselves into the Carrasco inquiry. Hobby actively pressed the legislature to deny the JCPR their funding request. The JCPR's overall funding was slashed by over 75 percent, causing the JCPR's annual budget to drop from $36,536 ($18,200 from each house) to $9,700. Staff salary, for instance, fell from $10,368 to $6,550, which meant that Albach would have to make serious cutbacks with his investigators. Far more damaging was the drastic cuts made in the travel budget. Even if the staff were willing to operate with fewer members and with less pay, a significant travel budget remained essential to allow the largely Austin-based committee staff to visit and inspect East Texas prisons. While the committee had requested $3,000 for staff travel, they received only a paltry $150. Such minimal funding hampered the JCPR's efforts to the point of irrelevancy.[76]

The public and political sentiment for prison reform withered under the shadow of carceral violence surrounding the Carrasco hostage crisis. Although the passage of prison reform along the lines of the JCPR's recommendations would have been a difficult political struggle, there was some indication that the Cruz-Beto court battles had exposed the TDC as a brutal system that needed some measure of reform. The legislature's 1973 passage of HB 1056 outlawing "supervisory and disciplinary authority" of one prisoner over another and the near-simultaneous creation of the JCPR and Citizens' Advisory Committee demonstrated that the public and the legislature were sympathetic to prisoner claims of rampant abuse and racial violence. Chet Brooks, Mickey Leland, Eddie Bernice Johnson, and other JCPR members had reason to believe they were gaining ground. However, the eleven-day Carrasco hostage crisis and the subsequent deaths of two innocent female staff members turned the public away from legislative prison reform. The political and public sympathy for the plight of prisoners that had been generated by court battles, press coverage, and JCPR hearings had suddenly diminished. As the JCPR chair, Senator Chet Brooks, noted, "the Carrasco affair provided an excuse to people that were hostile to the committee and gave them an excuse to stop coordinating. Inmate interviews were stopped, harassed."[77]

In the aftermath of a hostage siege by three nationally defiant Chicano prisoners seeking asylum in Cuba, the public's racial anxiety and fears of extending civil rights to prisoners effectively ended the hopes for legislative prison reform. A citizen letter to the *Austin American Statesman* said as much: "I feel Mr. Brooks [chairman of JCPR] used the ill fated prison break at Huntsville as a means to gain publicity through our most excited news media. Mr. Leland? Now what is his game? All his noise seems to be about prison reform (and I believe for Blacks only). I think that any group from our esteemed legislative group at Austin is a very poor choice to put in charge of prison reform."[78] Exhausted by controversy and under threat to lose funding, Mickey Leland resigned himself to the fact that the Carrasco affair had heightened the public's unease in hearing prisoner complaints of abuse. "It put the people of the State of Texas in a frame of mind that was already potentially there, but I think what has been enhanced is that punishment is better than rehabilitation. But I'm not going to mess with it any further. That incident . . . did so much damage to our committee that I would not like to refer to it anymore. I don't want any further damage done. I'd just like the dead to stay dead."[79]

In 1975 the legislature passed only one of the 160 recommendations from the JCPR and Citizens' Advisory Committee reports. In light of the growing racial animosity in Texas prisons, the 1975 state legislature repealed the 1927 statue that required racial segregation in Texas prisons, and they passed a largely symbolic law that prohibited discrimination of prisoners based on race. Even this measure, however, was largely due to the pending court case of *Lamar v. Estelle*, which charged that the TDC's racial segregation was unconstitutional and that its hiring practices were racially discriminatory. The hope for community corrections was dead, however. It died on the ramp leading to the Walls library with Carrasco. The opportunity to stem prison growth had darkened and then withered away under the shadow of carceral violence. The failure to mount a significant legislative reform package led to wider calls for law-and-order politics and set the stage for continued prison growth. Moreover, the JCPR's failure and the public response to the Carrasco incident fueled the TDC's resistance to prisoner claims for more humane treatment. It hardened the resolve of wardens and officers, who utilized the building tender system to renew control, discipline, and order. Within the prison, it served as notice to the prisoner community that their only hope for reform was wider prisoner mobilization and to turn away from the legislature and toward struggles in both the courts and the prison courtyard.

Chapter 8

Testimonios of Resistance

The Slave Narrative and the Prison Labor Strike of 1978

On December 18, 1865, the 13th Amendment to the US Constitution was ratified to abolish slavery. . . . That vulnerable institution has continued, however, in penitentiaries throughout the country. Texas Department of Corrections is probably the best example of slavery remaining in the nation today. . . . One gets a strong feeling that TDC exists not to punish offenders or deter others from committing crimes, not to rehabilitate criminals, but to perpetuate the plantation as the largest agribusiness operation in the state.

—Arnold Pontesso, U.S. Justice Department, 1978

Slavery, man, human slavery.

—anonymous Texas prisoner, *Corrections Magazine*, 1978

In 1969, David Resendez Ruíz was sent to the Eastham prison plantation and placed in the all-Mexican cell block known as P-line. After ten days on that wing, the captain of the unit called Ruíz into his office and told him that he would be moved to an all-white cell block, J-line, with five notorious building tenders that "will beat other prisoners on any orders from officers." After six months on J-line, Ruíz endured "cruel treatment and seeing countless prisoners beat up by said building tenders." After Assistant Warden McMillan denied Ruíz's repeated requests to be placed back on the Mexican American line, he was then moved to O-line where the assistant warden told Ruiz "that any little thing he got into he would be kill[ed]" under the fabricated charge of attempted escape. Ruíz had on his record a previous escape attempt and believed that this was no idle threat. In "great fear for his life," Ruíz was "driven to brutally mutilate both his arms to escape such treatment." At the hospital, the doctor stitched up Ruíz's arms without anesthesia for the pain. Angered by Ruíz's attempt at self-mutilation, the assistant warden and captain told Ruiz that "he would be surely killed now" and that "he would not live to see the next day." Cast into solitary confinement, "nude where [he was] forced to sleep on the cold concrete floor," a despairing Ruíz used a razor blade to mutilate his body and arms even further. The prison administration then moved Ruíz to the Wynn prison plantation under the watchful eye of

Warden Luther McAdams. Things only became worse for Ruíz, and in response to the "inhuman treatment" at the hands of McAdams and his building tenders, Ruíz then "brutally mutilated [cut] in two the Achilles tendon of his right foot." By holding his own body as hostage and subjecting it to self-harm, Ruíz both demonstrated the depth of his desperation and made use of one of his few means of protest against the racially hierarchical building tender system.[1]

Ruíz's tactics worked. He was transferred back to the Mexican American J-line at Eastham. Once back with his fellow Chicanos, Ruíz intervened in a fight on April 19, 1971, between an African American building tender who was wielding a "short handle axe" and a Mexican American prisoner who was of a slighter build than his opponent. Afterward, the prison administration gave the Black building tender, against whom Ruíz had defended his fellow Chicano prisoner, a "soft job," where he subsequently told the Chicanos that "he could kill any of the (3) Mexican Americans" and the assistant warden would see to it that no internal prison charges were filed. For Ruíz's intervention, however, the assistant warden placed him in forty days of solitary, where he received only one meal every three days, and that meal was never "more than (3) small spoons of food." He was caged nude for the first five days and given a pair of coveralls thereafter, but no "toothbrush, toothpaste, comb, towel, or soap to keep himself clean." For the next year, Ruíz would be placed in and out of solitary. Despite being caged in isolation, Ruíz managed to write the writ that evolved into the prisoners' rights case that put the entirety of the Texas prison plantation system on trial.[2]

On June 26, 1972, David Resendez Ruíz finished and notarized his twelve-page, handwritten complaint against the TDC. Ruíz's petition called attention to the prison's lack of medical care, the brutality of building tenders, and the practice of self-mutilation. The filing of Ruíz's writ in 1972 became the omnibus lawsuit *Ruiz v. Estelle*, the longest and largest prisoners' rights trial in the nation's history. It also started a mass movement within the prison that initiated a new phase for prisoners' rights in Texas. Though the legislature would fail in 1974 to enact any meaningful change, this caused the prisoners' rights movement to widen and expand its tactics to include massive resistance through work strikes and letter-writing campaigns. No longer just a few activist writ writers and their attorneys, between 1974 and 1981, the prisoners' rights movement had expanded to a mass movement that incorporated prisoners across the system. The movement's tactics utilized both the civil rights movement's call for civic inclusion and constitutional rights and the labor movement's tactic of achieving demands through work strikes. It also drew on Black Power and Chicano critiques against the state while making human rights a demand. For the prisoners, two decades of struggle had all built to this critical moment. Outside of prison and on the streets, Chicana/o and Black Power activism was beginning to wane by the mid-1970s.[3] But southern prisoners built on the lessons of Attica and Soledad to develop the very apogee of prisoners' rights in Texas during the mid- to late 1970s.

Across the East Texas prison plantation regime, the 1970s marked the high-water mark of radical and rights-based prisoner organizing. This mass movement assisted the litigation effort by documenting abuses through a massive letter-writing campaign that provided prisoner plaintiff attorneys and the courts with lengthy and detailed affidavits, depositions, and petitions. This collection of documented abuse was more than a legal project; it had grown into a political project. As organizers of an interracial alliance, African American and Chicano prisoners struck an alliance to make their slave-like condition legible to the public through the process of legal documentation as political testimony. This chapter, then, draws upon Mario T. García's oral history collection of the Chicano's generation, where *testimonios* are "collective in nature because they address collective struggles."[4] To that definition, this chapter adds the interracial and prison-made testimonies of resistance as "the politics of truth" that revealed the stark brutality that made the prison plantation function.[5]

Integral to the southern prisoners' rights campaigns was a language of resistance that claimed that southern prisons, in particular, were explicit examples of twentieth-century slavery.[6] In southwestern prisons, particularly in Texas, Mexican American prisoners, inspired by the Chicano movement, saw that the conditions of southern incarceration rendered both Black and brown prisoners as literal and legal slaves. As Cruz and Ruíz became mobilizing symbols to challenge the TDC in the courtroom, Black radical prisoners joined with a collection of Chicano and a small handful of white prisoners to organize fellow prisoners through interdependent prison societies of resistance that created a prison-made civil rights movement. These prisoners employed the language of Black Power and Chicano critiques even as they staked their rights-based claims for legal recognition on constitutional grounds.[7] To make their incarcerated conditions visible to the public, the prisoners' rights movement developed a two-pronged strategy that used mass protest labor tactics and Black and brown power critiques alongside civil rights cases and class-action lawsuits to demand public visibility.

The struggle for prisoners' rights centered on the visibility of the prisoners themselves and to make plain that their incarceration constituted coerced slave labor on prison plantations. They asked the courts to reconsider how the state punished those who committed a crime while also reminding the public of the prisoners' humanity and their constitutional rights. In all these cases, prisoners sought to be visible, both seen and heard, in a public campaign to elevate their voice in a crucial national debate over the growing power of the United States' rising carceral states. Indeed, prisoners of the 1970s and 1980s understood the dangers of mass incarceration before many on the outside realized it. As mass incarceration fueled racially disproportionate prison populations, the prison became a clear symbol of the exercise of stark and brazen racial oppression.[8]

The chapter begins with the story of David Ruíz and follows with several other Chicano testimonios. By telling Ruiz's story, this chapter considers the terror of racial violence, the necessity of self-defense, and the agony of self-mutilation. Prisoners employed a militant brand of self-defense that was spurred by gendered ideals of rough masculinity to confront the racial violence that they experienced at the hands of building tenders.[9] A reign of sexual violence and the constant threat of brutalization also resulted in the agonizing practice of self-mutilation, which stretched the very boundaries of "hidden transcripts" and "everyday resistance," where damaging one's own body was both a political act and a moment of deep despair and painful self-effacement. The chapter then broadens the movement to include the Black Panther Jonathan Eduardo Swift and a cadre of political organizers who spread the word of prisoner empowerment. Once the testimonies had developed into a mass movement, the prisoners planned the first ever systemwide prison labor strike just as the *Ruiz* case was going to trial. As Black and Chicano radical organizers, they waged a public campaign to make the conditions of the southern prison plantation visible by insisting that the Texas control penology and agribusiness model was built on a lie—that incarceration amounted to twentieth-century slavery. More than a powerful analogy, however, these radical prisoners pointed to the South's coerced agricultural labor demands, their internal control structures, and the routine nature of corporal punishment to make the case to the federal court and to the wider public that Texas prisoners were not slaves.

Tough with a Knife, Hell with a Writ: David Ruíz and Testimonios of Resistance

Born to migrant workers on May 15, 1942, and dying on November 12, 2005, David Resendez Ruíz spent all but eleven of his sixty-four years in captivity. Born the third youngest of thirteen children, Ruíz's family traveled daily from Austin, Texas, their home, to surrounding counties to work in the fields of large farmers and farm owners. When times were particularly tough, they would travel as far as Arizona, Colorado, Michigan, Minnesota, North Dakota, Oklahoma, and Wisconsin to find temporary work as "stoop laborers," but the return trip would always bring them home to Austin, within a transient labor network that the historian Marc Rodriguez named "the Tejano diaspora."[10] Ruíz experienced confinement at age eleven, when the state consigned him in 1953 to the Gatesville Reformatory School for Boys for stealing from shoeshine and newspaper boys. Ruíz returned to the same reformatory three times before the state finally tried him as an adult in 1959 for burglary and car theft, a charge for which he was found guilty and sentenced to a term of twelve years. He remained in Texas prison from 1960 until 1967, when he was released on parole. Ruíz thereafter met and married Rose Marie, but within the year he returned to prison for armed robbery, for which the state gave him a twenty-five-year sentence.[11]

Violence marked Ruíz's first stay in Texas prisons, particularly knife fighting. In his unpublished memoir, "Tough with a Knife, Hell with a Writ," Ruiz reflected on his early prison experience in the East Texas cotton fields and how he decided upon a path of violence as his first means of resistance:

> The field work was brutal, the first two weeks I barely made it day to day. At the end of each day I was completely exhausted. A work squad is combined of 25 or 30 prisoners and managed by a guard on horseback armed with a .38 pistol. Most guards were ignorant and did not know how to act in a humane manner toward the prisoners, most likely because they came from the backwoods of Texas. All guards used degrading language when speaking to or ordering a prisoner. The Chicanos were called "meskins," blacks were called "niggers," and whites "old thangs," with all kinds of sons of bitches added. Most guards carried long wood clubs or leather reins to beat the prisoners if they fail to stay up with squad of prisoners working on a line. The guards did not hesitate to knock a prisoner on the head with a club or reins if he could not stay up with the squad. I got several tests of the club and reins. When speaking to a guard out on the fields, the rules were, a prisoner took his cap or hat off and said "yes sur" or "no sur" when addressing the guards. . . . After several months of seeing all such misery, I made up my mind that I would oppose the prison system the only way I knew by rebelling and violence.[12]

In his first two years at the Ramsey farm (1960–61), Ruíz was involved in no less than ten fights with other prisoners. In perhaps the most striking example of his rage and violent past, he stabbed another Chicano prisoner over eighteen times. "I was stabbing blindly," recalled Ruíz. "And all I can remember is hearing the knife as it went in and crunched bones. I think I stabbed him in the neck and was holding his head up to go around and cut his head off. My foot was on his body." Ruíz only stopped when his fellow prisoners called out, "David, David, stop; he's already dead!"[13]

Ruíz not only inflicted violence on others; he also maimed himself. He mutilated himself no less than fifteen times before 1978, particularly in solitary. Ruíz routinely smashed the light bulbs of his solitary cell and often used the glass shards to slash his wrists and tendons, covering his cell and his body in blood. In the original writ that started his case, David Ruíz explained that self-mutilation was an act of desperation that he used to call attention to the brutality that prisoners experienced at the hands of the TDC and the BT system.[14] The BT system was complicated for Ruíz because many of the building tenders were drawn from the ranks of people he had known from his time in reform school. One of the head building tenders on his unit was a former friend from Gatesville, and Ruíz blamed the prison administrators for using the lure of power to turn his fellow convict and former friend against him. "They started working together to turn all the building tenders into that category of people," Ruíz recalled. "The one that started turning the building tenders . . . all over the system into snitches and beating up prisoners—abusing the other prisoners—that philosophy was wrought by Warden McAdams. He's the one that implemented the building tender system that turned them into nothing but sadists and snitches—cowards that depended on the officers to back them up so they could have that authority."[15]

Ruíz's first act of resistance was to participate in a brief 1961 work strike that occurred at Ramsey within the first few months of Dr. George Beto's directorship. Ruíz explained his participation in the work strike as the only means he had to resist the violence he experienced while working in the fields of prison labor:

> I knew it [the beatings by guards] was wrong and that's why I was rebellious. And that's why I participated when one of the initiators got the work stoppage, because I knew that I was giving them all I had. I would work like a slave every day to keep them off my back. And most of us did that, you know, so we wouldn't have any hassles. And then, the field guard, they was abusing his authority because he was impatient and accusing prisoners of not working and beating up somebody, and I mean, that horse tried to run you over. It was wrong. But, the only thing that I knew what to do is oppose him, and they had the guns, they had the men in power.[16]

For his participation in the strike, Ruíz was sent for the first time to solitary. When he returned from the fifteen-day starvation diet, the other Mexican American prisoners collected their commissary together to share with the returning prisoners. Ruíz recalled the solidarity of his fellow prisoners whenever someone returned from solitary: "Everybody would pitch in, you know, what he could, candy bar, a soda, a big bag of coffee, candy, so when you got out, they would give you that bag. If there was two or three of you, well, you all would split it."[17] Chicanos relied on this communitarian ethos to combat the contrasting acquisitiveness surrounding the self-aggrandizement of the building tender economy.

Reflecting on how he came to be a writ writer, Ruíz wrote that by the late 1960s he began to focus his rage on the building tender system, which he saw as the root of all the evils in the TDC: "I came to hate those prisoners who did the officers' dirty work mainly to receive extra privileges or a soft job and I did not like the weak prisoners much either because some would not even fight back because of fear of the outcome if they did."[18] When questioned by an Eastham guard as to why he engaged in such violent behavior toward building tenders, Ruíz responded with characteristic defiance: "I ain't a trouble maker, but I won't run from trouble. I will meet trouble half way and if forced upon. I will take orders from officers and not building tenders; and if I am ever assaulted by a building tender, book keeper or turnkey, they better kill me because I ain't taking no more beating and I been ready to die since the first day I entered this shithole prison."[19] Such defiance soon earned Ruíz a reputation of high respect and regard among prisoners, particularly the Chicanos, while the prison administration saw Ruíz as a "troublemaker" and "disturbed." As Ruíz's reputation grew, prison officials moved him from one prison farm to another, until finally, the TDC assigned Ruíz to Ellis, where he became one of Jalet's clients. He was also housed with the Eight Hoe group at Wynne, a maximum security unit, and home to an entire wing of prison activists and jailhouse attorneys. There Ruíz, who entered prison nearly illiterate, learned to turn his energies away from violence and toward legal redress, and he subsequently joined the ranks of a number of prisoners who had turned writ writing into an act of personal survival and political resistance.

After Fred Cruz found freedom, Jalet's clients were dispersed across the prison system, where they continued their writ writing. Ruíz was joined by a number of fellow Chicano and African American writ writers, including Salvador Gonzalez, Isaias Lara, Eduardo Salazar Mauricio, Ernesto Montana, Raul A. Rodríguez, David Robles, and Johnny Martínez. There was no single leader of this group, but they joined one another's suits as interracial solidarity between Black and brown prisoners. In a 1972 writ, Eduardo Mauricio made clear that "Chicano and Blacks have similar claims" concerning systematic racial abuse. Citing the system's segregation as the defining feature of plantation prison life, Mauricio charged that "Chicanos have suffered discriminatory and adverse effects stemming from racial classification, separation, and segregation" because "minorities are assigned the least promising job assignments . . . [which] subjects minorities to unequal basis with their Anglo counterparts." Because the TDC denied those claims and the existence of an abusive building tender system, these prisoners turned to civil rights attorneys and the courts to make themselves heard and their complaints of being caged on a plantation visible. By 1974, Mauricio had learned of southern prisoners' rights cases, particularly *Gates v. Collier* and the rampant abuses on Mississippi's Parchman prison plantation, and so he reached out to the attorney Roy Haber. Mauricio hoped that Haber would pursue a U.S. Code 1983 case in Texas based on a host of charges centering on racial humiliation and discrimination—including physical violence, denial of legal services, refusal to send mail, frequent strip down searches, and "racial slurs by officers that serves to build animosity" and "forcing prisoners to work beyond their physical conditions." Haber responded that he was too consumed with prisoners' rights cases in western states, but he forwarded Mauricio's letter to Judge William Wayne Justice of the Fifth Circuit.[20]

As a student of Fred Cruz, Mauricio displayed a similar thirst for knowledge and empowerment. Like Cruz, Mauricio converted from Catholicism to Buddhism, as he found Buddhism a better path for "seeking truth and for a change in my life" toward the Buddhist conceptualization of the four noble truths. Along with his religious conversion, Mauricio also became increasingly politicized through his appetite for new ideas. Beginning in the early 1970s, he requested from the University of California, Berkeley a series of lectures on political theory and social science, as well as courses on Chicano studies.[21] Mauricio characterized his radical turn toward greater politicization as a frustrated response against the TDC's intransigence, despite some legal victories. "I started getting more rebellious because we were fighting issues in the court and not seeing any outcome," Mauricio recalled. Instead, Mauricio looked to radicalization beyond the prison and turned toward "the Chicano community [that] was rising up in Brown consciousness."[22]

Chicana/o protest and politics outside of prison developed in relation to critical encounters with the burgeoning carceral state in Texas. The founding of the Mexican American Youth Organization (MAYO) on the St. Mary's University campus in San Antonio in 1967 had brought together a coalition between students and barrio street toughs and gang members as a civil rights organization that implemented voter registration drives, school walkouts, and political agitation against police brutality. By 1970, MAYO had flourished into a national and statewide organization with more than forty chapters across Texas.[23] The development of its political arm, the La Raza Unida Party (RUP), offered Mexican Americans a "third choice" of political parties when Ramsey Muñiz challenged the Democratic campaign of Dolph Briscoe in the 1972 and 1974 governor races.[24] Despite a strong showing with the Mexican American electorate, Muñiz received only 6 percent of the statewide vote. A carceral intervention ended this genuine challenge to two-party politics when a campaign of police surveillance of RUP resulted in the 1976 arrest of Muñiz for drug trafficking. The political excitement around La Raza Unida thus came to an abrupt halt with Muñiz's incarceration in a federal penitentiary.[25]

TDC activist Chicano prisoners watched these developments from their cells. As he became more politicized, Mauricio attempted to correspond with the Chicano leaders Corky Gonzales, Cesar Chavez, and Ramsey Muñiz before he too was incarcerated. Similarly, Chicano prisoners in the early 1970s unbounded their Texas incarceration through their political association with Maoist revolution and a Third World globalist critique of the Vietnam War that severed the historical tradition of Mexican American patriotism through military service in wartime. "So, I started getting more militant in my thinking, me personally," Maurico recounted. "I started subscribing to a radical publication by the name of *The Guardian* in New York, and then, through *The Guardian*, I started learning about other radical publications, so I started subscribing to *Peking Review* and *China Reconstructs*, directly from the People's Republic of China."[26] Armed with New Left literature, Mauricio and other Chicano prisoners saw the U.S. war in Vietnam through the lens of their own people's history with U.S. invasion, where the ramifications of the 1848 Treaty of Guadalupe Hidalgo rendered Mexican Americans as a colonized people without full citizenship or their former lands. In her study of Chicana/o activism during the Vietnam War, Lorena Oropeza offered the conclusion that "the Chicano claim to the land was an anticolonial struggle similar to the one that the Vietnamese were waging," which was a political critique that incarcerated Chicano prisoner activists also shared.[27]

Mauricio's writ writing and letters joined a host of prisoner complaints that had amassed on the desk of Judge Justice. In another 1974 prisoner complaint, Ellis prisoner Stanley Cedargreen forwarded to Judge Justice a "much needed judicial intervention for the humane treatment" of prisoners. In his letter, Cedargreen pointed out that despite the fact that House Bill 1056 banned the "TDC from using prisoners from acting in a disciplinary, supervisory, or administrative capacity" over other prisoners, "the prisoner-guard is still very much" at the heart of TDC operations. Cedargreen considered building tenders as an "elite group of prisoners" who retain "the liberty of misusing, abusing, and converting their 'power' for personal benefit." The "benefits" that building tenders accrued included "sexual needs, financial needs . . . the need to have access to outlets for inner hostilities, prejudices, and resentments," and especially "malicious suppression of minority identities and cultures (Negro-American and Mexican American)." The letter insisted that the federal court must intervene "to secure the enforcement of the law abolishing the prisoner guard system," and he further cited *Holt v. Sarver*'s argument that it does not require a compliant legislature to ensure a constitutional prison: "Let there be no mistake in the matter; the obligation of the respondents [Arkansas] to eliminate existing unconstitutionalities does not depend upon what the legislature may do. . . . If Arkansas is going to operate a penitentiary system, it is going to have to be a system countenanced by the Constitution of the United States."[28] While the TDC hoped to quiet these complaints, the uproar was only getting louder.

When Estelle dispersed Eight Hoe prisoners, he sent Lawrence Pope and David Ruíz to Retrieve, a largely African American and Chicano prison. The TDC moved Pope to an all-Black wing with the building tender L. D. Hilliard as his cellmate. Hilliard had previously been in charge of the protective custody wing that provided him open access to the younger prisoners who comprised the internal sex slave trade. Pope recalled that Hilliard was "one of the worst building tenders" and that "he carried two dirks in his belt that had been brought in by an officer from the free world." In his role as BT for those housed on the protective custody wing, Hilliard routinely used his position of power and "got all the sex he wanted, whether the prisoners wanted it or not." Pope saw his placement with Hilliard as an explicit racial and sexual threat from the TDC. Pope recalled the housing situation with some lingering anxiety: "Now this was putting a black person in a cell with a white person, and at that time the cell blocks were very rigidly segregated." Pope felt that the attempt to create carceral violence through interracial celling in an otherwise segregated system was just "another ploy to shut ol' Lawrence Pope up, so they put me over there in this all-black cell block. I was the only white person in there." Pope was able to avoid trouble as the other African American prisoners on that wing had little love for Hilliard, who falsely sold legal services to other prisoners as he pretended to be a writ writer to fellow Black prisoners. Hilliard routinely charged indigent Black prisoners their commissary items in exchange for the promise to write appeals that he never actually filed. As Pope recalled, Hilliard "was thoroughly hated by—just everybody, his own black people and—he had ripped them off." Meanwhile the TDC placed Ruíz in a solitary cell for nearly a year, when he was caught in 1973 bringing a spoon into his cell to construct a sharpened weapon. Pope recalled the effect of that year on Ruíz: "I think he was mentally affected by this one solid year of being in this cell, never going any place, never doing anything. It was while he was there that he drew up his lawsuit that became" the *Ruiz v. Estelle* lawsuit.[29]

Both the press and TDC attempted to cast such writ writing as a product of external influence and orchestration by liberal federal judges and radical civil rights attorneys. But Ruíz's writ was one of hundreds of writs that prisoners wrote themselves to initiate the machinery of law, rights, and justice on their own behalf. When Dan Balz of the *Washington Post* had suggested in an article about *Ruiz* that Frances Jalet-Cruz served as a "a lawyer who had become something of a den mother for jail house lawyers," the letter's presumptuousness and patronizing tone left Jalet-Cruz "disturbed and angered."[30] Jalet-Cruz defiantly wrote Balz to tell him that he had mischaracterized her "because of my womanhood and perhaps my age" and to remind him that while she was a respected civil rights attorney that she never initiated the prisoners' complaints. "I at no time 'helped' David Ruiz file papers," Jalet-Cruz retorted. "He never submitted any to me for that purpose. What I did was represent him in a habeas corpus case challenging his conviction."[31] Writ writing was a genuine form of political dissent that prisoners themselves initiated on their own behalf. Ruíz's writ was written within his everyday lived experience of carceral violence.

While David Ruíz spent his year in solitary writing his petition about past treatment, Judge William Wayne Justice was sorting through a host of prisoner petitions. As a federal judge, Justice oversaw the Eastern District of Texas and two of the TDC's thirteen prisons. Eastham was one of the two prisons in Justice's district, so when Ruíz filed his civil rights complaint on June 29, 1972, from Eastham, it went directly into Justice's hands. Justice had earned a reputation as an activist judge through his intervention in pressing four contentious public school desegregation cases in which public school systems in Tyler, Texas, openly refused court-ordered racial integration. He also issued unusual court orders that enforced such school discrimination issues as having a local high school hold a more racially inclusive cheerleader election and ordering Robert E. Lee High School to remove the Confederate flag and forsake its fight song, "Dixie." He gained even more notoriety as an activist judge when he presided over the case *Morales v. Turman*, which was a class-action suit filed by juvenile offenders against the Texas Youth Council (TYC).[32] The *Morales* charges against the TYC brought to court many of the same charges that prisoners had made against the TDC, including lack of access to attorneys and allegations of excessive corporal punishment. Justice ruled in favor of the juvenile offender in *Morales*, and this decision earned the interest of prisoners making similar pleas for court intervention against the TDC.[33]

Beginning with his appointment to the East Texas district in 1969, Justice oversaw a number of hearings on prisoner petitions that he found compelling, but he remained skeptical. Initially, Judge Justice responded to the many prisoner-initiated complaints with doubt because he had always believed the TDC's modernization narrative of good control, order, and efficiency. Justice admitted that his initial "attitude toward TDC at that time was probably similar to that of most Texans. I thought the system was efficient."[34] But as the prisoners' depositions, affidavits, and letters mounted, the Judge found that he "wasn't satisfied because what the prisoners were saying about getting beaten up and about inferior medical care and that kind of thing had the ring of truth about it." During a 1972 speech at Southern Methodist University's law school, Justice declared his willingness to consider prison class-action suits as a matter of civil rights: "Should prisons not aim to protect the public and to deter and rehabilitate the criminal without abandoning the civilized idea that we treat our fellow man, even those who have deviated from society's norm, with some dignity and compassion? . . . We would do less than our constitutional duty were we to refrain" from hearing state prison cases in federal court.[35]

Ruíz's twelve-page, handwritten petition caught Justice's eye as it explicitly addressed the brutality of the building tender system and the lack of medical care, two issues that made the TDC vulnerable to a legal argument that it operated an unconstitutional prison system. On April 12, 1974, Judge Justice consolidated six additional prisoner petitions with Ruíz's original petition as part of his orchestrated effort to develop a pending lawsuit against the TDC.[36] Justice also ordered the U.S. Department of Justice to appear as amicus curiae, and six months later it joined the suit as coplaintiffs.

In recognition of his prior work with Jalet, Justice also reached out to William Bennett Turner of the NAACP's Legal Defense Fund as the attorney for the prisoner plaintiffs. The NAACP LDF contacted Turner just as he was traveling the Himalayas and staying in Kathmandu, Nepal. Turner's initial reply to Justice, a handwritten note on the stationary of Hotel Yellow Pagoda, thought that prisoner rights cases "should be taken seriously," but because Turner did not expect to return for several months, he suggested Stanley Bass instead.[37] Justice had first met Turner during the 1972 conference at Southern Methodist University, and he had been impressed with Turner's persuasive argument that courts must reconsider prisoners' rights. Upon his return to the United States, however, Turner relented, and joined by Stanley Bass (a NAACP LDF attorney) and Sam Biscoe of Dallas, they undertook the prisoners' pleas as a section 1983 civil rights case. By 1974, Judge Justice granted Turner's motion to convert the case into a class-action lawsuit, *Ruiz v. Estelle*. Ruíz's initial petition now was a civil rights claim that represented the entire prison population of 15,000 against all of the TDC and its thirteen prisons. Upon learning of the class-action lawsuit, Director Estelle told an audience of criminal scientists at Sam Houston State University that the TDC represented "the finest large Department of Corrections in America," and his administration would firmly stand against such lawsuits that would only breed "institutional anarchy and . . . community terror."[38]

The inclusion of the Justice Department as amicus curiae provided politicized prisoners with another external source to make their claims publicly legible to the federal judiciary. As a new member of the writ-writing group, Johnny Valdez Martínez, held on a 145-year prison sentence for distributing narcotics, considered writ writing as a political act of collective resistance and solidarity shared between African American and Chicano prisoners. In an FBI memorandum from J. Stanley Pottinger, an assistant attorney general, to Clarence M. Kelly, the FBI director, the Civil Rights Division documented that Martínez and other writ writers were frequently "arrested and disciplined for writing to a staff member of the State Legislative Prison Reform Committee."[39] Martínez and his fellow writ writers believed that building tender violence was accelerating as the spread of writ writing documented more of the system's abuses. In a letter to Gail Littlefield of the Civil Rights Division, Martínez explained that state-orchestrated violence was accelerating "through scheme, design, and conspiracy (officials), this unit is being made ready to erupt in violence."[40] Following the pattern set by their handling of Fred Cruz and Muslim prisoners during the 1960s, the TDC's punitive response was to isolate Martínez from his fellow writ writers and move him to solitary, where he was subsequently assaulted by two white building tenders, one named "Peanuts," whose "crew cut hair . . . and a pot belly" made him look like a perverse Charlie Brown caricature, who hit Martínez repeatedly "with a blackjack, their feet and fists."[41]

When that beating failed to stop Martínez's writ writing, the TDC attempted to silence Martínez by employing a psychological diagnosis. In 1974, the FBI informed TDC assistant director D. V. McKaskle that they were conducting an investigation of Martínez's complaints. But the FBI shortly thereafter closed the case when the TDC delivered a statement from Martínez's father, who "stated that he saw no physical evidence of Johnny being beaten up as there were no bruises or marks visible . . . and also advised that Johnny had been treated for mental illness in 1964."[42] One of the prison's chief weapons against prisoners who complained to outside sources was to reframe political agitation as a state of "mental agitation" and antisocial behavior. Such dismissals drew upon a shift in psychiatric diagnosis that responded to 1960s-era civil rights and Black Power protests with "a diagnostic language" that associated Blackness with schizophrenia. TDC prison officials drew on a similar psychiatric discourse to dismiss prisoner politicization as what the historian and psychiatrist Jonathan Metzl has called "the protest psychosis."[43]

As politically conscious and well-read prisoners, writ writers were knowingly disdainful of such attempts to dismiss them as "mentally agitated." By 1974 their frustration centered on their shared skepticism that external political reform might yield any significant change. In a letter that summed up the writ writers' cumulative frustrations, Martínez impressed upon the Civil Rights Division that "the standard cover-up policy of the TDC" had narrowed the legislative options, leaving prisoners with the sole remaining hope of judicial intervention and their own prisoner mobilization.

> Legislators cannot provide us with the protection from TDC reprisals. The state attorney general refuses to enforce state law within the TDC. TDC employed attorneys refuse to help prisoner-victims file against the TDC. . . . Civil suits are being stolen from the writ room, TDC heads continue to take the word of unit officials that prison conditions are favorable. Inmate guards still have the authority to use brutality and terror tactics. . . . In many ways we, the TDC prisoners, are hanging off a cliff and TDC officials are stomping on our fingers with their cowboy boots.[44]

A Black Panther on the Cell Block: Johnny Swift's Campaign for Prison Mobilization and Organization

"Akeys! Comrades! Carnales! Brothers! Ndugus! The puppets of Wildcat's confinement has struck a subversive blow to Comrade [name stricken from record]. A comrade who asserted his rights. Our right! In a court of law so that the oppressive forces of this administration can be thrown asunder . . . So the prisoners of this slave camp, and all the slave camps of TDC can be liberated."[45] In 1973, this political tract greeted some of the Ramsey prisoners the day after the House had passed HB 1056, the bill that outlawed the use of building tenders in a supervisory or punitive capacity. One of the prison system's most active political organizers and tract writer was John Eduardo Swift, a self-avowed active member of the Black Panthers and a veteran of the Black Power movement with a 101-year sentence for the killing of H. C. "Jack" Kelly, board chairman of Merchant and Planter Bank, during a botched robbery attempt in Hearne, Texas.[46] Upon his arrest in neighboring Canadian County, Oklahoma, Sheriff Sonny Elliott told the gathered press that "Swift claims to be a Black Panther. I don't know whether he is or not, but I feel like he has been in close contact with them."[47] Within the first year of his arrival to the TDC, Swift began to organize other Black prisoners on what he called the "slave-plantation, Ellis," where he "was getting the place hot with a lot of people (Director, Reform Committee, etc.) snooping around and asking a lot of questions." When the Muslim prisoners on Ellis were repeatedly assaulted by building tenders who threatened sexual violence by routinely threatening to claim Muslim bodies as "whores," "girl boys" and "pussy fags," Swift documented a series of eighteen "atrocious, terroristic actions (barbarous beatings)." At the request of a badly beaten Muslim, desperate prisoners like Swift wrote the Nation of Islam, as well as State Representative Eddie Bernice Johnson.[48]

The TDC subsequently charged him with "agitating a mutiny," and they placed him in solitary on death row at the Ellis prison, even though Swift did not have a death sentence. Michael Jewell, a white prisoner and writ writer, recalled that Swift immediately became a political organizer from death row. "Johnny was much more than a writ writer. His forte was mentoring to other Blacks, even those under sentence of death. He exhorted them not to lay up on their asses and wait for the needle, but to study law and fight for their lives. And to write politicians and the media to tell their stories, and to complain of how they lived. Johnny survived the rigors of life on Seg [administrative segregation] by helping to keep others afloat."[49] Prisoner organizers implored other prisoners "to survey all surroundings consistently through scientific vigilance" and legal documentation.[50] Swift was one of many prisoners who mobilized and organized within the prison system a grassroots prisoners' rights movement. One prisoner's letter to Congresswoman Eddie Bernice Johnson made clear the author's association with Black radical politics: "I am a socialist who adheres to Marx-Mao-Fanon; an elite revolutionist . . . I have been a member of the Black Panthers for seven years to date."[51] The aim of this movement was to assist the writ writers and organize fellow prisoners to actively resist the building tender system through self-defense, collective organization, and a systemwide letter-writing campaign to judges, state legislators, the governor, the media, and civil rights attorneys. These prisoners joined the writ writers' legal efforts by creating incidents and demanding public attention for their cause. Their hundreds of letters, affidavits, and depositions became, in some cases, the material that the plaintiff attorneys used in making their argument against the TDC in *Ruiz v. Estelle*. Indeed, the movement had entered a new phase and incorporated mass mobilizing and organizing tactics aimed at assisting the attorneys and the court who were pursuing prisoner civil rights on their behalf.

The movement was aware that recent legislative measures, such as the bill that supposedly outlawed the authority of building tenders, were hamstrung by the public's wariness to support prisoner rights. "Yesterday a 'bill' was passed and made 'law' House Bill 1056 [outlawing BTs], but HB 1056, has not, and will not be recognized," the tract declared.[52] The tract called the placement of prisoners in administrative segregation a "political move" to subvert the JCPR inquiries. It accurately predicted that the TDC would use the 1973 Black uprising at Ramsey to gain legislative "support needed by this antagonistic, totalitarian system to be able to continue with their arbitrary power and subjugation and further to obliterate the truth." The tract charged that the Justice Department, the JCPR, and the Texas legislature were too meek and beholden to "political expediency" to use their "power and authority to eradicate our condition immediately."[53]

The various tracts argued that prisoners of all races must "unite immediately" to "struggle for liberation and self-determination that can only be carried out effectively by collective prisoners." Following the 1973 Black political organizing at Ramsey, the number of such tracts increased, and they encouraged fellow prisoners to organize a systemwide letter-writing campaign to state legislatures and the U.S. Department of Justice's Civil Rights Division. Its goal was to "raise at least 2,500 letters protesting these individuals and the use of administrative segregation." The objectives of the letter-writing campaign was to create an "abundance of letters [that] will mount the necessary pressure on the recipients and force them to abandon their belief in political expediency" while also "simultaneously forcing the identification of the prisoners' collective power base [the building tenders]."[54] Organizing from death row, Johnny Swift was one of the chief organizers who successfully encouraged prisoners across the system to respond with their letter writing, affidavits, and depositions as political testimonial.

The effort to politically organize prisoners beyond the confines of the prison plantation had assistance from Guadalupe Guajardo's 1972 writ to protect prisoner correspondence. Guajardo, another student of Fred Cruz and a Jalet client, was frustrated that his mail was censored and that the TDC had barred him from receiving Chicano movement literature and newspapers written in Spanish, particularly *Papel Chicano La Verbal*. He also charged that the TDC denied mailing of the U.S. Constitution, La Salle and Blackstone Law Courses, the *U.S. Reports, Federal Reporter, Federal Supplement*, and *Playboy*. His 1971 writ became a section 1983 civil rights trial, and in 1972 the court found that the TDC's interception of prisoner mail violated the First, Sixth, and Fourteenth Amendments and ordered injunctive relief that successfully limited the TDC's ability to censor and control prisoner mail.[55]

Once prisoners had the legal right to write external sources, they could expand the movement through letter writing and the circulation of political leaflets. Another political tract implored fellow prisoners to eschew individual problems and racial divisions through collective organization centered on their shared condition, which rendered prisoners of all colors as slaves:

> He can no longer stand and say, that's HIS problem! "We" can NO
> LONGER say it's NOT ME! Because every day ITS "YOU" and "ME" who
> is and always has been subjected to trumped up charges, to the same,
> that has befalled "HIM" will befall you and me!! . . . Let us start now!! Be
> MEN!!! And FIGHT!! The Struggle!! Must be joined by ALL! Akeys!
> Comrades! Carnales! Brothers! Ndugus! Arise, arise, Strike! For your
> lives and liberties. Now is the day and the Hour. Let every SLAVE on the
> Ramsey 1 SLAVE CAMP do this and the days of the "Slave Holder" are

numbered. . . . You cannot be more oppressed than you are. You cannot suffer greater cruelties than you have already. Let OUR motto be: Resistance! Resistance! Resistance![56]

One of the most daring aspects of the movement was its purposeful listing in political proclamations the names of building tenders and those fellow endangered "comrades" and "slaves" that the TDC held in solitary confinement and administrative segregation. In what had been an otherwise controlled prison environment, the listing of names of building tenders for all prisoners to see was a bold and dangerous act. Given the prison culture's critical reliance on traditions of respect to assure an individual's reputation, the situation must have been dire indeed and the political commitment deep for prisoners to put in writing that they were savagely beaten and raped. The petitions of Swift and other politicized prisoners implored their peers to expose building tenders by having the courage to name them specifically in their letters. Swift hoped to build the case for prison reform from within by supplying a host of names, incidents, and charges that could later be explored by the attorneys and the Justice Department during the *Ruiz* inquiries. Prisoners responded and their letters provided individual stories of racial and sexual violence and personal narratives of abuse. These letters contributed to a systemwide whistle-blowing operation that provided a host of full-length depositions, affidavits, and petitions.

The movement also attempted to restore a Black and brown power version of the convict code of prisoner loyalty against the prison administration. Sociologists have defined the "unwritten inmate code" as a cultural ethic of "convict loyalty," in which no prisoner may "snitch" on another prisoner. "Con loyalty," according to sociologies of the prison, normally created a cohesive "prison community" that set prisoners apart from prison administrators and guards.[57] Under the rule of building tenders, however, "con loyalty" had been torn asunder by privileging some prisoners as snitches and as prison administrators. Political organizers like Swift felt that the division of the prisoner population between privileged prisoners and the general population generated weakness. As one tract writer put it: "The situation as I see it, is very simple, you are either with us or against us, there is no middle ground." Political organizers therefore attempted to instill the subculture of the convict code and con loyalty as a political act to ensure collective organization. "We are all aware of snitches and the enormous power and influence they possess, but we continually display indifference and a dangerously self-defeating characteristic when we do nothing about them. They are able to operate and continue their subversive activities, openly in most cases, because we do much to encourage them. We must not cease our recognition of snitches, but actively censure, criticize, and condemn all snitches and any one that maintains friendly relations with them."[58]

Writing frequently to State Representative Eddie Bernice Johnson, they sought advice as to how Black Power prisoners might organize a racially segregated prison population with a long history of racial animosity. "By all the measurable indices," one prisoner wrote to Representative Johnson, "group consciousness among the Spanish-speaking minority is far below that of the Black community. The Panther Party has revealed that the Chicano community both admires and appreciates the heightened Black militance. But clearly, from an objective point of view, an alliance would be to the people's advantage."[59] Building on the work of Fred Cruz and David Ruíz, Swift's political tracts attempted to develop the jailhouse attorney network beyond a few select self-educated writ writers to construct a rank-and-file prisoner organization across racial lines, but mostly between Black and brown prisoners with a few key white radical prisoners like Stephen Blanchard and Lawrence Pope. In another letter supplying affidavit claims of physical abuse, the letter writer made clear that "your constitutional guarantees are advanced only when you constitute an active involvement toward the priority of unity. The common anger of apartheid between the minority ethnic groups" would only fulfill the prison's attempt to instill racial divisions and rivalries. Instead, the prisoner organizers attempted to eradicate "those petty jealousies and hostilities that exist between them. This is nothing more than another ploy in subterfuge that has been seeded by the oppressor."[60]

Swift, who had trained in the martial arts, was a proponent of collective self-defense, but he eschewed prison riots and random violence. In a February 1978 letter to Senator Chet Brooks, Swift wrote explicitly, "It is my opinion that *every* man has a *right to defend his life* when barbarically threatened." But, Swift acknowledged, he and his fellow prisoners had "only two essential weapons to challenge and struggle against repressivism and racism in prisons: political letters and civil rights suits. There is an extended measure, of course, brutal confrontation, but such, in my opinion, is born out of total desperation."[61] Swift and other prisoner organizers may not have embraced the idea of a full-scale prison riot, but he hoped that his organizing would create a prisonwide uprising of defiance, documentation, and exposure.

The letter-writing campaign hoped to bring public light and exposure to reveal the prison plantation's brutal truth. In another letter, a prisoner whose name was stricken from the prison record made clear how documentation for prisoners provided alternative narratives and hidden truths. The letter begins— "Salaam, it is with grief indeed that I am force[d] to send you the news" of a near fatal beating by one African American prisoner by six officials as "the forces of pig-sty-repression" had laid bare the bald truth of the TDC's prison plantation. "As beautiful as some remote romantics may endeavor to posit it [the TDC's agribusiness success narrative], the bestial pronouncement of racial repression is always ugly." The letter writer then implored his external contact to "contact the FBI immediately. Get a court order from a judge and visit [the beaten prisoner] as soon possible. His fear is great because his life is at stake. Your Panther servant will keep you informed. Contact Eddie Bernice Johnson Immediately."[62] Another letter sought to tie prisoner organizing with political organizing on the streets, but with an urgency that did not have time for political theorizing. In one letter to what may have been a Black Panther chapter (the addressee's name is stricken), the prisoner letter writer enclosed an affidavit of a series of solitary beatings and the attached letter speaks to the prisoner's desperation and urgency:

> As much as I would like to delve into the aspectual area of scientific socialism, the narrow-line of pig repression forbids me. I am hard press[ed] to emit as many letters of awareness I can in a short space of time. The prevailing situation here [Ellis] is critical indeed. . . . As I have stated to you in the past, I have great faith in your ability to mobilize your organization to and in our behalf. . . . Comrade, we need you now, while there is still a small vestige of life in our bodies. If an obit must be written, then let us dictate our own words. . . . My anger is great, but I refuse to let emotions sway me from the constructive role I seek. Don't forsake me when the lives of your brothers are hanging in the balance. Contact the FBI and respond to me.[63]

The movement hoped to inspire self-education among prisoners as a way of consciousness raising and to prepare these prisoners for writ-writing leadership roles, but it also inspired the collective organizing of prisoners who did not have the education or the inclination to become writ writers. Indeed, Swift's tracts and individual letters show his lingering fear that other prisoners might distance themselves from the fate of writ writers and that they might embrace instead the con colloquialism that each "man does his own time." In a population where few had more than a high school education and where self-esteem was often low, Swift attempted to instill confidence and inspire participation among all prisoners. "Of course not everyone is destined for leadership, nor is everyone qualified to file a writ, write to the legislature, news media, Judges, or the Justice Department, but anyone can help by offering stamps, writing materials, or the loan of a typewriter or a signature to a petition. . . . Anybody can be a hero."[64]

Swift was not alone in his political mobilization and organizing effort. Other prisoner organizers joined the movement, including such prisoner organizations as the Prisoner Solidarity Committee, Prisoners United, the Jailhouse Lawyers Association (JHLA), and Allied Prisoners Platform for Legal Equity (APPLE). These groups were typically small and composed of three or four core members who wrote tracts and petitions. For instance, the organization COPA was formed by the Black veterans of Ramsey and Retrieve's 1973 fight against building tenders. In one of its pamphlets, COPA exhorted to its members that their "struggle to secure our constitutional and human rights through prison reform" required that prisoners "must maintain the spirit and enthusiasm demonstrated the previous year in our collective efforts to eradicate the evil influence of the 'building tender' system." COPA hoped to expand prisoner consciousness from the small 1960s writ-writing group that mobilized legal campaigns to the more widespread political organizing during the decade of the 1970s that would create active prisoner resistance from the rank and file.

> We must keep the spirit alive through 1974 and expand it to combat all forms of injustice, oppression, and degradations. . . . We must intensify our effort in recruiting additional members to the struggle by establishing communications, coordination, and rapport between the different wings and extending the spirit of awareness. We must continue to actively support, in every way possible, the vanguard of the movement, the writ-writers, and all others who seek prison reform through protests, class-actions, affidavits, and letters to the legislature.[65]

These tracts were politically and legally astute and aimed to make documentation itself an act of consciousness raising. As one tract claimed,

> just because the legislature passed a bill to abolish the building-tender system does not mean that the system no longer exists. Its continued existence and essence was savagely manifested in segregation lock-up last year when several of our Black brothers and Chicanos were brutally attacked. Actually, the legislature merely set down the law and it is our responsibility to report all violations to the sponsors of bill . . . This issue will ultimately be resolved in court in the near future but we must be prepared to provide all relevant information in support of this cause to insure that the trial will result in the establishment of an enforcing code to this law.[66]

Prisoners then sent these tracts outside of the prison, and they also disseminated them among the general population. In a mass letter, titled "Dear Citizen," Ramsey prison's JHLA explained why their members had given up on politics and politicians and had turned instead toward the courts as a last-ditch effort to seek redress:

> For several years now, we have been attempting to raise the public's and the legislature's awareness to the adverse reality of prison life through letter-writing campaigns. As a result of these efforts, the Joint Committee on Prison Reform was selected by the 63rd Texas Legislature to investigate the many complaints of maltreatment issuing from the Texas Department of Corrections. . . . However, there is considerable lack of interest and some outright opposition among the more conservative elements of the Legislature regarding the Joint Committee's recommendation. As such, there is little chance that the 64th legislature will produce the legislation necessary to secure the standards urgently needed. Therefore, it is of paramount importance to the inmate writ-writers (jailhouse lawyers) to challenge the various unlawful practices, policies and procedures of the Texas Department of Correction through court litigation. . . . Court litigation is nevertheless the inmates' sole alternative outside of rioting and we have decided to continue our quest for reform and justice through this medium.[67]

Prisoner organizers had detailed plans for their organizations. The Revolutionary Vanguard Party Platform (RVP) adopted a Marxist framework and delineated an organizational plan that included an executive branch (party chairman, minister of defense, party secretary, and minister of domestic relationship, minister of international outreach), an intelligence unit (chief investigator, team leader, secretary), and a recruitment arm (field marshall general, head of recruiting, army secretary). The minister of interior, for instance, was tasked with documenting "all inner threats" and to stay "abreast of all incoming and outgoing populace to Ramsey" while keeping a log of all prisoners going to solitary and the injuries that they received at the hands of building tenders. The minister of domestic relationships was tasked to "make all families politically aware" of how the building tender system operated. It is not clear from the records how many prisoners actually joined the RVP, but the planning that went into its implementation demonstrated that prisoners in the 1970s were employing experienced political organizing from their free-world lives during the late 1960s.[68]

The JHLA included an executive board of prisoners and a citizens' coordinating committee. Its stated purpose was to write legal writs for indigent prisoners and to raise money for legal activities from out-of-prison and free-world contributors. The JHLA established a fund from its free-world board members that financed the payment of court filing fees, the purchase of law books, the photocopying of legal citations, typewriters, postage, stationery, and other legal material.[69] One of the distinctive characteristics of the letter-writing and legal campaign was the enormous amount of time and energy that such a campaign required. Without access to a mimeograph machine or a photocopier, prisoners typically hand copied the same letter and the same affidavit to as many as five different recipients. For many prisoners, these letters constituted assurance that they might survive the prison experience. The prisoner Michael Jewell expressed how his organizing efforts and political letter writing was motivated by a survival instinct:

> I had a list of a couple dozen people like Senator Brooks, Rep. Mickey Leland, Federal Judge Henry B. Gonzales, Judge Sarah T. Hughes, Patricia Gail Littlefield at the Civil Rights Division of the Justice Department, and the Sullivans at Texas CURE. Out of scores of people I wrote I retained these because I always asked them to write to W.J. Estelle and Warden Cousins to confirm or deny my allegations. This was critical to me because I wanted the officials to know that prominent outsiders were aware and interested in what they were doing. If nothing else, I am convinced that those who responded kept me alive and relatively unscathed.[70]

APPLE, meanwhile, was a hard-edged, left-wing political organization that issued such tracts as "Ally or Die," which was a proclamation issued to fellow "members of a totally enslaved class" in which "we are total slaves inside and disenfranchised wage-slaves outside." The prisoners Henry Lerma, David Edwards, and Carrol Maride formed Prisoners United, and they pressed prison reform by sending a series of signed petitions to state legislators. One petition, signed by twenty-eight prisoners, stated, "Since the introduction of the Bill (1056) TDC Administrative officials have intentionally and willfully closed their eyes and ears to this law and have further increased their building tender system as a means to make the conditions of confinement more oppressive than intended by law." Prisoners United charged that the TDC was "stretching the Constitution beyond its breaking point" and that "concealment, deception, and cover-up has become a way of life" within TDC culture.

> There are some of the undersigned who have witnessed, and have been victims of the injustices perpetrated against other inmates by building tenders. They saw there a contest thus produced which created bitterness, hatred, fear, revenge and ferocity that has seldom been equaled; they witnessed the whole framework of humanity shaken, justice denied, delay and brought into disrepute, crime stalking unreduced and

unpunished and the best interests of society shattered or crushed and they cannot remain silent.[71]

On December 28, 1975, the rhetoric and organizing escalated to attempted rebellion when fifteen African American prisoners, many of them Muslims, attempted to take over the Ellis prison with sharpened spoons. In 1975, Robert Cousins had taken over McAdams's role as the chief enforcer of prison discipline and was the Ellis warden. Working for Cousins was Major L. A. Steele, who had a reputation for violence against African Americans. The prisoner Michael Jewell recalled that Steele, who was six feet three and weighed well over 350 pounds, was one of the "most sadistic officials I ever had the displeasure of dealing with. He loved violence."[72] In an interview with the Justice Department consultant Arnold Pontesso, the Muslim prisoner Rester Ray Ballard told the investigators that "they were mistreating us, jumping on us, the building tenders and officers. We'd work all day in the fields and some of us they'd tell to catch the back gate so they could give us a [disciplinary] case, you know a field case for not working." Ballard contended that Black prisoners would get three to four days of cell restriction while white prisoners whom the TDC charged with the same offense would "get 2 or 3 hours cell restriction." Ballard felt that African American prisoners, particularly Muslims, were targets of racial violence. "I didn't ever see no white dude come out of the office all bloody, like he had been jumped on," Ballard argued. "The only thing I seen was just black dudes getting mistreated." Black prisoners had drawn up grievances and demands that the TDC remove Warden Cousins and Major Steele from the unit, which the TDC ignored.[73] A group of building tenders put down the failed rebellion by using "pipes and sticks" against the rebelling prisoners. The TDC placed the fifteen insurrectionists in solitary on three fifteen-day convictions for a total of forty-five days. The abortive efforts of the Muslims ended in further violence against the prisoners by building tenders, which served as a reminder that the onset of mass incarceration had been accelerating carceral violence.

Mass Incarceration: Making Carceral Violence Worse

Prisoner organizing was also a prisoner-initiated response to the mounting wave of mass incarceration that swept an increasingly disproportionate number of urban minorities into the nation's prisons. The prison environment from 1972 to the opening of the *Ruiz* trial in 1978 had grown more violent, overcrowded, and dependent on building tenders. Law-and-order politics and get-tough-on-crime policies contributed to the overcrowding. The call for law-and-order politics on the national level has its origin in the 1964 presidential campaign of Barry Goldwater and in the public's response to grow-ing crime rates in the 1960s.[74] A 1968 Gallup Poll, for instance, found that Americans saw crime and lawlessness as the single most pressing domestic problem.[75] In response to the public's perception of lawlessness, President Lyndon Johnson established the President's Commission on Law Enforce-ment and the Administration of Justice, which issued executive-level recom-mendations highlighting the nation's concern with the rising crime rate. Congress, meanwhile, enacted the Safe Streets and Crime Control Act of 1968, which offered federal monies to state and local government for innova-tive crime-prevention programs and further efforts at rehabilitation. At the same time, Congress in 1968 created the Law Enforcement Administrative Agency (LEAA) with a budget of over $8 billion for the development of ad-ditional police, courts, and prisons.[76] Moreover, embedded in Johnson's anti-poverty measures were federal programs that diminished urban Black communities' decision-making and introduced intrusive policing to inner-city neighborhoods.[77]

At the state level, Texas politicians followed suit and passed in 1967 a new penal code that restricted prisoner eligibility for parole only after serving one-third of their sentence. Previously, prisoners served only one-fourth of their sentence before they became eligible for parole. The 1967 law therefore kept prisoners in the TDC for longer periods. A decade later, a second law pro-pelled prison growth. A year before the *Ruiz* case was heard in federal court, Governor Dolph Briscoe passed a law-and-order crime package that extended prison stays for violent criminals. The 1977 state legislature's Senate Bill (SB) 152 stripped the good-time policy away from all prisoners who committed a felony with a deadly weapon. Before 1977, Texas state law allowed all con-victed prisoners, except those under the death penalty, to be considered for parole after they served one-third of their sentence or twenty years, which-ever was less. The new law stipulated that prisoners convicted with a violent felony serve "day for day" the first third of their sentence. Prisoners called it serving full "hard time" rather than good time. The law also diminished the judiciary's sentencing power. Prior to the 1977 law, both judges and juries had discretion to suspend sentences of less than ten years and to place defendants on probation. The Briscoe law, however, stripped judges of the power to grant probation for violent crimes.[78] Signaling a shift from prisoners' rights to vic-tims' rights, the bill also included restitution to the victims of a crime as a condition of parole. Before *Ruiz*, then, Texas was already well on its way toward mass incarceration.

When Briscoe first introduced his law-and-order crime package, he fre-quently cited the fact that 67 percent of offenders released from the TDC were arrested for a new offense within three years of their release.[79] Governor Briscoe was also responding to a shift in public sentiment that demanded longer prison sentences for convicted criminals. In a 1977 Texas Crime Poll of one thousand citizens conducted by Sam Houston State University's Criminology Department, 56 percent of respondents felt that prisoners should serve the full sentence and only 12 percent thought that violent prisoners should receive probation.[80] Even more compelling was the fact that 86 percent of those polled agreed that violent criminals should receive no probation. The issue of victims' rights also received a boost when 62 percent of respondents said that victims of crime were not treated fairly by the criminal justice system, while 75 percent of the respondents felt that the criminal justice system treated defendants and prisoners fairly.[81] Governor Dolph Briscoe reflected the public sentiment when he declared, "The time has come for Texans to demand the rights of the accused be no greater, extend no longer, be no more carefully defined than their own rights as citizens of Texas and of the United States. The time has come for government and the courts to announce the rights of the law abiding citizens."[82] An editorial in the *Herald* of Perryton, Texas, seemed to agree: "After all, the criminal has had his rights protected long enough. Now it's our turn."[83]

The 1967 change in the penal code and the 1977 crime package contributed to overcrowding in the prison system. With the passage of these two new laws, the total prisoner population more than doubled from 12,313 in 1970 to 29,886 by 1980. Not only was the prison population doubling, but the incarceration rate relative to the state's population growth had accelerated over the decade from 113 per 100,000 in 1967 to 210 by 1980. Many prisoners could expect to live in double- and triple-bunked cells meant for only one prisoner. As Ronald Reagan assumed the office of the presidency in 1980, Texas had more than 5,000 prisoners without beds and who slept nightly on the prison's hard, concrete floor.[84]

Correspondingly, mass incarceration also accelerated the TDC's reliance on building tenders, many of whom were white, to police and supervise the overcrowded cells and dormitories. In 1974, there were approximately 800 building tenders throughout the TDC, which made up 4.7 percent of the prisoner population of 17,000. By the end of the decade, however, there were 2,265 building tenders making up 9 percent of the 25,000 general prison population. Indeed, when the *Ruiz* case went to trial in 1978, the TDC employed one uniformed guard for every 12 prisoners, which was the lowest guard-to-prisoner ratio in the nation. Such an imbalance created an uneasy comparison to the national average of 1 guard for every 5 prisoners. The prisoner mobilization effort and the simultaneous increase in building tenders also led to more incidents of self-defense, violence, and unrest. The TDC reported that between 1970 and 1977 the number of annual prisoner infractions

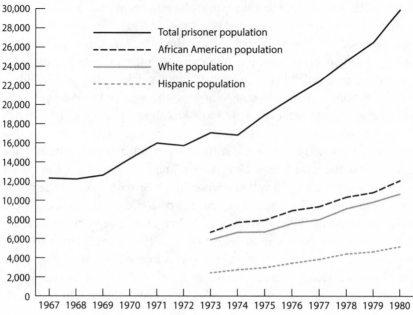

TDC population by racial classification, 1967–1980. Source: 1980 Annual Statistical Report, TCC, *Ruiz* Discovery, Overcrowding, 2004/015-31, *Ruiz*, CAH.

doubled from 124 to 234.[85] The overcrowding and expanded reliance on building tenders made for an explosive prison environment.

The Prisons as Slavery Narrative

As white prisoners policed, abused, and owned Black and brown bodies, the prisoners' rights movement fashioned a language of resistance that claimed that southern prisons, in particular, were explicit examples of twentieth-century slavery. While prisoners did not have the term *mass incarceration* to define their predicament, they knew from their lived experience that prison overcrowding accelerated TDC dependence on the building tender system, and as such they argued that carceral violence was getting worse. To counter the worsening conditions, prisoner organizing groups adopted similar language, whose purposeful tactic was to construct a counternarrative to the southern modernization "success story" by presenting their own narrative of a "backward" prison system tied to slave practices, racial brutality, and plantation labor. The prisoners reframed the control penology and agribusiness narrative with their own alternative narrative that cast the prison as a plantation and the prisoners as slaves. The rhetorical design to name all prisoners as slaves represented more than metaphorical rhetoric. For prisoners, it was a carefully crafted political design to enact consciousness raising by creating brotherhood across all racial lines that reminded prisoners that they shared the collective condition of dehumanization. In an attempt to break the "slave mentality," one letter writer expressed how the discovery of the prisoner as twentieth-century slave promised political conscious-ness and interracial unity. "I cannot overlook those repressive illegal methods of skullduggery that the oppressor in this 'plantation regime' have employed against certain unaware slaves here in past." References to the TDC as a "slavocracy" littered prisoner letters, which explicitly called attention to the southern practice of unpaid prisoner work as slave labor and the southern trusty system that accelerated the prison plantation's inter-nal sex slave ownership. Moreover, prisoners argued that their own agricul-tural stoop labor occurred on the grounds of former plantations and that their harvesting of cash crops was no different than the work of nineteenth-century slaves.

The universality of prison abuse in the U.S. South allowed prisoners of non–African American dissent, particularly Chicano prisoners, to share in the discourse that southern prisons created modern-day slavery. From 1973 to 1980, the number of Mexican Americans in Texas prisons more than dou-bled, from 2,442 to 5,168.[86] In view of this shared criminalization against people of color—both brown and Black—many politicized Chicano prison-ers drew on the Chicano movement to frame the conditions of southern pris-ons as a process of dehumanization that was shared by Mexican American and African American prisoners alike.[87]

Sympathetic white prisoners also employed the slave discourse as they ar-gued that the transition from freedom to debased plantation confinement rendered all prisoners, regardless of race, to the same condition. Thomas W. Shaw's September 1974 letter to State Senator Ron Clower, for instance, showed the ways in which prison stripped some Anglo prisoners of their in-tersectional masculinity and white skin privilege. "Men leave here every day who have been humiliated, belittled, abused, beaten up and reduced in man-hood," Shaw protested. "I never in my life realized until I entered this system, what it must be to be born BLACK, or be Spanish-American. However, since the system operates on the concept of slave master principles of 100 yrs. ago, I have found out for myself how it must feel to be black."[88] Anglo prisoners who felt that imprisonment cost them their "whiteness" often couched their critique of the prison system in a racialized language that employed crude racial epithets and a sense of loss over their previous racial entitlement.[89]

Outside of the South, the discourse that prisons constituted slavery was a metaphorical organizing principle that condemned the entire prison system as a form of U.S. apartheid, which could only be undone by rallying African

Americans to the prison abolitionist cause. In a variety of nonsouthern states, particularly California, Illinois, and New York, Black prisoners formed organizations and printed underground newspapers in hopes that the slavery discourse might galvanize African Americans across the nation toward collective action. In Illinois, for instance, the New Afrikan Prisoner Organization (NAPO) formed in the aftermath of prison uprisings at the Stateville and Joliet prisons, while in California the San Quentin Six, those men who were charged for the deaths of three guards and two prisoner trusties on the day of George Jackson's death, also employed the slavery discourse within a national context.[90]

Across the U.S. South, however, the charge that prisons constituted twentieth-century slavery had very literal physical manifestation. Southern prison farms forced unpaid prisoners to toil on former plantations in racially segregated work lines, where they picked the cash crop of cotton, worked under white prison bosses and convict drivers, and faced routine corporal punishment and state-orchestrated sexual assault. While Black Power outside of the South charged that African Americans went from the "prison of slavery to the slavery of prison," in Angela Davis's words, prisoners in the South underwent a distinct geographical imprisonment that made their legal condition as slaves of the state a visceral indictment against southern prison practices.[91] Southern prisoners' rights campaigns, therefore, sought a strategy that applied these metaphorical discourses to the physical geography of southern prison plantations, framing their contemporary incarceration as the living legacy of enslavement. By drawing analogies and comparisons between southern prison and slavery, southern prisoners knowingly confronted the TDC's modernization success story with the brutality and inhumanity of nineteenth-century slavery.[92]

The Prisoner Solidarity Committee (PSC), for instance, sent out a handbill titled "Texas Prisoners Resist Texas Slave System." The PSC's leader was Salvador Gonzalez, a writ writer and life-long friend of David Ruíz. The group's external sponsors beyond the prison were a collection of state representatives, labor unions, Texas farmworkers, La Raza Unida, Centro Aztlán, Brown Berets, Attica Brothers, the Mississippi Prisoners Defense Committee, and the Beat poet Allen Ginsburg.[93] One of their sponsors was the Brown Berets of Austin, whose very formation was aimed against police brutality and the carceral state after the Austin community became outraged over the death of twelve-year-old Santos Rodríguez in Dallas during a police interrogation involving a deadly game of Russian roulette.[94] As a former building tender himself, Gonzalez knew well the incentives and rewards of prisoner service to the state. Indeed, TDC prison officials had previously offered him the body of Steven Blanchard if he returned to his job and turned his back on writ writ-

In Ruiz lawsuit...

Prisoners resist Texas prison slave system

In 1924, the Committee on Prisons and Prison Labor condemned the Texas Prison System for inadequate medical care, unusual and brutal punishment, and for its unqualified personnel. Now 54 years later, it is 1978 and the Ruiz v. Estelle case is raising the same questions. Isn't it time for a change?

Slavery was abolished in 1865, but not in Texas prisons . . .

"On December 18, 1865, the 13th Amendment to the U.S. Constitution was ratified . . .

"That vulnerable institution was continued, however, in penitentiaries throughout the country. Texas Department of Corrections is probably the best example of slavery remaining in the nation today."

"The most overpowering impression is the immense size of the facilities and the well-kept farms of thousands of acres."

"One gets a strong feeling that TDC exists not to punish offenders or deter others from committing crimes, not to rehabilitate criminals, but to perpetuate the plantation as the largest agribusiness operation in the state."

Quoted from: Arnold Pontesso, U.S. Justice Department, Consultant, writing on "Ruiz v. Estelle"

What you can do to bring rights to prisoners in Texas

☐ We need people to help distribute leaflets to publicize the case.
☐ Arrange to have a member of our organization speak before your group, family, or friends.
☐ We desperately need contribution ($) for envelopes, stamps, paper, etc.
☐ Most importantly, we need people to attend the court sessions.

Please clip and return to: Prisoner Solidarity Committee, P.O. Box 52115, Houston, Tx. 77052   713-759-9714 713-926-8771

Name _____

Address _____

City/State/Zip _____

Partial list of sponsors

Ben T. Reyes, State Representative (Houston)/Carlos Truan, State Senator (Corpus Christi)/Ray Hill, Human Rights League (Houston)/Garland Jaggers, ‡Executive Director, Black Secretariat of the Roman Catholic Archdiocese of Detroit/Diane Goldberg, ‡AFSCME Local #140 (Detroit)/Demetrio Lucio, ‡AFSCME Local 1550 (Houston)/American Civil Liberties Union (Houston)/Lorenzo Cano, Harris County Raza Unida Party (Houston)/Antonio Orendain, Director, Texas Farmworkers Union/National Lawyers Guild (Houston)/La Raza Legal Alliance(Houston)/Rado Rosales, Brown Berets (Houston)/L.C. Dorsey, Associate Director of the Southern Coalition on Jails and Prisons, Inc./Ron Welch, Attorney, Mississippi Prisoners Defense Committee/Eddie Sandifer, Chairperson, Mississippi Alliance for Human Rights/Ruby Tobias, Mississippi Council on Human Relations/CASA-HGT (San Antonio)/Tom Soto, Prisoners Solidarity Committee and negotiator for Attica prisoners (New York)/Eduardo O. Canales, Director, Centro Aztlan (Houston)/Allen Ginsburg, Poet.
‡Organizations listed for identification purposes only.
(This brochure was produced in Sept. 1978 by the voluntary labor of members of the Prisoner Solidarity Committee.

Prisoner Solidarity Committee pamphlet declaring that "In Ruiz lawsuit, prisoners resist Texas prison slave system." By Prisoner Solidarity Committee, Frances Jalet-Cruz Papers, di_11637 and di_11638, Dolph Briscoe Center for American History, University of Texas at Austin.

ers. When Gonzalez refused, he and David Ruíz wrote a series of letters to state politicians that presented affidavits from fellow prisoners that offered a stark depiction of prison rape as state orchestrated and sexual enslavement. In a letter to state Senator Chet Brooks, Gonzalez implored the state legislature to respond to state orchestrated prison rape and rampant racism with constitutional and humane protections, "What is really happening in this prison, society refuses to believe, because they really believe in a humane world, and it is my prayer that the Legislature will investigate the conditions and operation of this prison and bring to light the many wrongs and dehumanizing conditions that exist here."[95] For prisoners motivated by the Chicano movement, the coerced ownership of one prisoners' body by another more priviledged prisoner violated what Tomás Almaguer has identified as a Chicano sexual cartography that configured masculinity through "gender/ sex/power . . . along the active/passive axis and organized through the scripted sexual role one plays [either *activos* or *pasivos*]."[96] State orchestrated prison rape at the hands of building tenders, however, threatened the Chicano prisoner's sense of individual sexual object choice, thus threatening the humanity of all prisoners and making a united front to expose such a rapacious system as sexual enslavement all the more urgent.

The eight-page handbill offered vivid pictures of southern prison labor hoeing cotton fields and picking the cotton harvest as cowboy-hat-wearing prison guard high riders bestrode on horseback above the laboring prisoners. The PSC acknowledged that the TDC had successfully constructed in the public's mind a modernization narrative, but the handbill countered that such a narrative hid the truth of Texas prisons that were "scarcely what a reasonable person would expect to find in 1978 in a state with a reputation for modern methods and proud structures." The handbill openly mocked TDC claims of modernity when it derisively stated that "the distance from the prison farms of East Texas to the NASA Space Center is greater than the distance from the Earth to the Moon." In response to the TDC's agribusiness narrative, the handbill charged that the conditions of southern incarceration in Texas "are the prison conditions of a century ago, of the pre–Civil War era. . . . It is scarcely what a reasonable person would expect to find in 1978 with a reputation for modern methods and proud structures." The TDC's rise as a model of southern correctional management to counter the rehabilitative model among prominent penologists and state prison managers was therefore contested in a public struggle over the prison's national image.

The PSC handbill provided a brief history of the Texas prison system, a letter of appeal from David Ruíz, and a summation of the issues in the *Ruiz* case. The PSC acknowledged that the JCPR had produced good and accurate reports of prison abuse but that "legislation has been passed with no punishment provided for its violation." Ruíz's letter, titled "An Appeal from Prison," stressed that the struggle for prisoners' rights crossed the boundary of prison walls and that the *Ruiz* case would be decided beyond the courtroom, where only "with strong public support we will succeed." Ruíz thought that the courtroom strategy must showcase the two decades of prisoner-initiated documentation "to shock the conscience of the vast majority of people." Ruíz's letter offered a personal message meant to remind the wider public that prisoners were more than criminals and that the prison system dehumanized prisoners and turned them into objects.

> Who are the prisoners in TDC? Some are white, some are brown, some are black. Almost without exception, we are the poor people of Texas; and without exception we are all human beings. I am sure that each of you realizes that each of us is human. We share the same feelings; we love, we feel joy, we feel pain, we know sorrow and we have dreams, hopes and desires for a better tomorrow. Progressive programs and humane treatment that may come about if this suit is won will surely encourage the inmates to participate in their rehabilitation with joy and hope.[97]

In the pamphlet, Ruíz never claimed that he was innocent of his robbery conviction, but he wanted the public to understand that the commission of a crime did not deny prisoners their humanity. "When you remember me, remember not one who desires evil and destruction, but a person whose only aims, hopes and desires are to improve, always to improve and to contribute to humanity." Accompanying his letter was a stark photograph of a line of prison guards in cowboy hats laughing as nude prisoners stripped of clothes and dignity filed by the bars and on to their cages. The handbill was part of a concerted public campaign to humanize prisoners and make carceral violence legible. As head of the PSC, Gonzalez offered to state Senator Chet Brooks what was perhaps the most eloquent summation of the southern prisons as slavery narrative: "No one wants to be enslaved. To be powerless, to be subject to the arbitrary exercise of pwer, to not be recognized as a human being, is to be a slave . . . an object, a number, or worse, a no-thing."[98]

A Peaceful Riot against the Prison Plantation: The Work Strike of 1978

The crowning phase of the movement, however, was the first ever system-wide prison labor strike in Texas. As the final act of prisoner organization, prisoners planned on the second day of the *Ruiz* trial to confront the prison plantation's power through a labor work strike. The prison strike started at Ellis prison, where an interracial planning committee included Alvaro

Luna Hernández and Johnny Swift as the two chief prisoner organizers. Before his conviction, Hernández styled himself as another tough pachuco who had first encountered police brutality in 1968 when at the age of sixteen he witnessed his friend Ervay Ramos shot in the back as he fled from Assistant Police Chief F. L. Powers during a traffic stop.[99] The U.S. Commission on Civil Rights documented the police shooting of Ramos in their 1970 report *Mexican Americans and the Administration of Justice in the Southwest* as a clear incident of police brutality.[100] For Hernández, this was a defining moment that revealed to him the degree to which the criminal justice system served as an agent of Chicano repression. Seven years later, Hernández, at the age of twenty-three, would be charged with the murder of an El Paso student, a crime that Hernández steadfastly denied.[101] Following his 1975 conviction, Hernández was sent to Ellis, where he embraced the prison culture's mind change and transformed himself by reading Chicano history and revolutionary political theory. In 1979, Hernández filed a First Amendment civil rights lawsuit to have access to *Torch-La Antorcha*, a bilingual publication of the Revolutionary Socialist League of New York. In the socialist magazine an article entitled "Texas Prisoners Oppose Klan Organizing" reported that the Ellis prisoners, likely under Frank Leahy's direction, were organizing a KKK chapter "with the encouragement of the guards." In opposition, the TDC claimed that the article should be prohibited because it was "designed to achieve a breakdown of prison through inmate disruption such as strikes or riot" because the prison was under a "powder keg situation."[102] As the *Ruiz* case neared its October 1978 opening day in court, Hernández worked with Swift and other prisoner organizers to coordinate a systemwide prison strike.

On October 4, 1978, the prisoners of the Ellis prison plantation turned the fields of coerced labor into a protest site. Nine prisoners refused to work and sat down in a work strike in support of the *Ruiz* trial. "On Oct 4th 8 comrades and myself threw off our cotton sacks while out in the cotton fields and told the overseer that we refused to work," one of the strikers, Butch Mendez, recalled. "All of us 9 quit at the same moment, for the same reason, which was to show our support for the brothers in court (David [Ruiz] vs. Estelle)." The TDC acted quickly to hide the rebellion as the nine strikers "were immediately whisked away on a bus so that others would not see us and join us." Following a hastily assembled "kangaroo court," the nine were placed on segregation. Butch Mendez and Marcelino Jaramillo were "charged as ringleaders agitating mutiny," and they had all their good time take away, reduced to the lowest third-class field status, and were sentenced to "two trips (15 days a trip) to solitary."[103] The TDC similarly charged Michael Jewell, a white prisoner and one of the first to strike, as a "mutineer," and they sentenced him to permanent segregation for acting as one of the group's leaders. While Jewell had written and disseminated tracts as a writ writer and political organizer, he felt that he "did no brilliant planning or organizing to accomplish the strike. I was just the match in the grass."[104] The price these prisoners paid for their participation in the strike was their chance at an earlier prison release.

But it was too late. The strike had spread. Despite the guards' sharp barks and insistent demands that the prisoners return to work, by midafternoon on October 4 another 408 prisoners sat down in solidarity. Sitting in the field at Ellis were several hundred prisoners refusing to work. Within the walled fence but outside of the building were another 150 to 200. On October 5, Mendez could see the strike's progress from the window of his segregation cell. "As men were on their way to work some 148 just sat down and refused to go to work. Chicanos, blacks, whites! It was a united front to show support for the trial. By the 6th there were close to 600 of us on strike here on Ellis. All in support of the trial."[105]

The strike spread within a day to the Darrington prison, where over three hundred prisoners turned from the field to march back toward their prison unit, only to be fired upon by the assistant warden, resulting in "superficial buckshot wounds" to three prisoners. As news of the work strike spread across the prison system, the prisons at Coffield, Ellis, Clemens, Darrington, Eastham, and Ramsey I and II also erupted into disturbances and work strikes throughout the next week. Out in the field at Eastham, the rank-and-file striker Eubanks remembered that "it wasn't a planned strike. There was kind of a rumored attempt at making—I say rumored attempt at planning it. There was guys going around talking for a couple of days before then, about man, we need to lay it down [term for strike]. We need to stop. We need to strike. Because the *Ruiz* case had just gone to trial."[106] The strike therefore had elements of frustrated spontaneity for some rank-and-file prisoners, but among prisoner organizers it was a carefully planned event coordinated with the opening of the *Ruiz* trial.

In all cases, the prisoners chose to begin the strike in the fields and not in the actual prison out of fear of what the building tenders might do. "It was generally accepted that beginning the strike in the fields was better than refusing to go to work from the building," recalled Eubanks. "The BTs (convict guards) controlled the building but not the fields. Plus, when an inmate went to work in the fields he was given what amounted to a large, heavy duty garden hoe, referred to as a 'aggie,' which could be used as either an offensive or defensive weapon."[107] Although the threat of violence and riot overshadowed the prison at all times, especially during a work strike, the first five days of the strike remained peaceful.

To keep state violence at bay, the prisoner organizers hoped that the media would cover the work buck and that statewide media coverage might keep the TDC from violent reprisal while they also hoped that television coverage would inspire more prisoners on other prisons to join them. "We'll use the media—their own media to spread the word to the other units," Hernández recalled, "and the other units hopefully will follow suit, and that's exactly what happened. I mean even the women at the Goree Unit—of course, Goree Unit was a women's facility then—even the women started to protest."[108] As the strike reached its second day, the prison guards refused to feed the prisoners and used hunger as a lure to get the prisoners back into the building. A fellow striker and white prisoner, Robert Mudd recalled the excitement of the media attention and yet also the strains of hunger: "A Channel 2 helicopter flew over at one point and we made signs with our black socks— they were giving us black socks back then, and we put 'No water—no food.' And they had set up video cameras up on the roof, and they were filming us, and they had this long pole with a microphone on it, and they would stick this microphone out over the yard when we were having meetings. Each—group had a representative—blacks had a representative, the whites had a representative, and the Mexicans had a representative."[109]

During these meetings, prisoners would have the opportunity to stand before their fellow prisoners to air grievances, keep the strike momentum, and pass the time. Hernández conceived of these impromptu strike speeches as "an extension of the prison reform movement, an extension of the civil rights movement, an extension of the political consciousness of a certain segment of society that were just thrown in the slammer and forgotten. And that's how we felt. And that's why we spoke about human rights and we spoke about revolution and we found inspiration in Attica. We found inspiration in George Jackson and with the things that he was saying." For Hernández, these meetings were the culmination of years of internal prison mobilization for a collective strike. "We tore the carts and everything and we had bonfires at night and it was beautiful. I mean, from the revolutionary prospective, I saw Attica. That's what I saw. Fires were going and then we would all have a chance to speak. You want to speak, get up there and just kind of lecture the people about, well, the importance of the struggle and why we have to do what we have to do." Indeed, the unity of the prisoners spread to even those that were not striking. When the prison administration refused to feed the striking prisoners, those prisoners who were not on strike inside the building broke the windows and passed food to the strikers.[110] Wilbur Collins, an African American prisoner on Ellis's death row who was known as "Wolf" for his temperament and "Kojak" for his shaved skull, recalled how even the death row prisoners contributed their food to the strikers. "It was beautiful, really, the total unity that was behind this. Because the guys on H 18, which was directly across from J-23 [death row], they passed blankets and food out. And they would bring a food cart to death row. On death row we would eat every other meal. Everyone on death row agreed. If we eat breakfast, we wouldn't eat lunch. We'd place our food on fix up trays and pass them across the hallway to the turnkey and they would pass them to the guys on H-18 and they would then pass them out the window to the back slab," where the strike was taking place.[111] As a prisoner on death row, Johnny Swift would have been among those that offered his food to the striking prisoners.

Moreover, the strike mixed previously segregated prisoner populations without incident and in peaceful racial solidarity. "There was no love loss among the races back then," Mudd recalled, "but at that point we were very unified in what we were doing as far as the strike. It was for the Ruiz trial, you know."[112] Hernández had a similar memory: "During those two weeks, there was no racial tension whatsoever, and there was black inmates, Hispanic inmates, white inmates, and it was just like solidarity there." But on Tuesday, October 10, the prisoners feared that they might be the victim of state violence when 1,500 prisoners on the Coffield prison barricaded themselves inside their cell blocks. These prisoners used blankets to tie their cell doors open, and they barricaded the openings to the cell blocks with mattresses, while also smashing TV benches, glass panes, mops, and brooms to make a series of lances from which they formed a defensive phalanx. In response, the TDC decided to storm the building, first using tear gas and then sending in corrections officers to quell the uprising. When the TDC stormed Coffield, the prisoners did not offer much resistance and surrendered. On the whole, prisoner unity in support of the Ruiz trial was such that it also kept the strikers from rioting or having violence break out among themselves. Hernández and his fellow prisoner organizers had watched the state violence unfold at the Attica and Soledad prisons, and they insisted that the southern prisoners' rights movement engage the prison plantation with a nonviolent strike at the locus of its power—the labor system. For Hernández, the fact that the prisoners remained nonviolent offered them an opportunity to showcase their humanity to the public. The fact that they had earned the public's interest and that the trial was shining a light on prisoner abuse showed that victory for the prisoners' rights movement was finally in reach:

We felt that we had TDC on the run, and of course, remember one of the objectives was to show the public our humanity. To show the public that hey, we're not animals. You know, we've got TDC on the run. We're in court. We've got one of the best judges in the country, William Wayne Justice. He's going to hear us. He's got right in here—inmates like us, or people who are oppressed, so everything's in our favor. Should we tear this place down? Should we try to take it over? And then we used the example of what the Muslim brothers tried to do when they tried to take over the [Ellis] building, and it didn't work. So, we'll just sit—we'll riot peacefully.[113]

By the end of the week, the "peaceful riot" and work stoppage had occurred on six of the prison system's fifteen units and had involved nearly 1,500 prisoners, approximately 15 percent of the total population of 29,000. Before it ended, it resulted in thirty-four prisoners and eighteen guards being injured.[114] The systemwide work stoppage occurred on the second day of the *Ruiz* trial, causing Robert DeLong, the general counsel for the TDC, to acknowledge that prisoner dissent had grown beyond a handful of writ writers to grip the entirety of the prison system. His words in a closed-door session speak to the southern prison administrators' great fear that prisoner uprisings had come south and that the southern prison plantation had lost its totalizing carceral power:

Never before in the history of TDC has there been a work stoppage that spread to more than one unit. This is the first time. . . . They [the prisoners] seem to have gained a feeling of support because nothing has been done, and severe measures have not been taken. We have attempted to discipline people on an individual basis with one disciplinary case of one inmate who has never had a disciplinary report before, and some have been punished severely trying to break the system, but the situation is not working. . . . They seem to believe or perceive it as helpful to the *Ruiz* case at this point. . . . There is obviously no question if things do get out of hand, the thing can be resolved, but force will have to be used, and hopefully that is what everybody is trying to avoid. We don't want to have another Attica or anything of that sort in Texas if it can be helped.[115]

From writ writing to prisoner organizing, the prisoners had now initiated the machinery of the law on their own behalf. Their testimonies of resistance and their campaign to make coerced prison labor legible as slave labor was seen and heard by the court and the public. Their struggle over two decades of prisoner resistance to the carceral state had culminated in a massive interracial strike against the prison plantation's most coveted tool of discipline— its coerced labor regime. In 1978, prisoners across Texas loudly declared that they were not slaves.

PART III

Collapse of the Prison Plantation and the Carceral Phoenix

Chapter 9

Stuck between Justice and the Carceral State

Ruiz v. Estelle *and the Politics of Mass Incarceration*

The 1978 work strike had put the TDC on notice: prisoners and their testimonies would shape the outcome of the trial of *Ruiz v. Estelle*. Previous narratives that have stressed the centrality of Judge Justice as the chief force that brought *Ruiz* to trial and almost single-handedly determined the outcome, be they critical narratives of unwanted federal court intervention or more triumphal narratives of judicial civil rights, have neglected the political transcript that prisoners provided through testimonies that put the southern prison plantation on trial.[1] Prisoner testimonials (testimonios) and their prison-made slavery discourse shaped public debate and the trial's eventual outcome. This chapter presents *Ruiz v. Estelle* through the lens of that prisoner testimony, which delivered a decisive victory for civil rights but which could not anticipate the politics of carceral federalism and mass incarceration that trapped prisoners in between federal justice and the carceral state.

Beginning in October 1978, *Ruiz* consisted of 159 days of trial from 349 witnesses, of which over 100 were TDC prisoners, and 1,565 exhibits as evidence, as well as lengthy expert testimony from activists, academics, psychiatrists, and penologists. The prisoners charged that the prison system violated the Eight and Fourteenth Amendments to the Constitution. As a totality-of-conditions case, the prisoners charged violations in overcrowding, security and supervision, health care, discipline, and access to the courts. As a case shaped by prisoner-initiated legal work, the chief subject of the trial was the building tender system. To make their case, the court heard testimony from many of the writ writers and prisoner organizers, including David Ruíz, Lawrence Pope, Ernest McMillan, Eddie James Ward, O. D. Johnson, Allen Lamar, Felipe Barbosa, Salvador Gonzalez, Ernesto Montana, Edward S. Mauricio, L. D. Hilliard, David Robles, and Lee Otis Johnson. With three pending civil rights cases of her own, Martha Quinlan, from the women's prison at Goree, joined the *Ruiz* suit as well and testified alongside the men. Members of the JCPR also provided testimony, including A. R. "Babe" Schwartz, Mickey Leland, and Eddie Bernice Johnson. Building tenders and prison guards were also deposed in testimony that sought to excavate the internal society and prison economy that building tenders constructed.

The trial centered on all the complaints that prisoners had made over two decades, including abuses of the building tender system, prison overcrowding, prison labor, inadequate health care, and denial of legal material. In his opening statement on behalf of the prisoners, William Bennett Turner immediately turned to the building tender system when he opened with the fact that "the TDC employs a relatively tiny staff" and "because there are so few, the TDC relies on force to an unnecessary degree in order to keep order." Worse, Turner continued, "because the system appears to pride itself on being inexpensive . . . it relies on inmates to supervise others." Turner promised the court to produce ample "testimony about assaults by building tenders, even a recent rape at knife point of one of our witnesses by a building tender." The case also put mass incarceration itself on trial as Turner promised to reveal "the unspeakable overcrowding," where the "indiscriminate use of long sentences and incarceration is practically the only response to conviction of crime." When it came to health care, Turner charged that the "TDC relies substantially on inmates to perform many medical services, ranging from dispensing drugs to taking x-rays, performing minor surgery," with the predictable result that the TDC exposed prisoners to "inadequate care, needless injured, careless administration of potent and debilitating drugs like thorazine." As for the perpetual denial of legal access, Turner framed it as both a constitutional violation and a politically prohibitive act, where "the evidence will show long-standing hostility by TDC officials toward any inmate who dares to make derogatory or critical statements about TDC policies or officers."[2] All these chief points of argument came first from the prisoners themselves through their many testimonies of resistance.

While the prisoners put racial and sexual violence on trial, the TDC's defense offered a prominent figure of Mexican American middle-class civil rights activism and politics whose own history was bound up in the Mexican American claim to full citizenship through the "whiteness" strategy. The TDC's defense was managed by Eduardo Idar Jr., Texas's assistant attorney general, a former veteran of the Mexican American Legal Defense and Education Fund, a veteran of World War II, and the scion of a prominent Mexican family at the forefront of the labor movement in early twentieth-century Mexico and Mexican American political and civil rights in the United States. Prominent members of the family included its patriarch and Ed Idar's grandfather, Nicasio Idar, who cofounded one of the first Mexican railway unions and who was editor of the critical labor newspaper *La Chroníca*; his uncle Clemente Idar, who was a prominent organizer of Mexican American labor under the American Federation of Labor (AFL); and his father Eduardo Idar, a cofounder of the League of Latin American United Citizens (LULAC).[3] As a patriotic member of the World War II–era Mexican American generation,

Ed Idar Jr. joined the U.S. Army during World War II, and for his service in China, he earned the Bronze Star and the Army Commendation Medal.[4] Following the war, Idar attended the University of Texas and thereafter met Dr. Hector P. García, who inspired Idar to join the newly founded American GI Forum, which campaigned for full Mexican American access to citizenship rights, particularly the GI Bill of Rights, which guaranteed educational access, medical benefits, and housing. Through his work at the American GI Forum, Idar pursued the whiteness strategy that sought to give Mexican Americans full citizenship benefits as white citizens, without addressing Jim Crow's racial inequality and segregation against African American people.[5] After receiving his law degree, he became a lead attorney for the Mexican American Legal Defense Fund from 1970 to 1974, where he worked on such important political cases as *Regester v. Bullock*, which challenged the reapportionment plan for the Texas House of Representatives and brought single-member districts for fairer representation. In 1974, Idar took the position of assistant attorney general for the state of Texas, where he defended the state in prominent police brutality cases. The historian Richard García captured Ed Idar's social outlook perfectly when he described the new Mexican American middle-class outlook "as ideologically pragmatic, Americanist in its patriotism, and acutely conscious of its civic obligation to all Mexican Americans regardless of class and status."[6] His role as the assistant AG and the lead counsel for the TDC's defense made perfect sense and provided the TDC with the image of what responsible civic Mexican American identity looked like as opposed to their attempt to cast the Mexican American and Black prisoner alliance as one rooted in lower-class lawlessness and criminality.

Indeed, Idar drew on the history of poor migrant Bracero conditions as a way to discredit the prisoners' claims that the prison plantation was inhumane. As a member of the American GI Forum (AGIF), Idar was an author of the 1953 landmark study *What Price Wetbacks?* The AGIF widely distributed the controversial report to Congress and the media, where congressmen could use its harsh conclusions to attack the Bracero program as a danger to Mexican American citizens and the nation as a whole.[7] In his opening statement defending the TDC, Idar called on his previous role in the AGIF study as his very first words in the trial were to equate the prisoners' complaints as trite compared to "wetback conditions." "In 1954," Idar opened, "I was part of a team that made a study of wetback conditions along the Texas border that started in El Paso. We wound up in Brownsville and we visited farms where wetbacks or illegal aliens were being worked. I saw wetback camps with women and children, some of those children literally starving to death, dysentery, diarrhea. . . . I have seen nothing of that sort in the many visits that I have made to the TDC facilities."[8] By comparing the prisoner to the migrant,

Idar drew on his past political work and deployed a dismissive strategy that was similar to the whiteness strategy that claimed Mexican American rights but not African American rights. Although different in content and not a claim to whiteness, his trial opening similarly dismissed prisoners' claims as facetious and undeserving of serious consideration when compared to the genuinely deplorable conditions that Mexican migrant workers experienced.

By opening with these analogies, both sides offered arguments that centered on a contemporary struggle over historical memory. Drawing on the Prisoner Solidarity Committee's handbill "In Ruiz Lawsuit . . . Prisoners Resist Texas Prison Slave System," David Vanderhoof opened for the Justice Department with a page directly out of the prisoner's complaint handbook when their opening statement equated the modern-day prison as beset with the same problems that the 1924 Committee on Prisons and Prison Labor had cited. Vanderhoof then cleverly concluded by telling the court about a friend who was a uniformed officer in Virginia whose "charges are permitted daily exercise. His charges are housed in an area greater than many prisoners. In fact, in some places in Texas we have three prisoners housed in a space less than the size of this table that counsel is sitting at, but my friend's charges are housed in greater space. His is an animal warden, a dog catcher in Fairfax, Virginia."[9]

In response, Idar offered the TDC's modernization narrative as he expressed dismay that Vanderhoof had ignored the TDC's reputation for progress as a modernizer for southern prison reform. "I can't imagine that they would make that kind of argument. There is nothing in this system that remotely resembles the conditions that existed in 1924," Idar admonished. Moreover, Idar insisted that the prisoner plaintiffs "are overlooking that Texas took the lead in reforming its prison system way before the United States ever thought about civil rights. . . . Texas started the movement toward prison reform" in the U.S. South. Beginning with a long historical view, Idar argued that the Texas prison reforms of 1948 took "some very significant steps in modernizing and updating its Texas prison system" and that "[Director O. B.] Ellis conducted a program of reform which was praised throughout the country." Idar then offered the TDC line of comparison between the Texan control penology model and the Californian rehabilitative model that in his eyes had lost "control" over its prisoners. He felt that the TDC had been unfairly "criticized very severely for, No. 1, its work ethic; No. 2, the strict discipline that it does enforce," but that "California, which relaxed the atmosphere in its prisons, cannot guarantee the health and the safety of an inmate in that system, as well as TDC can guarantee the health of an inmate living in TDC." Idar also openly refuted the prisoners' slave discourse by once again drawing on his Rio Grande experience with Mexican migrant workers. Idar countered the argument that "TDC operates the last slave plantation system in this country" with a knowing sneer: "Obviously, that particular expert and the attorneys for the United States have never been in South Texas, have never been in the Rio Grande Valley. They have never seen conditions under which free-world people have to work. . . . There is nothing that an inmate in TDC is required to do that some free-world person is not doing to help maintain him in prison." Rather than see agricultural work as slave labor, Idar attempted to reframe it as a "work ethic." He countered that "if it is a crime for the State of Texas for the people of Texas to require that somebody who has killed, who has raped, who has robbed at the point of a gun be required to work instead of going to school five days a week . . . I must confess that Texas is guilty of that, because the work ethic at TDC does require that every inmate do work."[10]

Informing and educating Ed Idar on all the key aspects of prisoner complaint was Dr. Bruce Jackson, whose relationship with the TDC stretched back to 1965 when Dr. Beto allowed Jackson to visit and record African American prisoner work songs, producing the 1965 album and book *Wake Up Dead Man*. As the TDC prepared for trial, Assistant Director McKaskle asked Jackson, then a professor at the University of Buffalo, New York, to visit the TDC and write a series of research memos investigating the chief prisoner complaints and suggesting how the TDC might counter them. Jackson visited every prison, with the sole exception of the new women's prison at Mountain View, and observed nearly every aspect of all the prisons, from the dining hall to field work. To keep the guards from knowing that he was observing them, he kept his distance and watched some interactions between prisoner and guard through binoculars. He read through piles of TDC statistical studies on race, disciplinary charges, incident reports on violence, use of force reports, and the 232-page deposition of the former TDC employee James Ekles that offered a whistle-blowing account of building tender abuse. In the course of his investigations, Jackson spoke to at least one warden at each prison and reported that "TDC staff gave me *everything* I asked for"; "when I asked hard questions, I got generally straight answers"; and TDC granted him "total freedom to look and poke as I wished" at any "files, stacks of papers, contents of rooms and boxes." When the curious correctional officer or prisoner asked what Jackson was doing, he simply told people that he was writing an article for *Texas Monthly*. But Jackson was conscientious in his investigation, and he actively attempted to "avoid talking with any inmates who were witnesses in Ruiz" because he did not want the TDC "accused of sending an undercover agent in to trap their informants (Wow: isn't that a reversal? All during the '60s, it was government undercover agents trying to trap *my* pals)."[11]

In general, Jackson felt that the racial dynamics had not changed since he had been there fifteen years earlier to study African American prison work songs. On the *Lamar v. Coffield* consent decree to racially integrate the TDC, Jackson thought that much of the racial intermixing was already ongoing naturally among the prisoners, and he remarked that he was "surprised to learn that prisons needed *Lamar* [the racial integration consent decision] to make this shift occur." On building tenders, Jackson offered his genuine and earnest belief that the "TDC does not use BT as thugs, the way it did in the pre-Beto days." Moreover, Jackson admitted that on the "charges of BTs pimping punks, selling favors, I can say nothing: I saw nothing like that going on, but it would be silly to expect things like that to go on when anyone was around." In his final assessment, Jackson saw the BTs as similar to "New York and California officials dealing through convict gang leaders, a practice which maintains the pattern of violence and even the organization of violence the convicts bring with them." Jackson thus saw BTs simply as snitches and concluded that "no prison can run without an adequate snitch system because without one the administrators are always working reactively, and late." The problem came when BTs "exert on their own initiative, with abuses of power on their part, and with illegal behaviors they get a pass or license for." To counter abuses that might occur due to the BTs' own volition, Jackson suggested that the TDC supply "statistics which prove that building tenders are written up and negatively sanctioned at exactly the same rate as the overall population." Such statistics would "neutralize to a significant extent the oft-repeated claim that building tenders/floorboys can get away with anything." Jackson suggested that "it would be very useful if you could bring some evidence that screening [by building tenders] is something usually done to *protect* inmates from charges brought by inexperienced guards, rather than something done to protect pets." Jackson's advice was not facetious, as he earnestly believed the TDC's claim that building tenders did not act on their behalf as "thugs."[12]

As for writ writers, Jackson suggested that the only way "you can neutralize the claim that they're punished for writing writs" is to show the "number of writ writers who have not been disciplined for anything in a long time." To Jackson's mind, "writ writers are the people who are challenging the system itself. They are exactly as dangerous as the wardens think." Although Jackson also made clear that their threat to administrative control "does not legitimize any special treatment or punishment for them." His recommendation was to identify "30 of the busiest writ writers" to show "that their current punishment pattern is no different from the punishment pattern they engendered before they got literary." In addition to his investigative reports and advice, Jackson also testified as an expert witness for the TDC. In his lengthy testimony, Jackson frequently compared the northern penitentiary with the TDC, and he offered statics and his own expert career observing prisons in a variety of states, north and south, to conclude that Texas simply ran a better, cleaner, safer, less violent, prison system. At one point, Jackson offered the sentiment that made many of the next day's newspaper headlines in Texas, when he told the court that "If I had to send my son to prison—I would do anything but send my son to prison—but if I had to, I would want it to be in Texas."[13]

Jackson's reports to Idar were thus conscientious and honest in his frank assessment of the prisoners' charges of abuse, of which he simply did not see much evidence. His reports and testimony in *Ruiz* demonstrated how little outsiders, even scholarly observers of prison culture and society, could discern about the reality of the prison plantation through the haze of the TDC's well-constructed modernization narrative. In 1978, his opinion of the TDC as a better prison system than the northern penitentiary had not really changed since he wrote his well-read 1968 *New York Times* piece "Our Prisons Are Criminal," where he concluded that "no prison in the United States really does its job. The best—like California and Texas—do what they can, but they are trapped in a conceptual nightmare created by outsiders who neither understand the prison's potential nor care very much about its limitations."[14] Years later when reflecting on his defense of the TDC, Jackson admitted in an oral history that his observations for the TDC were limited, because he could not see what was going on at night and because the very nature of outsider observation itself changes human behavior. "I never saw a convict fuck another convict, either, even though a lot of convicts were fucking other convicts. A lot of things just didn't happen when civilians were walking around the building. I don't have a doubt that when I set foot in the front of the building, every guard and building tender in the building knew I was walking around."[15]

The long, comprehensive *Ruiz* trial represented a remarkable legal effort that excavated the prison's internal society and economy. Prisoners testified about the racial hierarchy of the building tender system, the weapons that building tenders were allowed to keep, the many privileges that they received, the extensive brutality that they delivered against writ writers, and the bodies of other prisoners that they sexually assaulted as a matter of prison slave ownership. Their testimonies offered stark portrayals of brutality that cast the prisoners' conditions within the TDC as utterly desperate and thoroughly gruesome. To cite but one of many such examples, the testimony of twenty-six-year-old Euris Francis was particularly gruesome as he had lost both arms below the elbow while feeding silage into a trashing machine by hand, violating all safety procedures. Francis's ordeal only became more horrific when he nearly bled to death waiting for an ambulance to come from twenty miles away. Once finally at the hospital, another prisoner then proceeded to rape the defenseless Francis as other prisoners stood by and simply watched. "The man without the arms was crying," testified the prisoner witness Oscar Turner.[16]

When the press reported on such graphic rape narratives, they often portrayed the building tenders that preyed on the protective custody wing as "homosexuals" rather than as sexual predators. One *Houston Chronicle* headline on a warden's testimony characterized building tender rape as "both violent and homosexual" with a headline that blared "Gay Inmates Were Assigned as Porters, Warden Testifies."[17] The press thus conflated homosexuality itself as inherently criminal and violent rather than cast building tender rape as state-orchestrated assault. Testimony that recounted the torture and rape of the prisoner Gilbert by the building tenders Charley Robertson and Butch Ainsworth on K-line, known as the "Ku Klux Klan wing," on Eastham had the effect of silencing the courtroom. Ainsorth and Robertson wanted Gilbert's commissary that would provide them scrip for the commissary store. When he refused, "they [Ainsworth and Robertson] wrapped a wet blanket around him first, plugged an extension cord into a socket. The ends of the extension cord were uninsulated, and they stuck this energized electric cord to this wet blanket." When electrocution failed to convince Gilbert, the two BTs then "made him stand up in the commode . . . and placed the electrics wires to his body and into the water," causing Gilbert "to scream from extreme pain, to begin to tremble, even to cry, and to submit to the homosexual acts."[18]

Several prisoner testimonies characterized solitary as a space of physical torture and mental anguish. The writ writer Donald Whitt testified that solitary was "completely dark. Even in the daylight hours you couldn't see the sun. The windows had been painted, and you couldn't communicate with anyone. You couldn't hear anything. It was just total aloneness, I guess." Immersed in darkness, kept on a starvation diet, and mentally suffering from isolation's total deprivation, Whitt explained that self-mutilation provided a tortured moment of escape. "I was being beat up. Building tenders came into my cell, beat me up, and I was starving to death, and it was just an incredible situation. I had to find a way out of it, so I mutilated myself."[19]

Former building tenders testified that their actions were indeed state orchestrated. In an effort to intimidate the white prisoner Stephen Blanchard from siding with the mostly Black and brown writ writers, the building tender Jerry Ben Ulmer testified about the day that Blanchard was delivered by correctional officers (CO) to Ulmer's cell as a fellow building tender delivered a knife to Ulmer and directed him to terrorize Blanchard. "I cut Steve

Blanchard. I cut him both sides of the neck and both arms, and he was calling for the guard, and the guard came, and Major Maples came down there and numerous turnkeys came running down there. They took him out of the cell, and Major Maples smiled at me and said, 'Later.'"[20] When the torture failed, Blanchard was subsequently placed on an African American tank, where a head building tender had him raped. The building tender Bertrand Jerome Bennett testified that the building tenders had always been directed by the state: "I had my own personal slapjack and my own personal night stick, and both of these weapons were given to me by Warden Christian and Major Henderson. They would always know that these things were going on. . . . They gave the authority for it happen, and if any officers ever approached me because of what I was doing, that officer would actually get a mental whipping for interrupting or disturbing me from the job that the warden knew I was doing."[21] As head building tender for the Retrieve prison, Jerry Golden testified that his authority above COs was absolute: "Well, the major was my boss. The correctional officer didn't have the authority to— well, most correctional offices don't do nothing but what they are told anyhow. They don't have much authority, anyway."[22]

Prisoner testimonies also made conscious connections between the prisoner claims in *Ruiz* and Black Power struggles outside of prison. In 1968, Lee Otis Johnson's promotion of Black Power in Houston earned the ire of the city police, who arrested Johnson for having a single joint of marijuana. After the state railroaded Johnson with a thirty-year sentence, Black Power and Chicana/o advocates in Texas erupted over the sentence as a clear example of the inequities of police targeting and the racist nature of the criminal justice system. Once incarcerated within the TDC, Johnson wasted no time making common cause with the writ writers and the larger prisoner organization movement. In point of fact, Lee Otis Johnson did not serve thirty years for the marijuana charge but instead was incarcerated from 1970 to 1972.[23] But when he got out in 1972, his near-celebrity status over the marijuana charge earned the attention of the media, where in one live news segment Johnson made sure to "speak out about all the conditions I seen [in the TDC]." Johnson testified that the TDC's retribution for his TV news criticism came when he was incarcerated again in 1975. Upon his return to the TDC, Captain Wade, Warden McClintic, and Assistant Director McKaskle had a meeting with Johnson over his TV criticism, where they asked Johnson to weigh himself, telling him "you won't weigh that much no more. We're going to work you to death." Johnson offered testimony on the prison plantation labor system in blunt "prison language," where field work "means you going to work hard. They going to run up on you, tell you to speed up, tighten up, go to work, racial slurs, all kinds of names, derogatory name calling, and it's both mental and physical." Further, Johnson testified to the ways in which the TDC tried to divide the prisoner coalition through racial division and promises of rewards for the commission of carceral violence. Johnson offered testimony that on July 5, 1976, Major Steele at the Ellis prison approached him and offered to give him a real-world "big knife" to "kill that writ writing Meskin, Johnny Martínez" in exchange for the major arranging for Johnson to get an early parole. Unwilling to break the interracial alliance, Johnson refused, but he later saw Martínez head to the major's office and from there to the prison hospital.[24]

As a brother in Black Power, Eddie James Ward's testimony also offered repeated narratives of the TDC's embrace of Jim Crow–era white superiority as a means to degrade Black prisoners. At one point, Ward offered shocking testimony about the face-altering scars he received from four white building tenders, who assaulted him in the showers of administrative segregation. "When I was being attacked, my nose was cut halfway off and I was beat severely with blackjacks." Ward further testified about the day in 1973 when he was beaten bloody and nearly unconscious by building tenders, who then roughly shore off his Afro as a symbol to the other prisoners that only white power would reign on the prison plantation. "Inmate guard Brumbelow, he moves in and starts kicking me and stomping me, joining the officers. In fact, I was semiconscious, and they put my hands behind my back and run me into the brick wall, run me into the iron gate out in the hall, run me to the iron gate going into segregation, shoved me in the chair and told the inmate barber to cut all my hair off."[25] Black Power prisoners like Ward and Johnson hoped to strip down the prison's external appearance as a bucolic "farm" or as an efficient business "unit" and present the TDC as a space that ingrained and policed Jim Crow–era racial subjugation.

The courtroom also served as the public space to make the prison plantation's labor division legible through the slavery discourse. Another prisoner stated that he received beatings in the field because he could not pick cotton fast enough. He had trouble describing what it felt like to be so openly subjected to field whippings with blackjacks to his head by high riders and prisoner field drivers. "My head swelled up grotesquely and I had knots. My head was so tight that I couldn't lay it down. When I laid my head down, it was just a feeling of agony is all I can explain."[26] When the court questioned Mickey Leland about his criticism of prisoner field work as coerced "stoop labor," he offered a thoughtful rebuke that "there's something dishonorable or disillusioning" about the TDC's philosophy of field work as "rehabilitation" because "when the majority of the labor that is prescribed for these thousands of people—these many, many people who engage in this stoop labor are doing things that are not relative to the environment that they are going to return to. That's what is dishonorable."[27] As one of the 349 exhibits offered during the trial, the report by Arnold Pontesso, Oklahoma's former director of corrections and an administrator of the Federal Bureau of Prisons, showcased that the prisoners' slavery discourse had indeed shaped the *Ruiz* proceedings: "On December 18, 1865, the 13th Amendment to the US Constitution was ratified to abolish slavery. . . . That vulnerable institution has continued, however, in penitentiaries throughout the country. Texas Department of Corrections is probably the best example of slavery remaining in the nation today. . . . One gets a strong feeling that TDC exists not to punish offenders or deter others from committing crimes, not to rehabilitate criminals, but to perpetuate the plantation as the largest agribusiness operation in the state."[28]

Prisoner testimony called attention to the prison plantation's attempted political isolation and rabid denial of access to civil rights as prisoners were often severely punished and tortured simply for reaching out to attorneys and state elected politicians. Ward testified that when he was held on administrative segregation on October 18, 1974, he witnessed Warden Christian and his major and captain torture David Ruíz with mace after they discovered his whistle-blowing correspondence. "Several officer came up to the cell and told David to take his clothes off and stand upon something in the cell, and at this time they were shooting mace into the cell, all in there. They went in there and manhandled David and brought him out, and sprayed mace all around, and it got over into my cell."[29] Fellow Black prisoner Allen Lamar, whose lawsuit *Lamar v. Estelle* would desegregate Texas prisons, testified that when he assembled ninety detailed affidavits from fellow Black and Chicano prisoners on racially discriminatory policies that the TDC refused to mail them to the JCPR. As a result of his attempt to reach legislators, Lamar was charged with "inciting mutiny," his affidavits destroyed, and he was cast into the darkness of solitary.[30] The price for Lamar's correspondence with Frances Jalet was an attempt to kill him on the Ellis prison on January 3, 1978.[31]

As part of the trial, two women from Goree, Rosa Lee Knight and Martha Quinlan, offered the testimonies of women prisoners. As the most active and experienced writ writer among the women prisoners, Martha Quinlan had three litigation suits pending against the TDC, one having to do with access to the writ room and equal protection, a second on sex-based discrimination that charged that women prisoners faced discriminatory access to educational and rehabilitative programs, and a third on the overly restrictive rules on visitation. A politicized prisoner, Quinlan saw the male writ writers as allies in a broader struggle, and she thus enjoined the *Ruiz* suit. Quinlan and Knight testified on medical concerns having to do with other prisoners as medical staff performing intimate pelvic exams, how the key girl system operated, and how both women were targeted because of their sexual classification as "aggressive homosexuals." In her testimony, Quinlan offered a very different account of women tenders that lacked the carceral violence that surrounded the abusive powers of their male counterparts. Quinlan described the work of key girls as follows: "They are awakened at 5:00 in the morning, handed a set of key that gives them access to every inmates' cell in that cell block. Their job is to open—to let inmates in and out of their cells, keep the living area clean, to count the laundry, keep the showers clean and also to report any disciplinary infractions to the officers." Unlike the male building tenders, Quinlan noted the absence of carceral violence among the women and the fact that the key girls and women tenders received no other privileges than the line prisoners—"other than their cell is open the entire time from five in the morning until ten in the evening five day a week, and then two nights a week they are open until 11:00 P.M. in the evening. They have free access of the cell block."[32] Free access and unrestricted movement within the prison, however, was a valuable privilege when prison restricted freedom itself.

It was the women's sexuality, however, that elicited some testimony on abuses against women prisoners. When first incarcerated, Quinlan had a good job as an "inmate bookkeeper" overseeing the stores of the kitchen. But after she complained that the other women were dragging the heavy sacks loaded with raw vegetables across the ground, making them wet and prone to rotting, she was then immediately given what she believed was a punitive job assignment to mop the hall from midnight to 1:00 A.M. each night. Although the state questioned that single hour of work as a "soft job," Quinlan curtly responded, "It's a pretty soft if you liked to be locked up all the time. I am locked up all the rest of the time" in the isolated single-cell wing for "aggressive homosexuals." As such, Quinlan testified that she was a victim of a bad classification system because she did not self identify as a lesbian. When the TDC countered that she had admitted during the classification intake interview to "being a homosexual," Quinlan corrected them: "I admitted to the fact that I had at one time in my life engaged in a homosexual relationship, yes. I did not admit to being a homosexual, because I am not a homosexual."

However, that did not stop the TDC from classifying her as such, and they used the classification of "aggressive homosexual" as a weapon against her writ writing. To keep women from writ writing, the TDC moved the Goree writ room, where prisoners did legal work, which was sixty by forty feet wide, to a small thirteen-by-thirteen-feet room meant to accommodate as many as thirty women attempting to do their legal work at the same time. With no desks, women did their legal work out in the hall and on their laps. On one occasion, the room's lack of space forced Quinlan to the hall to discuss with her fellow writ writer Wanda Moore how the Supreme Court's decision in

Wolf v. McDonnell, which declared that there was "no iron curtain" that separated prisoners from civil rights, might affect their pending comprehensive U.S. Code 1983 lawsuit against the TDC. The TDC immediately charged Quinlan with "talking outside the writ room," which carried a two-week cell lockdown with no privileges. But the TDC's rationale for this no-hall-talking rule was actually "to prevent use of the library for couples who were homosexual partners to meet with each other." With great frustration, Quinlan explained the power of the "aggressive homosexual" charge to silence writ writing: "Anyone and everyone is viewed as a homosexual or a potential homosexual," Quinlan testified, "and this was done to prohibit them from talking together, because they felt that anyone using the law library or going any place for that matter are using it for homosexual purposes."[33] Quinlan thus revealed to the court that the TDC used the label of "aggressive prison lesbianism" as an excuse to silence the legal and political work of women prisoners.

Male Chicano prisoners testified how the prison plantation system frequently targeted them because the smaller population of Mexican Americans meant that there were fewer Mexican American building tenders. One prisoner recounted how the prison derisively mimicked the treatment that Mexican migrants might find in overcrowded border crossings: "There are two lines going into solitary, and the officers in both lines had long clubs, and they were running the Chicanos in there one at a time down that line beating them with these clubs and hollering, 'Mexican, find a hole; Mexican, find a hole,' and they had four cells with the doors open, you know, so they could run in, and they just stacked them in there. I think it was 28 or 29 of them in those four cells. They stacked all of them in those four cells." The writ writer Johnny Martínez described how Chicano prisoners' legal papers would go missing from their lockers and how TDC guards and BTs had the power to simply destroy the writ-writing attempt to legally document abuses. After working days on a case, Martínez was allowed to bring some crucial affidavits back to his cell to continue his legal work, when one guard "went to reading them, and he didn't like the nature of the affidavits, and he took those and tore them up and threw them in the wastebasket, but stating, 'You sorry Meskin, you sorry Meskin, you're trying to make trouble for this poor old white man.'"[34]

Among the prisoners, David Ruíz testified first, over the course of two days on October 3 and 4, 1978. Ruíz recounted nearly a decade of brutality against him, the many thwarted attempts to reach attorneys and politicians for help, the isolation of solitary confinement, and the debilitating despair of self-mutilation. Ruíz testified that he repeatedly tried to reach outside observers because he knew that the TDC would deny his claims of building tender abuse. Over his decade of legal struggle, Ruíz received visits from Representative Ron

Waters, Chris Miller, and State Representatives Mickey Leland and Eddie Bernice Johnson. Ruíz explained that he chose self-mutilation as many as fifteen times over the course of his incarceration because "my only way out was to mutilate if I wasn't going to discontinue my relationship with Ms. Cruz [as his attorney]." Ruíz conveyed to the court that painful self-mutilation was the only relief he could feel from the mental anguish and torture of solitary confinement. "When I've been placed in solitary time after time [repeated fifteen-day allotments], I get to feeling that I might get to reach the point where my mind, you know, might just blow up, and to keep my sanity and to escape solitary confinement, I mutilate myself to get out of that."[35]

TDC cross-examination attempted to depict Ruíz as schizophrenic. TDC lawyers hoped to sow doubt that Ruíz's testimony could possibly be true as they twisted Ruíz's words about suffering "mental anguish" when in solitary as clear evidence of schizophrenia. On cross-examination, TDC attorneys asked Ruíz if he "hear[s] voices that aren't there sometimes" and sees "things that aren't there sometimes?" "Do you feel any strange tensions or do you have anything that leads you as an individual to think that there might be something wrong with your mental process?"[36] In mocking disbelief, Ruíz wryly responded that he was not qualified to make a psychological diagnosis on himself but that he still suffered headaches from a significant blow to his head that he received from building tenders in 1971. In point of fact, Ruíz had no medical history of schizophrenia whatsoever. The TDC's attempt to impeach his testimony and truthfulness with the false suggestion that he suffered from schizophrenia drew upon a post-1960s trend in psychology to pathologize political dissent from minorities as a matter of "protest psychosis."[37] Despite their best efforts, however, the TDC could not cast doubt on Ruíz's testimony, which documented over a decade of prison abuse with a clear-eyed matter-of-fact approach.

As the two sides prepared for a courtroom trial, some prisoners grew concerned about the choice of Ruíz as the movement's figurehead. Judge Justice chose Ruíz's petition from many similar writs and affidavits to serve as the catalyst for a class-action lawsuit on behalf of all prisoners, though it could have just as easily been any of the other writ writers. In an oral history, Johnny Martínez confided that "Ruíz liked to fight more than write writs. He was a fighter all the time."[38] Upon reflection, William Bennett Turner acknowledged that Ruíz was no great writ writer, but that he had a personal strength that allowed him to endure the prison's carceral violence. "I noticed the mutilations on his body the first time I saw him," Turner recalled in an oral history. "That's how he dealt with solitary confinement—he would self mutilate. His reputation among the prisoners as a jail house lawyer was undeserved. But he had superhuman ability to take punishment and to remain calm in the face of being targeted. He could handle that in a way that most other human beings couldn't. But he was not a resourceful, creative jail house lawyer the way Fred Cruz was, for example, or Lawrence Pope. David viewed himself as a martyr and a leader of men."[39] The choice of Ruíz as figurehead for the prisoners' rights movement was therefore burdened with his past history of prison violence and self-mutilation. Ruíz, however, brought personal charisma and pachuco charm to the movement, and during the court case he took on the role of an outlaw media darling.

But when the TDC could not discredit Ruíz in the courtroom, they turned to familiar practices of carceral power and outright manipulation to discredit him from within the Houston jail. As the two sides prepared for trial, little known charges came to light that Ruíz had allegedly sexually assaulted an eighteen-year-old prisoner on November 12, 1978, at the Harris County Detention Center while waiting to testify in his case. In a letter to Governor Bill Clements, the prisoner Emiliano Figueroa Magana offered to testify that Ruíz was a "revolutionary" who "almost killed me when I refused to allow him to attack me sexually."[40] The eighteen-year-old Magana offered Andres Hernandez, a fellow prisoner with a fifty-year murder sentence, to serve as witness to the incident. "Since David Ruíz has many followers," Magana worried, "Andres and I are in constant danger. If we are not free soon, we will withdraw our charges." Magana promised that "once set free, we will continue our charges against David Ruíz." Upon learning of Magana's charges and his testimony in return for freedom, the prisoner plaintiff attorney, William Bennett Turner, wrote to the governor's office. "We have learned that there were certain correspondence between the alleged victim, Emiliano Figueroa Magana, and the governor's office," Turner wrote. "I am writing to ask that you furnish us with copies of all correspondence."[41] When Magana learned that he would remain in prison and that "there is nothing that can be done until after the appeal" and that it would take "at least two years," he dropped his charges. "I don't think I want to continue testifying the case against David Ruiz, and I'm going to drop the charges against him," Magana promised.[42]

Some suspected that Magana's charges were similar to the false allegations of Donald Lock and Freddie Dreyer that were made seven years earlier against Frances Jalet in the case *Dreyer v. Jalet*. Indeed, Magana later admitted that he was approached while in the jail by an "Anglo man in civilian clothes," whom he could not identify. Magana claimed that he was told that Ruíz was to be placed in his cell and that Magana should then claim rape in return for his freedom. "I was to compose a story that he [Ruíz] tried to sexually abuse me or that he tried to kill me," Magana admitted in his 1981 testimony.[43] Magana's false allegation against Ruíz shows the extent of corruption within prison and the ways in which sexual violence or even the allegations of sexual violence were used as a weapon against writ writers who were, themselves, trying to expose the sexual violence of the southern trusty system on the prison plantation.

Another TDC source that attempted to cast false aspersions against the writ writers came from Frank X. Leahy, the writ writer that had tried to blow the whistle during the Carrasco hostage crisis and the same prisoner who had founded the AOKKK and wrote a legal brief to oppose racial integration plans in *Lamar*. Despite his racism, Leahy was a talented writ writer, causing Turner to request that Leahy testify in *Ruiz*. Leahy was transferred to the Houston jail along with the other writ writers, but after being celled with them, Leahy found that they became "pretty vindictive and abusive" when it was clear that Leahy "was no longer huing the party line," which left Leahy with "confused feelings and emotions of disgust and contempt." Thereafter, Leahy refused to testify but denied the charges from other writ writers that he had "sold out," that he had been granted any favor from the TDC, or that he removed himself as a witness under any threat from TDC or building tenders. Nonetheless, he wrote a poisoned pen letter to Robert DeLong, TDC's general counsel, requesting a deal. Leahy's letter had particular venom for Ruíz because he felt that "David appeared to me to be totally consumed by his own image to the total detriment of the litigation." He charged that Ruíz was "no great brain," that his espousal of "socialist and Marxist politics" was a "front," and that among the writ writers it was "common knowledge that Eduardo Mauricio was the actual 'worker' of the bunch and the most legally talented writ writer." He further charged that Ruíz cared only about three things: "(1) his clothes, (2) sex, (3) publicity, good or bad." Leahy offered the vituperative charge that during the trial Ruíz focused most often on letters he received from girls and that on his way back to the jail at night, he often bragged to the other testifying prisoners "about what 'kid' he can get that night and hoping some 'new meat' came in. The next morning on the way back to Court he discusses what he 'got' last night and what women might be in court that day." Leahy argued that in their conversations "sex is a predominate theme—to a ridiculous point" and that there "are some fellows definitely being abused" among the testifying prisoners. He further confided that the Black and Chicano writ writers falsely imagined themselves as part of what Black Power prisoners Allen Lamar and Lee Otis Johnson called a "revolutionary brotherhood" that was, in truth, being financially supported in a near conspiracy by Houston's Socialist Workers Party, which "was a Marxist group with close ties emotionally and philosophically to the Cuban 'revolutionary movement.'" Leahy disdainfully wrote, "Everyplace I looked, I was staring at a sign or scrawl: 'Viva Cuba,' 'Viva la Revolution Socialista,' and 'Viva Estelle: P.S. (with some statement in Spanish that my friends tell me translates 'until I get mine.')" More pointedly, he wrote, "With regard to their Marxist philosophies, I would certainly like to see how that squared with their sexual abuse of their 'brothers' and the conniving and thieving and preoccupation with material goods." Ed Idar kept a copy of Leahy's letter, but there is no further documentation that TDC acted on it. However, it is possible that Leahy's letter provided TDC with the rationale to convince Emiliano Figueroa Magana to make false and trumped-up charges against Ruíz during the trial. In exchange for Leahy's "tell-all" indictment against the writ writers, Leahy asked only that he be allowed to withdraw from his upcoming *Ruiz* testimony and that once he returned to TDC's custody, he be moved to another cell with Darald Stone as a cellmate, who "is a turnkey and works for Major Ramsey, is trusted by Major Ramsey, and happens to also be a very loyal friend of mine."[44] From Cruz to Ruíz, TDC turned to the prison practice of false allegations from snitches, who were offered privileges for their compliance.

After 159 days of trial, Judge Justice had to decide if the Texas prison system was "the best example of slavery remaining in this country," as prisoners and Arnold Pontesso of the Justice Department contended, or if the TDC was "superb, a worthy state counterpart to the well-administered and progressive federal bureau of prisons," as Fred Wilkinson, the former director of the Federal Bureau of Prisons, put it.[45] The stark difference between the model image of the TDC and the reality of prison life as alleged by prisoners pointed to a monumental clash between TDC's modernization narrative and the prisoners' plantation slave discourse. Indeed, the trial represented a clash of cultures and ideologies between southern claims of modernity that rested on productive labor and the prisoners' claims to constitutional civil and human rights. As Judge Justice noted in the conclusion to his memorandum opinion, "the trial of this action lasted longer than any prison case—and perhaps any civil rights case—in the history of American jurisprudence. In marked contrast to prison cases in other states, the defendant prison officials have refused to concede that any aspect of their operations were unconstitutional, and vigorously contested the allegations of the inmate class on every issue."[46]

On December 12, 1980, Judge Justice ruled in favor of the prisoners with a damning indictment of the Texas Department of Corrections. The court concluded that Texas prisons were overcrowded and understaffed, that prisoners had poor medical and mental health care, and that prisoners were exposed to wanton abuse and frequent violence by guards and other prisoners. After what was then the longest civil rights trial in U.S. judicial history, the court declared "their aggregate effects upon TDC prisoners undeniably contravene the constitution." Justice's opinion was a lengthy 249 double-spaced pages with 219 footnotes. Its critique was a sharp rebuke and a public indictment of the postwar southern prison system that the TDC had pioneered. Justice did not take up the language of the prisoners' slave discourse narrative and never once referred to Texas prisoners as "slaves" nor the prison system as a "plantation." On the prisoner's claim that their labor constituted "neo-slavery," Turner admitted that "the prisoner complaint of neo-slavery was a point of discussion" in their trial preparation because "it was so obviously tied to plantation work that the topic came up frequently, but we didn't have any claim in the case that it violated the involuntary servitude clause of the U.S. Constitution."[47] But Judge Justice's pointed denunciations of the TDC drew heavily on the prisoners' decade-long documentation effort to reveal how the southern prison labor regime operated.

On prison overcrowding and the encroachment of mass incarceration, Justice took up the prisoners' holistic approach that overcrowding "exercises a malignant effect on all aspects of inmate life." Justice described the cells, which measured seven and a half feet long and three feet wide for a total of twenty-two and a half square feet, as so cramped that "an average man can stand in the center of the cell and touch both walls with outstretched arms." The dormitories received an even more dire assessment as "shocking," where two rows of double-decker bunks lined the room just inches from the next bed, "resembling one giant bed." The practice of triple-celling prisoners in spaces meant for one or two had the effect of accelerating "predatory activities," where "TDC inmates are routinely subjected to brutality, extortion and rape." Drawing on the prisoners' long-standing complaint of an internal prison slave trade and sex economy, Justice made the case that prison overcrowding resulted in accelerated rates of prison rape. "Some of the most heinous examples have occurred in triple-celling situations, where two-on-one confrontations practically guarantee the capitulation of the abused third cellmate." The first waves of mass incarceration had overwhelmed the prison, and the subsequent overcrowding created "severe psychological harm and physical discomfort," where prisoners experienced "rampant violence" and the "appalling consequences" of prison rape. "Crowded two or three to a cell or closely packed dormitories, inmates sleep with the knowledge that they may be molested or assaulted by their fellows at any time."

Justice eschewed the TDC's southern modernization narrative and embraced the prisoners' complaint that the southern prison was a racialized labor system. Justice's decision cited that guards were rural and white, while prisoners were increasingly urban minorities coerced to work in cotton fields as agricultural labor. Moreover, he employed the prisoners' political charge that the labor regime privileged white prisoners. Justice cited that the correctional officers routinely "favored [white] inmates such as 'politicians' and 'building tenders'" but "keep a close watch on [black and brown] 'writ writers.'" In Idar's defense of the control penology model, he pointed to the fact that Texas had the nation's lowest murder rate, but Justice countered with words that mirrored what the prisoners had long since maintained. "While inmates may not be subject to murder at excessive rates, that does not relieve their well-founded apprehension of extortion, assault, and rape." Rather than measure prisons through the southern efficiency metric, Justice instead held that effective field work was entirely dependent upon "routine brutality" that only met productivity goals by coercing prisoner labor under constant threat of corporal punishment. Indeed, the court found that "the frequency of prison guard violence makes it apparent that brutality against inmates is nothing short of routine." Justice held that "inmates must live not only in fear of their fellow inmates, but of their keepers as well." Such a work environment created "a climate of fear and apprehension by reason of the constant threat of violence." Citing the prisoners' successful legal documentation campaign, Justice maintained that the "record is replete with credible evidence of inmates being unreasonably and unmercifully beaten with fists and clubs, kicked, and maced by the officers."

The court's assessment of solitary affirmed what Frances Jalet and Fred Cruz had tried to show in the previous decade. Judge Justice maintained that solitary and administrative segregation were nothing short of a "nightmarish condition" that created "severely negative and pernicious psychological effects." The court cited solitary's utter darkness, rank unsanitary conditions, and starvation diet, which "attempts to starve its most troublesome inmates into abject submission." Justice framed the effect of solitary as physical pain and as a psychological deprivation that resulted in such torture that desperate prisoners sought relief through self-mutilation. The judge cited the practice of "standing on the wall" and "hanging from the bars" as further evidence of carceral torture.

The fact that the building tender system stood at the very center of the judge's blunt assessment showed the degree to which the prisoners themselves shaped the court's decision. Despite the TDC's dismissal that "convicts always lie," the judge agreed with the decades-old prisoner complaint that building tenders "do the guards' 'dirty work,' serving as enforcers of the ranking officers' will in the living areas, and harassing, threatening, and physically punishing inmates perceived as troublemakers." Moreover, building tenders had engaged in "rampant callous utilization of arms" that "allows them to engage in acts of marked brutality toward other prisoners," which included torture, beating, and maiming of other prisoners with impunity. Justice noted the routine nature of "needless, savage brutality against inmates who are already subdued." The BTs' close relationship to senior prison staff meant that "inmates who feel threatened cannot necessarily communicate their fears to prison officials" because only prisoners with a "special relationship with guards are able to make his straits known to officers without fear of being re-taliated against by other inmates." Justice concluded that the building ten-der system was indeed state orchestrated and that their state-sanctioned ac-tions gave them "actual or implied immunity" to abuse other prisoners. At a minimum, the court concluded that the state had at least "partial blame for the abuses of building tenders" and that "similar culpability attaches to other high-level TDC officials, all of whom allow the building tender system, with its systemic abuses, to be perpetuated."

Justice drew upon the prisoners' legal documentation campaign to reveal the inner working of a prison plantation society and internal economy that depended on racialized privilege, coercive labor, and sexual slavery. Judge Justice highlighted that the building tenders' "great contact with prison of-ficials permits them the opportunity to arrange or influence job and housing changes, and to sell their influence over such matters to other inmates." In his decision, Justice even went so far as to point to how building tenders used their position to gain intelligence on other prisoners to fuel the internal prison economy: "Certain building tenders are able to view general inmates' files and use the information to operate extortion, prostitution, and usury schemes." Within the internal prison plantation economy, Justice maintained that the "free market situation does not prevail" and that the building tenders' eco-nomic "puissance in this respect extends to causing the loss of privileges (e.g., the right to go to the commissary, favorite job or housing assignments) or even the infliction of physical punishment."

In his conclusion, Justice wrote an opinion that could have come from the pages of a prisoner writ. Justice concluded that "the climate in TDC was one of fear and trepidation, engendered by the occurrence of frequent physical and sexual assaults, intimidation, bribery, and rule by threats and violence." Justice's memorandum opinion conveyed the tumultuous nature of the trial, and his words revealed that the prisoners' decade-long effort to bring the TDC's brutality to light had finally succeeded:

> It is impossible for a written opinion to convey the pernicious conditions
> and the pain and degradation with which ordinary inmates suffer within
> TDC prison walls—the gruesome experiences of youthful first offenders
> forcibly raped; the cruel and justifiable fears of inmates, wondering
> when they will be called upon to defend themselves against the next
> violent assault; the sheer misery, the discomfort, the wholesale loss of
> privacy for prisoners housed with one, two, or three others in a forty-
> five-square-foot cell or suffocating packed together in a crowded
> dormitory; the psychological suffering and wretched physical stress
> which must be endured by those sick or injured who cannot obtain

David Ruíz in victory, 1978. Courtesy of Alan Pogue.

adequate medical care; the sense of abject helplessness felt by inmates arbitrarily sent to solitary confinement or administrative segregation without proper opportunity to defend themselves or to argue their causes; the bitter frustration of inmates prevented from petitioning the courts and other governmental authorities from relief from perceived injustices.[48]

With this decision, prisoners made the southern prison plantation's labor regime legible to the wider public and the federal court. The TDC's southern modernity and efficiency narrative had successfully been countered by the prisoners' public campaign to expose Texas prisons as a form of plantation labor and dehumanizing slavery. Their victory in *Ruiz* resounded across the nation's courts and in its prisons. Civil rights had indeed come to the cell block and planted its legacy behind prison walls. But like so many struggles against the U.S. carceral state, the moment of victory was fleeting.

Carceral Massive Resistance in the Age of Mass Incarceration: The Political Stalemate over Ruiz

In the immediate aftermath of the 1980 *Ruiz* decision, the prisoners' courtroom victory was stuck over a political struggle between the state and the federal system. Prisoners were at the mercy of a variation on "massive resistance," where the TDC resisted federal court intervention at every turn. Making matters worse, as mass incarceration was now fully taking hold, the prisons were becoming more and more overcrowded and prone to violence. Trapped between the court and the state, prisoners had fewer external political allies as the 1980s dawned. Both Democrats and Republicans vied openly with one another over which party was the "toughest" on crime, meaning they were equally hostile to the *Ruiz* decision. Acting within the new law-and-order politics of mass incarceration, the TDC made a political appeal to the public to reject court-ordered reform, and system administrators stubbornly refused to acknowledge the abuse of the building tenders as the state repeatedly sought to overturn the ruling. Over the course of the first six months after the ruling, Director Estelle repeatedly criticized the federal court. He used the media to complain that Justice believed "lying inmates" over hardworking correctional officers and TDC officials. Estelle vehemently charged that Justice's ruling "read like a cheap dime-store novel" and that the memorandum opinion displayed a "crass, gross, almost incredible lack of literary skills."[49]

As the TDC resisted Justice's court order, the prisoners were caught in the middle of a political tug-of-war between the Republican governor William P. Clements and the Democratic attorney general Mark White over which of them would emerge as the law-and-order candidate that might resist the *Ruiz* ruling. The acrimony and struggle over who controlled state prison management particularly served the purposes of Attorney General Mark White as he prepared himself to challenge Clements in the upcoming 1982 election for governor. White had been the attorney general during the *Ruiz* proceedings, and he remained a steadfast force in resisting the 1980 decision. Signaling a political shift from prisoners' rights to victims' rights, Attorney General Mark White warned that *Ruiz* created "a very serious and dangerous situation" that "has given prisoners the mistaken notion that they don't need to obey the rules and regulations of the prison system." White criticized the *Ruiz* ruling as an unwanted federal intervention into state affairs, and he openly charged that Judge Justice "was one of these federal officials [who] takes the side of the prisoners" and "wants them all to have private rooms." Sharpening his law-and-order bone fides, White churlishly growled to the press that "too many people are crying tears for the prisoners and not for the victims. . . . I'm sick and tired of hearing from the little whining devils."[50]

Some in the public shared White's view of the *Ruiz* ruling and denounced the imposition of the federal judiciary into their state government. In an editorial letter to the press, one angry citizen cited the Article 10 of the Constitution. "This amendment [*sic*, article] means," insisted the writer, "that the prison system of Texas is nobody's business but Texas' and Texans'—and the federal government has no authority to interfere." A similar letter in the *Houston Post* suggested that the newspaper print the entire U.S. Constitution as "obviously Judge Justice has not read it. Otherwise, he would know that the federal government has specific limits to its power, and that constitutional amendments, not a judge's ruling, is required to grant it more power."[51] Another letter provided an even more abrupt suggestion: "Only nine federal judges have ever been impeached. Let's make Federal Judge Wayne Justice No. 10."[52] In some quarters, resentment drew on the public's growing animosity over the imposition of federal power over state control. As one letter writer put it, "The Civil War was lost by the seceding states, but this should not mean that we lost our Constitution."[53] Judge Justice's sweeping condemnation of the Texas prison system stirred lingering southern resentment and anger at federal power and its enforcement of civil rights issues.

Despite the growing political firestorm over litigated prison reform, the TDC still faced the power of a court order, and the prison system had little choice but to make some concessions. On March 3, 1981, the TDC reluctantly agreed to a consent decree that implemented a plan to meet Justice's ruling in the areas of health care, terms and conditions of solitary confinement, use of chemical agents, work safety and hygiene, and disciplinary hearings for administrative segregation. The building tender system, however, remained unaddressed, and the TDC continued to claim that it did not exist as a power structure within the prison. In an obvious attempt to disguise the BTs, the TDC renamed the system as support service inmates (SSIs), who were only supposed to engage in minor custodial duties. Their actual duties, power, and social system within the prison remained the same, despite the court order.

Although often cited for its decision to dismantle the building tender system, the intent of *Ruiz* had always been to reduce the size of the prison population to stem the growing tide of mass incarceration. In April 1981, Judge Justice issued a remedial order demanding that the TDC reorganize its prison system by constructing new, smaller prisons near urban communities. These prisons would house no more than 500 prisoners and would be within fifty miles of a metropolitan area with a population of at least 200,000. The order barred the TDC from building large prisons in the traditional East Texas region where prisoners had toiled in agricultural labor. Justice's 1981 remedial order thus sought to institute what legislative prison reform failed to do in 1974 with the JCPR's and Citizens' Advisory Committee's recommendations. Attorney General Mark White was aghast at the order and predicted that it would cost the state as much $4 billion to decentralize and reorganize Texas prisons according to Justice's new designs.[54] The TDC appealed Judge Justice's decision to the Fifth Circuit Court of Appeals in New Orleans on June 1, 1981.

The court of appeals issued a mixed decision on June 23, 1982. The appeals court reaffirmed the *Ruiz* decision that the TDC operated an unconstitutional prison that violated the Eighth Amendment's prohibition against "cruel and unusual punishment" and that TDC denied prisoners due process and full access to the courts. It also upheld Justice's prison ruling limiting each prison in the TDC to 95 percent of its total capacity. But the Fifth Circuit also agreed with the state's claim that Justice's court-ordered remedies were too intrusive. The court thus concluded that reorganizing Texas prisons into smaller, decentralized prisons in urban areas was beyond the federal court's power. Moreover, it concluded that the federal court had no power to insist that the TDC reduce its overcrowded prison population through increased use of parole, accelerated good time, and weekend furloughs. As the prisoner plaintiff attorney William Bennett Turner put it, the Fifth Circuit Court of Appeals "gave each side half a loaf."[55] The appeals court couched its decision in medical language and argued that Justice's remedial order "administers a massive curative dose" when "a lesser therapeutic measure" would suffice.[56] While the TDC declared victory regarding the appeals decision, the Fifth Circuit did uphold Justice's fundamental conclusion that the TDC operated unconstitutional prisons.

Judge Justice was thus free to take additional measures to ensure that the TDC carried out his orders to dismantle the building tender system. Justice responded by ordering a special master, Vincent Nathan, to routinely investigate the prison and implement full compliance. Nathan, a former law professor at the University of Toledo and a court-appointed former special master for prisons in Ohio and Georgia, assembled a staff of investigators who made 142 investigative trips in its four months of operation. These investigations resulted in a series of reports that confirmed that the SSI title was simply a euphemism and that the building tender system continued despite the court order.

After a tumultuous year, the TDC filed on January 25, 1982, a motion to discharge the special master for "gross misconduct." Attorney General Mark White charged that the disturbances across the prison system were due not to the continuation of the building tender system but to the intrusion of federal authorities into the state institution. "The activities of the special master and his staff," White charged, "are clearly the cause of inmate disturbances at TDC." Governor Clements agreed that the special master and his staff had "invaded the prisons" and that they were acting as "father confessor" to the prisoners and "causing real unrest."[57] Insisting that Judge Justice's effort to curb the onset of mass incarceration made the federal judiciary "mouthpieces for convicts," White exemplified the split over carceral federalism when he called on the Reagan Administration's Justice Department to desert *Ruiz* as plaintiff alongside the prisoners. "I'm sure President Reagan doesn't really know that his department is advocating private rooms for prisoners," White bitterly told the press. He countered with a plea to Reagan to instruct his attorney general to abandon the case because it violated his view of states' rights. "The federal government continues and will continue to persist in its demand for private rooms for prisoners," complained White. "To the state, this is simply not negotiable."[58] In a TDC memorandum notifying wardens of the effort to oust Vincent Nathan and his investigative staff, Estelle argued that the "officious and intrusive" investigation endangered the "safety and security of our units."[59] Indeed, the TDC's dismissal motion accused the special master's office of "undermining discipline and fostering unrest" and "scheming with inmates to thwart prison discipline." The state's recriminations against the special master mirrored Beto's argument a decade earlier that Jalet was fomenting riot and revolt through her legal actions. Outside influence, according to the TDC, impaired control and challenged order.

Meanwhile, Judge Justice fired back when he escalated the pressure on the TDC by calling a seven-day contempt hearing on the building tender system on March 15, 1982. During the hearing, streams of building tenders and general population prisoners testified that building tenders still ruled the cell blocks. The prison board, meanwhile, had lost its longtime chairman, H. H. Coffield, who had reigned over the board from 1955 until his retirement in 1977. The absence of a strong figure on the board allowed Jim Estelle to take "up the void." As one anonymous board member protested, "He [Estelle] very autocratically ran the entire system, including the Board."[60]

The 1978 election of Bill Clements as governor, however, had caused a shift in board members from entrenched Democrats to Republicans with less allegiance to the TDC's past record of economic success. Clements's appointment of Harry Whittington and Robert Gunn to the board brought two

Republican voices of dissent who questioned the TDC's standard denials. Whittington, who would later become known as the victim of Vice President Dick Cheney's errant shotgun fire during a hunting mishap in February 2006, pursued his own investigations into the building tender system by questioning guards and prisoners through private inquiries. "The staff kept denying we had them," Whittington told the press upon reflection of his skepticism. "They kept saying that building tenders were just inmates who swept the floors. But these guys had keys. If I came into prison as a new inmate and saw some guy with a key, I would know he had some kind of authority. . . . But nobody would admit the system existed and when we finally did settle it, we agreed in May of 1982 to hire 4,000 guards. That turned out to be 3,000 short, so that tells you who was running the system."

In May 1982 the board, under pressure from the prisoners and the public, approved an agreement to dismantle the building tender system. The consent decree barred SSIs (formerly BTs) from having weapons of any kind and strictly limited their duties to clerical and janitorial work. More effective was the clear stipulation that compelled the TDC to deny 60 percent of the current SSIs their building tender positions. The new prisoners selected as SSIs had to have a nonviolent record and no record of sexual assault. The court accelerated compliance for the prisons with the worst record of building tender abuse, namely, Eastham, Ellis, and Ramsey. These prisons had to comply by January 1, 1983, whereas the rest of the system had to comply by January 1985.[61]

The 1982 building tender consent agreement marked the beginning of the end for the old TDC order. The TDC dismissed and forced into early retirement a number of old practitioners of the control penology model. Estelle fired Warden R. M. Cousins, the protégé of McAdams and a career TDC employee for twenty-eight years, in October 1983 when Cousins ordered his guards to beat the prisoner Charles Richard Bell, a convict who had attempted to escape. The field officers at Coffield prison whipped Bell with horse reins, leaving marks across his back, and they used their horse to trample him with hooves to the bare ground. Cousins gave the order against Bell when he told his men to "do something to his ass" over a prison radio that was heard by prisoners, leaving Estelle with little choice but to dismiss the longtime warden. Donna Brobry, William Bennett Turner's partner in the *Ruiz* litigation, remarked in hopeful reflection to the press: "I hope the obviously deserved termination of this warden ushers in a new period where violence and brutality by prison guards is no longer tolerated."[62]

To make matters worse, the court-appointed special master had appointed monitors whose reports revealed that the TDC continued to flout *Ruiz* and that the prison was a chronically violent institution. In 1983, the eighty-two-

"Talking Ruiz and Prisoners' Rights" at CURE's 7th Annual Convention, David Ruíz
and O. D. Johnson representing African American and Mexican American prisoners,
and Marilyn Jones and Charlie Sullivan of CURE, 1981. Courtesy of Alan Pogue.

page special master's report on prison abuse and violence, written by the
court-appointed monitor Paul T. Belazis, was leaked to the press. The special master's office had received 670 complaints of abuse between December 1982 and August 1983. The report stated that "guard brutality to prisoners
was routine and that high ranking officers were not only aware of the brutality but condoned such actions." In the aftermath of the report, 107 officers
were disciplined and 2 wardens were fired outright, and a number of wardens
from the Ellis, Beto, and Estelle era simply retired.[63]

Exhausted and embattled by his tug-of-war with the court, prisoners, and
state politics, Estelle announced his retirement two weeks prior to Cousins's
firing. Although Estelle was scheduled to serve for another six months, a series of mismanagement charges arose that forced him to leave only four days
after he fired Cousins. The source of those charges was Lawrence Pope, the
former writ writer and prominent member of Eight Hoe. Pope stayed active
in prison reform, and he joined CURE upon his release. The notoriety of the
Ruiz case, the increasing prison population, and worried family members
with loved ones in prison caused CURE's ranks to swell. By 1977, CURE
boasted 1,500 members, and by 1985 the organization had grown to 2,500
members. In 1986, Charlie and Pauline Sullivan established CURE as a national organization headquartered in Washington, DC. Pope was CURE's

first formerly incarcerated hire, and he brought with him to CURE's office seventeen carefully filed boxes of prison documentation. From CURE's local Austin office, Pope wrote dozens of "poison pen" letters to state officials, politicians, and the TDC administration that continued the prison tradition of documenting abuses through open, public testimony. "Prison reform," Pope resolutely claimed, "is my life. It's what I am all about."[64]

In his new position, Pope found a news article that mentioned Estelle's holding in a land company known as Ten-K Inc., which also had a $2.7 million construction contract with the TDC. Pope reported that information to the prison board member Harry Whittington and State Representative Ray Keller, chairman of the House Law Enforcement Committee. Keller's committee launched an investigation into the TDC's financial dealings, and they found evidence of corruption, graft, and serious financial mismanagement.[65] The committee agreed that Estelle's construction contract to Ten-K was unethical. It concluded that cost overruns in TDC construction may have cost state taxpayers "tens of millions of dollars." It also cited an estimated $1.8 million in prison equipment that was missing, including such items as a deep fat fryer and a Caterpillar tractor. Moreover, the committee discovered that TDC officials kept two accounting ledgers, one that was given to the legislature and another that was kept from state officials that calculated the actual perks of employees. Keller angrily concluded that these discoveries were either "the end product of total incompetency or they're deliberate, neither one of them is acceptable." On his departure, Estelle resigned himself to his fate as he told the press, "I have tried to serve Texas with competence, integrity and all the sense of duty I possess."[66] But as he bid the press core farewell, he could not hide his lingering resentment: "I am not feeling sorry for myself. I'm just angry. Character assassination and guilt by association are not new to this world."[67] Within a year of Estelle's bitter resignation, four assistant directors resigned or retired and five career TDC wardens departed.

———

In the 1970s, the world of Texas prisons was in conflict. The prisoners themselves had brought attention to their cause and thrown the old prison order into crisis. Writ writers like Fred Cruz started a civil rights revolution in Texas prisons, which civil rights, Black Power, and Chicano advocates advanced through prison mobilization, organization, and legal documentation. Their public-outreach campaign earned the interest of the civil rights attorneys Jalet and Turner, and it provoked a sense of moral indignity and outrage from Judge Justice. Their cumulative efforts were thus part of a national shift in criminal law that placed Texas at the center of a national debate over prisoners' rights of citizenship and legal recognition.

The success of an interracial prisoners' rights movement to confront the prison plantation demonstrated how resistance to the carceral state required historical intersections from the labor movement, the civil rights movement, Black Power, and the Chicano movement. Their collective resistance during the late 1970s demonstrated that struggles over civil rights and radical critiques were far from being beset by a "decade of nightmares" and activist declension. Indeed, those prisoners who were veterans of the civil rights and Black Power movements felt that their struggle behind bars was intrinsically linked to their organizing experience out in the streets of free society. An analysis of the prisoners' rights movement as part of the civil rights movement also highlights how incarceration and carceral violence upholds white superiority in a post–Jim Crow South. Prisoners confronted the prison's system of racial and sexual brutalization through nonviolent means in the courts and through massive letter-writing campaigns that hoped to generate external political support. Moreover, the *Ruiz* trial and all the writ writing and testimonios that led up to it highlighted the crucial and leading role of Chicano prisoners, who drew on their own history of racial oppression against Mexican Americans within a southwest internal colonization framework. Legal documentation was more than an exercise in legality; for prisoners, the very act of legal documentation represented a political and collective act of dissent (the testimonio) as well as a constitutional claim of defiance for their civil rights.

The old southern prison plantation order had fallen, but the carceral phoenix was already arisen anew, shifting the very ground under prisoners' feet. From the prison plantation's ashes arose the new militarized prison of the 1980s ready to make war on what they viewed as the prisoner insurgent.

Chapter 10

War on the Prison Insurgent

Prison Gangs, the Militarized Prison,
and the Persistence of Carceral Violence

On Saturday, April 4, 1981, Major Billy Max Moore and Warden Wallace Pack took the prisoner Eroy Brown down to the bottoms riverbed just outside of the Ellis prison at Turkey Creek, a tributary of the Trinity River in Walker County.[1] Brown was an African American prisoner with two prior terms in the TDC. He was also a trusty, Moore's bookkeeper, a minor writ writer, and a tire shed foreman. In his position as tire shed foreman, Brown gave tires, tubes, butane bottles, and free repair to Moore's friends, many of them TDC employees, at the state's expense. When Pack denied Brown a weekend furlough to celebrate his thirtieth birthday at home, he became increasingly agitated and wrote to his sister that "these white folks got me with rocks in my jaws always working!! Working the shit out of me and steadily keep denying me for furlough."[2] In his frustration, Brown spent the morning of April 4 complaining of "all he had done for Moore" to his fellow prisoners who worked in the tire shed. As he vented his frustration, Brown even threatened to tell of Moore's tire giveaway.

Upon overhearing Brown's veiled threat of exposure, the prison guard Bill Adams subsequently ordered Brown into the truck for "running his head" (talking too much) about the tire operation. Because it was Saturday, Major Moore was fishing along the Trinity River when Adams found him and told him what Brown had said. Moore and Adams turned on Brown, cursed him, beat him, and forced him out of his shoes while stomping on his bare feet with their heavy boots. "Mr. Adams went on hitting me and every time I raised up, he would stomp on my feet," Brown recounted. "They kept hitting me and kicking me there, and I started weeping then."[3] Moore then called to the Ellis prison on the radio and asked Warden Wallace M. Pack to join them. Upon Pack's arrival, Adams left the area to return to his duties. Meanwhile, Brown noticed that the warden was carrying a snub-nosed .38-caliber pistol, which no prison guard or official was supposed to have within the prison. Moore grabbed Brown and swung him around to the side of the car and made him place his hands on the car top and spread his legs. Pack then came around from the back of the car and aimed the pistol at Brown's head directly against his exposed temple. Moore and Pack then attempted to handcuff Brown as they cursed him with a series of racial epithets and threatened him for "running his head."

Just as Moore fastened the iron handcuff around Brown's left wrist and as he attempted to place the other handcuff on the right wrist, a struggle ensued over the gun that ended with two shots being fired, one of them into Eroy's foot and another directly into the head of Major Moore, which killed him instantly. The fight between Pack and Brown continued for several more minutes as they struggled for the gun that had fallen in the nearby creek. During the struggle, Pack was shot in the elbow, and Brown repeatedly pressed the warden's face into the creek and a nearby mud-filled ditch. Yet the fight continued. "He just kept on wanting to fight," Brown claimed. "He kept on. Man, I begged and I pleaded with him. He just kept on."[4] His face pressed into muddied water, Warden Pack suffocated and died in a roadside ditch with Eroy Brown's hands pressed against his neck and shoulders.[5] Later that afternoon, a spokesman of the Ellis prison told the huddled press that had come to the prison on reports of a murder, "We've got a situation here . . . in the bottom."[6]

———

"Blood in, blood out." That's what senior gang leaders told Virgil Henry Barfield when he joined the Texas Aryan Brotherhood (AB). That meant, quite bluntly, that Barfield had to kill to get into the prison gang and that only his own death could release him from his prison-made gang bond. In the spring of 1985, AB leaders had directed Barfield to attack and kill Calvin Massey, who was only twenty-one years old, because Massey had given a witness statement against an AB member for the murder of another prisoner. Informants, African Americans, and Mexican Americans held the highest spots on AB hit lists, and, as the press put it, "right behind them were gang members who wanted out."[7] In preparation for the murder, AB members at the Darrington prison had plotted with Barfield about how the hit might take place, as they hid a ten-inch homemade knife, a shank, in the recreation yard for Barfield to use on the planned day of the murder. In a perversion of the writ writing of the prisoners' rights movement, the AB members had even preselected "witnesses" who would testify that Barfield acted in self-defense because AB members planned to plant a shank on Massey as well. The AB even went so far as to type up fabricated affidavits and witness testimony before the murder was to even occur.

On March 19, 1985, Barfield, in full view of an undisguised video surveillance camera, acted upon his orders, as he chased Massey around the dayroom openly wielding his shank, while other AB members frantically attempted to bar the door from correctional officers. During the subsequent trial, the medical examiner testified that "Massey received 42 stab wounds to his body, including two stab wounds to the back and numerous 'defense-type' wounds to his hands and arms, and four fatal wounds—one to the right lung, one to the heart, one to the right carotid artery, and one to the left jugular vein."[8] In the aftermath of the brazen prison gang hit, the press reported that "any one of the four wounds to the chest area would have been enough" to kill Massey and that so vicious were the forty-two slash wounds that Barfield had left Massey's body "filleted like a fish." One prisoner witness who had turned against the prison gang later testified that he saw Barfield just before the murder and that "he [Barfield] smiled—everything was set to take out the hit on Massey." As he committed the murder, Barfield brazenly looked up to the undisguised surveillance video camera and smiled directly into the lens. Once found guilty of the murder, Barfield spent the next twenty years in total isolation within a twenty-three-hour, seven-days-a-week cage that held prisoners in the system's new prison-within-a-prison known as administrative segregation.[9]

———

These two stories of prison murder, Eroy Brown's claim of self-defense against two white high-ranking prison officials and Virgil Barfield's gang-initiated hit, reflect how TDC prisons transitioned from state violence against prisoners to gang-initiated and racially motivated violence among the prisoners themselves in a carceral version of 1980s outsourcing and neoliberalism. From Chicago's P Stone Rangers to the Young Lords, the rise of dissident street gangs during the late 1960s occurred alongside the development of Black Power and El Moviemento, where urban gang formation represented an important organizational stepping stone in the process of urban racial politicization.[10] What is absent in narratives of urban gang formation is the ways in which incarceration and imprisonment shaped urban gang formation and racial politicization. Moreover, the existing literature frames gang formation within nonsouthern urban cityscapes and focuses most often on the social organization of urban people of color outside of the U.S. South and Southwest.[11] This chapter addresses that absence through an analysis of social change within the Texas prison system from writ writing and prison mobilization against the southern plantation model to gang formation and racialized balkanization.

Within the rural Texas prison milieu, the rise of white rural supremacist organizations supplanted the rule of building tenders. The sociologists Ben M. Crouch and James W. Marquart situated the development of prison gangs within what they call an "authority vacuum," where a new prisoner social organization "restructured inmate society, increased inmate-inmate violence, and [fomented] the rise of prisoner gangs." Crucial to their sociological account was the conclusion that "the court's dismantling of TDC's traditional and white-dominated control structure encouraged many minority (as well as many white) prisoners to press their apparent advantages" with the result that "not only did blacks effectively take over in many cell-blocks, but they also began to exploit white prisoners." Such sociological critiques of court-ordered intervention frame any disruption of stability, authority, and order as pejorative social chaos.[12] For Marquart and Crouch, the prisoners' rights movement and the *Ruiz* decision hewed to the "paradox of reform" argument that contends that "although court-ordered reform may improve conditions for prisoners, it promotes inmate-inmate violence in the process," and such prison violence is often cast as Black and brown prison violence run amok against hapless white prisoners.[13]

This chapter, however, contends that the new prison violence was due to mass incarceration, overcrowding, an attempt to reassert white privilege through gang outsourcing, and the militarized prison where gangs functioned as prison insurgents and correctional officers became counterinsurgent forces. The formation of the neo-Nazi and KKK white gangs attempted prison assassinations for radical white supremacist ends as an effort to stem the victories of civil rights in both the courtroom and the prison courtyard. As a result of white, rural prison gang formation with the aim of stabilizing the crumbling white supremacy of southern prisons, African American prisoners formed gangs of their own in response to white nationalist gangs as both a matter of group protection and as a means to compete for the illicit underground economy of the prison. This chapter reconsiders the sociological "paradox of reform" and "authority as good social order" argument by demonstrating that the shift from prison mobilization for prisoners' rights to racialized balkanization must be understood within the onset of mass incarceration, where Texas became the nation's most incarcerated state. In Texas, the decade of the 1980s caused the very ground to shift underneath the feet of prisoners who had defeated the old southern system only to see the new prison arrangement of vastly overcrowded prisons, cell isolation, administrative segregation prisons, gang warfare, and privatization. The persistence of carceral violence after the *Ruiz* decision did not occur because the prisoners' rights movement interrupted social order. Rather, the prison system itself remains an inherently violent space that consciously changes the shape, form, and modalities of its punishment regime as a way to perpetually reproduce new arrangements of carceral violence and power.

The Bottoms of the Prison Plantation:
The Race Trial of Eroy Brown

As the state waged its ongoing struggle with the federal court, the trial for the murders of Warden Wallace M. Pack and Major Billy Max Moore resurrected many of the charges in the *Ruiz* case. There was no mystery as to who killed the two TDC employees. The prisoner Eroy Brown had confessed to shooting Major Moore in the head and drowning Warden Pack. Never before in the history of the Texas prison system had a prisoner killed a warden, and no security staff employee of the prison had been shot by a prisoner since 1900, except for the Carrasco hostage crisis of 1974 in which two civilian librarians died. In response to the charges, Brown declared that it was "self-defense, all the way." His pending defense trial threatened to renew the *Ruiz* charges concerning racial violence that had only just concluded in Judge Justice's decision four months earlier. The ensuing defense trial of Eroy Brown thus drew media attention and public fascination across the state. It also contributed to the political environment of unrest within the prison community, and it affirmed reactionary fears among law-and-order politicians and some in the public that federal intervention into the state's prison system ultimately resulted in lawlessness, violence, and misrule.

Brown's defense team sought to shift the onus of the deaths from Brown to the way in which the prison system fostered racial violence. Brown's attorneys included William T. Habern, a trial attorney at thirty-one, whose father was a former Texas prisoner, and Craig Washington, one of the celebrated People's Five minority candidates elected to the state senate in 1973. Habern was a criminal attorney and the former executive director of the Texas Criminal Defense Lawyers Project, which was the educational arm of the Texas Criminal Defense Lawyers Association (TCDL). He thought of himself as the inside "producer" of the Brown defense but that Washington remained "the leading man and the star."[14] The son of a union organizer, Washington was an outspoken member of the People's Five, who joined such post–civil rights minority politicians as Eddie Bernice Johnson and Mickey Leland in protesting how the TDC administered its prisons and treated minority prisoners. Washington's eloquence promised that the Brown case would garner widespread press coverage.

As the two sides prepared for trial, Washington held numerous press conferences in which he contended that Eroy Brown was a "victim of a system." "In my judgment," declared Washington, "the prison system is part and parcel of the trial. I find very little difference between the people who enforce the laws and the people who break the laws."[15] Washington's partner in Brown's defense, William Habern, agreed that "it will come down to a story about the bottoms. It's no secret our case is a self-defense case. The bottoms is a place where people are taken to be beaten."[16] Prisoners had long claimed that the bottoms riverbed was the site of unofficial "head strummings," where TDC guards had beaten and disciplined prisoners. The TDC vehemently denied that such practices ever occurred and dismissed them as a series of tall tales and convict lore. The prisoner Alan Wade Johnson disagreed, however. He wrote to the press editor of a local newspaper: "Why do the officials go to pains to disclaim any knowledge of what happens in the river bottoms at the Ellis and other units of TDC, when at one time or another they have used the place too? Among us inmates it's a well-known place where inmates are reprimanded—by severe beatings."[17] During the trial, Aubrey Eugene Komurke, who also testified during the *Ruiz* and *Guajardo* trials, defined the "bottoms" as a punitive space outside of the law and prying eyes: "The bottoms generally means the area away from the building, specifically, the river bottoms. Most of the units, the farm units which I have been on, or assigned, are bordered by one of the rivers. The bottoms refers to that area, but it is actually in effect, any area away from the building proper. Any area some distance from the living area."[18] The "bottoms" analogy also carried a double meaning in African American prison work songs. It symbolized not only the geographic place of the river bottoms but also the prisoners' sense of being at society's very bottom.

The Eroy Brown defense also resurrected the decade-long struggle between writ writers and building tenders. Pack's appointment as warden of Ellis just weeks before the incident reflected his loyalty as a career TDC employee with nineteen years of service. He rose steadily through the ranks after his initial appointment as a correctional officer in 1961. He had been promoted to lieutenant in 1964, made captain by 1966, became a major in 1967, and an assistant warden in 1977. Pack had served as Warden "Beartracks" McAdams's major at the Ellis and Wynne Units when the TDC was at the height of its struggle to silence writ writers. During the trial, the defense called former writ writers and activist prisoners, who testified about Pack's reliance on building tenders. The former prisoner and writ writer Alvin Slaton, for instance, testified that in 1969 Pack stood by while two building tenders beat the prisoner Harold Melvin Blunt with blackjacks until blood spluttered on the ceiling. Slaton then testified that Pack and the building tenders returned six hours later and placed Blunt in a straitjacket and hung him from the cell bars. Slaton was a former Jalet client and a writ writer, and he had served time with Fred Cruz. He also was the prisoner who shot and killed McAdams's head building tender Robert Barber when both were out of prison in 1972. Although Slaton revealed scars on his wrists during the trial from what he claimed were handcuff scars left by Pack, the prosecution under cross-examination revealed that Slaton was a frequent self-mutilator who had scars up his entire arm from his stays in mental institutions in both the state and federal penitentiary.[19] Fourteen prisoners, meanwhile, refused to testify for fear of retribution.[20] Unlike the *Ruiz* case, there was no protection from the federal court and the presiding judge declared eight prisoners in contempt of court for refusing to testify after they were subpoenaed by the defense.[21] Dr. George Beto also returned to the fray when he testified for the prosecution. Beto called Pack a "deeply religious" man whom he considered nonviolent and benevolent. Moreover, Beto testified that he named Pack as an officer at the Wynne Treatment Center for mental patients because he "observed that Pack was particularly gifted in helping prisoners with mental problems."[22] Beto denied receiving any prisoner complaints about Pack and denied the claims made by such prisoners as Slaton. Washington and Habern, however, attempted to place Pack's reputation on trial as a TDC employee who engaged in the system's tradition of racial violence.

The prosecution pinned its hopes on maintaining the trial's focus on the day of the murders. In their hope for a conviction, Pack's family hired Mike Hinton as special prosecutor to help the beleaguered Walker County district attorney Mike Ward. Hinton highlighted Eroy Brown's criminal past and the fact that two long-standing TDC employees had died at the hands of a three-time convicted criminal. The state attempted to demonstrate that Brown was angry for not getting his furlough because he wanted to get out for a weekend sexual encounter. Hinton also argued that Brown was a habitual three-time criminal who was high and drunk that morning from marijuana and "chock" (prison-made alcohol), although Brown's blood tests for alcohol were negative. Two prisoners, Levi Dusan and James Soloman, testified that from the banks of the river they were able to witness the event. They both testified that Brown was able to break Moore's hold, grab Pack's pistol, and shoot Moore directly and intentionally. One of the two prisoners testified that he then saw Brown chase Pack to a drainage ditch, which caused the two men to fall while struggling.[23]

The defense hoped to place the TDC on trial rather than Brown. During the closing arguments on February 26, 1982, the courtroom held a packed house, with white prison guards from Huntsville seeking punitive justice on one side of the aisle and African Americans from Galveston hoping for restorative justice on the other. Self-defense, in Washington's telling, became more than a simple legal strategy—it was an inherent right. "What if you are an inmate at TDC and you know about people coming up missing at the bottoms?" Washington asked the jurors in his closing argument. "And all of a sudden Major Moore does a flip job on you and handcuffs you. From Eroy Brown's standpoint, they didn't do it to scare him, they did it to kill him. That is the quintessential manifestation of the case—it's kill or be killed. I think a dog on the street has a right of self-defense." The case also centered on a racial appeal that equated Texas prisons with slavery. The defense painted race onto the legal canvas of the Brown trial by having a series of African American prisoners testify for Brown, which contrasted with the nearly all-white cast of TDC officials and investigators who testified for the state. Brown's testimony was filled with the memory of what Pack and Moore had said to him that day, and his testimony highlighted how their language was littered with racial epithets and threats. In one instance, Brown testified how the two TDC employees referred to their ability to continue old racial hierarchies through racial violence: "Mr. Moore said, 'Nigger, you ain't going to be able to tell no one what goes on here. We still do away with niggers like you down here.'"[24] Indeed, during his closing statements Washington adopted the "slave imagery" that prisoner protestors had used to make their case during the *Ruiz* trial. "There was no marijuana," insisted Washington. "He [Brown] was out there for one reason, for 'running his head' about Master Moore." Washington closed with a personal plea that attempted to humanize Brown: "Follow the truth, follow the law and you'll walk him [Brown] home. Let justice be done though heaven may fall."[25]

Worried by the defense's largely successful effort to refocus the trial on the TDC rather than on the murders of Pack and Moore, Special Prosecutor Hinton charged that the "TDC has been on trial because the reputation of two of their finest has been completely assailed. We have been hearing the trial of [Warden] Wallace Pack. It's been a long time since we heard anything about the state versus Eroy Brown. I have never heard anything so despicable in my life as a layman or a lawyer." Hinton characterized the testimony of prisoners as "scurrilous innuendos" made "by people who could care less about the meaning of an oath." Hinton closed by charging that "Wallace Pack has been dragged through worse slime than that in which he ended up dead."[26]

The jury, composed of seven men and five women, three African Americans and one Mexican American, ended in deadlock 10–2 in favor of Brown's acquittal, and the case was declared a mistrial.[27] Brown was tried again for Pack's murder in November 1982, and a jury of six whites, four African Americans, and two Mexican Americans acquitted him. He was tried for yet a third time for the shooting of Billy Max Moore, and an all–Mexican American jury found him not guilty. Brown completed the remainder of his sentence and was free for less than six months before he was arrested again for armed robbery of a 7-eleven convenience store. He spent his fourth prison term in the federal penitentiary for fear of retribution in the TDC.

Outside of the prison, Brown's acquittal in the deaths of two high-ranking TDC employees caused a political backlash. It signaled that the *Ruiz* decision had given prisoners the false belief that they could disrupt the otherwise controlled and ordered universe of Texas prisons. The Brown case reflected the public's growing disenchantment with the courts, and it contributed to a rising law-and-order chorus demanding that state control of prisons remain with the state legislature and bureaucracy. Within the prisons, however, Brown's acquittal represented a challenge to the traditional pattern of racial violence by prison officials against African American prisoners. Brown was not known as a Black Power veteran or an open advocate of self-defense, but his actions signaled to others that the old order upheld through racial violence and hierarchy was crumbling. The Brown trial inaugurated the TDC's worst year for work strikes, racial disorder, and uprisings since the 1930s.

The Violence of Mass Incarceration: The Battle of Tent City, Work Strikes, and Carceral Assassinations

Within the prison, the prisoners themselves were hopelessly locked within the political struggle over *Ruiz* even as they were literally locked inside an overcrowded and increasingly volatile system. Their hopes for outside relief from the courts and the legislature were frustrated at every opportunity. Following the sweeping *Ruiz* ruling, prisoners sensed that the ground had shifted underneath the TDC's feet and that the uneasy "peace" between guards and prisoners was in jeopardy of descending into chaos. Prisoners therefore pressed for a resolution to the crisis through the only remaining means available to them: uprisings and work strikes. Within the first year of Justice's 1980 decision, the state witnessed a wave of prison work stoppages, minor riots, and unrest that rippled through the Texas prison system. Although TDC recorded only six major disturbances between 1973 and 1980, the prison system experienced eleven such disturbances in the first six months of 1981 alone. Three weeks after Eroy Brown killed the Ellis prison major and warden, 2,208 prisoners out of a total population of 3,050 prisoners staged a massive work strike at Ellis. The strike was due to frustration with the TDC's lack of complicity to the court order, overcrowding, and the fear of racial reprisal stemming from the Brown case. Following the *Ruiz* case, prisoners also felt a moment of opportunity to press their claim for more humane treatment, and once again the work strike seemed the natural means of protest to gain public attention.

Despite the roiling tensions, the strike remained peaceful. The prisoners demanded that the state replace Director James Estelle and the TDC's entire administrative staff. The strike had started with a press story's coverage of the overcrowded conditions and the number of prisoners sleeping on the floor. The story quoted the forty-five-year-old guard G. P. Hardy's callous assessment: "Hell, these people were brought up in crowded homes. They are used to crowds. These people were raised by prostitutes and slept on the floor."[28] Hardy's comment may have prompted the strike, but the conditions for unrest had more to do with the TDC's thumbing its nose at the *Ruiz* court order.

As another guard noted, Ellis was a "short fuse, a stick of dynamite" just ready to go off. "They've [the inmates] been wanting to do it [stage a work stoppage] for a long time. That newspaper story just set it off," noted another guard.[29]

Indeed, the Ellis strike was a planned and orchestrated event that was put into motion by a prison organization called the First Inmate Reform Strike in Texas (FIRST). FIRST distributed a pamphlet that initially called for a work strike on April Fools' Day 1981, but after the date passed, another pamphlet called for the strike to occur "later in the month." The pamphlet announcing the strike had no author, although its language and design is similar to the work of the Black Panther veteran Johnny Swift. Swift had remained at Ellis during the *Ruiz* hearings, and sometime in the mid-1970s, the TDC moved him from general population to the administrative segregation wing on Ellis's death row, even though he was not scheduled for execution, which was part of the TDC's strategy to isolate and segregate prisoners who attempted political organization and "agitation."

But following the *Ruiz* decision, the prisoners' rights movement had lost many of its writ-writing leaders. By 1981, the original writ writers and prisoner activists had departed, leaving the prisoners' rights movement to a new generation of prisoner activists. Following the *Ruiz* trial, Judge Justice had ordered the TDC to allow all *Ruiz* prisoner witnesses who wished to transfer to the federal penitentiary system to do so. Within the prison, this transfer meant the loss of eighty-one writ writers and activists who represented the intelligentsia of the prisoners' rights movement and included those with the most experience in prison organizing and mobilizing. Despite the loss of the original writ writers, prisoners remained inspired by the 1978 strike, and they attempted to carry that spirit into the new decade of the 1980s.

Materialist needs and political demands related to full compliance with *Ruiz* prompted the 1981 strike. FIRST aimed its organizing tract against what it called "Estellism," which it defined as the TDC's stubborn reluctance to obey the court order and instead enforce its rule through a "reactionary dictatorship of a petty-bourgeois, who think cruelty is the cornerstone of rehabilitation." FIRST implored that it was "the task of all inmates to free themselves from Estelle" and that prisoners "must be made conscious of themselves as a political force." FIRST called on all prisoners, "Blacks, Browns, Yellows, Reds, and Whites" and "gays and straights," to ally and "rally the support of families, friends, sympathizers, legal and political groups" to once again press for prison politicization. "What is to be done?" the pamphlet queried in its Leninist tone: "Strike! Of course. We the inmates must strike! We must pose an inmate general strike, and, perhaps an inmate culture strike! We must not participate in any kind of work for the prison system whatsoever. We must bring all field work to a complete halt, stop all factory work, stop all kitchen work, stop all laundry work, stop all office work, stop all hospital work, stop building all new prisons and bring all inside and outside work to a complete halt! Take to your cells and dormitories and sit completely down."[30]

In preparation for the strike, FIRST organized prisoners and established communes in the wing and cell blocks of all TDC prisons. "Each wing and dormitory should agree upon selecting at least two inmates from its class to represent them," the pamphlet instructed. "For instance, if there's Blacks, Chicanos, Indians, Whites or others living in a cell-block or dormitory to say, the Blacks should have two Black inmates represent them, two Chicano inmates representing the Chicanos, same applies for the Indians, Whites, and Others. And those selected inmates should work together as one. They must educate and organize every inmate possible in their wing or dormitory." Moreover the commune leaders had to be "politically bright and strong willed" and they had to coordinate with other commune leaders from wing to wing and cell block to cell block. The pamphlet initially called for a letter-writing campaign, but it acknowledged that in the aftermath of *Ruiz* that letter writing had become futile and that prisoners had to accelerate their political demands through a general work strike.[31]

The pamphlet stressed, however, that FIRST was "not a revolutionary uprising; it is not a radical movement; and it is not to overthrow the prison system!" Rather, it was a program that had both political designs to achieve the ouster of Estelle and material interests aimed at gaining prisoner privileges to survive within the prison plantation that refused to comply with *Ruiz*. Survivalist and practical concerns centered on prisoners' desire to wear and buy free-world clothes, shoes, jewelry, and tape recorders. The pamphlet also called for empowerment politics by demanding such "rights of identity" as the ability to grow a prisoner's hair and to wear whatever cultural garb they wished. Moreover, the strike demanded minimal pay for prison labor. But as a politically astute organization, FIRST hoped to ameliorate the public's growing concern for victims' rights by offering half of their proposed pay to their victims. FIRST demanded "the rights of all inmates to be paid at least $1 an hour for all labor, and a program should be set up so the inmate can pay restitution to the victim . . . but no more than half of an inmate's pay can be entitled to at least 50 cents an hour."[32]

During the April 29 general strike, the Ellis strikers were joined by 15 prisoners at Eastham and 32 prisoners at Darrington. On June 25, 70 prisoners in the typing pool of the Wynne prison refused to go to their jobs. On August 11 a parolee and a prisoner at the Wynne prison filed a federal court lawsuit claiming that they had been bitten and permanently scarred while working as "dog boys" to train TDC guard dogs. On August 18, 20 Ellis prisoners began a hunger strike to protest working conditions. On September 30, 2 prisoners on Retrieve prison mutilated themselves with razor blades in protest when a building tender assaulted a prisoner in solitary confinement. The following day, the prison's lieutenant placed 9 building tenders in the hall before the lunchtime meal. When those building tenders assaulted the same prisoner on his way to the meal, 200 to 300 prisoners rushed to his support by smashing windows and refusing to return to their cells. By October 2, 190 Retrieve prisoners "violently resisted" the attempt to press them back into their cells by guards and building tenders. On the same day, there was a 113-prisoner stoppage at Ramsey II. By October 19, 160 Ellis prisoners began a month-long work stoppage. On November 18 and 19, 9 prisoners and 4 officers were injured at the Darrington prison when 500 prisoners set fires, fought with guards, and broke windows.[33]

The biggest battle, however, was what prisoners called "the battle of tent city," a two-hour uprising at Eastham. Overcrowding had reached such a critical level that in the fall of 1981 Governor William P. Clements agreed to a TDC plan to house prisoners in vast "tent cities" that sprawled just outside of prisons that were too full to house any more prisoners. By the fall of 1981 there were 1,200 men housed in tents, and at its height the tent population ultimately reached nearly 4,000. The Eastham prison maintained one of the prison system's largest tent cities. On the morning of November 20, 2 building tenders harassed 6 Chicano prisoners. The other prisoners in the yard struck back and fought the building tenders back into the main building. A full-scale uprising broke out in the prison yard, where some 270 prisoners torched the tents and used mattresses as barricades. The fire spread quickly across the yard, and the smoke billowed above the prison. Inside the building, meanwhile, 60 guards formed a riot squad to quell the mayhem. The main shock troops, however, were not TDC employees but 150 building tenders assembled under the head building tender Sonny Evans, who ordered his men to tie white bandannas around their heads to differentiate building tender from prisoner during the ensuing melee. The building tenders were armed and carried trash can lids as shields and pipes, clubs, and weight lifting bars as weapons.

The former TDC captain Keith Price described the moment before the charge as if it was the last seconds before a pitched military battle. "The adrenaline's really flowing," Price recalled. "Flowing so much it's spooky."[34] As the guards and building tenders stormed the compound, those prisoners who were part of the uprising scattered and attempted to head back into the building.[35] Blocking their way, however, was a line of building tenders, who had formed a "whupping line" that created a gauntlet through which the prisoners had to pass to get back inside the building. In an exposé story titled "Inside America's Toughest Prison," *Newsweek* reported what happened next: "As they tore the ubiquitous white cloth made in the prison factory, the tenders growled, a kind of primal cry. . . . The only way to the safety of the gym was down that gauntlet, and the rioters, now edging toward panic, began running through. Prisoner Ronnie Roland was inside the main building as the 'whupped' staggered in. 'Some of the guys you couldn't recognize, and a lot were unconscious. I wasn't sure if they was alive or dead.' The inmates who could walk staggered back to the cell blocks, the others were carried inside to wait for ambulances." One of the prisoners reported how he experienced that day's violence: "There were guards and inmates with clubs lined up against this fence with room to get by. We was told to run down the fence and if we was not fast enough the clubs was used. This was when I was hit in the head."[36] Rather than reestablishing BT power, however, the "battle of tent city" became instead the building tenders' last gasp and final violent demonstration of their waning reign on a southern prison plantation, whose sun had already set.

In the midst of the political deadlock amid prison overcrowding, a post-*Ruiz* campaign of carceral retribution and assassination overtook the prison. In 1982, the carceral violence that marked Texas prisons claimed the life of one of the most outspoken prisoner organizers of the prisoners' rights movement. On August 8, 1983, the death row prisoner James Demouchette, notorious for having killed three other prisoners and stabbing a guard, moved without escort from his cell on Ellis's death row past three gated doors that were normally locked. He then found Johnny Swift, the Black Panther and prisoner organizer, in the dayroom, where he was awaiting a legal visit. Demouchette approached, accusing Swift of "back-biting," and then stabbed Swift with a particularly large shank. According to the prisoner witness Clayton B. Phillips, "he [Swift] knocked the shank out of James Demouchette's hand but he had already been stabbed several times and then he fell to the floor." Once his victim fell to the ground, Demouchette continued to stab Swift's prone and motionless body. The prisoner Michael Jewell, also housed on death row at the time, recalled that Swift's death was widely rumored among the prisoners as an orchestrated hit: "On the day Johnny Swift was murdered, the picket officer, who was barred off from the wing, opened Demouchette's door with no escort present, allegedly for him to shower. Demouchette left his cell fully clothed and armed with what early accounts called a 'free world Buck knife.' The gates on all three landings were conveniently left unlocked, as was the Day Room door. . . . I know Johnny never suspected trouble and never saw it coming. He didn't have a chance to defend himself."[37] The prisoner witness Phillips also questioned the murder when he recounted the assault to the press: "the fact that Demouchette left out of his cell for over half an hour leave no doubt in my mind that the whole incident was set up to get inmate Johnny Swift killed." Phillips openly questioned why Demouchette, who had a history of attacking officers and stabbing prisoners, had been allowed out of his cell: "Why was he allowed to be in possession of such an extraordinary 'shank'? This was not your average homemade prison knife which he used."[38] Wilbur Collins, another prisoner on death row during Swift's murder, held a similar conviction that Swift's murder could not have occurred without some level of administrative help. "Somehow, allegedly, accidentally," Collins bitterly recalled, "someone had forgotten to close Demouchette's cell. Demochette came out of his cell . . . climbed from one row to three row up the stairs, and there is supposed to be locked doors at 1 row stairs and another locked door at 2 row stairs to prevent the guys at 2 row from going to 3 row. Both of these doors was unlocked. . . . Swift was set up."[39]

The news of Swift's murder hit the prisoners' movement hard. Only sixteen months before Swift's murder, Alvaro Luna Hernandez, one of the chief political organizers of the 1978 work strike, had written a court-appointed *Ruiz* monitor that Demouchette had "constantly threatened Chicanos while he was in solitary confinement for stabbing another inmate." Prisoners were so concerned about Demouchette's threats against Chicano and Black prisoners that they managed to contact Mickey Leland, now a newly elected U.S. congressional representative. Representative Leland requested that Judge Justice transfer the threatened prisoners out of Ellis, but no court order ever delivered them away from Demouchette's threatening presence. Following Swift's murder, fourteen prisoner activists composed a memorial tribute that reflected on Swift's work as a prison mobilizer and a prison Black Panther. His fellow activist prisoners mourned Swift as "a real and unrelenting warrior for prisoner's human and civil rights, an excellent teacher and dreadfully feared organizer of fellow prisoners, a strongly effective legal advocate."[40] As one of the prisoners who testified in *Ruiz*, Martha Quinlan had been transferred to the federal prison in 1979 and then released in 1982, but she continued to fight for prisoners on the outside through CURE and through her avid correspondence with Lawrence Pope, who also was free from prison. In their correspondence over Swift's murder, Quinlan confessed to Pope that the news about Swift's murder "came as a terrible blow and I'm still rocking from its force." She explained how the prison assassination exemplified the desperate and precarious moment for the prisoners' movement:

I am filled with a tremendous sense of loss and struck to the core with an admixture of hate, anger, and anguish. The hatred, I must come to grips with, arises out of the cauldron of injustices and indignities heaped upon us prisoners by own keepers which reduces the weak among us to a level of primitiveness where all social mores are totally ignored. Hence, come the anger at/over those weak minded—mindless really—individuals who play those of us who dare to stand up, who dare to refuse to be reduced to the level of an animal.[41]

In the aftermath of the *Ruiz* decision, those *Ruiz* witnesses and prisoner organizers that remained in the TDC faced the threat of outright assassination and death under suspicious circumstances. Carl Reed Jr., for instance, died on October 5, 1979, after his throat was cut by a suspected building tender even though Reed was asleep at the time in a locked cell. Julio Nieto, also a *Ruiz* witness, was taken from his hospital bed for a minor rule violation and placed into solitary confinement where he died of a diabetic coma on July 29, 1979. Gus Fiest Jr., a volunteer witness who never had the chance to testify, was beaten to death in October 1979. The *Austin American Statesman* reported that a building tender, Warden Christian, and Major Lawson were suspected in the deaths and remarked that "both Christian and Lawson have been the subjects of frequent, inconclusive FBI charges of beating prisoners." Steven Thompson, another *Ruiz* witness who was twenty-seven at the time and had been in prison since he was sixteen, was stabbed to death on October 16, 1981, by the building tender Carl Venter.[42] The Prisoners Defense Committee report went on to cite eleven more deaths due to "suicide" or neglected medical conditions resulting in fatal epileptic seizures, heart attacks, and one prisoner activist who died when he did not receive medical care after his appendix ruptured. In light of these deaths, Martha Quinlan wrote a desperate letter to civil rights attorneys involved in the *Lamar* racial integration consent decree, explaining how the ongoing assassination and "hit" campaign of carceral violence within the prisons was silencing prisoners out of stark fear.

> Given the present situation in TDC, it does not surprise me to know that you have not received a single complaint from any prisoner currently incarcerated in TDC in regards to the *Lamar* rules. There are few inmates left in TDC who will "buck the system" in the face of so much bloodletting. Something "bad" has happened to all those who have. One-by-one, they been murdered, brutally assault and/or out. Samuel James Jackson, a plaintiff in the instant case, was "hit" last July and survived only through the grace of God. I have in my possession letters from present TDC inmates which state that everyone is afraid to even file an administrative grievance complaint. The risk of retaliation is too high.[43]

Quinlan thoughtfully closed her letter with a political plea that civil rights attorneys not "turn your head, heart and mind aside" and seek "an easy way out" by giving up on the prisoners, despite how carceral violence had frightened so many into silence. "As things stands now, the legislature, the people, and the courts, of Texas are more than aware that the difficult choice must finally be made" between political surrender and continued civil rights litigation. "Eliminating one evil [the BT system] does not always guarantee that good will replace it. However, experience has shown that men and women are made not better, but worse, by punitive treatment designed to hurt and humiliate them. Society, you, and I—all of us—ought to profit from that experience. . . . For without any commitment, on anyone's part, the TDC, you, we, and the society which created it, will continue a downhill slide to hell!"[44]

Whether these deaths were orchestrated conspiracy or random prison violence and medical neglect amid strange circumstance, the loss of these prisoners robbed the prison community of its most astute, politically aware, and involved members. Johnny Swift's murder, in particular, silenced the prison's loudest voice for active prisoner organization and mobilization.[45] As the body count mounted and the number of writ writers dwindled after post-*Ruiz* release, the prisoners' rights movement began to fracture.

In 1985, Martha Quinlan took the reins of the Texas chapter of CURE from Charlie and Pauline Sullivan as they established a national CURE lobby in Washington, DC. The media responded with such headlines as "Ex-Con Hopes to Establish Record as Effective Lobbyist," but Quinlan persisted by letting the public know that she now acted for prisoner rehabilitation as well as serving as the very symbol of how the prisoners' rights movement reconstituted prisoners as political citizens. "I'm well aware of the fact that I probably will be rejected by any number of people, but that will not stop me," Quinlan defiantly told the press. "I think it's important that they do know that [about her prison record]. Otherwise, how will they know that I do know what I'm talking about?"[46] When asked about Quinlan's new political role as an "ex-con," Charlie Sullivan retorted with a politicization-as-rehabilitation narrative: "Texans like to see a success story, and I think Martha is a success story. One reason we felt Martha could make a contribution is that the Legislature doesn't see people walking the hall who have turned their lives around. . . . I think Martha is a symbol that these people are salvageable and we shouldn't give up on them."[47] Like many of the politicized prisoners, Quinlan may have left the prison, but the prison never left her. "There's something deep down inside of me that will not leave the Texas Department of Corrections situation the way I found it," she admitted to the press. "So much so that I'll do whatever it takes to turn the system around. I recognize the need in any society for a prison system, but it does not have to be the way it is in Texas."[48]

In her new role, Quinlan wanted to turn the prisoners' rights movement away from civil rights litigation and toward political lobbying and state-level legislation. "I felt we had exhausted the court remedies on conditions in TDC," she told the media. "As a consequence, I felt the only way to go beyond that for additional relief was through the Legislature. My job will be to lobby the legislature, to persuade them that there are many things they should do to change the negative impact in the Department of Corrections."[49] To spread her new agenda to the prisoners still within the TDC, Martha Quinlan took her message to Ray Hill's *Prison Radio Show*, a weekly favorite for prisoners, for an on-air interview. Quinlan related to the listeners that "the climate in the courts today is such that they are not returning favorable decisions for the inmates." After the comprehensive decision in *Ruiz*, she felt that "we've topped out our litigative opportunities" and that "further changes are going to have to come from the legislature."[50] But to politicized prisoners still within the TDC, lobbying the legislature was a middle-class strategy to "cozy up" to the powerful for modest reforms, which they viewed as a betrayal of civil rights litigation that made demands in the court room, not political requests. In a pair of open letters shared with prisoners' rights advocates both within prison and without, Albert Arande and Alvaro Luna Hernández, now the "inside chairman" of the Committee for Prison Reform and Defense of Human Rights, vehemently opposed Quinlan's "new assessment," which Hernández criticized as "totally wrong—tactically, strategically, legally, morally, politically, and otherwise." In a strongly worded condemnation, Hernández minced no words:

> You have come out and openly discredited and negated the importance of resorting to the legal struggle (litigation) with your statement to the prison you have consciously or unconsciously (it is hard for anyone to presume that your statement was made unconsciously on account of your intellect) performed a disservice to the prison (working class) movement and have rendered a great service to the forces of reaction [TDC]. Against this I will not stay silent and will resolutely oppose your "tactics" and "strategies" since they are not based on rationale, logic, or principle. In fact, your statements have only caused anger and confusion amongst prisoners. Of course, I do not negate the importance of working with Legislature on prison reform issue since every little bit helps, but to come out and negate the importance of the legal struggle is pure narrow-mindedness, bankruptcy and political apostasy on your part.[51]

These letters demonstrated a number of post-*Ruiz* fractures within the movement centered on class, gender, and racial friction. For instance, Hernández charged that Quinlan had "retrogressed in the last few months," a somewhat bitter allusion to her newfound freedom, and that her middle-class lobbying work with CURE threatened "containment of the movement along political opportunist lines." Albert Arande was even more blunt in naming Quinlan's reformist political vision as reducing her to a "handmaiden for the bourgeois." "I am still in this beast," Arande angrily recounted. "You are removed, do you want lies or to be ignored and esteemed as you were remembered; is revolution wrong today for you because of yesterday's 'removal.'"[52] Similarly, Hernández considered her former "advocacy of 'class struggle'" as "now all of a sudden intoxicated with legislative lobbying" that amounted to "legislative drunkenness and personal ambition," which foreclosed "the advocacy of resorting to other [more radical] methods of reformist and revolutionary struggle—litigation in efforts to remedy wrongs and expose the class contradictions" of white privilege within prison. For politicized Chicano prisoners like Arande and Hernández, the only way forward was to continue class-action lawsuits despite the *Ruiz* victory because prisoners "continue to suffer one of the most brutal repression and exploitation (prison slavery) in the TDC that the legislative will not even attempt to remedy or touch with a ten-foot pole."

Personally wounded, Quinlan wrote them both back, telling them, "You disappoint me, and hurt me greatly," while she sharply criticized their letters as patronizing and denying her independence from them because she was a woman. She found both letters as an "erroneous, misconstrued version of what I am all about." She was especially angry at the charge from working-class Chicano prisoners that she had been co-opted in exchange for middle-class comfort and media adoration. "You, who claim to be well-grounded in Marxist thought and support the concept of self-determination for the Third World countries appear incapable of recognizing it for an individual!!"[53] As the most well known and prominent activist prisoners among the women, Quinlan wondered aloud whether the criticism from male prisoners was a form of patriarchial silencing. "Could it be that you, and others, resent the fact that I appear not to have aligned myself with you? Are you all resenting the fact that I seek no direction from any of you? Do you resent my not reporting any activities to and all continuously?" With some venom in her pen, she closed by emphasizing her freedom and independence to pursue gains for "the movement" as she saw best:

> My dear comrade . . . it is good to learn that you recognized my abilities. I'm delighted to know that you aren't giving up on me . . . you cannot possibly lose me simply because I never BELONGED to you in the first place.

> I belong to the dream I have. It's the dream we all share. It's the dream which animates us all. The dream has us all dancing—moving about in order it into a form which has substance. My commitment is to that task . . . Do not sell me short. Still struggling, Martha.[54]

In response to the fiery and open exchanges, Lawrence Pope admitted to Aubrey Komurke, a released Black Power advocate and writ writer, that Pope initially offered a vigorous defense of Quinlan but then thought better of it. Pope was angry and frustrated that under Quinlan CURE had praised Mark White "even though he has always been the enemy, perhaps more so than even Estelle and Beto since he was AG and opposing us so drastically in *Ruiz vs Estelle*." Although Pope and Quinlan had shared a long and friendly exchange, he resigned himself to the fact that "she had changed drastically from the litigious, fiery person that came through in her letters while she was inside." He noted that Quinlan was "at odds" with Johnny Martínez, who now was running a prisoners' rights group from San Antonio, as well as with Chicano prisoners still inside. "She seems to be determined to abandon her old friends while she was inside," Pope lamented. He even went so far as to suggest that perhaps Quinlan had accepted an offer of parole from Ruben Montemayor, the hostage negotiator during the Carrasco hostage crisis, when he recounted how Quinlan once told him that Montemayor had suggested that she "cease my legal activities; adapt to the system; and quietly do my time."[55] There is no other evidence, however, that any such deal was ever made.

Nonetheless, the political intransigence, the law's inability to rush change, the growing and deadly level of prison violence, the dangerous overcrowding due to mass incarceration, and the sheer exhaustion over the struggle for prisoners' rights had taken its toll, and the movement was beginning to fracture. Things would only get worse as the prison turned toward militarization to stem the prisoner insurgency.

The Sunbelt Carceral Regime: From Southern Prison Plantation to the Militarized Prison

After an interim period with D. V. "Red" McKaskle serving as acting director, Governor Mark White and the TDC prison board replaced Estelle by hiring as its new director Raymond K. Procunier, who had been a state prison director for the Virginia, California, and Utah prison systems. Appointed by Governor Ronald Reagan as California's prison director in 1967 and remaining in that position until 1975, Procunier had overseen the state prison's response to the Soledad Brothers and the death of George Jackson at the hands of California correctional officers. Procunier's directorship over the California prison system also promised to bring a tough, seasoned prison administrator to Texas, who combatted prison radicalism, prisoners' rights lawsuits, and the rise of organized prison gangs. While California's prison director, the system faced a number of lawsuits, including *Raymond K. Procuier v. Robert Martínez, et al.*, which was a class-action lawsuit similar to Texas's *Guadarajo v. Estelle* case, as *Procunier v. Martínez* successfully challenged California's mail censorship regulations and the ban against the use of law students and legal paraprofessionals to conduct attorney-client interviews with prisoners.[56]

But the Texas Prison Board was especially eager to hire Procunier because of his role as assistant director of New Mexico's prison system, where he had served in the aftermath of the nation's most deadly prison riot in 1980 at Santa Fe. In the Santa Fe riot prisoners initiated a horrific bloodletting of snitches, in which the rioters tortured, raped, dismembered, decapitated, or burned alive their fellow prisoners. During that tumultuous riot, prisoners took twelve officers hostage, murdered thirty-three fellow prisoners, and injured more than two hundred.[57] While a disturbing example of prison violence, the riot should be seen as a response to the legal struggle over prisoners' rights, on the one hand, and the worsening of prison conditions, on the other.

Following a 1976 collective prison work strike in New Mexico, prison officials there initiated a divisive and dangerous surveillance program known as "snitching," which rewarded prisoner informers with better housing, improved classification, furlough and parole, and sometimes cash and drugs. When a prisoner refused to be an informant, however, prison officials threatened punishment by giving them a "snitch jacket," which endangered their lives as it falsely labeled them as an informant to the general prison population. Snitches, meanwhile, routinely made false allegations to gain state rewards. Desperate to alleviate snitching and prison overcrowding, the prisoner Kevin Duran, a civil rights veteran and Vietnam War protester, filed a section 1983 civil rights suit in the District of New Mexico against the prison system and the governor of New Mexico. In 1977, his legal efforts were combined with those of the ACLU's National Prison Project. The result was a federal consent decree, *Duran v. Apodaca*, meant to alleviate poor prison conditions. However, state prison officials resisted and the snitch system and prison overcrowding continued unabated.[58] Even the nation's most disquieting prison riot must therefore be placed within the historical context of the struggle over prisoners' rights and the encroachment of mass incarceration and a more punitive prison. When viewing the Santa Fe riot in hindsight, Duran aptly surmised, "We all knew something was bound to happen. The state was moving too slow."[59]

To bolster Procunier's credentials as a new breed of Sunbelt prison administrator, the TDC countered domestic prisoner insurgency with increasing militarization. Lane McCotter, who was handpicked by George Beto and rumored to serve as Procunier's successor after his two-year contract ended, joined Procunier as deputy director.[60] McCotter was a career military officer, retiring as a colonel in the U.S. Army, and he had served as former U.S. Army commandant of the Disciplinary Barracks at Fort Leavenworth, Kansas, and as a military police officer in the Eighteenth Military

Police Brigade during his 1968–69 tour in Vietnam. To take up the TDC's offer, McCotter turned down a senior position in the army's Command and General Staff College. During his tour in Vietnam, Colonel McCotter had supervised military police combat operations and had overseen the confinement of U.S. prisoners and prisoners of war.[61] When asked by the press about the wisdom of appointing a military officer to a senior TDC position, Hardy Rauch, director of standards for the American Correctional Association, told the press that "the style of management and operations and dealing with personnel and inmates in prisons is very comparable to a military situation" and that the blending of military and correctional justice practices would put Texas in alignment with the "national standard for operations."[62] Command Sergeant Major Robert Gooding, who had worked alongside McCotter at Fort Leavenworth, summarized why Texas had selected Colonel McCotter: "From what I understand, he's what you (Texas) need . . . Either you run it (a prison) or they (prisoners) run it, and we run it here. He'll do that in Texas."[63] McCotter's arrival to the TDC thus brought a seasoned military veteran to oversee the transition from the southern prison plantation model to a get-tough military approach that employed the tactics and ideology of counterinsurgent thought to the domestic prison.

Procunier and McCotter advocated a wholesale "prison restructuring" that envisioned a militarized, bureaucratic hierarchy of regional directors.[64] Together, Procunier and McCotter promised to clean house in the face of *Ruiz*, and they offered a "tough justice" vision for prison management. As a prison administrator from outside of the U.S. South, Procunier was able to successfully navigate and more easily accept the *Ruiz* consent decree. "In my opinion," Procunier admitted, "Texas spent too much time saying 'Ain't it [the *Ruiz* decision] awful' without realizing it is the law and it can't be changed. A lot of people felt that some miracle was going to happen and it was going to go away." William Bennet Turner, the NAACP LDF attorney for the prisoners in the *Ruiz* case, described Procunier as a "progressive on prison overcrowding," but he also characterized him as "a no-nonsense prison guy. He's no bleeding-heart liberal and realizes there are tough *hombres* in prison, and he's not going to put up with any nonsense from them." Comparing Procunier to Jim Estelle, Turner thought that "Procunier is a very outspoken, direct, blunt and honest man. Estelle . . . is so close-mouthed and uncommunicative, you never know where you are. With Procunier, you know where you are all the time." When it came to the *Ruiz* decision, Turner thought that Procunier would "not tolerate a good deal of the stuff Estelle was not willing to do anything about."[65]

Procunier implemented his plans with one eye focused on complying with the special master's oversight, while also implementing a tightly controlled modernized prison regime that moved beyond southern traditions. Procunier's plans included a new prisoner classification system, an effort to segregate the "most volatile inmates into six of the state's 27 prison units," and boosting the guard force with one thousand new correctional officers that the new administration claimed would be trained to discern "the difference between necessary force and abuse." Such "necessary force" included "nightsticks, taser guns, tear gas and all that." Having learned from the 1971 Attica uprising and New Mexico's 1981 brutal prison riot, Procunier firmly told the press that "if we have a riot or disturbance, it should be put down immediately because there is no room for negotiation during a period of insurrection." "What we have to establish in this department is that we are the tougher of the two groups [prisoners and guards]," explained Procunier. "Once we get that established, we won't have to prove it."[66]

The end of Estelle's administration and the demise of building tenders resulted in an upheaval in the correctional officer structure. Previously, the TDC drew its ranks from the local rural community, where they had employed largely white guards and officers. These guards received not only their basic pay but such emoluments from the prison as housing, food, haircuts, domestic service, and laundry services. Most of these services, which the Joint Committee on Prison Reform estimated to be worth as much as $18,000 a year, came to a halt under the *Ruiz* decree.[67] Beginning in 1978, the TDC had initiated a massive affirmative-action hiring program to employ urban minorities. Moreover, the TDC settled a sex-discrimination lawsuit in 1982, which required that women employees must constitute at least 14.3 percent of the prison's security staff. TDC guards had no union of their own, although the Texas State Employees Union (TSEU) had tried to recruit from the prison, and their wages remained low through the 1980s.[68] Sociologists contended that the new and untested guards and the introduction of female security personnel contributed to an increase in guard-to-prisoner contraband, charges of sexual exchange, and drug trafficking.[69] Procunier's new administration also promised to "clean house," and during 1984 he fired several longtime employees for beating allegations, including Warden David Christian, who had served the TDC for nineteen years and was one of the perpetrators of the Father's Day incident of 1973 as Retrieve's assistant warden.[70] These changes caused the prison guard staff to expand drastically. Indeed, the number of security staff more than tripled from 2,500 in 1979 to 9,000 by 1985.[71] The sociologists Ben M. Crouch, also a former TDC guard, and James W. Marquart argued that the influx of new guards, particularly women and minorities, "undermined the traditional officer subculture" that had so characterized the pride of TDC since the Ellis reforms of 1948.[72] On the other hand, the inclusion of female and minority correctional officers represented an opportunity for the TDC to move away from their nearly all-white guard structure rooted in southern labor disciplinary practices.

Lockdown: Declaring War on the Domestic Prisoner Insurgent and Organized Prison Gangs

In 1983, classication sociologist Salvador "Sam" Buentello encountered his first prison gang member. As a Mexican American with a father who had worked at the Sugarland prison factory, Buentello was similar to many TDC COs with familial ties to the prison. But because of his Mexican American heritage, Buentello felt that he was "an outsider, because there weren't many Hispanics there and there was a lot of nepotism and a lot of cliques" that he simply could not access. His move to the Classification Department, however, allowed him to use his Spanish to communicate and build a rapport with Mexican American prisoners.[73] Working as a sociologist for the TDC's Classification Department, Buentello interviewed all incoming prisoners on their family background, their convictions, and their past social history. When he interviewed a new incoming TDC prisoner from California, Buentello discovered the startling revelation that he was a member of the Texas Syndicate (TS). Buentello was shocked when the prisoner told him that he expected trouble from the TS. "My antenna said we don't have gangs in Texas, never heard of them," Buentello told himself. "But I knew by looking at the expression on his face that he was thinking 'here is another individual who is never going to believe an inmate.' And when I saw that look, I said okay tell me about it."[74]

Following the prisoner interview, Buentello spent much of the next two years building a database on three-by-five index cards of suspected TS gang members by collecting information from classification interviews, prison wardens, correctional officers, and eventually gang informants. Initially, the intelligence gathering was a one-man operation, but as gang membership rose, the incidents of prisoner violence multiplied. "In 1984, when we started to see a huge increase in homicides, that's when people started to take notice," Buentello said. "My boss, S.O. Woods, said 'keep an eye on these guys,' and we would give feedback to the unit, and it kept going that way. There was no system, it could be a major, a warden, a guard, communicating to me, but it wasn't until the war of 1985 that we got organized."[75] What started as a one-man operation from classification, soon developed into the TDC's unnamed gang intelligence unit with Buentello as the lead investigator.

Gangs first came to Texas through California's prison system. Prior to the 1980s, Texas gang affiliation was nearly nonexistent. But as Lawrence Pope pointed out in his work as a prisoner organizer, "there is another 'gang' among TDC inmates which is not generally recognized as such, especially by TDC officials. That is the building tender system."[76] Building tenders operated with official sanction, even if their acts were largely unrecorded as unofficial punishments, while prison gangs were a prisoner-initiated organization that the TDC prison administration had never encountered before. The TS, initially known among its many Spanish-speaking members as El Syndicato Tejano, was founded in 1974 at San Quentin prison in California. In his first gang interview with a TS member, Buentello discovered that "they joined (TS) first in California, and then they made their way into Texas, but they were really low key (before the 1980s), because they knew the building tenders would be on top of them."[77] The TS formed out of self-protection from California's gang system that targeted outsiders, particularly Tejanos. As one California-based TS member put it, "the Tejanos must stick together in prison, especially in California."[78] By 1983, TS members imprisoned in the TDC began to surface.

The TS structure was militarized and hierarchical but also democratic. The top of the military hierarchy was a president and vice president for every state chapter. Beneath the state leadership was a paramilitary hierarchy within each prison. At the top of every prison was the chairman—known alternately as La Pabra, La Billa, La Tabla, or El Jefe. His job was to preside at *juntas* (meetings), where the gang members held an electoral process for "voting on hits, recruiting, and business." The second in command was the vice chairman, known alternately as El Visa, El Sequndo, Capitan, and his job was to convey messages from El Jefe and to "keep his soldiers/*carnales* in line. He settles all the arguments and disputes, serves as gang spokesman." Lieutenants formed the next rank, and these men served as executive officers who had to "keep his soldiers/*carnales* in line. He settles all the arguments and disputes." Sergeants served as gang secretaries and communication officers who "mostly handles the mail. He makes sure all the *carnales* read the in-coming mail of other carnales. . . . He also sees to it that all have a weapon." Beneath the sergeants were squad leaders, whose job included managing the day-to-day operations of his squad, which were all gang members on his cell block, while being in charge of everyone's weapon, hiding places, and new-member indoctrination. The bottom rank were soldiers who acted as prison drug dealers and carried out ordered hits of prison assassination. Although the TS had a military hierarchy, it made its decisions through a semidemocratic voting process. As an original California gang member and gang informant to the TDC put it, "Although there are ranks, everyone has to vote and before any action can be taken it must be unanimous."[79]

For Tejanos isolated in California's prison system, the gang offered more than protection; it also represented ethnic pride and above all *respeto* (respect), which was the base currency of prison survival and status. In prison, respect was the lifeblood of survival. It was what made you known by other prisoners when you had nothing else. In the course of interviewing a variety of gang members over two decades, Buentello summarized the notion of prisoner respect as a survivalist feature of prison life: "In prison, respect was everything. Their code is they're going to carry themselves with respect. Respect is the key word in my opinion. Everything boils down to that. If you look at me wrong, you disrespect me, if you don't look at me, you disrespect me. If you ask me a question when I didn't want you to talk to me, that's disrespect. Everything's respect, disrespect. I don't know how many times I've interviewed individuals who are involved in an assault or murder and when you ask them why, 'So, he disrespected me.'"[80]

The TS recruited among isolated prisoners to construct a fraternity of *carnalismo* (brotherhood). In their founding anthem, the TS relayed to prospective recruits how gang membership offered the pride and protection of carnalismo. "I'm a member with great pride in what I represent. My members are the same about dedication and alone I'm counted with them. We're Texans and Texas is our native land. . . . Hand in hand, arm in arm, we're all one and the same. In heart, in soul, and spirit, we're all brothers."[81] The rules of membership grew over the years to over twenty key regulations, but the initial eight rules centered on instilling a sense of carnalismo.

1. Be A Texan
2. Once carnal always a carnal.
3. Never let a carnal down.
4. Right or wrong, a carnal is always right
5. Carnales come first, The Texas Syndicate comes first
6. All Carnales will respect each other
7. All Carnales will wear the Texas Syndicate tattoo
8. Do not reveal our thing

To demonstrate the potency of their organization, the TS stabbed a California prisoner multiple times and threw him from the fifth floor of a cell block because he had reportedly "disrespected" Tejanos with the words "*tejas aqui mamaba* [all Texans suck]."[82] With this incident, the TS announced their power.

Additional regulations added during the transition to Texas prisons focused on expansion while retaining the gang's close-knit sense of brotherhood and respect. One of these regulations, for instance, made it a rule that "a member will carry himself with respect at all time and abide by all the rules forever." Other new regulations centered on expansion made recruitment a personal responsibility, as anyone who developed a new recruit would be "forever responsible for the prospective members' action should he become a

El Syndicato Tejano (Texas Syndicate, TS) gang sigil tattoo. Photograph from author's private collection.

member." Expansion was also collective and democratic, as every new member must be voted on by "every member on every unit." To retain gang cohesion beyond the prison, each member was required to "stay in contact with at least one member" after his release. More ominously, members directed to make a hit had two weeks to carry out their assassination or "he will be hit himself."

The TS's growth within the TDC was slow during the prisoners' rights and building tender era of the 1970s, but the following decade provided fruitful ground for expansion. By 1983 there were only 188 known or suspected members of the TS out of a prison population of 37,745, which represented less than 1 percent of the total population. Within two years, however, there were 813 known and suspected members of eight gangs throughout the TDC out of a total population of 39,411, or 2.175 percent of the total population. In 1984, there was an average of 5 members for every 1,000 prisoners. Within one year, however, there was an average of 18 members for every 1,000 prisoners.[83] TS members included mostly Tejano prisoners, but some whites were allowed to join the gang as a measure of protection against California gangs.

By the mid-1980s the TS was facing competition from the rise of the Mexican Mafia in Texas. To swell their ranks, the TS decided in 1986 to expand their base to include Puerto Ricans, Cubans, and other Latin Americans as prospective members, while banning any future white members. Moreover, the TS had initially prohibited any member who was a former turnkey, building tender, or porter because they wanted no members who had past affiliations working for "the man" (administration) as snitches or convict guards. But when it came to light that several of the leadership had, in fact, once served as BTs, the membership opened in 1986 to allow former BTs and porters. The TS recruited mostly older recidivist prisoners—first offenders comprised only 44 out of 226 members in 1986. Members younger than twenty-six years old accounted for only 55 members out of 226. TS members were incarcerated for a variety of felony convictions, including robbery (56), homicide (54), kidnapping (3), burglary (46), sex related (11), drugs (10), assault (8), and larceny (11). Most of the members came from the cities of Houston (44), San Antonio (32), Dallas (15), Corpus Christi (14), and El Paso (10). By 1986, the Texas prisons that had the most TS members were the old prison plantations ("farm units"), including Coffield (18), Darrington (36), Ellis (16), Eastham (28), Ferguson (13), Ramsey II (14), Retrieve (33) and Wynne (26).

As the gang grew, their communications methods became more complex. Initially, the TS relied on the chain bus, which delivered transfers and new incoming prisoners, to communicate to the small number of members, but with swelling numbers the TS turned to affiliates or sympathizers who might carry messages between different prisons or wings. By 1985, they perfected their method of communication by having one senior prisoner held at the central Walls prison near Huntsville coordinate messages from prisoners who might carry them from different prisons after having self-mutilated or purposefully eaten something to make them sick enough to receive a transfer to the Walls hospital wing. While in the hospital, the injured or sick prisoner could transmit his information to the senior member, who could then relay that message onto its intended recipient. The hospital wing thus became a "secret hub of gang communications." While the desperate tactic of self-mutilation had once been an act of truth telling and temporary escape during the era of building tenders, during the mid-1980s transition to the gang and militarized prison the act of self-mutilation became a twisted means of ordering assassinations.[84]

Once the TS perfected the logistical system for messages, they turned to a series of clandestine secret codes to cleverly disguise the meaning of their words. Because one of their members was nearly blind and familiar with Braille, the TS drew upon Braille to deliver hidden communiques to its soldiers. The TDC gang intelligence report explained how the code operated: "To use Braille code, a letter . . . would be very general and would not discuss gang activity. After the letter was written, dots signifying words used in the Braille code were added on at various points in the letter so as not to draw attention to the mailroom personnel." The Braille dots would appear above letters and convey such messages as "The Hit Is On" within a normal-looking letter that only discussed a fellow prisoner going on bench warrant. Another method was the number code, which assigned numbers to letters in an alphabet so that every time a number appeared in the letter it corresponded to a letter in the alphabet to spell out hidden messages. To keep the TDC from learning the system, the gang used a key code that was often revealed to them through the date of the letter. For instance, the key for a letter might be "Sunday January 4"—making 4 the beginning key for *a*, and every other number would correspond to a letter in the alphabet (5 equaling *b*, etc.). Other more complicated codes might put the key in the first sentence, with one example reading, "Sorry to be 3 weeks in answering," meaning twenty-one days, with 21 representing the beginning of the key for letter *a*. Throughout the letter, every numerical expression would then equal a letter, such that one seemingly innocuous letter that discussed the weather actually contained a coded message: "Hit Unit Warden." Other methods of code included the use of invisible ink made with Alka Seltzer, Visine, vitamin E, or crushed Sudafed tablets on which gang members would write coded messages on the back of regular letters. The letters then cued readers that the letter in question was the one that contained invisible ink. In one intercepted letter, any words containing "foods" became the new code for future letters: "Ese Te! The key work for the coding is 'food'!! When a letter says something about 'chowtime'—'refin'-'comida'-'menudo'-'Frijoles conqueso'-any letter than about 'planton' or 'refin' is an indication there is a letter on the reverse side. If I say 'Pelon' you're really gaining weight with those 'sloppy joes' there's the key I'm talking about!" The TS's advanced messaging and secret code system provided their organization an advantage in recruitment, drug proliferation, and assassination, which proved especially valuable when the Texas Syndicate initiated an intraracial gang war in 1985.[85]

By 1986, the TS granted most of white members the opportunity to form their own organization, the Texas Mafia, with 110 members. Other prisoner gangs formed during the critical gang formation years of 1984 to 1985, and included the Texas Aryan Brotherhood (white and distinct from the national Aryan Brotherhood) with 287 members, the Mexican Mafia with 351 members, Nuestro Carneles (Mexican American) with 47 members, the Mandingo Warriors (African American) with 66 members, the Self Defense Family (majority African American and interracial) with 107 members, and the Hermanos De Pistolero (Latina/o) with 21 members.[86] These gangs operated with a paramilitary structure that issued orders, made hits, and attempted to control an expanding prison drug trade. Nationally, the Justice Department estimated that in 1985 the nation's prisons had a total of 12,634 prison gang members divided between 114 individual gangs spread throughout 29 state prison systems, with the highest number of prison gang members known to be incarcerated in the states of Illinois (5,300), Pennsylvania (2,400), and California (2,050).[87] But as Buentello's fledgling gang intelligence operation in Texas had demonstrated, the attempt to make numerical estimations of gang affiliation was often difficult to determine as "gang intelligence" was a relatively new prison management tool for many states during the mid-1980s.

As prison gangs took root across the TDC system, new kinds of carceral violence began to accelerate. Between 1983 and 1986, assaults on guards increased by 565 percent. In 1983, there were a total of nine homicides in TDC, and four of those murders were suspected gang hits. In the following year, however, TDC experienced a total of twenty-five prison homicides, of which twenty were known to be gang related. In 1985, TDC experienced a record twenty-seven prison homicides, of which twenty-three were known to be gang related. From 1984 to 1986, nearly 83 percent of all prison homicides were known or suspected to be gang related. While homicides increased, assaults and stabbings accelerated even more. In 1984 and 1985, 693 prisoners were stabbed and 52 murdered.[88]

In addition to the drug trade, prison gangs controlled some of the sex trade operation and required prisoners that they considered weak to pay extortion money for protection. When prisoners refused to pay such exorbitant protection fees, the result could be gang-directed prison rape. In 1984, Steve Fryer refused to pay protection money to the gangs and remained instead in his cell while issuing complaints to Ferguson prison administrators that his cell door would not lock. As retribution for failure to pay protection money, four prisoners came to his cell late in the night on May 16, 1984, and raped him repeatedly. In a harrowing description, Fryer related to the press that he believed that gangs had organized the assault and that the prison administration had willingly looked the other way. "I was hollering most of the time, but there wasn't a guard that would answer. After four or five (sexual assaults), I passed out. When I looked up, there were a lot of people standing around like they wanted to do it too."[89] Fyer spent five months at Ferguson before he was transferred to Wynne, and during that time he claimed that he witnessed four rapes, heard two, and knew of ten others.

When the media began to take notice of gangs in 1984, the TDC initially responded by blaming gang organization on urban minorities who preyed on otherwise innocent white prisoners. "What we have here," the prison board chairman Robert Gunn told the press, "was a situation where blacks were taking advantage of the whites and asking for protection. We had naïve country white boys alongside city-smart blacks and that is the battle that is being fought now."[90] Such sentiments played into racial stereotypes of the "tricky" Black city dweller and inverted the reality of prison life under the building tender system of white authority and domination over African American prisoners.

The development of gang activity centered on the drug trade within prison, but it also had a relationship to the crumbling of the old racial structure that had previously been secured by the building tender system. Although the ranks of building tenders included all races, white prisoners were particularly advantaged by the BT system as they reigned over the prison system as head building tenders. The building tender system's collapse diminished the power and prestige of white prisoners. In response, white prisoners turned toward gang organization as a means to reassert their prior dominance. In point of fact, the founding of the Texas Aryan Brotherhood as separate from the California and national counterpart was bound up in the *Ruiz* decision. The Aryan Brotherhood Texas (ABT) was based on the California Aryan Brotherhood, which had been active since the late 1960s. The Texas Aryan Brotherhood, however, existed as its own organization apart from the national AB with its network headquartered in California. According to Buentello's intelligence gathering, the California AB, which founded the gang, had followed the *Ruiz* testimony in the news, and they felt that "there was a lot of testimony about the whites being taken advantage of by building tenders and the Aryan Brotherhood in California felt like, 'hey you guys don't deserve to be Aryan Brotherhood because you wouldn't take care of your own kind and you didn't stand up to the building tenders, as far as we're concerned, you don't have what it takes to be one of us.'"[91] The prison's first official memorandum that acknowledged the existence of the Aryan Brotherhood was issued in late 1984.[92] In TDC's AB intelligence report, Buentello concluded that the national and California-based Aryan Brotherhood did not consider the Texas AB as part of the national gang organization because the Texan AB was "considered to be too soft and easily intimated by prison officials" and that they didn't "have their heart right." As a result, the gang intelligence report concluded that the Texas AB overcompensated with "an usual amount of ferociousness" as an attempt to "make a name for themselves in TDC as well as other state and federal institutions."[93] As a separate gang entity, the Texas Aryan Brotherhood was ruled by a council, or steering committee, who made gang laws, anointed new members, and ordered hits on other gang members or individual prisoners. The sociological researchers Terry Pelz, Mary Pelz, and James Marquart have concluded that the AB was responsible for as much as 32 percent of all prisoner homicides in the TDC in 1984 and for 40 percent of all gang homicides.[94]

White rural gangs in Texas formed in the hopes of restoring the power of white superiority in the face of minority activism and civil rights agitation. One Aryan Brotherhood member stated that the dismantling of the building tender system "brought about the beginning of the AB . . . because the Black inmates, being in the position of numerical superiority, used this superiority

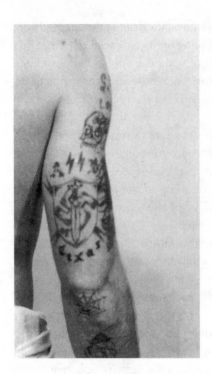

Aryan Brotherhood gang sigil tattoo. Photograph from author's private collection.

of numbers and the fear it caused among most white inmates to start robbing and sexually assaulting the weaker inmates."[95] Without fear of reprisal from building tenders, minority prisoners asserted themselves and disrupted the system's racial order.

However, the Texas AB did not form as a defensive organization to protect themselves from other gangs so much as to enact violence against African Americans in their "holy quest" to renew the system of white superiority that they felt the civil rights revolution had imperiled. The Brotherhood's Creed adopted the position that "brotherhood" was forged through fearless defiance. "An Aryan Brother is without care, he walks where the weak, the heartless won't dare, and if by chance he should stumble and lose control, his brother will be there, to help reach his goal." To reach the organization's "goal" of white superiority, the AB creed promised that only violent ferocity would resurrect the imperiled "white nation." "For an Aryan Brother, death holds no fear, vengeance will be his through his brothers still here." Only the brother's death, especially if their life was taken in the "holy cause" of defending white superiority, released a brother from his bond. "For the brotherhood means just what it implies, a brother's a brother, till his brother dies. So a brother am I and always will be even after my life its taken from me." Aryan Brotherhood tattoos featured a shield on which the swastika was emblazoned with a dagger superimposed over the Nazi-era symbol to connote the "race war" that the AB promised. Atop the dagger was a crown that symbolized their claim to defend the rightful reign of white superiority. Over the shield, the words "AB of Texas" were tattooed alongside a pair of lightning bolts of Nazi Germany's Schutzstaffel (SS). When an AB member received an order to hit another prisoner, even if it was one of his "brothers," he had to make good on the assassination, or he would become the next target. From 1984 to 1987, six of the twenty-four AB homicides were AB members killing their own "brother."[96]

Among white gangs, the murder of African American and Chicano prisoners became a "holy cause" to regain the "lost status" of white power within Texas prisons. AB members circulated pamphlets, leaflets, and drawings that promised a return to power for white prisoners. One prisoner in particular exemplified the murderous nature of this racial struggle, and his words evoked the violence of committing murder in a perverse sexualized analogy: "The smell of fresh human blood can be overpowering but killing is like having sex. The first time is not so rewarding, but it gets better and better with practice, especially when one remembers that it's a holy cause."[97]

The AB organization of the 1980s organized itself around the geographic division of the East Texas prison corridor that included the tripartite North, Central, and South Divisions. The governing body was a five-member steering committee (SC) called the "Supreme Court," composed of the president and the northern, central, and southern judges. Beneath the steering committee were captains of each geographic division, followed by individual prison lieutenants and then the soldiers at each prison. Unlike the TS, the AB had no real democratic traditions, and the SC ruled gang business through committee fiat and dictate, which then were passed on to the regional judges and from there on down to the individual prison captains. When a captain was transferred to another prison, he lost his rank and became another soldier, so as not to create violent competition for leadership positions. To recruit members, the AB developed a tight "kite" organization of passing notes among members in different prisons across the system, even expanding their reach beyond prison bars by placing advertisement in such popular motorcycle magazines as *Easy Rider*.[98]

Through his networks of remaining writ writers, Lawrence Pope, now out of prison, attempted to document that the Texas AB had members who were former building tenders and that the AB had launched a secret campaign in 1984 and 1985 to hunt down and murder writ writers, prison organizers, and any African American prisoner who embraced civil rights. To cite but one of Pope's cases of targeted white gang violence against Black civil rights organizers, Roy Lynn Boozer, an African American prisoner, was stalked and eventually killed by the AB member Gary Brown on June 17, 1984. In a letter to Lane McCotter, Lawrence Pope forwarded an affidavit by fellow writ writer Oss Smith, an African American prisoner, that "Brown stabbed unsuspected Roy Lynn Boozer in the back while he was eating at the dining table. When Ray Lynn Boozer fall to the floor Gary Brown got down on Roy Lyn Boozer and stabbed him several more times." But this was no random act of prison gang violence; rather, it was a racially targeted assassination meant to silence Black prisoner politicization. The affidavit pointed out that "Ray Lynn Boozer was a writ-writer working in cooperation with the Office of the Special Master. He was a prison reform advocate in opposition of racism, the practice of racial discrimination, and persecution. He was also organizing a work strike at the time he was killed."

To combat the carceral violence of the Aryan Brotherhood, prisoner organizers attempted to fight back with the legal tools that they used to combat the TDC during the 1970s. The prison organizers documented AB assaults, wrote affidavits that named gang members, and attempted to enlist the support of their political allies by sending their documentation to civil rights attorneys, the *Ruiz* special master, and aligned politicians. In one affidavit, Oss Smith charged that the AB member Anthony Archer, known as "Slim," was an ex–building tender and an informant to the TDC. The affidavit claimed that Archer was actively "working in conspiracy with these white racist inmates that are killing blacks." The affidavit then followed Swift's tradition of naming the names of building tenders by suppling a list of twenty-nine white prisoners, with their prisoner number, who were suspected of being AB members.[99]

Pope collected several affidavits that even claimed that the AB had simply replaced the BT system as informants for the TDC and that the AB's assassination campaign was a TDC conspiracy, or at least provided for the TDC the convenient eradication of Black prisoner organizers that threatened state control over the prison system. Johnny Martínez, now out of the TDC and running the Prisoners' Rights Coalition out of San Antonio, filed the civil rights suit, *The Prisoners' Rights Coalition v. Texas Department of Corrections and the Aryan Brotherhood*. The suit alleged that a coalition of prisoners' rights organizations "have joined efforts concretely under one umbrella for the sole purpose of preserving circumstantial and concrete evidence to Governor Mark White and the upcoming legislative session pursuant to a conspiracy to murder certain inmates" by the Aryan Brotherhood and with the full knowledge of the TDC guards within the administrative segregation wing.[100] Another affidavit by a different prisoner made its claim even clearer: "TDC officials use these Aryan Brotherhood members to do their 'dirty work' by allowing them to harass, threaten, physically injure, and kill Black inmates perceived as troublemakers. These black inmates perceived as troublemakers are inmates that organize work strikes, inmates that write writs, inmates that work in cooperation with the Office of the Special Master, inmates that is prison reform advocates in opposition of racism, the practice of racial discrimination, and persecution."

To make their case, Pope cited the use of prisoner segregation, which was the new punitive tool in the kit box of the Procunier/McCotter administration that isolated prisoners in solitary security wings known as administrative segregation (Ad Seg). On these Ad Seg wings, the TDC placed African American writ writers and political agitators alongside Aryan Brotherhood members, who then initiated attacks whenever the opportunity presented itself. On April 2, 1985, for instance, AB members colluded with TS members to take a guard hostage on the administrative segregation wing so that they could initiate a hit on Charles Young, an African American writ writer, who barely survived with thirty-four stab wounds requiring two colostomies. In his letter of denunciation to McCotter, Pope recounted the incident as a perverse response to the *Lamar* court order to racially integrate Texas prisons. "Your officials On Ramsey 1, Darrington and many other units, especially in segregation areas, carefully placed black inmates in *very* close proximity to the ABs . . . Yes, your Ramsey I officials did a GREAT job of integrating Charles Young right in among the ABs so they could almost kill him. And how many other black inmates had a been integrated right among the ABs and others in the so-called 'protective custody' or administrative segregation, only to be stabbed or killed by their enemies?"[101]

But unlike the prisoners' rights movement, there was little legal ground that prisoners who documented gang violence might possibly gain against organizer prison gangs. While Pope and Martínez claimed that the Texas AB merely replaced the BTs as outsourced white violence and prison control, the TDC's gang intelligence report maintained that all prospective members had "to pass a rather intense and strident review of his past history to insure that the prospect is not or even been a building tender, turn-key, informant, etc."[102] The allegations against the TDC as a collaborator in white racial violence was almost impossible to prove. The TDC simply countered that they placed those AB members on Ad Seg to halt gang violence, not promote it. Yet the prisoners' practice of legal documentation did leave behind new testimonies of resistance and documentation of carceral violence.

The Aryan Brotherhood, meanwhile, mocked the practice of writ writing and civil rights legal work when they issued assassination orders as disguised legal correspondence. Due to the *Guajardo* decision, genuine legal correspondence was protected from TDC letter monitoring. Because of that decision, prison gangs took advantage by disguising assassination orders as civil rights cases. In 1984, Buentello's gang intelligence operations managed to intercept one such coded "legal correspondence." Portions of the letter follow: "In reference to the class action *Ruiz v. Procunier,* a recent Supreme Court ruling has taken place and it is by order of the court that inmate John V. Montes replace Ronnie Evans in . . . coordinating the present litigation . . . This is the result of an "en bana" (unanimous) opinion of the Court and there seem to be a mistaken opinion that such Court orders are appealable. This is *not* the case! The Supreme Court defines the law as the law is, and so it stands." The coded letter deceptively communicated that Montes was to replace Evans as the hitman for the assassination ("the present litigation") and that no AB member so designated as the assassin could deny the order, which was disguised as "a Supreme Court ruling."[103]

As the white gangs attempted to restore racial superiority through murder and white terror, African American prisoners responded by forming such self-defense groups and racially integrated gangs as the Self Defense Family, whose name speaks to its purpose. In retaliation for the AB's murderous campaign against those African Americans who pursued civil rights, the Self Defense Family filed a class-action lawsuit of their own that charged the TDC with assisting the AB with political and racially motivated assassinations of Black prisoners.[104] Many African American prisoners felt that the years of racial subservience had added to a lingering sense of bitterness in the 1980s. "Yeah, we got an attitude towards whites," one Black prisoner admitted to the sociological researchers James Marquart and Ben Crouch. "Why not? The reason I say this is because the whites have always more or less run this farm [Eastham]. This place has always been a white boy's farm, so our attitude is kind of bitter. We washed the floors around here long enough and seen the white boys make trusty quicker than any of us. Yeah, we got a bad attitude awright. So what about it?"[105] Of course, African American prisoners were involved in the drug trade too, and groups like the Mandingo Warriors competed with the other gangs for their share of narcotics traffic. The demise of the building tenders, the removal of writ writers and activists from the TDC, the outright murder of remaining writ writers and prisoner organizers, the strained effort to racially integrate a formerly southern prison plantation, and the rise of racial gangs created a new prison society and culture centered on racial competition and militarization.[106]

Gang warfare during the mid-1980s contributed to unprecedented levels of prison violence and hastened the mounting prison crisis. As brutal as the building tender system had been, murders were rare in the control model as Texas maintained the nation's lowest murder rate. Indeed, the TDC recorded only seventeen murders during the entire decade of George Beto's administration (1961–71).

Mexikanemi (Mexican Mafia), Soldiers of Aztlán, gang sigil tattoo. Photograph from author's private collection.

Only thirteen months into his two-year contract, Director Raymond Procunier announced his retirement. "I just run out of gas. I'm tired. . . . I never anticipated this—resigning—but I never anticipated the magnitude of this job either. This system is about three or four systems in one." Telling the press that he could "only go to the trough so many times," Procunier resigned with the confession that "this job is 10 or 50 times more difficult that I had anticipated. Probably 100 times would have been more accurate." In sympathy with Procunier's exhaustion, the prison board chairman Robert Gunn compared managing the TDC in the post-*Ruiz* environment to "a person who has been in a massive car wreck" and that he believed Procunier's short directorship had seen Texas "through the recovery."[107] In the hopes of controlling and stemming the unrest, the TDC quickly promoted Lane McCotter as its new director. It was rumored that McCotter had been Governor White's first choice all along.[108]

During the Labor Day weekend of 1985, four prisoners were killed in a twenty-four-hour period when a full-scale intraracial "gang war" erupted when the TS secretly declared war against the Mexican Mafia over gang recruitment and a drug trade that had gone bad.[109] As with the origins of the TS, the Mexican Mafia originated in the California prison system, but much earlier, during the late 1950s. In 1985, Tejano prisoners received permission from the California branch to form their own chapter, known as the Mexikanemi (the Soldiers of Aztlan), or La EMI, while California prisoners retained the name La EME. As self-styled prison insurgents, La EMI adopted a top-down hierarchical structure, with a president and vice president over the statewide organization and generals over distinct prison regions, lieutenants over individual prisons, and sergeants operating as the coordinator of gang hits and the underground drug trade. La EMI adopted similar "blood in, blood out" rules as the TS and other gangs of the mid-1980s, but they openly forbade "homosexuals" as members, and their twelve membership rules stressed respect as a signifier of their racial cohesion and pride, requiring that when any member received disrespect that "all members of the MEXIK-ANEMI will unite to destroy the person or the other group completely."[110] "Soldiers of Aztlan," the Texas Mexican Mafia's symbol for tattoo art drew on Mexican nationalism, as they adopted Mexico's eagle and a snake over a flaming circle with crossed knives to demonstrate their willingness to take up violence to defend their fellow carnales. The Mexican Mafia imagined themselves as insurgent revolutionaries, who pursued revolution and antiauthoritarianism through criminal organization. One La EMI member proudly declared that his gang status should be seen as a revolutionary response to a long history of Anglo oppression against Mexicans and Mexican Americans in the U.S. Southwest and along the U.S.-Mexico border. "The Mexican mafia believes that they are God's people, that's why they call themselves 'Soldiers of Aztlan.' They believe that this land belongs to Mexico because it was forcibly taken away by the capitalistic American government. The Mexican people in this land are consistently suppressed by the white Americans. So in the name of unity and honor, the MEXIKANEMS view themselves as having the responsibility of liberating this land through whatever illegal means necessary since legitimate means are not available."[111]

While La EMI offered racial cohesion for Mexican Americans, they openly declared in their rules for membership that their end goal was crime and profit from criminality: "The Mexikanemi is a criminal organization and therefore will participate in all aspects of criminal interests for monetary benefit." Unlike the more exacting selection process for TS membership, the Mexikanemi more easily recruited younger members from "homeboy" networks without the same level of scrutiny and rejection as the more selective TS. The allure of racial cohesion and pride, the safety of organized protection, the promise of respect, looser membership rules, and the temptation of profit made the Mexican Mafia grow to become the prison system's largest gang, with 294 members, within its first year.

Threatened by the Mexican Mafia's rapid expansion, the TS planned during the month of August 1985 to initiate an intraracial gang war against La EMI. Over Labor Day weekend, the TS struck, and by the end of the long weekend, four La EMI members were killed by TS gang hits. According to

TDC gang intelligence, "while the Mexican Mafia was trying to write one another to find out what was happening," the TS had used its "superior communication system" to relay a series of planned hits to its members. The Mexican Mafia had a numbers advantage as they had more members, but the TS's well-oiled communication system provided greater organizational cohesion and an ability to make good on hits with frightening speed. The TS even utilized Ray Hill's popular Houston radio program, the *Prison Show*, that had a strong enough broadcast to reach most Texas prisons with the coded message: "All Carnales should eat M&M candies (in reference to Mexican Mafia) first chance they get." According to one gang informant, this hidden radio message through popular media delivery initiated the kill code for an all-out, systemwide gang war.[112] In the first year of the war, the TS had the upper hand resulting in eight Mexikanemi fatalities from deadly stabbings, while the Mexican Mafia had not managed to kill a single TS member. The four deaths of Labor Day weekend had capped a tumultuous year of prison violence in which Texas had the highest number of homicides among the nation's five largest prison systems. By September 1985, Texas had twenty-six homicides while California, known for its gang violence, had six homicides, and the states of New York and Florida had only one each.[113]

In response to the intraracial gang violence, Director McCotter issued his own public declaration of "war" on the prison gangs by placing 17,000 prisoners on lockdown.[114] During his press briefing on the Labor Day gang crisis, McCotter told the media that "open gang warfare between some of our racially motivated gangs" was accelerating at an "alarming level." Buentello's gang intelligence report on the TS recommended that "this war has also demonstrated that the Texas Syndicate as well as other disruptive gangs should remain in lock-up status due to their unpredictability in regards to violence and to prevent another repeat of the rash of homicides related to the Texas Syndicate/Mexican Mafia war."[115]

In the course of his war, McCotter fully embraced a militarized approach to prison management. Turning to military tactics and borrowing from recent developments in urban police departments, McCotter implemented the formation of SWAT-like prison guards based on military units, named Special Operations Response Teams (SORT). SORT generally consisted of six-man teams, including a sniper and a negotiator. These paramilitary guards answered directly to McCotter and dressed in black or dark blue combat fatigues and wore steel-toed combat boots, carried steel riot batons, and became notorious among prisoners for inflicting physical abuse without any outward or observable physical signs of violence. As one prisoner put it, "There isn't a time when SORT comes down here that someone doesn't get the hell beat out of him."[116]

"Through These Gates Enter the Finest Correctional Officers," SORT Paramilitary
Tactical Team, 1986. Robert R. McElroy/Getty Images.

McCotter also advanced the use of Ad Seg and what became known as
"super" segregation cell blocks. These were cordoned-off cell blocks with individual cells, known among prisoners as a series of "prisons within prisons."
Arizona was the first state to develop the super-maximum prison in 1986,
where every cell is an isolation cell, and California quickly adopted the model
for its overpopulated prison system.[117] Texas, however, built wings of high
"threat security" for total cell isolation on the old prisons that also held the
general population. The development of Ad Seg wings locked away those
prisoners that TDC accused as a "security threat" in a single cell that measured nine by six feet with very little to no material allowed in the stark cell
that consisted of only a toilet and often a built-in concrete bunk. Once moved
to Ad Seg, prisoners were locked in their cell twenty-three hours a day, seven
days a week. Their one daily hour outside of the cell required them to parade
down a line of wire mesh cages before being allowed to exercise. Sleep deprivation was part of Ad Seg's torturous nightly routine, as glaring hall lights
with florescent bulbs shined into cells twenty-four hours a day, and the rau-
cous sounds of other prisoners and their radios blared at all hours of the night.
Food was slipped through the cell's bars or placed in a revolving metal slot in
the steel door. Living in isolated "supermax" cell conditions caused prisoners to experience extreme psychological distress and to develop such
conditions as severe sleep deprivation, self-mutilation, auditory and visual
hallucinations, depression, and anxiety.[118]

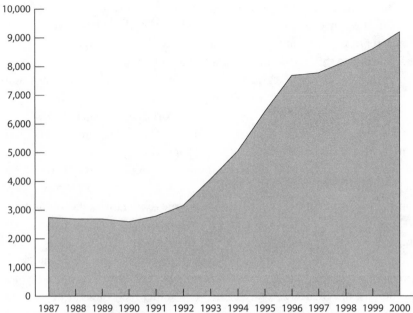

Ad Seg population, 1987–2000. Source: Open Records Request, Texas Department of Criminal Justice (TDCJ), in author's possession.

Ad Seg cages and militarized CERT team, Coffield prison, 2000. Courtesy of Andrew Lichtenstein.

During the 1980s, the onset of mass incarceration exacerbated the prison's racialization by convincing prison authorities that the "new breed" of prisoners represented a home-grown domestic "savage" or "insurgent" who could only be tamed through domestic paramilitarism. In 1983, there were 345 prisoners in administrative segregation, but under McCotter's regime the population of Ad Seg increased fivefold to 1,860. By 1987 those housed in Ad Seg increased to 3,055, while prisoner homicides dropped in 1986 to five.[119] Most of the assaults, however, happened on the Ad Seg wings, where caged prisoners used common items, such as rolled paper, to fashion spears, spikes, and other dangerous weapons that they shot with deadly efficiency through the wire mesh of their new cages. Despite Ad Seg's promise of "protection," prisoners moving out of their cells required a large rolling metal sheet, known as "the wall" or "the shield," which prevented prisoners in other cells from shooting deadly darts as they moved down the corridor. The mounting prison population and the embrace of militarized prisons to combat prison gangs created new kinds of savagery as the prison devolved into a barely contained wilderness of violence. As one reasonable, but incisively thoughtful, prisoner put it, "I cannot fault his (McCotter's) administration for locking us down, but I do fault the militarism. . . . It was a real shock to see the prison guards running around with combat boots on and their pants legs tucked inside the boots. Where did they think they were, over there in Vietnam, fighting in the bush? This is prison, but I thought it was a battlefield."[120] In the post-Vietnam era, McCotter's mid-1980s paramilitary regime treated prisoners as if they were home-grown insurgents in a "war" that might allow McCotter and the TDC to attain the victory at home that eluded the U.S. military in Vietnam.[121]

McCotter's heavy hand, however, was called into question when several prisoners died in custody under violent circumstances, causing Judge William Wayne Justice to threaten to fine the state $1,000 a day if improvements were not made. In a March 1986 memorandum to all wardens, McCotter announced a new policy that all newly received prisoners were to gain the highest good-time status of state-assured trusty (SAT) 4, which allowed them to earn forty days toward their sentence for every thirty served.[122] Previously, incoming prisoners were given a classification that allowed them to earn only twenty days of good time for thirty days served. Such an action provoked the ire of Bill Clements, who was running again for governor in 1986 in a renewal of the 1982 campaign between White and Clements. Promising that he wanted "action and not talk" about controlling prisons, combined with tougher and longer sentences, Clements promised to fire McCotter if elected, to put in his own people on the prison board, and to enact a "complete restructuring of the Texas criminal justice system."[123] Clements won, and McCotter resigned under extreme political pressure.

The trajectory of Lane McCotter's career after the TDC embodied significant shifts in prison management from custodial to military practice, to the privatization of the prison, and to the ways in which domestic and military prisons influenced one another. After his departure from the TDC in 1987, McCotter became cabinet secretary of the New Mexico Corrections Department from 1987 to 1992 and director of the Utah Department of Corrections from 1992 until 1997, when McCotter resigned his post following the controversy that erupted from the death of Michael Valent, a schizophrenic prisoner whom the prison guards bound naked to a restraint chair for over sixteen hours for refusing to take a pillowcase off his head. Although the prison administration claimed that Valent died at the hands of other prisoners, a videotape surfaced that showed otherwise. Valent's death resulted from blood clots that formed in his immobilized legs and blocked an artery to his heart. McCotter thereafter followed the trend toward the privatization of prisons and became the director of Corrections Business Development for the private, Centerville, Utah, based prison and education company Management & Training (MTC). In view of McCotter's successful management of the nation's third-largest privatized prison company, Attorney General John Ashcroft selected McCotter in 2003 as one of three advisers sent to establish the U.S. military prison Abu Ghraib in Iraq. Although McCotter never managed Abu Ghraib, his role as a consultant resulted in debate on the floor of the U.S. Senate. "There are many questions begging for answers," remarked New York's Senator Chuck Schumer. "Mr. McCotter's selection also raises serious questions about the role that was played by civilian advisers in setting prison policies, designing training programs for prison guards and directly influencing the environment in which the horrible abuses at Abu Ghraib took place." McCotter's role in Texas and later in Abu Ghraib shows the circular and shared practices between the U.S. military and domestic prisons. When the two were blended, they forged violent narratives that falsely cast prisons as battlegrounds, wars, and savage internal frontiers.[124] By the mid-1980s, such deceptive narratives had become prison policies that fashioned the militarized prison that made war on its own prison population as prisoners were reimagined as prison insurgents contained only by the newly fashioned cages of total cell isolation.

"The Largest Prison Construction Program in the History of the World": *Ruiz* and the Construction of Texas's New Carceral State

As new waves of carceral violence swept over the prison, Governor Clements, now in his second gubernatorial administration, struck a political bargain

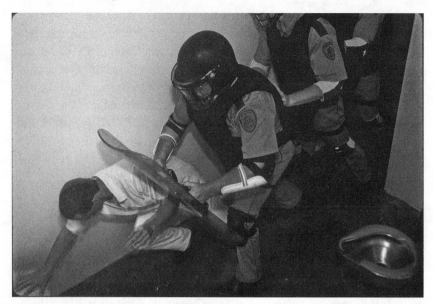

Ad Seg cell search by militarized CERT team, Coffield prison, 2000. Courtesy of Andrew Lichtenstein.

between compliance with *Ruiz* and building the new architecture for the militarized carceral state. Wary of a political fight over a prison system constructed by Democrats, the Republican Clements simply moved away from the pattern of denial and resistance to the court-ordered reforms of its prison system. Instead, he embraced the coming changes and offered an uncharacteristic olive branch to Judge Justice. Clements suggested a "meeting of the minds" between the plaintiff attorneys and the state in Judge Justice's chamber. The protagonists in the near decade-long struggle emerged from the January 9, 1987, meeting with a series of compliance agreements that satisfied all parties. In his State of the State address to the 70th Legislature, Clements declared peace: "The lawsuit is over. . . . We must get in compliance as quickly as possible. We have no choice." Federal oversight of Texas state prisons continued until 2002, but the ongoing warfare between Justice and the state in the courtroom and in the court of public opinion had ceased. By 1989 Judge Justice closed the special master's office after nearly a decade of direct supervision.

Compliance with *Ruiz*, however, suited Clements's broad law-and-order vision.[125] Within thirty days after he took office, Clements sought a $12.6 million emergency appropriation to begin compliance with Justice's order that forbade the TDC from housing more than 95 percent of its capacity prison population. Rather than restricting prison population, however, Clements

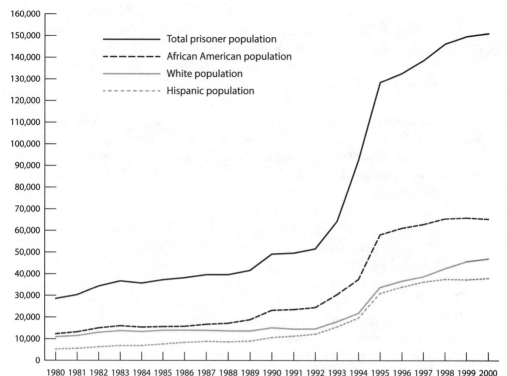

TDC population, 1980–2000. Source: Open Records Request, Alicia Frezia King to Robert Chase, December 5, 2008, Texas Department of Criminal Justice (TDCJ), in author's possession.

used this court order as rationale to build more prisons so that the TDC would not have to release its prisoners. Clements used the crisis over *Ruiz* compliance to ask the 1987 legislature for funds to create eight thousand new beds at a cost of $213 million. Clements promised that "one way or another, we will build more prisons."[126]

Clements was indeed true to his promise. In three years under his second term as governor, Clements proposed and received legislative approval for 24,000 new beds for incoming prisoners with a $547 million price tag ($213 million in 1987 for 8,000 beds and $324 million in 1989 for 11,000 beds).[127] Public-supported bonds, rather than new taxes, paid for these new prisons. His successful passage of his criminal justice plan included the punitive measures of mandatory hard time over good time for recidivists, parole on the condition of compulsory drug testing and treatment, asset seizure for drugs dealers, a uniform crime database, and lengthy prison terms for aggravated assault with a deadly weapon against a police officer.[128] Charles Terrell, the head of Clements's Texas Criminal Justice Task Force, recalled the astounding success of the Clements program and how it was a joint effort by lobbying interests, the legislature, and the public: "We passed 29 pieces of anti-crime legislation that set the tone for the future. We set into movement the largest prison construction program in the history of the world. By our group, by the governor alone? Hell, no. You have to have people in leadership positions; the public's got to support it with votes on bond issues; but he [Clements] set it into motion and it has carried forward."[129] Indeed, from 1987 to 1993 the state legislature allocated nearly $3 billon for new state prisons. Between 1993 and 1996, Texas built twenty-six new prisons and purchased six private facilities housing five hundred men each.

The new wave of prison construction heralded the future for prisons in Texas within a new geography and a new physical structure of control. The new prisons were built across the state, including in West Texas, outside of the old agricultural corridor of Houston and Huntsville. These new prisons abandoned the postwar "telephone pole" design for a modular pod design that provided near comprehensive surveillance aimed against "riot control."[130] Meanwhile, new internal gang law injunctions sentenced prisoners to a wave of new "convictions within a conviction" and incarcerated them in solitary Ad Seg cells constructed of reinforced concrete that created the new militarized system of "prisons within prisons."[131] Since the *Ruiz v. Estelle* decision, Texas has held more prisoners in private prisons than any other state: 18,720 in 2006.[132] This suggests that the turn to privatized prisons in the U.S. South may have been one way for state legislatures to circumvent the power and oversight of federal courts.[133]

Clements proposed that to manage such a vastly expanded prison system that the TDC and the state's probation and parole offices join together under a new administrative rubric as the Texas Department of Criminal Justice (TDCJ), which was enacted on September 1, 1989. This consolidation fit Clements's political vision and made good on his campaign promises to law-and-order groups that prison management and parole would operate in a coordinated fashion so as to avoid early release of violent offenders and to deliver punitive sentences with longer prison time. The administration of TDCJ was handed over to James Lynaugh, who had taken over the administrative reins of the TDC in 1987 after McCotter's dismissal. Lynaugh, a career accountant with the state's controller office, offered a new order of bureaucratic efficiency and practical business acumen. "The TDC is a $400 million-a-year operation. That is a business," Lynaugh flatly proclaimed to the press on the day of his appointment.[134] By 1995, Clements's prison-building plan resulted in nine prisons of the new "cookie cutter" and "supermax" security design.[135] It was indeed "the largest prison construction program in the history of the world."

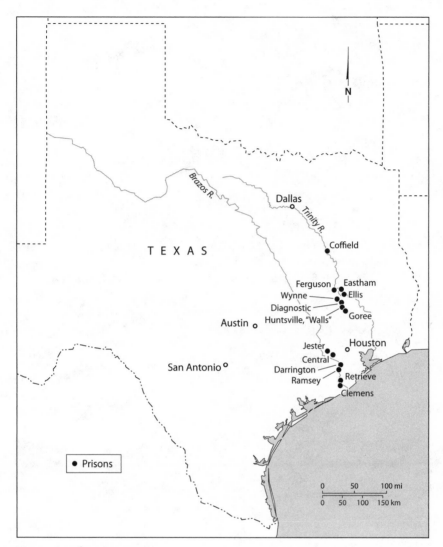

Texas prison locations, 1978

Since the *Ruiz* decision of 1980, the Texas prison system has grown from a population of 30,000 prisoners on fourteen prison plantations to five times that size by 1999 in ninety-one prisons. By 1999, Texas had outpaced California with the largest prison population in the country: 163,190. By century's end in the year 2000, the incarceration rate in Texas for Latina/os was twice as high as that for whites (1,152 Latinos per 100,000 residents compared to 694 for whites). The state incarcerated African Americans, meanwhile, at five times the rate of whites in Texas (3,734 per 100,000).[136] In the two decades

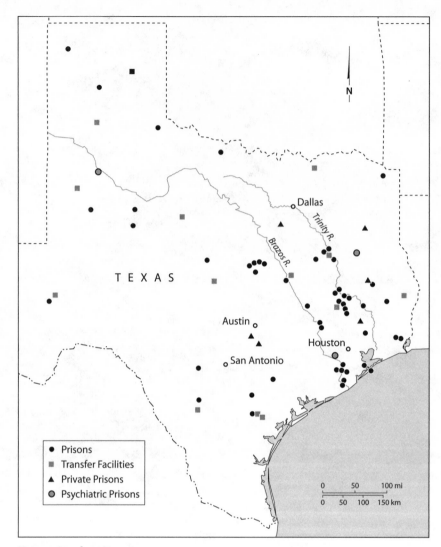

Texas prison locations, 2019

since Governor Clements brokered the 1987 "peace" with Judge Justice, Texas had fashioned the nation's largest carceral state.

When reflecting on the impact of the *Ruiz* litigation on the modern-day prison in Texas, the TDCJ typically responds with its new modernization narrative. Scott McCown, who defended the state during *Ruiz* as an assistant attorney general, offered the conclusion that "the Ruiz litigation transformed our prison from a backwards Southern plantation-style system into a modern penal system." In his estimation, Turner acknowledged that the case could not stem mass incarceration, but he considered *Ruiz* "a success in bringing the rule of the law into the prison so that they couldn't any longer run it like a slave plantation. They had to have rules and it became bureaucratized and that's a mixed blessing, but it was no longer a lawless operation."[137] Similarly, Carl Reynolds, the TDCJ's general counsel from 1993 to 2005, offered a parallel sentiment: "It was an important lawsuit for Texas to come to grips with, [now] running a modern prison system."[138] Just as the postwar reforms constructed a modernization narrative of agribusiness efficiency and control while ignoring coerced labor and state violence, the post-*Ruiz* prison was cast as one that left behind its past as a prison plantation in favor of the new modernization narrative centered on "high-threat security" and a new regime of militarized control over the prisoner insurgent.

The Persistence of Carceral Violence

While the prisoners' rights movement of the 1970s was organized along interracial lines, the mid-1980s generation of prisoners reorganized into a balkanized racial prison, where prisoners of each racial group collected together to wage a war of survival on each other, as mass incarceration made prisons dangerously overcrowded and contributed to new levels of carceral violence. The violence was both intraracial, as with the Mexikanemi and Tejano Syndicato "war" of 1985, and interracial, as demonstrated by the Aryan Brotherhood's 1984–86 campaign to exterminate through political and racial assassination African American writ writers and "civil rights agitators." In reflection of the difference between the politicized prisoner society of the 1970s and the viciousness of mid-1980s gang warfare, the former writ writer and current prisoner Stephan Blanchard wistfully aired his regret and a personal sense of defeat:

> I was so sad at what we'd wrought, . . . [In being part of *Ruiz*] I thought I would have the opportunity to build a prison system of meaning and instead we chose cannibalism, and the gangs came. And the violence came with gangs. And we started feeding on ourselves—just animals feeding on ourselves. Instead of the residual idealism of the rights movement, all that we had tried to accomplish—I felt defeated, and we didn't do anything, but set it up for tyranny in another form. And it was the letter tyranny, the EME, the TS, the AB, the AC, the ANs—all the gangs, and their letters of hate. And we created a monster that's grown to this 160 something thousand bed monstrosity. Why we just failed. We got rid of the building tenders, that's all that we did. And they've been replaced by staff—not as overtly brutal, but more subtle—more psychological oriented in a state that doesn't care. And among prisoners that don't care.[139]

Critics of the *Ruiz* decision have frequently blamed the intervention of the federal court and Justice's ruling for the rise of gangs in Texas. The *Ruiz* case, they argue, had created a social breakdown within prison society, diminished the guard's subculture, and created such agitation among prisoners that many felt entitled to confront their keepers through violence, riot, and misrule.[140] Sociologists have appraised the building tender system as a "co-option of the kept" where elite prisoners served as "negotiators" for guards and an extension of security staff. While such approaches have acknowledged the brutality that the *Ruiz* case revealed, their appraisal of building tenders tends to cast them in the role of elite "mediators" and "managers" who only became "out of control" when the prison system grew too large in the mid- to late 1970s.[141] But prisoners had been complaining about the building tenders and documenting abuse throughout the postwar period, particularly during the mid-1960s, before the prison system experienced the massive prison expansion of the post-1977 period. Building tenders had always been abusive and the construction of cell blocks accelerated their power and gave them enclosed and partially hidden space for secreted abuse. Moreover, the perpetual abuse of building tenders came to light only as the civil rights revolution and Black and brown movements for empowerment made its way into prison to testify, document, and demand public legibility of state prison abuse.

Gangs in Texas arose alongside mass incarceration, and while gangs engaged in a power struggle over prisoner society, the *Ruiz* case did not create overcrowded prisons and the conditions of violence.[142] While Judge Justice attempted to reduce the prison population, the southern brand of carceral massive resistance, whether coming from the Democrats or the new Republicans, attempted to ignore and then outright thrawt the court's intention to counter mass incarceration. Moreover, to suggest that *Ruiz* created gangs is to diminish the power that building tenders had within prison society. Although building tenders drew their ranks from all races in their effort to control racially segregated cell blocks, it was white prisoners who held the most influence and power with white prison officers. When the warden, assistant warden, or major had a problem on his hands, he frequently turned to such white head building tenders as Sonny Evans, Jack Friday, Butch Ainsworth, or Robert Barber to solve the problem. Building tenders therefore ruled prison society through the physical enforcement of white superiority and racial hierarchy. Contextualizing gang violence within the two-decade struggle over prisoners' rights demonstrates that the gangs did not simply evolve in a power vacuum due to an interruption of social order but rather that the "social order" of prisons, whether directed by the state or by the prisoners themselves, is upheld through the persistence of carceral violence.

Epilogue

Steel on Steel: The Legacy of Ruiz

The legacy of *Ruiz* demonstrated that prisoner-initiated political organization and litigation could successfully challenge the core practices of abusive prison regimes of control. Southern prisoners, in particular, took note and pursued similar federal court interventions into the management of southern prisons. Leading up to *Ruiz* and in the decade thereafter, federal courts found eight of the eleven states of the U.S. South as having unconstitutional prisons.[1] In some of these cases, other southern states faced the combination of prisoner-inspired civil rights suits alongside prisoner organizing.

In Tennessee, for instance, prisoner litigation and mobilization campaigns worked in tandem to deliver public exposure of southern prison abuse. During the mid-1970s, Tennessee prisoners filed a series of lawsuits against the Tennessee Department of Corrections based on claims of overcrowding, filthy and unsanitary living conditions, and physical abuse and rampant violence. Across the state's prison system, Tennessee housed prisoners in "high density cells," which offered each person less than sixty square feet per prisoner. A total of 92 percent of the state's prisoners were confined in such units. Only Florida, with 94 percent of its prisoners in overcrowded cells, had a higher rate. In 1979, Tennessee had a total prison population of 5,549 evenly split between white prisoners (51.74 percent) and Black prisoners (48.36 percent), which represented an increase in total population of 130 percent over the total in 1957.[2] Tennessee's overcrowded prison system also had the highest per capita violent death rate in the country for 1984. Tennessee led the nation in violent deaths, with 111 per 100,000 prisoners. The next highest rate was Texas with 68.1 per 100,000 prisoners. The national average was 29.4 violent deaths per 100,000 prisoners. State corrections officials reported 8 violent deaths in Tennessee prisons in 1984 alone.[3] Such violent conditions, the prisoners claimed, violated the Eighth Amendment's protections against "cruel and unusual punishment."

During the same year of the *Ruiz* trial, the Tennessee trial court ruled in 1978 against the Department of Corrections. The state appealed the cases, however, to the Tennessee Court of Appeals and Tennessee Supreme Court. When the Tennessee Supreme Court abstained from issuing a decision, the federal judiciary stepped into the legal fray. In 1980, the U.S. district court combined the cases on appeal into a class-action suit on behalf of the prisoners and appointed attorneys on their behalf, resulting in the prisoner-inspired class-action lawsuit known as *Grubbs v. Bradley*. Within two years, the prisoners were victorious when, in 1982, the U.S. district court ruled in the *Grubbs* case that specific prison "conditions and practices amount to cruel and unusual punishment in violation of the Eighth and Fourteenth Amendments to the United States Constitution and Article I, Sections 16 and 32 of the Tennessee Constitution."[4] The case cited seven specific conditions and practices that the court determined amounted to cruel and unusual punishment, which focused largely on rampant brutality at the hands of the guards, extremely unsanitary living conditions, poor facility maintenance, and a widespread problem of overcrowding and double and triple celling prisoners in spaces meant for single prisoners. Between 1982 and 1985, the federal court system ruled in three different trials that the Tennessee prison system maintained unconstitutional conditions. But after winning their court case, prisoners found that the state did very little to respond to the court's dictates.

Despite their victory, however, Tennessee prisoners experienced a period of intransigence as Governor Lamar Alexander's Plan for the Eighties offered a law-and-order approach that passed tougher sentencing laws, sending more and more prisoners into a vastly overcrowded system. Lamar's Plan for the Eighties centered on renewing southern prison labor. "All able-bodied prisoners in Tennessee's adult penal system will work and most inmate rehabilitation programs will be canceled," stipulated Lamar's plan.[5] The plan decried spending on prisoners and declared that "taxpayers' money for general education or job training program will be spent first on law-abiding citizens who are deserving of taxpayers' support." In response to the governor's "Plan for the Eighties," a group of ten politically active Muslim prisoners presented an alternative plan under their foundational belief that the governor's plan was nothing less than a "get tough policy" that "has manifest itself as a failure." The alternative plan presented to the commissioner of corrections, Ernest Pellegrin, centered on early release, a "living skills" educational program, a more diversified and better educated correctional staff to make up for an annual turnover rate of nearly 45 percent, and more modern job training to contrast the southern prison labor model where "in a age of micro chips and high tech, most of the inmates are forced to do unproductive or crude field labor."[6]

Prisoner activism came on the heels of a three-day work strike by 269 prisoners at the Fort Pillow prison in July 1983. In an eleven-page typed recounting of the strike, "What Really Happened at Fort Pillow," the Muslim prisoner Ron Lewis Freeman offered a litany of reasons for the strike: "the heat, lack of proper medical care, the food, the heavy coveralls they must wear, the low pay of eleven dollars a month, the insect bites they endure daily, the menacing shotgun-toting guards, the lack of educational or vocational training, and the fact that they are forced to work or be punished." Once the prisoners burned their coveralls, the striking prisoners were met by a "large contingent of riot gear-equipped, shotgun carrying guards" led by a "rather large, no nonsense, militaristic officer, who seemed to be in all his glory, leading a vicious club-swinging charge into a passive group of non-violent protestors," who were then cordoned off into a small encampment in an unshaded part of the recreation yard that was surrounded by barbed wire and a semicircle of shotgun-wielding correctional officers. After three nights and days in ninety-degree summertime heat, each dawn made the sun "the hot enemy of comfort." Freeman offered a vivid description of mounting prisoner desperation during the three-day strike: "The anxiety, depression, stress and strain continued to mount amongst the inmates. The fetid odor of human urine and feces hung over the compound, flies replaced mosquitos of the previous night, and the discomfort of human unwashed bodies and unbrushed teeth made matters that much worse. It was obvious that if something wasn't done soon, this was going to be a day of disaster by one means or another. The feeling of impending doom was too strong to ignore." The feeling of disaster was soon borne out, as on the strike's third day prisoners finally relented and decided to end the strike. But when four prisoners came forward to wave their white shirts in the air to surrender, the surrounding correctional officers fired on them, wounding all four in a spray of buckshot. In the aftermath of the shooting, the Tennessee Department of Corrections (TDOC) offered scant information to the media and insisted that the wounded prisoners suffered only "ricochet" wounds from buckshot that had hit the ground as warning shots, despite the policy to only fire warning shots into the air.[7] The *Tennessean* staff writer Dwight Lewis offered an op-ed that graded the Tennessee prison system as a "flat F—for information about the work stoppage" that resulted in an "almost total loss of credibility."[8] The prisoner Freeman similarly scoffed at the TDOC version of events, claiming the "ricochet theory to be an out-and-out lie" that was tantamount to "Kent State and Attica relived." Freeman wrote up his detailed account so that "full truth is disclosed, and some of the injustices inherent in Tennessee's prison system have been once more challenged in the federal court system."[9] Indeed, the state's massive resistance to the *Grubbs* decision had accelerated labor tensions, and Alexander's get-tough Plan for the Eighties brought the prison temperature to a boiling point. When the state legislature in 1985 decided to return its prisoners from a blue denim uniform to a striped convict uniform that harkened back to the era of convict lease, the prisoners revolted, gathered their retro convict uniforms

"Remember Attica!!" Red-painted flag by prisoners during 1985 Tennessee prison hostage crisis. Courtesy of the Nashville Public Library, Special Collections.

together, burned them, and engaged in a systemwide prison uprising that resulted in a hostage situation similar to the one that New York's Attica prisoners created in 1971.

In Tennessee, prisoner mobilization campaigns expanded the slave resistance discourse to include modern-day struggles over the history and collective memory of the convict lease. During the 1985 Tennessee hostage crisis, however, prisoners avoided the bloodbath that Attica prisoners experienced as the Tennessee prisoners offered to return their hostages peacefully in return for the opportunity to have a live television news conference so that prisoners could make the public aware that federal court orders were ignored by the state and that prison conditions continued to dangerously deteriorate, with the nation's second-highest rate of prison overcrowding and highest rate of prison violence.[10] "In the Alexander administration, corrections have taken a back seat," the prisoner Marty Phillips angrily told the press. "We, who have become a political football, seek public attention to a public dilemma. It's not the stripes that caused the rioting and it's just not the food. It's the whole

nutshell."[11] Another organizing prisoner, Mike Garrard, repeatedly reminded the press that the prison administration refused to comply with
court orders meant to alleviate the deplorable conditions of rampant violence and overcrowding. "Do you remember when this court situation began? 1975 . . . yet it's the same rhetoric and the prison system hasn't improved
despite winning the 1982 lawsuit." "It wouldn't blow up all over the state
unless something was drastically wrong," the prisoner Marty Phillips
agreed.[12] With even more frustration, fellow striker Mike Garrard summed
up the striking prisoners' lack of patience with the state's massive resistance
to prisoners' rights and the *Grubbs* decision: "Inmates done tried things the
right way. We done sued the Department of Corrections and beat them. But
the federal courts are playing games with us. When you can't get justice in
court, the last resort is physical force and violence." But as fellow striker
James Bragg empathized, violence was "not, I repeat, not what the inmates
want. We are not animals, and we will not be treated like animals." One sign
in particular connected the southern prisoners' rights movement to northern resistance, while also reminding both the prisoners and their keepers to
learn from the tragedies of the past. In hand-painted, sharp red letters that
dripped down a drop cloth spread over the front of the Walls prison, the sign
offered the simple but poignant admonition: "Remember Attica!" Drawing
on prison administrators' fears of an Attica South, the Tennessee prison
hostage crisis was also an integral part of the legacy of *Ruiz* and the effort by
prisoners to combine litigation with prisoner organization to make prison
abuse legible to the public as both a legal and political struggle.

Indeed, an essential part of the legacy of *Ruiz* is the ongoing political struggle over prisoner litigation and organization. Foes of prisoner organization
acknowledged this critical connection when Congress wrote the Prison Litigation Reform Act (PLRA), which was a national and congressional response to *Ruiz* and the advance of national prisoner litigation that demanded
that prisoners have civil and human rights. But the thirty-year era of federal
court intervention on behalf of the prisoners' rights movement came to an
abrupt end in 1995. In the wake of the "conservative revolution" of 1994, the
conservative members of the new 104th Congress considered how it might
curb "frivolous prison lawsuits," restrict the power of "liberal Federal
judges," and return control of prisons to state legislatures. In 1995 Senate
majority leader Bob Dole and Arizona senator John Kyl introduced the
PLRA, an act intended to "discourage frivolous and abusive prison lawsuits"
and to return the control of the prisons to "responsible parties," meaning
state government.[13]

PLRA sought to diminish the prisoner's ability to file lawsuits in federal court by restricting the fees that attorneys could accrue from their

representation. PLRA stipulated that prisoner plaintiff attorneys could not be awarded an hourly rate greater than 150 percent of what court-appointed attorneys made in criminal cases. Additionally, the total attorney fee could not exceed more than 150 percent of the final judgment, no matter how small the final award. Moreover, the attorney fee must first be derived from up to 25 percent of the prisoners' damage award. By stipulating that relief in a civil action "extend no further than necessary to correct the violation of the Federal right of a particular plaintiff or plaintiffs," the PLRA also restricted the power and scope of federal intervention. The PLRA restricted the duration of federal relief by terminating the court's involvement automatically two years after the court order, unless the court issued a written finding saying explicitly that the violation of rights had continued. It also empowered the state prison defendant by allowing the state prison system to request termination after two years. Whenever the state filed a termination motion, the court granted a stay on relief and federal oversight until the court ruled on the motion within thirty days.

The PLRA was also aimed at prisoners themselves as it required prisoners to exhaust "such administrative remedies as are available," which meant that they had to file a formal grievance within the prison and lose all their appeals before they could petition the federal court. More importantly for prisoners of limited means, as so many prisoners often are, the PLRA restricted appeals in forma pauperis, which had previously allowed prisoners to file a civil rights complaint without paying associated fees, some of them quite costly. Under the new law, prisoners with trust fund accounts or who were paid nominal wages for their labor had to pay some of the fees. Indigent prisoners labored under a "three strikes" rule, which barred indigent prisoners from free filing if they had three prior lawsuits dismissed.[14] Finally, the PLRA limited the amount of fees that a court-appoint monitor (special master) could expect to receive.

If Texas writ writers had labored under such a restrictive law, prisoners like Fred Cruz, who filed many unsuccessful writs before being heard, would have been silenced. During the *Ruiz* era, prisoner litigants could attract high-profile attorneys like the NAACP's William Bennett Turner not only because of the justice of their cause but because Turner could eventually expect a fair award, which he eventually received from the state at more than one million dollars. When state prison systems resisted litigation, as Texas did during *Ruiz*, the plaintiff attorney had to absorb all expenses and wait on their award until court resolution, which was a costly endeavor. Moreover, the ability of the state to request termination after two years meant that state intransigence and noncompliance, as Texas had experienced in the *Ruiz* case, would be rewarded with the prospect of repeated stays of the order and early termination. The PLRA was thus carefully aimed at limiting the ability of prisoners ever again to file a civil rights complaint as comprehensive, sweeping, and lasting as the *Ruiz* litigation.[15]

Despite the PLRA's attempt to silence prisoners, the past decade has seen mounting prisoner and immigrant detention resistance that has been ongoing for nearly a decade.[16] Much of the prisoner organizing has come out of the U.S. South and has centered its critique on incarceration's racial disparities, prison labor, and the denial of constitutional and human rights. One of the earliest sites of resistance was the Pecos Insurrection or "Motin," as it was called by its participants, at the Reeves County Detention Complex in Texas, a for-profit immigrant detention center owned by the GEO Group. The strike at Reeves occurred from December 2008 to 2009 after the prison administration punitively placed Jesus Manuel Galindo, an immigrant detainee who suffered from epilepsy, in "*la celda de castigo*," a solitary dungeon wing, where he died from lack of medical care.[17] Then, in Georgia, a massive statewide prison work strike in 2010 became one of the largest prison strikes in U.S. history until it was repressed by Georgia's Department of Corrections, who responded with solitary confinement for its leaders, reported beatings, and prisonwide lockdowns.[18] Two years later, Georgia prisoners started another wave of protest through a forty-four-day hunger strike organized by the prisoner group United Nations Against the Machine. An even larger hunger strike occurred the very next year in July 2013 at California's Pelican Bay State Prison.[19] By 2014, the Free Alabama Movement (FAM) had learned of the Georgia prison strikes, and they were subsequently inspired to initiate a similar work strike at St. Clair and Holmon prisons. As one cofounder, Melvin Ray, put it, striking prisoners wanted to reveal to the public that Alabama was "running a slave empire" and "incarcerating people for free labor."[20] In the spring of 2016, the Industrial Workers of the World's Incarcerated Workers Organizing Committee (IWW-IWOC) in Texas initiated a springtime prison work strike in April on seven prisons, and the prison administration countered the strike with a punitive three-week lockdown.[21]

In such a political context, growing prisoner resistance earned national attention when in 2016 prisoners mounted the first ever nationwide prison strikes. "In one voice, rising from the cells of long term solitary confinement, echoed in the dormitories and cell blocks from Virginia to Oregon, we prisoners across the United States vow to finally end slavery in 2016." Meant to rattle and prick the nation's conscience by connecting human atrocities past and present, these were the words that announced a national prison strike on September 9, 2016—a precipitous date forty-five years to the day of the Attica prison uprising of 1971.[22] In their announcement of the strike, the IWW-IWOC and FAM named their protest as a "Call to Action Against Slavery in America" and declared, "We will not only demand the end to prison slavery, we will end it ourselves by ceasing to be slaves."[23] During the three-week strike, an estimated 24,000 prisoners in over twenty-nine prisons across at least twenty-three states refused to work. Despite the size and scope of the first ever nationwide prison strike, the national mainstream press provided scant coverage, with some national press finally providing coverage in the strike's third week.[24] Most of the news of the strike came from radio and web-based news gathering sources that provided one of the few forums for the prisoners' voice.[25] The strikers' demands varied from state to state and included unionization, fair wages, better medical treatment, access to legal aid, and an end to degrading conditions, including corporal punishment and prolonged stays in solitary confinement. But the shared goal among all was to draw attention to the continued use in U.S. prisons of slave labor and to the fact that incarceration itself is neoslavery. A total laboring prison population of nearly 900,000 people is coerced to work for a $2 billion-a-year prison industry. The average daily wage is $0.93. Yet up to 80 percent of these meager wages can be withheld for reasons such as "room and board." Four states, all in the South, pay no wages at all: Alabama, Arkansas, Georgia, and Texas. Indeed, while Texas prisoners work without any pay whatsoever, Texas Correctional Industries, a for-profit corporation operated by the Texas Department of Criminal Justice, posted nearly $89 million in profits during 2014.[26] Thanks to Beto's 1962 prison-made goods law, coerced and entirely unpaid prisoner labor continues to benefit the state as public universities are one of the biggest purchasers of prison-made products. In 2019, for instance, public universities in Texas purchased $383,874 in merchandise from Texas Correctional Industries (TCI). The state universities buying prisoner-made products includes the University of Texas Medical Branch ($107,409); Sam Houston State University ($96,893); Trinity Valley Community College ($42,341); Texas A&M ($14,098); the University of Texas, Austin ($4,161); the University of Texas, San Antonio ($2,250); Texas Tech University ($1,956); as well as a host of other state universities relying on coerced and unpaid prisoner labor.[27]

Much of the organizing for this strike came out of the South, particularly from the Free Alabama Movement, the Free Mississippi Movement, and the End Prison Slavery in Texas movement. "These strikes are our method for challenging mass incarceration," Kinetik Justice, a founder of FAM and prisoner at Holman prison in Alabama, told the press. Justice explained the rationale for a labor strike: "We understood that our incarceration was pretty much about our labor and the money that was being generated through the prison system." As a result, prisoners "began organizing around our labor and used it as a means and a method in order to bring about reform in the Alabama prison system." By beginning the nationwide strike on September 9, the forty-fifth anniversary of the Attica prison uprising, the prisoners aligned themselves with the long historical arc of prisoners' rights movements that stretches from the mid-1960s until today. Looking back at nearly a decade of mounting prisoner resistance, Siddique Abdullah Hasan, a prisoner at Ohio's Lucasville prison, told the press why the prisoners adopted a labor-centered and prisons-as-slavery discourse. "We've tried hunger strikes and filing grievances with courts," Siddique Abdullah Hasan said of prior resistance campaigns. "But since super-economic exploitation is what keeps these prisons alive, we decided a labor strike is the way to go."[28]

Another nationwide strike with southern legal and labor origins but collectively national occurred in 2018. Jailhouse Lawyers Speak (JLS), an organization of prisoners for prisoners meant to provide legal aid and training to fight cases and conditions of confinement, organized prisoners across the country for a nationwide strike after seven prisoners were killed when isolated together among rival gangs, and when violence broke out, the prison administration idly waited for nearly seven hours before finally intervening.[29] In their statement on the strike, prisoners called attention to the idea that they suffer social death and that prisons today are "warzones." "Prisoners understand they are being treated as animals," read the statement. "Prisons in America are a warzone. Every day prisoners are harmed due to conditions of confinement. For some of us it's as if we are already dead, so what do we have to lose?"[30] Among the ten demands, one of the most prominent was their demand for "an immediate end to prison slavery" in exchange for "the prevailing wage in their state." Understanding that gang laws target prisoners of color in "prisons within prisons," such as Texas's Ad Seg or California's supermaximum prisons, the prisoners called for "an immediate end to racist gang enhancement laws targeting Black and Brown humans." As an organization that grew out of the prisoners' rights movement for civil rights and legal change, the JLS also demanded that "the Prison Litigation Reform Act must be rescinded, allowing imprisoned humans a proper channel to address grievances and violations of their rights."

The nationwide strikes of 2016 and 2018 draw upon a history of prisoner resistance to craft a renewed historical analogy of incarceration as slavery and slave labor. The strikes call attention to coerced labor, state violence, and the denial of civil rights as a contradiction of both the prisoners' citizenship and their humanity. These were contradictions that Texas prisoners understood all too well, as four decades earlier they built upon the inspirations of Attica and Soledad to craft the prisons-as-slavery critique through civil rights litigation and the work strike.

The legacy of *Ruiz*, then, is to offer prisoner organization and litigation as part of an ongoing political struggle. Within Texas, the prisoners' rights movement of 1965 to 1985 accomplished the unthinkable by challenging the prison plantation's labor division and control regime. Indeed, *Ruiz* and the wider prisoners' rights movement eradicated the southern prison plantation, state-enforced racial segregation and the trusty guard system and diminished the work discipline regime of agricultural stoop labor. By the mid-1980s, the prisoners had upended nearly all the aspects that made Texas prisons uniquely southern. By 1989, for instance, industrial work and sales had grown to an astounding $51 million. By 1990, however, cotton production had plummeted from its height in 1965 as valued at $12.1 million as compared to the TDC's 1990 total cotton production value of only $388,000 (inflation adjusted to 2018 dollars).[31] The prisoners' defiant declaration that "we are not slaves" and their testimonies of resistance documented and made publicly legible the abuses of the southern prison labor regime that otherwise would have remained hidden. Since the *Ruiz* decision, however, the collapse of the southern prison plantation was quickly replaced by the new carceral regime centered on the militarized prison and its Ad Seg supermax conditions. Due to the concerted "carceral massive resistance" political effort against the federal court's design in *Ruiz* to curb mass incarceration, Texas has more than tripled its incarceration rate from 208 in 1980 to its height in 2000 of 754. Such high rates of incarceration place Texas at the forefront of mass incarceration for both the U.S. South and the nation. Since the post-1980 era of mass incarceration, southern states have consistently yielded the nation's highest incarceration rates. At the height of mass incarceration in 2009, for instance, states outside of the U.S. South had an average incarceration rate of 361 while the U.S. South had an astounding average incarceration rate of 577. Mass incarceration is, without a doubt, a national crisis, but the regional history of struggle over prison conditions and prisoners' rights in the U.S. South played a critical political role in the infamous rise of Texas as a national and regional leader in human caging. The prison system that Texas fashioned after the *Ruiz* case ended the prison plantation's labor control model, and what emerged from its ashes was neither the rehabilitative and human warehouse penitentiary of the antebellum northeast nor the plantation prison farm model of the old U.S. South. Instead, Texas was in the forefront of a new prison Sunbelt landscape that embraced the militarized super-maximum prison and the employment of a new set of tools to enact new modalities of carceral violence against the people that are chained to the cages that mass incarceration has created.

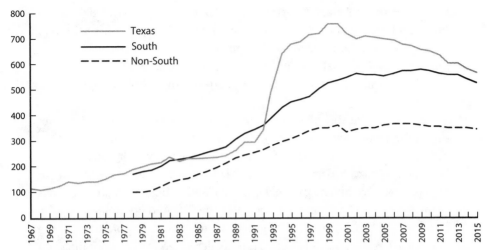

Texas Department of Corrections incarceration rate compared to southern and non-southern states, 1967–2015. Source: Compilation of data from Joshua Aiken, "Era of Mass Expansion: Why State Officials Should Fight Jail Growth." Table 4: Jail and prison incarceration rates by state over time. Prison Policy Initiative Report, May 31, 2017. https://www.prisonpolicy.org/reports/jailsovertime_table_4.html; Peter Wagner, "Tracking State Growth in 50 States." Figure 3: Regional State Prison Incarceration Rates. Prison Policy Initiative Report, May 8, 2014. https://www.prisonpolicy.org/reports/overtime.html.

The prisoners who initiated the prisoners' rights movement were people whose lives were bound up in incarceration's dehumanization, as each of them carried the weight of their past bondage beyond the prison. All prisoners who testified in *Ruiz* were placed in federal custody as protection, and then within a few years of the court decision, they were released. But while free from prison, none of them could ever escape the dehumanization that they experienced. Many of them had only a fleeting moment of freedom before they returned to the TDCJ for parole violations and new crimes. Eddie James Ward, a proponent of Black Power, was released in 1980 and returned to prison, this time in the federal system, in 1990 for a drug possession charge. He then was incarcerated within the TDCJ once again after a visit to his brother's home landed him in the middle of a drug bust that violated his parole. Guadalupe Guajardo was released before the *Ruiz* case in 1975 but was sentenced to the TDC again for assault in 1986 and again with a parole violation in 1994. Alvaro Luna Hernández was freed from prison in 1991, and after moving to Houston he continued his political connection to the Chicana/o movement as he founded and directed the new National Movement of La Raza, where he organized the Texas community behind the effort to successfully overturn the conviction of the Mexican national Ricardo Aldape Guerra, who had been falsely convicted of shooting a police officer and subsequently slated for execution on Texas's death row. Yet in 1996 Hernández returned to the TDCJ after a visit from Sheriff Jack McDaniel under questionable circumstances ended with an armed confrontation that led to Hernández's conviction for aggravated assault.

Some politicized prisoners avoided another encounter with the TDCJ, but their life's work remained challenging incarceration and criminal justice. True to the business card that he carried at all times, which described Ray Hill's profession as "citizen provocateur," Hill remained a lifelong advocate for both prisoners' rights and gay rights, as he helped to found such organizations as the Montrose Counseling Center, the Montrose Activity Center, the Gay and Lesbian Switchboard, the Montrose Clinic, and the Conference for the Futures of Lesbian, Gay, Bisexual, Transgender, Intersexed, Questioning and Allied Residents of the Houston Metropolitan Area. His *Prison Radio Program* on KPFT Houston 90.1 was a community-building staple for nearly three decades, where incarcerated people could listen to discussions on prison reform, as well as the call-in portion of the show, where prisoners heard shout-outs from friends and family members. Sadly, Ray Hill died on November 24, 2018, causing the *Houston Chronicle* to eulogize Hill as a "Houston icon and civil rights activist."[32]

Aware of the historic nature of the prisoners' rights movement and the precarious need to document prison abuse, Lawrence Pope culled together his files and maintained a well-documented collection of newspaper clippings, affidavits, and letters on writ writers, abused prisoners, TDC guards and officials, building tenders, gang members, prison construction, and prison privatization. Prior to his death from a heart attack in 1988, he conducted an eight-hundred-page oral history with the archivist John Wheat, and he donated his papers to the University of Texas at Austin's Briscoe Center for American History. To the last, he was the prison movement's documentarian and archivist.

Martha Quinlan followed her political and personal transformation to remain as head of CURE, Texas, for almost a decade. "As I grew older, I examined myself and decided I was just going in a circle," she explained upon self-reflection. "I decided my life had to have a purpose. I'd spent a major part of it in prison and felt I had accumulated a vast store of knowledge that should be shared. I found out I was not so bad a person and could do something with my life."[33] Eduard Maurciano, who, like Fred Cruz, had converted to Buddhism and become a politicized Chicano activist, would later become evangelicized and a Christian minister after his release from TDC. Ernest

McMillan never again returned to the TDC, and his community organizing work outside of prison aimed to make sure that young African American men didn't have to face incarceration. After working for a time as congressional aide to Eddie Bernice Johnson, McMillan founded in 1984 the Fifth Ward Enrichment Program, a nonprofit, community-based youth-development initiative to foster mentoring for young men as an alternative to gang membership. McMillan continued directing that successful community program for the next twenty-five years.

David Ruíz and Fred Cruz struggled their entire lives over their encounter with incarceration. Within a few years of his release, Cruz's old demons came back to haunt him. Jalet helped Cruz find positions as a paralegal with several firms, but Cruz found his efforts frustrated because he never managed to shake his addiction to heroin. Despite his freedom and marriage to Jalet, Cruz relapsed, and his addiction to heroin slowly eroded his marriage and his legal talents. In 1977, only five years after their marriage, Jalet and Cruz divorced. After his divorce from Frances, Fred Cruz met and married Isabelle Irene Cruz, with whom he had two more children. To escape from Texas and all that surrounded his time in the TDC, Cruz and his new family moved to Minneapolis–St. Paul, Minnesota. Cruz's talent and ambition remained frustrated, however, by his inability to get a job as a lawyer or paralegal due to his prior convictions. On many days, he felt the pain of incarceration and the darkness of solitary creeping back into his life. His daughter, Margarite Frances Cruz, named for Frances Jalet, recalled how her father would frequently go to a separate room, sit in the dark, for hours, alone, meditating or revisiting the pain of solitary's darkness. In 1987, Fred Cruz was found dead at forty-seven of a drug overdose. "His anger over it all," Margarite Frances Cruz recalled, "all that isolation, not having human contact, none, really affected him to the point he would sit alone in a room in darkness and meditate. He would be there for hours. Because he was so used to being in solitary, almost as if there was too much noise around him, too many things, as if he was going to a different place."[34] During happier moments, Cruz would sit at his daughter's bedside, and strum his guitar to lull her to sleep, so she could dream of better things.

In his final years, before his death from cancer in November 2005, David Resendez Ruíz, still locked behind Texas prison bars, seemed to grasp that his legacy of prisoners' rights would live much longer than he would. Following the trial, the court transferred most *Ruiz* witnesses into the federal prison system for their own protection. Ruíz was paroled in July 1981, but while he left prison, he felt the criminal justice system never left him alone. Over the next four years he had frequent encounters with law enforcement in a policing effort that he believed was yet another retributive conspiracy for his civil rights work against the TDC. In November 1981, Austin police charged him with armed robbery of the Scoot Inn, but he was acquitted a year later when during his trial another man openly confessed to the robbery. In 1982 he was charged with possession of marijuana, but that too was dismissed. Then in 1984 he was charged in yet another robbery along with two other suspects as well as a second case for gun possession when he allegedly brandished a gun at his apartment complex manager. Bob Looney, Ruíz's attorney, told the press that "this is the latest in a long series of attempts to frame David Ruíz. I wouldn't be surprised to hear a country and western song called "Let's Pin It On David Ruiz" playing on the radio." On January 30, 1985, he was found guilty of perjury when he testified that he had lied in a 1984 parole hearing. In his typical defiant fashion, Ruiz told the press that the twenty-five-year sentence to return to the TDCJ was unfair and that "they didn't try [President] Nixon for perjury."[35] David Ruíz, however, could not escape his lifetime of institutionalization, and he ended his chance for freedom when he returned to the TDC in 1986 for armed robbery.[36] Despite his personal failings, Ruíz understood that his role in Texas prison reform was historic and that it would be documented in future histories.[37] Ruíz's memoir claims that as a result of the trial he spent 4,825 hours in solitary confinement, received 214 "brutal beatings," suffered 104 attempts by TDC officials to persuade him to make a deal and drop all legal proceedings in return for his freedom, served 1,460 days in isolation, suffered over 75 false accusations by Texas prison officials, and, perhaps the most painful for Ruíz, was refused release from solitary confinement for the funeral of his father, despite prison regulations that allowed a prisoner to attend a parent's funeral services.

Toward the end of his life, Ruíz spent his remaining two years attempting to prove that the TDC knew of the cancer that was eating his body but denied him medical treatment until it was too late. Over time, Ruíz retreated from prison reform, although he continued to seek legal redress for what he suspected was the TDC's intentional medical negligence aimed at ending his life while still in prison. As the years passed, Ruíz developed an interest in poetry and drawing. His artwork depicted revolutionary images of Zapata, modern images of Chicanos with their defiant fists in the air, and proud images of Native American chieftains and shamans. Like his artwork, Ruíz's unpublished poem, "Steel on Steel," is punctuated with a sense of abiding pride, anger, and irony.[38] The poem depicts Ruíz's imaginary conversation with a TDC guard. His words connect past and present by conveying his sense that the effort to reveal the hidden world of Texas prisons was indeed historic. More than historic, his efforts at prison reform carried for Ruíz the irony that history would ultimately judge the prison system that had judged him so unfairly all his life.

Steel on Steel

BY DAVID R. RUÍZ

Night Shadows dance on the wall,
I hear the sound of steel on steel
Echo and re-echo
Through these cold cells.

Officials pace the catwalks,
Counting and recounting,
"Ruiz, are you there?"
Yes, I am still here.
You laugh. I hear it
Echo and re-echo
Through these sad cells.

"Ruiz, what do you see,
alone in that cell at night?"

I see your face without its mask,
I see ships full of Blacks in chains,
I see the slaughter of my
Ancestors—
Mexicans and Indians,
I see you steal their lands,
You sit on the face of the poor
In the free world you lock us in
With the sound of steel on steel
That echoes and re-echoes
Through these lonely cells.

I see you try to break us
See you isolate and kill,
Then call us killers,
Call us violent so we escape
A little while: drink, drug
Ourselves, for which you
Lock us in again, the
Sound of steel on steel
Echoes and re-echoes
Through these bitter cells.

"Ruiz, you just one Meskin. You
lost your youth, your hair is gray.
What do you think you gained?"

I'm the *huevon* Mexican, cell-taught,
Self-taught, the original writ-writer,
Chained up and locked down
For a lifetime. I'm the Mexican
Who never gave up, who fought till
Every prisoner, guard, and lawyer
In America knows me.
I taught myself to use your tools: I'm Ruiz,
Unbroken for all your torture,
All your shackles and steel on steel
That echoes and re-echoes
Through these dark cells.

When the Eagle killed the Serpent
A Nation was born; where the people rise
My Nation is born: I am
Whole in The People's Nation.
The People will judge you, not me.
You are the one trapped in the sound of steel on steel
Which echoes and re-echoes through these empty cells.[39]

To survive incarceration's dehumanization, these people engaged in mind change and *concientización* to achieve both personal transformation and political solidarity. As Bruce Franklin astutely put it, the prisoner organization and activism around prisoners' rights represented the moment when "the political activist [was] thrust into prison, and the common criminal thrust into political activism. The distinction between these two groups tends to dissolve as the definition of crime, from both sides of the law, becomes increasingly political."[40] And yet the fact that prison rendered all these politicized people so deeply scarred and marked that they either returned to prison or left prison without ever being free from it demonstrates how carceral power attempts human elimination. After visiting Attica in 1990, Michel Foucault concluded that incarceration can only ever produce a "curious mechanism of circular elimination: society eliminates by sending to prison people whom prison breaks up, crushes, physically eliminates; the prison eliminates them by 'freeing' them and sending them back to society. . . . The state in which they come out insures that society will eliminate them once again, sending them to prison." The persistence of carceral violence clings to the prison, in all its guises and shapes, and thus it fulfills Foucault's admonition that prison itself functions as a "prodigious stomache" that "consumes in order to eliminate that which has already been eliminated."[41]

Yet the fact that the prisoners so effectively dismantled the southern prison plantation is no small historical example of effective movement politics, prisoner organization, and litigation as radical demand. Their collective testimonials showed their humanity, their legal right to constitutional protections, and the unconstitutionality of prisons that were run like slave plantations. Moreover, the fact that the prison refashioned itself so quickly into a space that changed the nature but not the fact of carceral violence only speaks to the prison's immunity to even the greatest victory aimed at genuine reform. But as Robin D. G. Kelley has pointed out, we cannot evaluate social movements solely on a narrow metric of "success" or "failure" to realize "their visions rather than on the merits or power of the visions themselves . . . as it is precisely these alternative visions and dreams that inspire new generations to struggle for change."[42] This is never more true than in the current struggle over mass incarceration, which connects distinct campaigns across time through history's memory of how to confront the carceral state. The hope for the future is to draw on the past to remember how collective resistance requires alliances both within prisons and throughout society. The historical lineage of resistance continues as long as prisoners remain what they name as "slaves" and as long as carceral violence clings to the prison. The struggle for true reform and indeed prison abolition is yet to come.

Acknowledgments

Writing a book on state violence, coerced labor, and the demand for prisoners' rights inevitably forces both the writer and its reader to encounter prison life as a site of terror, power, pain, and anguish but also as one of individual transformation and collective community. I could not have countenanced such a project without accumulating great intellectual and personal debt to a great many people. Indeed, my development as a scholar owes much to the faith of those who believed in this project when it faced its most difficult obstacles. I owe a special debt of gratitude to my former teachers. Although they have left this world, the scholarly model, example, and teachings of Lawrence Levine, Roy Rosenzweig, and Ira Berlin have always stayed with me, and their influence can be seen throughout these pages.

While pursuing my doctorate in the History Department at the University of Maryland, College Park, I benefitted from a number of supportive, thoughtful, and challenging teachers who provided a model of scholarship and intellectual engagement that made my graduate career one of constant growth and development. I am especially grateful to my committee members, Ira Berlin, James B. Gilbert, John Laub, and Sonya Michel, all of whom supported my development as a scholar by asking me to stretch my thinking in ways that I did not always anticipate but from which I always benefited. Jim Gilbert was always quick to share with me his wisdom and insight into U.S. culture, particularly valuable as I plumbed the depths of internal prison societies and culture. I appreciated the times he invited me to share a meal and talk about my research whenever he came to Houston, where I was working. My dissertation advisor Gary Gerstle went far beyond the pale as an advisor to help me develop as a scholar, writer, and researcher. Gary offered a wealth of trenchant advice, intellectual guidance, incisive editorial assistance, personal support, and an unwavering belief in this study. His mentorship, intellectual critique, professional example, and friendship have always encouraged and inspired me.

The research and writing of this book would not have been possible without the generous financial support of a number of universities and institutions. Academic centers and university institutions that supported the research and writing of this book include the Clements Center for Southwest Studies at Southern Methodist University, the Center for Historical Analysis at Rutgers University, the Postdoctoral Fellowship in African American Studies at Case Western Reserve University, and the Institute for the Humanities at the University of Connecticut, Storrs. The scholars in each of those institutions provided invaluable support, intellectual feedback, seminars, and manuscript workshops. I cannot thank them enough for granting me the time to bring this project to fruition and for supporting my academic career. Thank you to Andrea Boardman, Ruth Ann Elmore, Andrew R. Graybill, Benjamin Johnson, and Sherry L. Smith at the Clements Center for Southwest Studies. While at SMU, David Weber welcomed my work into the fold of borderlands and western history, and I will be forever grateful that he, Ben Johnson, and Sherry Smith encouraged me to lean "West" in my work on carceral histories. At the Clements Center, a number of scholars provided invaluable feedback during a manuscript workshop, including Curtis Austin, William Bush, George Díaz, Raphael Folsom, David Rex Galindo, Alex Lichtenstein, Angie Marian Nozalda, and John Weber. As one of the postdoctoral fellows at Case Western Reserve University's postdoctoral fellowship for African American history, I am especially grateful to the indefatigable and brilliant Rhonda Y. Williams, who encouraged me to connect scholarship to activism and activism to people. At the Center for Historical Analysis at Rutgers University, the scholarly gathering around "Narratives of Power" yielded amazing conversations and unexpected connections. Thanks to Caroline Brown, Mark Chambers, Abosede George, Sandra Russell Jones, Ibram X. Kendi, and Andrew Urban. Thank you to Debra Gray White and Donna Murch for hosting me as a fellow and for encouraging me to connect my work to critical narratives of power. Thanks also to Michel P. Lynch and Alexis L. Boylan at the Institute for the Humanities at the University of Connecticut for hosting my work as a research fellow and for creating such dynamic dialogue with other resident fellows, particularly Leo J. Garofalo, Anna Mae Duane, Mark Healey, Daniel Hershenzon, Daniel Silvermint, Christine Sylvester, and Dimitris Xygalatas. Thanks also to Stephen Sloan and Thomas Charlton at the Institute of Oral History at Baylor University for transcribing my oral histories. Thank you to the outstanding list of scholars who have read and provided comments on early draft chapters or as conference papers, including Dan Berger, Ibram X. Kendi, Julily Kohler-Hausman, Michelle Nickerson, Natalie Ring, Nikh Singh, Donna Haverty-Stacke, Yohuru Williams, and Timothy Stewart Winter. I am especially grateful for the invitation from Mario T. García to present a chapter of this book at the Sal Castro Memorial Conference on the Emerging Historiography of the Chicano Movement held at the University of California, Santa Barbara. The conference provided an opportunity to present this work to Chicana/o scholars and I am thankful for their thoughtful and incisive feedback, particularly Ben Olguín and David Montejano who shared some valuable thoughts on sources. Thanks also to Garth Davies, Stephen Tuck, and Robin D. G. Kelley, then the Harold Vyvyan Harmsworth Visiting Professor of American History, for hosting a most valuable talk and ensuing conversation on the research for this book at Oxford University's Rothermere American Institute.

To the University of North Carolina's press, I am eternally gratefully to an amazing collection of scholars and top-notch editors. Rhonda Y. Williams and Heather Ann Thompson were more than exemplary press series editors for the Justice, Power, and Politics series at UNC, Chapel Hill. Both of them guided this project as incredibly thoughtful and incisive editors, while also offering their unyielding support and wise guidance of my work and academic path. Brandon Proia was simply the best possible editor that an author could imagine. He offered thoughtful revisions with great patience and personal aplomb. As my manuscript reviewers for UNC, Mary Ellen Curtain and Max Krochmal provided a wealth of insightful suggestions for revision that were simply invaluable. I thank them for helping me to see critical directions and needed paths for this manuscript to follow. Thanks also to Michael Taber for providing such a thorough and well-conceived index. Thanks also to the book production staff at

Westchester Publishing Services, especially to Michelle Witkowski who was endlessly patient and incredibly thorough.

The assistance and expert knowledge of archivists made possible my research. John Wheat, Brenda Gunn, Evan Hocker, Aryn Glazier, and Amy Bowman at the Dolph Briscoe Center for American History (CAH) at the University of Texas at Austin were particularly helpful in tracking down the *Ruiz* trial transcripts and for their detailed knowledge of the CAH collections. Thanks especially to Evan Hocker, who helped track down some last-minute requests from the Jalet-Cruz and Pope papers. Few know the papers of the Texas Department of Correctional Justice better than archivist Laura Saegert at the Texas State Library and Archives. Laura was also especially helpful in my effort to file state-level requests for information and for alerting me to newly released material from the attorney general's office on the *Ruiz* case. Thanks also to Jim Willett and Sandy Rogers of the Texas Prison Museum, who shared with me the museum's collection of oral histories. I am deeply indebted to Bruce Jackson, Alan Pogue, and Andrew Lichtenstein for the use of their incredible photographs of Texas prisons and prison life.

I thank my colleagues in the History Department at Stony Brook University for supporting my work, engaging my ideas, and stretching my thinking on this project. Thanks especially to Michael Barnheart, Herman Lebovics, Paul Gootenberg, Lori Flores, Gary Marker, April Masten, Donna Rilling, Nancy Tomes, Chris Sellers, and Erik Zolov for their intellectual encouragement. At Stony Brook University, I am appreciative of funding grants to conduct research and present my work at academic conferences, which were made possible through awards from the Research Initiative Grant of the Faculty in the Fine Arts, Humanities, and Lettered Social Sciences; and the President's Distinguished Travel Grant. A special thanks to Gary Marker, who, when serving as chair of the Department of History, graciously supported the conference From the Color Line to the Carceral State, where I shared my work alongside other pioneering scholars of the field. Thanks also to Stony Brook University librarian Jennifer DeVito for providing research assistance navigating databases on legal cases. Many thanks to the graduate students who acted as research assistants for this book, including Mia Brett, Jordan Hellin, and Yalile Suriel.

Other scholars shared resources and ideas. Thank you to Susanne Mason, who shared with me seventeen of her interviews with prisoners that she conducted in service to her award-winning documentary, *Writ Writer: One Man's Journey for Justice.* I also owe great gratitude to Robert Perkinson, who graciously shared with me access to rare sources and who welcomed new research on a similar topic.

I also owe a profound debt of gratitude to the long list of people who shared with me their life stories, personal experiences and insights, and the fortitude that they acquired through the turbulence and violence of incarceration. Telling their stories required many of them to revisit painful experiences that they probably would have otherwise left untold but which none of them could ever quite forget. I thank them for sharing even the most painful of memories. I want to thank especially those people who shared with me their personal papers and letters, most especially Robert Lee Mudd, Alvaro Luna Hernández, Guadalupe Guajardo, Danny Grundstrum, Ray Hill, Michael Jewel, and Ernest McMillan. Marie Ruíz, widow of David Ruíz, was especially kind to share with me the unpublished writings, artwork, poetry, and papers of her late husband. Margarite Frances Cruz, the daughter of Fred Cruz, provided me some personal insights on what happened to Fred after he left the TDC, and I thank her for sharing those personal memories. I dedicate this book to the people incarcerated in Texas who made possible my research and who insisted that institutions of criminal justice acknowledge and observe the U.S. Constitution, civil rights, and the demands of social justice.

A great debt of thanks is also owed to William Habern for sharing with me the private defense papers of Eroy Brown. Bill and Connie Habern also made possible my oral histories by sharing with me their home as I traversed the prison system and the state of Texas. Few people are as knowledgeable about the Texas prison system as Bill Habern, and even fewer can grill a steak or smoke a fish so well. Thank you to the Haberns for sharing their home, company, wine, and good conversation. Without Ray Hill and the long reach of his Houston-based *Prison Radio Program*, I would not have been able to make contact with many prisoners. It is because of Ray's program that I was able to begin a correspondence with current prisoners that eventually resulted in a series of oral histories. I am sorry that he did not have the opportunity to see this project become a book, but his imprint is on it, nonetheless. My conversations with Danny Grundstrum were also particularly helpful in navigating the rough contours of prison society, argot, and culture. Dwight Rawlinson wrote many letters of introduction for me to other prisoners and opened the doors to prisoner correspondence and interviews that otherwise might have been closed.

This book is also dedicated to my parents, who shared with me their love of books, intellectual inquiry, and education. As life-long teachers and writers, they nurtured me not only with their love but with a steady diet of reading similar books together, taking long hikes and exploring nature, and by having marvelously good and sometimes hilariously funny dinner conversations late into many an evening. In 1970, they dedicated their poetry anthology on nature, *The Wind is Round*, to me as "their infant son, so that all the wonders of nature are his to enjoy." I now return the honor and dedicate this book to them. Many thanks are also owed to my godparents, Wendy Mackenzie, Sandy Cortesi, and Hoagland Keep, for their life-long guidance, friendship, and constant support. From first grade to first book, my life-long friends Greg Calvan, Bart Clake, Adam Cohen, Joel Dancy, C. B. Dexter, Erika Kan, Elizabeth Kan, Ken Lopez, and John Staren have always always acted like family and given my work their steadfast belief. As my spouse, Gloria Rios provided her personal support, good advice, clever wit, and ever present compassion. The sacrifices she made so that I might complete this project are always on my mind and deeply appreciated. I also thank the Rios family, particularly my wise father-in-law, Mr. Rene A. Rios, for their support over the years. Kay Bartlett, my aunt, supported me with her humor, love, and warmth. My father, John Terry Chase, a life-long teacher, writer, and educator, provided me intellectual encouragement and wisdom to become a scholar in my own right. I am greatly saddened that my mother, Sara Hannum Chase, did not live to see me finish this book, but her spirit and the ever present memory of her wit, courage, friendship, generosity, and love inspired me to complete the journey that she helped me start.

Notes

Introduction

1. "3 Inmates Injured by Warning Shots from Prison Guards," *Dallas Times Herald*, October 9, 1978; "TDC Head Refuses Comment on Prisoner Strike," *Dallas Times Herald*, October 10, 1978; "Convicts in Other Facilities Join Prison Work Stoppage," *Fort Worth Star Telegram*, October 11, 1978; "Texas Prisons: Overcrowded, Edgy, and Under Fire," *Dallas Times Herald*, October 15, 1978; "Riot by 1,500 Inmates Acknowledged," *Houston Chronicle*, October 19, 1978.

2. Butch Mendez, Ellis Unit, Inmate number 256311, to State Senator Chet Brooks, Chairman, Joint Committee on Prison Reform, December 15, 1978, Papers of Ron Chet Brooks, Texas State Archives and Library (hereafter cited as Brooks, TSLA), box 1999/136.

3. For both analytical and narrative accounts of the prison disturbances of the late 1960s and early 1970s, see Silberman, *Criminal Violence, Criminal Justice*; Wicker, *Time to Die*; Colvin, *Penitentiary in Crisis*; Useem and Kimball, *States of Siege*; and Jacobs, *Stateville*.

4. New York State Special Commission on Attica, *Attica*.

5. Robert DeLong, Testimony of Julian Griego and In-Chambers Conference, October 16, 1978, David R. Ruiz et. al. vs. W. J. Estelle Jr. et. al., Center for American History, University of Texas at Austin (hereafter cited as CAH), MAI 8/J-92.

6. On the "residual powers" of the Tenth Amendment in the framing of the U.S. Constitution, see Rakove, *Original Meanings*, 192. On policing powers, see Gerstle, *Liberty and Coercion*.

7. On the development of the convict lease as both central to Jim Crow and part of the New South modernization project, see Ayers, *Vengeance and Justice*; Lichtenstein, *Twice the Work*; Curtain, *Black Prisoners*; Shapiro, *New South Rebellion*; Mancini, *One Dies, Get Another*; Myers, *Race, Labor and Punishment*; and Oshinsky, *"Worse than Slavery."*

8. On the centrality of prison labor to a variety of southern state prison systems, see Miller, *Hard Labor*; Lichtenstein, *Twice the Work*; Carleton, *Politics and Punishment*; Oshinsky, *"Worse than Slavery,"* 135–56; Taylor, *Brokered Justice*.

9. For the persistence of Texas prison labor as the mainstay of southern incarceration even during the Great Depression, see Blue, *Doing Time*. For a survey of prison labor in Texas from the era of convict leasing to the late twentieth century, see Perkinson, *Texas Tough*.

10. "Texas Prison System Changes Afford New Hope for Inmates," *Houston Chronicle*, February 21, 1954; and George Beto, "The Case for Prisons," *Texas Police Journal*, August 1964, George Beto Collection, Sam Houston State University (hereafter cited as Beto, SHSU), 1-4/45.

11. For statistics concerning the size of New York's prison system in 1971, see New York State Special Commission on Attica, *Attica*. For comparative statistics on Texas, California, and New York prisons in 1978, see "Texas Prisons 1975–Present," Vertical Files, newspaper clippings, CAH.

12. Slotkin, *Regeneration through Violence*, 5, 7.

13. On the use of enslaved African Americans who worked as "field drivers" in Texas cotton fields during the antebellum period, see Campbell, *Empire for Slavery*, 115–33.

14. On the Warren court's embrace of rights-based decisions, see Epps, *Rights Revolution*; Horwitz, *Warren Court*; and Tani, *States of Dependency*.

15. Robinson v. California, 370 U.S. 660 (1962).

16. On African American Muslims in the United States, see Baer, *Black Spiritual Movement*; Lincoln, *Black Muslims in America*; Marsh, *From Black Muslims*; McCloud, *African American Islam*; Curtis, *Black Muslim Religion*; Banks, *Black Muslims*. On Muslims in California's prison system, see Cummins, *Rise and Fall*, 63–92. On Malcolm X's prison term as a transformative experience, see Malcolm X, with Haley, *Autobiography of Malcolm X*. On the Nation of Islam and Black Power after Malcolm X, see Taylor, "Nation of Islam," 177–98. For an account of Muslim prisoners organizing in New York prisons through legal suits during the 1950s and early 1960s, see Felber, "'Shades of Mississippi,'" 71–95.

17. For a narrative history of the origins of the *Cooper* case and its aftermath, see Losier, "'Strictly Religious Reason[s],'" 19–38.

18. Wolff v. McDonnell, 418 U.S. 539 (1974).

19. On the increase in the number of prisoner rights lawsuits between 1966 and 1984, see *Annual Report of the Director of the Administrative Office of United States Courts* for each year. Thomas, *Prisoner Litigation*, 61.

20. Arkansas: Pugh v. Locke, 406 F. Supp. 318 (M.D. Ala. 1976); Holt v. Sarver, 300 F. Supp. 825 (E.D. Ark. 1969); Alabama: Holt v. Sarver (Holt II), 309 F. Supp. 362, 365 (E.D. Ark. 197); Mississippi, Gates v. Collier, 349 F. Supp. 881 (N.D. Mississippi, 1972), aff'd, 501 F.2d 1291 (5th Cir. 1974); South Carolina: Plyler v. Evatt, C.A. No. 82-876-0 (D.S.C. January 8, 1985); Texas: Ruiz v. Estelle, 503 F. Supp. 1265 (S.D. Tex. 1980). Other "totality of conditions" cases in the U.S. South included Tennessee Grubbs v. Bradley, 552 F. Supp. 1052 (M.D. Tenn. 1982); Mississippi, Gates v. Collier, 349 F. Supp. 881 (N.D. Mississippi, 1972), aff'd, 501 F.2d 1291 (5th Cir. 1974).

21. Costello v. Wainwright, 397 F. Supp. 20 (M.D. Fla. 1975); Small v. Martin, No. 85-987-CRT (E.D. N.C. 1988); Hubert v. Ward, No. C-E-80-414-M (W.D. N.C. 1985), thirteen road and farm camps.

22. Gilmore, *Golden Gulag*; Lichtenstein, "Flocatex," 113–25; Lynch, *Sunbelt Justice*; Perkinson, *Texas Tough*; Schoenfeld, *Building the Prison State*; Janssen, "Sunbelt Lock-Up."

23. Justice Policy Institute, "Texas Tough?"

24. Association of Correctional Administrators and Yale Law School's Arthur Liman Public Interest Program, "Aiming to Reduce Time-In-Cell."

25. Perkinson, *Texas Tough*, 8.

26. On the litigation and its effects on the prison system from the perspective of the courts and attorneys involved in the cases, see Martin and Ekland-Olson, *Texas Prisons*; and Kermer, *William Wayne Justice*.

27. Feeley and Rubin, *Judicial Policy Making*, 46.

28. For a courtroom perspective of the trial through the perspective of David Ruíz, William Wayne Justice, and William Bennett Turner, see Perkinson, *Texas Tough*, 251–85, 274.

29. Schlanger, "Beyond the Hero Judge," 1994–2036. Marie Gottschalk has made the same argument. "The dense network of interest groups and organizations that initially gave the prisoners' rights issue such traction and developed in complicated ways that ultimately hastened the rise of the carceral state." Gottschalk, *Prison and the Gallows*, 166. See also Guetzkow and Schoon, "If You Build It," 401–32.

30. Schoenfeld, *Building the Prison State*, 91.

31. Schoenfeld, 4.

32. Prison scholars adopting this critique of the *Ruiz* decision include DiIulio, *Governing Prisons*; and Horton and Nielson, *Walking George*.

33. On the sociological and criminological approach to the prison administration as "co-opted" by building tenders, see Crouch and Marquart, *Appeal to Justice*. On the effect of *Ruiz* on prisoner control after 1980, see Marquart and Crouch, "Judicial Reform and Prisoner Control," 557–86.

34. On legal and policy scholarship that celebrates court-ordered intervention, but from the perspective of the courts, civil rights attorneys, and judges, see *Yale Law Journal*, "Beyond the Ken," 506–58; Chayes," Role of the Judge," 1281; Feeley and Hansom, "Impact of Judicial Intervention"; and Filter, *Prisoners' Rights*. For work that offers a more critical perspective of federal court orders as unwanted intrusions against otherwise steady state management, see DiIulio, ed., *Courts, Corrections*; and DiIulio, *Governing Prisons*.

35. Goluboff, *Lost Promise*, 5.

36. While the historical literature on citizenship is vast, critical works that shape my thinking on citizenship and historical processes that have included and excluded certain groups over time include Gerstle, *American Crucible*; Kerber, *No Constitutional Right*; Schudson, *Good Citizen*; Smith, *Civic Ideal*; Canaday, *Straight State*; Jacobson, *Whiteness*; Glenn, *Unequal Freedom*.

37. On conscientización, see Mendoza, *raúlsalinas*, 16. On "mind change" as personal and political transformation to achieve revolutionary politics and societal change, see Spencer, *Revolution Has Come*.

38. García, *Chicano Generation*, 4.

39. On testimonios as "the politics of truth," Beverly, *Testimonio*. For testimonios as revealing truths about the brutality of Latin American regimes, see Gugelberger, *Real Thing*.

40. Mendoza, *raúlsalinas*, 17.

41. Abu-Jamal, *Jailhouse Lawyers*, 32.

42. Lamar v. Coffield, 352 F. Supp. 1081 (S.D. Tex. 1972). For a policy analysis of racial integration of Texas prisons, see Trulson and Marquart, *First Available Cell*.

43. For critical assessments of the problems that historians of oral history face when separating memory from history, see Thompson, *Voice of the Past*, esp. Grele, "Movement without Aim," chap. 4; Portelli, "What Makes Oral History," chap. 6; and the Popular Memory Group, "Popular Memory," chap. 7. See also Maze, "Memory Theory," 275–96; and Gluck, "Narrative Theory," 384–410.

On oral history as a social movement to document those often ignored by traditional methods of historical documentation, see Perks and Thompson, *Oral History Reader*, esp. Bornat, "Oral History," chap. 16; and Schragger, "What Is Social," chap. 24. On the value of oral histories for criminologists and those studying criminal justice, see Laub, "Talking about Crime," 29–42.

44. On the ways in which the "rebel archive" reveals people and practices that have been eliminated through incarceration, see Hernández, *City of Inmates*, 199–220.

45. Scott, *Seeing Like a State*.

46. Berger, *Captive Nation*, 6.

47. Cummins, *Rise and Fall*, ix.

48. Jacobs, *Stateville*.

49. Kalinich, *Inmate Economy*; and Wright, "Violent and Victimized," 103–22.

50. On the cultural production of prison radicalism, see James, *Imprisoned Intellectuals*; Rodríguez, *Forced Passages*. For legal accounts, see Filter, *Prisoners' Rights*; DiIulio, *Courts, Corrections*; and Feely and Rubin, *Judicial Policy Making*.

51. Berger, *Captive Nation*, 5.

52. Berger, "From Dachau with Love," 355–84.

53. Thompson, *Blood in the Water*, 561.

54. Berger, 3.

55. Berger, *Captive Nation*, 12, 15.

56. Childs, *Black Incarceration*, 5.

57. Childs, *Black Incarceration*, 11, 16.

58. Berger, *Captive Nation*, 14.

59. Thompson, "Blinded," 74–98. For the ways in which Progressive era social scientists developed an "unscientific use of the statistical method" to fashion the link between blackness and criminality, see Muhammad, *Condemnation of Blackness*.

60. Berlin, "Evolution of Afro-American Society," 44–78.

61. Berlin and Morgan, *Cultivation and Culture*, 1–2.

62. On Thompson's conceptualization of "the criminalization of urban space," see Thompson, "Why Mass Incarceration Matters," 703–34.

63. For work on Latina/os in prison, see Oboler, *Behind Bars*; Davidson, *Chicano Prisoners*; Díaz-Cotto, *Gender, Ethnicity*; Díaz-Cotto, *Chicana Lives*; and Olguín, *La Pinta*. For work that considers Latina/o critical resistance in federal prisons, particularly among Puerto Ricans, see Gomez, "'Nuestras vidas,'" 67–98.

64. For recent work on urban Chicana/o protest movements in Texas, see Montejano, *Quixote's Soldiers*; Behnken, "'Dallas Way,'" 1–29; Dulaney, "Whatever Happened," 66–95; Rossinow, *Politics of Authenticity*; De León, *Ethnicity in the Sunbelt*; and Behnken, *Fighting Their Own Battles*.

65. García, *From the Jaws*.

66. On the political evolution of pachucos and los vatos within the Chicana/o movement, see Montejano, *Quixote's Soldiers*, 30–79. On community control and the rejection of "whiteness" as an assimilation strategy for education in Texas, see San Miguel Jr., *Brown, Not White*.

67. On Chicano student activism and their struggle to gain local community and political control in urban spaces, see Acuña, *Occupied America*; Navarro, *Mexican American Youth Organization*; Navarro, *Cristal Experiment*; García, *United We Win*;

Gómez-Quiñones, *Chicano Politics*; Gómez-Quiñones, *Mexican Students*; Chavez, *¡Mi Raza Primero!*; Vigil, *The Crusade for Justice*. For accounts written by Chicano activists of the period, see García, *Chicanismo*; and Muñoz, *Youth, Identity, Power*.

68. On Mexicans and Mexican Americans in the U.S. South, see Wiese, "Mexican Nationalisms, Southern Racisms," 749–77; Fink, *Maya of Morgantown*; Weise, *Corazon de Dixie*; Guerrero, *Nuevo South*.

69. Hernández, *City of Inmates*, 9. On state violence and policing within the borderlands, see Hernández, *Migra!*. On similar traditions of state violence in policing the U.S. frontier, see Graybill, *Policing the Great Plains*; Graybill, "Rural Police," 253–80; and McGrath, *Gunfighters, Highwaymen, and Vigilantes*.

70. For work that considers interracial organizations in the context of Black and brown power as well as civil rights rebellions, see Ogbar, *Black Power*; Wilson, "Invisible Cages," 191–222; Barber, "Leading the Vanguard," 223–51; Leonard, "'Interest of All Races,'" 309–41; Araiza, "In Common Struggle," 200–223; and Jackson, *From Civil Rights*.

71. For recent accounts of the coalition between the Chicano movement and African American protest struggles of the late 1960s and 1970s, see Mariscal, *Brown-Eyed Children*, 15, 45; and Pulido, *Black, Brown, Yellow*.

72. For recent work that simultaneously demonstrates moments of interracial cooperation and conflict during the late 1960s, see Mantler, *Power to the Poor*; and Araiza, *To March for Others*. For work that stresses conflict over attempts at interracial organizing, see Behnken, *Fighting Their Own Battles*; and Foley, *Quest for Equality*.

73. On the changing racial perceptions of Mexican Americans in Texas, see De Leon, *They Call Them Greasers*; Foley, *White Scourge*; and Montejano, *Anglos and Mexicans*. On state repression and Mexican Americans in the Southwest, see Rosenbaum, *Mexicano Resistance*; Hoffman, *Unwanted Mexican Americans*; García, *Operation Wetback*; Balderrama, *Decade of Betrayal*; Hernández, *Miagra!*

74. On the whiteness strategy for Mexican American civil rights, see Kaplowitz, "Distinct Minority," 192–222; Kaplowitz, *LULAC*.

75. For historians that stress racial contestation between African American civil rights struggles and Mexican American "whiteness" politics, see Behnken, *Fighting Their Own Battles*; Foley, *White Scourge*; López, *Racism on Trial*; Guglielmo, "Fighting for Caucasian Rights," 1212–37.

76. Both "Mexican American Generation" and "Chicano Generation" are terms that Mario Garcia coined.

77. On the collapse of interracial movements by 1974, see Mantler, *Power to the Poor*; Araiza, *To March for Others*; and Behnken, *Fighting Their Own Battles*.

78. For an account of Texas civil rights struggles that stresses difference between Mexican Americans and African Americans, see Behnken, *Fighting Their Own Battles*, 3. On multiracial coalition in Texas, see Krochmal, *Blue Texas*, 8.

79. For alternative masculine identities within the Chicano movement due to a repositioning of masculinity during the Vietnam War, see Oropeza, *¡Raza Si! ¡Guerra No!*.

80. Gross, *Colored Amazons*; Hicks, *Talk with You*; Kunzel, *Criminal Intimacy*; McGuire, *At the Dark End*; LeFlouria, *Chained in Silence*; Haley, *No Mercy Here*; Freedman, *Redefining Rape*; Block, "Rape without Women," 849–68; and Block, *Rape and Sexual Power*.

81. Canaday, *Straight State*; Stein, *Sexual Injustice*; Johnson, *Lavender Scare*; Luibhéid, *Entry Denied*.

82. McGuire, *At the Dark End*, xx.

83. Thurma, "Lessons in Self-Defense," 52–71; and Thurma, "'Prison/Psychiatric State,'" 26–51.

84. For work that connects gang organization to community control, the Black Power movement, and movements for racial pride and identity among Puerto Ricans, see Venkatesh and Levitt, "'Are We a Family,'" 427–62; Jeffries, "From Gang-Bangers," 288–304; Hagedorn, *World of Gangs*; Venkatesh, *Gang Leader*; and Fernandez, "Young Lords," 60–82.

85. For recent scholarship on northern urban gang organization as a stepping stone for power movements, see Diamond, *Mean Streets*; Venkatesh and Levitt, "'Are We a Family'"; Jeffries, "From Gang-Bangers"; Hagedorn, *World of Gangs*; Venkatesh, *Gang Leader*; Rios, *Punished*; and Fernandez, "Young Lords."

86. On the construction of blackness and whiteness as a matter of northern urban cityscapes, see Sugrue, *Urban Crisis*; Hirsch, *Making the Second Ghetto*; Davis, *City of Quartz*; and Hagedorn, "Race Not Space," 194–208.

87. On a corresponding effort to draw upon anti-insurgent thought for domestic policing, see Schrader, "More Than Cosmetic Hanges."

88. Schlanger, "Civil Rights Injunction," 550–630; Schlanger, "Inmate Litigation," 1555–1706; Schoenfeld, *Building the Prison State*; Hughett, "Silencing the Cell Block."

89. For the "law and order" conservative politics narrative, see Flamm, *Law and Order*; and Parenti, *Lockdown America*. On political backlash among conservative African American leaders, see Fortner, *Black Silent Majority*. For the critical policy and new political history of the carceral state, see Murakawa, *First Civil Right*; Hinton, *War on Poverty*; and Kohler-Hausmann, *Getting Tough*.

90. Murakawa, *First Civil Right*; Kohler-Hausman, *Getting Tough*; Hinton, *War on Poverty*; Weaver, "Frontlash," 230–65.

91. The top ten state incarceration rates per 100,000 are (1) Louisiana, 719; (2) Oklahoma, 704; (3) Mississippi, 619; (4) Arkansas, 598; (5) Arizona, 569; (6) Texas, 553; (7) Missouri, 532; (8) Kentucky, 527; (9) Georgia, 506; (10) Alabama, 486. See "State-by-State Data," Sentencing Project, accessed July 29, 2019, https://www.sentencingproject.org.

92. These numbers are compiled from the 1972–1979 LEAA annual reports providing the totals for Parts B, C, and E of all grant allocations to the states—the Juvenile Justice Allocations were not counted in the total. LEAA, 4th Annual Report of the Law Enforcement Assistance Administration, Fiscal Year 1972 (Washington, D.C.: U.S. Department of Justice, 1980), 99–101.

93. LEAA Annual Reports, 1969–1979.

94. Schulman, *Seventies*; Jenkins, *Decade of Nightmares*; Cowie, *Stayin Alive*; and Fortner, *Black Silent Majority*.

95. On the vibrancy of 1970s-era movement history, see Berger, *Hidden Seventies*; Thompson, *Blood in the Water*; Spencer, *Revolution Has Come*; and Orleck, *Storming Caesars Palace*.

96. On the 1970s as a formative decade that linked political retreat from welfare with the embrace of "get tough" politics that included mass incarceration, see Kohler-Hausmann, *Getting Tough*.

97. On the transition between prisoner solidarity to prison gangs in California, see McCarty, "Blood in, Blood Out," 245–78. For a national overview of prison gang violence, see Parenti, *Lockdown*.

98. Gilmore, *Golden Gulag*; Wacquant, *Punishing the Poor*; Wacquant, *Prisons of Poverty*.

99. In his assessment of the three states with the nation's highest rates of imprisonment—Florida, California, and Texas—historian Alex Lichtenstein fashioned the term "Flocatex" to describe the regional merger of political and prison economies within a broader Sunbelt. Through the lens of political economy, Lichtenstein argued that the rise of Flocatex as the nation's forerunner for the carceral regime mirrored transformations in U.S. capitalism where "explosive growth in the nonindustrial sector of the economy, the privatized ideal of a weak state, and the determined fiscal austerity in the area of social goods" fashioned the Sunbelt. Lichtenstein, "Flocatex," 125.

Chapter 1

1. Legislative Committee on Investigation of State Penitentiaries and the Farm System, Report on Texas Prisons, Beauford Jester papers, TSLA (hereafter cited as Jester, TSLA), box 4-14/113.

2. Canaday, *Straight State*, 95.

3. On the expulsion of homosexuality from New York City during the 1930s, see Chauncey, *Gay New York*, 9, 331–54.

4. D'Emilio, "Homosexual Menace," 226–40; Chauncey, "Postwar Sex Crime Panic," 160–78; D'Emilio, *Sexual Politics, Sexual Communities*, 41–53; Corber, "Lesbian Visibility," 6–7; Johnson, *Lavender Scare*.

5. Kunzel, *Criminal Intimacy*, 87.

6. On the nineteenth-century response to homosexuality as "a species," see Kunzel, *Criminal Intimacy*, 51; Foucault, *History of Sexuality*.

7. The impetus behind the legislative effort to restrict convict labor came from two sources: the progressive movement to end the South's convict lease system and northeastern labor organizations who felt that profitable convict labor threatened free labor and collective organization. For the protest of organized labor, particularly in the Northeast, against convict labor, see Gildemeister, *Prison Labor and Convict*.

8. When these laws were challenged, the U.S. Supreme Court twice upheld their constitutionality with unanimous decisions. See Whitfield v. Ohio, 297 U.S. 431–41 (1936); and Kentucky Whip and Collar Company v. Illinois Central Railroad Company, 299 U.S. 334 (1937).

9. Jones Jr., *Prison Labor*.

10. For the northern emphasis on the rehabilitative prison and reformatories, see Rothman, *Conscience and Convenience*; Pisciotta, *Benevolent Repression*; Rafter, *Partial Justice*; and Garland, *Punishment and Welfare*. On New York's adoption of the "new penology" during the Progressive era, see McLennan, *Crisis of Imprisonment*; and McLennan, "Punishment's 'Square Deal,'" 597–619. It is important to note that while Progressive and New Deal–era federal law constricted convict labor, it obviously did not end prison work altogether. Some state systems, particularly California, blended together rehabilitative programs with a continuing emphasis on prison labor through

firefighting and forest camps. For California's emphasis on "bibliotherapy," group therapy, and education, see Cummins, *Rise and Fall*, 1–62. On California's attempt to instill civic duty through forestry and firefighting camps for prisoners, see Janssen, "'Jungle' Met the Forest." 702–26.

11. Thompson, *Blood in the Water*, 29.

12. In 1940, southern prisons employed 33,272 prisoners out of a total prison population (both male and female) of 53,804 prisoners. Northeastern prison states, however, employed only 9,886 prisoners out of a total prison population of 31,665 (both male and female). For the purposes of this chapter, southern prison systems included the states of Alabama, Arkansas, Florida, Georgia, Kentucky, Louisiana, North Carolina, South Carolina, Tennessee, Texas, Virginia, and West Virginia. Northeastern states included Connecticut, Delaware, Maine, New Hampshire, New Jersey, New York, Pennsylvania, Rhode Island, and Vermont. Both male and female prisoners were included in the total number of prisoners. See Jones, Jr., *Prison Labor*; Bair, *Prison Labor*.

13. Jones Jr., *Prison Labor*; and Austin MacCormick, "Alabama Prison System," Report of the Osbourne Association, Inc., MacCormick papers, box 7, Sam Houston State University (hereafter cited as MacCormick, SHSU).

14. U.S. Department of Justice, *Attorney General's Survey*, 34.

15. Ferguson, "The History of the Arkansas Penitentiary," MacCormick, SHSU, box 2, folder 5.

16. "Report of the Osbourne Association, Inc. on the Alabama Prison System: Summary of Findings," 1949, MacCormick, SHSU, box 7, folders 5 and 6.

17. On industrial prison labor during the Depression, see Blue, *Doing Time*.

18. On the development of the plantation state-run cash crop, see Perkinson, *Texas Tough*, 177–214. On the Rusk penitentiary and the experiment in industrial prison labor, see Lucko, "Prison Farms," 289–348; Perkinson, *Texas Tough*, 118–20. On the development of the convict lease in Texas, see Walker, *Penology for Profit*; Lucko, "Prison Farms," 191–239; Perkinson, *Texas Tough*, 83–131.

19. "Texas Prison System Runs Gauntlet of Bad and Best in Nation's Penal Institutions," *Tyler Courrier-Times*, December 20, 1947.

20. "Behind the Walls," *Daily Times Herald*, December 20, 1947; "Overcrowding and the 'Tanks' Are the Source of Many Problems Found in Texas Prison System, *Tyler Morning Telegraph*, December 29, 1947; "Poor Housing, Pay for the Guards," *Houston Post*, September 13, 1948.

21. "Texas Prison System Runs Gauntlet of Bad and Best in Nation's Penal Institutions," *Tyler Courrier-Times*, December 20, 1947.

22. Austin MacCormick, Report on Texas Prisons, 1947, Jester, TSLA, box 4-14/113.

23. Anonymous prisoner, quoted in Jackson, *Wake Up Dead Man*, 9.

24. Texas Prison System, *Annual Report*.

25. State Legislature, Special Committee on Penitentiary, Report (Austin, 1871), TSLA.

26. *Report of the Commission Appointed by the Governor of Texas to Investigate the Alleged Mismanagement and Cruel Treatment of the Convicts* (Houston: A. C. Gray, State Printer, April 10, 1875).

27. On trustees overseeing field labor in Mississippi, see Oshinsky, *"Worse than Slavery,"* 140–50.

28. On the continued practice of trusty guards after the abolition of convict leasing, see Board of Prison Commissioners, *Annual Report* (Austin, unpublished, 1914), printed in Texas State Legislature, Senate Penitentiary Investigating Committee, supplementary documents (Austin, 1915), TSLA, box 4-2/1594b.

29. Albert Race Sample's memoir, *Racehoss: Big Emma's Boy*, provides a chilling tale of sexual violence and brutality on Texas prison farms from 1955 to 1972. As an African American prisoner housed in a segregated dormitory, Sample's memoir is one of the few prison memoirs that reveal the raced space of Texas prison farms. For an account of prison life in the postwar period from the perspective of an African American prisoner, see Sample, *Racehoss*, 164–65. On the building tender system in the 1930s before the postwar reforms, see Blue, *Doing Time*, 102–9.

30. Prison society and the power of building tenders during the postwar period is the topic of chapter 4 of this study.

31. Diaz, "Cultural Resilience."

32. Blue, "Hard Time," 79. Blue argued that the 1936 classification plan created a racial "universe" in Texas prisons that "produced social inequality even with the egalitarian vision that the New Deal era promised."

33. Kunzel, *Criminal Intimacy*, 87.

34. Folder "Rodeo Program 1939," describes the classification plan, Texas Department of Correctional Justice, Texas State Library Archives (hereafter cited as TDCJ, TSLA), box 1998/038-404.

35. Ayers, *Vengeance and Justice*, 207.

36. For the ways in which "white skin privilege" conferred racial identity and power, see Roediger, *Wages of Whiteness*; Ignatiev, *Irish Became White*; Hale, *Making Whiteness*; Lipsitz, *Possessive Investment in Whiteness*; and Delgado and Stefancic, *Critical White Studies*. For studies showing how the racial category of "whiteness" could change over time or even be lost for an individual or ethnic group, see Jacobson, *Whiteness*; and Foley, *White Scourge*.

37. For an administrative and political account of the effort to turn back prison reform in the 1930s, see Lucko, "Counteracting Reform," 19–30; and Crow, "Texas Penal System," 43–44. For a cultural history of Texas punishment and prisons in the 1930s, see Blue, *Doing Time*.

38. For the Texas tradition of slave punishment, particularly the use of the lash, see Campbell, *Empire for Slavery*, 103–8, 145–53.

39. Anonymous prisoner, Jackson, 9.

40. Anonymous prisoner, Jackson, 9.

41. Anonymous prisoner, Jackson, 25.

42. Anonymous prisoner, Jackson, 25.

43. Anonymous prisoner, Jackson, 1.

44. In 1947, the year of Texas prison reforms, the total prison population numbered 5,700 on twelve prison units, which included one walled penitentiary and eleven prison farms encompassing a total acreage of 73,010. "Texas Prison System Runs Gauntlet of Bad and Best in Nation's Penal Institutions," *Tyler Courier-Times*, December 20, 1947; Annual Report of the Texas Prison Board to the Governor, Honorable Coke Stevenson, Texas Department of Corrections, 1945 and 1946; Texas Department of Corrections, *20 Years of Progress*.

45. Crouch and Marquart, *Appeal to Justice*, 24.

46. "Texas Prisons Called Humanity's Junk Pile," *San Antonio Express*, November 18, 1948.

47. On suicide and self-destruction among the enslaved during the Middle Passage, see Rediker, *Slave Ship*, 17–19, 212–13, 289–91; and Brown, *Reaper's Garden*.

48. Van Dyke, "Investigation of Self-Mutilation," 64, 90, 98.

49. R.C. Koeninger, "What about Self-Mutilation?" *Prison World*, March–April 1951; Texas, Annual Reports, 1940–1942.

50. Anonymous prisoner, Jackson, 9.

51. *Texas Department of Corrections, 20 Years of Progress* (Huntsville, 1967), 98; "8-Time Loser Admits Decapitating Convict," *San Antonio Express*, December 16, 1948; H. Heinecks, "Either Him or Me, Convict Declares in Describing Beheading at Prison," *Fort Worth Star Telegram*, December 16, 1948.

52. Carl Luther McAdams oral history with Cynthia Linzy, October 26, 1987, Texas Prison History Museum.

53. The Tyler news article highlighted the difference between the proponents and opponents of the prison system as running the "gauntlet of bad and best" in the nation. "Texas Prison System Runs Gauntlet of Bad and Best in Nation's Penal Institutions," *Tyler Courrier-Times*, December 20, 1947.

54. "No. 2 of a Series: The Need for Adequate Housing; Overcrowding and 'The Tanks' Are the Source of Many Problems Found in Texas Prison System," *Tyler Morning Telegraph*, December 29, 1947.

55. "Prison Gang Chiefs Served by Valets," *New York Times*, January 25, 1934, 3; "Welfare Island Raid Bares Gangster Rule over Prison; Weapons, Narcotics Found," *New York Times*, January 25, 1934, 3; "MacCormick Raids Welfare Island," *New York Herald Tribune*, January 25, 1934, 9.

56. For a description of the raid against Welfare Island prison's segregation wing for prisoners it classified as homosexual, see Chauncey, *Gay New York*, 92–95. In her study, Regina Kunzel found that MacCormick's raid was emblematic of a shift among criminologists in their approach to prison homosexuality from "habit forming" to "subject-forming" that "challenged notions of sexual identity and fixity at the time of their supposed solidification." Kunzel, *Criminal Intimacy*, 80.

57. U.S. Federal Bureau of Investigation, *Uniform Crime Reports*, vol. 17, no. 2, Annual Bulletin, 1946, 90; U.S. Federal Bureau of Investigation, *Uniform Crime Reports*, vol. 18, no. 2, Annual Bulletin, 1947, 80–83, 87.

58. "Texas Prison System Runs Gauntlet of Bad and Best in Nation's Penal Institutions," *Tyler Courrier-Times*, December 20, 1947.

59. For Osborne's efforts to instill citizenship through mutual welfare leagues and convict government in New York's prison system, see McLennan, "Citizens and Criminals," 242–338. For an analysis that considers gender and Osborne's role in formulating progressive notions of "political manhood," see Murphy, *Political Manhood*, chap. 5.

60. On McCormick's career in penology, see Robert J. Wright, "Austin H. MacCormick: A Memorial Statement," *Corrections Today* (January–February 1980), 60–61; R. M. Yoder, "Trouble Shooter of the Big House," *Saturday Evening Post*, May 12, 1951, 19–21.

61. On the North's predominance in fashioning the reformatory movement and the rehabilitative ideal during the Progressive period, see Rothman, *Conscience and Convenience*; Colvin, "Applying Theories"; and Pisciotta, *Benevolent Repression*.

62. Austin MacCormick, "The Future of Correctional Work in America," in MacCormick, SHSU, box 4, folder 14.

63. Gilbert, *Cycle of Outrage*.

64. Freedman, "'Uncontrolled Desires,'" 83–106; D'Emilio, "Homosexual Menace."

65. Kunzel, *Criminal Intimacy*, 87.

66. Austin MacCormick, Report on Texas Prisons, 1947, Jester, TSLA, box 4-14/113.

67. Austin MacCormick, Report on Texas Prisons, 1947, Jester, TSLA, box 4-14/113.

68. Austin MacCormick, Report on Texas Prisons, 1947, Jester, TSLA, box 4-14/113.

69. Austin MacCormick, Report on Texas Prisons, 1947, Jester, TSLA, box 4-14/113.

70. "Minutes of the Texas Prison Board," TDCJ, TSLA (March 1944–July 1945), 677.

71. Steve J. Martin and Sheldon Ekland-Olson's landmark study of Texas prisons and litigation provided a valuable overview of the MacCormick report, but their analysis focused on practical issues of management and does not fully deconstruct how MacCormick's report revealed the modernization impulse nor the report's focus on space and sexuality. See Martin and Ekland-Olson, *Texas Prisons*, 15–18. See also Horton and Nielsen, *Walking George*, 50–52.

72. Austin MacCormick, Report on Texas Prisons, 1947, Jester, TSLA, box 4-14/113.

73. Austin MacCormick, Report on Texas Prisons, 1947, Jester, TSLA, box 4-14/60.

74. MacCormick's fear that one bad prisoner could act as a "poison" to the larger prison body builds on what the historian Michael Meranze has termed "mimetic corruption." Meranze's study of the development of prisons in Philadelphia argued that reformers established the penitentiary in the early nineteenth century because they feared that criminals would literally infect the body politic and normal citizens. Meranze defined this fear as "mimetic corruption," which, in his words, was "where the very presence of embodied criminality overwhelmed spectators' virtue and led them to identify with and replicate criminality." In this way, "the body was not only subject to various penal technologies; its very presence and materiality had the capacity to disrupt the orderly dissemination of virtue." Just as Philadelphia's early national prison reformers used the language of disease and social contagion to construct prisons, so too did MacCormick rely on a similar medically inspired dialect to argue for the creation of cells and confined spaces for Texas prisoners. See Meranze, *Laboratories of Virtue*, 8–9.

75. "No. 2 of A Series: The Need for Adequate Housing; Overcrowding and 'The Tanks' Are the Source of Many Problems Found in Texas Prison System," *Tyler Morning Telegraph*, December 29, 1947.

76. For work on the role of the state in the suppression of gay culture into "the closet" during the twentieth century, see D'Emilio, *Sexual Politics, Sexual Communities*; D'Emilio, *Making Trouble*; Chauncey, *Gay New York*; Berubé, *Coming Out under Fire*; Kennedy and Davis, *Boots of Leather*. On the Cold War's political culture and the effort to persecute and expunge homosexuals from the federal government, see Johnson, *Lavender Scare*; Dean, *Imperial Brotherhood*; Smith, "National Security," 307–37; and Cuordileone, *Manhood*.

77. On the ways in which "moral panics" infuse political culture, see Rubin, "Thinking Sex," 3–44; Rogin, *Ronald Reagan*.

78. Johnson, *Lavender Scare*, 11.

79. Kunzel, *Criminal Intimacy*, 87.

80. Austin MacCormick, Report on Texas Prisons, 1947, Jester, TSLA, box 4-14/113.

81. Austin MacCormick, Tape Transcription, March 3, 1947, Jester, TSLA, box 4-14/113.

82. Austin MacCormick, Report on Texas Prisons, 1947, Jester, TSLA, box 4-14/113.

83. Austin MacCormick, Report on Texas Prisons, 1947, Jester, TSLA, box 4-14/113.

84. See de Certeau, *Practice of Everyday Life*; Scott, *Domination*; and, Kelley, "'Not What We Seem,'" 75–112.

85. Austin MacCormick, Report on Texas Prisons, 1947, Jester, TSLA, box 4-14/113.

86. Legislative Committee on Investigation of State Penitentiaries and the Farm System, Report on Texas Prisons, Jester, TSLA, box 4-14/113.

87. "Prisons Rotten System, Says One of Board," *Fort Worth Press*, March 5, 1948; "Texan Brawls Like a Baby after Tour of the State's Prison Farms," *Jacksonville Journal*, March 4, 1948; "Convicts Live in Stinking Filth," *Wichita Falls Record News*, April 23, 1948.

88. Legislative Committee on Investigation of State Penitentiaries and the Farm System, Report on Texas Prisons, Jester, TSLA, box 4-14/113.

89. As Nayan Shah demonstrated in his study of the spatial and racial formation of Chinatown in turn-of-the-century San Francisco, public health officials articulated a language of contamination and "strategies of containment," which allowed the state to control, segregate, and racialize social space. MacCormick adopted a similar language when he described Texas prison conditions. See Shah, *Contagious Divides*.

90. Mrs. Lillie B. Atchison to Beauford Jester, Jester, TSLA, box 4-14/113.

91. Mrs. Frank Riley to Beauford Jester, Jester, TSLA, box 4-14/113.

92. Mrs. Frank Riley to Beauford Jester, Jester, TSLA, box 4-14/113.

93. Legislative Committee on Investigation of State Penitentiaries and the Farm System, Report on Texas Prisons, Jester, TSLA, box 4-14/113.

94. S. E. Barnett to M. Riley Wyatt, September 1947, Jester, TSLA, box 4-14/113.

95. S. E. Barnett to M. Riley Wyatt, September 1947, Jester, TSLA, box 4-14/113.

96. Legislative Committee on Investigation of State Penitentiaries and the Farm System, Report on Texas Prisons, Jester, TSLA, box 4-14/113.

97. Legislative Committee on Investigation of State Penitentiaries and the Farm System, Report on Texas Prisons, Jester, TSLA, box 4-14/113.

98. Legislative Committee on Investigation of State Penitentiaries and the Farm System, Report on Texas Prisons, Jester, TSLA, box 4-14/113.

99. State Representative Sam Sellars to Beauford Jester, Jester, TSLA, box 4-14/113.

100. The subject of spatial formation and how it changed relations of power within Texas prisons is explored further in chapter 4. For geographical scholarship that discusses spatial formation and relations of power, see Soja, *Postmodern Geographies*, 6; Davis, *City of Quartz*; Foucault, "Of Other Spaces," 22–27; Foucault, "Questions on Geography," 63–77; Gregory and Urry, *Social Relations*; Harvey, *Condition of Postmodernity*, esp. 201–39.

Chapter 2

1. Jack Kyle, interview with the author, June 25, 2005, transcribed by the Institute of Oral History, Baylor University, Waco, Texas (hereafter cited as IOH, Baylor).

2. "Texas Prison System Runs Gauntlet of Bad and Best in Nation's Penal Institutions," *Tyler Courier Times*, December 20, 1947; Austin MacCormick to O. B. Ellis, June 14, 1949, Jester, TSLA, box 4-14/113.

3. For a narrative account of "control penology," see Perkinson, *Texas Tough*, 230–50.

4. On the anti-convict-lease movement in Texas, see Walker, *Penology for Profit*; and Perkinson, *Texas Tough*, 132–76.

5. On convict leasing as an archaic labor system, see Woodward, *Origins*; Wright, *Old South, New South*; Daniel, *Breaking the Land*; and Carleton, *Politics and Punishment*.

6. Lichtenstein, *Twice the Work*, xvi. See also Mancini, *One Dies, Get Another*; and Blackmon, *Slavery by Another Name*.

7. Fierce, *Slavery Revisited*; Curtin, *Black Prisoners*; Myers, *Race, Labor and Punishment*; Shapiro, *New South Rebellion*; and Oshinsky, *"Worse than Slavery."*

8. Miller, *Hard Labor*, 18. See also Carleton, *Politics and Punishment*. For histories of Parchman prison farm, see Oshinsky, *"Worse than Slavery"*; and Taylor, *Brokered Justice*.

9. Zieger, *Life and Labor*, 2. On the postwar South and its transitional labor system and economy, see Zieger, *Southern Labor in Transition*; Cobb, *Industrialization and Southern Society*; Fite, *Cotton Fields No More*; Wright, *Old South, New South*; Bartley, *New South*; Gregory, "Southernizing," 135–54; Schulman, *From Cotton Belt*; and Applebome, *Dixie Rising*.

10. J. Edgar Hoover to Austin MacCormick, June 1947, MacCormick papers, SHSU, box 1, folder 8.

11. The political historian George Green aptly called the 1946 political campaign between Beauford Jester and Harold Rainey as a choice between Jester as the "establishment" candidate and Rainey as "the last truly liberal candidate in the state's history to have any significant press support." Green, *Establishment in Texas Politics*, 95. For the struggle between Rainey and the University of Texas Board of Regents, see Green, *Establishment in Texas Politics*, 83–89; Rainey, *Tower and the Dome*; Dugger, *Our Invaded Universities*; Cox, "Rainey Affair."

12. Austin MacCormick to Governor Beauford Jester, Western Union telegram, August 28, 1947, Jester, TSLA, box 4-14/113.

13. Austin MacCormick, Tape Transcription, March 3, 1947, Jester, TSLA, box 4-14/113.

14. W. C. Windsor to Beauford Jester, "Prison Board, 1947" Jester, TSLA, box 4-14/60.

15. Shelby County Penal Farm (monograph), 1946, SHSU.

16. W. Flower, "Texas Solution Seen in Model Penal Farm," *Dallas Morning News*, December 4, 1947.

17. Letter from W. C. Windsor, chairman of Texas Prison Board, November 1947, Prison Board Minutes, TSLA.

18. "Prison System, Newspaper Comment," Jester, TSLA, box 4-14/60; Texas Prison Board, Jester, TSLA, box 4-14/113.

19. *Commercial Appeal*, Memphis, November 26, 1947.

20. "Milestone in Prison History," *Tyler Morning Telegraph*, November 27, 1947.

21. "State Prison Program," *Dallas Morning News*, December 7, 1947.

22. Texas Department of Correctional Justice, Texas Prison Board, "A Program for the Improvement of the Texas Prison System," Huntsville, 1945, 1998/038-127.

23. *The Tyler Daily*, Newsclippings, 1947, Prison Board Minutes, TSLA.

24. "Give Ellis a Chance," *Houston Press*, March 4, 1948.

25. Austin MacCormick to O. B. Ellis, June 14, 1949, Jester, TSLA, box 4-14/113.

26. For an analysis of the 1952–53 riots, see McGee, *Riots and Disturbances*; MacCormick, "Behind the Prison Riots," 18–19; Sykes, *Society of Captives*; and McKelvey, *American Prisons*, chap. 13.

27. Texas Department of Corrections, *20 Years of Progress*.

28. "Texas Prison System Changes Afford New Hope for Inmates," *Houston Chronicle*, February 21, 1954.

29. George Beto, "The Case for Prisons," *Texas Police Journal*, August 1964, Beto, SHSU, 1-4/45.

30. Wainwright, *Annual Report, 1976–1977*.

31. Ellis quoted in Ray Holbrook, "Former Tennessean Revolutionizes Texas Prison System," *Nashville Tennessean*, February 21, 1954.

32. Texas Department of Corrections, *20 Years of Progress*.

33. Frierson, a native of Haskell County's open farmlands, graduated from Texas A&M and was hired by Ellis in 1949, and he remained a career TDC employee for over twenty years. "Texas's Biggest Farmer," *Houston Chronicle Magazine*, February 15, 1959; Walter B. Moore, "Grows Almost Everything: Texas' Biggest, Best Farmer in Prison," *Dallas Morning News*, January 23, 1969.

34. Texas Department of Corrections, *20 Years of Progress*.

35. Ray Holbrook, "Former Tennessean Revolutionizes Texas Prison System," *Nashville Tennessean*, February 21, 1954.

36. Don Reid Jr., "The Prisons: In Seven Years They've Gone from Bad to Good," *Houston Post*, January 30, 1955.

37. Dick West, *Dallas News*, June 3, 1955.

38. On Cunningham and the Sugarland operation, see Perkinson, *Texas Tough*, 83–85, 97–100; Andrews, "Historic Foundations."

39. Blue, *Doing Time*, 78, 81.

40. In 1940, Texas consumed 1,511,860 pounds of steel to produce 3,455,700 license plates. Blue, *Doing Time*, 82.

41. The canning operation turned out spinach greens at a total cost of $2.13 a case (six number 10 cans), a case of corn for $2.86, and a case of green beans for $2.28. Gayle McNutt, "Reduce Waste in Prison Labor, Study Groups Urge," *Houston Post*, September 1, 1962.

42. Don Reid Jr., "New Prison Unit for Young Offenders Opens," *Houston Post*, June 18, 1962.

43. O. B. Ellis, *Annual Report to the Texas Prison Board* (1949), TSLA.

44. Testimony of John Albach, Staff Director for the Joint Committee on Prison Reform, CAH, *Ruiz* Special Master, MAI 8/J88; Joint Committee on Prison Reform, Texas Legislature, "Final Report of the Joint Committee on Prison Reform, 63rd Legislature, December 1974."

45. Testimony of John Albach, Staff Director for the Joint Committee on Prison Reform, CAH, *Ruiz* Special Master, MAI 8/J88.

46. Testimony of John Albach, Staff Director for the Joint Committee on Prison Reform, CAH, *Ruiz* Special Master, MAI 8/J88.

47. "To Protect Society from the Criminal and the Criminals from Each Other: The Five-Point Prison Plan," O. B. Ellis memorandum, Prison Board minutes, February 1948, TDCJ, TSLA.

48. CURE Report, authorized by CURE member Gonzalo Barrientos and by Bruce Hupp, Brooks, TSLA, CURE file, 1991/068-29.

49. Billy Wayne McCarter, oral history with Susanne Mason, October 20, 1997, in author's possession and used here with permission of Susanne Mason.

50. Jack Kyle, interview with the author, June 25, 2005, IOH, Baylor.

51. U.S. Department of Commerce, *Sixteenth Census*, 761; U.S. Department of Commerce, "Census Population: 1980," 45–101.

52. The number of new arrivals in 1971 for each county was as follows: Harris, 1,331; Dallas, 1,205; Tarrant, 407; Bexar, 379; Travis, 218; McLennan, 149; Nuece, 111; Jefferson, 104. See George Beto, "Outline of Address: The Complexion of the Texas Prison Population," 1970, Beto, SHSU, 1-4/38.

53. In *Condemnation of Blackness*, Khalil Gibran Muhammad revealed how scientific racism imbued the very development of criminal science with racial bias where social statisticians relied upon the "unscientific use of the statistical method" to fashion an enduring link between blackness and criminality. Muhammad, *Condemnation of Blackness*, 64. On the racialized bias of intelligence testing for juvenile delinquents, particularly how such scientific tests "racialized, criminalized, and pathologized" Mexican American youths, see Chávez-García, *States of Delinquency*.

54. On slavery and social death, see Patterson, *Slavery and Social Death*, 13. Brown, "Social Death," 1231–49, 1233. On the power of geographic dislocation during the Middle Passage and in the internal slave trade, see Miller, *Way of Death*; Thomas, *Slave Trade*; Rediker, *Slave Ship*; Johnson, *Soul by Soul*; and Tadman, *Spectators and Slaves*.

55. Arthur Johnson, oral history conducted by author, March 20, 2008, IOH, Baylor.

56. Unpublished excerpt from Robert Lee Mudd's prison memoir, in the author's possession.

57. On the planting season for cotton harvesting in East Texas during antebellum slavery, see Campbell, *Empire for Slavery*, 118–22.

58. On the use of enslaved drivers as the predominant form of field labor management in antebellum Texas, see Campbell, *Empire for Slavery*, 127–28.

59. Jerry Quate, oral history conducted by the author, March 12, 2007, IOH, Baylor.

60. Lawrence Pope, oral history conducted by John Wheat, Lawrence Pope papers, CAH (hereafter cited as Pope, CAH), 318. On the use of enslaved African Americans who worked as "field drivers" in Texas cotton fields during the antebellum period, see Campbell, *Empire for Slavery*, 57.

61. Crouch's fieldwork led him to work "undercover" in the Texas prison system as a guard. Crouch argued that prison guards in Texas operated under different social norms and rules. Those that worked in the field operated less formally and ruled prisoners through "the boot," whereas those that worked in the building relied on more formal measures of discipline and operated by "the book." See Crouch and Marquart, "'Book vs. the Boot," 207–24.

62. Robert Lee Mudd, unpublished prison writings and private papers, in the author's possession.

63. Eubanks, oral history, IOH, Baylor.

64. Anonymous prisoner, quoted in Jackson, *Wake Up Dead Man*, 35.

65. Guadalupe Guajardo interview with the author, March 8, 2007, IOH, Baylor.

66. For a definition of Pachuca/os argot, see Hernández, *Chicano Satire*, 21–22.

67. On Pachuca/os argot as cultural resistance to policing and prisons, see Montejano, *Quixote's Soldiers*, 30–55; Olguín, *La Pinta*, 176–208; Alvarez, *Power of the Zoot*.

68. Anonymous prisoner, quoted in Jackson, *Wake Up Dead Man*, 9.

69. Texas Department of Correctional Justice, Texas Prison Board, O. B. Ellis, "A Program for the Improvement of the Texas Prison System," (Huntsville, 1948), TDCI, 1998/038-127.

70. For the Progressive-era origins of parole and indeterminate sentencing, see Rothman, *Conscience and Convenience*, 43–82. On the Progressive-era reformatory movement, see Pisciotta, *Benevolent Repression*. As part of the postwar prison reform effort, the Texas Legislature in 1947 passed the Adult Probation Law, which removed the practice of the suspended sentence in favor of a formal system of probation and created the Texas Board of Pardons and Parole to oversee the newly established parole system. The 1957 law, passed with the full support of Ellis and the TPS, created the Division of Parole Supervision, which provided a much stronger enforcement capacity for the Board of Pardons and Parole. On the creation of the probation and parole system in Texas see, Horton and Turner, *Lone Star Justice*, 274–78, 303–7.

71. Under executive clemency the governor could issue a pardon, and a prisoner was freed from the remainder of his sentence and regained full citizenship. In 1893, the legislature passed a law that created a two-member Board of Pardons Advisors to alleviate the governor's office from the burden of reviewing clemency pleas. In 1929, the executive clemency was reformed yet again when the legislature replaced the Board of Advisors with a Board of Pardons and Parole whose members were appointed by the governor and then ratified by the senate. The 1957 law, passed with the full support of Ellis and the TPS, created the Division of Parole Supervision, which provided a much stronger enforcement capacity for the Board of Pardons and Parole.

72. "Texas Department of Corrections Rules and Regulations," chap. 2, sec. 2.52, cited in Van Mendoza, "Labor and Industry Working Paper," Joint Committee on Prison Reform.

73. "Texas Department of Corrections Rules and Regulations," chap. 2, sec. 2.52, cited in Van Mendoza, "Labor and Industry Working Paper," Joint Committee on Prison Reform.

74. Beto, untitled speech, Beto, SHSU.

75. Kelley, "'We Are Not,'" 75–112, 76. On "infrapolitics" and the transcripts of both the powerful and the oppressed, see Scott, *Domination*; Scott, *Weapons of the Weak*;

and Scott, *Moral Economy*; de Certeau, *Practice of Everyday Life*. Kelley's call for histories of infrapolitics pointed to the work of Lila Abu-Lughod to underscore how such work must do more than reveal the agency of the oppressed by also revealing where and how hegemonic powers attempt to exert repression and domination.

76. Abu-Lughod, "Romance of Resistance," 41–55.

77. Perkinson, *Texas Tough*; Blue, *Doing Time*, 91–95.

78. Bruce Jackson interview with the author, April 26, 2008, IOH, Baylor.

79. On the African American practice of work songs both during antebellum slavery and in the early twentieth century, see Levine, *Black Culture*. For work on the musical and political import of prison work songs in Texas, see Jackson, *Wake Up Dead Man*; Blue, "Beating the System," 56–70. Jackson collected the majority of the prison work songs at the Ramsey, Ellis, and Wynne prisons.

80. Lyrics to "In the Bottoms" can be found in Jackson, *Wake Up Dead Man*, 217.

81. Lyrics to "Jody" quoted in Jackson, *Wake Up Dead Man*, 172.

82. Anonymous prisoner, quoted in Jackson, *Wake Up Dead Man*, 18.

83. Sample, *Racehoss*, 165.

84. Anonymous prisoner, quoted in Jackson, *Wake Up Dead Man*, 19.

85. Anonymous prisoner, quoted in Jackson, *Wake Up Dead Man*, 10.

86. Levine, *Black Culture*, 215, 202–17, 233–70; Jackson, *Wake Up Dead Man*, 30.

87. Michael Jewell to Senator Chet Brooks, July 1977, Brooks, TSLA, Michael Jewell file, 1999/136-21.

88. Kelley, "'We Are Not,'" 78.

89. Campbell, *Empire for Slavery*, 123.

90. See Brown, with Gaines, *Joyce Ann Brown*; Gregory, "Persistence and Irony."

91. Dr. George Beto to All Wardens, October 14, 1965, TDC memorandum no. 14-65, TDCJ, 1998/038-62; Ellis's 1951 memorandum to all wardens is repeated and copied in Dr. Beto's 1965 memorandum.

92. "55 Texas Prison Officials Said to Use Black Houseboys," *Houston Chronicle*, February 13, 1976.

93. Charlie Combs interview with the author, June 5, 2006, IOH, Baylor.

94. Charlie Combs interview with the author, June 5, 2006, IOH, Baylor.

95. Benny Wade Clewis, oral history with Susanne Mason, in author's possession and used here with Susanne Mason's permission.

96. E. R. Cass to Gordon Peters; and E. R. Cass to Allan Shivers, April 17, 1953, Prison Board Minutes, July 1953, TDCJ, TSLA, 1998/038-9.

97. A. Frank Lee to Austin MacCormick, January 8, 1969, MacCormick, SHSU, box 2, folder 1.

98. Austin MacCormick, "Report of a Study of the Louisiana State Penitentiary," July 1964, MacCormick, SHSU, box 4.

99. Albert Woodfox, *Solitary*, 25.

100. Austin MacCormick, "Report of a Study of the Louisiana State Penitentiary," July 1964, MacCormick, SHSU, box 4.

101. Austin MacCormick to George W. Healy, October 15, 1968, MacCormick, SHSU, box 2, folder 1.

102. Austin MacCormick, "Report of a Study of the Arkansas State Penitentiary, 1967," MaCormick, SHSU, box 4.

103. Austin MacCormick to O. B. Ellis, November 2, 1954, entirety of letter in Texas Board Meeting Minutes, TDCI, TSLA, 1998/038-9 and 14998/038-10.

104. Ellis, "The President's Page"; Ellis, "Correctional Growth," 6–8, 30–33.

105. Austin MacCormick to Dr. George Beto, February 28, 1968, Prison Board minutes, February 1968, TDCJ, TSLA, 1998/038-13.

106. Dr. George Beto quoted in Copeland, "Department of Corrections," 232.

107. Kevin Krajick, "Profile Texas," *Corrections Magazine*, 1978, 13.

108. At the end of Beto's tenure, the agribusiness Texas prison empire included 15,000 beef and dairy cattle, 17,000 hogs, 112,000 chickens, 3,000 turkeys, 345 horses, 290 mares, 10,000 cultivated catfish, and 387 man-hunting dogs. Annually, the farms yielded 819,490 dozen eggs, 83,500 pounds of cheese, four million pounds of potatoes, 3,500 bales of cotton, and 500,000 bushels of corn. Stan Redding, "Prison Work Programs Protect Inmate and Taxpayer," *Houston Chronicle*, July 9, 1970.

109. Dr. George Beto, untitled speech, Beto, SHSU, box 4/15.

110. "13,000 Inmates Call Him 'The Man,'" *Lutheran Layman*, October 1, 1965.

111. John Barbour, "America's Prisons Overflowing, but Texas Makes Them Work," *Houston Chronicle*, October 23, 1977.

112. "Former California Official Praises TDC as the 'General Motors' of Prisons," *Dallas Morning News*, August 2, 1979.

113. Fudge to Jim Estelle, April 15, 1974, Cushing Memorial Library, Texas A&M University, Estelle papers, *Ruiz* file.

114. Kevin Krajick, "Profile Texas," *Corrections Magazine*, March 1978, 13.

115. Dr. George Beto, "Address to the Southern Prisons Association," keynote address, New Orleans, Louisiana, April 1964, Beto, SHSU, and in author's possession.

Chapter 3

1. Affidavit, anonymous Texas prisoner, Brooks, TSLA, 1999/136-20.

2. David Ruiz to W. J. Estelle, July 10, 1978, Brooks, TSLA, 1999/136-20.

3. Horton and Nielson, *Walking George*.

4. Sykes, *Society of Captives*, 277.

5. Clemmer, *Prison Community*, 152

6. Chauncey, *Gay New York*, 9.

7. Benny Wade Clewis, oral history with Susanne Mason, 1997, in author's possession and used here with permission of Susanne Mason.

8. Before 1980, the exception to the "telephone pole" design was the Coffield Unit, built in 1965. Coffield was designed in a series of spokes that extended outward from the central building. At the time, it was the prison's largest unit, with a capacity to hold 4,000 prisoners. The prison was named for the prominent prison board member H. H. Coffield.

9. Michael Wayne Eubanks interview with the author, March 13, 2007, IOH, Baylor; Alvaro Luna Hernández, interview with the author, March 23, 2007, IOH, Baylor; Steven Blanchard, interview with the author, March 14, 2007, IOH, Baylor; Robert Lee Mudd, interview with the author, March 30, 2007, IOH, Baylor; Jerry Quate, interview with the author, March 6, 2007, IOH, Baylor; Walter Siros, interview with author,

June 15, 2005, IOH, Baylor; Walter Siros, interview with the author, June 15, 2006; Cecil Norris (former Texas prisoner from 1959 to 1979), interview with the author, June 18, 2006; Larry Casey (longtime Texas prisoner), letter to the author, June 18, 2006; Michael Eubanks (Texas prisoner since 1977), letter to the author, April 2, 2006.

10. Billy "Redbird" McCarter, oral history with Susanne Mason, October 20, 1997, in author's possession and used here with permission of Susanne Mason.

11. Robert King, *From the Bottom of the Heap: The Autobiography of Black Panther Robert Hillary King*, first draft of manuscript different from what was published, Amistad Research Center, Tulane University.

12. Winfred Rembert, *All Me: The Life and Art of Winfred Rembert*, documentary, interview provided to author.

13. Lawrence Pope, oral history conducted by John Wheat, 317, Pope, CAH, box 4C982.

14. The following chapter relies on oral histories, courtroom testimonies, court-monitored prisoner interviews, and legal affidavits to show how the internal prison economy operated. But for explicit testimony that shows the privileges of BTs, see the following trial transcripts. On the building tender's ability to have single cells and choice of cell assignment and cell partner, see David A. Christian at 149, 288, CAH, *Ruiz v. Estelle* Collection, Office of the Special Master, Vincent Nathan, Papers, 1979–92 (hereafter cited as *Ruiz* Special Master), MAI 8/J93; William Forrest at 1, *Ruiz* Special Master, MAI 9/J91; Hill at 12, *Ruiz* Special Master, MAI 8/92; James Lagermaier at 41–42, *Ruiz* Special Master, MAI 8/J98; Walter Harvey Ballard at 32, 36, *Ruiz* Special Master, MAI 8/J88; Francisco Guerra at 21–22, *Ruiz* Special Master, MAI 8/J91. On the BTs' ability to have more personal property, including clothes, stereos, and pets, see John Albach at 118, 207, *Ruiz* Special Master, MAI 8/J88; Arnold E. Pontesso at 113–14, *Ruiz* Special Master, MAI 8/J94; Jeters at 78–82, *Ruiz* Special Master, MAI 8/J102; David A. Christian at 103, *Ruiz* Special Master, MAI 8/J96; Francisco Guerra at 51–52, *Ruiz* Special Master, MAI 8/J91. On the BTs' close relationship to top prison officials, particularly assistant wardens and majors, see John Albach at 118, 207, *Ruiz* Special Master, MAI 8/J88; Arnold E. Pontesso at 113–14, *Ruiz* Special Master, MAI 8/J94; Jeters at 78–82, *Ruiz* Special Master, MAI 8/J102; David A. Christian at 103, *Ruiz* Special Master, MAI 8/J96; Francisco Guerra at 51–52, *Ruiz* Special Master, MAI 8/J91. On the BTs' access to weapons, ability to "run a store," manage a sex trade, and freely engage in prison rape, see James Eckles at 24–31, 42–44, 45–48, 234–35, 239–41, *Ruiz* Special Master, MAI 8/J-91; Guerrant at 14, 50, 87, *Ruiz* Special Master, MAI 8/J-92; Francisco Guerra at 18–19, 161–63, 165–70, *Ruiz* Special Master, MAI 8/J-91; Rosa Lee Knight at 24, *Ruiz* Special Master, MAI 8/J102; Paul Crosson at 28, 29, 72–73, *Ruiz* Special Master, MAI 8/9-96; Simonton at 27-30, *Ruiz* Special Master, MAI 8/J-88; Gibson at 46, 134, *Ruiz* Special Master, MAI 8/J-92; Eddie James Ward at 143, *Ruiz* Special Master, MAI 8/J-95; Hubbard at 150–53, *Ruiz* Special Master, MAI 8-92; Lovelace at 49–52, *Ruiz* Special Master, MAI 8/J-98; Robles at 32, 97, 113–14, *Ruiz* Special Master, MAI 8/J-99; Oscar Turner at 35, *Ruiz* Special Master, MAI 8/J-99.

15. Frank X. Leahy to Faye Morris and Michael E. Chase, August 27, 1977, Brooks, TSLA, 1991/136-23.

16. Frank X. Leahy to Faye Morris and Michael E. Chase, August 27, 1977, Brooks, TSLA, 1991/136-23.

17. "First Monitor's Report of the Factual Observations to the Special Master," General Counsel Office for the Texas Department of Correctional Justice (GC-TDCJ), *Ruiz*, TSLA, 2004/016 (hereafter cited as *Ruiz*, TSLA).

18. Testimony of Bertrand Jerome Bennett, *Ruiz* Special Master, MAI 8/J-88.

19. Michael Wayne Eubanks, oral history conducted by the author, March 13, 2007, IOH, Baylor.

20. "First Monitor's Report of the Factual Observations to the Special Master," *Ruiz*, TSLA, 2004/016.

21. Walter Siros, oral history conducted by the author, June 15, 2005, IOH, Baylor.

22. Hal Husbands, oral history with Susanne Mason, June 6, 1998, in author's possession and used here with permission of Susanne Mason.

23. Robert M. Cousins, oral history with Susanne Mason, June 8, 1998, in author's possession and used here with permission of Susanne Mason.

24. GC-TDCJ, "Inmate Statements," W. David Arnold interviews, *Ruiz*, TSLA, 2004/016-1.

25. Testimony of James Lagermaier, *Ruiz* Special Master, MAI 8/J98.

26. Benny Hudson, interview with W. David Arnold, September 21, 1981, *Ruiz* Special Master, 93-458/38; and GC-TDCJ, "Inmate Statements," W. David Arnold interviews, *Ruiz*, TSLA, 2004/016-1.

27. William Michael Smith (Inmate Number 307856), to the Southern District Court of Texas, August 15, 1981, *Ruiz* Special Master, 93-458/38; and GC-TDCJ, "Inmate Statements," W. David Arnold interviews, *Ruiz*, TSLA, 2004/016-1.

28. "Building Tender System: Supplemental Report," working paper by John Albach, Joint Committee on Prison Reform, *Ruiz* Special Master, MAI 8/J-85.

29. Transcript of interview, W. David Arnold report, *Ruiz* Special Master, 94-458/5; and in author's possession.

30. "Building Tender System: Supplemental Report," working paper by John Albach, Joint Committee on Prison Reform, *Ruiz* Special Master, MAI 8/J-85.

31. Article 6184L of the *Revised Civil Statutes of Texas* established that prisoners with a good prison record might gain additional time off of their initial sentence for every day served in prison. Article 6184l, *Revised Civil Statues of Texas*; Wayne Oakes, Committee Staff, Joint Committee on Prison Reform, "Custody and Security Working Paper," *Ruiz* Special Master, MAI 8/J-85.

32. Testimony of James Eckles, *Ruiz* Special Master, MAI-8/J91.

33. Letter from Steve Blanchard, inmate number 213745, to Gail Littlefield, attorney, Civil Rights Division, United States Department of Justice, November 24, 1973, TSLA, Papers of State Senator Ron Clower, box 1981/217-93.

34. Testimony of Francisco Guerra Jr., *Ruiz* Special Master, MAI-8/J2.

35. Walter Siros, oral history conducted by the author, June 15, 2005, IOH, Baylor.

36. The principles and rules of good time can be found in, Article 6184l, *Revised Civil Statues of Texas*; and Wayne Oakes, Committee Staff, Joint Committee on Prison Reform, "Custody and Security Working Paper," *Ruiz* Special Master, MAI 8/J-85.

37. Testimony of Stephan Thompson, *Ruiz* Special Master, MAI 8/J-92.

38. The descriptions of such punishments were made by a variety of prisoners; see Frances Jalet, "The Ellis Report," November 6, 1968, in author's possession, with permission by Robert Reps Perkinson, who received a copy of the confidential report from the personal papers of the attorney William Bennett Turner; Lawrence Pope, oral history conducted by John Wheat, Pope, CAH, 366.

39. Benny Wade Clewis, oral history with Susanne Mason, February 22, 1991, in author's possession and used here with permission of Susanne Mason.

40. Sample, *Racehoss*, 141.

41. Benny Wade Clewis, oral history with Susanne Mason, February 22, 1991, in author's possession and used here with permission of Susanne Mason.

42. Sample, *Racehoss*, 149.

43. Lawrence Pope, oral history conducted by John Wheat, Pope, CAH, 364.

44. Michael Eubanks, oral history with the author, March 13, 2007, IOH, Baylor.

45. Testimony of Francisco Guerra, *Ruiz* Special Master, MAI 8/J-91.

46. Charlie Combs, interview with the author, June 5, 2006, IOH, Baylor.

47. "Building Tender System: Supplemental Report," working paper by John Albach, Joint Committee on Prison Reform, *Ruiz* Special Master, MAI 8/J-85.

48. Hal Husbands, oral history with Susanne Mason, June 6, 1998, in author's possession and used here with permission of Susanne Mason.

49. Willett and Rozelle, *Warden*; Brandi Grissom, "Looking Back on Life as a Death House Warden," *New York Times*, March 26, 2011.

50. Jim Willet, interview with the author, June 20, 2005, IOH, Baylor.

51. Jim Willet, interview with the author, June 20, 2005, IOH, Baylor.

52. "Transcript of Inmate Interviews," conducted by W. David Arnold, TDCJ, TSLA, *Ruiz* General Counsel Papers, 2003/016-1-10; Benny Hudson (TDC #247579) interview with W. David Arnold, September 21, 1981, *Ruiz* Special Master, 93-458/38.

53. Dreyer v. Jalet, 349 F. Supp. 452 (1972).

54. Cecil Alexander, oral history with Susanne Mason, May 1999, in author's possession and used here with permission of Susanne Mason.

55. Benny Hudson (TDC #247570) interview with W. David Arnold, September 21, 1981, *Ruiz* Special Master, 94-458/5.

56. Anonymous building tender prisoner quoted in Kevin Krajik, "Is TDC the Paragon of Prison Systems . . . Or a Slave Plantation?" *Corrections Magazine*, 23, 7–23.

57. Frank X. Leahy to Faye Morris and Michael E. Chase, August 27, 1977, Brooks, TSLA, 1991/136-23.

58. U.S. Department of Justice, *Sourcebook*; Bruce Jackson to Alvin J. Bronstein, November 23, 1978, Clements Papers, Texas A&M; "Readings on Violence," Treatment Directorate Research and Development Division, TDC, Special Project No. 16, May 77, Texas A&M, Clements Papers, box 10.

59. C. L. McAdams, "Report of the Wynne Treatment Center," TDC, held in the private collection of the law firm Habern, O'Neill, and Pawgan, Huntsville, Texas, and in author's possession.

60. Sample, *Racehoss*, 145.

61. In the course of my research, I sent out a questionnaire to over one hundred prisoners in the Texas prison system that had been confined since at least 1975. My 2005

appearance on Houston's KPFT *Prison Radio* program allowed me to begin correspondence with prisoner activists still in Texas prisons. I received forty responses to my questionnaire, and I have drawn on some of that material here, particularly the following: Walter Siros, interview with the author, June 15, 2006; Cecil Norris (former Texas prisoner from 1959 to 1979), interview with the author, June 18, 2006; Larry Casey (longtime Texas prisoner), letter to the author, June 18, 2006; Michael Eubanks (Texas prisoner since 1977), letter to the author, April 2, 2006.

62. Testimony of Kenneth Hayes, October 30, 1978, *Ruiz* Special Master, MAI 8/92.

63. James Lagermaier testimony, December 21, 1978, and April 3, 1979, *Ruiz* Special Master, MAI 8/J98.

64. Michael Eubanks, oral history with the author, March 27, 2007, IOH, Baylor.

65. Walter Siros, oral history conducted by the author, June 15, 2005, IOH, Baylor.

66. On middle-class gender identity and the nineteenth century's "crisis" of the middle class, see Bederman, *Manliness and Civilization*, 5–20; Rotundo, *American Manhood*, 223–27, 244–46. On the postwar period's development of the other-directed, supposedly feminized, "organizational" man, see Potter, *People of Plenty*; Frazier, *Black Bourgeoisie*; Galbraith, *Affluent Society*; Riesman, *Lonely Crowd*; Marcuse, *One-Dimensional Man*; Bell, *Cultural Contradictions of Capitalism*. For a critique of the middle-class anxiety over masculinity during the 1950s, see Gilbert, *Man in the Middle*. On the role that consumption, domesticity, and suburbanization played in forming male identity and middle-class gender roles, see Cross, *All-Consuming Century*; May, *Homeward Bound*; and Weiss, *To Have*.

67. On working-class violence and its connection to honor and masculinity, see Gorn, "Good-Bye Boys," 388–410; Wyatt-Brown, *Southern Honor*; Kaplan, "New York City Tavern," 591–618; Gallant, "Honor, Masculinity," 359–82; Spierenburg, "Masculinity, Violence, and Honor," 1–29; Chudacoff, *Age of the Bachelor*, 227–28; Gorn, *Manly Art*, 185–96; D'Cruze, "Unguarded Passions," 14–16; Conley, *Melancholy Accidents*, 18; Adler, *First in Violence*, esp. 26–44. On the development of a working-class masculinity as a counternarrative to the middle-class ideal during the postwar period, see Lipsitz, *Time Passages*; Slotkin, *Gunfighter Nation*; McNally, *Frankie Goes to Hollywood*; Lipsitz, *Rainbow at Midnight*; Gilbert, *Cycle of Outrage*; Wilson, *American Tough*.

68. Arthur Johnson (a.k.a. Haneef Pasha), interview with the author, March 20, 2007, IOH, Baylor.

69. Steven Blanchard, oral history with the author, March 14, 2007, IOH, Baylor University.

70. Ray Hill, *Rebels, Rubyfruit and Rhinestones*, 213.

71. Ray Hill, interview with author, November 8, 2005, IOH, Baylor.

72. On the need to connect antigay work with antiracist work, see Berubé, "How Gay Stays White," 225.

73. On the difference between prison's assigned and sexualized gender roles and the post-Stonewall effort to create among prisoners, "lessons in being gay," see Kunzel, "Lessons in Being Gay," 11–30; Kunzel, *Criminal Intimacy*, 191–224.

74. Ray Hill, oral history with the author, November 8, 2005, IOH, Baylor.

75. "Treatment of the Mentally Ill and the Mentally Retarded—Working Paper," submitted to the Joint Committee on Prison Reform, by Jim Gibson, committee staff, *Ruiz* Special Master, MAI 8/J-85.

76. Ray Hill, oral history with the author, November 8, 2005, IOH, Baylor.

77. Quote attributed to Alan Pogue during a conversation, with his permission, while in Austin, Texas, viewing his photography of Texas prisons, September 17, 2015.

78. Michael Eubanks, oral history with the author, March 27, 2007, IOH, Baylor.

79. On the practice of issuing and making prison-made "marriage" and "divorce" certificates among female prisoners, see Propper, *Prison Homosexuality*, 1–9, figs. 1-1 and 1-2 showing examples of marriage certificates.

80. Sample, *Racehoss*, 181–82.

81. Floyd Patterson, oral history with Susanne Mason, in author's possession and used here with permission of Susanne Mason.

82. Michael Chase to Jim Estelle, December 14, 1976, "Frank Leahy file," Brooks, TSLA, 1991/136-23; Michael E. Chase and Frank X. Leahy, "Defendants' Request for Stay of the Proceeding," Wynne Unit Disciplinary Committee, "Frank Leahy file," Brooks, TSLA, 1991/136-23.

83. Dundes, "'Jumping the Broom,'" 324–39; Parry, "Married in Slavery Time," 273–312.

84. Ray Hill, oral history with the author, November 8, 2005, IOH, Baylor.

85. Donald Tucker, "Punk's Song," excerpt, private papers of David Ruiz, in the author's possession.

86. Ray Hill, oral history with the author, November 8, 2005, IOH, Baylor.

87. Donald Tucker, "Punk's Song," emphasis in original.

88. Rideau and Sinclar, "Prisoner Litigation," 1061–76.

89. King, *From the Bottom*, unpublished first draft manuscript, Amistad,10.

90. Albert Woodfox, *Solitary*, 26.

91. Rideau, "Prison," 54, 60–61, 51–78.

92. Rideau, "Prison," 54.

93. Floyd Patterson, oral history with Susanne Mason, in author's possession and used here with permission by Susanne Mason.

94. Patterson and Conrad, *Scottsboro Boy*.

95. On James Dunn and his sexual enslavement, see Wilbert Rideau and Billy Sinclair, "Prison: The Sexual Jungle," *The Angolite*, Amistad Archives, Tulane University.

96. Rideau, "Prison," 61.

97. Woodfox, 26.

98. Novak v. Beto, 320 F. Supp. 1206 (S.D. Tex. 1970).

99. I am indebted to Ethan Blue's exploration of building tenders' cultural power during the Great Depression as an expression of Bourdieu's "symbolic capital." In his analysis of Texas prison culture during the Depression, Blue termed the building tenders' sexual violence as "statecraft." During the postwar period, however, the state relied on building tenders more than ever to uphold their modernization narrative, while at the same time the construction of cells allowed more informal rewards to accrue. When civil rights revolution erupted within Texas prisons, the first line of defense for the state was the informal power of building tenders to quell dissent and prisoner organizing. For an analysis of building tenders during the 1930s drawn from Bourdieu, see Blue, *Doing Time*, 102–9.

100. Former Building Tender letter to David W. Arnold, Office of the General Counsel, "Inmate Statements," W. David Arnold interviews, TDCJ, TSLA, 2004/016-1-10.

101. Jerry Quate, oral history with the author, March 12, 2007, IOH, Baylor.

102. Chauncey offered this definition for the relationship between "punks" and "wolves" in the public culture of New York City before 1929: "Punk generally genoted a physically slighter youth who let himself be used sexually by an older and more powerful man, the wolf, in exchange for money, protection, or other forms of support." On the construction of the "third sex," see Chauncey, *Gay New York*, 47–64. On "husbands, wolves, and punks" in the public space of New York City before 1929, see Chauncey, *Gay New York*, 88, 86–97. Unlike the rapacious world of the prison, the presence of violence was minimal in Chauncey's explorations of male relationships of sexual exchange in urban space.

103. Jerry Quate, oral history with the author, March 12, 2007, IOH, Baylor.

104. Testimony of Bobby Taylor, *Ruiz* Special Master, MAI 8/J-95.

105. John Makeig, "Man Alleges Vendetta by Police, then Convicted of Burglary," *Houston Chronicle*, March 16, 1986; Terri Cook, "Ainsworth's 99-year Prison Term Affirmed," *Galveston News*, February 8, 1986; Joel Kirkpatrick, "'Butch' Ainsworth Wounded," *Galveston Daily News*, April 28, 1984; Rebecca Galvan, "Gay Inmates Were Assigned as Porters, Warden Testifies," *Houston Chronicle*, May 23, 1989.

106. Lawrence Pope to David Arnold, re: violations of building tender agreement, Pope, CAH, 4C771; Lawrence Pope to Board of Corrections, re: William "Butch" Ainsworth (213700), Pope, CAH, 4C771.

107. Judge William Wayne Justice, memorandum opinion, *Ruiz v. Estelle*, Papers of Frances Jalet-Cruz, CAH, 94/042-16.

108. "Michael Jewell file," Brooks, TSLA, 1999/136-21.

109. For scholarship on the rarity of rape in prison, see Davis, "Sexual Assaults," 102–13. As a reflection of the paucity of reliable statistical data on prison rape, the George W. Bush administration signed into law on September 4, 2003, the Prison Rape Elimination Act of 2003 (P.L. 108–79), which requires the Bureau of Justice Statistics (BJS) to collect data on sexual assault within correctional facilities as part of an effort to "eliminate" prison rape. See U.S. Department of Justice, Office of Justice Program, "Data Collection for the Prison Rape Elimination Act of 2003,." June 30, 2004, Bureau of Justice Statistics, Status Report. For an account that does not consider sexual trade in prison as rape, see Fleisher and Kienert, *The Myth of Prison Rape*.

110. For sociological studies that view prison rape through the lens of individual pathology and cultural systems of prison hypermasculinity, see Lockwood, *Prison Sexual Violence*; Nacci and Kane, "Sex and Sexual Aggression," 46–53; Wooden and Parker, *Men behind Bars*; and Wright, "Violent and the Victimized," 103–22.

111. For sociological studies of prison homosexuality, see Buffum, *Homosexuality in Prison*; Fishman, *Sex in Prison*; Kirkham, "Homosexuality in Prison," 325–44; Weiss and Friar, *Terror in the Prisons*. For work that considers consensual homosexual relationships among female prisoners, see Propper, *Prison Homosexuality*.

112. For an analysis that considers underreporting of male rape, see Eigenberg, "Rape in Male Prisons," 145–66.

113. Anonymous prisoner to W. David Arnold, Monitor, October 31, 1981, TDCJ, TSLA, *Ruiz* General Counsel Papers, 2004/016-1-10.

114. Freedman, *Redefining Rape*, 5.

115. Akers, Hayner, and Gruninger, "Homosexual and Drug Behavior"; Bartollas, Miller, and Dinitz, "White Victim"; Buffum, "Racial Factors in Homosexuality"; Carroll, *Hacks, Blacks, and Cons*; Carroll, "Humanitarian Reform"; Danziger, "Sexual Assaults"; Davis, "Sexual Assaults"; Zeringer, "Sexual Assaults."

116. Scacco, *Rape in Prison*, 62.

117. Rundle quoted in Rideau, "Prison: The Sexual Jungle."

118. On the "deprivation model," see Sykes, *Society of Captives*; Goffman, "Characteristics of Total Institutions"; Akers, Hayner, and Gruninger, "Homosexual and Drug Behavior"; Akers, Hayner, and Werner, "Prizonization in Five Countries"; and Giallombardo, *Society of Women*.

119. For works emphasizing the "importation model," see Irwin and Cressey, "Thieves, Convicts"; Irwin, *Prisons in Turmoil*; Schrag, "Some Foundations"; and Schwartz, "Pre-institutional vs. Situational Influence."

120. Kunzel, *Criminal Intimacy*, 189

121. *Ruiz* trial transcript, MAI 8/J-91, CAH.

122. James Adams to Chet Brooks, September 12, 1977, Brooks, TSLA, 1999/136-8.

123. Steven Blanchard, oral history with the author, March 14, 2007.

124. Steven Blanchard, oral history with the author, March 14, 2007.

125. In addition to sexual intimidation and rape, physical violence was also used against Blanchard to scare him away from joining the civil rights litigation. During the *Ruiz* trial, Jerry Ben Ulmer testified that Major John Holmes of the Ramsey unit solicited Ulmer in the summer of 1975 to "scare off" some *Ruiz* witnesses. A convict guard provided Ulmer with a knife that he then used to slash Blanchard about the neck and arms. When the state attorney Harry Walsh asked Ulmer: "Why didn't you kill Blanchard?" he was met with a mocking response: "Why take his life," testified Ulmer, "when all you want to do is scare him off." After slashing Blanchard, Ulmer testified that he met Major Holmes and the "the major smiled and just said 'later.'" Ulmer testified that he was not punished for this act of violence. Ulmer's testimony shows how building tenders understood that violence was an acceptable form of intimidation and control, while murder was unnecessary. *Houston Chronicle*, October 7, 1978, news clippings, Brown collection, in author's possession.

126. Testimony of Salvador Gonzalez, *Ruiz* Special Master, MAI 8/J-91.

127. Huggins, "Study of Family Units," 79–85.

128. Final Report of the Joint Committee on Prison Reform, 63rd Legislature, December 1974, in author's possession.

129. Saralee Tiede, "Inmate Protest Conditions in Women's Prisons; Goree Warden Disputes Charges of Bad Food, Mental Harassment," *Dallas Times Herald*, April 2, 1978.

130. Saralee Tiede, "Inmate Protests Conditions in Women's Prison; Goree Warden Disputes Charges of Bad Food, Mental Harassment," *Dallas Times Herald*, April 3, 1978.

131. Esther Chavez, committee staff, "Women in Prison in Texas," working paper submitted to the Joint Committee on Prison Reform (JCPR), *Ruiz* Special Master, MAI 8/J103.

132. Final Report of the Joint Committee on Prison Reform, 63rd Legislature, December 1974, in author's possession.

133. Conviction data as of September 1, 1973, from the chart "Table 7: Major Offenses of Inmate Population," compiled by TDC for the JCPR and in Esther Chavez, commit-

tee staff, "Women in Prison in Texas," working paper submitted to the JCPR, *Ruiz* Special Master, MAI 8/J103.

134. Sentencing data as of September 1, 1973, from the chart "Table 12: Sentence Length of Inmate Population," compiled by TDC for the JCPR and in Esther Chavez, committee staff, "Women in Prison in Texas," working paper submitted to the JCPR, *Ruiz* Special Master, MAI 8/J103.

135. Prior incarcerations in TDC data as of September 1, 1973, from "Table 9: Prior Confinements in TDC of Inmate Population," compiled by TDC for the JCPR and in Esther Chavez, committee staff, "Women in Prison in Texas," working paper submitted to the JCPR, *Ruiz* Special Master, MAI 8/J103.

136. Prior incarcerations in other states as of September 1, 1973, from "Table 12: Sentence Length of Inmate Population," compiled by TDC for the JCPR and in Esther Chavez, committee staff, "Women in Prison in Texas," working paper submitted to the JCPR, *Ruiz* Special Master, MAI 8/J103.

137. Prior confinement data in reformatories as of September 1, 1973, from "Table 10: Prior Confinements in Reformatories of Inmate Population," compiled by TDC for the JCPR and in: Esther Chavez, committee staff, "Women in Prison in Texas," working paper submitted to the JCPR, *Ruiz* Special Master, MAI 8/J103.

138. Demographical data on age drawn from "Table 1: Age Groups of the Inmate Population" compiled by TDC for the JCPR. Esther Chavez, committee staff, "Women in Prison in Texas," working paper submitted to the JCPR, *Ruiz* Special Master, MAI 8/J103.

139. Final Report of the Joint Committee on Prison Reform, 63rd Legislature, December 1974, 80, in author's possession.

140. Final Report of the Joint Committee on Prison Reform, 63rd Legislature, December 1974, 82, in author's possession.

141. Esther Chavez, committee staff, "Women in Prison in Texas," working paper submitted to the JCPR, 16, *Ruiz* Special Master, MAI 8/J103.

142. Esther Chavez, committee staff, "Women in Prison in Texas," working paper submitted to the JCPR, 16, *Ruiz* Special Master, MAI 8/J103.

143. Esther Chavez, committee staff, "Women in Prison in Texas," working paper submitted to the JCPR, *Ruiz* Special Master, MAI 8/J103.

144. Esther Chavez, committee staff, "Women in Prison in Texas," working paper submitted to the JCPR, *Ruiz* Special Master, MAI 8/J103.

145. Freedman, "Prison Lesbian," 397.

146. Saralee Tiede, "Inmate Protests Conditions in Women's Prison: Goree Warden Disputes Charges of Bad Food, Mental Harassment," *Dallas Times Herald*, April 2, 1978; Miriam Korshak, "Do Demands of Equality Include Right to Get into More Trouble?," *Houston Chronicle*, November 24, 1974; and Quinlan file, news clippings, Pope, CAH, 4C825.

147. Testimony of Rosa Lee Knight, October 24, 1978, *Ruiz* Special Master, MAI 8/J102.

148. Miriam Korshak, "Do Demands of Equality Include Right to Get into More Trouble?" *Houston Chronicle*, November 24, 1974.

149. On "collective trauma" and its cultural power to impart communal identity, see Alexander et al., *Collective Trauma*, 22; and Robben and Suarez-Orozco, *Cultures under*

Siege. For a critique on the problematic application of "cultural trauma" to historical analysis, see Kansteiner, "Genealogy," 193–22. For a historically based application of "collective trauma" to slavery and the formation of Black identity, see Eyerman, *Cultural Trauma*. For its application to the civil rights movement and a sense of shared identity towards community mobilization, see McGuire, "'It Was Like,'" 906–31.

150. Kunzel, "Situating Sex," 255, 253–70.

151. Testimony of Lionel W. Lippman, *Ruiz* Special Master, MAI 8/J-102.

Chapter 4

1. "Minutes of the Texas Board of Corrections" (1966), 3733, November 27, 1966, TDCJ, TSLA, box 1998/038-13.

2. Octavio Paz, *Labyrinth of Solitude*, 14.

3. Montejáno, *Quixote's Soldiers*, 23.

4. García, *Rise of the Mexican*, 310.

5. Montejáno, *Quixote's Soldiers*, 23–24.

6. Rudy Portillo, oral history with Susanne Mason, February 9, 2003, in author's possession and used here with permission of Susanne Mason.

7. Rios, *Punished*, xv.

8. Alvarez, *Power of the Zoot*, 8.

9. Victor Rios applied infrapolitics as a way to circumvent what he called "racialized punitive social control," which he defined as a system of ubiquitous and racially targeted punishment that constituted "the process by which individuals come to feel stigmatized, outcast, shamed, defeated or hopeless." Criminalization, according to Rios, enacted punishment against youths of color, while the youths themselves embraced their criminalization and reframed it as a paradoxical dissident political culture. Such a paradoxical dialectic stretched the boundaries of state legibility because, as Rios astutely observed, the youths "had gained redress for the punitive social control they had encountered by adopting a subculture of resistance based on fooling the system and by committing crimes of resistance, which made no sense to the system but were fully recognizable to those who had been misrecognized and criminalized." Rios, *Punished*, xv, 123.

10. On the racialization that occurs through "intelligence" testing that is often biased against Mexican Americans, see Chávez-García, "Intelligence Testing," 193–229; Blanton, "From Intellectual Deficiency," 39–62; Blanton, *Strange Career*; Valencia, *Chicano Students*.

11. William Gates, TDC clinical psychologist, quoted in Ethan Watters, "The Love Story That Upended the Texas Prison System," *Texas Monthly*, October 11, 2018.

12. Rudy Portillo, oral history with Susanne Mason, February 9, 2003, in author's possession and used here with permission of Susanne Mason.

13. Rudy Portillo, oral history with Susanne Mason, February 9, 2003, in author's possession and used here with permission of Susanne Mason.

14. In 1961, 117,368 Bracero workers came to Texas of a total number 291,420 entering the United States. On the Bracero program in Texas, see Scruggs, "Bracero Program," 251–64; and Galarza, *Spiders in the House*.

15. On the transnational experience of Bracero workers, see Cohen, *Braceros*. On the end of the Bracero program, see Flores, "Town Full," 124–43. On the dissident culture,

civil rights activism, and labor politics of Bracero workers in the Salinas valley, California, see Flores, *Grounds for Dreaming*.

16. On "policing Mexicano mobility" before the age of mass incarceration, see Hernández, "Crimes and Consequences," 421–44; Hernández, *U.S. Border Patrol*, 46.

17. On the changing racial perceptions of Mexican Americans in Texas, see De León, *They Call Them Greasers*; Foley, *White Scourge*; and Montejano, *Anglos and Mexicans*.

18. Trulson and Marquart, *First Available Cell*, 80–81.

19. Diaz, "Cultural Resilience and Resistance."

20. *Annual Report of the Prison Board*, 1946, 37–38, TSLA.

21. Guadalupe Guajardo, interview with the author, March 8, 2007, IOH, Baylor.

22. Rudy Portillo, oral history with Susanne Mason, February 9, 2003, in author's possession and used here with permission of Susanne Mason.

23. Beto's master's thesis in history was titled "The Marburg Colloquy of 1529: A Textual Study," and his dissertation was titled "Arguments Found in the Literature for the Continued Existence of the Protestant Church–Related Liberal Arts College." Additionally, he completed his PhD language requirement in Latin, which was a reflection of the six years of Latin he received as part of the classical liberal arts curriculum of Concordia College.

24. Texas Prison Board Meeting Minutes, March 1957, TDCJ, TSLA, 1998/038-10.

25. For a biographical account of Beto's life and his role in fashioning control penology, see Horton and Nielson, *Walking George*.

26. Ruffin v. Commonwealth 62 Va 790 (1871).

27. Ruffin v. Commonwealth, 21 Gratt. 790, 62 VA 790 (1871).

28. Wallace, "*Ruffin v. Virginia*," 333–42.

29. Fradella, "Meritorious Claims," 24–55. On federalism as the lynchpin for the emerging "hands off" doctrine, see "Constiutional Rights of Prisoners: The Developing Law," 985–1008.

30. On the legal evolution of "civil death," see McLennan, "Convict's Two Lives," 191–219.

31. Avery v. Everett, 18 N.E. 148 (NY 1888).

32. The number of prisoners' rights cases that cited *Ruffin v. Commonwealth* before 1964 include the following cases: Huffaker v. Commonwealth, 98 S.W. 331, 332 (Ky. 1906); Karnes v. Commonwealth, 99 S.E. 562, 564 (Va. 1919); State v. Griffith, 107 S.E. 302, 303 (W. Va. 1921); Frankel v. Woodrough, 7F.2d 796, 798, C.C.A.8 (Neb. 1925); State v. Dignam, 171 S.E. 527, 528 (W. Va. 1933); Moss v. Hyer, 171 S.E. 527, 528 (W. Va. 1934); Reynolds v. Milk Commission of Virginia, 177 S.E. 44, 47 (Va. 1934); Reynolds v. Milk Commission of Virginia, 179 S.E. 507, 517 (Va. 1935); Hager v. Homuth, 276 N.W. 668, 672 (N.D. 1937); Howell v. Com., 46 S.E. 2d 37, 41 (Va. 1948); Sigmon v. U.S. 110F. Supp. 906, 907 (Va. 1953); Nibert v. Carroll Trucking Co., 82 S.E. 2d 445, 452 (W. Va. 1954); Duncan v. Ulmer, 191 A.2d 617, 622 (Me. 1963).

33. State v. Dignan, 181 S.E. 527, 114 W. VA 275 (W. Va. 1933).

34. Anderson v. Salant, L.R.A. 1916D, 651, 38 R.I. 463, 96A. 425 (R.I. 1916).

35. Moss v. Hyer, 172 S.E. 795 (W. Va. 1934).

36. Westbrook v. State, 133 Ga. 578 (1909).

37. Westbrook v. State, 133 Ga. 578 (1909).

38. Westbrook v. State, 133 Ga. 578 (1909).

39. The literary scholar Dennis Childs sees *Westbrook* as "the law's very disavowal of neoslavery" while simultaneously "re-chattelize[ing] the 'free' black civil subject." As Davis put it, the court saw Westbrook's whipping as an "unlawful invasion" only within a circumscribed ruling that offered "a backdoor normalization of the very condition of possibility for Westbrook's torture and James Davis's biological death—that is, the chain-gang system itself." Childs, *Slaves of the State*, 51–52.

40. Coffin v. Reichard, 143 F.2d 443 (1944).

41. United States ex rel. Atterbury v. Ragen, 237 F.2d 953 (7th Cir. 1956) cert. denied, 353 U.S. 964 (1957).

42. Trop v. Dulles, 356 U.S. 86 (1958).

43. Monroe v. Pape, 365 U.S. 167 (1961).

44. Section 1983 of the Civil Rights Act of 1871 stipulates that "every person who, under color of any statue, ordinance, regulation, custom, or usage of any State or Territory subjects, or causes to be subjected, any citizen of the United States or other person within the jurisdiction thereof to the deprivation of any rights, privileges, or immunities secured by the Constitution and laws shall be liable to the party injured in an action at law, suit in equity, or other proper proceeding for redress."

45. Robinson v. California, 370 U.S. 660 (1962).

46. Jones v. Cunningham, 371 U.S. 236 (1963).

47. On the Supreme Court's historic rejection of the "hands off" doctrine and its embrace of prisoners as citizens with a right to be heard in court, see *Yale Law Journal*, "Beyond the Ken"; Fliter, *Prisoners' Rights*; DiIulio, *Courts, Corrections*; Mushlin, "Prison Reform Revisited, 395–417; and Feely and Rubin, *Judicial Policy Making*.

48. Cooper v. Pate, 378 U.S. 546 (1964). On the ways in which the law circumscribed prisoner aims through the legal "translation" of their claims, see Losier, "'Strictly Religious Reasons,'" 19–38.

49. Wolff v. McDonnell, 414 U.S. 539 (1974), 555–56.

50. *Annual Report of the Director of the Administrative Office of United States Courts* for each year. Thomas, *Prisoner Litigation*, 61.

51. On the mid-twenteith-century "rights revolution" in U.S. law, see Epps, *Rights Revolution*; Horwitz, *Warren Court*; Mackenzie and Weisbrot, *Liberal Hour*; and Tani, *States of Dependency*.

52. For cases that challenged the all-white democratic primary in Texas, see Nixon v. Herndon, 273 U.S. 536 (1927); Nixon v. Condon, 286 U.S. 73 (1932); Grovey v. Townsend, 295 U.S. 45 (1935).

53. On the struggle over the all-white primary in Texas, see Hine, *Black Victory*; Hine, "Blacks and the Destruction," 43–59; and Behnken, *Fighting Their Own Battles*, 18–21. Smith v. Allwright, 321 U.S. 649 (1944); Sweatt v. Painter, 339 U.S. 629 (1950).

54. Behnken, *Fighting Their Own Battles*, 72–83.

55. For historians that stress racial contestation between African American civil rights struggles and Mexican American "whiteness" politics, see Behnken, *Fighting Their Own Battles*; Foley, *White Scourge*; López, *Racism on Trial*; Guglielmo, "Fighting for Caucasian Rights."

56. In re Rodriguez, 81 F. 337 (1897); Delgado v. Bastrop ISD, No. 388 Civil, Final Judgment (1948); Hernandez v. Texas, 347 U.S. 475 (1954); Hernandez v. Driscoll (CISD), Civil Action No. 1348 (S.D. Texas 1957).

57. García, *Viva Kennedy*; Gómez-Quiñones, *Chicano Politics*; Rodriguez Jr., *Henry B. Gonzalez*; Sloane, *Gonzalez of Texas*; Flynn, *Henry B. Gonzalez*.

58. Behnken, *Fighting Their Own Battles*, 27.

59. Frantz Fanon quoted in diary of Fred Cruz, 1967, Papers of Frances Jalet-Cruz, CAH, 94-042/2.

60. In his account of race and nationalism, Gary Gerstle discerns two simultaneous political traditions—civic nationalism and the more exclusionary power of racial nationalism. He defined civic nationalism as "a kind of democratic univeralism that can take root anywhere" that locates "the transformative power of the United States not in God but in the nation's core political ideals, in the American belief in the fundamental equality of all human beings, in every individual's inalienable rights to life, liberty, and the pursuit of happiness, and in a democratic government that derives its legitimacy from the people's consent." Gerstle, *American Crucible*, 4.

61. Diary of Fred Cruz, 1967, Papers of Frances Jalet-Cruz, CAH, 94-042/2.

62. On the ways in which El Movimento cast Mexican Americans within the dialectic of internal colonialism, see Almaguer, "Study of Chicano Colonialism," 137–42; Lopez, *Racism on Trial*; Muñoz, *Youth, Identity, Power*; Navarro, *Mexican American Youth Organization*; Oropeza, *Raza Si! Guerra No!*; Arturo, *Testimonio*; Pulido, *Black, Brown*; and Marsical, *Brown Eyed Children*.

63. On "bibliotherapy" as intellectual uplift, see Cummins, *Rise and Fall*, 21–32.

64. Berger, *Captive Nation*, 61.

65. Spencer, *Revolution Has Come*, 51.

66. On Thomas X Cooper's legal challenge against the Stateville Penitentiary for the state's denial of his religious freedoms, see Jacobs, *Stateville*, 52–73; and Gilmore, "States of Incarceration," chap. 6, 224–82.

67. Glenn McCarthy, a millionaire oilman, established the Shamrock Hotel on South Main Street in Houston.

68. Testimony of George Beto, *Dreyer v. Jalet*, Beto, SHSU, 1-2/1.

69. Between 1970 and 1978, compulsory prison education at Windham resulted in the granting of more than 10,000 high school diplomas or equivalency certificates. In 1965, Beto launched a two-year junior college program allowing prisoners an associate's degree by taking college-level courses in the prison through Alvin, Lee, Brazosport, and Henderson County junior colleges. Four-year college programs became available by 1966, and in 1969 the first prisoner earned a bachelor's degree, followed by another 18 prisoners by 1978. In its first year, the Windham School District had a budget of two million dollars, and it employed a school superintendent, 6 principals, 174 classroom teachers, 34 vocational teachers, 4 counselors, and 8 librarians and nurses. After the initial allotment, the prison system provided only space, utilities, and maintenance, while school costs were paid by state educational agencies. In an estimation of Beto's educational and vocational training program, Dr. Garland S. Wollard, the director of education for the U.S. Bureau of Prisons, extolled the educational improvements: "Texas is definitely providing the leadership that most of the states should follow in establishing educational and vocational programs within their prisons." Horton and Nielsen, *Walking George*, 131; Kevin Krajick, "Is TDC the Paragon of Prison Systems . . . or a Slave Plantation?" *Corrections Magazine*, March 1978, 6–23; Steven Gettinger, "The Windham School District," *Corrections Magazine*, March 1978, 14–15; Stan Red-

ding, "Texas Prison Training Among Best: Convict Program Ranges from Job Skills to College." *Houston Chronicle*, July 8, 1970.

70. Hoping to implement a religious program centered on Christianity, Beto initiated in May 1963 a major revision in the religious program by augmenting the chaplains' standards to insist that chaplains must have college and seminary degrees. Moreover, Beto sought the support of the Texas Council of Churches to boost its funding of prison chaplains, and he awarded PIP points to those prisoners who attended religious services. Horton and Nielsen, *Walking George*, 135.

71. "Beto Describes Fred Cruz Cruz as Nonconformist," *Houston Chronicle*, May 26, 1972.

72. From 1935 to 1941, McAdams served as a guard at the Wynne Farm. He was promoted to assistant warden at Wynne upon his return in 1948, and he became the warden at Ramsey in 1951 and stayed at that position until 1961 when George Beto handpicked him to oversee the construction of the Ellis unit from 1961 to 1964. McAdams then became the first warden at Ellis from 1964 until 1969, when he was transferred to Wynne where he remained warden until his retirement in 1971. Application of Employment by Carl Luther McAdams, Open Records request, TDCI, March 14, 2019.

73. "Warden McAdams' Career Traces Colorful TDC History," by Doug Murdock, news clipping, C. L. "Beartracks" McAdams file, Texas Prison History Museum, hereafter referred to as "TPHM"; "Big Beartracks McAdams Works a Miracle While Building a Prison," *Houston Chronicle*, 1963, McAdams file, TPHM; "Change at Ramsey: Smither Unit to Acquire Warden McAdams in May," March 1961, McAdams file, TPHM; Carl L. McAdams resume, compiled by Wilma Manos and Beverly Johnson, TPHM.

74. Carl Luther McAdams, oral history with Susanne Mason, August 9, 1996, in author's possession and used here with permission of Susanne Mason.

75. Carl Luther McAdams, oral history with Susanne Mason, August 9, 1996, in author's possession and used here with permission of Susanne Mason.

76. Diary of Fred Cruz, 1967, Papers of Frances Jalet-Cruz, CAH, 94-042/2.

77. Anonymous prisoner to Walter White, November 14, 1947, Jester, TSLA.

78. Homer B. Adams v. O.B. Ellis, 194 F.2d 483; and Sigel v. Ragen, 180 F.2d 785, cert. denied, 339 U.S. 990, reh'g denied, 390 U.S. 847; Prison Board Meeting Minutes, TDCJ, TSLA, September 1954.

79. Johnson v. Avery, 252 F. Supp. 783 (M.D. Tenn. 1966); Johnson v. Avery, 382 F.2d 353 (6th Cir. 1967).

80. Diary of Fred Cruz, 1967, Papers of Frances Jalet-Cruz, CAH, 94-042/2.

81. Diary of Fred Cruz, 1967, Papers of Frances Jalet-Cruz, CAH, 94-042/2.

Chapter 5

1. On grassroots struggles to address income inequality that stretched the boundaries of Great Society antipoverty programs, see Korstad and Lelouids, *To Right These Wrongs*; Orleck and Hazirjian, *War on Poverty*; Orleck, *Storming Caesars Palace*. For a political account of how liberals structured workfare into antipoverty federal program, such as Aid to Dependent Children (ADC), see Mittlestadt, *From Welfare to Workfare*.

2. Diary of Fred Cruz, 1967, Papers of Frances Jalet Cruz, CAH, 94-042/2.

3. Fred Cruz to Frances Jalet, fifteen-page hand-written letter, in author's possession.

4. Cruz v. Beto, Appendix volume 4, 77-1641, Defendants' Exhibit 55, Beto, SHSU.

5. Carl Luther McAdams, oral history with Susanne Mason, August 9, 1996, in author's possession and used here with permission of Susanne Mason.

6. Cruz v. Beto, Appendix volume 4, 77-1641, Defendants' Exhibit 55, Beto, SHSU.

7. Fred Cruz to Frances Jalet, fifteen-page hand-written letter, in author's possession.

8. Frances Jalet to Anthony G. Amsterdam, November 6, 1968, "The Ellis Report," in author's possession.

9. Frances Jalet to Anthony G. Amsterdam, November 6, 1968, "The Ellis Report," in author's possession.

10. Frances Jalet to Anthony G. Amsterday, November 6, 1968, "The Ellis Report," in author's possession.

11. Frances Jalet to Anthony G. Amsterdam, November 6, 1968, "The Ellis Report," in author's possession.

12. In addition to seeing Malcom's role in the Hinton assault as a public critique against police brutality, Manning Marable also cast it as the event that "set in motion the forces culminating in Malcolm's inevitable rupture with the Nation of Islam" as it made the NOI's future growth contingent on "its being immersed in the black community's struggles of daily existence." Marable, *Race, Reform, and Rebellion*, 129.

13. Essiem-Udom, *Black Nationalism*, 378; Marable, *Race, Reform, and Rebellion*, 60.

14. On Muslims in America, see Baer, *Black Spiritual Movement*; Lincoln, *Black Muslims in America*; Marsh, *From Black Muslims*; McCloud, *African American Islam*; Curtis, *Black Muslim Religion*; Banks, *Black Muslims*. On Muslims in California's prison system, see Cummins, *Rise and Fall*, 63–92. On Malcolm X's prison term as a transformative experience, see Malcolm X, *Autobiography of Malcolm X*. On NOI and Black Power after Malcolm X, see Taylor, "Elijah Muhammad's."

15. Felber, "'Shades of Mississippi,'" 141.

16. Prison Board Meeting Minutes, March 1961, TDCJ, TSLA, 1998/38-11.

17. Testimony of George Beto, Drever v. Jalet, Beto, SHSU, 1-2/1; "Prison Hits at Muslim Recruiting," *Austin American Statesman*, July 11, 1963.

18. Billy "Redbird" McCarter, oral history conducted by Jim Willett, May 22, 2003, TPHM.

19. Lawrence Pope, oral history conducted by John Wheat, Pope, CAH, box 4C982.

20. Carl Robbins, interview with Susanne Mason, in author's possession and with permission of Susanne Mason.

21. Al Slaton, oral history with Robert Perkinson, July 2002, in author's possession and used with Robert Perkinson's permission.

22. Carl Luther McAdams, oral history with Susanne Mason, August 9, 1996, in author's possession and used here with permission of Susanne Mason.

23. Frances Jalet to Anthony G. Amsterdam, November 6, 1968, "The Ellis Report," in author's possession.

24. Floyd Patterson, oral history with Susanne Mason, in author's possession and used here with permission of Susanne Mason.

25. Billy Wayne McCarter, oral history with Susanne Mason, October 20, 1997, in author's possession and used here with permission of Susanne Mason.

26. Frances Jalet to Anthony G. Amsterdam, November 6, 1968, "The Ellis Report," in author's possession.

27. Frances Jalet to Anthony G. Amsterdam, November 6, 1968, "The Ellis Report," in author's possession.

28. Frances Jalet to Anthony G. Amsterdam, November 6, 1968, "The Ellis Report," in author's possession.

29. William Bennett Turner interview with the author, September 30, 2019.

30. Novak v. Beto, 320 F. Supp. 1206 (S.D. Tex. 1970).

31. "Jail House Lawyers Lose Right to 'Practice,'" *Houston Post*, October 14, 1970; Fred Harper, "Use of Solitary in Texas Prisons Upheld by Judge," *Houston Chronicle*, prisons news clipping file, CHA.

32. Woolsey v. Beto, 450 F. 2d 321 (1976); Rocha v. Beto, 449 F. 2d 741 (1971).

33. Arsenault, *Freedom Riders*; Farmer, *Lay Bare the Heart*, 22–23.

34. Roy S. Haber, interview with the author, March 15, 2018.

35. Gates v. Collier, 349 F. Supp. 881 (1972). For Haber's thoughts on the "last vestige" of state-sponsored slavery, see Janine Robben, "Profiles of the Law: Lessons from Parchman Farm," *Oregon Bar Bulletin*, January 2007, https://www.osbar.org/publications/bulletin/07jan/profiles.html.

36. On Jackson's role for making Black oppression visible, see Berger, *Captive Nation*, 91–138.

37. For a more critical assessment of how the New Left "constructed" George Jackson as a revolutionary hero, see Cummins, *Rise and Fall*, chap. 7, 151–86.

38. Berger, "'From Dachau with Love'.

39. Thompson, *Blood in the Water*, 561.

40. George Beto, "The Case for Prisons," speech given at the annual Texas Police Conference in El Paso, 1964, reprinted in *Texas Police Journal*, Beto, SHSU.

41. In his testimony in *Dreyer v. Jalet*, Beto referred to prison reformers as "liberal do-gooders." Dreyer v. Jalet, 1972.

42. George Beto to Richard Daley, August 30, 1968, Beto, SHSU.

43. Cruz v. Beto, 405 U.S. 319 (319).

44. Testimony of George Beto, Novak v. Beto, 320 F. Supp. 1206, 1209 (1970).

45. Karen Northcott, "Another Planet," *Texas Observer*, July 7, 1972.

46. "Wanted Man Found Shot," *Austin American Statesman*, September 23, 1973.

47. Al Slaton, oral history with Susanne Mason, October 18, 1997, 2002, in author's possession and used here with permission of Susanne Mason.

48. "Defendant Likely to Testify Today in Murder Trial Here," *Austin Statesman*, March 14, 1973.

49. "Summations Begin in Al Slaton Trial," *Austin Statesman*, March 15, 1973.

50. Al Slaton, oral history with Susanne Mason, October 18, 1997, 2002, in author's possession and used here with permission of Susanne Mason.

51. Dreyer v. Jalet, Beto, SHSU, 1-2/1.

52. Dreyer v. Jalet, Beto, SHSU, 1-2/1.

53. Martin and Ekland-Olson, *Texas Prisons*, 56.

54. Judge Carl O. Bue opinion in *Dreyer v. Jalet*, quoted in Northcott, "Another Planet."

55. Fred Harper, "Mrs. Cruz Exonerated on Conspiracy Charge," *Houston Chronicle*, September 19, 1972.

56. George Beto to Wardens of TDC, memorandum, November 8, 1963, Beto, SHSU, 1-2/1. The entire memorandum reads as follows: "To all wardens: Gentleman, recently there was an unauthorized use of building tenders in the Department. All of you are familiar with the long standing policy of the Department of Corrections as far as the use of building tenders or wing attendants is concerned. I would at this time unequivocally reiterate that policy. While it is no prohibition against the use of wing attendants or building tenders, at no time are inmates to be used to perform duties in the area of punishment and discipline. This responsibility rests and must continue to rest solely with custodial officers."

57. Hans Toch, "Books in Review: *Governing Prisons: A Comparative Study of Correctional Management*," *Society*, May/April 1989.

58. Horton and Nielson, *Walking George*, 143.

59. For Beto's role in the Arkansas prison investigation, see Gilmore, "States of Incarceration," 159–61.

60. "Prison Potential Far Exceeds Actuality, Investigators Told," *Arkansas Gazette*, April 30, 1967.

61. Dreyer v. Jalet, Beto, SHSU, 1-2/1.

62. George Beto quoted in DiIulio, *Governing Prisons*, 112.

63. Martin and Ekland-Olson, *Texas Prisons*, 38.

64. Memorandum to all Wardens from Dr. George Beto, Dreyer v. Jalet, 349 F. Supp. 452, 488 (1972), Plaintiffs' exhibit, Beto, SHSU, 1-2/1.

65. Frances Jalet to Alice Daniel, January 6, 1972, letter in author's possession.

66. *Cruz v. Beto II* included the following members of Eight Hoe: Fred Cruz, James E. Baker, Felipe Barbosa, Guadalupe Guajardo, Allen L. Lamar, Edward S. Mauricio, Herman G. Miller, Ernesto R. Montana, Roger Earl Pirkle, Lawrence C. Pope, David Robles, David Ruiz, Alvin D. Slaton, Amado Soto, and Anthony M. Zilka.

67. Rudy Portillo, oral history with Susanne Mason, February 9, 2003, in author's possession and used here with permission of Susanne Mason.

68. Eduardo Mauricio, oral history with Susanne Mason, August 29, 1998, in author's possession and used here with permission of Susanne Mason.

69. Joe Morgenstern, "The Banker Who Robbed Banks," *New York Times Magazine*, November 12, 1989, 55–56, 73–75.

70. Lawrence Pope, oral history conducted by John Wheat, 317, Pope, CAH, box 4C982.

71. Lawrence Pope, oral history conducted by John Wheat, 317, Pope, CAH, box 4C982.

72. Lawrence Pope, oral history conducted by John Wheat, 317, Pope, CAH, box 4C982.

73. Lawrence Pope, oral history conducted by John Wheat, 317, Pope, CAH, box 4C982.

74. Lawrence Pope, oral history conducted by John Wheat, 317, Pope, CAH, box 4C982.

75. Lawrence Pope, oral history conducted by John Wheat, 317, Pope, CAH, box 4C982.

76. Guadalupe Guajardo, interview with the author, March 8, 2007, IOH, Baylor.

77. See Lamar v. Coffield, 951 F. Supp. 629 (S.D.Tex.); Guajardo v. McAdams, 349 F. Supp. 211 (1972) and Guajardo v. Estelle, 580 F.2d. 748 (1978); Corpus v. Estelle, 409 F. Supp. 1090 (1975) and Corpus v. Estelle, 551 F.2d. 68 (1977).

78. "Former Prison Boss Ordered to Pay Inmates," *Houston Chronicle*, March 20, 1976.

79. Lawrence Pope, oral history conducted by John Wheat, 317, Pope, CAH, box 4C982.

80. According to Cruz's letter to Beto, Bartola Mendez was expected to be released from Goree sometime in 1968. Fred Cruz to George Beto, May 18, 1968, Jalet-Cruz papers, CAH, 94/042/1.

81. Fred Cruz to Frances Jalet, fifteen-page handwritten letter, in author's possession.

82. Montejano, *Quixote's Soldiers*, 58.

83. Montejano, *Sancho's Journal*.

84. On the Chicano youth movement, see Muñoz, *Youth, Identity, Power*; García, *United We Win*; and Navarro, *Mexican American Youth Organization*.

85. Fred Cruz, "Pagina de Fred Cruz: Remember the Prisoners," Papal Chicano, June 1–7, 1972, Jalet-Cruz papers, CAH, 94/042/1.

86. Following the Mexican Revolution of 1910, Mexicans that had migrated to the U.S. and Mexican Americans that had resided in the U.S. since the 1948 Treaty of Guadalupe Hidalgo, retained a strong sense of Mexcian pride and nationalism. This cultural connection across the U.S.–Mexico border constructed what historians have called "México de Afuera," which was a cultural tradition that retained Mexicano national identity among Mexican and Mexican American communities living and working in the U.S. through a widely circulating Spanish-language press, cultural and musical traditions, Catholic church services, and political awareness of events in Mexico and along the U.S.–Mexican border. On the Spanish-language press in this period, see Chacon, "The Chicano Immigrant Press," 48–54. On México de Afuera within carceral states, see Hernandez, "Scorpion's Tale," and Diaz, "Cultural Resilience."

87. Fred Cruz, "Remember the Prisoners," *Chicano Times*, 1972, Mario Marcel Salas papers, University of Texas, San Antonio (UTSA).

88. Floyd Patterson, oral history with Susanne Mason, 1999, in author's possession and used here with permission of Susanne Mason.

Chapter 6

1. On the role of self-defense during the civil rights movement in the U.S. South, see Hill, *Deacons for Defense*; Tyson, *Radio Free Dixie*; Umoja, *We Will Shoot Back*; Crosby, *Little Taste of Freedom*; Cobb Jr., *This Nonviolent Stuff'll*.

2. On the rising tide of Black Power protest against police brutality in Houston, see Behnken, *Fighting Their Own Battles*, 154–65, 164.

3. On California's prison camp and conservation program in the postwar period, see Janssen, "Convict Labor, Civic Welfare," 455–509.

4. Martin and Ekland-Olson, *Texas Prisons*, 60.

5. A TDC file from the early 1970s titled "California's prison radicalism" records a series of documents that reflect TDC's growing concern that Texas prisoners might look to California and New York for radical inspiration. Prison administrators looked to military and intelligence experts for advice on how they might quash prison uprisings and prisoner revolution. Among these documents was an unclassified paper for the CIA by FBI special agent Thomas J. Deakin titled "The Legacy of Carlos Marighella: Tactical and Theoretical Antecedents of Urban Guerilla Warfare in the United States." Another was a paper by Richard H. Ichord delivered to the FBI national symposium, 1974, entitled "The American Penal System: A Revolutionary Target." Other documents in the file included reports on the Attica uprising and the Vietnam Veterans against the War–Winter Soldier Organization Newsletter on the San Quentin Six, the six Black and Chicano defendants charged with the murder of three white guards and two white prisoners in San Quentin in 1971.

6. "Lifer," *Houston City Magazine*, April 1982, 81.

7. "Montana's Loss Is Texas's Gain," press clipping file, unnamed newspaper and no date, Clements papers, Texas A&M University.

8. "Prison System Gets Good Man," press clipping file, unnamed newspaper and no date, Clements papers, Texas A&M University.

9. Lawrence Pope, oral history conducted by John Wheat, Pope, CAH, box 4C982.

10. Ernest McMillan, interview with the author, March 4, 2009.

11. McMillan v. Estelle, testimony of Bobby Taylor.

12. Norma Adams Wade, "Activism Sparked by Son: Eva McMillan Joined Civil Rights Crusade," *Dallas Morning News*, February 11, 1988.

13. Ernest McMillan, oral history with the author, April 4, 2007, IOH, Baylor.

14. Ernest McMillan, oral history with the author, April 4, 2007, IOH, Baylor.

15. Jeffries, *Bloody Lowndes*, 4. For other key works on SNCC's voter registration drives in the South, see Hogan, *Many Minds, One Heart*, 56–92, 143–82; Carson, *In Struggle*; and Payne, *I've Got the Light*.

16. For an analysis that considers McMillan's role in the OK Supermarket demonstration as part of a local Dallas trend that rejected SNCC and militant violence, see Behnken, "'Dallas Way'"; Behnken, *Fighting Their Own Battles*, 165–67. Behnken concludes that "clearly SNCC was unwelcome in Dallas" and that "the lack of violence in Dallas . . . suggests at the very least that scholars have overemphasized the role of violent behavior in racial change in the civil rights movement." An analysis of the prisoner rights movement, however, shows the ways in which McMillan and former SNCC members continued to forge a vibrant interracial movement in Texas. For an account of the OK Supermarket demonstration as "symbolic of how the civil rights movement in Dallas remained fractured," see Dulaney, "Whatever Happened."

17. Ernest McMillan to Eva McMillan, cited in "Collins, Now Released from Prison, Vows Fight against Parole System," *Black Panther Speaks*, January 1973, in Salas papers (UTSA).

18. Ernest McMillan, interview with the author, March 4, 2009.

19. "CURE: Poor, Yes, but Determined," *Austin American Statesman*, February 21, 1977; Jon Standefer, "Couple Core of Prison Reform Lobby," *Houston Post*, February 27, 1977. In May 1975, CURE held a constitutional convention. CURE's objective as stated in its constitution was to convince legislators and the public that "crime can most ef-

fectively be diminished by providing errants with information on existing rehabilitative programs, by promoting the creation of additional rehabilitative programs, by developing correctional alternatives, by illustrating to errants that members of our society and government are concerned with their problems and by convincing errants that change can be more effectively accomplished through the exercise of their constitutional rights of free speech, freedom to associate, freedom to petition the government for a redress of grievances and other orderly activity rather than through crime and violence." By 1977, CURE boasted 1,500 members, and by 1985 the organization had grown to 2,500 members; it became a national organization for rehabilitation headquartered in Washington, DC. New York Prison Association, Grenader Special Collections, State University of New York, Albany, CURE, box 68, series 7; "The Constitution of Citizens United for Rehabilitation of Errants," Pope, CAH.

20. Charles and Pauline Sullivan, oral history with the author, August 15, 2010.

21. Fred Cruz, testimony before Committee on Criminal Jurisprudence, House of Representatives, 63rd Legislature, March 28, 1973.

22. George Beto to Wardens of TDC, memorandum, November 8, 1963, Beto, SHSU, 1-2/1.

23. W. J. Estelle to Chet Brooks, October 15, 1973, read in its entirety into the testimony of Eddie Bernice Johnson, *Ruiz* Special Master, MAI 8-J102.

24. David D. Allen to H. H. Coffield, December 20, 1972, Board of Corrections, general correspondence, November, December 1972, TDCJ, TSLA, 1998/038-55.

25. On Jordan and Texas liberalism, see Curtain, "Reaching for Power," 211–32.

26. Norma Adams Wade, "Activism Spared by Son: Eva McMillan Joined Civil Rights Crusade," *Dallas Morning News*, February 11, 1988.

27. "'The Walls Outside Are Beautiful, But' . . . Prison Life, Brutality Apall Black Lawmakers," *Houston Forward Times*, July 7, 1973, Mickey Leland Papers and Collection Addendum, Texas Southern University, 2015.

28. Eddie Bernice Johnson, *Ruiz* Special Master, MAI 8/J-102.

29. Statement to the Press, Joint Committee on Prison Reform, July 20, 1973, *Ruiz* Special Master, MAI 9/J103, CAH.

30. "'The Walls Outside are Beautiful, But' . . . Prison Life, Brutality Apall Black Lawmakers," *Houston Forward Times*, July 7, 1973, Mickey Leland Papers and Collection Addendum, Texas Southern University, 2015. "Legislators Call for Probe into Alleged Prison Beating," *Dallas Morning News*, September 14, 1973.

31. "Legislators Call for Probe into Alleged Prison Beating," *Dallas Morning News*, September 14, 1973; "'The Walls Outside are Beautiful, But' . . . Prison Life, Brutality Apall Black Lawmakers," *Houston Forward Times*, July 7, 1973, Mickey Leland Papers and Collection Addendum, Texas Southern University, 2015.

32. TDC Memorandum No. 201, June 29, 1973, TDCJ, TSLA.

33. "'Mutinous Situation': Prisons Chief Upholds Beatings of 10 Inmates," *Houston Chronicle*, July 31, 1973.

34. "Estelle Back in Inmates Interview Ban in Beatings Case," *Houston Chronicle*, July 18, 1973.

35. McMillan v. Estelle, testimony of W. J. Estelle Jr.

36. Bobby L. Taylor to W. J. Estelle Jr., interoffice memorandum, June 18, 1973, TDCJ, TSLA, 1980/020-31.

37. Bobby L. Taylor to W. J. Estelle Jr., interoffice memorandum, June 18, 1973, TDCJ, TSLA, 1980/020-31.

38. McMillan v. Estelle, testimony of W. J. Estelle Jr.

39. Joint Committee on Prison Reform, Hearings of November 15, 1973; McMillan v. Estelle, Findings of Fact and Conclusion of Law.

40. Allen L. Lamar et al. v H.H. Coffield et al., Civil Action, No. 72-H-1393.

41. Allen Lamar's personal narrative can be found in Trulson and Marquart, *First Available Cell*, 92–106, 99, 100.

42. Fanon, *Black Skin*.

43. Allen Lamar, "Imperialism Means Imprisonment," in Jalet-Cruz papers, CAH, 94/042/25.

44. Allen L. Lamar et al. v H. H. Coffield et al., Civil Action, No. 72-H-1393, consent decree.

45. Francis X. Leahy v. W. J. Estelle, Texas Department of Correction, et al., 371 F. Supp. 951 (1974).

46. Ruth Eyre, "Jailhouse lawyer makes his mark, gains funds, support from family," *Dallas Times Herald*, August 4, 1976; Don Mason, "Convict lawyer takes his own case to court," August 8, 1976, *Dallas Mornign News*.

47. Dudley Lynch, "Profiles: Frank Leahy, Jailhouse Lawyer," Brooks, TSLA, 1991/136-23.

48. Frank Leahy to Chet Brooks and Charles and Pauline Sullivan, July 13, 1979, Brooks, TSLA, 1991/136-23.

49. Frank X. Leahy to Steven Renfro, administrative assistant to Chet Brooks, April 9, 1979; Frank Leahy to Chet Brooks and Charles and Pauline Sullivan, July 13, 1979, Brooks, TSLA, 1991/136-23.

50. Trulson and Marquart, *First Available Cell*, 109.

51. Trulson and Marquart, 110.

52. Payne, "View from the Trenches," 146.

53. "Confidential Staff Report," John Albach, Staff Director, JCPRR, memorandum to members of JCPR from John Albach, "Tension at the Ramsey Unit," May 23,1974, *Ruiz* Special Master, MAI 8/J-99.

54. "Confidential Staff Report," John Albach, Staff Director, JCPRR, memorandum to members of JCPR from John Albach, "Tension at the Ramsey Unit," May 23,1974, *Ruiz* Special Master, MAI 8/J-99.

55. Eddie James Ward, oral history with the author, March 22, 1007, IOH, Baylor.

56. Eddie James Ward, oral history with the author, March 22, 1007, IOH, Baylor.

57. On the politicizing impact of the Vietnam War on some veterans, see Moser, *New Winter Soldiers*; Appy, *Working-Class War*; and Terry, *Bloods*.

58. On community building by the BPP and the launching of the Breakfast Program, see Spencer, *Revolution Has Come*, 85–86; Murch, *Living for the City*. On Houston's PP2 and their effort to engage the local community in clothing drives, food pantries for the impoverished, and health clinics, see Behnken, *Fighting Their Own Battles*, 163.

59. Ward, oral history with the author, March 23, 2007, IOH, Baylor.

60. Don Fisher, "Ward: A Radical View from 101 Years Alone," *Austin Today*, December 1975, 32–38.

61. Don Fisher, "Ward: A Radical View from 101 Years Alone," *Austin Today*, December 1975, 32–38.

62. Eddie James Ward, oral history with the author, March 22, 2007, IOH, Baylor.

63. Ward, interview with the author, March 23, 2007, IOH, Baylor.

64. Steve Estes's study of Black masculinity during the civil rights and Black Power concluded that the era's "quixotic quest for manhood" resulted in a "masculinist rhetoric used by both sides [that] served to obscure the questions of racial and economic equality that lay at the heart of the original struggle." However, my work considers how alternative and more protective masculinities evolved within the framework of state-orchestrated prison rape. My framing of Black masculinity as a communitarian network to protect fellow prisoners' bodies draws on Darlene Clark Hine's anthology that removes Black manhood as pathology and places it in historical context alongside violence and oppression. On Black masculinity during the civil rights and Black Power era, see Steve Estes, *I Am a Man*, 8; Hine and Jenkins, *Question of Manhood*.

65. Woodfox, *Solitary*, 93.

66. "Confidential Staff Report," John Albach, Staff Director, JCPRR, memorandum to members of JCPR from John Albach, "Tension at the Ramsey Unit," May 23, 1974, *Ruiz* Special Master, MAI 8/J-99.

67. "Confidential Staff Report," John Albach, Staff Director, JCPRR, memorandum to members of JCPR from John Albach, "Tension at the Ramsey Unit," May 23, 1974, *Ruiz* Special Master, MAI 8/J-99.

68. Florentino G. Rangel to Ron Clower, State Senator, District 9, February 17, 1974, Ron Clower papers, TSLA, 1981/217-93.

69. Steven Blanchard to Senator Ron Clower, November 11, 1973, Ron Clower papers, TSLA, 1981/217.

70. Steven Blanchard, interview with the author, March 14, 2007, IOH, Baylor.

71. Ward v. Estelle, C.A. 73-H-1721, SD/Tex, Houston Division.

72. Stockard and Ward never married, but they did carry their in-prison romance to the "free world" for a brief time in the early 1980s. Ward, interview with the author, March 23, 2007, IOH, Baylor; Janet Stockard, conversation with the author, October 16, 2008.

73. Ward, interview with the author, March 23, 2007, IOH, Baylor; Janet Stockard, conversation with the author, October 16, 2008.

74. "Officials 'Plot' Client's Murder" and "Impending Bogus Riot Allegedly Schemed to Cover Deaths," *Austin American Statesman*, July 4, 1974.

75. "In the Fields," *The Angolite*, 1973, Amistad Research Center, Tulane University.

76. King, unpublished first draft, *Amistad*, 10.

77. Sinclair v. Henderson, 331 F. Supp. 1124 (E.D. La. 1971).

78. Sinclair v. Henderson, 425 F.2d 125, 126 (5th Circuit 1970).

79. For an overview of prisoner litigation in Louisiana, see Rideau and Sinclair, "Prisoner Litigation."

80. "Panthers Defy New Orleans Police," *San Antonio News*, November 20, 1970.

81. Woodfox, 82. On the NYC jail uprisings, see Toussaint Losier, "Against 'Law and Order' Lockup: The 1970 NYC Jail Rebellions," *Race & Class* 59, no. 1 (2017): 3–35.

82. Herman Wallace to Elayn Hunt, Director of Corrections, June 7, 1973, box 1, folder 15, ACLU of Louisiana records (hereafter cited as ACLU), Special Collections, Tulane University.

83. Gilbert Montegut to unknown recipient, ACLU, Tulane University, box 1, folder 15.

84. King, unpublished first draft of manuscript, Amistad Center, Tulane University, 9.

85. Elie v. Henderson, 340 F. Supp. 958 (E.D. LA. 1972).

86. Alvin J. Bronstein, Offender Rights Litigation: Historical and Future Developments, Prisoners' Rights Sourcebook, 9–10 (1980), in author's possession.

87. Alvin J. Bronstein to David Hunter, January 4, 1973, American Civil Liberties Union Papers, Mudd Special Collections Library, Princeton University, box 1089, folder 5. For the development of the National Prison Project and its operations in North Carolina, see Hughett, "Safe Outlet."

88. Robert C. Coney to Captain Butler and Warden Dees, Louisiana Department of Corrections, July 10, 1973, Elie v. Henderson, 340 F. Supp. 958 (E.D. LA. 1972).

89. Robert C. Coney letter to Louisiana Department of Corrections, September 30, 1971, Elie v. Henderson, 340 F. Supp. 958 (E.D. LA. 1972).

90. David L. Clark testimony to Louisiana Department of Corrections, August 27, 1971, Elie v. Henderson, 340 F. Supp. 958 (E.D. LA. 1972).

91. Rideau and Sinclair, "Prisoner Litigation," 1070–71.

92. Rideau and Sinclair, "Prisoner Litigation," 1070–71.

93. Erwin James, "37 Years of Solitary Confinement: The Angola Three," *Guardian*, March 10, 2010; Campbell Robertson, "Last 'Angola 3' Inmate Freed after Decades in Solitary," *New York Times*, December 12, 2017.

Chapter 7

1. United States v. Nixon, 418 U.S. 683 (1974). On July 24, the U.S. Supreme Court ruled by unanimous decision that President Richard M. Nixon could not cite executive privilege to protect tape recordings pertaining to Watergate from congressional subpoena.

2. "Violence Built Carrasco Legend," *San Antonio Express and News*, August 4, 1975, 2A, 3A.

3. "Carrasco's Story: Violence and Dope," *San Antonio Express and News*, July 28, 1974; Barios, *Fred Gómez Carrasco*; "Violence Built Carrasco Legend," *San Antonio Express and News*, July 29, 1975, 6A; "Carrasco Demands Weapons," *San Antonio Express and News*, July 25, 1973, 6A. "Who Was Carrasco Nobody Remembers," *San Antonio Express*, August 4, 1974. "Carrasco Talkative on the Phone," *San Antonio Express*, July 26, 1974; "Carrasco Refuses Offers," *San Antonio Express*, July 27, 1974.

4. For an account that offers Carrasco as Mexican borderland drug kingpin, see McKinney, *Fred Gomez Carrasco*. For a journalistic view of Carrasco as violent criminal, see Harper, *Eleven Days in Hell*. For hostage narratives, see House, *Carrasco Tragedy*.

5. Olguín, *La Pinta*, 178; Montejano, *Quixoite's Soldiers*, 213.

6. In her formulation of Tijerina as "memory entrepenur," Oropeza draws upon the scholarship of Elizabeth Jelin's work on political transitions in Latin American countries from dictatorships to democracies to define "memory entrepreneur" as "people who apply the full force of their personality and persuasive power to bring forth a new—

or formerly suppressed—version of the past in service of a political cause." Oropeza, "Chicano History," 49–67; Jelin, *State Repression*.

7. On rethinking the borderland in a broader carceral framework, see Chase, "Rethinking Carceral Networks."

8. "El Plan de Aztlán." On the rejection of the whiteness strategy, see Gómez-Quinones, *Chicano Politics*. On the turn away from the whiteness strategy, especially in Texas, see Behnken, *Fighting Their Own Battles*, 170–94.

9. Testimony of John Albach, *Ruiz v. Estelle*, *Ruiz* Special Master, MAI 8/J88.

10. Testimony of John Albach, *Ruiz v. Estelle*, *Ruiz* Special Master, MAI 8/J88.

11. Final Report of the Joint Committee on Prison Reform, 63rd Legislature, December 1974.

12. "Treatment of the Mentally Ill and the Mentally Retarded—Working Paper," submitted to the Joint Committee on Prison Reform, by Jim Gibson, committee staff, *Ruiz* Special Master, MAI 8/J-85.

13. "Medical Study on the Use of Tranquilizing Drugs on Homosexuality," Prison Board meeting minutes, in author's possession.

14. Gilmore, "States of Incarceration," 153.

15. On the legal development of the *Holt v. Sarver* court case in Arkansas, see Feeley and Rubin, *Judicial Policy Making*, 51–80; and Gilmore, "States of Incarceration," 116–223; Holt v. Sarver, 309 F. Supp. 362 (1970); and, Holt v. Sarver II, 442 F. 2 d. 304 (1971).

16. "Racial Practices under criticism," *Houston Chronicle*, December 22, 1974; Final Report of the Joint Committee on Prison Reform, 63rd Legislature, December 1974.

17. Carl Freund, "Behind These Walls, Huntsville: A Mirror," *Houston Chronicle*, November 28, 1974.

18. Final Report of the Joint Committee on Prison Reform, 63rd Legislature, December 1974.

19. Kathi Miller, "Lawmaker Gloomy on Prison Reform," *Star Telegram* (Austin), December 9, 1974.

20. "Citizen's Advisory Committee Final Report," released November 25, 1974, *Ruiz* Special Master, MAI 8/J103.

21. "Citizen's Advisory Committee Final Report," released November 25, 1974, *Ruiz* Special Master, MAI 8/J103.

22. "Citizen's Advisory Committee Final Report," released November 25, 1974, *Ruiz* Special Master, MAI 8/J103.

23. "Citizen's Advisory Committee Final Report," released November 25, 1974, *Ruiz* Special Master, MAI 8/J103.

24. Kathi Miller, "Lawmaker Gloomy on Prison Reform," *Star Telegram* (Austin), December 9, 1974.

25. "Citizens Group Asks Prison System Change: Effective Rehabilitation Sought," *Houston Post*, November 27, 1974.

26. George Carmack, "End of a Prison's Dark Ages," *San Antonio Express*, January 27, 1974.

27. "Footing the Bill," *Dallas Morning News*, December 9, 1974.

28. "Bars to Reform," *Houston Post*, December 6, 1974.

29. "Prison Reform Panel Rapped," *Houston Post*, December 18, 1974.

30. Testimony of John Albach, *Ruiz v. Estelle*, *Ruiz* Special Master, MAI 8/J88.

31. Testimony of Mickey Leland, *Ruiz v. Estelle*, *Ruiz* Special Master, MAI 8/J102.

32. "Prison Reform Panel Rapped," *Houston Post*, December 17, 1974.

33. "Houston Lawyer Raps Citizen Panel on Prison Reform," *Houston Chronicle*, November 2, 1974.

34. "Prison Reform Movement Needs to Accentuate the Positive," *San Antonio Express and News* editorial, September 22, 1974.

35. "Citizen Prison Committee Sizzles," *San Antonio Light*, September 22, 1974.

36. "Prison Reform Movement Needs to Accentuate the Positive," *San Antonio Express and News* editorial, September 22, 1974.

37. "Citizen Prison Committee Sizzles," *San Antonio Light*, September 22, 1974.

38. "Brief Psychological Summary of Inmate Frederico Gomez Carrasco," Estelle papers, *Ruiz* case files, Texas A&M University.

39. Hobsbawm, *Primitive Rebels*; Hobsbawm, *Bandits*.

40. On "policing Mexicano mobility" before the age of mass incarceration, see Hernández, "Crimes and Consequences"; Hernández, *Migra!*, 46; Diaz, *Border Contraband*.

41. The hostages were the employees Glen D. Johnson, Ronald W. Robinson, Aline V. House, Novella M. Pollard, Linda G. Woodman, Elizabeth Y. Beseda, Julia C. Standley, Bertha M. Davis, Ann Fleming, Bobby G. Heard, and Anthony Branch; Father Joseph O'Brien; and four prisoners, Martin Quiroz, Henry Escamilla, Steve Robertson, and Florencio Vera.

42. Tommy Miller and Larry Cooper, "Standoff at Huntsville Prison Ends with Four Dead," *Houston Chronicle*, July 25, 1974.

43. Carrasco hostage tapes, TDC, TSLA, 1998/038-405, tapes 1, 24.

44. Carrasco hostage tapes, TDC, TSLA, 1998/038-405, tape 65.

45. Carrasco hostage tapes, TDC, TSLA, 1998/038-405, tape 12, side A.

46. Carrasco hostage tapes, TDC, TSLA, 1998/038-405, tape 2, side A.

47. Carrasco hostage tapes, TDC, TSLA, 1998/038-405, tape 2, side B.

48. Carrasco hostage tapes, TDC, TSLA, 1998/038-405, tape 2, side B.

49. Carrasco hostage tapes, TDC, TSLA, 1998/038-405, tape 36, side B.

50. Carrasco hostage tapes, TDC, TSLA, 1998/038-405, tape 19, side A.

51. Carrasco hostage tapes, TDC, TSLA, 1998/038-405, tapes 24, 12.

52. Carrasco hostage tapes, TDC, TSLA, 1998/038-405, tape 2, side B.

53. Carrasco hostage tapes, TDC, TSLA, 1998/038-405, tape 27, side A.

54. Carrasco hostage tapes, TDC, TSLA, 1998/038-405, tape 27, side A.

55. Carrasco hostage tapes, TDC, TSLA, 1998/038-405, tape 2, side A.

56. Carrasco hostage tapes, TDC, TSLA, 1998/038-405, tape 2, side B.

57. Carrasco hostage tapes, TDC, TSLA, 1998/038-405, tape 2, side A.

58. Carrasco hostage tapes, TDC, TSLA, 1998/038-405, tape 2, side A.

59. Texas Rangers, "Report on Attempted Escape," Huntsville, Texas, July 24–August 3, 1974, Houston, 1974, in author's possession; "Supplier of Guns to Carrasco to Get Life in Prison, Jury Says," *Austin American Statesman*, February 13, 1976.

60. Two of the hostages claimed that law officers fired first, while another hostage claimed that the first gunshots came from the prisoners. See "Carrasco Questions," *Texas Observer*, September 6, 1974, 1–3.

61. For a narrative account of the siege, see Harper, *Eleven Days in Hell*.

62. Carrasco hostage tapes, TDC, TSLA, 1998/038-405, tape 15, side A.

63. "Prison Shootout Ranked," *Houston Post*, December 12, 1974.

64. Carrasco tapes, TDCJ, TSLA, 199/113, audio 40.

65. Paredas, *Folklore and Culture*, 28.

66. Olguín, *La Pinta*, 176.

67. Ricardo Sánchez's testimonio, "Cabalgado como bestia" (Corralled like a beast), can be found in Olguín, *La Pinta*, 194.

68. *Chicano Times*, "Reflections on Chicano Folkheroes," August 2, 1974.

69. "ACLU Seeks Release of Autopsies, Videotapes of Prison Gun Battles," Carrasco news clippings, Ed Idar papers, Benson Latin American Collection, University of Texas at Austin; "Rangers' Rogers to Spearhead Prison Probe," Carrasco news clippings, Ed Idar papers, Benson Reading Room, University of Texas at Austin.

70. Frank X. Leahy to Oscar H. Mauzy, Senator, August 8, 1974, Papers of Ron Cloward, TSLA, 1981/217-93.

71. "Carrasco Questions," *Texas Observer*, September 6, 1974.

72. "Supplier of Guns to Carrasco to Get Life in Prison, Jury Says," *Austin American Statesman*, February 13, 1978; Harper, *Eleven Days in Hell*, 300.

73. Frank X. Leahy to Senator Ron Clower, Papers of Ron Clower, TSLA, 1981/217-93; "Carrasco Inquiry Court Suffers from Cover-Up," *San Antonio Express*, December 18, 1974.

74. "House Panel Won't Drop Carrasco Investigation," *San Antonio Light*, September 27, 1974.

75. "Huntsville Hostage Blasts Critics of Prison," news clipping, Ed Idar papers, Benson Latin American Collection, University of Texas at Austin.

76. "Hobby Denies Blocking Problem," *Austin American Statesman*, August 30, 1974.

77. "Prison Probers Protest," *San Antonio Express*, September 19, 1974.

78. Letter to the editor, *Austin American Statesman*, August 30, 1974.

79. Kathi Miller, "Lawmaker Gloomy on Prison Reform," *Forth Worth Star Telegram*, November 23, 1974.

Chapter 8

1. David R. Ruiz, Inmate Number 198698, vs. Billy G. McMillan, Assistant Warden, Frank McCarty, Captain, and Warden E. Z. Harelson, Eastham Unit, Texas Department of Corrections, United States District Court, Tyler Division. This item is the original writ, which became *Ruiz v. Estelle* in 1974 after it was joined by several other prisoner complaints. Original writ from David Ruiz's private papers, currently in author's possession.

2. Original writ from David Ruiz's private papers, currently in author's possession.

3. On the collapse of interracial movements by 1974, see Mantler, *Power to the Poor*; Araiza, *To March for Others*; and Behnken, *Fighting Their Own Battles*. On the ways in which violence had disrupted the Black Panther Party by 1974, see Austin, *Up against the Wall*. On the BPP's shift to community survival during the mid- to late 1970s, see Spencer, *Revolution Has Come*, 143–76.

4. García, *Chicano Generation*, 4.

5. On testimonios as "the politics of truth," Beverly, *Testimonio*.

6. Davis, "From the Prison," 74–95; and Wacquant, "From Slavery," 41–60.

7. My thinking on the ways in which the southern prisoners' rights movement blended Black Power demands, civil rights legal work, and labor protest traditions draws on Peniel Joseph's that characterizes the civil rights and Black Power era as a mutually reinforcing "complex mosaic rather than mutually exclusive and antagonistic movements." For a historical interpretation that stresses the connections and similarities between civil rights protest and Black Power demands, see Joseph, *Black Power Movement*, 8.

8. On post-1960s prison radicalism in California, see Berger, *Captive Nation*; Berger, *Hidden Seventies*. On prison radicalism in Illinois, see Losier, "Prison House of Nations."

9. On self-defense and the question of violence in the civil rights and Black Power movement, see Tyson, *Radio Free Dixie*; Hill, *Deacons for Defense*; Austin, *Up against the Wall*. New scholarship has also begun to consider how gender and sexuality shaped civil rights and the Black Power movement; see D'Emilio, *Lost Prophet*; Green, *Battling the Plantation Mentality*; and Estes, *I Am a Man!*

10. On the impact of internal diasporic migration as fomenting Chicana/o radicalism, see Rodriguez, *Tejano Diaspora*. For the migratory pattern and working conditions of Tejano cotton harvesters during this period, see Vargas, *Labor Rights*, 18–27.

11. Eric Hartman, "David Ruiz: Profile of a Writ Writer," *Texas Observer*, September 22, 1978, 6–7.

12. Ruiz, "Tough with a Knife," in author's possession, given with permission of Rose Marie Ruiz on David Ruiz's death in 2006.

13. Ruiz, "Tough with a Knife."

14. Original writ from David Ruiz's private papers, currently in author's possession.

15. David Ruiz, oral history with Robert Reps Perkinson, 2004, in author's possession and with permission of Robert Perkinson.

16. David Ruiz, oral history with Robert Reps Perkinson, 2004, in author's possession and with permission of Robert Perkinson.

17. David Ruiz, oral history with Robert Reps Perkinson, 2004, in author's possession and with permission of Robert Perkinson.

18. Ruiz, "Tough with a Knife."

19. Ruiz, "Tough with a Knife."

20. "Inmate Affidavits," *Ruiz* Special Master, 94-458/32.

21. Roy S. Haber to William Wayne Justice, November 4, 1974; Eduardo Mauricio to Roy S. Haber, undated, *Ruiz* Special Master, 94-458/32.

22. Eduardo Mauricion, oral history with Susanne Mason, August 29, 1998, in author's possession and used here with permission of Susanne Mason.

23. On MAYO's San Antonio origins and its alliance with *los vatos* street gang members, see Montejano, *Quixote's Soldiers*, 49–79; and Navarro, *Mexican American Youth Organization*.

24. In 1972, Muniz received 214,072 votes (6.3 percent) and a bit less in 1974 with 190,000 votes. But as David Montejano pointed out, Muniz carried 20 percent of the votes in south and west Texas, which had large Mexican American populations. See Montejano, *Quixote's Soldiers*, 222.

25. David Montejano's *Quixote's Soldiers* comes the closet to adopting a carceral framework when he placed Muniz's political decline as a result of police surveillance, where Muniz's subsequent incarceration at Fort Leavenworth federal penitentiary did not end his political journey, as Muniz served his time as a "mexicano political prisoner" and part of the "new Mexika movement." But Montejano also casts Muniz's incarceration within the framing of a "wrong turn" for the Chicana/o movement as a whole. Taking up a carceral framework, however, would make Muñiz's incarceration as integral to systematic racial oppression that responded to a genuine Chicana/o political threat with the power of carceral force. On the demise of Muñiz and La Raza Unida as a political force, see Behnken, *Fighting Their Own Battles*, 179–85; and García, *United We Win*.

26. Eduardo Mauricio, oral history with Susanne Mason, August 29, 1998, in author's possession and used here with permission of Susanne Mason.

27. Oropeza, *¡Raza Si! ¡Guerra No!* 95.

28. Stanley Cedargreen to William Wayne Justice, December 16, 1974, *Ruiz* Special Master, 94-458/32.

29. Lawrence Pope, oral history with John Wheat, Pope papers, 4C981 & 4C982, CAH.

30. Dan Balz, "A Common Felon in an Uncommon Case," *Washington Post*, December 15, 1981.

31. Frances Jalet Cruz to Dan Balz, February 3, 1982, in author's possession.

32. Morales v. Turman, 326 F. Supp. 667 (E.D. Tex. 1991).

33. Kemerer, *William Wayne Justice*, 145–81.

34. Kemerer, *William Wayne Justice*, 358–58.

35. Justice, "Prisoners Litigation," 720.

36. The other prisoner complaints consolidated into the *Ruiz* civil suit included L. D. Hilliard, Ernesto Montana, Herman Randall, Leandro Pado, O. D. Johnson, and Arthur Winchester. The titles of the consolidated complaints were Soto v. Estelle, no. 5594; Hilliard v. Estelle, No. TY-73-CA-20; Winchester v. Estelle, No TY-73-CA-32; Randall v. Estelle, No. TY-73-CA-103; Pardo v. Estelle, No. TY-73-CA-207; and Johnson v. Estelle, No. TYp73-260. Order of Judge Justice, David R. Ruiz v. W. J. Estelle, Civil Action No. 5523, *Ruiz* Special Master, MAI 8/J103.

37. William Bennett Turner to William Wayne Justice, April 25, 1974, *Ruiz* Special Master, 94-458/32.

38. W. J. Estelle, "Prisons-Power-Politics," lecture, Sam Houston State University, June 12, 1974, Estelle papers, box 3, folder 14, Texas A&M.

39. J. Stanley Pottinger, Assistant Attorney General, Civil Rights Division, to Director, FBI Memorandum, July 31, 1974, personal papers of Johnny Martínez, in author's possession; oral history with Johnny Martínez, April 21, 2018, in author's possession.

40. Johnny V. Martínez to Patricia Gail Littlefield, U.S. Department of Justice, Civil Rights Division, July 22, 1974, personal papers of Johnny Martínez, in author's possession.

41. FBI Memorandum, February 6, 1974, personal papers of Johnny Martínez, in author's possession.

42. Civil Rights Section, Federal Bureau of Investigation, FBI memo, February 6, 1974, personal papers of Johnny Martínez, in author's possession.

43. Metzl, *Protest Psychosis*.

44. Civil Rights Section, Federal Bureau of Investigation, FBI memo, February 6, 1974, personal papers of Johnny Martínez, in author's possession.

45. Prisoner political tract, prisoner correspondence and writings, *Ruiz*, TDCJ, TSLA, Office of the Special Counsel, 2004/016-55.

46. Swift was implicated with three others—Lee Murray Jurode, Joann Adams, and Robert Duron—in a home burglary attempt that became violent and ended with the triple murders of H. C. Kelley; his wife, Reola Kelly; and daughter Kelly Stovall. The four had broken into Kelly's home and demanded that he open the bank for them, and when he refused, it became violent. Among the four accomplices, Swift was charged and convicted for the murder of H. C. Kelly and the murder of their accomplice Robert Duron, whose body was discovered after the bungled robbery in Oklahoma. "Hearne is Stunned by Slaying of Hearne Family," *Hearne Democrat*, May 25, 1972; "Three Killing Suspects Arrested in Oklahoma," *Hearne Democrat*, May 25, 1972; "Swift Is Found Guilty of Murdering R. Duron," *Hearne Democrat*, November 9, 1972; "Criminal Appeals Court Upholds Swift Sentence, *Hearne Democrat*, May 30, 1974.

47. "Two Murder Suspects Are Returned to County Briefly," *Hearne Democrat*, June 1, 1971.

48. Letter to Eddie Bernice Johnson, TDCJ, TSLA, Office of the Special Counsel, 2004/016-55.

49. A seventeen-page letter to the author, Michael Jewell to Robert Chase, November 1, 2008, in author's possession.

50. Prisoner correspondence, May 29, 1974, inmate correspondence and writings, *Ruiz*, TDCJ, TSLA, Office of the Special Counsel, 2004/016-55.

51. Prisoner letter to Eddie Bernice Johnson, inmate correspondence and writings, *Ruiz*, TDCJ, TSLA, Office of the Special Counsel, 2004/016-55.

52. Prisoner political tract, inmate correspondence and writings, *Ruiz*, TDCJ, TSLA, Office of the Special Counsel, 2004/016-55.

53. Prisoner political tract, inmate correspondence and writings, *Ruiz*, TDCJ, TSLA, Office of the Special Counsel, 2004/016-55.

54. Inmate writings and correspondence, *Ruiz*, TSLA, 2004/016-55.

55. The case was first filed as Guajardo v. McAdams, 349 F. Supp. 211 (S.D. Tex. 1972). Once TDC lost the case, it went through appeal and became Guajardo v. Estelle, 432 F. Supp. 1373 (S.D. Tex. 1977). Guadalupe Guajardo, interview with the author, March 8, 2007 IOH, Baylor.

56. Inmate writings and correspondence, *Ruiz*, TDCJ, TSLA, Office of the Special Counsel, 2004/016-55.

57. See Clemmer, *Prison Community*, 152.

58. Prisoner political tract, inmate correspondence and writings, *Ruiz*, TDCJ, TSLA, Office of the Special Counsel, 2004/016-55.

59. Prisoner political tract, inmate correspondence and writings, *Ruiz*, TDCJ, TSLA, Office of the Special Counsel, 2004/016-55.

60. Unnamed prisoner letter, June 3, 1974, *Ruiz*, TSLA, 2004/016-55. Unnamed prisoner letter, June 3, 1974, *Ruiz*, TSLA, 2004/016-55.

61. Johnny E. Swift to Chet Brooks, February 2, 1978, Brooks, TSLA, 1999/136-20.

62. The six prisoner officials named in the beating were Captain Steele, Captain Blacek, Lieutenant Cathy, Sergeant Fulton, Officer Thornton, and an unknown officer. Unnamed prisoner letter, June 3, 1974, *Ruiz*, TSLA, 2004/016-55.

63. Unnamed prisoner letter, June 3, 1974, *Ruiz*, TSLA, 2004/016-55.

64. Unnamed prisoner letter, June 3, 1974, *Ruiz*, TSLA, 2004/016-55.

65. Inmate writings and correspondence, *Ruiz*, TSLA, 2004/016-55.

66. Inmate writings and correspondence, *Ruiz*, TSLA, 2004/016-55.

67. Inmate writings and correspondence, *Ruiz*, TSLA, 2004/016-55.

68. Inmate writings and correspondence, *Ruiz*, TSLA, 2004/016-55.

69. Letter announcing formation of JHLA and "Duties and Responsibilities of Citizen Members of JHLA," inmate writings and correspondence, *Ruiz*, TSLA, 2004/016-55.

70. Michael Jewell to Robert Chase, November 1, 2008, a seventeen-page letter to the author in author's possession.

71. Inmate political tract, inmate writings and correspondence, *Ruiz*, TSLA, 2004/016-55.

72. Michael Jewell to Robert Chase, November 1, 2008, a seventeen-page letter to the author in author's possession.

73. Ruiz, 2004/016-55, Unit Inspections, Inmate Interviews, 1976; "Texas Department of Corrections: Inspection of Security and Control Procedures in All Institutions, July–August, 1976," by Fred T. Wilkinson, Corrections Consultant, *Ruiz*, CAH, 2004/016-55.

74. On the historical and political development of "law and order" campaigns at the national level, see Flamm, *Law and Order*; Perlstein, *Before the Storm*; and Goldberg, *Barry Goldwater*.

75. Reported in Cronin, Cronin, and Milakovich, *U.S. v. Crime in the Street*, 60, 69; Useem and Kimball, *States of Siege*, 15.

76. On the role of the LEAA and its impact on crime and the expansive criminal justice system, see Feeley and Sarat, *Policy Dilemma*; Parenti, *Lockdown America*.

77. Hinton, *War on Poverty*.

78. The violent crimes included aggravated kidnapping, aggravated rape, aggravated sexual abuse, and aggravated robbery or use of a deadly weapon other than a firearm during the immediate flight from a felony.

79. "Briscoe for Curbing Convicts' Release," *Houston Chronicle*, April 8, 1976.

80. "Texas Crime Poll," Fall 1977 survey, Texas Criminal Justice Center, Sam Houston State University, Papers of Ron Clower, TSLA, 1981/217-125.

81. Those numbers shift slightly when race was considered. Among white respondents, 77 percent felt that the criminal justice system treated defendants fairly, while only 65 percent of Black and 68 percent of Mexican Americans agreed. Moreover, only 18 percent of whites felt that defendants were not treated fairly, while 31 percent of both Black and Mexican American respondents felt that defendants were treated unfairly.

82. "Get Tougher on Criminals," *Register* (Gatesville, TX), July 12, 1976.

83. "Anti-Crime Bill," *Herald*, July 26, 1976.

84. 1980 Annual Statistical Report, TDC; "Overcrowding," *Ruiz* discovery, *Ruiz* Special Master, 2004/015-31.

85. "Shortage of Guards Is a Major Problem in State's Prison System," *Houston Chronicle*, September 9, 1978. Texas Research League, *Houston Chronicle*, September 9, 1978.

86. "Overcrowding," *Ruiz* discovery, *Ruiz* Special Master, 2004/015-31.

87. Mariscal, *Brown-Eyed Children*. On Chicano prison mobilization, see Díaz-Cotto, *Gender, Ethnicity*; Gómez, "'Nuestras Vidas'"; and Chase, "Self Taught, Cell Taught," 836–61.

88. Thomas W. Shaw, Ellis to Ron Clower, September 30, 1974, Papers of Ron Clower, TSLA, 1981/217-93.

89. For a historical evaluation of white slavery, see Peck, "White Slavery and Whiteness," 41–63.

90. Berger, *Captive Nation*; Losier, "Prison House of Nations."

91. Davis, "From the Prison," 74–95.

92. "Prisoners Resist Texas Prison Slave System," handbill, Prisoner Solidarity Committee, in author's possession.

93. Its sponsors included State Representative Ben Reyes of Houston, State Senator Carlos Traun of Corpus Christi, Ray Hill of the Human Rights League, Gargland Jaggers of the Black Secretariat of the Roman Catholic Archdiocese of Detroit, Diane Goldberg of AFSCME Local 140 (Houston), Demetrio Lucio of AFSCME Local 1550 (Houston), Lorenzo Cano, Harris County Raza Unida Party (Houston), Antonio Orendain of the Texas Farmworkers Union, Rado Rosales of the Brown Berets (Houston), L. C. Dosey of the Southern Coalition on Jails and Prisons, Ron Welch of the Mississippi Prisoners Defense Committee, Eddie Sandifer of the Mississippi Alliance for Human Rights, Ruby Tobias of the Mississippi Council on Human Relations, Tom Soto of the Prisoner Solidarity Committee, representatives of Attica prisoners, Eduardo O. Canales of Centro Aztlan, and the Beat poet Allen Ginsburg.

94. For protest against police brutality in Austin, see Mike Kelley, "Austinite Files Suit Claiming Police Violated Civil Rights," *Austin American Statesman*, January 24, 1973; Robert Faulk, "Chicanos Consider Police 'Harassment,'" *Daily Texasn*, January 24, 1973. On the Rodriguez police murder, see "Handcuffed Boy, 12, Shot Dead in Squad Car by Dallas Officer," *New York Times*, July 25, 1973; *Dallas Morning News*, July 25–30; November 14–20, 1973; July 21, 2013; *New York Times*, October 18, 1973; *Texas Observer*, July 7, 1978. Vertical Files, CAH.

95. Salvador Gonzalez to Senator Chet Brooks, July 29, 1773, copies also provided to Senator Ron Clower and Senator Bill Meier, Clower papers, TSLA, 1981/217-93.

96. Almaguer, "Chicano Men," 77, 75–100. In a more recent update, Almaguer reconsidered the strict binary between activos and pasivos as conferring cultural notions of hetero or homosexuality. Vidal-Ortiz et al., "Revisiting *Activos* and *Pasivos*," 253–73.

97. "Prisoners Resist Texas Prison Slave System," handbill, Prisoner Solidarity Committee, in author's possession.

98. Salvador Gonzalez to Senator Chet Brooks, July 29, 1973, Papers of Ron Clower, TSLA, 1981/217-93.

99. "Officer Shoots Alpine Youth," *Odessan American*, June 11, 1968; "Alpine Teenager Shot in Chase," *Waco-News Tribune*, June 13, 1968; "Alpine Police Officer Resigns," *Odessan American*, June 17, 1968.

100. U.S. Commission on Civil Rights, *"Mexican Americans.*

101. George Hackler, "Charged Two Alpine Men with Beard Murder," *Alpine Avalanche*, September 25, 1975.

102. Alvaro L. Hernández, Jr. v. W.J. Estelle, Jr., 788 F. 28 1154 (5th Cir. TX. 1986).

103. Butch Mendez, Ellis Unit, inmate number 256311, to State Senator Chet Brooks, Chairman, Joint Committee on Prison Reform, December 15, 1978, Brooks, TSLA, box 1999/136.

104. A seventeen-page letter to the author, Michael Jewell to Robert Chase, November 1, 2008, in author's possession.

105. Butch Mendez, Ellis Unit, inmate number 256311, to State Senator Chet Brooks, Chairman, Joint Committee on Prison Reform, December 15, 1978, Brooks, TSLA, box 1999/136.

106. Michael Wayne Eubanks, oral history with the author, March 27, 2007, IOH, Baylor.

107. "Strike at Eastham," unpublished letter and account of the 1978 strike, Michael Eubanks (Texas prisoner since 1977), letter to the author, April 2, 2006.

108. Alverro Luna Hernández, oral history with the author, March 23, 2007, IOH, Baylor.

109. Robert Mudd, oral history with the author, March 30, 2007, IOH, Baylor.

110. Alverro Hernández, oral history with the author, March 23, 2007, IOH, Baylor.

111. Wilbur Collins, oral history with the author, March 21, 2007, IOH, Baylor.

112. Robert Mud, oral history with the author, March 30, 2007, IOH, Baylor.

113. Alverro Hernández, oral history with the author, March 23, 2007, IOH, Baylor.

114. "3 Inmates Injured by Warning Shots from Prison Guards," *Dallas Times Herald*, October 9, 1978; "TDC Head Refuses Comment on Prisoner Strike," *Dallas Times Herald*, October 10, 1978; "Convicts in Other Facilities Join Prison Work Stoppage," *Fort Worth Star Telegram*, October 11, 1978; "Texas Prisons: Overcrowded, Edgy, and Under Fire," *Dallas Times Herald*, October 5, 1978; "Riot by 1,500 Inmates Acknowledged," *Houston Chronicle*, October 19, 1978.

115. Robert DeLong, Testimony of Julian Griego and In-Chambers Conference, October 16, 1978, *David R. Ruiz, et. al. vs. W.J. Estelle, Jr., et. al.*, *Ruiz* Special Master, MAI 8/J-92.

Chapter 9

1. For a court room account, see Martin and Ekland-Olson, *Texas Prisons*, 113–68; Perkinson, *Texas Tough*, 214, 251–85. For a critical account of the legal ramifications of Ruiz as disasterous federal intervention, see DiIlulio, *Governing Prisons*; Feeley and Rubin, *Judicial Policy Making*; and Crouch and Marquart, *Appeal to Justice*.

2. William Bennett Turner, opening statement, *Ruiz v. Estelle*, October 2, 1978, MAI 8/J101, CAH.

3. On the Idar family's role in Mexican and Mexican American labor unions, see Zamora, *Mexican American Worker*, 61–63, 97–98. On Eduardo Idar's role in cofounding LULAC, see Márquez, *LULAC*, 17.

4. On shifting generational ideologies from the immigrant to the Mexican American generation, see García, "Americans All"; García, *Mexican Americans*.

5. On Idar's role in formulating the whiteness strategy through his work in the GI Forum, see Behnken, *Fighting Their Own Battles*, 31–35, 43–44, 65–66.

6. García, *Rise of the Mexican*, 310.

7. On the political influence of *What Price Wetbacks?*, see Flores, *Grounds for Dreaming*, 76.

8. Ed Idar, opening statement, *Ruiz v. Estelle*, October 2, 1978, MAI 8/J101, CAH.

9. David Vanderhoof, opening statement, *Ruiz v. Estelle*, October 2, 1978, MAI 8/J101, CAH.

10. Ed Idar, opening statement, *Ruiz v. Estelle*, October 2, 1978, MAI 8/J101, CAH.

11. Bruce Jackson to Ed Idar, September 25, 1978, eleven-page, single-spaced, typed letter/report, Idar papers, box 31, folder 2-5, Benson Center. Other letters from Jackson to Idar providing his advice and observations include September 11, 1978, and September 27, 1978.

12. Bruce Jackson to Ed Idar, September 25, 1978, eleven-page, single-spaced, typed letter/report, Idar papers, box 31, folder 2-5, Benson Center. Other letters from Jackson to Idar providing his advice and observations include September 11, 1978, and September 27, 1978.

13. Testimony of Bruce Jackson, *Ruiz* Special Master, MAI 8/J102.

14. Bruce Jackson, "Our Prisons Are Criminal: Not One of Them Really Does Its Job," *New York Times*, September 22, 1968.

15. Bruce Jackson, interview with the author, April 26, 2008, IOH, Baylor.

16. John M. Crewdson, "Inmates Tell of Texas Prison Brutality," *New York Times*, November 11, 1978.

17. "Gay Inmates Were Assigned as Porters, Warden Testifies," *Houston Chronicle*, May 23, 1979.

18. Lawrence Pope to David Arnold, regarding violations of building tender agreements, Pope, CAH, 4C771; Lawrence Pope to Board of Corrections, regarding William "Butch" Ainsworth (213700), Pope, CAH, 4C771.

19. Donald Whitt, testimony, November 7 and 8, 1978, *Ruiz* Special Master, MAI 8/J101.

20. Jerry Ben Ulmer testimony, *Ruiz* Special Master, MAI 8/J95.

21. Testimony of Bertrand Jerome Bennett, December 12, 1978, *Ruiz* Special Master, MAI 8/J95.

22. Tesimony of Jerry Golden, December 20 and 21, 1978, *Ruiz* Special Master, MAI 8/J92.

23. Lee Otis Johnson had several terms in TDC. His first term was 1965 to 1965, where he served his time mostly at the Ramsey prison. His second term was from 1970 to 1972 and then he received a third sentence in 1975. Testimony of Lee Otis Johnson, April 10, 12, 26, and 29, 1979, *Ruiz* Special Master, MAI 8/J102.

24. Testimony of Lee Otis Johnson, April 10, 12, 26, and 29, 1979, *Ruiz* Special Master, MAI 8/J102.

25. Testimony of Eddie James Ward, December 11 and 12, 1978, *Ruiz* Special Master, MAI 8/J95.

26. George F. Wilson, November 8 and 9, 1978, *Ruiz* Special Master, MAI 8/J95.

27. Testimony of George Thomas (Mickey) Leland, November 21, 1978, *Ruiz* Special Master, MAI 8/J98.

28. Expert Report Security, Arnold Pontesso, Prepared for U.S., Plaintiff-Intervenor, filed February 18, 1977, *Ruiz* Special Master, MAI 8/J10.

29. Testimony of Eddie James Ward, December 11 and 12, 1978, *Ruiz* Special Master, MAI 8/J95.

30. Testimony of Allen Lamar, October 5, 1978, *Ruiz* Special Master, MAI 8/J98.

31. Trulson and Marquart, *First Available Cell*, 125.

32. Testimony of Martha Quinlan, November 15 and 16, 1978, *Ruiz* Special Master, MAI 8/J99.

33. Testimony of Martha Quinlan, November 15 and 16, 1978, *Ruiz* Special Master, MAI 8/J99.

34. Testimony of Johnny Valdez Martínez, November 22, 1978, *Ruiz* Special Master, MAI 8/J94.

35. Testimony of David Ruíz, October 3 and 4, 1978, *Ruiz* Special Master, MAI 8/J99.

36. Testimony of David Ruíz, October 3 and 4, 1978, *Ruiz* Special Master, MAI 8/J99.

37. On the medicalization discourse that associated schizophrenia with Black protest, see Metzl, *The Protest Psychosis*.

38. Johnny Martínez, interview with the author, April 19, 2018.

39. William Bennett Turner interview with the author, September 30, 2019.

40. Emiliano Figueroa M. and Andres Hernadez to Governor William Clements, translated by Good Neighbor Commission, May 1, 1979; Emiliano Figueroa Magana to Governor William Clements, February 29, 1979, Governor Clements Records, General Counsel's File, *Ruiz*, Texas A&M University, box 21, folder 64.

41. William Bennett Turner to David Dean, Counsel to the Governor, June 3, 1980, Governor Clements Records, General Counsel's File, *Ruiz*, Texas A&M University, box 21, folder 64.

42. Emiliano Figueroa Magana to William LaRowe, no date given, Governor Clements Records, General Counsel's File, *Ruiz*, Texas A&M University, box 21, folder 64.

43. "Accuser Testifies Ruiz Target of 'Put-Up' Story," *Houston Post*, January 7, 1981.

44. Frank X. Leahy to Rachel Rivers and Robert E. DeLong, November 26, 1978, Idar papers, 21.12, Benson Center.

45. Expert Report Security, Arnold Pontesso, Prepared for U.S., Plaintiff-Intervenor, filed February 18, 1977; "Inspection of Security and Control Procedures in all Institutions," Fred T. Wilkinson, prepared for the TDC, filed March 10, 1977.

46. Judge William Wayne Justice, memorandum opinion, Papers of Frances Jalet-Cruz, 94/042-16.

47. William Bennett Turner interview with the author, September 30, 2019.

48. Judge William Wayne Justice, memorandum opinion, Papers of Frances Jalet-Cruz, 94/042-16.

49. "Prison Director Lambasts Judge Justice's Partiality, Literary Skills," *San Antonio Express*, February 21, 1982; William P. Barrett, "Lifer," *Houston City Magazine*, April 1982, 75.

50. Saralee Tiede, "Texas Prisons: A Wave of Inmate Unrest," *Dallas Times Herald*, November 22, 1981.

51. Letter to the editor, *Houston Post*, January 29, 1981.

52. "Sound-Off: Texas Prison Texas' Business, He Says," news clipping file, Brown defense, in author's possession.

53. "Sound-Off: Texas Prison Texas' Business, He Says," news clipping file, Brown defense, in author's possession.

54. Richard Vara, "Texas Told to Cut Prison Population or Reject Inmates," *Houston Post*, April 21, 1981; Felton West and Richard Vara, "White Says Decision Likely to Cost State Millions," *Houston Post*, December 13, 1980.

55. Turner quoted in Martin and Ekland-Olson, *Texas Prisons*, 217.

56. Ruiz v. Estelle, 679 F.2d 1115 (5th Cir. 1982), p. 1132.

57. "Unrest on the Rise: Upsurge in Prison Rioting Results from Reform Order, Officials Say," *Austin American Statesman*, November 23, 1981; "Judge's Order Blamed: Jails 'Dangerous,'" *Odessan American*, November 23, 1981; "State Claims Court Order Causes Prison Unrest," *El Paso Times*, November 29, 1981.

58. Felton West, "White issues call for Reagan to intervene in Texas' fight against prison reform order," undated news clipping file, CAH.

59. Interoffice communication, Estelle to All Wardens, January 25, 1982, TDCJ, in author's possession.

60. Unnamed board member quoted in Crouch and Marquart, *Appeal to Justice*, 140.

61. "TDC Board Votes to Dismantle BT System," *Houston Post*, April 17, 1982.

62. "Warden Fired for Telling Guards to Beat Prisoner," *Dallas Times Herald*, October 12, 1983.

63. "The Prisoners Defense Committee Report on Brutality and Torture in The Texas Department of Corrections," Prisoners Defense Committee, 1983, "Brutality file," Pope, CAH.

64. Candice Hughes, "Prison-Reform Work Gives Banker a Break with the Past," *Austin American Statesman*, August 30, 1982.

65. "Mattox Assigns Lawyers to Audit Probe," *Houston Chronicle*, December 17, 1983; "TDC Investigating Payroll Practices," *Houston Chronicle*, January 27, 1983; "TDC Finances: Out of Control," *Houston Post*, January 22, 1984.

66. David Hanners, "Estelle Angry over Wrongdoing Allegations," *Dallas Morning News*, February 3, 1984; "Abuses of TDC Perks Uncovered," Associated Press news clipping, Brown papers, in author's possession; "Estelle Ends Job Quietly," news clipping, Brown papers, in author's possession.

67. David Hanners, "Estelle Angry over Wrongdoing Allegations," *Dallas Morning News*, February 3, 1984.

Chapter 10

1. What follows is Brown's claim as to how events that day transpired drawn from his own testimony. Eroy Brown testimony, second trial, November 2, 1982, 56, Brown Defense papers, Lawfirm of Habern, O'Neil, and Pawgan (hereafter cited as Brown Defense), copy in author's possession and with permission of William T. Habern.

2. "Inmate's Letter Hint of Anger Building Up in Him," *Dallas Times Herald*, April 12, 1981.

3. Eroy Brown testimony, second trial, November 2, 1982, 56, Brown Defense.

4. Eroy Brown testimony, second trial, November 2, 1982, 56, Brown Defense.

5. For a narrative account of the murder and the subsequent three murder trials against Eroy Brown, see Berryhill, *Trials of Eroy Brown*.

6. "TDC Ellis Warden, Supervisor Slain," *Houston Post*, April 5, 1981.

7. Monty Fowler, "Aryan Brotherhood: Veil of Secrecy Ripped from Brutal Prison Gang," *Brazosport Facts*, September 14, 1986.

8. Barfield v. State of Texas, Court of Appeals of Texas, Houston (1st Dist.), No. 01-86-00932-CR, February 4, 1988.

9. Dane Shiller, "Years-Long Isolation of Inmates under Attack in Texas 5," *Houston Chronicle*, August 16, 2011.

10. In his complex study of Chicago's gang formation, blackness, and whiteness, the historian Andrew Diamond demonstrated that "the politicization of black identity went hand in hand with the politicization of white identity," and he offered the provocative conclusion that "gangs were the most effective (and arguably the only) grassroots organizations capable of bringing such solidarities into existence." Diamond, *Mean Streets*, 226, 232. For work that connects gang organization to community control, the Black Power movement, and movements for racial pride and identity among Puerto Ricans, see Venkatesh and Levitt, "Are We a Family'"; Jeffries, "From Gang-Bangers"; Hagedorn, *World of Gangs*; Venkatesh, *Gang Leader*; and Fernandez, "Young Lords." In his study of Chicago's P-Stone Rangers, Will Cooley critiqued the historical approach that "credit[s] gangs for intensifying racial consciousness during the northern phase of the Civil Rights Movement." On this historiographical debate over gang and racial politicization, see Cooley, "'Stones Run It,'" 911–32; Gilfoyle, Diamond, and Cooley, "Revisiting Gangs," 803–11.

11. An important exception in urban gang and racial politicization historiography is David Montejano's study of San Antonio, where barrio gangs create an alliance with student organizations to foment a southwest urban Chicana/o movement. Montejano, *Quixote's Soldiers*.

12. For pioneering work on prison order and authority as the necessary social stability that the prisoners' rights movement disrupts, see Jacobs, "Prisoners' Rights Movement," 429–70; Jacobs, *Stateville*.

13. Crouch and Marquart, *Appeal to Justice*, 191, 192.

14. William T. Habern, interview with the author, November 5, 2005, IOH, Baylor.

15. Stan Jones, "Inmate Is a 'Victim' of System," *Ft. Worth Star Telegram*, November 8, 1991.

16. "Trial May Give Glimpse of Life in Texas Prisons," news clipping file, Brown Defense; "Prison Murder Called a Case of Self-Defense," *Daily Sun*, November 22, 1981, in author's possession.

17. Alan Wade Jonson, TDC 255182, letter to the editor, newspaper clipping, Brown Defense, in author's possession.

18. Testimony of Aubrey Eugene Komurke, February 15, 1982, *State of Texas v. Eroy Brown*, Brown Defense, in author's possession.

19. Slaton had been confined in a federal penitentiary, an Oklahoma penitentiary, and a mental institution in Missouri. "Brown Trial: Defense Witnesses Say Warden Had Reputation for Violence toward Inmates," *Houston Post*, February 17, 1982; "Brown

Witness Admits Mutilation, but Sticks to Story," *Dallas Time Herald*, February 24, 1982.

20. "8 Inmate Witnesses Declared in Contempt for Refusing to Testify at Brown Trial," *Houston Post*, February 16, 1982.

21. The prisoners included Ben W. Lacy II, Kenneth M. Pallend, Robert L. Dunbar, Clinton R. Derry, David R. Waller, Dale Lee Tedenick, Joe B. Peacock, and Victor H. Ramirez.

22. "TDC Officials Say Pack Not Violent," *Houston Post*, February 24, 1982.

23. Richard Vara, "Defense to Call First Witness in TDC Inmate Trial Today," *Houston Post*, news clippings, Brown defense, in author's possession.

24. Brown testimony, second trial, Brown Defense, in author's possession, 98.

25. Patti Kilday, "Brown Jury Hears Final Arguments," news clipping, Brown Defense, in author's possession.

26. Patti Kilday, "Brown Jury Hears Final Arguments," news clipping, Brown Defense, in author's possession.

27. "Brown Murder Case Ends in Mistrial," *Galveston Daily News*, March 5, 1982; Richard Vara and Steve Olafson, "Brown Case Ends in Mistrial," *Houston Post*, news clipping, Brown Defense, in author's possession.

28. Glenn Smith, "Officials Not Sure Yet of Reasons for Work Stoppage by 2,200 at Ellis Unit," *Houston Chronicle*, April 30, 1981.

29. Glenn Smith, "Officials Not Sure Yet of Reasons for Work Stoppage by 2,200 at Ellis Unit," *Houston Chronicle*, April 30, 1981. See also Bill Deener, "Inmate Strike at Ellis Prison Eases as 600 Answer Morning Work Call," *Dallas Morning News*, May 1, 1981; Glenn Smith, "Mood after Ellis Unit Work Stoppage Is Quiet but Tense," *Houston Chronicle*, May 7, 1981.

30. "FIRST Edition 1981, March, Critique of the Estelle Program," TDCJ, TSLA, Director's Office, July–November 1982, 1998/038-60.

31. "FIRST Edition 1981, March, Critique of the Estelle Program," TDCJ, TSLA, Director's Office, July–November 1982, 1998/038-60.

32. "FIRST Edition 1981, March, Critique of the Estelle Program," TDCJ, TSLA, Director's Office, July–November 1982, 1998/038-60.

33. "Internal Violence, Disturbances, and Escapes," Warden's meeting, February 3, 1984, TDCJ, in author's possession; "Inmates Strike at Ellis Prison as 600 Answer Morning Work Call," *Dallas Morning News*, May 1, 1981; "Mood after Ellis Unit Work Stoppage Is Quiet but Tense," *Houston Chronicle*, May 7, 1981; "Prison Riot Inquires Guard, 15 Inmates," *Houston Chronicle*, October 3, 1981; "Disturbances Reported at 2 TDC Prison Units," *Houston Post*, October 1981, newsclipping file, in author's possession; "400 TDC Inmates Riot at Darrington Facility," *Houston Chronicle*, November 20, 1981; "Error Let Inmates Out, Riot Followed," *Houston Post*, newsclippings, in author's possession; "Texas Prison System: A Rough Year for TDC, and No Relief in Sight," *Houston Chronicle*, December 6, 1981.

34. Aric Press, "Inside America's Toughest Prison," *Newsweek*, October 6, 1986.

35. Aric Press, "Inside America's Toughest Prison," *Newsweek*, October 6, 1986.

36. Anonymous inmate, quoted in Martin and Ekland-Olson, *Texas Prisons*, 204.

37. Michael Jewell, seventeen-page typewritten letter to the author, November 1, 2008.

38. Doug Freelander, "Inmates Say Reform Advocates Not Getting Whole Story," *Houston Post*, November 20, 1983.

39. Wilbur Collins, interview with the author, March 27, 2007, IOH, Baylor.

40. Doug Freelander, "Inmates Say Reform Advocates Not Getting Whole Story," *Houston Post*, November 20, 1983.

41. Martha Quinlan to Lawrence Pope, August 10, 1983, "Quinlan file," Pope, CAH, 4C825.

42. Martha Quinlan to Lawrence Pope, August 10, 1983, "Quinlan file," Pope, CAH, 4C825.

43. Martha Quinlin to Scott J. Atlas (Vinson and Elkins), April 5, 1982, "Martha Quinlan," Pope, CAH, 4C825.

44. Martha Quinlin to Scott J. Atlas (Vinson and Elkins), April 5, 1982, "Martha Quinlan," Pope, CAH, 4C825.

45. In the course of this research, I submitted several open-record requests to TDCJ to receive information on John Eduardo Swift's prison record and his death, which received some media attention at the time as a sensational prison murder. Despite supplying Swift's official prisoner number, his prison location, and the period of his incarceration, TDCJ was not able to locate any records on John Eduardo Swift or on his murder on Ellis's death row.

46. "Ex-Con Hopes to Establish Record as Effective Lobbyist," *San Antonio Light*, January 13, 1985.

47. "Ex-Con Hopes to Establish Record as Effective Lobbyist," *San Antonio Light*, January 13, 1985.

48. "Ex-Inmate Says She Can't Leave Troubles of State Prisons Behind," *Dallas Morning News*, September 2, 1984.

49. "Ex-Inmate Says She Can't Leave Troubles of State Prisons Behind," *Dallas Morning News*, September 2, 1984.

50. Conversation between Ray Hill and Martha L. Quilin, March 25, 1984, excerpts from KPFT Prison Radio Show, Pope, CAH, 4C825.

51. Alvaro Luna Hernández to Martha Quinlan, April 16, 1984, "Martha Quinlan," Pope, CAH, 4C825.

52. Albert Aranda to Martha Quinlan, March 26, 1984, "Martha Quinlan," Pope, CAH, 4C825.

53. Martha Quinlan to Albert Aranda, March 20, 1984, "Martha Quinlan," Pope, CAH, 4C825.

54. Martha Quinlan to Albert Aranda, March 30, 1984, "Martha Quinlan," Pope, CAH, 4C825.

55. Lawrence Pope to Aubrey Komurke, November 9, 1985, Martha Quinlan," Pope, CAH, 4C825.

56. Raymond K. Procunier v. Robert Martínez, et al., 416 U.S. 396 (94 S. Ct. 1800, 40 L.Ed.2d 224), 1974.

57. For a narrative account of the New Mexico riot, see Morris, *Devil's Butcher Shop*. The sociologist Mark Colvin has argued that the New Mexico riot occurred because of a shift in prison management and prison society in which prisoner leaders were stripped of power by new administrative designs. Colvin's analysis concluded that "accommodation" to prisoner leadership actually produced a "stable" prison society and

deterred riot. He concluded, "As accommodations, which had induced prisoner leaders' cooperation and given them sources of nonviolent power over other inmates, are dissolved, inmate leaders are no longer able to provide a stabilizing or cohesive influence over the inmate social structure. Relations among inmates themselves become more coercive as nonviolent sources of power dry up and are replaced with violence." The Texas prison case, however, provides a different example where "accommodation" to "inmate leadership" kept order at the price of a despotic and violent reign of southern trusty power. Colvin, *Penitentiary in Crisis*, 40.

58. Duran v. Anaya, formerly V. Apocada v. King, Civil No. 77-721-C, U.S. District Court, New Mexico. Colvin, *Penitentiary in Crisis*.

59. "Duran Warned State Pen Was a Time Bomb," *Albuquerque Journal*, November 9, 1997.

60. McCotter's first experience with TDC occurred in 1970 as he was earning his master's degree in criminology and sociology at Sam Houston State University. While enrolled in the master's program, McCotter accepted an internship with TDC while Beto was in the last year of his directorship.

61. "New TDC Chief Called Outspoken, Innovative," *Dallas Morning News*, May 22, 1984; "Deputy Director Has Military Background," May 22, 1984, news clipping file, in author's possession.

62. Anne Reifenberg, "Deputy Prisons Director Has Military Background," *Dallas News*, May 22, 1984.

63. Anne Reifenberg, "Deputy Prisons Director Has Military Background," *Dallas News*, May 22, 1984.

64. Linda Anthony, "Prison Restructuring Urged by 2 Officials," *Austin American Statesman*, November 8, 1984.

65. Bruce Nichols, "New TDC Chief Called Outspoken, Innovative," *Dallas News*, May 22, 1984.

66. "TDC Director Vows Get-Tough Policy to Reestablish Order," *Houston Chronicle*, May 25, 1984.

67. Testimony of John Albach, Staff Director for the Joint Committee on Prison Reform, *Ruiz* Special Master, MAI 8/J88.

68. TSEU started its unionizing drive in 1984, and by 1986 they had unionized two thousand TDC employees. Marquart and Crouch, *Appeal to Justice*, 178.

69. On the relationship between female guards and male inmates and its impact on prison society, see Zimmer, *Women Guarding Men*; and Pollock, *Sex and Supervision*. On changes within the Texas prison guard subculture during this period, Crouch and Marquart, "Becoming a Prison Guard," 63–110; and Crouch, "Book vs. the Boot." On the increase in drug traffic due to new guards, see Crouch and Marquart, *Appeal to Justice*, 158–59, 189–91.

70. "6 Prison Officers Fired in Inquiry on Beating Claims," *Austin American Statesman*, February 7, 1984.

71. Crouch and Marquart, *Appeal to Justice*, 155.

72. Crouch and Marquart, *Appeal to Justice*, 179. Crouch and Marquart's research on the demise of the officer and guard subculture was based on oral histories with guards and on a random sample of 460 prisoners in eight TDC units. Their work remains the most comprehensive source on the guard subculture and is cited here as such.

73. Salvador Buentello, oral history interview with the author, August 8, 2018.

74. Salvador Buentello, oral history interview with the author, August 8, 2018.

75. Salvador Buentello, oral history interview with the author, August 11, 2018; Salvador Buentello, "The Texas Syndicate," Texas Department of Corrections, confidential report, 1985.

76. Lawrence Pope to Ann Lents, Vinson & Elkins, November 2, 1985, "Gangs File," Pope, CAH, 4C797.

77. Salvador Buentello, oral history interview with the author, August 11, 2018.

78. Anonymous gang member to Salvatore Buentello, ten-page, single-spaced memo, "El Syndicato Tejano, Texas Syndicate," undated, in author's possession.

79. Anonymous gang member to Salvatore Buentello, ten-page, single-spaced memo, "El Syndicato Tejano, Texas Syndicate," undated, in author's possession.

80. Salvator Buetello, interview with the author, August 7, 2018.

81. Salvador Buentello, Vice-Chairman, State Classification Committee, "Texas Syndicate: A Review of Its Inceptions, Growth in Violence, and Continued Threat to the Texas Department of Criminal Justice," Confidential Report (Huntsville: Department of Correctional Justice, 1986), in author's possession.

82. Anonymous gang member to Salvatore Buentello, ten-page, single-spaced memo, "El Syndicato Tejano, Texas Syndicate," undated, in author's possession; Salvador Buentello, Vice-Chairman, State Classification Committee, "Texas Syndicate: A Review of Its Inceptions, Growth in Violence, and Continued Threat to the Texas Department of Criminal Justice," Confidential Report (Huntsville: Department of Correctional Justice, 1986), in author's possession.

83. Salvador Buentello, Vice-Chairman, State Classification Committee, "Texas Syndicate: A Review of Its Inceptions, Growth in Violence, and Continued Threat to the Texas Department of Criminal Justice," Confidential Report (Huntsville: Department of Correctional Justice, 1986), in author's possession.

84. Salvador Buentello, Vice-Chairman, State Classification Committee, "Texas Syndicate: A Review of Its Inceptions, Growth in Violence, and Continued Threat to the Texas Department of Criminal Justice," Confidential Report (Huntsville: Department of Correctional Justice, 1986), in author's possession.

85. Salvador Buentello, Vice-Chairman, State Classification Committee, "Texas Syndicate: A Review of its Inceptions, Growth in Violence, and Continued Threat to the Texas Department of Criminal Justice," Confidential Report (Huntsville: Department of Correctional Justice, 1986), in author's possession.

86. The data on gang membership is derived from Robert Fong's study. Fong, "Comparative Study," 11.

87. Camp and Camp, *Prison Gangs*.

88. Salvador Buentello, Vice-Chairman, State Classification Committee, "Texas Syndicate: A Review of Its Inceptions, Growth in Violence, and Continued Threat to the Texas Department of Criminal Justice," Confidential Report (Huntsville: Department of Correctional Justice, 1986), in author's possession.

89. Mary C. Bounds, "Guards Stop Caring," *Dallas News*, September 30, 1984.

90. "Racial Tensions Blamed in Surge of TDC Violence," *Houston Chronicle*, August 9, 1984.

91. Salvator Buentello, interview with the author, August 7, 2018.

92. Sonny Buentello issued the memorandum that acknowledged the Texas AB. His early intelligence work on gang activity informed the work of the sociologists Terry and Mary Pelz and James Marquart in their pioneering study of the Texas AB. It also informs my own brief summary of racial gangs in Texas. Buentello's memorandum read as follows: "Recently, an illegal organization has emerged within the Texas Department of Corrections, which in some respects can be considered an 'off-shoot' of the 'Aryan Brotherhood' organization which can be found in various other states." Pelz, Marquart, and Pelz, "Right-Wing Extremism," 23–37, 27.

93. Salvatore Buentello, "The Aryan Brotherhood," Gang intelligence report, 1985, in author's possession.

94. Pelz, Marquart, and Pelz, "Right-Wing Extremism," 23–37.

95. Pelz, Marquart, and Pelz, "Right-Wing Extremism," 28. One of the authors of the Texas AB study was a former TDC employee, which provided these sociologists with access to over 3,000 letters from and to Aryan Brotherhood members during the period 1984 through 1991. Their pioneering work on the AB provided the words of AB members that are cited here.

96. Pelz, Marquart, and Pelz, "Right-Wing Extremism," 60.

97. Pelz, Marquart, and Pelz, "Right-Wing Extremism," 31.

98. Salvatore Buentello, "The Aryan Brotherhood," Gang intelligence report, 1985, in author's possession.

99. Aryan Brotherhood file, Pope, CAH, 4C773.

100. "The Prisoners' Rights Coalition v. Texas Department of Corrections and the Aryan Brotherhood," AB Gang file, Pope, CAH, 4C773.

101. Lawrence Pope to O. L. McCotter, October 17, 1986, Aryan Brotherhood file, Pope, CAH, 4C773.

102. Salvatore Buentello, "The Aryan Brotherhood," Gang intelligence report, 1985, in author's possession.

103. Aryan Brotherhood Coded Letter, November 20, 1984, in author's possession through the personal collection of Salvador Buentello.

104. Pelz, "Aryan Brotherhood."

105. Anonymous prisoner, Crouch and Marquart, *Appeal to Justice*, 193.

106. On the impact of racial integration in Texas prisons during the 1990s, see Trulson and Marquart, "Caged Melting Pot," 743–82; and Trulson and Marquart, "Racial Desegregation," 233–55.

107. Linda Anthony, "Top Aide Named Prison Chief as Boss Resigns," *American Austin Statesman*, June 18, 1985.

108. Martin and Ekland-Olson, *Texas Prisons*, 243.

109. Mary C. Bounds, "LOCKDOWN: Prison Gang Wars on Rise: Texas Chief Orders Prompt Lockdown," *Dallas Morning News*, September 10, 1985; Salvador Buentello, Vice-Chairman, State Classification Committee, "Texas Syndicate: A Review of Its Inceptions, Growth in Violence, and Continued Threat to the Texas Department of Criminal Justice," Confidential Report (Huntsville: Department of Correctional Justice, 1986), in author's possession.

110. Fong, "Comparative Study," 74.

111. Fong, "Comparative Study," 75.

112. Salvador Buentello, Vice-Chairman, State Classification Committee, "Texas Syndicate: A Review of Its Inceptions, Growth in Violence, and Continued Threat to the Texas Department of Criminal Justice," Confidential Report (Huntsville: Department of Correctional Justice, 1986), in author's possession.

113. Dale Rice, "Prison Gangs Grow Deadly," *Dallas Times Herald*, September 15, 1985.

114. "Lockdown: New TDC Director Brings 'Ultimate Control' to State's Violence Plagued Prison System," *Tyler Morning Telegraph*, August 26, 1984.

115. Salvador Buentello, Vice-Chairman, State Classification Committee, "Texas Syndicate: A Review of Its Inceptions, Growth in Violence, and Continued Threat to the Texas Department of Criminal Justice," Confidential Report (Huntsville: Department of Correctional Justice, 1986), in author's possession.

116. "Team of Last Resort," *Houston Chronicle*, October 21, 1985; "Special Squads to Help Guard Unruly Inmates," *Austin American Statesman*, August 31, 1984.

117. Lynch, *Sunbelt Justice*; Reiter, "Path to Pelican Bay."

118. Social scientists and psychologists have named the effects of "super-maximum" cell isolation as "SHU syndrome," where "perceptual changes, affective disturbances, cognitive difficulties, disturbing thought content and impulse control problems that immediately subside following release from such confinement." O'Keefe et al., "One Year Longitudinal Study." Haney and Lynch, "Regulating Prisons," 477, 478-566.

119. Fong, "Comparative Study," 15; Camp and Camp, *Corrections Yearbook*; Les Layman, "Offender Classification," 47.

120. "N.M. Recycles McCotter," *Coalition for Prisoners' Rights Newsletter, Vol. 12*, April 1987, "McCotter file," Pope, CAH, 4C884.

121. On the role of militarism in a post-Vietnam age, the "savage frontier" in U.S. imagination and culture, and the crisis of "victory culture," see Bacevitch, *New American Militarism*; Slotkin, *Gunfighter Nation*; Gibson, *Warrior Dreams*; and Englehardt, *End of Victory Culture*. On the application of military practices to criminal justice and prison management, see Christianson, "Correctional Law Developments," 243–47. On a corresponding effort to draw upon anti-insurgent thought for domestic policing, see Schrader, "More Than Cosmetic Hanges."

122. "TDC Staff, Early Release Policy under Attack," *Dallas Times Herald*, October 24, 1986.

123. "Candidates Offer Prison Solutions," *Houston Chronicle*, October 30, 1986; "McCotter Should Be Fired, Clements Says," *Huntsville Item*, October 24, 1986.

124. For McCotter's role in the death of Michael Valent, see "Fade Back to the Sixteenth Century: Restraints at the Utah State Prison," Jensie Anderson, ACLU Staff Attorney, *ACLU Reporter*, Summer 1997. For McCotter's role in Iraq, see Department of Justice, "Department of Justice"; "Ex-Head of TDCJ Set Up Iraq Jail: Checkered Career Raises Questions," *Houston Chronicle*, May 14, 2004. For Senator Schumer's criticism of McCotter's role in Abu Ghraib, see "Schumer: Prison Official with Checkered Past Put in Power at Abu Ghraib," press release, May 13, 2004, Office of Senator Charles E. Schumer, New York.

125. Clements was not alone in this kind of political arrangement, as a similar compromise was sought after prisoner litigation in Florida. See Schoenfeld, *Building the Prison State*.

126. "Clements Vows Prison Woes to End by '91," *Houston Post*, October 6, 1987.

127. "Clements Touts $1 Billion Prison-Building Program," *Dallas Times Herald*, October 6, 1987; "Clements Vows Prison Woes to End by '91," *Houston Post*, October 6, 1987; "Prison Growth Proposal May Ease Overcrowding," *San Antonio Express*, July 8, 1987.

128. Barta, *Bill Clements*, 369.

129. Barta, *Bill Clements*, 370.

130. On the first of these prisons, the Michael prison, see Perkinson, *Texas Tough*, 314–15.

131. On the development of gang sentences and placement on Ad Seg in the 1990s through the 2000s, see Burman, "Resocializing and Repairing," 105–29.

132. As of November 30, 2008, TDCJ holds 15,185 prisoners in private facilities out of a total inmate population of 156,070. Alicia Frezia-King to Robert Chase, December 5, 2008, Open Records Request, TDCJ, in author's possession.

133. The 1989 state legislature heralded the new regime of prison management by passing Senate Bill 251, which sanctioned privately owned companies to operate privatized prisons. SB 251 authorized the state to contract with private firms and counties for the construction, management, maintenance, and operation of minimum- and medium-security private prisons that housed fewer than five hundred inmates. These prisons had to be operated at no less than 10 percent less than what it would cost for state operation. In 1987, TDC contracted with Corrections Corporation of America (CCA), the nation's largest privatized prison firm, founded in Nashville, Tennessee, in 1984, and with Beacon-Wackenhut, the world's largest security firm, to operate four five-hundred-man prerelease centers that housed minimum- and medium-security inmates within two years of their release dates. For a journalistic narrative of prison privatization within Louisiana and its ties to Texas, see Bauer, *American Prison*.

134. Martin and Ekland-Olson, *Texas Prisons*, 247.

135. These "super-maximum" prisons are Stiles, Clements, Robertson, Allred, Telford, Hughes, Polunsky, Connally, and McConnell. Alicia Frezia-King to Robert Chase, December 5, 2008, Open Records Request, TDCJ.

136. Human Rights Watch, "Race and Incarceration"; Ziedenberg and Schiraldi, "Race and Imprisonment in Texas"; Coyle, "Texas Criminal Justice System."

137. William Bennett Turner interview with the author, September 30, 2019.

138. Janet Elliot, "Inmate Who Fought for Prison Reform Dies," *Houston Chronicle*, November 15, 2005.

139. Steven Blanchard, interview with the author, March 14, 2007, IOH, Baylor.

140. Prison scholars adopting this critique of the *Ruiz* decision include DiIulio, *Governing Prisons*; and Horton and Nielson, *Walking George*.

141. On Marquart and Crouch's approach to building tenders as "co-opted" inmates, see Crouch and Marquart, *Appeal to Justice*, chap. 3. For their argument that the building tender system became "out of control" due to prison expansion in the mid-1970s, see Crouch and Marquart, *Appeal to Justice*, 114–16. On the effect of *Ruiz* on prisoner control after 1980, see Marquart and Crouch, "Judicial Reform."

142. On the impact of overcrowding on prison violence in Texas, see Ekland-Olson, "Crowding, Social Control," 389–422.

Epilogue

1. These included six "totality of conditions" cases in Alabama, Arkansas, Mississippi, South Carolina, Tennessee, and Texas, while Georgia and Louisiana had comprehensive orders against their flagship maximum security prisons. Florida and North Carolina also faced sweeping court orders on overcrowding and the unconstitutionality of the southern prison dormitory and housing barracks at road work camps. Arkansas, Pugh v. Locke, 406 F. Supp. 318 (M.D. Ala. 1976), and Holt v. Sarver, 300 F. Supp. 825 (E.D. Ark. 1969); Alabama, Holt v. Sarver (Holt II), 309 F. Supp. 362, 365 (E.D. Ark. 197); Mississippi, Gates v. Collier, 349 F. Supp. 881 (N.D. Mississippi, 1972), aff'd, 501 F.2d 1291 (5th Cir. 1974); South Carolina, Plyler v. Evatt, C.A. No. 82-876-0 (D.S.C. January 8, 1985); and Texas, Ruiz v. Estelle, 503 F. Supp. 1265 (S.D. Tex. 1980). Other "totality of conditions" cases in the American South included Tennessee, Grubbs v. Bradley, 552 F. Supp. 1052 (M.D. Tenn. 1982); and Mississippi, Gates v. Collier, 349 F. Supp. 881 (N.D. Mississippi, 1972), aff'd, 501 F.2d 1291 (5th Cir. 1974); Costello v. Wainright, 397 F. Supp. 20 (M.D. Fla. 1975); Small v. Martin, No. 85-987-CRT (E.D. N.C. 1988); and Hubert v. Ward, No. C-E-80-414-M (W.D. N.C. 1985), thirteen road and farm camps.

2. Tennessee Department of Corrections (TDOC) Annual Report, 1978–1979, *Grubbs Case* (RG#321), Tennesse Public Library, roll 6, box 7, folder 27.

3. Patricia Templeton, "State Prisons' Rate for Death by Violence Highest in Country," *Nashville Benner*, November 2, 1985.

4. Grubbs v. Bradley, 552 F. Supp. 1052 (M.D.Tenn. 1982).

5. Dwight Lewis, "Earlier Prison Problems Left Unresolved," *Tennesseean*, July 7, 1985.

6. Karim Aziz Abdullah, "Prisoners Plan for the TDOC," Tennesse Department of Corrections Records (RG#277), roll 2, box 2, folder 22.

7. Dwight Lewis, "Correction Overhaul Begins, 4 Advanced," *Tennessean*, August 6, 1983; Woody Baird, "Striking Prisoners Calm down at Ft. Pillow," *Daily New-Journal*, July 14, 1983.

8. Dwight Davis, "Correction Department Ommissions Damage Credibility," *Tennessean*, July 20, 1983.

9. Ron Lewis Freeman, "What Really Happened At Fort Pillow," Tennessee Department of Correction Records (RG#277), Tennessee Public Library, roll 2, box 2, folder 22.

10. Patricia Templeton, "State Prisons' Rate for Death by Violence Highest in Country," *Nashville Benner*, November 2, 1985.

11. Patricia Templeton, "State Prisons' Rate for Death by Violence Highest in Country," *Nashville Benner*, November 2, 1985.

12. "Inmate Killed after Tennessee Prison Riots End," United Press International, July 3, 1985.

13. S. 1279, 104th Congress (1995), The Prison Litigation Reform Act (PLRA); Prison Litigation Reform Act of 1995, Pub. L. No. 104-134, 110 Stat. 1321.

14. On the courts' response to the PLRA and its restrictions, see Belbot, "Prison Litigation Reform Act."

15. On the practical effect of PLRA on the filing of prisoner lawsuits in federal court, see Clarke, "Barring the Federal Courthouse," 301–14.

16. For an overview of this twenty-first-century history of prisoner resistance, see IWW, Houston Incarcerated Workers Organizing Committee, "Incarcerated Workers Take the Lead: Prison Struggles in the United States, 2008–2016," political pamphlet in author's possession.

17. Forest Wilder, "The Pecos Insurrection: How a Private Prison Pushed Inmates to the Brink," *Texas Observer*, October 8, 2009.

18. Sarah Wheaton, "Prisoners Strike in Georgia," *New York Times*, December 12, 2010.

19. Benjamin Wallace-Wells, "The Plot from Solitary," *New York Magazine*, February 26, 2014, accessed May 1, 2018, http://nymag.com/news/features/solitary-secure-housing-units-2014-2/.

20. Bowers, "Challenging Prisons." As a new prisoner, Asur's mentor was Richard "Mafundi" Lake, a Black Panther, and part of his political awakening included the profound influence of Stokely Carmichael's *Ready for Revolution*.

21. "Texas Inmates Strike for Better Conditions," *Austin Chronicle*, April 4, 2016.

22. On the strike's historical connection to the Attica prison uprising of 1971, see Robert Chase, "Slaves of the State Prison Uprisings and the Legacy of Attica," *Boston Review*, November 11, 2016, accessed May 31, 2019, http://bostonreview.net/law-justice/robert-chase-slaves-state-prison-uprisings-and-legacy-attica.

23. For the full announcement of the nationwide prison strike, see IWW Incarcerated Workers Organizing Committee, "Announcement of Nationally Coordinated Prisoner Workstoppage for Sept. 9, 2016," accessed October 12, 2016, https://iwoc.noblogs.org/post/2016/04/01/announcement-of-nationally-coordinated-prisoner-workstoppage-for-sept-9-2016/; and "National Prisoner Workstoppage: STOP SLAVERY—Sept 9 2016," https://freealabamamovement.wordpress.com/national-prison-strike-sept-9-2016?iframe=true&theme_preview=true.

24. For mainstream news coverage, see Tom Kutsch, "Inmates Strike in Prisons Nationwide over 'Slave Labor' Working Conditions," *Guardian*, September 9, 2016; E. Tammy Kim, "A National Strike against 'Prison Slavery,'" *New Yorker*, October 3, 2016; Jaweed Kaleem, "'This Is Slavery': U.S. Inmates Strike in What Activists Call One of the Biggest Prison Protests in Modern History," *Los Angeles Times*, October 28, 2016.

25. For online news gathering sources, see James Kilgore, "'We're Freedom Fighters': The Story of the Nationwide Prison Labor Strike," Truthout, accessed September 18, 2016, http://www.truthout.org/news/item/37644-we-re-freedom-fighters-the-story-of-the-nationwide-prison-labor-strike; Ivan Stamenkovic, "The Largest Prison Strike in History Is Being Ignored by Major Media," September 26, 2016, accessed October 12, 2016, http://countercurrentnews.com/2016/09/largest-prison-strike-history-ignored-major-media/; Rebekah Barber, "Nationwide Prison Strike Draws Attention to Unpaid Labor," Facing South: A Voice for a Changing South, September 16, 2016, accessed October 13, 2016, https://www.facingsouth.org/2016/09/nationwide-prison-strike-draws-attention-unpaid-labor.

26. Rebekah Barber, "Nationwide Prison Strike Draws Attention to Unpaid Labor," Facing South: A Voice for a Changing South, September 16, 2016, accessed October 13, 2016, https://www.facingsouth.org/2016/09/nationwide-prison-strike-draws-attention-unpaid-labor.

27. Open Records Request from TDCJ to Robert T. Chase, September 16, 2019.

28. Jaweed Kaleem, "'This Is Slavery': U.S. Inmates Strike in What Activists Call One of the Biggest Prison Protests in Modern History," *Los Angeles Times*, October 28, 2016.

29. For a close narrative of the national prisoner strike, its origins in South Carolina, and an analysis of its demands, see Toussaint Losier, "The 2018 National Prison Strike: A Movement Making Its Mark," Verso, August 27, 2018, accessed August 28, 2018, https://www.versobooks.com/blogs/3993-the-2018-national-prison-strike-a-movement-making-its-mark; Ed Pilkington, "US Inmates Stage Nationwide Prison Labor Strike over 'Modern Slavery,'" *Guardian*, August 21, 2018.

30. Ed Pilkington, "US Inmates Stage Nationwide Prison Labor Strike over 'Modern Slavery,'" *Guardian*, August 21, 2018.

31. In 1965 dollars, TDC's cotton production was valued at $1,522,021.40. In 1990 dollars, TDCJ's cotton production was valued at $201,806. Texas Department of Corrections, Annual Report, 1965; Texas Department of Correctional Justice, Annual Report, 1990.

32. Keri Blakinger, Alyson Ward, and Allan Turner, "Ray Hill, a Houston Icon and Civil Rights Activist, Dies at 78," *Houston Chronicle*, November 24, 2018.

33. News clipping, *Houston Post*, December 9, 1984, "Quinlan file," Pope, CAH, 4C825.

34. Margarite Frances Cruz, telephone conversation with the author, March 6, 2019.

35. Pete Wittenberg, "Accuser testifies Ruiz target of 'put-up' story," *Houston Post*, April 7, 1981; Pete Wittenberg, "Sex abuse attempt count against Ruiz dropped," *Houston Post*, January 8, 1981; "Man who stated prison suit faces new robbery charge," *San Antonio Express*, June 24, 1982; "Ruiz charged with possession of marijuana," *Austin-American Statesman*, March 2, 1982; Dick Stanley, "State to answer Ruiz assertion of conspiracy," *Austin-American Statesman*, June 28, 1982; Jim Phillips, "Ruiz faces prison again after losing parole vote," *Austin-American Statesman*, September 7, 1983; Joe Vargo, "Prison activist Ruiz is charged in attempted slaying of Austenite," April 29, 1984; Joe Vargo, "Prison activist Ruiz charged in gun violation," June 11, 1984; "Ruiz calls gun charge conspiracy by officers," *Austin-American Statesman*, June 12, 1984; Jerry White, "Activist Ruiz is defended," *Austin-American Statesman*, September 27, 1984; Mike Cox, "Prison reformer David Ruiz held on felony charges," *Austin-American Statesman*, September 9, 1984; "Jerry White, "Ex-prison activist Ruiz sentence to 25 years," *Austin-American Statesman*, January 31, 1985. The security guards were all-white and were called freeman.

36. "Ruiz Convicted of Aggravated Robbery," *Austin American Statesman*, December 7, 1985.

37. David Ruíz, "Tough with a Knife," unpublished memoir, in author's possession.

38. There are several drafts of this unpublished poem in David Ruíz's personal papers. What follows is a poem titled "third draft," and it appears to be the final copy.

39. "Steel on Steel," unpublished poem by David Ruíz (there are at least three different versions), in author's possession and given with permission of his widow, Marie Ruíz.

40. Franklin, *Prison Literature*, 242.

41. Foucault and Simon, "Michel Foucault on Attica," 26–34, 27.

42. Kelley, *Freedom Dreams*, vii.

Bibliography

Archival Sources and Oral Histories

Manuscript Collections and Archives

Dolph Briscoe Center for American History, University of Texas at Austin
    Briscoe, Dolph, Texas Governor, Papers
    Citizens United for the Rehabilitation of Errants (CURE) Papers
    Jalet, Frances T. Freeman, Papers, 1966–86
    Pope, Lawrence, Papers, 1961–89
    Ruiz v. Estelle Collection, Office of the Special Master, Vincent Nathan, Papers, 1979–92
    Vertical Files
        Prisons: news clippings, vertical file
        Jails: news clippings, vertical file
        Criminal Justice: news clippings
Benson Latin American Collection, University of Texas at Austin
    Idar, Ed, Papers
Texas A&M University
    Clements, William P., Texas Governor, Papers
    Estelle, James, Papers
Texas State Archives and Library (TSLA), Austin, Texas
    Brooks, Chet, Senate, Texas Legislature Papers
    Clower, Ron, Senate, Texas Legislature Papers
    Daniel, Price, Texas Governor, Papers
    Hobby, William Petus, Jr. Lieutenant Governor, Papers
    Jester, Beauford, Texas Governor, Papers
    Carrasco Hostage & Escape, Files
    Shivers, Allan, Texas Governor, Papers
    Texas Department of Criminal Justice (TDCJ), Papers
        Administrative correspondence and subject files, 1961–62, 1967–69, 1974–76
        Administrative correspondence, Board of Corrections, 1949, 1955, 1958–64, 1967–74, 1976
        Administrative correspondence, insanity of inmates, 1950–54, 1960–64
        Convict ledgers, 1854–1970
        In service training materials, 1975
        Ruiz litigation files and court records, 1966, 1978–87
        Rules, regulation, and procedural manuals, 1947–91
        Texas Prison Rodeo Photographs, 1935–84
        Texas Prison Rodeo Programs, 1941–86

TDCJ Photographs Collection, 1940–85
TDCJ-*Ruiz*, General Counsel's Office, *Ruiz* litigation files
White, Mark, Texas Governor, Papers
Texas Southern University
  Leland, Mickey, Papers
Sam Houston State University, Huntsville, Texas
  Beto, George, Papers
  MacCormick, Austin, Papers
Grenader Special Collections, State University of New York, Albany
  New York Prison Association
Tennessee State Library and Archives
  Tennessee Department of Corrections
    Grubbs Lawsuit Records
  Tennessee Department of Corrections Records
Tulane University, Louisiana
  Armistad Research Center
    The Angolite (Angola prison newspaper)
    Robert Hillary King, unedited typescript autobiography
  Special Collections
    ACLU of Louisiana Records
      Box 1: The Angola Four, 1973 (Folder 15)
      Box 2: Black Muslims (Folder 15, 16)
      Joseph, Frankie V. v. Louisiana State Penitentiary et al., 1973–1974 (Folder 22)

Published Documents and Reports

Director. *Annual Report of the Director of the Administrative Office of United States Courts.* Washington D.C.: Government Printing Office, 1966 and 1984.
Association of State Correctional Administrators and Yale Law School's Arthur Liman Public Interest Program. "Aiming to Reduce Time-In-Cell: Reports from Correctional Systems on the Numbers of Prisoners in Restricted Housing and on the Potential of Policy Changes to Bring About Reforms." November, 2016. https://law.yale.edu/system/files/area/center/liman/document/aimingtoreducetic.pdf and https://law.yale.edu/system/files/documents/pdf/Liman/asca_iman_2018_restrictive_housing_revised_sept_25_2018_-_embargoed_unt.pdf.
"Citizen's Advisory Committee Final Report." Released November 25, 1974.
Coyle, Michael J. "Latinos and the Texas Criminal Justice System." National Council of La Raza, 2003, Statistical Brief, no. 2.
Wainwright, Louie L. *Secretary, Annual Report, 1976–1977.* Florida Department of Offender Rehabilitation. http://edocs.dlis.state.fl.us/fldocs/dcor/retro_ar/1976-1977.pdf, accessed March 15, 2018.
Joint Committee on Prison Reform, Texas Legislature. "Final Report of the Joint Committee on Prison Reform, 63rd Legislature, December 1974."
Houston Incarcerated Workers Organizing Committee. "Incarcerated Workers Take the Lead: Prison Struggles in the United States, 2008–2016." (Pamphlet in

author's possession). https://itsgoingdown.org/incarcerated-workers-take-lead
-prison-struggles-united-states-2008-2016.

Human Rights Watch Press Backgrounder. "Race and Incarceration in the United
States." New York, New York: Human Rights, 2002.

Jones, Richard P. *Prison Labor in the United States,* Bulletin No. 698, U.S.
Department of Labor, Bureau of Labor Statistics. Washington, D.C.: U.S.
Government Printing Office, 1941).

Justice Policy Institute. "Race and Imprisonment in Texas: The Disproportionate
Incarceration of Latinos and African Americans in the Lone Star State." Jason
Ziedenberg and Vincent Schiraldi, researchers.

Kaplan, Dana, Vincent Schiraldi, and Jason Ziedenberg. "Texas Tough: An Analysis
of Incarceration and Crime Trends in the Lone Star State." *Justice Policy Institute,*
October 1, 2000. http://www.justicepolicy.org/research/2062, and http://www
.justicepolicy.org/uploads/justicepolicy/documents/texas_tough.pdf.

O'Keefe, Maureen L., Kelli J. Klebe, Alysha Stucker, Kristin Sturm, and William
Leggett. "One Year Longitudinal Study of the Psychological Effects of
Administrative Segregation." U.S. Department of Justice report, 2011, 5. Accessed
June 1, 2018, https://wwwncjrs.gov/pdffiles1/jij/grants/232973.pdf.

*Report of the Commission Appointed by the Governor of Texas to Investigate the
Alleged Mismanagement and Cruel Treatment of the Convicts.* Houston: A. C. Gray,
State Printer, April 10, 1875.

U.S. Commission on Civil Rights. "Mexican Americans and the Administration
of Justice in the Southwest." Washington, D.C.: Government Printing Office,
1970.

U.S. Department of Commerce. "Census Population: 1980." Washington, D.C.:
United States Government Printing Office, 1983.

U.S. Department of Commerce. *Sixteenth Census of the United States: 1940,
Population, Vol. II, Part 6.* Washington, D.C.: U.S. Government Printing Office,
1943.

Texas Department of Corrections. *20 Years of Progress.* Huntsville, 1967.

———. *Texas Department of Corrections: A Brief History.* Huntsville, 1968.

———. *30 Years of Progress.* Huntsville, 1977.

———. *Annual Reports.* Huntsville, 1944–90.

U.S. Department of Justice. *The Attorney General's Survey of Release Procedures Vol.
V: Prisons.* Leavenworth, KS: Federal Prison Industries, 1940.

U.S. Department of Justice. "Department of Justice Sends 25 Advisors to Iraq
in Support of Provisional Authority Effort to Reconstruct Criminal System."
www.usdoj.gov/archive/opa/pr/2003/May/03_ag_267.htm, accessed July 29,
2019.

U.S. Federal Bureau of Investigation. *Uniform Crime Reports* 17, no. 2. Annual
Bulletin. Washington D.C.: Government Printing Office, 1946.

———. *Uniform Crime Reports* 18, no. 2. Annual Bulletin. Washington D.C.:
Government Printing Office, 1947.

Ziedenberg, Jason, and Vincent Schiraldi. "Race and Imprisonment in Texas: The
Disproportionate Incarceration of Latinos and African Americans in the Lone
Star State," Justice Policy Institute.

Unpublished Documents and Reports

Jalet, Frances. "The Ellis Report," November 6, 1968, in author's possession
Joint Committee on Prison Reform (JCPR) unpublished working papers
   Access to Legal Materials
   Building Tender System, supplemental report
   Coffield Unit: A New Prison for Texas
   Counseling
   Custody and Security
   Education and Recreation Fund
   Homosexuality in Texas Department of Corrections
   Medical Care
   Labor and Industry
   Personnel
   Prison Disciplinary Procedures
   Prisoner Classification
   Prisoner Education
   Rehabilitation
   Report on Investigation of Incident at Ramsey I, November 8, 1973
   Confidential Staff Report: Tension at the Ramsey Unit
   Treatment of the Mentally Ill and the Mentally Retarded
   Women in Prison in Texas

Private Papers (unpublished and in author's possession)

Norwood Andrews. "Historic Foundations of Prison Privatization: Sugar and
   Convict Lease in Texas." Unpublished paper, in author's possession.
David Ruiz, private papers and memoir, with permission of Ruiz family and in
   author's possession.
David Ruiz, "Tough with a Knife, Hell with a Writ," unpublished memoir.
Robert Lee Mudd, prisoner activist, private papers, in author's possession.
Johnny Martínez, prisoners activist, private papers, in author's possession.
Defense Papers of Eroy Brown, with permission of William T. Habern and in
   author's possession.

Newspapers

Albuquerque Journal
Austin American Statesman
Chicano Times
Corpus Christi Caller-Times
Dallas Morning News
Dallas Times Herald
Denison Times Herald
Express-News
Echo (Huntsville)

Fort Worth Star Telegram
Galveston Daily News
Houston Chronicle
Houston Post
Houston Press
Huntsville Item
Nashville Tennessean
New York Times
New York Times Magazine

Newsweek
Odessan American
Papal Chicano
San Antonio Express
San Antonio Express-News
San Antonio Light
San Antonio News
Star Telegram
Texas Monthly

Texas Observer
The Black Panther: Newspaper of the
  Black Panther Party
Tyler Courrier-Times
Tyler Morning Telegraph
Waco-News Tribune
Washington Post
Washington Times
Wall Street Journal

Oral Histories Conducted by the Author

(held at Baylor University's Institute for Oral History)
Barnes, Lewis [current TDC prisoner], March 22, 2007
Beavers, Lanny [current TDC prisoner], March 14, 2007
Blanchard, Steven [current TDC prisoner], March 14, 2007
Breeden, Clarence [current TDC prisoner], March 9, 2007
Buentello, Salvador [former assistant director of the Security Threat Group
    Management office, TDCJ], August 10, 2018
Casey, Larry [current TDC prisoner], March 25, 2007
Collins, Wilbur [current TDC prisoner], March 21, 2007
Combs, Charlie [former correctional officer], June 5, 2006
Elder, Arthur [current TDC prisoner], March 29, 2007
Emerson, Wesley [current TDC prisoner], March 6, 2007
Eubanks, Michael [current TDC prisoner], March 13, 2007
Gilabert, Ana Lucia [current TDC prisoner], April 2, 2007
Grundstrum, Daniel [former TDC prisoner], March 25, 2007, April 1 and 3, 2007
Guajardo, Guadalupe [current TDC prisoner], March 8, 2007
Haber, Roy, [prisoners' rights attorney], March 2018
Habern, William [criminal defense attorney for Eroy Brown], November 5, 2005
Hernández, Alvaro Luna [current TDC prisoner], March 23, 2007
Hill, Ray [former TDC prisoner], November 8, 2005
Hurt, Chuck [current TDC prisoner], June 19, 2006
Jackson, Bruce [folklorist and English professor], April 26, 2008
Johnson, Daniel [current TDC prisoner], March 6, 2007
Kyle, Jack [former warden and assistant director], June25, 2005
Limbocker, Daryle [current TDC prisoner], March 22, 2007
Martínez, Johnny, [former TDC prisoner] May 2018
McCray, Robert [current TDC prisoner], March 5, 2007
McMillan, Ernest [former TDC prisoner], April 4, 2007
Mitchell, Robert [current TDC prisoner], March 28, 2007
Mudd, Robert [current TDC prisoner], March 28, 2007
Nance, Sherry [current TDC prisoner], April 2, 2007
Norris, Zeke [former TDC prisoner], June 22, 2005
Pasha, Haneef (a.k.a. Arthur Johnson) [current TDC prisoner], March 20, 2007

Quate, Jerry [current TDC prisoner], March 12, 2007
Scribner, Allyn [current TDC prisoner], March 29, 2007
Siros, Walter [former TDC inmate], June 5, 2005
Sullivan, Charlie [former Priest and co-founder of CURE], June 2011
Sullivan, Pauline [former Nun and co-founder of CURE], June 2011
Turner, William Bennet [prisoners' rights attorney, NAACP Legal Defense Fund],
    August 2019
Ward, Eddie James [former TDC prisoner], March 23, 2007
Willett, Jim [former TDC prison warden], June 5, 2005

Oral Histories Conducted by Other Researchers

Alexander, Cecil [former TDC prisoner], May 1999.
Alva, Carlos [former TDC prisoner], February 9, 2003. *
Anderson, James "Wildcat" [former assistant warden], May 7, 2005, Texas Prison
    History Museum, Huntsville.
Beto, George [former TDC director], conducted by Janye Craiq, December 1984,
    Texas Prison History Museum, Huntsville.
Bowers, Devon Douglas. "Challenging Prisons: An Interview with the Free Alabama
    Movement." Interview with Asur, TruthOut.com.
Briggs, David [former TDC prisoner], June 7, 1998. *
Clewis, Benny Wade [former TDC prisoner], February 22, 1991. *
Clewis, Benny Wade, October 21, 1997. *
Cousins, Robert [former TDC warden], June 8, 1998. *
Cousins, Robert, December 17, 1998. *
Crews, D'Anne [O. B. Ellis's secretary], undated oral history, Texas Prison History
    Museum, Huntsville.
Husbands, Hal [former TDC warden], June 6, 1998. *
Killbuck, Robert [Ellis prison correctional officer], undated oral history, Texas
    Prison History Museum, Huntsville.
Martínez, John V. [former TDC prisoner], February 9, 2003. *
Mauricio, Eduardo [former TDC prisoner], August 29, 1998. *
McAdams, Carl Luther [former TDC warden], August 9, 1996. *
McAdams, Carl Luther. "Beartracks" [former warden], oral history conducted by
    Cynthia Linzy, October 26, 1987, Texas Prison History Museum, Huntsville.
McAdams, Carl Luther. "Beartracks," undated oral history conducted by Susanne
    Mason.
McCarter, Billy Wayne "Redbird" [former TDC prisoner], October 20, 1997. *
McCarter, Billy Wayne "Redbird" [current TDC prisoner], conducted by Jim
    Willett, May 22, 2003, Texas Prison History Museum, Huntsville.
Mercado, Erasmo [former TDC prisoner], February 9, 2003. *
Patterson, Floyd [former TDC prisoner]. *
Portillo, Rudy [former TDC prisoner], February 9, 2003. *
Powell, Johnny Raymond [former TDC prisoner], conducted by Jim Willett,
    December 18, 2003, Texas Prison History Museum, Huntsville.
Robins, Carl [former TDC prisoner]. *

Ruiz, David [TDC prisoner], conducted by Robert Perkinson, with Robert Perkinson's permission.

Slaton, Al [former TDC prisoner], October 18, 1997. *

Slaton, Al, 2002. *

Slaton, Al [former TDC prisoner], conducted by Robert Perkinson, with Robert Perkinson's permission.

Woodman, Linda [Carrasco hostage and former warden], conducted by Jim Willett, Texas Prison History Museum, Huntsville.

*Partial list of transcripts of interviews produced by Susanne E. Mason for the production of the historical documentary *Writ Writer*. All transcripts are copyright © Susanne E. Mason and are used here by permission of Susanne E. Mason. Any other reproduction of this material is strictly prohibited.

Secondary Sources

Abu-Jamal, Mumia. *Jailhouse Lawyers: Prisoners Defending Prisoners v. The U.S.A.* San Francisco: City Lights, 2009.

Acuña, Rodolfo. *Occupied America: A History of Chicanos.* New York: Pearson Longman, 2002.

Adler, Jeffrey S. *First in Violence, Deepest in Dirt: Homicide in Chicago.* Cambridge, MA: Harvard University Press, 2006.

Alexander, Jeffrey C., Eyerman, Bernhard Giesen, Neil J. Smelser, Piotr Sztompka. *Collective Trauma and Collective Identity.* Chicago: University of Chicago Press, 2004.

Alvarez, Luis. *The Power of the Zoot: Youth Culture and Resistance During World War II.* Berkeley: University of California Press, 2008.

Applebome, Peter. *Dixie Rising: How the South Is Shaping American Values, Politics, and Culture.* New York: Harcourt Brace, 1996.

Appy, Christian. *Working-Class War: American Combat Soldiers and Vietnam.* Chapel Hill: University of North Carolina Press, 1993.

Araiza, Lauren A. *To March for Others: The Black Freedom Struggle and the United Farm Workers.* Philadelphia: University of Pennsylvania Press, 2013.

Arsenault, Raymond. *Freedom Riders: 1961 and the Struggle for Racial Justice.* Oxford: Oxford University Press, 2011.

Austin, Curtis. *Up against the Wall: Violence in the Making and Unmaking of the Black Panther Party.* Fayetteville: University of Arkansas Press, 2006.

Ayers, Edward L. *Vengeance and Justice: Crime and Punishment in the Ninetieth-Century American South.* Oxford: Oxford University Press, 1984.

Bacevitch, Andrew J. *The New American Militarism: How Americans Are Seduced by War.* Oxford: Oxford University Press, 2003.

Baer, Hans A. *The Black Spiritual Movement: A Religious Response to Racism.* Knoxville: University of Tennessee Press, 1984.

Bair, Asatar P. *Prison Labor in the United States: An Economic Analysis.* New York: Routledge, 2008.

Balderrama, Francisco E. *Decade of Betrayal: Mexican Repatriation in the 1930s.* Albuquerque: University of New Mexico Press, 1995.

Barios, Gregg, ed. and trans. *Fred Gómez Carrasco: Memories of My Life*. Los Angeles: Posada, 1979.

Barta, Carolyn. *Bill Clements: Texian to His Toenails*. Austin, TX: Eakin Press, 1996.

Bartley, Numan V. *The New South, 1945–1980: The Story of the South's Modernization*. Baton Rouge: Louisiana State University Press, 1985.

Bauer, Shane. *American Prison: A Reporter's Undercover Journey into the Business of Punishment*. New York: Penguin, 2018.

Bederman, Gail. *Manliness and Civilization*. Chicago: University of Chicago Press, 1995.

Behnken, Brian D. *Fighting Their Own Battles: Mexican Americans, African Americans, and the Struggle for Civil Rights in Texas*. Chapel Hill: University of North Carolina Press, 2011.

Bell, Daniel. *The Cultural Contradictions of Capitalism*. New York: Basic, 1976.

Berger, Dan. *The Hidden Seventies: Histories of Radicalism*. New Brunswick, NJ: Rutgers University Press, 2010.

———. *Captive Nation: Black Prison Organizing in the Civil Rights Era*. Chapel Hill: University of North Carolina Press, 2015.

Berger, Dan, and Toussaint Losier. *Rethinking the Prison Movement*. New York: Routledge, 2018.

Berlin, Ira, and Morgan, Philip D. *Cultivation and Culture: Labor and the Shaping of Slave Life in the Americas*. Charlottesville: University Press of Virginia, 1993.

Berryhill, Michael. *The Trials of Eroy Brown: The Murder Case that Shook the Texas Prison System*. Austin: University of Texas Press, 2011.

Berubé, Allan. *Coming Out under Fire: The History of Gay Men and Women in World War II*. New York: Free Press, 1990.

Beverly, John. *Testimonio: On the Politics of Truth*. Minneapolis: University of Minnesota, 2004.

Blackmon, Douglas. *Slavery by Another Name: The Re-enslavement of Black Americans from the Civil War to World War II*. New York: Doubleday, 2008.

Blanton, Carlos K. *The Strange Career of Bilingual Education in Texas, 1936–1981*. College Station: Texas A&M Press University Press, 2004.

Block, Sharon. *Rape and Sexual Power in Early America*. Chapel Hill: University of North Carolina Press, 2006.

Blue, Ethan. *Doing Time in the Depression: Everyday Life in Texas and California Prisons*. New York: New York University Press, 2012.

Brown, Joyce, with Jay Gaines. *Joyce Ann Brown: Justice Denied*. Chicago: Noble, 1990.

Brown, Vincent. *The Reaper's Garden: Death and Power in the World of Atlantic Slavery*. Cambridge, MA: Harvard University Press, 2008.

Buffum, Peter C. *Homosexuality in Prison*. Washington, D.C.: U.S. Department of Justice, Law Enforcement Assistance Administration, 1972.

Camp, George, and Camille Camp. *Prison Gangs: Their Extent, Nature and Impact on Prisons*. Washington, D.C.: U.S. Department of Justice, 1985.

———. *The Corrections Yearbook*. New York: Criminal Justice Institute, 1983–1987.

Campbell, Randolph B. *An Empire for Slavery: The Peculiar Institution in Texas, 1821–1865*. Baton Rouge: Louisiana State University Press, 1989.

Canaday, Margot. *The Straight State: Sexuality and Citizenship in Twentieth-Century America*. Princeton, NJ: Princeton University Press, 2009.

Carleton, Mark T. *Politics and Punishment: The History of the Louisiana State Penal System*. Baton Rouge: Louisiana State University Press, 1971.

Carroll, Leo. *Hacks, Blacks, and Cons: Race Relations in a Maximum Security Prison*. Lexington, MA: D. C. Heath, 1974.

Carson, Clayborne. *In Struggle: SNCC and the Black Awakening of the 1960s*. Cambridge, MA: Harvard University Press, 1981.

Chauncey, George. *Gay New York: Gender, Urban Culture, and the Making of the Gay Male World, 1890–1940*. New York: Basic, 1994.

Chavez, Ernesto. *¡Mi Raza Primero! Nationalism, Identity, and Insurgency in the Chicano Movement in Los Angeles*. Berkeley: University of California Press, 2002.

Childs, Dennis. *Slaves of the State: Black Incarceration from the Chain Gang to the Penitentiary*. Minneapolis: University of Minneapolis Press, 2015.

Chudacoff, Howard P. *The Age of the Bachelor: Creating an American Subculture*. Princeton, NJ: Princeton University Press, 1999.

Clemmer, Donald. *The Prison Community*. Boston: Christopher Publishing, 1940.

Cobb, Charles E., Jr. *This Nonviolent Stuff'll Get You Killed: How Guns Made the Civil Rights Movement Possible*. New York: Basic, 2014.

Cobb, James C. *Industrialization and Southern Society, 1877–1984 (New Perspectives on the South)*. Lexington: University Press of Kentucky, 1984.

Cohen, Deborah. *Braceros: Migrant Citizens and Transnational Subjects in the Postwar States and Mexico*. Chapel Hill: University of North Carolina Press, 2011.

Colvin, Mark. *The Penitentiary in Crisis: From Accommodation to Riot in New Mexico*. Albany: State University of New York Press, 1992.

Conley, Carolyn. *Melancholy Accidents: The Meaning of Violence in Post-Famine Ireland*. Lanham, MD: Lexington, 1999.

Cowie, Jefferson. *Stayin Alive: The 1970s and the Last Days of the Working Class*. New York: New Press, 2012.

Cronin, Thomas E., Tania Z. Cronin, and Michael E. Milakovich. *U.S. v. Crime in the Street*. Bloomington: Indiana University Press, 1981.

Crosby, Emilye. *A Little Taste of Freedom: The Black Freedom Struggle in Claiborne County, Mississippi*. Chapel Hill: University of North Carolina Press, 2005.

Cross, Gary. *An All-Consuming Century: Why Commercialism Won in Modern America*. New York: Columbia University Press, 2000.

Crouch, Ben M., and James W. Marquart. *An Appeal to Justice: Litigated Reform of Texas Prisons*. Austin: University of Texas Press, 1989.

Cummins, Eric. *The Rise and Fall of California's Radical Prison Movement*. Stanford: Stanford University Press, 1994.

Cuordileone, K. A. *Manhood and American Political Culture in the Cold War*. New York: Routledge, 2005.

Curtain, Mary Ellen. *Black Prisoners and Their World: Alabama, 1865–1900*. Charlottesville: University of Virginia, 2000.

Curtis, Edward E. *Black Muslim Religion in the Nation of Islam, 1960–1975*. Chapel Hill: University of North Carolina Press, 2006.

D'Emilio, John. *Sexual Politics, Sexual Communities: The Making of the Homosexual Minority, 1940–1970*. Chicago: University of Chicago Press, 1983.

———. *Making Trouble: Essays on Gay History, Politics and the University*. New York: Routledge, 1992.

———. *Lost Prophet: The Life and Times of Bayard Rustin*. New York: Free, 2003.

Daniel, Pete. *Breaking the Land: The Transformation of Cotton, Tobacco, and Rice Cultures since 1880*. Urbana: Illinois University Press, 1985.

Davidson, Theodore R. *Chicano Prisoners: The Key to San Quentin*. New York: Holt, Rinehart, and Winston, 1974.

Davis, Mike. *City of Quartz: Excavating the Future in Los Angeles*. New York: Vintage, 1992.

De Certeau, Michel. *The Practice of Everyday Life*. Translated by Steven Randall. Berkeley: University of California Press, 1984.

de León, Arnold. *They Call Them Greasers: Anglo Attitudes towards Mexicans in Texas, 1821–1900*. Austin, University of Texas Press, 1983.

———. *Ethnicity in the Sunbelt: Mexican Americans in Houston*. College Station: Texas A&M University Press, 2001.

Dean, Robert. *Imperial Brotherhood: Gender and the Making of Cold War Foreign Policy*. Amherst: University of Massachusetts Press, 2001.

Delgado, Richard, and Jean Stefancic, eds. *Critical White Studies: Looking Behind the Mirror*. Philadelphia: Temple University Press, 1997.

Diamond, Andrew J. *Mean Streets: Chicago Youths and the Everyday Struggle for Empowerment in the Multiracial City, 1908–1969*. Berkeley: University of California Press, 2009.

Diaz, George. *Border Contraband: A History of Smuggling across the Rio Grande*. Austin: University of Texas Press, 2015.

Díaz-Cotto, Juanita. *Gender, Ethnicity, and the State: Latina and Latino Prison Politics*. Albany: State University of New York Press, 1996.

———. *Chicana Lives and Criminal Justice: Voices from El Barrio*. Austin: University of Texas Press, 2006.

DiIulio, John. *Governing Prisons: A Comparative Study of Correctional Management*. New York: Free Press, 1987.

———. *Courts, Corrections, and the Constitution: The Impact of Judicial Intervention on Prisons and Jails*. Oxford: Oxford University Press, 1990.

Donald, Walker. *Penology for Profit: A History of the Texas Prison System, 1967–1912*. College Station: Texas A&M University Press, 2000.

Dugger, Ronnie. *Our Invaded Universities*. New York: W. W. Norton, 1974.

Englehardt, Tom. *The End of Victory Culture: Cold War America and the Disillusioning of a Generation*. New York: Basic, 1995.

Epps, Charles. *The Rights Revolution: Lawyers, Activists, and Supreme Courts*. Chicago: University of Chicago Press, 1998.

Essiem-Udom, E. U. *Black Nationalism: The Search for Identity in America*. Chicago: University of Chicago Press, 1962.

Estes, Steve. *I Am a Man! Race, Manhood, and the Civil Rights Movement*. Chapel Hill: University of North Carolina Press, 2005.

Eyerman, Ron. *Cultural Trauma: Slavery and the Formation of African American Identity*. New York: Cambridge University Press, 2001.

Fanon, Frantz. *Black Skin, White Masks*. Translated by Richard Philcox. New York: Grove Press, 2008 (original publication, 1952).

Farmer, James. *Lay Bare the Heart: An Autobiography of the Civil Rights Movement*. New York: New American Library, 1985.

Feeley, Malcolm M., and Edward Rubin. *Judicial Policy Making and the State: How the Courts Reformed America's Prisons*. London: Cambridge University Press, 2000.

Feeley, Malcolm M., and Austin Sarat. *The Policy Dilemma: Federal Crime Policy and the Law Enforcement Assistance Administration*. Minneapolis: University of Minnesota Press, 1980.

Fierce, Milfred C. *Slavery Revisited: Blacks and the Southern Convict Lease System, 1865–1933*. New York: Africana Studies Research Center, 1994.

Filter, John A. *Prisoners' Rights: The Supreme Court and Evolving Standards of Decency*. Westport, CT: Greenwood, 2001.

Fink, Leon. *The Maya of Morgantown: Work and Community in the Nueva New South*. Chapel Hill: University of North Carolina Press, 2007.

Fishman, J. F. *Sex in Prison*. London: John Lane, Bodley Head, 1951.

Fite, Gilbert C. *Cotton Fields No More: Southern Agriculture, 1865–1980*. Lexington: University Press of Kentucky, 1984.

Flamm, Michael W. *Law and Order: Street Crime, Civil Unrest, and the Crisis of Liberalism in the 1960s*. New York: Columbia University Press, 2005.

Fleisher, Mark S., and Jessie L. Kienert. *The Myth of Prison Rape: Sexual Culture in American Prisons*. Lanham, MD: Rowman and Littlefield, 2009.

Flores, Lori A. *Grounds for Dreaming: Mexican Americans, Mexican Immigrants, and the California Farmworker Movement*. New Haven, CT: Yale University Press, 2016.

Flynn, Jean. *Henry B. Gonzalez: Rebel with a Cause*. Austin: Eakin, 2004.

Foley, Neil. *The White Scourge: Mexicans, Blacks, and Poor Whites in Texas Cotton Culture*. Berkeley: University of California Press, 1999.

———. *Quest for Equality: The Failed Promise of Black-Brown Solidarity*. Cambridge, MA: Harvard University Press, 2010.

Fortner, Michael Javen. *Black Silent Majority: The Rockefeller Drug Laws and the Politics of Punishment*. Cambridge: Harvard University Press, 2015.

Franklin, Bruce H. *Prison Literature in America: The Victim as Criminal and Artist*. Westport, CT: Lawrence Hill, 1978.

Frazier, Franklin E. *Black Bourgeoisie*. Glencoe, IL: Free, 1957.

Freedman, Estelle B. *Redefining Rape: Sexual Violence in the Era of Suffrage and Segregation*. Cambridge: Harvard University Press, 2013.

Galarza, Ernesto. *Spiders in the House and Workers in the Field*. Notre Dame, IN: Notre Dame Press, 1970.

Galbraith, John Kenneth. *The Affluent Society*. Boston: Houghton Mifflin, 1958.

García, Ignacio. *United We Win: The Rise and Fall of La Raza Unida Party*. Tucson: University of Arizona Press, 1989.

———. *Chicanismo: The Forging of a Militant Ethos among Mexican Americans*. Tucson: University of Arizona Press, 1997.

———. *Viva Kennedy: Mexican Americans in Search of Camelot*. College Station: Texas A&M University Press, 2000.

García, Juan R. *Operation Wetback: The Mass Deportation of Mexican Undocumented Workers in 1954*. New York: Praeger, 1980.

García, Matt. *From the Jaws of Victory: The Triumph and Tragedy of Cesar Chavez and the Farm Worker Movement*. Berkeley: University of California Press, 2012.

García, Mario T. *Mexican Americans: Leadership, Ideology, and Identity, 1930–1960*. New Haven, CT: Yale University Press, 1989.

———. *The Chicano Generation: Testimonios of the Movement*. Berkeley: University of California Press, 2015.

García, Richard A. *Rise of the Mexican American Middle Class: San Antonio, 1929–1941*. College Station: Texas A&M University Press, 1991.

Garland, David. *Punishment and Welfare: A History of Penal Strategies*. Hants, UK: Gower, 1985.

Gerstle, Gary. *American Crucible: Race and Nationalism in the Twentieth Century*. Princeton, NJ: Princeton University Press, 2001.

———. *Liberty and Coercion: The Paradox of American Government; from the Founding to the Present*. Princeton, NJ: Princeton University Press, 2015.

Giallombardo, Rose. *Society of Women: A Study of a Women's Prison*. New York: Wiley, 1966.

Gibson, William. *Warrior Dreams: Paramilitary Culture in Post-Vietnam America*. New York: Hill and Wang, 1994.

Gilbert, James. *A Cycle of Outrage: America's Reaction to the Juvenile Delinquent in the 1950s*. New York: Oxford University Press, 1986.

———. *Man in the Middle: Searching for Masculinity in the 1950s*. Chicago: University of Chicago Press, 2005.

Gildemeister, Glen A. *Prison Labor and Convict Competition with Free Workers in Industrializing America, 1840–1890*. New York: Garland, 1987.

Gilmore, Ruth Wilson. *Golden Gulag: Prisons, Surplus, Crisis, and Opposition in Globalizing California*. Berkeley: University of California Press, 2007.

Glenn, Evelyn Nakano. *Unequal Freedom: How Race and Gender Shaped American Citizenship and Labor*. Cambridge, MA: Harvard University Press, 2004.

Goldberg, Robert Alan. *Barry Goldwater*. New Haven, CT: Yale University Press, 1995.

Goluboff, Risa. *The Lost Promise of Civil Rights*. Cambridge, MA: Harvard University Press, 2007.

Gómez-Quiñones, Juan. *Mexican Students Por La Raza*. Austin: Relampago, 1978.

———. *Chicano Politics: Reality and Promise*. Albuquerque: University of New Mexico Press, 1990.

Gorn, Elliot. *Manly Art: Bare-Knuckle Prize Fighting in America*. Ithaca, NY: Cornell University Press, 1986.

Gottschalk, Marie. *The Prison and the Gallows: The Politics of Mass Incarceration in America*. Cambridge: Cambridge University Press, 2006.

Graybill, Andrew. *Policing the Great Plains: Rangers, Mounties, and the North American Frontier, 1875–1910*. Lincoln: University of Nebraska Press, 2007.

Green, George Norris. *The Establishment in Texas Politics: The Primitive Years, 1938–1957*. Westport, CT: Greenwood, 1979.

Green, Laurie Beth. *Battling the Plantation Mentality: Memphis and the Black Freedom Struggle*. Chapel Hill: University of North Carolina Press, 2007.

Gregory, Derek, and John Urry. *Social Relations and Spatial Structures*. London: Macmillan; New York: St. Martins, 1985.

Gross, Kali. *Colored Amazons: Crime, Violence, and Black Women in the City of Brotherly Love, 1880–1910*. Durham, NC: Duke University Press, 2006.

Guerrero, Perla M. *Nuevo South: Latinas/os, Asians, and the Remaking of Place*. Historia USA. Austin: University of Texas Press, 2017.

Gugelberger, Georg. *The Real Thing: Testimonial Discourses and Latin America*. Durham, NC: Duke University, 1996.

Hagedorn, John M. *A World of Gangs: Armed Young Men and Gangsta Culture*. Minneapolis: University of Minnesota Press, 2009.

Hale, Grace Elizabeth. *Making Whiteness: The Culture of Segregation in the South, 1890–1940*. New York: Pantheon, 1998.

Haley, Sarah. *No Mercy Here: Gender, Punishment, and the Making of Jim Crow Modernity*. Chapel Hill: University of North Carolina Press, 2016.

Harper, William T. *Eleven Days in Hell: The 1974 Carrasco Prison Siege in Huntsville, Texas*. Denton: University of Texas Press, 2004.

Harvey, David. *The Condition of Postmodernity: An Enquiry into the Origins of Cultural Change*. Cambridge, MA: Blackwell, 1990.

Hernández, Guillermo. *Chicano Satire: A Study in Literary Culture*. Austin: University of Texas Press, 1971.

Hernández, Kelly Lytle. *Migra! A History of the U.S. Border Patrol*. Berkeley: University of California Press, 2010.

———. *City of Inmates: Conquest, Rebellion, and the Rise of Human Caging in Los Angeles, 1771–1965*. Chapel Hill: University of North Carolina Press, 2017.

Hicks, Cheryl. *Talk with You Like a Woman: African American Women, Justice, and Reform in New York, 1890–1935*. Chapel Hill: University of North Carolina, 2010.

Hill, Lance E. *Deacons for Defense: Armed Resistance and the Civil Rights Movement*. Chapel Hill: University of North Carolina Press, 2004.

Hine, Darlene Clark. *Black Victory: The Rise and Fall of the White Primary in Texas*. Millwood, NY: KTO, 1979.

Hine, Darlene Clark, and Earnestine Jenkins, eds. *A Question of Manhood: A Reader in U.S. Black Men's History and Masculinity*. Bloomington: Indiana University Press, 1999.

Hinton, Elizabeth. *From the War on Poverty to the War on Crime: The Making of Mass Incarceration in America*. Cambridge, MA: Harvard University Press, 2016.

Hirsch, Arnold. *Making the Second Ghetto: Race and Housing in Chicago 1940–1960*. Chicago: Chicago University Press, 1983.

Hobsbawm, Eric. *Bandits*. New York: Delacorte, 1969.

Hobsbawm, Eric. *Primitive Rebels: Studies in Archaic Forms of Social Movement in the 19th and 20th Centuries*. New York: W. W. Norton & Company, 1959.

Hoffman, Abraham. *Unwanted Mexican Americans in the Great Depression: Repatriation Pressures, 1929–1939*. Tucson: University of Arizona Press, 1974.

Hogan, Wesley. *Many Minds, One Heart: SNCC's Dream for a New America*. Chapel Hill: University of North Carolina Press, 2007.

Horton, David M., and George R. Nielson. *Walking George: The Life of George John Beto and the Rise of the Modern Texas Prison System*. Dallas: University of North Texas Press, 2005.

Horton, David M. and Ryan K. Turner. *Lone Star Justice*. Austin, TX: Eakin, 1999.

Horwitz, Morton J. *The Warren Court and the Pursuit of Justice*. New York: Hill and Wang, 1998.

House, Aline. *The Carrasco Tragedy: Eleven Days of Terror in the Huntsville Prisons*. Waco, TX: Texian Press, 1975.

Ignatiev, Noel. *How the Irish Became White*. New York: Routledge, 1995.

Irwin, John. *Prisons in Turmoil*. Boston: Little Brown, 1980.

Jackson, Bruce. *Wake Up Dead Man: Afro-American Worksongs from a Texas Prison*. Boston: Harvard University Press, 1972.

———. *Wake Up Dead Man: Hard Labor and Southern Blues*. Atlanta: University of Georgia Press, 1999.

Jackson, Thomas F. *From Civil Rights to Human Rights: Martin Luther King, Jr., and the Struggle for Economic Justice*. Philadelphia: University of Pennsylvania, 2007.

Jacobs, James. *Stateville: The Penitentiary in Mass Society*. Chicago: University of Chicago Press, 1977.

Jacobson, Matthew Frye. *Whiteness of a Different Color: European Immigrants and the Alchemy of Race*. Cambridge, MA: Harvard University Press, 1999.

James, Joy. *Imprisoned Intellectuals: America's Political Prisoners Write on Life, Liberation, and Rebellion*. Lanham, MD: Rowman and Littlefield, 2003.

Jeffries, Hasan Kwame. *Bloody Lowndes: Civil Rights and Black Power in Alabama's Black Belt*. New York: New York University Press, 2009.

Jelin, Elizabeth. *State Repression and the Labors of Memory*. Minneapolis: University Minnesota Press, 2003.

Jenkins, Philip. *Decade of Nightmares: The End of the Sixties and the Making of Eighties America*. Oxford: Oxford University Press, 2008.

Johnson, David K. *The Lavender Scare: The Cold War Persecution of Gays and Lesbians in the Federal Government*. Chicago: University of Chicago Press, 2004.

Johnson, Walter. *Soul by Soul: Life Inside the Antebellum Slave Market*. Cambridge, MA: Harvard University Press, 1999.

Joseph, Peniel. *The Black Power Movement: Rethinking the Civil Rights–Black Power Era*. New York: Routledge, 2006.

Kalinich, David B. *The Inmate Economy*. Lexington, MA: Lexington, 1980.

Kaplowitz, Craig A. *LULAC, Mexican Americans, and National Policy*. College Station: Texas A&M University Press, 2005.

Kelley, Robin D. G. *Freedom Dreams: The Black Radical Imagination*. Boston: Beacon Books, 2002.

Kemerer, Frank R. *William Wayne Justice: A Judicial Biography*. Austin: University of Texas Press, 1991.

Kennedy, Elizabeth Lapovsky, and Madeline Davis. *Boots of Leather, Slippers of Gold: The History of a Lesbian Community*. New York: Routledge, 1993.

Kerber, Linda. *No Constitutional Right to Be Ladies: Women and Obligations of Citizenship*. New York: Hill and Wang, 1998.

Kohler-Hausmann, Julily. *Getting Tough: Welfare and Imprisonment in 1970s America*. Princeton, NJ: Princeton University Press, 2017.

Korstad, Robert Rodger, and James L. Lelouids. *To Right These Wrongs: The North Carolina Fund and the Battle to End Poverty and Inequality in 1960s America*. Chapel Hill: University of North Carolina Press, 2010.

Krochmal, Max. *Blue Texas: The Making of a Multiracial Democratic Coalition*. Chapel Hill: University of North Carolina Press, 2016.

Kunzel, Regina. *Criminal Intimacy: Prison and the Uneven History of Modern American Sexuality*. Chicago: University of Chicago Press, 2009.

LeFlouria, Talitha L. *Chained in Silence: Black Women and Convict Labor in the New South*. Chapel Hill: University of North Carolina Press, 2015.

Levine, Lawrence W. *Black Culture and Black Consciousness: Afro-American Folk Thought; from Slavery to Freedom*. New York: Oxford University Press, 1978.

Lichtenstein, Alex. *Twice the Work of Free Labor: The Political Economy of Convict Labor in the New South*. New York: Verso, 1996.

Lincoln, Eric C. *The Black Muslims in America*. Grand Rapids, MI: William B. Eerdmans, 1994.

Lipsitz, George. *Time Passages: Collective Memory and America Popular Culture*. Minneapolis: University of Minnesota Press, 1990.

———. *Rainbow at Midnight: Class and Culture in the 1940s*. Urbana: University of Illinois Press, 1994.

———. *The Possessive Investment in Whiteness: How White People Profit from Identity Politics*. Philadelphia: Temple University Press, 1998.

Lockwood, Daniel. *Prison Sexual Violence*. New York: Elsevier, 1980.

López, Ian Haney. *Racism on Trial: The Chicano Fight for Justice*. Cambridge, MA: Harvard University Press, 2003.

Luibhéid, Eithne. *Entry Denied: Controlling Sexuality at the Border*. Minneapolis: University of Minnesota Press, 2002.

Lynch, Mona. *Sunbelt Justice: Arizona and the Transformation of American Punishment*. Stanford, CA: Stanford Law Books, 2010.

Mackenzie, G. Calvin, and Robert Weisbrot. *The Liberal Hour: Washington and the Politics of Change in the 1960s*. New York: Penguin, 2008.

Mancini, Matthew J. *One Dies, Get Another: Convict Leasing in the American South, 1866–1928*. Columbia: University of South Carolina Press, 1996.

Mantler, Gordon K. *Power to the Poor: Black-Brown Coalition and the Fight for Economic Justice, 1960–1974*. Chapel Hill: University of North Carolina Press, 2013.

Marable, Manning. *Race, Reform, and Rebellion: The Reconstruction in Black America, 1945–1982*. Jackson: University of Mississippi Press, 1984.

Marcuse, Herbert. *One-Dimensional Man: Studies in the Ideology of Advanced Industrial Society*. Boston: Beacon, 1964.

Mariscal, George. *Brown-Eyed Children of the Sun: Lessons from the Chicano Movement, 1965–1976*. Albuquerque: University of New Mexico Press, 2005.

Márquez, Benjamin. *LULAC: The Evolution of a Mexican Political Organization*. Austin: University of Texas, 1993.

Marsh, Clifton E. *From Black Muslims to Muslims: The Transition from Separatism to Islam, 1930–1980*. Metuchen, NJ: Pathfinder, 1984.

Martin, Steve, and Sheldon Ekland-Olson. *Texas Prisons: The Walls Came Tumbling Down*. Austin: Texas Monthly Press, 1987.

May, Elaine Tyler. *Homeward Bound: American Families in the Cold War Era*. New York: Basic, 1989.

McCloud, Aminah Beverly. *African American Islam*. New York: Routledge, 1995.

McGee, Richard A. *Riots and Disturbances in Correctional Institutions*. Washington, D.C.: American Prison Association, 1952.

McGrath, Roger D. *Gunfighters, Highwaymen, and Vigilantes: Violence on the Frontier*. Berkeley: University of California Press, 1984.

McGuire, Danielle L. *At the Dark End of the Street: Black Women, Rape, and Resistance—a New History of the Civil Rights Movement from Rosa Parks to the Rise of Black Power*. New York: Vintage, 2010.

McKelvey, Blake. *American Prisons: A History of Good Intentions*. Montclair, NJ: P. Smith, 1977.

McKinney, Wilson. *Fred Gomez Carrasco: The Heroin Merchant*. Austin, TX: Heidleberg, 1975.

McLennan, Rebecca. *The Crisis of Imprisonment: Protest, Politics, and the Making of the American Penal State, 1776–1941*. Cambridge: Cambridge University Press, 2008.

McNally, Karen. *When Frankie Goes to Hollywood: Frank Sinatra and American Male Identity*. Chicago: University of Illinois Press, 2008.

Mendoza, Louis G., ed. *raúlsalinas and the Jail Machine: Selected Writings by Raúl Salinas*. Austin: University of Texas Press, 2006.

Meranze, Michael. *Laboratories of Virtue: Punishment, Revolution, and Authority in Philadelphia, 1760–1835*. Chapel Hill: University of North Carolina Press, 1996.

Metzl, Jonathan M. *The Protest Psychosis: How Schizophrenia Became a Black Disease*. Boston: Beacon, 2009.

Miller, Joseph. *Way of Death: Merchant Capitalism and the Angolan Slave Trade, 1730–1830*. Madison: University of Wisconsin Press, 1988.

Miller, Vivien M. L. *Hard Labor and Hard Time: Florida's "Sunshine Prison" and Chain Gangs*. Gainesville: University Press of Florida, 2012.

Mittlestadt, Jennifer. *From Welfare to Workfare: The Unintended Consequences of Liberal Reform, 1945–1965*. Chapel Hill: University of North Carolina Press, 2005.

Montejano, David. *Anglos and Mexicans in the Making of Texas, 1836–1986*. Austin: University of Texas Press, 1987.

———. *Quixote's Soldiers: A Local History of the Chicano Movement, 1966–1981*. Austin: University of Texas Press, 2010.

———. *Sancho's Journal: Exploring the Political Edge with the Brown Berets*. Austin: University of Texas Press, 2012.

Morris, Roger. *The Devil's Butcher Shop: The New Mexico Prison Uprising*. Albuquerque: University of New Mexico Press, 1988.

Moser, Richard. *New Winter Soldiers: GI and Veteran Dissent During the Vietnam Era*. New Brunswick, NJ: Rutgers University Press, 1996.

Muhammad, Khalil Gibran. *The Condemnation of Blackness: Race, Crime and the Making of Modern Urban America*. Cambridge, MA: Harvard University Press, 2010.

Muñoz, Carlos. *Youth, Identity, Power: The Chicano Movement*. New York: Verso, 2007.

Murakawa, Naomi. *The First Civil Right: How Liberals Built Prison America*. Oxford: Oxford University Press, 2014.

Murch, Donna. *Living for the City: Migration, Education, and the Rise of the Black Panther Party in Oakland, California*. Chapel Hill: University of North Carolina Press, 2010.

Murphy, Kevin P. *Political Manhood: Red Bloods, Mollycoddles, and the Politics of Progressive Era Reform*. New York: Columbia University Press, 2008.

Myers, Martha A. *Race, Labor and Punishment in the New South*. Columbus: Ohio State University Press, 1998.

Navarro, Armando. *Mexican American Youth Organization: Avant-Garde of the Chicano Movement in Texas*. Austin: University of Texas Press, 1995.

———. *The Cristal Experiment: A Chicano Struggle for Community Control*. Madison: University of Wisconsin Press, 1998.

New York State Special Commission on Attica, *Attica: The Official Report of the New York State Special Commission on Attica*. New York: Praeger, 1972.

Oboler, Suzanne. *Behind Bars: Latino/as and Prison in the United States*. New York: Palgrave McMillan, 2009.

Ogbar, Jeffrey O. G. *Black Power: Radical Politics and African American Identity*. Baltimore: Johns Hopkins University Press, 2004.

Olguín, B. V. *La Pinta: Chicana/o Prisoner Literature, Culture, and Politics*. Austin: University of Texas Press, 2010.

Orleck, Annelise. *Storming Caesars Palace: How Black Mothers Fought Their Own War on Poverty*. Boston: Beacon, 2005.

Orleck, Annelise, and Lisa G. Hazirjian, eds. *The War on Poverty: A New Grassroots History, 1964–1980*. Athens: University of Georgia Press, 2011.

Oropeza, Lorena. *¡Raza Si! ¡Guerra No! Chicano Protest and Patriotism during the Viet Nam War Era*. Berkeley: University of California Press, 2005.

Oshinsky, David. *"Worse than Slavery": Parchman Farm and the Ordeal of Jim Crow Justice*. New York: Free, 1996.

Paredas, Americo. *Folklore and Culture on Texas American Border*. Austin: University of Texas, 1993.

Parenti, Christian. *Lockdown America: Police and Prisons in the Age of Crisis*. New York: Verso, 1999.

Patterson, Haywood, and Earl Conrad Patterson. *Scottsboro Boy: The Story That America Wanted to Forget*. New York: Doubleday, 1950.

Patterson, Orlando. *Slavery and Social Death: A Comparative Study*. Cambridge, MA: Harvard University Press, 1982.

Payne, Charles. *I've Got the Light of Freedom: The Organizing Tradition and the Mississippi Freedom Struggle*. Berkeley: University of California Press, 1995.

Paz, Octavio. *The Labyrinth of Solitude*. New York: Grove Press, 1961.

Perkinson, Robert. *Texas Tough: The Rise of America's Prison Empire*. New York: Metropolitan, 2010.

Perks, Robert, and Alistair Thompson, eds. *The Oral History Reader*. New York: Routledge, 1998.

Perlstein, Rick. *Before the Storm: Barry Goldwater and the Unmaking of the American Consensus*. New York: Hill and Wang, 2001.

Pisciotta, Alexander W. *Benevolent Repression: Social Control and the American Reformatory-Prison Movement*. New York: New York University Press, 1994.

Pollock, Joycelyn M. *Sex and Supervision: Guarding Males and Female Inmates*. Westport, CT: Greenwood, 1986.

Potter, David M. *People of Plenty: Economic Abundance and the American Culture*. Chicago: University of Chicago Press, 1954.

Propper, Alice M. *Prison Homosexuality: Myth and Reality*. Lexington, MA: Lexington, 1981.

Pulido, Laura. *Black, Brown, Yellow and Left: Radical Activism in Los Angeles*. Los Angeles: University Press of California, 2006.

Rafter, Nicole Hahn. *Partial Justice: Women in State Prisons, 1800–1935*. Boston: Northeastern University Press, 1985.

Rainey, Howard. *The Tower and the Dome*. Boulder, CO: Pruett, 1977.

Rakove, Jack N. *Original Meanings: Politics and Ideas in the Making of the American Constitution*. New York: Alfred A. Knopf, 1996.

Rediker, Marcus. *The Slave Ship: A Human History*. New York: Penguin, 2007.

Riesman, David, Nathan Glazer, and Reuel Denney. *The Lonely Crowd: A Study of the Changing American Character*. New Haven, CT: Yale University Press, 1950.

Rios, Victor M. *Punished: Policing the Lives of Black and Latino Boys*. New York: New York University Press, 2011.

Robben, Antonius C. G. M., and Marcelo Suarez-Orozco, eds. *Cultures under Siege: Collective Violence and Trauma*. Cambridge: Cambridge University Press, 2000.

Rodríguez, Dylan. *Forced Passages: Imprisoned Radical Intellectuals and the U.S. Prison Regime*. Minneapolis: University of Minnesota Press, 2006.

Rodriguez, Eugene, Jr. *Henry B. Gonzalez: A Political Profile*. New York: Arno, 1976.

Rodriguez, Marc Simon. *The Tejano Diaspora: Mexican Americanism and Ethnic Politics in Texas and Wisconsin*. Chapel Hill: University of North Carolina, 2011.

Roediger, David. *Wages of Whiteness: Race and the Making of the American Working Class*. New York: Verso, 1997.

Rogin, Michael Paul. *Ronald Reagan, the Movie and Other Episodes in Political Demonology*. Berkeley: University of California Press, 1987.

Rosales, Arturo F., ed. *Testimonio: A Documentary History of the Mexican American Struggle for Civil Rights*. Houston: Arte Publico, 2000.

Rosenbaum, Robert J. *Mexicano Resistance in the Southwest: "The Sacred Right of Self-Preservation."* Austin: University of Texas Press, 1981.

Rossinow, Doug. *The Politics of Authenticity: Liberalism, Christianity, and the New Left in America*. New York: Columbia University Press, 1999.

Rothman, David J. *Conscience and Convenience: The Asylum and Its Alternatives in Progressive America*. New York: Aldine de Gruyter, 1980.

Rotundo, E. Anthony. *American Manhood: Transitions in Masculinity from the Revolution to the Modern Era*. New York: Basic, 1993.

Sample, Albert R. *Racehoss: Big Emma's Boy*. New York: Ballatine, 1984.

San Miguel, Guadalupe, Jr. *Brown, Not White: School Integration and the Chicano Movement in Houston*. College Station: Texas A&M University Press, 2001.

Scacco, Anthony M. *Rape in Prison*. Springfield, IL: C. C. Thomas, 1975.

Schoenfeld, Heather. *Building the Prison State: Race and the Politics of Mass Incarceration*. Chicago: University of Chicago Press, 2018.

Schudson, Michael. *The Good Citizen: A History of American Civic Life*. New York: Free, 2011.

Schulman, Bruce J. *From Cotton Belt to Sunbelt: Federal Politics, Economic Development, and the Transformation of the South, 1938–1980*. Oxford: Oxford University Press, 1991.

———. *The Seventies: The Great Shift in American Culture, Society, and Politics*. New York: Da Capo, 2002.

Scott, James C. *The Moral Economy of the Peasant: Rebellion and Subsistence in Southeast Asia*. New Haven, CT: Yale University, 1976.

———. *Weapons of the Weak: Everyday Forms of Peasant Resistance*. New Haven, CT: Yale University Press, 1985.

———. *Domination and the Arts of Resistance: Hidden Transcripts*. New Haven, CT: Yale University Press, 1990.

———. *Seeing Like a State: How Certain Schemes to Improve the Human Condition Have Failed*. New Haven, CT: Yale University Press, 1990.

Sears, James T. *Rebels, Rubyfruit and Rhinestones: Queering Space in the Stonewall South*. New Brunswick, NJ: Rutgers University Press, 2001.

Shah, Nayan. *Contagious Divides: Epidemics and Race in San Francisco's Chinatown*. Berkeley: University of California Press, 2001.

Shapiro, Karen A. *A New South Rebellion: The Battle against Convict Labor in the Tennessee Coalfields, 1871–1896*. Chapel Hill: University of North Carolina Press, 1998.

Silberman, Charles E. *Criminal Violence, Criminal Justice*. New York: Random House, 1978.

Sloane, Todd A. *Gonzalez of Texas: A Congressman for the People*. Evanston, IL: John Gordon Burke, 1960.

Slotkin, Richard. *Regeneration through Violence: The Mythology of the American Frontier, 1600–1860*. Middletown, CT: Wesleyan University Press, 1973.

———. *Gunfighter Nation: The Myth of the Frontier in 20th Century America*. New York: Atheneum, 1992.

Smith, Rogers M. *Civic Ideal: Conflicting Visions of Citizenship in U.S. History*. New Haven, CT: Yale University Press, 1999.

Soja, Edward W. *Postmodern Geographies: The Reassertion of Space in Critical Social Theory*. London: Verso, 1989.

Spencer, Robyn. *The Revolution Has Come: Black Power, Gender, and the Black Panther Party in Oakland*. Durham, NC: Duke University Press, 2016.

Stein, Marc. *Sexual Injustice: Supreme Court Decisions from Griswold to Roe*. Chapel Hill: University of North Carolina Press, 2010.

Sugrue, Thomas J. *Origins of the Urban Crisis: Race and Inequality in Postwar Detroit*. Princeton, NJ: Princeton University Press, 1996.

Sykes, Gresham. *Society of Captives: A Study of a Maximum Security Prison*. Princeton, NJ: Princeton University Press, 1958.

Tadman, Michael. *Spectators and Slaves: Masters, Traders, and Slaves in the Old South*. Madison: University of Wisconsin Press, 1989.

Tani, Karen M. *States of Dependency: Welfare, Rights, and American Governance, 1935–1972*. Cambridge: Cambridge University Press, 2016.

Taylor, William Banks. *Brokered Justice: Race, Politics, and Mississippi Prisons, 1778–2002*. Columbus: Ohio State University Press, 1993.

———. *The Black Muslims*. Philadelphia: Chelsea House, 1997.

Terry, Wallace. *Bloods: An Oral History of the Vietnam War, by Black Veterans*. New York: Random House, 1984.

Thomas, Hugh. *The Slave Trade: The Story of the African Slave Trade, 1440–1870*. New York: Simon and Schuster, 1999.

Thomas, Jim. *Prisoner Litigation: The Paradox of the Jailhouse Lawyer*. Totowa, NJ: Rowman and Littlefield, 1988.

Thompson, Heather. *Blood in the Water: The Attica Uprising of 1971 and Its Legacy*. New York: Pantheon, 2016.

Thompson, Paul. *The Voice of the Past: Oral History*. 3rd ed. Oxford: Oxford University Press, 2000.

Tibbs, Donald F. *From Black Power to Prison Power: The Making of Jones v. North Carolina Prisoners' Labor Union*. New York: Palgrave Macmillan, 2012.

Trulson, Chad R., and James W. Marquart. *First Available Cell: Desegregation of the Texas Prison System*. Austin: University of Texas Press, 2009.

Tyson, Timothy B. *Radio Free Dixie: Robert F. Williams and the Roots of Black Power*. Chapel Hill: University of North Carolina Press, 1999.

Umoja, Akinyele O. *We Will Shoot Back: Armed Resistance in the Mississippi Freedom Movement*. New York: New York University Press, 2013.

Useem, Bert, and Peter Kimball. *States of Siege: U.S. Prison Riots, 1971–1986*. Oxford: Oxford University Press, 1989.

Valencia, Richard R. *Chicano Students and the Courts: The Mexican American Legal Struggle for Educational Equality*. New York: New York University Press, 2004.

Vargas, Zaragosa. *Labor Rights Are Civil Rights: Mexican American Workers in Twentieth-Century America*. Princeton, NJ: Princeton University Press, 2005.

Venkatesh, Sudhir. *Gang Leader for a Day: A Rogue Sociologist Takes to the Streets*. New York: Penguin, 2008.

Vigil, Ernesto. *The Crusade for Justice: Chicano Militancy and the Government's War on Dissent*. Madison: University of Wisconsin Press, 1999.

Wacquant, Loïc. *Prisons of Poverty*. Minneapolis: University of Minnesota Press, 2009.

———. *Punishing the Poor: The Neoliberal Government of Social Insecurity*. Durham, NC: Duke University Press, 2009.

Weber, John. *From South Texas to the Nation: The Exploitation of Mexican Labor in the Twentieth Century*. Chapel Hill: University of North Carolina Press, 2015.

Weise, Julie. *Corazon de Dixie: Mexico and Mexicans in the U.S. South Since 1910*. Chapel Hill: University of North Carolina Press, 2015.

Weiss, Carl, and James Friar. *Terror in the Prisons: Homosexual Rape and Why Society Condones It*. New York: Bobbs-Merrill, 1974.

Weiss, Jessica. *To Have and to Hold: Marriage, the Baby Boom, and Social Change*. Chicago: University of Chicago Press, 2000.

Wicker, Tom. *A Time to Die*. New York: Quadrangle, 1975.

Willett, Jim, and Joe Rozelle. *Warden: Prison Life and Death from the Inside Out.* Albany: Bright Sky, 2004.

Wilson, Rupert. *American Tough: The Tough-Guy Tradition and American Character.* Westport, CT: Greenwood, 1984.

Wooden, Wayne S., and Jay Parker. *Men behind Bars: Sexual Exploitation in Prison.* New York: Da Capo, 1982.

Woodward, Vann C. *Origins of the New South, 1877–1913.* Baton Rouge: Louisiana University Press, 1951.

Wright, Gavin. *Old South, New South: Revolutions in the Southern Economy Since the Civil War.* New York: Basic, 1986.

Wyatt-Brown, Bertram. *Southern Honor: Ethics and Behavior in the Old South.* New York: Oxford University Press, 1982.

X, Malcolm, with Alex Haley. *The Autobiography of Malcolm X.* New York: Ballantine, 1964.

Zamora, Emilio. *The World of the Mexican American Worker in Texas.* College Station: Texas A&M University Press, 1993.

Zieger, Robert H., ed. *Southern Labor in Transition, 1940–1995.* Knoxville: University of Tennessee Press, 1997.

———. *Life and Labor in the New New South.* Gainesville: University Press of Florida, 2012.

Zimmer, Lynn E. *Women Guarding Men.* Chicago: University of Chicago Press, 1986.

Articles and Chapters

Abu-Lughod, Lila. "The Romance of Resistance: Tracing Transformations of Power through Bedouin Women." *American Ethnologist* 17, no. 1 (February 1999): 41–55.

Akers, Ronald L., Norman S. Hayner, and Werner Gruninger. "Homosexual and Drug Behavior in Prison: A Test of the Functional and Importation Models of the Inmate System." *Social Problems* 21 (1974): 411–22.

———. "Prisonization in Five Countries: Type of Prison and Inmate Characteristics." *Criminology* 14, no 4 (February 1977): 527–54.

Almaguer, Tomás. "Toward the Study of Chicano Colonialism." *Aztlan* 2 (Spring): 137–42.

———. "Chicano Men: A Cartography of Homosexual Identity and Behavior." *differences: A Journal of Feminist Cultural Studies* 3, no. 2 (1991): 75–100.

Anderson, Jensie. "Fade Back to the Sixteenth Century: Restraints at the Utah State Prison" *ACLU Reporter* (Summer 1997).

Araiza, Lauren A. "In Common Struggle against a Common Oppression: The United Farm Workers and the Black Panther Party, 1968–1973." *Journal of African American History* 94, no. 2 (Spring 2009): 200–223.

Barber, David. "Leading the Vanguard: White New Leftists School the Panthers on Black Revolution." In *In Search of the Black Panther Party*, edited by Jama Lazerow and Yohura Williams, 223–51. Durham, NC: Duke University Press, 2006.

Bartollas, Clemens, and Stuart J. Miller, and Simon Dinitz. "The White Victim in a Black Institution." In *Treating the Offender: Problems and Issues*, edited by Marc Riedel and Pedro A. Vales. New York: Praeger, 1977.

Behnken, Brian D. "The 'Dallas Way': Protest, Response and the Civil Rights Experience in Big D and Beyond." *Southwestern Historical Quarterly* 140, no. 1 (July 2007): 1–29.

Belbot, Barbara. "Report on the Prison Litigation Reform Act: What Have the Courts Decided So Far?" *Prison Journal* 4, no. 3 (September 2004): 290–316.

Berger, Dan. "'From Dachau with Love': George Jackson, Black Radical Memory, and the Transnational Political Vision of Prison Abolition." In *Caging Borders and Carceral States: Incarcerations, Migrant Detentions, and Resistance*, edited by Robert T. Chase, 355–84. Chapel Hil, NC: University of North Carolina Press, 2019.

———. "Prison Radicalism and the Long Shadow of George Jackson, 1960–2012." In *Sunbelt Prisons and Carceral States: Incarceration, Immigration Detention/Deportation, and Resistance*, edited by Robert T. Chase and Norwood Andrews. Chapel Hill: University of North Carolina Press, forthcoming.

Berlin, Ira. "Time, Space, and the Evolution of Afro-American Society on British Mainland North America." *American Historical Review* 85, no. 1 (February 1980): 44–78.

Berubé, Allan. "How Gay Stays White and What Kind of White It Stays." In *My Desire for History: Essays in Gay Community Labor History*, edited by John D'Emilio and Estelle B. Freedman, 202–232. Chapel Hill: University of North Carolina Press, 2011.

Blanton, Carlos Kevin. "From Intellectual Deficiency to Cultural Deficiency: Mexican Americans, Testing, and Public School Policy in the American Southwest, 1920–1940." *Pacific Historical Review* 72, no. 1 (February 2003): 39–62.

Block, Sharon. "Rape without Women: Print Culture and the Politicization of Rape, 1765–1815." *Journal of American History* 89, no. 3 (2002): 849–68.

Blue, Ethan. "Beating the System: Prison Music and the Politics of Penal Space." In *Isolation: Place and Practices of Exclusion*, edited by Alison Bashford and Carolyn Strange, 56–70. London: Routledge, 2003.

Bornat, J. "Oral History as a Social Movement." In *The Oral History Reader*, edited by Robert Perks and Alistair Thomson, 189–205. London: Routledge, 1998.

Brown, Vincent. "Social Death and Political Life in the Study of Slavery." *American Historical Review* 114, no. 5 (December 2009): 1231–49.

Buffum, Peter C. "Racial Factors in Homosexuality." In *Male Rape*, edited by Anthony M. Scacco Jr., 104–6. New York: AMS, 1982.

Carroll, Leo. "Humanitarian Reform and Biracial Sexual Assault in a Maximum Security Prison." *Urban Life* 5 (January 1977): 417–37.

Chacon, Ramon. "The Chicano Immigrant Press in Los Angeles: The Case of 'El Heraldo de Mexico, 1916–1920." *Journalism History* 4, no. 2 (Summer 1977): 48–54.

Chamberlain, Mary. "Narrative Theory." In *Handbook of Oral History*, edited by Thomas L. Charlton, Lois E. Myers, and Rebecca Sharpless, 384–410. Lanham, MD: Altamira, 2006.

Chase, Robert T. "Self Taught, Cell Taught: Urban Chicanos in Rural Prisons." *Journal of Urban History* 41, no. 5 (September 2015): 836–61.

———. "Carceral Networks: Rethinking Reason and Connecting Carceral Borders." In *Caging Borders and Carceral States: Incarcerations, Migrant Detentions, and Resistance*, edited by Robert T. Chase, 1–54. Chapel Hill: University of North Carolina Press, 2019.

Chauncey, George. "The Postwar Sex Crime Panic." In *True Stories from the American Past*, edited by William Graebner, 160–78. New York: McGraw-Hill, 1993.

Chávez-García, Miroslava. "Intelligence Testing at Whittier School, 1890–1920." *Pacific Historical Review* 76, no. 2 (May 2007): 193–229.

Chayes, Abram. "The Role of the Judge in Public Law Litigation." *Harvard Law Review* 89, no. 7 (May 1976): 1281–316.

Christianson, Scott. "Correctional Law Developments: Prison Labor and Unionization—Legal Developments." *Criminal Law Bulletin* 14, no. 3 (1978): 243–47.

Clarke, Matthew T. "Barring the Federal Courthouse to Prisoners." In *Prison Nation: The Warehousing of America's Poor*, edited by Tara Herviel and Paul Wright, 301–14. New York: Routledge, 2003.

Colvin, Mark. "Applying Theories to the Rise and Consolidation of the Penitentiary in the Northeast." In *Penitentiaries, Reformatories, and Chain Gangs: Social Theory and the History of Punishment in Nineteenth-Century America*, 109–27. New York: St. Martin's, 1997.

Cooley, Will. "'Stones Run It': Taking Back Control of Organized Crime in Chicago, 1940–1975." *The Journal of Urban History* 37, no. 6 (October 2011): 911–32.

Corber, Robert J. "Lesbian Visibility in *All About Eve*." *GLQ: A Journal of Lesbian and Gay Studies* 11, no. 1 (January 2005): 1–22.

Crouch, Ben M., and James W. Marquart. "On Becoming a Prison Guard." In *The Keepers: Prison Guards and Contemporary Corrections*, edited by Ben M. Crouch, 63–110. Springfield, IL: Charles C. Thomas, 1980.

———. "'The Book vs. the Boot': Two Styles of Guarding in a Southern Prison." In *The Keepers: Prison Guards and Contemporary Corrections*, edited by Ben M. Crouch, 207–24. Springfield, IL: Charles C. Thomas, 1980.

Curtain, Mary Ellen. "Reaching for Power: Barbara C. Jordan and Liberals in the Texas Legislature, 1966–1972." *Southwestern Historical Quarterly* 108, no. 2 (October 2004): 211–32.

D'Cruze, Shani. "Unguarded Passions: Violence, History, and the Everyday." In *Everyday Violence in Britain, 1850–1950*, edited by Shani D'Cruze, 1–26. Harlow, UK: Longman, 2000.

D'Emilio, John. "The Homosexual Menace: The Politics of Sexuality in Cold War America." In *Passion and Power: Sexuality in History*, edited by Kathy Peiss and Christine Simmons, 226–40. Philadelphia: Temple University Press, 1989.

Danziger, Peter L. "Sexual Assaults and Forced Homosexual Relationships in Prison: Cruel and Unusual Punishment." *Albany Law Review* 36 (1971): 428–38.

Davis, Alan J. "Sexual Assaults in the Philadelphia Prison System." In *Corrections: Problems and Prospects*, 2nd ed., edited by D. Peterson and C. Thomas, 102–13. Englewood Cliffs, NJ: Prentice-Hall, 1968.

———. "Sexual Assaults in the Philadelphia Prison System and Sheriff's Vans." *Trans-Action* 6 (December 1968): 8–17.

Davis, Angela. "From the Prison of Slavery to the Slavery of Prison." In *The Angela Y. Davis Reader*, edited by Joy James, 74–95. Malden, MA: Blackwell, 1998.

Diaz, George. "Cultural Resilience and Resistance: The World of Mexican Prisoners in Texas." In *Caging Borders and Carceral States: Incarcerations, Migrant*

Detentions, and Resistance, edited by Robert T. Chase, 149–69. Chapel Hill: University of North Carolina Press, 2019.

Dulaney, Martin. "Whatever Happened to the Civil Rights Movement in Dallas, Texas?" In *Essays on the American Civil Rights Movement*, edited by W. Marvin Dulaney and Kathleen Underwood, 66–95. College Station: Texas A&M University Press, 1993.

Dundes, Alan. "'Jumping the Broom': On the Origin and Meaning of an African American Wedding Custom." *Journal of American Folklore* 109, no. 433 (Summer 1996): 324–39.

Eigenberg, Helen M. "Rape in Male Prisons: Examining the Relationship between Correctional Officers' Attitudes toward Male Rape and their Willingness to Respond to Acts of Rape." In *Prison Violence in America*, 145–66.

Ekland-Olson, Sheldon. "Crowding, Social Control, and Prison Violence: Evidence from the Post-*Ruiz* Years in Texas." *Law and Society Review* 20, no. 3 (1986): 389–422.

"El Plan de Aztlán." In *Takin' It to the Streets: A Sixties Reader*, edited by Alexander Bloom and Wini Breines, 151–53. Oxford: Oxford University Press, 2015.

Ellis, O. B. "The President's Page." *American Journal of Correction* 20, no. 5 (September–October 1958).

———. "Correctional Growth through Co-operative Effort," presidential address, 1959, *American Journal of Correction* 21, no. 5 (1959): 6–8, 30–33.

Feeley, Malcolm M., and Roer A. Hansom. "The Impact of Judicial Intervention on Prisons and Jails: A Framework for Analysis and a Review of the Literature." In *Courts, Corrections, and the Constitution: The Impact of Judicial Intervention on Prisons and Jails*, edited by John DiIulio, 12–46. New York: Oxford University Press, 1990.

Felber, Garrett. "'Shades of Mississippi': The Nation of Islam's Prison Organizing, the Carceral State, and the Black Freedom Struggle." *Journal of American History* 105, no. 1 (June 2018): 71–95.

Fernandez, Johanna. "The Young Lords and the Postwar City: Notes on the Geographical and Structural Reconfigurations of Contemporary Urban Life." In *African American Urban History Since World War II*, edited by Kenneth Kusmer and Joe W. Trotter, 60–82. Chicago: University of Chicago Press, 2008.

Flores, Lori. "A Town Full of Dead Mexicans: The Salinas Valley Bracero Tragedy of 1963, a Collision of Communities, and the End of the Bracero Program." *Western Historical Quarterly* 44, no. 2 (Spring 2013): 124–43.

Flynn, Frank T. "The Federal Government and the Prison-Labor Problem in the States," *Social Science Review* 24, nos. 1 and 2 (March and June 1950).

Foucault, Michel. "Questions on Geography." In *Power/Knowledge: Selected Interviews and Other Writings 1972–1977*, edited by Colin Gordon, 63–77. New York: Pantheon, 1980.

———. "Of Other Spaces." *Diacritics* 16, no. 1 (Spring 1986): 22–27.

Foucault, Michel, and John K. Simon. "Michel Foucault on Attica: An Interview." *Social Justice* 18, no. 3 (45), Attica: 1975–1991, A Commemorative Issue (Fall 1991): 26–34, 27.

Fradella, Henry F. "In Search of Meritorious Claims: A Study of the Processing of

Prisoner Civil Rights Cases in a Federal District Court." *Justice System Journal* 21, no. 1 (1999): 23–55.

Freedman, Estelle. "'Uncontrolled Desires': The Response to the Sexual Psychopath, 1920–1960." *Journal of American History* 74, no. 1 (June 1987): 83–106.

———. "The Prison Lesbian: Race, Class, and the Construction of the Aggressive Female Homosexual." *Feminist Studies* 22, no. 2 (Summer 1996): 397–423.

Gallant, Thomas W. "Honor, Masculinity, and Ritual Knife Fighting in Nineteenth-Century Greece." *American Historical Review* 105 (April 2000): 359–82.

García, Mario T. "Americans All: The Mexican American Generation and the Politics of Wartime Los Angeles, 1941–1945." In *The Mexican American Experience: An Interdisciplinary Anthology*, edited by Rodolfo O. De La Garza. Austin: University of Texas, 1985.

Gilfoyle, Timothy, Andrew Diamond, and Will Cooley. "Revisiting Gangs in the Post–World War II North American City: A Forum." *Journal of Urban History* 38, no. 4 (June 2012): 803–11.

Goffman, Erving. "On the Characteristics of Total Institutions: The Inmate World." In *The Prison: Studies in Institutional Organization and Change*, edited by Donald Cressey. New York: Holt, 1961.

Gomez, Alan Eladio. "'*Nuestras vidas corren paralelas*'": Chicanos, *Independentistas*, and the Prison Rebellions in Leavenworth, 1969–1972." In *Behind Bars: Latino/as and Prison in the United States*, edited by Suzanne Oboler, 67–98. New York: Palgrave McMillan, 2009.

Gorn, Elliot J. "Good-Bye Boys, I Die a True American." *Journal of American History* 74, no. 2 (September 1987): 388–410.

Graybill, Andrew. "Rural Police and the Defense of the Cattleman's Empire in Texas and Alberta, 1875–1900." *Agricultural History* 79 (Summer 2005): 253–80.

Gregory, James N. "Southernizing the American Working Class: Post-War Episodes of Regional and Class Transformation." *Labor History* 39, no. 2 (May 1998): 135–54.

Grele, R. J. "Movement without Aim: Methodological and Theoretical Problems in Oral History." In *The Oral History Reader*, edited by Robert Perks and Alistair Thomson, 38–52. London: Routledge, 1998.

Guetzkow, Joshua, and Eric Schoon. "If You Build It, They Will Fill It: The Unintended Consequences of Prison Overcrowding Legislation." *Law and Society Review* 49, no. 2 (2015): 401–32.

Guglielmo, Thomas A. "Fighting for Caucasian Rights: Mexicans, Mexican Americans, and the Transnational Struggle for Civil Rights in WWII Texas." *Journal of American History* 92, no. 4 (March 2006): 1212–37.

Hagedorn, John M. "Race Not Space: A Revisionist History of Gangs in Chicago." *Journal of African American History* 92, no. 2 (Spring 2006): 194–208.

Haney, Craig and Mona Lynch, "Regulating Prisons of the Future: A Psychological Analysis of Supermax and Solitary Confinement," *New York University Review of Law and Social Change* 23, no. 4, (1997): 477, 478–566.

Hernández, Kelly Lytle. "The Crimes and Consequences of Illegal Immigration: A Cross-Border Examination of Operation Wetback, 1943 to 1954." *Western Historical Quarterly* 37, no. 4 (Winter 2006): 421–44.

———. "Scorpion's Tale: A Borderlands History of Mexican Imprisonment in the Sunbelt." In *Caging Borders and Carceral States*, edited by Robert Chase. Chapel Hill: University of North Carolina, 2019, 125–48.

Hine, Darlene Clark. "Blacks and the Destruction of the Democratic White Primary, 1935–1944." *Journal of Negro History* 62, no. 1 (January 1977): 43–59.

Hoffman, Alice M., and Howard S. Hoffman. "Memory Theory: Personal and Social." In *Handbook of Oral History*, edited by Thomas L. Charlton, Lois E. Myers, and Rebecca Sharpless, 275–96. Lanham, MD: Altamira, 2006.

Hughett, Amanda. "A Safe Outlet for Prisoner Discontent: How Prison Grievance Procedures Stymied Inmate Organizing during the 1970s," *Law and Social Inquiry*, forthcoming.

Irwin, John, and Donald Cressey. "Thieves, Convicts, and the Inmate Culture." *Social Problems* 10, no. 2 (Autumn 1962): 142–55.

Jacobs, James B. "The Prisoners' Rights Movement and Its Impact, 1960–1980." In *Crime and Justice: An Annual Review of Research Vol. 2*, edited by N. Morris and Michael Tonry, 429–70. Chicago: University of Chicago Press, 1980.

Janssen, Volker. "When the 'Jungle' Met the Forest: Public Work, Civil Defense, and Prison Camps in Postwar California." *Journal of American History* 96, no. 3 (December 2009): 702–26.

———. "Sunbelt Lock-Up: Where the Suburbs Met the Super-Max." In *Sunbelt Rising: The Politics of Space, Place, and Religion*, edited by Michelle Nickerson and Darren Dochuk, 217–39. Philadelphia: University of Philadelphia Press, 2011.

Jeffries, Judson. "From Gang-Bangers to Urban Revolutionaries: The Young Lords of Chicago." *Journal of the Illinois State Historical Society* 96 (2003): 288–304.

Justice, William Wayne. "Prisoner's Litigation in the Federal Courts." *Texas Law Review* 31 (1973): 720.

Kansteiner, Wulf. "Genealogy of a Category Mistake: A Critical Intellectual History of the Cultural Trauma Metaphor." *Rethinking History* 8, no. 2 (2006): 193–221.

Kaplan, Michael. "New York City Tavern Violence and the Creation of a Working-Class Male Identity." *Journal of the Early Republic* 15, no. 4 (Winter 1995): 591–617.

Kaplowitz, Craig A. "A Distinct Minority: LULAC, Mexican American Identity, and Presidential Policy Making, 1965–1972." *Journal of Policy History* 15, no. 2 (2003): 192–222.

Kelley, Robin D. G. "'We Are Not What We Seem': Rethinking Black Working Class Opposition in the Jim Crow South." *Journal of American History* 80 (June 1993): 75–112.

Kirkham, G. "Homosexuality in Prison." In *Studies in the Sociology of Sex*, edited by James M. Henslin, 325–44. New York: Appleton-Century-Crofts, 1971.

Kohler-Hausmann, Julily. "'The Attila the Hun Law': New York's Rockefeller Drug Laws and the Making of the Punitive State." *Journal of Social History* 44, no. 1 (Fall 2010): 71–95.

Kunzel, Regina. "Situating Sex: Prison Sexual Culture in the Mid-Twentieth Century United States." *GLQ* 8, no. 3 (2002): 255, 253–70.

———. "Lessons in Being Gay: Queer Encounters in Gay and Lesbian Prison Activism." *Radical History Review* 100 (Winter 2008): 11–30.

Laub, John H. "Talking about Crime: Oral History in Criminology and Criminal Justice." *Oral History Review* 12 (1984): 29–42.

Leonard, Kevin A. "'In the Interest of All Races': African Americans and Interracial Cooperation in Los Angeles during and after World War II." In *Seeking El Dorado: African Americans in California*, edited by Lawrence de Graaf, Kevin Mulroy, and Quintard Taylor, 309–41. Seattle: University of Washington Press, 2001.

Lichtenstein, Alex. "Flocatex and the Fiscal Limits of Mass Incarceration: Toward a New Political Economy of the Postwar Carceral State." *Journal of American History* 102, no. 1 (June 2015): 113–25.

Loïc, Wacquant. "From Slavery to Mass Incarceration: Rethinking the 'Race Question' in the U.S." *New Left Review* 13 (January–February 2002): 41–60.

Losier, Toussaint. "Against 'Law and Order' Lockup: The 1970 NYC Jail Rebellions." *Race & Class* 59, no. 1 (2017): 3–35.

———. "'. . . For Strictly Religious Reason[s]': *Cooper v. Pate* and the Origins of the Prisoners' Rights Movement." *Souls: A Critical Journal of Black Politics, Culture, and Society* 15, nos. 1–2 (July 2013): 19–38.

Lucko, Paul M. "Counteracting Reform: Lee Simmons and the Texas Prison System, 1930–1935." *East Texas Historical Journal* 30, no. 2 (1992): 19–30.

MacCormick, Austin H. "Behind the Prison Riots." *Annals of the American Academy of Political and Social Science* 293, no. 1 (May 1954): 17–27.

Marquart, James, and Ben Crouch. "Judicial Reform and Prisoner Control: The Impact of *Ruiz v. Estelle* on a Texas Penitentiary." *Law and Society Review* 19, no. 4 (1985): 557–86.

McCarty, Heather. "Blood in, Blood Out: The Emergence of California Prison Gangs in the 1960s." In *Caging the Border and Intersecting Carceral States: New Histories of Incarceration, Immigration Detention/Deportation, and Resistance*, edited by Robert T. Chase, 245–78. Chapel Hill: University of North Carolina Press, 2019.

McGuire, Danielle. "'It Was Like All of Us Been Raped': Sexual Violence, Community Mobilization, and the African American Freedom Struggle." *Journal of American History* 91, no. 3 (December 2004): 906–31.

McLennan, Rebecca "Punishment's 'Square Deal': Prisoners and Their Keepers in 1920s New York." *Journal of Urban History* 29, no. 5 (2003): 597–619.

———. "The Convict's Two Lives: Civil and Natural Death in the American Prison." In *America's Death Penalty: Between Past and Present*, edited by David Garland and Michael Meranze, 191–219. New York: New York University Press, 2011.

Mushlin, Michael B. "Prison Reform Revisited: The Unfinished Agenda." *Pace Law Review* 24, no. 2 (Spring 2004): 395–417.

Nacci, P. L., and T. R. Kane. "Sex and Sexual Aggression in Federal Prisons." *Federal Probation* 48, no. 1 (1984): 46–53.

Oropeza, Lorena. "The Heart of a Chicano History: Reies López Tijerina as a Memory Entrepreneur." *The Sixties: A Journal of History, Politics, and Culture* 1, no. 1 (June 1967): 49–67.

Parry, Tyler D. "Married in Slavery Time: Jumping the Broom in Atlantic Perspective." *Journal of Southern History* 81, no. 2 (May 2015): 273–312.

Payne, Charles. "The View from the Trenches." In *Debating the Civil Rights Movement*, edited by Steven F. Lawson and Charles Payne. New York: Rowman & Littlefield, 2006.

Peck, Gunther. "White Slavery and Whiteness: A Transnational View of the Sources of Working-Class Radicalism and Racism." *Labor: Studies in Working-Class History of the America* 1, no. 2 (2004): 41–63.

Pelz, Mary E., James W. Marquart, and C. Terry Pelz. "Right-Wing Extremism in the Texas Prisons: The Rise and Fall of the Aryan Brotherhood of Texas." *Prison Journal* 71, no. 2 (Fall–Winter 1991): 23–37.

Reiter, Keramet. "The Path to Pelican Bay: The Origins of the Supermax Prison in the Shadow of the Law, 1982–1989." In *Caging Borders and Crossing Carceral States: Immigration Detentions, Incarcerations, and Resistance*, edited by Robert Chase, 303–40. Chapel Hill: University of North Carolina Press, 2019.

Rideau, Wilbert. "Prison: The Sexual Jungle." In *The Angolite: The Prison News Magazine*, (November–December 1979), 51–78. Amistad Research Center, Tulane University.

Rideau, Wilbert, and Billy Sinclair. "Prisoner Litigation: How it Began in Louisiana." *Louisiana Law Review* 45, no. 5 (May 1985): 1061–76.

Rubin, Gayle. "Thinking Sex: Notes for a Radical Theory of the Politics of Sexuality." In *The Lesbian and Gay Studies Reader*, edited by Henry Abelove, Michèle Aina Barale, and David M. Halperin, 3–44. New York: Routledge, 1993.

Schlanger, Margo. "Inmate Litigation." *Harvard Law Review* 116, no. 2 (April 2003): 1555–1706.

———. "Civil Rights Injunction over Time: A Case Study of Jail and Prison Court Orders." *New York University Law Review* 81, no. 2 (2006): 550–630.

Schrader, Stuart. "More Than Cosmetic Hanges: The Challenges of Experiments with Police Demilitarization in the 1960s and 1970s" *Journal of Urban History* (April 2017).

Schragger, S. "What Is Social in Oral History." In *The Oral History Reader*, edited by Robert Perks and Alistair Thomson, 284–300. London: Routledge, 1998.

Schwartz, Barry. "Pre-institutional vs. Situational Influence in a Correctional Community." *Journal of Criminal Law, Criminology and Police Science* 62 (1971): 532–42.

Scruggs, Otey M. "Texas and the Bracero Program, 1942–1947." *Pacific Historical Review* 32, no. 3 (1963): 251–64.

Smith, Geoffrey S. "National Security and Personal Isolation: Sex, Gender, and Disease in the Cold-War United States." *International History Review* 14, no. 2 (May 1992): 307–37.

Spierenburg, Peter. "Masculinity, Violence, and Honor." In *Men and Violence: Gender, Hope, and Rituals in Modern Europe*, edited by Pieter Spierenburg. Columbus: Ohio State University Press, 1998.

Taylor, Ula. "Elijah Muhammad's Nation of Islam: Separatism, Regendering and a Secular Approach to Black Power after Malcolm X (1965–1975)." In *Freedom North: Black Freedom Struggles outside the South, 1940–1980*, edited by. Jeanne F. Theoharis and Komozi Woodard, 177–98. New York: Palgrave McMillan, 2003.

Thompson, Heather Ann. "Blinded by a 'Barbaric' South: Prison Horrors, Inmate Abuse, and the Ironic History of American Penal Reform." In *The Myth of Southern Exceptionalism*, edited by Matthew D. Lassiter and Joseph Crespino, 74–98. Oxford: Oxford University Press, 2010.

————. "Why Mass Incarceration Matters: Rethinking Crisis, Decline, and Transformation in Postwar American History." *Journal of American History* 97, no. 3 (December 2010): 703–34.

Thurma, Emily. "Against the 'Prison/Psychiatric State': Anti-Violence Feminisms and the Politics of Confinement in the 1970s." *Feminist Formations* 26, no. 2 (Summer 2014): 26–51.

————. "Lessons in Self-Defense: Gender Violence, Racial Criminalization, and Anticarceral Feminism." *Women's Studies Quarterly* 43, nos. 3 and 4 (Fall/Winter 2015): 52–71.

Trulson, Chad, and James Marquart. "Racial Desegregation and Violence in the Texas Prison System." *Criminal Justice System* 27, no. 2 (2002): 233–55.

————. "The Caged Melting Pot: Toward an Understanding of the Consequences of Desegregation in Prisons." *Law and Society Review* 36, no. 4 (2002): 743–82.

University of Pennsylvania Law Review. "Constitutional Rights of Prisoners: The Developing Law." *University of Pennsylvania Law Review* 110, no. 7 (May 1962): 985–1008.

Venkatesh, Sudhir Alladi, and Steven D. Levitt. "'Are We a Family or a Business?' History and Disjuncture in the Urban American Street Gang." *Theory and Society* 29, no. 4 (2000): 427–62.

Vidal-Ortiz, Salvador, Carlos Decena, Héctor Carillo, and Tomás Almaguer. "Revisiting *Activos* and *Pasivos*: Toward New Cartographies of Latino/Latin American Same Sex Desire." In *Latina/o Sexualities: Probing Powers, Passions, Practices and Policies*, edited by Marysol Asencio, 253–73. New Brunswick, NJ: Rutgers University Press, 2010.

Wallace, Donald H. "*Ruffin v. Virginia* and Slaves of the State: A Nonexistent Baseline of Prisoners' Rights Jurisprudence." *Journal of Criminal Justice* 20, no. 4 (1992): 333–42.

Wiese, Julie M. "Mexican Nationalisms, Southern Racisms: Mexicans and Mexican Americans in the US South, 1908–1949," *American Quarterly* 60, no. 3 (September 2008): 749–77.

Williams, Yohuru. "Introductory Comment: White Tigers, Brown Berets, Black Panthers, Oh My!" In *In Search of the Black Panther Party*, edited by Jama Lazerow and Yohuru Williams, 191–222. Durham, NC: Duke University Press, 2006.

Wilson, Joel. "Invisible Cages: Racialized Politics and the Alliance between the Panthers and the Peace and Freedom Party." In *In Search of the Black Panther Party*, edited by Jama Lazerow and Yohuru Williams, 191–222. Durham, NC: Duke University Press, 2006.

Yale Law Journal. "Beyond the Ken of the Courts: A Critique of Judicial Refusal to Review the Complaints of Convict." *Yale Law Journal* 72, no. 3 (1963): 506–58.

Weaver, Vesla. "Frontlash: Race and the Development of Punitive Crime Policy," *Studies in American Political Development* 21 (Fall 2007), 230–65.

Wright, Kevin. "The Violent and Victimized in the Male Prison." In *Prison Violence in America*, edited by Michael C. Braswell, Reid H. Montgomery Jr., and Lucien X. Lombardo, 103–120. Cincinnati, OH: Anderson, 1994.

Zeringer, B. D. "Sexual Assaults and Forced Homosexual Relationship to Prison: Cruel and Unusual Punishment." *Albany Law Journal* 36 (1972): 428–38.

Dissertations and MA Theses

Burman, Michelle Lynn. "Resocializing and Repairing Homies within the Texas Prison System: A Case Study on Security Threat Group Management, Administrative Segregation, Prison Gang Renunciation and Safety for All." PhD diss., University of Texas at Austin, 2012.

Copeland, Craig. "The Evolution of the Texas Department of Corrections." MA thesis, Sam Houston State University, 1980.

Cox, Alice. "The Rainey Affair: A History of the Academic Freedom Controversy at the University of Texas, 1938–1946." PhD diss., University of Denver, 1960.

Crow, Herman Lee. "A Political History of the Texas Penal System, 1829–1951." PhD diss., University of Texas, 1964.

Felber, Garrett A. "'Those Who Say Don't Know and Those Who Know Don't Say': The Nation of Islam and the Politics of Black Nationalism, 1930–1975." PhD diss., University of Michigan, 2017.

Fong, Robert. "A Comparative Study of the Organizational Aspects of Two Texas Prison Gangs: Texas Syndicate and Mexican Mafia." PhD diss., Sam Houston State University, 1987.

Gilmore, Kim. "States of Incarceration: Prisoners' Rights and US Prison Expansion after World War II." PhD diss., New York University, 2005.

Gregory, Jan Howe. "Persistence and Irony in the Incarceration of Women in the Texas Penitentiary, 1907–1910." MA thesis, Rice University, 1994.

Huggins, Denise Walker. "A Study of Family Units Formed in Female Correctional Facilities in the State of Texas." PhD diss., Texas Women's University, 2001.

Hughett, Amanda Bell. "Silencing the Cell Block: The Making of Modern Prison Policy in North Carolina and the Nation." PhD diss., University of North Carolina, 2017.

Janssen, Volker. "Convict Labor, Civic Welfare: Rehabilitation in California's Prisons, 1941–1971." PhD diss., University of California, San Diego, 2005.

Layman, Les. "Offender Classification in Texas State Prisons." MA thesis, Sam Houston State University, 2003.

Losier, Touissaint. "Prison House of Nations: Police Violence and Mass Incarceration in the Long Course of Black Insurgency in Illinois, 1953–1987. PhD diss., University of Chicago, 2014.

Lucko, Paul. "Prison Farms, Walls, and Society: Punishment and Politics in Texas, 1848–1910." PhD diss., University of Texas at Austin, 1999.

Pelz, Mary E. "The Aryan Brotherhood in Texas: An Analysis of Right-Wing Extremism in Texas Prisons," Ph.D. diss., Sam Houston State University, 1988.

Van Dyke, Paul. "Investigation of Self-Mutilation at the Texas Prison System in Terms of the Minnesota Multiphasic Personality Inventory and Other Measures." MA thesis, University of Texas at Austin, 1953.

Laws/Court Cases

Allen L. Lamar et al. v. H.H. Coffield et al., Civil Action, No. 72-H-1393.
Alvaro L. Hernandez, Jr. v. W. J. Estelle, Jr., 788 F. 28 1154 (TX. 5th Circ. 1986).
Atterbury v. Ragen, 237 F.2d 953 (7th Cir. 1956) *cert. denied*, 353 U.S. 964 (1957).

Coffin v. Reichard, 143 F.2d 443 (1944).

Cooper v. Pate 378 U.S. 546 (1964).

Corpus v. Estelle, 409 F. Supp. 1090 (1975).

Corpus v. Estelle, 551 F.2d 68 (TX. 5th Cir. 1977).

Costello v. Wainwright, 397 F. Supp. 20 (M.D. Fla. 1975).

Cruz v. Beto, 405 U.S. 319 (1972).

Delgado v. Bastrop ISD, No. 388 Civil, Final Judgment (1948).

Dreyer v. Jalet, 349 F. Supp. 452 (S.D. Tex. 1972).

Elie v. Henderson, 340 F. Supp. 958 (E.D. LA. 1972).

Gates v. Collier, 349 F. Supp. 881 (N.D. Mississippi, 1972), *aff'd*, 501 F.2d 1291 (5th Cir. 1974).

Grovey v. Townsend, 295 U.S. 45 (1935).

Grubbs v. Bradley, 552 F. Supp. 1052 (M.D. Tenn. 1982).

Guajardo v. Estelle, 432 F. Supp. 1373 (S.D. Tex. 1977).

Guajardo v. Estelle, 580 F.2d 748 (1978).

Guajardo v. McAdams, 349 F. Supp. 211 (S.D. Tex. 1972).

Hernandez v. Driscoll (CISD), Civil Action No. 1348 (S.D. Tex. 1957).

Hernandez v. Texas, 347 U.S. 475 (1954).

Holt v. Sarver, 300 F. Supp. 825 (E.D. Ark. 1969).

Holt v. Sarver, 309 F. Supp. 362, 365 (E.D. Ark. 1970).

Holt v. Sarver II, 442 F.2d 304 (1971).

Homer B. Adams v. O.B. Ellis, 194 F.2d 483.

Hubert v. Ward, No. C-E-80-414-M (W.D. N.C. 1985).

In re Rodriguez, 81 F. 337 (1897).

Johnson v. Avery, 252 F. Supp. 783 (M.D. Tenn. 1966).

Johnson v. Avery, 382 F.2d 353 (6th Cir. 1967).

Jones v. Cunningham, 371 U.S. 236 (1963).

Kentucky Whip and Collar Company v. Illinois Central Railroad Company, 299 U.S. 334 (1937).

Lamar v. Coffield, 353 F. Supp. 1081 (S.D. Tex. 1972).

Lamar v. Coffield, 951 F. Supp. 629 (S.D. Tex. 1996).

Leahy v. Estelle, 371 F. Supp. 251 (N.D. Tex. 1974).

Gates v. Collier, 349 F. Supp. 881 (N.D. Mississippi, 1972), *aff'd*, 501 F.2d 1291 (5th Cir. 1974).

Monroe v. Pape, 365 U.S. 167 (1961).

Morales v. Turman, 326 F. Supp 667 (E.D. Tex. 1971).

Nixon v. Condon, 286 U.S. 73 (1932).

Nixon v. Herndon, 273 U.S. 536 (1927).

Novak v. Beto, 320 F. Supp. 1206, 1209 (S.D. Tex. 1970).

Plyler v. Evatt, C.A. No. 82-876-0 (D.S.C. January 8, 1985).

Pugh v. Locke, 406 F. Supp. 318 (M.D. Ala. 1976).

Raymond K. Procunier v. Robert Martínez, et al., 416 U.S. 396 (94 S. Ct. 1800, 40 L. Ed. 2d 224), 1974.

Robinson v. California, 370 U.S. 660 (1962).

Rocha v. Beto, 449 F. 2d 741 (Tex. 1971).

Ruiz v. Estelle, 503 F. Supp. 1265 (S.D. Tex. 1980).

Sigel v. Ragen, 180 F.2d 785, *cert. denied*, 339 U.S. 990, *reh'g denied*, 390 U.S. 847.

Sinclair v. Henderson, 331 F. Supp. 1123 (E.D. La. 1971).

Sinclair v. Henderson, 425 F.2d 125, 126 (5th Cir. 1970).

Small v. Martin, No. 85-987-CRT (E.D. N.C. 1988).

Smith v. Allwright, 321 U.S. 649 (1944).

Sweatt v. Painter, 339 U.S. 629 (1950).

Trop v. Dulles, 356 U.S. 86 (1958).

United States v. Nixon, 418 U.S. 683 (1974).

Whitfield v. Ohio, 297 U.S. 431-41 (1936).

Wolff v. McDonnell, 418 U.S. 539 (1974).

Woolsey v. Beto, 450 F.2d 321 (Tex. 1976).

Index

Page numbers in italics signify graphics.

Browning, O'Neal, 231
Buddhism, 176, 186, 199, 280
Bue, Carl O., 203, 205
Buentello, Salvador "Sam," 362–63, 364, 369, 374, 468n92
building tenders (trusties): as armed, 4, 108, 111–12, 319; beatings and assaults by, 108, 111, 112, 219, 234–35, 239, 276, 285, 286, 305, 351; Beto defense of, 98, 203–4, 444n56; as control and discipline mechanism, 38, 101, 103–4, 109, 119; and convict code, 117, 289–90; convicted murderers as, 179–80; as "defenders" of weaker prisoners, 118–19, 122; dismantling of institution, 334, 335–36, 361; dress of, 113; filing of false charges by, 120; and gangs, 109, 164, 363, 369, 388; House Bill banning, 224–25, 254, 270–71, 281, 286, 287; immunity for, 121–22, 139, 140, 329–30; and internal prison economy, 123–25, 137, 156; JCPR on, 254–55; Lamar on, 230; and mass incarceration, 294–95, 297–98; and Muslims, 190, 286; number of, 110, 114; porters, turnkey, and floor boys beneath, 109–10; power and authority of, 103, 105, 107–23, 388; and prison administrators, 121–22; prisoner debts to, 124–25; prisoner organizing against, 191–92, 286, 289, 304–5; and prison guards, 114–15, 117–18, 361–62; and prison labor, 98, 119; punishments administered by, 112, 114–16, 117, 124–25; and racial hierarchy, 5, 108–9, 179, 192–93, 207; rapes and sexual violence by, 4–5, 22, 102, 108, 136–40, 141, 143, 230, 237–38, 276, 318, 319, 433n99; renamed support service inmates, 110, 333; rewards and perks of, 108, 113, 114; Ruíz on, 279; and *Ruiz v. Estelle* case, 105, 284, 311, 312, 316, 318–19, 329–30; and sex trade, 125–32, 136–39; spatial control by, 103, 190; TDC defense of, 224, 280, 297–98; used to quell dissent, 234–35, 274, 279, 305, 433n99; *Ward v. Estelle* suit against, 241;

at women's prison, 22–23, 150–51, 153–54, 322
Burk, G. W., 268–69
Burton, Jim, 253
Bush, Cecil, 225
Bush, George W., 7, 434n109

California prison system: cost of, 3, 66; funding for, 25; gangs in, 362–64, 368, 375–76, 377; and George Jackson shooting, 242, 358; prison labor in, 33–34, 73, 417–18n10; prison radicalism in, 217, 446n5
Campbell, Leavy, 231
Canaday, Margot, 21–22, 32, 58
Captive Nation: Black Prison Organizing in the Civil Rights Era (Berger), 15
carceral dialectic, 14
carceral massive resistance, 9, 27, 388, 398
carceral violence: and building tender system, 105, 111, 120, 143, 202, 322; criminality reproduced by, 193; documentation of, 14, 373; and field labor, 77–78, 79; and gangs, 342, 368, 370, 371–72, 373–74; homicides, 43, 121–22, 343, 352–55, 368, 372, 373–75; as integral to prison society, 136; interracial unity against, 21, 184, 282; and masculinity, 135–36; and mass incarceration, 295–98, 332, 343, 348–58, 387; persistence of, 343, 387–88, 404–5; and prison construction program, 381; resistance to, 164–65, 216, 234–42, 251, 264, 303, 339; as state-orchestrated, 4, 11, 14, 16, 22, 26, 103, 104, 140, 141, 155, 230, 300, 318; used as threat, 320, 321, 354, 374, 435n125. *See also* Rape and sexual violence
Carrasco, Frederico "Fred" Gómez: biographical information, 259–60; as cultural folk hero, 249, 251, 260–61, 267; demands presented by, 261–62; execution of, 266, 268–69; nationalist framework presented by, 261–64; and prisoner issues, 262–65, 267–68

Fudge, Lewis, 99
Futrell, J. M., 34

Galindo, Jesus Manuel, 395
gang formation, 23–24, 342, 463n10
gangs, prison, 362–77; and building
  tenders, 109, 164, 363, 369, 388; and
  drug trade, 369, 374; list of, 367;
  membership in, 362–63, 364, 367;
  and prison violence, 342, 370,
  373–74; rapes by, 368–69; rise of,
  342–43, 363, 388; tattoos of, 12–13,
  365, 370, 370–71, *375,* 376; warfare
  between, 25, 375–77, 387. *See also*
  Aryan Brotherhood, Texas; Mexican
  Mafia; Texas Syndicate (TS)
García, Hector P., 313
García, Mario T., 10, 20, 275
García, Richard, 160, 313
Garrard, Mike, 393
Gates, Nazareth, 196
gay and lesbian prisoners, 115, 126–32,
  140, 152–54. *See also* Homosexuality
gender identity, 104, 135–36
Georgia prison system, 99, 170, 416n91,
  471n1; prisoner labor in, 107, 396;
  statewide work strike in, 395
Gerstle, Gary, 440n60
Gilbert (prisoner), 139, 318
Gilbert, James, 46
Gilmore, Ruth Wilson, 26
Ginsburg, Allen, 300
Goffman, Erving, 142
Golden, Jerry, 319
Goldwater, Barry, 296
Goluboff, Risa, 10
Gonzalez, Corky, 250, 281
Gonzalez, Henry B., 173, 294
Gonzalez, Mariano "Dalou," 197
Gonzalez, Salvador, 144, 155, 231, 279,
  303, 311; as PSC leader, 300, 302
Gooding, Robert, 360
good-time law, 81–82, 98, 101, 114
Goree State Prison, 39, 144–54; classifica-
  tion process at, 146, 152; history of,
  145–46; key girls at, 151, 153–54;

lesbianism and "aggressive homosexuals"
  at, 152–54, 321–22; policies and
  programs at, 145–46; prison labor at,
  149–50; racial hierarchies and discrimi-
  nation at, 147–48, 149–50, 151–52;
  trusty system at, 22–23, 150–51, 152–53;
  work strike at, 306
Gottschalk, Marie, 413n29
Great Society, 24
Green, George, 423n11
Gross, Kali, 21
Guajardo, Guadalupe, 80, 164, 210,
  288, 399
Guajardo, Juan, 213
guards. *See* prison guards
Guerra, Francisco, Jr., 113, 117
Guerra, Ricardo Aldape, 400
Gunn, Robert, 355, 375

habeas corpus writs, 159, 166, 170, 171,
  283
Haber, Roy S., 195–96, 280
Habern, William T., 344–45, 346
Haley, Sarah, 21
Hall, Anthony, 225
Hall, Lawrence James, 265
Hampton, Carl, 216
Hardy, G. P., 348
Harlem prison, 89, 162, 164–66, 177
Hasan, Siddique Abdullah, 397
Hawes-Cooper Bill, 33, 417n8
Hayes, Kenneth, 123
health conditions, 57. *See also* medical
  care
Heidegger, Martin, 174
Henderson, Major, 319
Henley, William Earnest, 174
Hermanos De Pistolero, 367
Hernández, Alvaro Luna, 353, 356–57,
  399–400; and 1978 work strike, 303–4,
  306–7
Hernandez, Andres, 325
Hernandez, Joe, 240
Hernández, Kelly Lytle, 12, 20, 163, 260
Hicks, Cheryl, 21
Hicks, Tommy, 197

prison reform movement, 63–64, 100, 228, 306; and contagion language, 49–50, 421n74; legislative response to, 53–58; and public sentiment, 270–71; scholarship on, 8–9. *See also* Joint Committee on Prison Reform; prisoner organizing

prison work strikes. *See* work strikes

privatized prisons, 7, 381, 384, 470nn132–33

probation, 81, 426n70

Procunier, Raymond K., 358–59, 360–61, 375

P Stone Rangers, 342

psychiatric hospitals, 71, 252–53

Pulido, Laura, 20

"punks": and building tenders, 123, 233; defined, 132–33; distinguishing, 132, 434n102; punk/slave dynamic, 135–37, 138, 140; punk wings, 126, 128–29, 138, 252–53

Punk's Song, A (Donaldson), 132

Quate, Jerry, 138

Quinlan, Martha, 23, 323; on assassination of prisoner activists, 353–55; at Goree prison, 153–54; as head of CURE, 355, 356, 400; and movement strategy, 356–58; *Ruiz* trial testimony by, 311, 321–23

Quiroz, Martin, 268, 452n41

racial classification system, 39, 55

racial segregation, 109, 142, 144, 147–48, 179, 212, 247–48, 253, 279–80, 282; at agricultural prison farms, 1, 38–40, 41, 77; and building tender system, 108–9; court challenges to, 173, 231; elimination of in Texas prisons, 11, 271, 398; JCPR critique of, 252, 253–54, 256; Lamar challenge to, 229–34; against Mexican Americans, 13, 38–39, 160, 164, 173, 207, 279

Ragan, Joe, 171

Ramos, Ervay, 304

Ramsey prisons, *76*, 109, 288; building tenders at, 113, 121; prisoner organizing at, 286–87, 288–89, 293–94; "punk wing" at, 128–29, 130; rebellion at, 234–35, 287; Ruíz at, 277–79; work strikes at, 278, 305

Rangel, Florentino G., 239–40

Rao, Joseph, 43–44

rape and sexual violence: by building tenders, 4–5, 22, 102, 108, 136–40, 141, 143, 230, 237–38, 276, 318, 319, 433n99; as control and domination, 32, 104, 133; definition of, 141; and prison gangs, 368; resistance to, 22, 143; *Ruiz v. Estelle* case on, 318, 328–29, 330; scholarship on, 21–23, 141–43; and sexual identity, 132–33, 135–36; and slavery discourse, 133–34; as state-orchestrated, 4, 11, 16, 22, 26, 103, 104, 140, 141, 155, 230, 300, 318; statistics on, 140–42, 434n109

Rape in Prison (Sacco, Anthony), 142

Rauch, Hardy, 360

Ray, Melvin, 395

Ray, Tommy, 236–37

Reagan, Ronald, 297, 358

Redwine, Charles, 42–43

Reed, Carl, Jr., 354

Reeves County Detention Complex, 395

rehabilitation, 13, 33–34, 80; MacCormick on, 45–46, 48

Rembert, Winfred, 107

Retrieve prison, 38, 52, 131, 178, 282, 366; building tenders at, 54–55, 282, 319, 351; Father's Day Incident at, 218–19, 226, 361

Revolutionary Vanguard Party Platform (RVP), 293

Reyes, Benny, 225

Reynolds, Carl, 387

Rideau, Wilbert, 133–34, 247

Rios, Victor, 161, 437n9

Ripley, Frank, 54–55

Rivera, Daniel, 250

Robbins, Carl, 190

Robertson, Charles, 102, 139, 143, 155, 318

Robinson, H. E., 177

285, 328, 345; by Cruz, 159–60, 166, 174, 177, 180; and Eight Hoe Squad, 205–10, 217, 218, 229; legal cases around, 181, 182, 229, 231; and PLRA, 393–94; and prison organizing, 285, 291, 292–93, 300–302, 305, 308, 349, 355; racial animosity used against, 207, 254; and Ruíz, 274, 276–79, 282–84; and *Ruiz v. Estelle* testimony, 311, 316–17, 319, 321–28; solitary confinement used against, 160, 177, 180, 285, 318; TDC attempts to silence and curb, 177, 181, 187, 189, 193, 279, 281, 282–83, 285–86, 316, 323, 345; in women's prison, 321–23

Wyatt, M. Riley, 55

Wynne, Lawrence, 235

Wynne prison, 39, 53, 54, 71, 122, 346, 368; Eight Hoe at, 205, 218; work strike at, 350

Wynne Treatment Center, 71, 122

Young, Charles, 373

Young Lords, 342

Zieger, Robert, 62

Index of Cases